INSIDE JAVA

KARANJIT S. SIYAN, PH.D.
JAMES L. WEAVER
JIM MATHIS
LUKE CASSADY-DORION

CONTRIBUTIONS BY CRAIG OLAGUE

New Riders Publishing, Indianapolis, Indiana

Inside Java

By Karanjit S. Siyan, Ph.D. and James L. Weaver

Published by:
New Riders Publishing
201 West 103rd Street
Indianapolis, IN 46290 USA

Printed in the United States of America 1 2 3 4 5 6 7 8 9 0

Library of Congress Cataloging-in-Publication Data

`***CIP data available upon request***`

Warning and Disclaimer

This book is designed to provide information about Java. Every effort has been made to make this book as complete and as accurate as possible, but no warranty or fitness is implied.

The information is provided on an "as is" basis. The authors and New Riders Publishing shall have neither liability nor responsibility to any person or entity with respect to any loss or damages arising from the information contained in this book or from the use of the disks or programs that may accompany it.

Publisher *Don Fowley*
Associate Publisher *David Dwyer*
Marketing Manager *Mary Foote*
Managing Editor *Carla Hall*

Product Development Specialist
Sean Angus

Acquisitions Editor
Nancy Maragioglio

Senior Editors
Sarah Kearns
Suzanne Snyder

Development Editor
Naomi Goldman

Project Editor
Gina Brown

Copy Editors
Krista Hansing
Wendy Garrison
Cricket Harrison

Technical Editor
Jim Mathis
Andrew Trieger

Software Specialist
Steve Flatt

Software Acquisitions
Pete Bitar

Acquisitions Coordinator
Stacy Merkel

Administrative Coordinator
Karen Opal

Cover Designer
Sandra Schroder

Cover Illustration
© Sally Wern Comport/SIS

Cover Production
Aren Howell

Book Designer
Sandra Schroder

Production Manager
Kelly Dobbs

Production Team Supervisors
Laurie Casey
Joe Millay

Graphics Image Specialists
Steve Adams, Kevin Cliburn, Wil Cruz, Tammy Graham, Oliver Jackson

Production Analyst
Erich J. Richter

Production Team
Lori Cliburn, Kim Cofer, William Huys Jr, Rowena Rappaport

Indexer
Chris Barrick

About the Authors

Karanjit S. Siyan is president of Kinetics Corporation. He has authored international seminars on Solaris & SunOS, TCP/IP networks, PC Network Integration, Windows NT, Novell networks, and Expert Systems using Fuzzy Logic. He teaches advanced technology seminars in the United States, Canada, Europe, and the Far East. Dr. Siyan has published articles in *Dr. Dobbs Journal, The C Users Journal, Databased Advisor,* research journals, and is actively involved in Internet research. Karanjit has worked with computer languages such as C/C++, Pascal, LISP, Algol, Ada, MSL, CMS-2, Jovial, Java and other languages for many years, and has written compilers for a number of these languages. Karanjit holds a Ph.D in Computer Science. Before working as an independent consultant, Karanjit worked as a senior member of technical staff at ROLM Corporation and as a software developer and technical manager on numerous projects. As part of his consulting work, Karanjit has written a number of custom compiler and operating system development tools. His interests include UNIX-based, NetWare-based, Windows NT-based, and OS/2-based networks. He is actively involved in the application of many computer science disciplines, such as networks, operating systems, programming languages, databases, expert systems, and computer security. Dr. Siyan holds certification credentials for Windows NT and holds a Master CNE and ECNE certification for Novell-based networks. He has written numerous books. Karanjit Siyan is based in Montana where he lives with his wife.

Jim Weaver (`jlweaver@netusa1.net`) has designed and developed many business, manufacturing, and engineering applications during the last 15 years, both as an independent consultant and as a Senior Systems Engineer for EDS. Jim is currently involved in Internet research, focusing on technologies that enable applications to use the Internet (and corporate intranets) as an execution platform. He is also beginning to focus on Java-based agents that can roam the Internet. He loves to play the guitar, but doesn't spend nearly enough time doing it. Jim and his wife Julie live in Indiana and have two children.

Trademark Acknowledgments

Dedications

Jim Weaver's Dedications

This book is dedicated to Julie, Lori, and Kelli for all their support.

Acknowledgments

Karanjit S. Siyan's Acknowledgments

One of the more pleasurable tasks of being an author is to thank the people responsible for the success of a book. My heartfelt thanks to my wife Dei for her love and support. I wish to thank my father, Ahal Singh, and my mother Tejinder; my brothers Harjeet, Jagjit; my sisters Kookie and Dolly. Thanks also to Margaret Cooper Scott, Cathryn and Bob Foley, Craig and Lydia Cooper, Robert and Janie Cooper, Heidi and Steve Bynum, Barbara and Edward L. Scott (Scotty), and Jacquelyn McGregor for their love and support. Special thanks to Mother, Saint Germain, El Morya Khan, Bhagwan Krishna and Babaji. Without their spiritual support, this book would not have been possible.

I want to thank Bob Sanregret and Anders Amundson, who initially got me interested in writing teaching materials about computers. I also wish to thank the many people at Learning Tree for their help and support on various projects. In particular I would like to thank John Moriarty, Rick Adamson, Dr. David Collins, Eric Garen, Marti Sanregret, Richard Beaumont, Mark Drew, David O'Neil, and Robin Johnston. Boyd Badten created, at a very short notice, the graphic image files for the animation applet discussed in this book. Thanks Boyd!

I wish to thank Marta Partington and Naomi Goldman for their help in developing this book. Special thanks to Don Fowley, Jim LeValley, Sean Angus, Gina Brown, Nancy Maragioglio, and Krista Hansing for their help with this book. I also wish to thank Drew and Blythe Heywood for their friendship, support, and encouragement throughout the many years it has been my pleasure to know them.

Jim Weaver's Acknowledgments

Thanks to all the people at New Riders that worked so hard to make this book a reality. A special thanks to Sean and Nancy for giving me the opportunity to co-author this book, and to Gina Brown, Naomi Goldman, Krista Hansing, and Jim Mathis for their expertise and diligence in editing. I also appreciate Colin for recommending me to New Riders.

Thanks to Julie Weaver, Lori Weaver, Kelli Weaver, Marilyn Prater, Walter Weaver, and Ken Prater for their love and support. Thanks to God who always manages to make things in my life "work together for good."

Congratulations and thanks to the past and present members of the JavaSoft team. They have produced technology that is enabling a revolution in the Information Technology industry, and is fun to use as well!

Contents at a Glance

Table of Contents

CHAPTER 1

Introduction to Java

Java is a new programming language from Sun Microsystems. Java has a number of characteristics that make it suitable for use with Internet applications, such as the World Wide Web, although it is not limited exclusively to the Internet. Java's cross-platform portability is very attractive, which makes it a good choice for many internal corporate networks. The Java language has also been used for the development of large scale software systems. This experience suggests that the language can be used as a general purpose tool for writing business and scientific logic. Java's support for rich classes and object inheritance enables a programmer to reuse existing code and to write complex applications quickly.

The Java Language

The origins of the Java language can be traced to an attempt by software engineers years ago to write portable software for controlling consumer electronics devices, such as ovens, toasters, TVs, VCRs, lights, telephones, pagers, set-top boxes, personal digital assistants, and so on. In April 1991, a group of Sun Microsystem employees began working on a project with the code name "Green." The goal of the Green project was to develop a system for developing consumer electronics' logic. The Sun Microsystem employees quickly realized that there were no standards in consumer electronics as to which type of processor was actually used. To simplify development for consumer electronics, these Sun employees needed a platform-independent environment.

James Gosling (creator of the UNIX EMACS editor and NeWS window system) at Sun Microsystems initially attempted to extend the C++ language. This was considered to be too much effort and not an avenue that would yield the best results. Therefore, work began on a new language for the Green project called Oak. The name Oak came to James Gosling when he saw an oak tree outside his window as he was entering the directory structure for the new language. Later on, the name Oak had to be discarded because it was a name already used by an older language. After many hours of brainstorming, inspiration struck one day after the team members visited a local coffee shop. Therefore, contrary to popular belief, Java is not an acronym for "Just Another Vague Acronym." There were four elements to the Oak development platform: the language Oak, an operating system code named GreenOS, a user interface, and a PDA-like device code named *7. The name "*7" came from the telephone sequence used to answer any ringing phone in the Sand Hill offices where the Green project members had their offices. The *7 device was envisioned as a generic control device that could be sold to consumer electronic manufacturers who could incorporate it into their products. The user interface consisted of a full-color animated representation of a home (or office) where appliances could be manipulated by touching the screen.

In 1993, the Green team, now incorporated into a Sun Microsystems spin-off called "FirstPerson, Inc.," made a bid for the Time-Warner TV trial where many homes were supposed to have experimental video on demand hardware for testing. By June 1993, however, Time-Warner had selected Silicon Graphics, Inc. over the Green team's proposal. In 1994, another deal with the company 3DO fell through, and the prospects of new marketing partners looked bleak. FirstPerson's public launch was cancelled, and the newly formed corporation dissolved. Half the Green team members went to work for Sun Interactive to work on digital video servers; the other half went back to the parent Sun company to work on multimedia and network-based computing.

While all this was happening to the Green team, the Web was gaining larger acceptance, particularly with the development of powerful GUI Web clients that gave the user considerable flexibility and navigational power. At this time it was becoming apparent that Internet growth was being fueled by the World Wide Web. Sun Microsystems realized the potential for using the Oak technology and developed the WebRunner browser, later renamed HotJava.

The development of the *7 device and the Video On Demand (VOD) technologies helped to mature the Java language. The Java compiler, which was first written in C, was later rewritten in Java by Arthur Van Hoff. Compilers are complex pieces of software, and the rewrite of the Java compiler in the Java language demonstrated the general purpose nature of Java.

On May 23, 1995 the Java environment was announced by Sun Microsystems at SunWorld '95. The flurry of activity and interest in Java that followed is a testimony of the interest and promise that this technology holds for the future of network computing.

Popular browsers, such as the Netscape Navigator and Internet Explorer, incorporate Java-based technology. These browsers can run Java programs that are downloaded from remote Web servers. Java programs for the Web are called Java *applets*. The description of Java applets is embedded in the HTML pages as URL addresses. Because the URL addresses can refer to any computer on the network, the HTTP protocol and the HTML language can be used to distribute code for execution on the intranet or the Internet.

Special Features

Sun describes its Java language as a simple, distributed, interpreted, secure, architecturally neutral, portable, high-performance, multithreaded, and dynamic language. That is a lot of adjectives, and some people may even classify them as buzzwords.

Some of these buzzwords have also been used to describe other languages, but what makes Java unique is that it is the first language that can be used for writing general purpose programs, as well as programs designed specifically for use on internets and intranets. When used for Internet or intranet applications, Java programs are typically used while viewing Web pages in conjunction with using a tool such as a Web browser. Java programs that are designed to be run within a Web browser are called applets. General purpose Java programs that can be run stand-alone, outside a Web browser, are called Java applications. You will learn more about the distinction between these ways of writing programs as you progress through this book.

Simplicity of Use

Java was designed with the intent of keeping the language simple but powerful enough to perform network computing tasks for the Web. This simplicity and power is also helpful in developing applications for intranets. To meet the goal of simplicity, the designers of the language kept the number of language constructs small. This makes it easier for people to learn the language, yet keeps the compilers smaller and easier to implement.

The designers also based the language on the C/C++ syntax. A large body of competent C/C++ programmers exists, and these people would find the language easy to migrate to and to learn. Some of the features of C/C++ were deliberately removed to keep the Java language simple and secure. As an example, the Java language does not support goto statements; instead it provides exceptional handling, labeled break and continue, and finally, statements. The C/C++ language header files have been removed. There are no #include preprocessor statements in Java; instead, the Java import statement is used to selectively import a Java class or all classes in the specified package.

To support the development of large software in a modular fashion, the concept of package is used. A *package* is a collection of Java code grouped together because of similarity of function.

Other differences with C/C++ include the removal of support for data structures such as struct and union. A similar concept can be implemented by the class construct. Also operator overloading and multiple-inheritance capabilities of C++ have been eliminated to keep the Java language simple.

One of the biggest changes from C/C++ is the removal of the direct use of pointers. Although pointers in C/C++ are very powerful mechanisms, they require discipline to use them correctly and to ensure that the code that uses them is bug free. Real life experience from maintaining C/C++ code suggests that the use of pointers in C/C++ creates error prone programs. Java automatically handles referencing and dereferencing of language objects. This frees you from the problems of dangling reference pointers, invalid pointer references, memory leaks, and so on. Objects are created dynamically and garbage collection is performed automatically in the background by the Java environment. Incorrect use of memory allocation is another common source of error in C/C++ programs. By having the Java environment perform this automatically, memory type errors are reduced.

Even though the Java language has been simplified in comparison with C/C++, it comes with a very rich set of predefined classes to perform I/O, network, and graphic operations. This makes the Java language easy and powerful enough for developing network-enabled intranet applications.

Object-Oriented Nature

Java is an object-oriented language. In this language, all programs and data always exist in the context of objects. An *object* is a collection of data and the programs that operate on it. The programs are written specifically for the data that resides in the object and are called object methods. In fact, one of the parameters to the method is the object itself (referred to in the Java language by a special reserved word called "this"). As the name "method" suggests, the object methods are the mechanism used to operate on the data held in the object. The data and the methods describe the state of the object.

The notion of an object in Java is implemented by the class construct. The use of classes is so fundamental to the Java language that it is not possible to write a Java program that does something meaningful without using the class construct.

Code reuse is supported in Java by using object inheritance. A class can be derived from another class. This process is called inheritance or subclassing. The Java language comes with useful predefined class hierarchies. At the very top is the special class Object. This is the root class from which all other classes become subclasses. By default, a newly created class always inherits from the root class Object, even though you may not explicitly define a class that you inherit from. The predefined Java class hierarchies provide the richness of the Java environment.

In fact, the biggest learning curve in Java does not come from the language syntax or the language semantics, both of which are relatively straightforward and easy to learn. The biggest challenge lies in becoming familiar with the predefined class hierarchies and the methods and their purpose. Of course, you could always start from scratch and reinvent a new set of class hierarchies to replace the existing rebuilt hierarchies, but you would be a lot less productive.

By using inheritance, you can always use the concept of code reuse and subclass existing class hierarchies. Where the desired class hierarchies are not adequate or available, you can always create your own.

A Distributed Language

Java was designed to support applications that run on a network. This network could be the Internet or corporate intranets. Java provides network capabilities by using a predefined language package called Java.net. This package contains many classes to simplify network communications between applications running on different computers on a network. By using Java, you can access remote or local files with equal ease. In addition, a virtual circuit network connection is supported by the language, which can be used to build distributed client/server software for intranets.

An Interpreted Language

The Java compiler does not produce the machine language instructions that make up the executable Java program. Instead, the Java compiler produces an intermediate code called byte codes. The Java byte codes are read by a Java interpreter and executed by it using an internal model of an abstract machine. The Java interpreter, and the implementation of this abstract machine, are called the *Java Virtual Machine* (JVM).

The Java byte code is an architecturally neutral representation of the program. Because the Java program is executed by interpreting the Java byte codes, the Java language is interpretive. In an interpretive environment the standard "link" phase of patching together the object modules to form a binary executable set of machine instructions vanishes. The linking phase is replaced by the loading of the new class into the Java environment. Interpretive environments, such as Java, support rapid prototyping and program development.

Just In Time (JIT) compilers are also available for those applications that cannot afford the overhead of an interpretive execution of Java code. These JIT compilers translate the byte code into the machine language instructions of the computer on which the program is run. This leads to significant improvements in performance. Of course, the output of the JIT compilers is no longer architecturally neutral.

A Robust Language

When programmers talk about robustness in a language, they mean the support for eliminating error prone constructs both at compile and runtime. Java is a strongly typed language, which means that well-defined rules have been established on how objects are to be used. You cannot assign, for example, a floating point number to an integer value without a loss in precision. The compiler will catch this and other similar errors at compile time. You can explicitly force certain types of objects into others by an explicit type conversion (casting) or by writing conversion programs, but this is an explicit action that has to be performed by the programmer and will not be done automatically by the Java language.

The Java memory model performs automatic garbage collection, thus eliminating another important class of runtime errors. Pointers are not directly supported, and this eliminates pointer-related runtime errors such as inadvertent data overwrites and memory corruption. The Java interpreter also performs runtime checks, such as ensuring that array and string accesses are within the bounds of the array size.

Java supports explicit exception handling in the language, which gives the programmer an additional tool to write robust programs. Besides the predefined exceptional conditions that indicate potential problems, the programmer can define his or her own exceptions.

A Secure Language

Because Java code is expected to run in a networked environment with untrusted host computers, the language was designed with security as a major goal. Java code, which resides at a Web server, can be downloaded and run within the Java Virtual Machine provided by the Web browser. There is nothing to prevent viruses and other malicious programs from masquerading as legitimate code and causing damage to the client computer or other computers on the network.

A technique many virus programs use to cause damage is to get hold of machine resources by the clever manipulation of address variables such as pointers. This is one of the reasons the Java designers decided not to support pointers in the language, which also eliminates a major security risk.

Memory allocation and layout of classes are done transparently by the Java environment. Because the programmer does not have access to the memory layout, he or she cannot know the actual memory layout that is used. This makes it difficult for virus programs to access the internal data structures of the Java program.

Before a Java program is interpreted, the Java runtime system performs a byte-code verification. Byte-code verification is a formal process in which mathematical algorithms are used to ensure that the program is not violating system integrity. Additionally, programs that are loaded from across the Net are loaded in a separate name space than local classes. This prevents a malicious Java applet from replacing standard Java classes.

Java anticipates and protects against traditional techniques used to cause the program to misbehave. It cannot, however, guarantee or claim a 100 percent fool-proof environment. A number of malicious and wily hackers will see in Java a new challenge to overcome. As these cases come up, Sun Microsystems will have to plug the security holes and stay one step ahead of these hackers.

Although security is important in an Internet environment, it is less so than in the intranet environment. The primary reason for this is that intranets have less exposure to malicious users than the Internet. Because Java is designed to provide a safe execution environment on the Internet, it can certainly meet the needs of most intranets.

Architecturally Neutral

A compiled Java program produces byte code that is interpreted in the Java Virtual Machine. The byte code is independent of any specific processor type and machine architecture. Use of the byte code enables the Java code to run on any machine that supports the Java Virtual Machine and Java interpreter.

The architectural neutrality of Java is important for intranets because it enables program code to be written just once in Java. The same program code can then run across a variety of different client or server platforms. Figure 1.1 shows the same Java applet code downloaded into different client platforms.

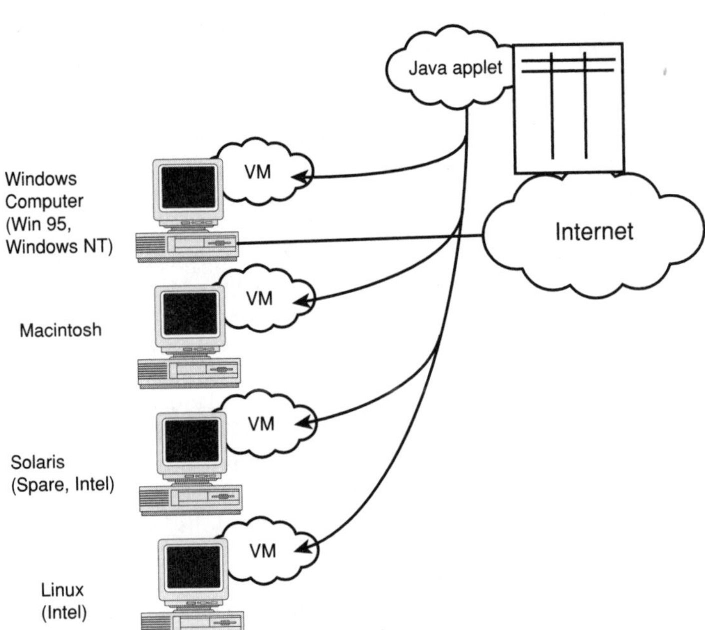

Figure 1.1
Java code executing in a platform independent environment.

Currently, many organizations spend a great deal of effort and money trying to cover every possible platform they need to support. With different versions of UNIX, Windows NT, Windows 95, OS/2, and Macintosh computers, it is a challenge to write software that can run on all these platforms. Java goes a long way toward helping with this challenge.

A Portable Platform

Because Java code is architecturally neutral, it can be run on any platform. The code needs to be written once, and the byte code can then be distributed to different platforms and run unchanged. A constant source of portability problems in other languages is the difference in implementation of the size of basic language types such as integers, characters, and floating point numbers.

You need, for example, to know whether or not a basic integer type is 16 bits long or 32 bits long. In Java, all basic types have the same size regardless of the platform on which they run. An integer type in Java, for example, is always a signed 32-bit value whether it runs on a UNIX machine or on an OS/2 machine. The use of a standard definition of an integer type avoids errors, such as overflow or underflow, that typically arise due to an incorrect assumption made on the size of the basic types.

Because Java applets are GUI-based and can be multithreaded, Java programs can run only on those environments that have these features. It would be difficult, for example, to have Java code run on MS-DOS machines that do not support a GUI interface or multitasking.

A High-Performance Vehicle

Java is high performance compared to other scripting languages such as the varieties of Basic and Visual Basic languages, shell scripts, and Perl. It is, however, about 20 times slower than the C language. For many interactive applications the speed of Java is adequate.

If you want to make the speed of Java comparable with C, you will have to use Just In Time compilers. Examples of JIT are available from several vendors, such as Sun, Borland, Symantec, and so on. Web browsers are licensing JIT compilers to provide accelerators to improve the performance of applets. The Java byte code was designed to provide a quick translation from the byte code format to the machine instructions for processors. So the performance of byte codes converted to machine instructions is comparable to C/C++ programs.

A Multithreaded Language

Java is one of the few languages (Ada is another) that provides support for multitasking in the form of multithreading within the language itself. This means that you can write Java programs where multiple threads are executing simultaneously. A thread is an independent line of execution through a program. Threads can be used to implement a level of parallelism in the program. Each thread performs a specialized function. With several threads running, several parallel activities are taking place. On a single processor machine, the threads will each have to have their turn at executing on the CPU, so it only appears as if the threads are executing simultaneously. In reality, each thread runs for a duration of time before it is pre-empted and another thread gets a chance to run. On a multiprocessor machine, threads can be simultaneously executing on different processors. To prevent threads from tripping over each other when critical operations are being performed, you can specify critical regions by using the synchronized keyword.

Most programs that use some form of multitasking or multithreading make low-level calls for system services to the operating system on which they run. Because of differences in system service calls, these programs are not portable to different operating system types. With Java, however, you can write a multithreaded program that could run without alteration on different machines and operating system types.

A Dynamic Language

Java is a dynamic language in the sense that it loads the classes it needs as they are needed. You can determine at runtime which class an object belongs to by checking the run-type information associated with the class. The runtime class definitions make it easy to perform dynamic linking of classes.

Summary

In this chapter you have been introduced to the features of the Java language. Java is a new programming language from Sun Microsystems and has a number of characteristics that make it suitable for use with Internet applications such as the World Wide Web. The features of the Java language were discussed without going into the details of the elements of the language so that you can have a broader understanding of what Java can do for you. A key aspect of the Java language is that it is not limited to being used exclusively on the Internet. Java's cross-platform portability is very attractive and makes it a good choice for many internal corporate networks.

CHAPTER 2

Getting Started with Java

This chapter will discuss what a Java program is and how to write a simple program. The goal of this chapter is to show a quick overview of the basic elements of the language without overwhelming you with the details and the power of the language. After you understand the basic concepts of how a simple Java program is written, you will have an easier time grasping some of the more complex concepts covered in later chapters.

This chapter does not assume that you are a professional programmer. If you have had some prior background experience in programming such as BASIC, Pascal, Ada, or even C/C++, many of the programming concepts in this chapter will be a review. This chapter, however, will introduce to you some of the basic elements of the language.

At the end of this chapter, you should be able to write some simple but useful programs. To achieve this goal, this chapter will concentrate on some of the Java program basics such as variables and constants, control flow, and the basics of input and output. Some of the other concepts such as object-oriented programming and design class structures are important for writing larger programs. But these have been deliberately left out in this chapter on getting started with Java.

Although this approach will give you an understanding of how to write simple Java programs, there are some disadvantages to this way of teaching. One disadvantage is that you may be misled as to what you can accomplish with Java because you will not be presented with the full power of Java. You should also be aware that some of the examples have been contrived, because the full power of the Java language is not presented here. Another disadvantage of this overview approach to programming in Java is that later chapters will repeat some of these concepts, albeit in greater detail.

There are several ways to compile your Java program, both free and commercial. Throughout this book the examples will use the command line compiler supplied with the Java Developers Kit (JDK). The examples will also be using the Java Virtual Machine that comes with the JDK to run the Java programs. There are also commercial programs for compiling Java such as Symantec's Visual Café and Microsoft's Visual J++.

Getting Started with Writing a Simple Program

First, make sure that you have installed the JDK or your Java compiler as described in the product documentation. In the section that follows, you will write the program that will print out the following words:

```
Hello, world! I am a simple Java program!
```

To be able to print this text with a Java program, you must learn the following elements:

- The basic structure of a Java program
- How system output is performed in the language
- How to create/edit this program
- How to compile the Java program
- How to run the Java program

In essence, these same steps will be used for even more complex and larger programs. So after you understand how to perform these steps for a simple Java program, you will have mastered larger Java programs as well.

Creating, Compiling, and Running a Simple Java Program

The following is an example of a simple Java program.

```
class HelloWorld
{
    public static void main(String args[])
    {
        System.out.println("Hello, world! I am a simple Java program!");

    }
}
```

To use this sample program, you must save the Java program in a text file. The name of the file must end with a "java" extension. With the current release of the Java language, you must save the program with the same name as the class name Hello-Java. The *class name* is the name that follows "class" in the preceding program and describes the program fragment that is placed in the brackets {} as illustrated next:

```
class classname
{
      ...

}
```

The name of the file, in the previous example, must be HelloWorld.java to match the class name of HelloWorld. Class names in Java are case-sensitive. To compile and run this program, you must change the class name to helloworld. In Java, because class names are case-sensitive, the following class names are all distinct:

```
class HelloWorld
{
      ...
}

class helloworld
{
      ...
}
class helloWorld
```

```
{
    ...
}
```

Notice that because Java file names end with a four-letter "java" extension, you cannot use an MS-DOS editor for creating these file names. MS-DOS file names are limited to three characters.

File names are also case-sensitive under UNIX. Under Windows NT and Windows 95, however, file names are not case-sensitive, even though the case is preserved when creating file names. This means that if you try to create a file name, such as helloWorld.java in a directory that already has a file named HelloWorld.java, you will not be able to create a separate file name. In practical terms, this means that in the Windows NT and Windows 95 environments, you must use class names that will not lead to conflicts in unique file names if the Java programs are kept in the same directory.

To create the Java text file, create a file called HelloWorld.java by using a text editor. You can use any text editor that can work with long file names to create and save this file.

The next step is to compile the test program. You can compile the program by using the javac command line compiler. Bring up a command prompt window and change to the directory in which you saved the HelloWorld.java file. Type "javac HelloWorld.java" and you should see output similar to figure 2.1.

Figure 2.1
Compiling the HelloWorld program from the command line.

To execute the compiled program, pass the class name as a parameter to the Java Virtual Machine, java. Figure 2.2 shows the output of running the HelloWorld program from the command line.

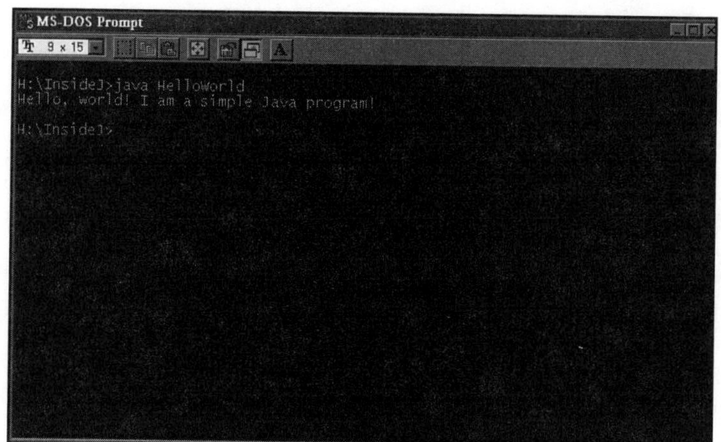

Figure 2.2
Running the HelloWorld program from the command line.

Understanding the Structure of a Java Program

The HelloWorld Java program illustrates the basic structure of a Java program.

```
class HelloWorld
{
     public static void main(String args[])
     {
             System.out.println("Hello, world! I am a simple Java program!")

     }
     }
```

The following sections describe the structure and meaning of this simple Java program. Interestingly enough, to explain this simple Java class, you need to understand several programming language concepts and the concept of objects in Java.

The Class Structure

Notice that the program code for the HelloWorld program is embedded in the following syntax:

```
class classname
{
     Rest of program code
}
```

In Java, a class is used to define a piece of program code. It begins with the reserved word class followed by the name of the class (*classname*) and then by the brace characters {}. The program code is placed in the brace characters {} that follow the class statement. In Java, the brace characters {} and the program code inside them are called a program *block*.

A reserved word, such as class, has a special meaning in the Java language and cannot be used for programmer-defined data variables and functions. Other reserved words in the HelloWorld Java example are public, static, and void.

All Java programs containing program code must have at least one class. Within this class is the actual data and program code that operates on the data. The class mechanism is used in Java to describe the notion of an *object.*

Simple Java Objects

An object is a collection of data and programs that operate upon that data. Figure 2.3 shows a conceptual representation of an object. In this figure, the data is shown in the central core of the object. Surrounding the data, in this figure, are programs that operate upon the data. Programs defined within an object that operate upon the data in the object are called *methods.* In other object-oriented languages such as Small Talk, a language developed at Xerox Palo Alto Research, the methods are also called *messages,* and therefore some of the Java documentation refers to the programs that operate on data within an object as messages.

Figure 2.3

Conceptual representation of an object.

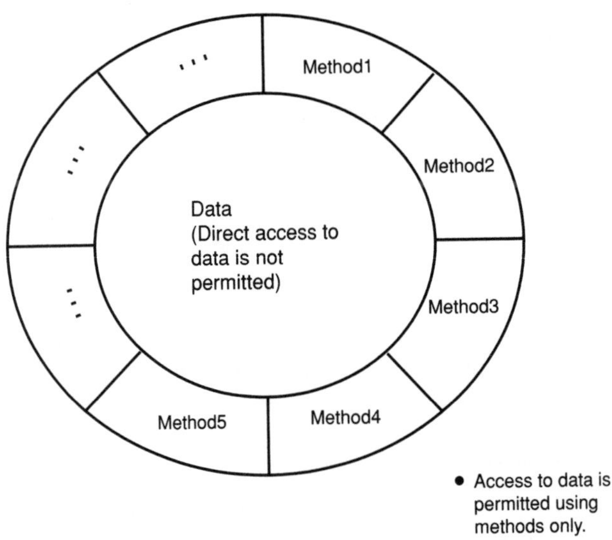

Causing the program in the object to be run is called *invoking a method, calling a method,* or *sending a message* to the object. Conceptually, the idea is that when a method is invoked for the object, or when a message is sent to the object, the program code alters the state of the object that is represented by data in the object (see fig. 2.4).

It is not always necessary for a method to modify the data in an object; the method could simply return the current values of the data in the object, or perform some other logic. A method in a Java class corresponds to the functions, procedures, or subroutines in other programming languages such as C, Pascal, BASIC, Fortran, and so on. A major difference is that a method in the Java language is always defined within a class or within the syntax of a class, whereas a function, procedure, or subroutine does not have this association with the object. A Java method has access to all data defined in the class. Other methods outside the class do not automatically have access to the data in the class, unless explicitly granted such access (see fig. 2.5). You will learn more about methods and classes in later chapters in this book. At this point, only the basic meaning of a Java class is sufficient for understanding simple Java programs being introduced.

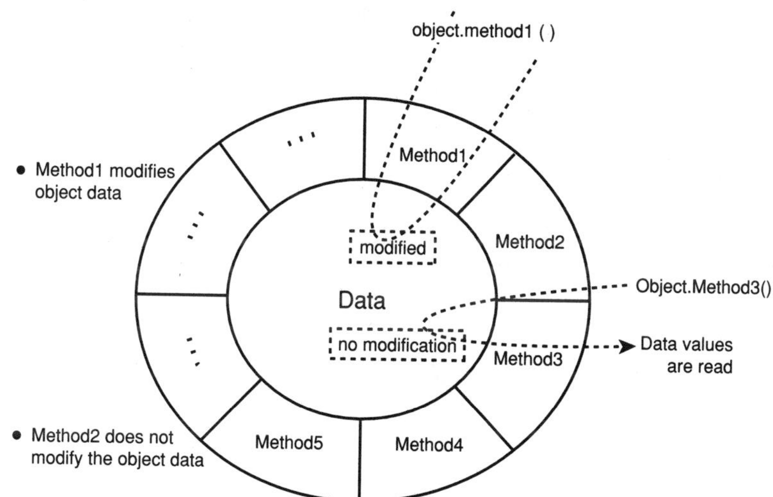

Figure 2.4

Invoking a method or sending a message to an object.

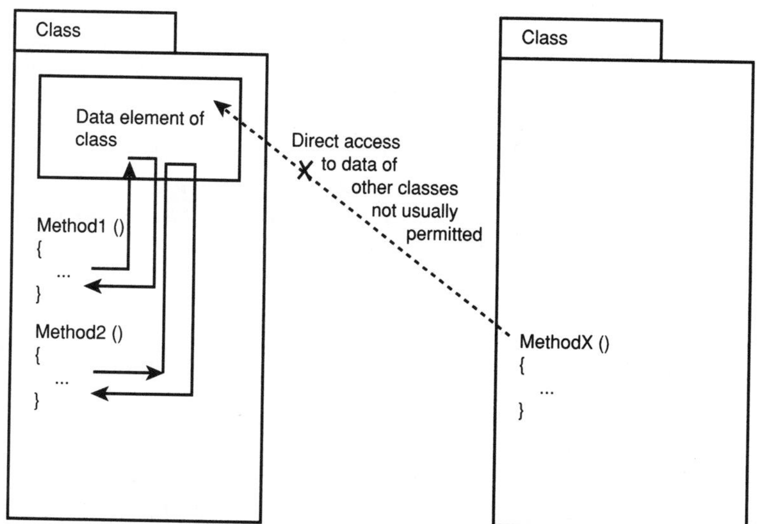

Figure 2.5

Methods accessing data in class.

Coming back to the HelloWorld program, you may notice that the HelloWorld program is a trivialized form of a Java object. HelloWorld class contains no data, and the class contains only one method called "main."

The Definition of the main Program Method

When a Java application is run, control is transferred to the method called "main." Normally, you can assign any name to the methods in a class, but the name "main" is special, because it is the name reserved for the method to which initial program control is transferred when a Java program is run. The method main is defined as follows:

```
public static void main(String args[])
{
      Rest of program code for main
}
```

To communicate data with a method, you pass *arguments* to the method. Arguments are also called *parameters*. Arguments, or parameters, are placeholders that describe the actual data that is passed to the method. Arguments follow the method name and are enclosed in parentheses.

Note Arguments or parameters are used as placeholders for passing data to methods.

Immediately following the method name and arguments is a block of code enclosed in braces {}. In the example of the main method there is only a single argument definition inside the parentheses:

```
String args[]
```

The String refers to a built-in class defined in the Java language that is used to contain string data. The Java language defines several useful built-in classes for types of data and functions that are used frequently in many Java programs. In this case, the String built-in class is particularly useful for describing string data. String data is a sequence of characters and is typically used to describe text data, such as messages. String data is represented as a sequence of characters enclosed in quotes. You can see an example of string data in the class HelloWorld:

```
"Hello, world! I am a simple Java program!"
```

The use of args immediately following Strings defines the name of the placeholder for the type of data to be passed to the method. The brackets [] following the args define the argument args to be a reference to an array. Therefore, the argument args that are to be passed are an array of Strings. You will learn more about arrays later on, but for now consider an array as an ordered list of elements—in the case of args, each element of the array is of type Strings. The first element of args, for example, could be the string "To" and the second element could be "be." Figure 2.6 shows an example of an array of strings that could be passed to the main method.

There is nothing special about the name args used in the main method. You can replace it with another valid variable name, such as the one shown in the following example:

```
public static void main(String str v[])
{
     Rest of program code for main
}
```

If your code in the body of the main program needs to reference the argument passed to main, you must ensure that you use the new name str_v instead of the name args. You will find, however, that as a convention, most Java code uses the name args as the argument for the main program.

Who supplies the array of strings that are passed to the method main? The Java runtime environment passes the string data specified on the command line when the HelloWorld Java program is invoked as an array of strings. Consider, for example, the following invocation of the Java program:

```
> jview HelloWorld To be or not to be!
```

In this case, the method main will pass the following array of strings:

```
"To", "be", "or", "not", "to", "be!"
```

In the body of the main method (that is, code included in the braces {}), no further reference is made to args in the simple example of the HelloWorld program, which was discussed earlier. You must still, however, specify the args parameter as an array of strings, even though your program may not actually use the string.

The main method is preceded with a number of modifiers such as public, static, and void. As mentioned previously, these modifiers are reserved words in the Java language and cannot be used as variable names.

The modifier public before a method name makes the method "callable" to Java code outside the class. In the HelloWord example, there is no other Java code outside the class HelloWorld, but the caller, in this case, is the Java runtime environment. The Java runtime environment contains the Java Virtual Machine that processes the Java byte code and the Java runtime library code needed for running a Java program. The use of the reserved word public before a method name makes the method publicly available or callable to any "user" or "client" of the class. The "user" or "client," in this case, is not a human person; it actually refers to any other program code that is defined outside the class.

The class defines the object; however, it does not create the actual object. A created object occupies space in computer memory. The class only defines a template for the object. To create the actual object, you must use the class name to create the object. The following is an example of creating an object from the class HelloWord:

```
HelloWorld    hwobj;
```

The preceding statement creates the object hwobj from the class (or template) definition HelloWorld. This process of creating an object from a class definition is called creating an *instance* of the object or *instantiating* a class. After you have created a real object, you can invoke the public methods (methods such as main that have a public modifier) by using a notation such as the following:

```
hwobj.main("To", "be" "or", "not", "to", "be!");
```

The preceding example shows how a method in a class is invoked. The general syntax of invoking a method is as follows:

```
objectname.methodname(arguments);
```

The *objectname* refers to the name of the object, such as hwobj; *methodname* refers to the name of the method, such as main; and *arguments* refers to the list of arguments passed to the method.

In general, one must create an instance of the object before invoking its method. The method is then associated with data inside the object. Creating an object from a description of the object is called instantiating the object. The class definition of an object is the description of the object.

Sometimes you would like to call a method, such as main, without first creating an instance of the class HelloWorld. You can do this by using the modifier static in defining the method. In the example of the main method defined in class HelloWorld, the modifier static is used to indicate that the main method can be invoked without defining an instance of the class such as hwobj. Assuming the example of the arguments passed in figure 2.6, the Java runtime environment is able to invoke main by using the equivalent of the following syntax:

```
HelloWorld.main("To", "be" "or", "not", "to", "be!");
```

Notice that HelloWorld is the name of the class and not the name of an instantiated object. It is possible to call `main()` in this manner because a method defined with a reserved word static is associated with all instances of the object of a class, and can be invoked by using the following syntax:

```
classname.methodname(arguments);
```

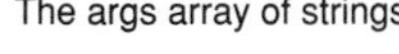

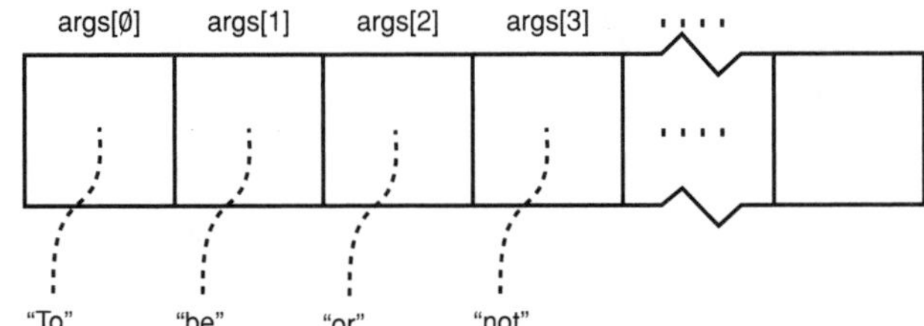

Figure 2.6

Example of array of strings passed to main method.

The *classname* refers to the name of the class; *methodname* refers to the name of the method, and *arguments* refers to the list of arguments passed to the method.

The final modifier that is used with the definition for main is void. In Java all methods are expected to return a value. Many situations arise, however, when a method performs a piece of logic but does not need to return anything. In these cases, you must use the modifier void before the method name, thereby indicating that no value is expected to be returned by the method.

Printing Output and Program Summary

So far you have learned all aspects of the HelloWorld class except the single code statement in the main method:

```
System.out.println("Hello, world! I am a simple Java program!");
```

The preceding statement invokes the println method defined in the built-in System class. The println method prints the string to the standard output device, which is usually the computer monitor. After printing the string, the println method outputs the new-line character, which causes the cursor to be positioned on the next line on the computer screen.

Notice that to use the method println, there was no instance of the System class defined in the class HelloWorld. This is because all methods in the System class are static and can be invoked by specifying the class name alone.

Figure 2.7 shows a summary of the program elements of a simple Java program, such as the HelloWord class described in this section. This summary is by no means a complete outline of a Java program.

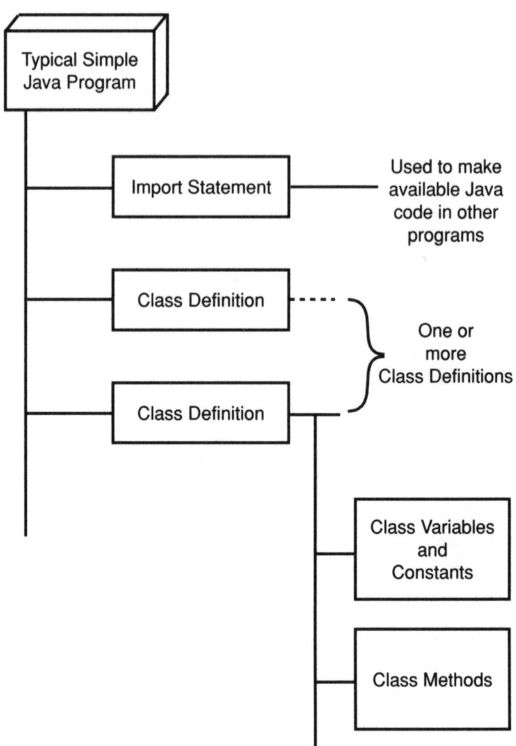

Figure 2.7
Summary of a simple Java program.

Introducing Variables and Simple Arithmetic

Now that you know how to write a simple Java program, consider a program that does something a little more interesting. In this section you will learn how simple Java variables are defined and how they can be used in Java statements to build logic. You will learn about the different ways to comment a program, how to assign values to variables, and how to create simple types of loop statements. Later chapters will cover these issues in greater detail.

Writing a Temperature Conversion Program

As a first attempt, you will learn how to write a program that will print out a table of Celsius temperatures and their equivalent Fahrenheit temperatures. The program starts with a Celsius temperature of –40 degrees, the temperature at which the Celsius and Fahrenheit temperature scales are equal, and continues to print out the

Fahrenheit temperature equivalent at intervals of 10 degrees until a temperature of 100 degrees Celsius is reached. Note that symbols +, *, and / when used in an arithmetic expression have the usual meanings of addition, multiplication, and division that are used in most programming languages.

The following contains the complete program code.

Listing 2.1

```
Line=================Java Source=================
/**
8 TempConvCF: Program to convert from Centigrade to
* Fahrenheit.
*
* Author: Karanjit S.G.S. Siyan
*/

class TempConvCF
{
    public static void main(String args[])
    {
        int     lowest, highest;    // lowest and
                                    // highest temperature
        int     delta;              // temperature increment

        float   fahrT, centT;       // Fahrenheit and
                                    // Centigrade vars

        // Initialize the variables
        lowest = -40;
        highest = 100;
        delta = 10;

        /* Print title */
        System.out.println("Centigrade\tFahrenheit");

        /**
        * Set up a loop to print a table of
        * Centigrade to Fahrenheit conversion.
        */
```

continues

Listing 2.1, Continued

```
        centT = lowest;
        while (centT <= highest)
        {
            fahrT = (float) ((9.0/5.0)*centT + 32.0);
            System.out.println(centT+"\t\t"+fahrT);
            centT = centT + delta;

        } // end while

    ) // end main

} // end TempConvCF
```

On the CD

Please note that the line numbers in listing 2.1 and other listings in this book are shown for discussion purposes and are not part of the language syntax. If you plan on typing in these programs, you should omit the line numbers. To run this program, you can copy the file TempConvCF.java from the CD-ROM into a new directory and build the project. The steps for performing this are outlined in detail for the JDK earlier in this chapter. When the program is run, it produces the output shown in figure 2.8.

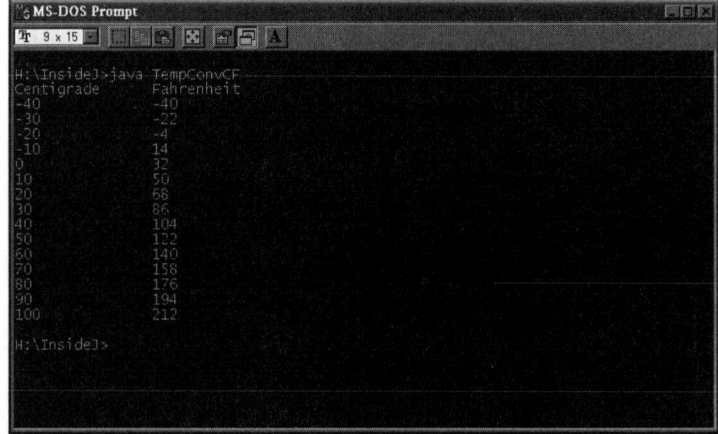

Figure 2.8
Output of temperature conversion program.

Overview of Program Code TempConvCF

Among the first points you should notice in the program listing 2.1 is the liberal use of comments. In Java, comments are used to document the program. Blank lines are used to space the lines and to make the program more readable or improve its aesthetic appeal. Indentations are used to indicate the nesting of statements.

You will notice in listing 2.1 that three styles of comments exist. The program begins with the comments of the following type:

```
/**
 * TempConvCF: Program to convert from Centigrade to
 * Fahrenheit.
 *
 * Author: Karanjit S. G. S. Siyan
 */
```

Later on you also see a comment of the following type:

```
/* Print title */
```

From a language syntax point of view, these two comment types are nearly identical in the sense that they both comment out the enclosing text. The first comment type is used with an extra asterisk after the initial /*, whereas the second comment type does not have the extra asterisk. Both comment types end with a closing */. Tools are available, however, with many Java development kits that enable the extraction of comments that begins with a /** and ends with a */. An example of this is the javadoc tool that is available in JDK 1.1.

If you have major sections of program logic that you would like to document and be reported by the Java document analysis tool (javacdoc), you should enclose them with a /** and */. Any other comment type such as the /* */ will not be reported by the document analysis tool.

Javadoc is a very powerful documentation tool that can be used to automatically generate documentation for packages, classes, interfaces, exceptions, methods, and variables. Documentation will only be generated for public and protected aspects of objects in accordance with the basic object-oriented principle of encapsulation. To prepare your objects for autogenerated documentation, surround your comments with the /** */ comment delimiters. Many parameters may be used to create more meaningful documentation, for more information about these refer to the online documentation.

After you are ready to generate documentation for your object simply type **javadoc objectname**. If, for example, you wanted to autogenerate documentation for the java.net package you would type **javadoc java.net.***.

If you do not want to use autogenerated documentation you may want to avoid the use of the /** */ and /* */ comment delimiters. A problem with the these delimiters is that one may, during the process of editing the program text, accidentally delete the ending */, or place it in the wrong location. In this case, entire sections of programs may get accidentally commented out. In many cases, this will cause syntax errors to be generated, but this is not guaranteed and, in the worst case, the program may compile just fine, but have missing functionality or incorrect logic.

A safer form of comment would be to use the // characters to start the comment. The end-of-line character on that line, or end of file, automatically terminates the comment so that it is impossible to inadvertently leave the comment unterminated. In listing 2.1 you can see examples of this type of comment on lines 12–17 that describe the use of program variables.

Also, notice the use of comments on the closing brace (}) used to indicate the end of syntax element of the program. The while statement on lines 32–38, for example, has the form:

```
while (centT <= highest)
{
        ...

} // end while
```

The // end while at the end of the closing brace (}) for the while loop is optional, and is used by the author as a matter of style to visually and clearly indicate the end of the statement. In a large program that is literally littered with hundreds of closing braces, it can become difficult to figure out which closing brace ends which type of statement, especially when the statements are heavily nested and span several pages of text. You'll notice similar comments that end the main function definition and the class definition:

```
        } // end main

  } // end TempConvCF
```

Notice the use of blank lines in the program to group statements into logical units for easier reading and comprehension of the program. Again, this is an issue of style, and highly recommended by the author.

Lines 12–17 of listing 2.1 define the variables that must be used. A variable must be defined before it can be used. The general syntax of defining a variable is the following:

```
type var1{, varN ;
```

The *type* is one of the Java basic types or a class name defined in the program. In listing 2.1, you can see examples of the basic types such as int and float. The int type represents a range of integers, and float represents floating point values. Besides these basic types, Java defines other basic types such as byte, short, long, double, and char.

The *var1, varN* are one or more variables that can follow the type name. The declaration of variables ends with a semicolon. The notation {,*varN*} means zero or more occurrences of whatever is inside the braces. The braces are used as *meta-characters* and are not part of the syntax.

For Java basic types, the compiler automatically allocates space for variables of that type. As mentioned earlier, class names can also be used to replace *type*. If class names are used, the variables become the names of the object of that class type. The Java compiler does not automatically create space for these class objects. Therefore, unlike the case of Java basic types, class objects have to be instantiated using additional code.

Notice that several variables can be defined by listing them on the same line. In listing 2.1, a comment is placed next to each variable definition, further describing what the variable represents. The variables that are used should be suggestive of the values that they contain and their use.

Variables that are defined by method are called *local variables*, and exist only for the duration of the method invocation. When the method invocation returns to the caller who called the method, the local variables "disappear." They disappear in the sense that you cannot access these variables from the caller program. These variables are called local because they have a meaning only inside the method when that method is being executed. When these variables are defined without the qualification of the reserved word static, the space allocated for these variables is released when the method exits.

If the qualifier static is used, the variable is allocated space at compile time; that is, before the program is run and before the method is called. The space for a static local variable is not released when the method exits. So a subsequent invocation of the method can still reference the value that the variable was set to in a previous invocation of the method. However, because the static variable is local to the method, only the program code in the method can access this variable.

Lines 19–22 of listing 2.1 are examples of assignment statements. Assignment statements and declarations must terminate in a semicolon. You can place several assignment statements on the same line. For example, lines 19–22 can also be written as the following:

```
lowest = -40; highest = 100; delta = 10;
```

Generally speaking, such a placement of assignment statements is not recommended because it makes such programs look dense and cluttered and a little harder to read.

Also note that in listing 2.1, the variables are defined first and then the assignment statements are used to set their values. Definitions can occur anywhere an assignment statement occurs, although it is common to see definitions of variables grouped together in the beginning, while statements, such as assignment statements that reference them, occur later in the program. It is also possible to initialize a variable when defining the variable. For example, you can define the variable delta and initialize it by using the following statement:

```
int delta = 10;
```

You can then eliminate the statement on line 22 that sets the value of delta to 10.

The main program logic is in lines 32–38, which describe a while loop that performs the conversion of Centigrade values to their equivalent Fahrenheit values. The formula that is used to provide this conversion is the following:

$F = \frac{9}{5} C + 32$

C is the temperature in the Centigrade scale, and *F* is the temperature in Fahrenheit.

Dissection of Program Code TempConvCF

The following is a line-by-line dissection of the program in listing 2.1:

Lines 1–7: This is the main comment preceding the program code. Notice that it uses the /** */ form of the comment so that it can be reported in the document analysis tool.

Lines 8–9, 42: This is the definition of the class. The name of the class is TempConvCF. Therefore, the file name that contains this class should be named TempConvCF.java. The body of the class is placed between the braces { } on lines 9 and 42.

Lines 10–11,40: These lines contain the definition of the only method in this class. This program is being developed as a Java application and not an applet. As such it must contain the definition of function `main()`. As explained during the discussion of the HelloWorld program earlier in the chapter, the function main must be qualified with reserved words public, static, and void.

Lines 12–17: These contain the variable definitions. The variable lowest and highest define the low and high values of the centigrade values that will be converted. The variable delta is the increment in temperature that is used for generating the centigrade values between lowest and highest. A type of int is used to describe these variables because an int is a 32-bit signed number and has a value ranging from –2147483648 to 2147483647. This is big enough for the values we have in mind and is in fact an overkill for this example. Later on you will learn about other Java data basic types that are smaller in size and that would be adequate for this example. These variables fahrT and cenT are floating point variables that represent Fahrenheit and Centigrade values.

Lines 19–22: These lines are the assignment statements, and are used to set the value of the variables *lowest, highest,* and *delta.*

Lines 24 and 25: These are used to print out the title of the Centigrade and Fahrenheit columns. Notice the use of the \t character in the string that is displayed. This generates a tab character. When you use the \ character, you are escaping the character value that follows. This means that the character value that follows must be treated specially. In the case of \t, the letter 't' that follows the backslash (\) indicates that the character should be treated as a tab. Similarly, \n means the line feed character, \f means the form feed character, and so on.

Lines 27–31: The statement on line 31 is used to initialize the centT variable to the lowest variable. Although the lowest is of type int, and centT is of type float, an automatic conversion is done of the int value to a float value when this assignment is performed. A float value is much larger than an int value so it can easily accommodate any type of int value that may be assigned to a float variable.

Lines 32, 33, 36, 38: The while loop repeatedly executes the body of statements within its opening ({) and closing braces (}) until the condition specified in the while statement evaluates to false. In this example it means that the statements between lines 32–38 will be repeatedly executed as long as the centT variable is less or equal to highest. When the centT variable has a value that is greater than the highest variable, control will be transferred to the statement after line 38. It is important that if you want the program to exist, the while test condition centT <= highest must evaluate to false. This is done by ensuring that centT is incremented by a positive value delta on line 36 within the body of the while loop.

Line 34: This assignment statement performs the computation that converts Centigrade value to the Fahrenheit value. Notice the use of the (float) immediately preceding the expression on the right-hand side of the assignment statement. This syntax denotes that the compiler must perform a type conversion. The result of an arithmetic expression involving floating point value is always a double. A double is a floating point value that has a larger precision than a float type. The compiler will generate an error message if you assign a double floating point value to a variable defined as a float type because this could result in a loss of precision if the double floating point value is very large. So the use of the (float) before the arithmetic expression tells the compiler that it is safe to perform the conversion to a float value. If the double value is indeed very large, a loss of precision will occur, and you will get a truncated value assigned to the float variable.

Line 35: This line prints out the Centigrade and the equivalent Fahrenheit values. The `System.out.println()` function expects a string argument. The expression centT+"\t\t"+fahrT is converted to a string. The "+" operator in this context represents string concatenation and not arithmetic addition. Therefore, the value of centT and fahrT are converted to string values by the compiler, and these are then concatenated with two tabs ("\t\t") in the middle to form a string value that is then passed to the `println()` method. Note that the "+" operator is overloaded, in the sense that depending on the context, it can mean arithmetic addition or string concatenation. Java, in general, does not permit operator overloading. This example is one of the few instances where there is built-in operator overloading defined.

Summary

In this chapter, you learned to write a simple Java program. You also learned to create a Java text file and use the javac compiler to compile the program.

You also learned how to write a more complex program that used local variables, assignment statements, a while loop, and print statements to display a table of Centigrade values and the equivalent Fahrenheit values.

The goal of using simple sample programs is to show you a quick overview of the basic elements of the language without overwhelming you with the details and the power of the Java language. Later chapters will cover more complex concepts.

CHAPTER 3

Experimenting with Java Data Types and Variables

In the previous chapter, you learned how to write a simple Java application. You were introduced to the concepts of types and variables, and you saw an example that used two of Java's basic types: the int and float types. This chapter will discuss in detail other basic types in the Java language, the types of arithmetic operations that can be performed, the type of data that can be represented, and how you can mix and match data types. In addition, you will learn to use one of Java's predefined Math class methods. At the end of this chapter, you will be able to write Java programs of increased complexity.

Overview of Java Data Types

Data types are used to represent the format and structure of data. Most programs end up performing some operation on data that is represented in the program by data types. In general, you can think of a data type as a description or template of how the data is to be represented when the program is running. Typically, this data is stored in the computer's memory when the program executes, and not on secondary storage, such as a hard disk or a file on the network.

It is important to remember that Java data types are templates for data. The actual data is referenced by using variable identifiers in the language. Consider, for example, the following variable definition:

```
int  delta;
```

The int is the data type and the delta is a variable of type int. The int is the template that is used by the Java compiler to allocate space in memory for a variable called delta (see fig. 3.1). The number of bytes and the range of values represented by the data type int is controlled by the attributes of that data type. In the Java language, int describes a 4-byte signed integer, and therefore the variable delta is allocated 4 bytes of memory, and it can have a signed value ranging from –2**32 to 2**32; that is, from –2147483648 to 2147483647. In figure 3.1, the fact that int is a template is denoted by a dotted line box representing the data type, and the actual space is allocated only when the variable delta is defined. This is indicated by a solid line box.

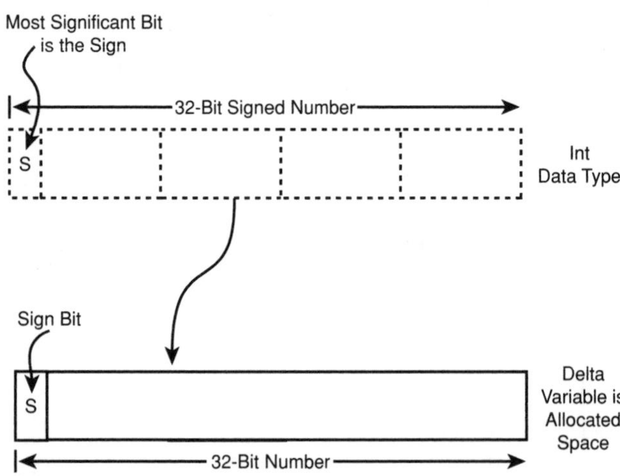

Figure 3.1
Data type template and variable.

Java's built-in data types can be defined in terms of four categories (see fig. 3.2). These categories are listed as follows:

- integer
- floating point
- character
- Boolean

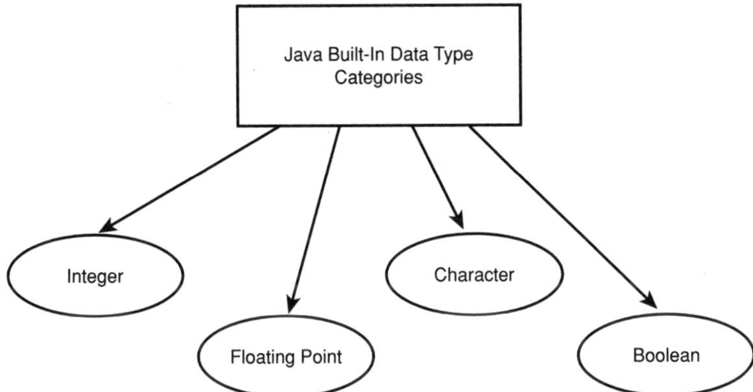

Figure 3.2

Java built-in data type categories.

The integer and floating point categories consist of further subcategories that describe the actual Java data types that are used in the language.

The built-in data types described here are not objects. Objects are encapsulating data, such as the data types discussed in this chapter (see fig. 3.3). Each of these objects are typically encapsulated by one or more methods that act on the encapsulated data. Figure 3.3 also shows a comparison between objects and Java data types. The example shown is that of the Integer object and the Java data type int. The object Integer is the name of a class that is predefined in the Java language. This Integer object is defined by using the class syntax, and it defines methods that operate on the data representation of the integer. If, for example, you create an instance of the object Integer, you can call the methods such as `parseInt()` to convert a string representation of the integer to the Java int data type. Because `parseInt()` is a static method, you could invoke its methods by using the class name Integer. The following code fragment shows an example of how the static method `parseInt()` can be used to convert the string "314159" to an int data type:

```
int  ivalue;
ivalue = Integer.parseInt("314159");
```

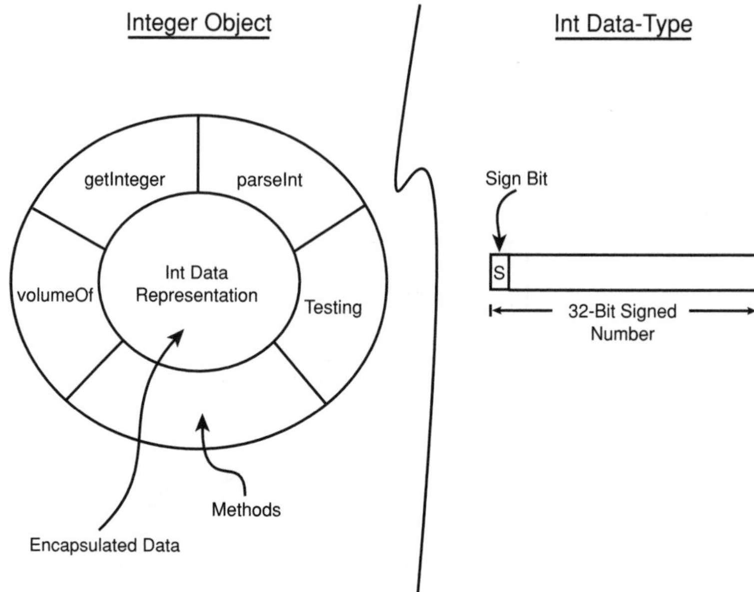

Figure 3.3
Objects and Java data types.

Variable Names and Identifiers

A variable's name is described by an identifier such as delta, in the example in the previous section. Identifiers are names for language entities such as variables, classes, and so on. An identifier in Java can be a sequence of unicode characters of *any* length. For practical reasons, you may not want to abuse this lack of limitation in the length of an identifier. Defining a variable, for example, whose name is 500 characters will not only make the program difficult to create, but also create significant difficulties for anyone who is trying to understand and modify the program.

Some limitations exist on the characters that you can use to create the identifier. A Java identifier must begin with a letter, followed by any combination of letters and digits. A letter is set consisting of letters a–z, A–Z, the underscore (_), and dollar ($) characters. If the unicode characters defining the scripts of other languages are used, then the letter acquires a broader meaning and can include glyphs from scripts such as Russian, Devanagari, Gurumukhi, Korean, Chinese, Farsi, Japanese, and so on.

Java Reserved Words

Although identifiers can be any combination of letters, some combination of letters are reserved, and are therefore called *reserved words* or *keywords*. The words int, float, and class, for example, that you encountered earlier are used in the Java language to define the data types of integer, floating point, and the class construct respectively. These reserved words cannot be used for programmer defined names, such as names for variables and objects.

Table 3.1 defines a list of reserved words in the Java language. A number of additional words appear to be language keywords, but actually are literal values. These are the following words:

```
null  false  true
```

The word null is used as a value for an object variable that has not been instantiated (or defined). The words false and true are values for a boolean data variable. Because these literals are similar to constants such as 314, 7.12, 'c' and so on, they are not included in table 3.1. Even though these literal words are not formally defined as the language reserved words, you cannot use them as programmer defined names.

TABLE 3.1
Reserved Words in Java

abstract	double	int	super
Boolean	else	interface	switch
break	extends	long	synchronized
byte	final	native	this
case	finally	new	throw
catch	float	package	throws
char	for	private	transient
class	goto	protected	try
const	if	public	void
continue	implements	return	volatile
default	import	short	while
do	instanceof	static	

Examining the Java Language Built-In Data Types

As mentioned in the previous section, Java has four categories of built-in data types. Built-in data types are also called Java *primitive data types* or *basic data types.* This section will discuss the built-in Java data types in greater detail.

Examining the Integer Data Type

The integer data type consists of four data types of different sizes and ranges (see fig. 3.4). All integer data types are signed integers and are expressed by using two's complement notation. This means that if the number of bits that make up the integer are *n*, the most significant bit is used for the sign bit and the remaining *n*–1 bits are used to represent the value (see fig. 3.5). Therefore, the minimum negative value of such a number is –2**(*n*–1), and the maximum positive value is 2**(*n*–1) –1.

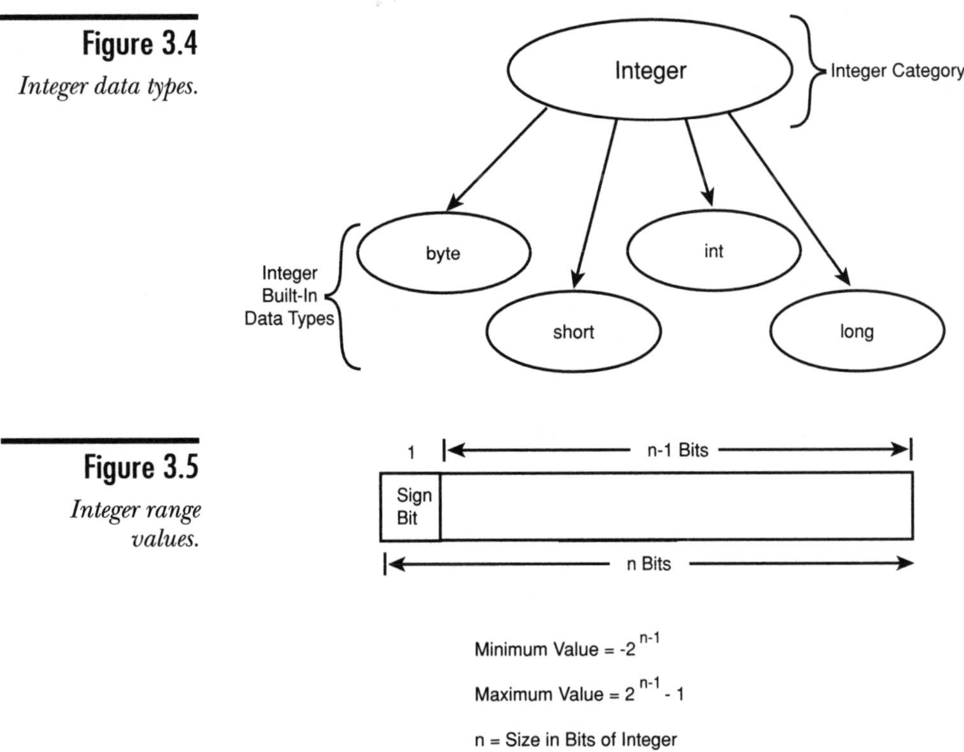

Figure 3.4 *Integer data types.*

Figure 3.5 *Integer range values.*

Table 3.2 shows the different integer data types, their bit size, and their range of values.

TABLE 3.2
Integer Data Types

Integer Type	Bits Width	Range
byte	8	–128 to 127
short	16	–32768 to 32767
int	32	–2147483648 to 2147483647
long	64	–9223372036854775808 to 9223372036854775807

The reason for defining so many different integer data types is to give the programmer flexibility in dealing with integer values of varying ranges and memory requirements. For very small integer values within the range of –128 to 127, for example, a byte representation would be adequate. Integers that are smaller in bit size also take up less space. The memory savings may be small if you are using just a few integer types. But if you are defining an array of, say 1000 integers, then the choice of which integer type to use can have an impact on the amount of memory allocated for the integer array.

Note Integer types are always signed in Java. If you are used to a language like C/C++, there are no unsigned qualifiers. You must use table 3.2 to decide if the integer data type can adequately represent the range of numbers.

Table 3.3 shows a comparison of the amount of space used for integer arrays of 1000 elements. If you blindly use a type of int, as many programmers do out of habit, when an integer type of byte is adequate, you will allocate 4000 bytes instead of 1000 bytes.

TABLE 3.3
Comparison of Space Used for an Integer Array of 1000 Elements

Integer Type	Amount of Space Used (Bytes)
byte	1000
short	2000
int	4000
long	8000

When arithmetic operations are performed, values that are of type byte or short are evaluated internally as int before the arithmetic operation is performed. If a literal of type int is assigned to a byte or short value, and the value is within the range of the data type that is being assigned to, the integer literal is treated as a byte or short, respectively.

Integer literals, the values that are used to express the range of values for an integer, are written as a sequence of decimal, octal, or hexadecimal digits. The following integer literals, for example, have the same value:

```
42   051     0x2A     0X2a
```

The first number, 42, is a decimal integer literal—it is based on the decimal number system. Integer literals that are preceded with a leading 0 (zero) are in octal number notation, and use a base of 8. Lastly, integer values that are preceded with a 0x or 0X are in hexadecimal notation, and use a base of 16. In the hexadecimal notation the digits corresponding to the decimal value of 10, 11, 12, 13, 14, 15 are written as A, B, C, D, E, F. You can also use lowercase letters.

Integer literals are assumed to be of type int, unless they end in the letter L or l (el). Therefore, the examples of the literals mentioned earlier are all type int. Because the letter l (el) can be easily confused with the digit 1 (one), it is best to use the L notation for long literals.

Consider some examples of defining integer variables that are in the IntEval.java file on the CD-ROM. This program is reproduced in listing 3.1.

Listing 3.1

```
Line=================Java Source=================
/**
 * IntEval: Test program to examine
 * syntax errors for integer evaluation.
 *
 * Author: Karanjit S.G.S. Siyan
 */
class IntEval
{
    public static void main(String args[])
    {
        // Example 1
        int        a;
        short      b,c,d;
```

```
14          int          e,f = 2314;
15          byte         g = -45, h;
16
17          // Assigning to an int
18          a = g * f;
19
20          // Assigning to a short
21          b = g * f;
22
23          // Example 2
24
25          long    i, j;
26          int     k = 10000000000, el = 3;
27
28          // Assign to an int
29          a = k * 4L;
30
31          // Assign to a long
32          i = k * 4L;
33
34
35      } // end main
36
37 } // end IntEval
```

Consider the following definitions in listing 3.1 (lines 12–15):

```
    int                          a;
    short                        b,c,d;
    int                          e,f = 2314;
    byte                         g = -45, h;
```

The first definition defines an int variable, a, with no initial value. The second example defines variables b, c, d of type short. No initial values are set for the short variables. The third example defines int variables e and f and initializes the value of f to 2314. Notice that this value is within the range of the int value. The fourth example defines byte variables g and h, and initializes variable g to –45. Notice that –45 is a literal of type int, but the assignment to a byte is permissible because it is in the range of value for the byte type.

Now, consider the following assignment statement in listing 3.1 (line 18):

```
a = g * f;
```

The variable g is of type byte with an initial value of –45. The compiler converts this internally to an int and multiplies it with the value of the int value 2314 in variable f. The result is an int of value –104130 that is within the range for an int data type.

Consider the next assignment statement in listing 3.1 (line 21):

```
b = g * f;
```

As before, the g * f expression will evaluate to an int of value –104130. This value, however, is being assigned to a short data type, and it is outside the range of the short data type. This statement will therefore produce an error message on compilation.

Next, consider the definitions on lines 25 and 26:

```
long    i, j;
        int     k = 10000000000, el = 3;
```

Line 25 defines long variables i and j, and line 26 defines int variables k and el initialized to 10000000000 and 3. Now consider the following assignment statement on line 29:

```
a = k * 4L;
```

The constant 4L causes the entire right-hand side expression to evaluate to long. The left-hand side of the assignment is an int, which is smaller in size than a long; therefore, the compiler produces an error message.

Consider the same expression (k * 4L) assigned to variable i which is of type long on line 32:

```
i = k * 4L;
```

The above assignment statement as the right-hand side and left-hand side of the assignments are both of type long.

Figure 3.6 shows the result of compiling IntEval.java with JavaC.

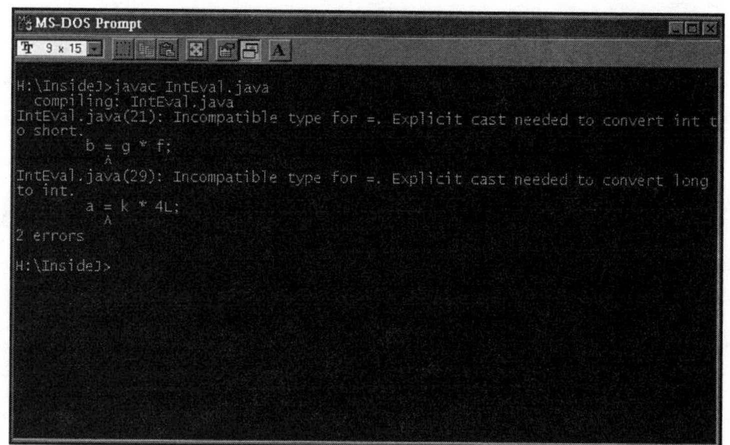

Figure 3.6
Compiling IntEval.java with JavaC.

Notice that the two error messages that are produced are on lines 21 and 29:

```
IntEval.java(21): Incompatible type for =. Explicit cast needed to convert int
to short.
        b = g * f;
          ^
IntEval.java(29): Incompatible type for =. Explicit cast needed to convert long
to int.
        a = k * 4L;
          ^
2 errors
```

Besides the standard division, multiplication, addition, and subtraction operations that can be performed on integers, a number of other operations exist. These operators apply to all the integer data types such as byte, short, int, and long. These are explained next.

The increment (++) and decrement operators (– –) are unary operators and apply to single integer values. The ++ operator increases the value of its operand by one, and the – – operator decreases the value by one.

When the ++ operator is placed after the operand, it increments the operand *after* its value has been used. When the ++ operator is placed *before* the operand, it increments the operand before using its value. When the ++ operator is placed after the operand, it is called *postfix* increment, and when it is placed before the operand it is called *prefix* increment.

Similarly, when the -- operator is placed after the operand, it decrements the operand *after* its value has been used. When the -- operator is placed *before* the operand, it decrements the operand before using its value. When the -- operator is placed after the operand, it is called *postfix* decrement, and when it is placed before the operand it is called *prefix* decrement.

Consider the following example:

```
int  ival1 = 10;
int  ival2 = 20;
int  ival3;
ival3 = ival1++;        // Postfix increment
ival3 = ++ival1;        // Prefix increment
ival3 = ival2--;        // Postfix decrement
ival3 = --ival2;        // Prefix decrement
```

After evaluating the first assignment statement, the value of ival3 is 10 and the value of ivall is 11.

After the second assignment statement, the value of ival3 and ivall are both 12.

After evaluating the third assignment statement, the value of ival3 is 20 and the value of ival2 is 19.

After the fourth assignment statement, the value of ival3 and ival2 are both 18.

The complement operator (~) is also an unary operator and performs a bitwise complement of the bits in the integer value. It converts each 1-bit into a 0-bit, and each 0-bit to a 1-bit.

Consider the following example:

```
byte bval1 = 5;
byte bval2;
bval2 = ~ bval1;
```

The bit representation of the byte value 3 is the following:

00000101

The assignment statement performs a complement of each of the bits. This results in the following value:

11111010

Remember, that integers are signed numbers in Java. Therefore, this number is in two's complement notation, and evaluates to the value of –6.

Note For an *n* bit number in two's complement, whose individual bits are b*n*, b*n*–*1*, ...b2, b1 with b*n* as the most significant bit, the value is represented by the following:

–b*n** 2**(*n*–1) + b*n*–*1** 2**(*n*–2) + ... + b2 * 2 + b1

Other bitwise operators for integers are the *bitwise OR* (|) , *bitwise AND* (&), *bitwise XOR* (^). These operators operate on the corresponding bits on each of its operands.

The OR operator produces a 1, unless each of its bit operands is a 0, in which case the result is a 0. The AND operator produces a 0, unless each of its bit operands is a 1, in which case the result is a 1. The XOR operator produces a 0, if each of its operands has the same value; otherwise, it produces a 1.

Consider the following example:

```
byte bval1 = 6;
byte bval2 = 14;
byte bval3;
bval3 = bval1 | bval2;
bval3 = bval1 & bval2;
bval3 = bval1 ^ bval2;
```

The bit representation of the value in bval1 and bval2 are the following:

```
bval1 =         00000101
bval2 =         00001110
```

The value of bval3 in the first assignment statement that uses the bitwise OR (|) can be calculated as shown:

```
bval1 =         00000101
bval2 =         00001110
--------------------------------------
bval3 =         00001111        = 15 decimal
```

The value of bval3 in the second assignment statement that uses the bitwise AND(&) can be calculated as shown:

```
bval1 =       00000101
bval2 =       00001110
-----------------------------------
bval3 =       00000100         = 4 decimal
```

The value of bval3 in the third assignment statement that uses the bitwise XOR(^) can be calculated as shown:

```
bval1 =       00000101
bval2 =       00001110
-----------------------------------
bval3 =       00001011         = 11 decimal
```

There are a number of shift operators for integers. These are the *left shift* (<<), *right sign shift* (>>), and *right zero fill shift* (>>>) operators. These operators have the following general syntax:

operand op bitsToShift

Here *op* is one of the <<, >>, >>> operators.

Consider the following example:

```
byte bval1 = -6;
byte bval2;
byte bval3;
bval2 = bval1 << 2;
bval3 = bval2 >> 2;
bval3 = bval2 >>> 2;
```

The bit representation of bval1, which has a value of –6, in two's complement notations is the following:

11111010

The first assignment statement shifts this value of bval1 by 2 bits. The resulting value assigned to bval2, is therefore –24:

11101000

Notice, that each left shift by 1 bit is equivalent to multiplying the original value by 2.

In the second assignment statement, the value of bval2 is shifted to the right by 2. Bit positions in the high order bit are filled with the sign bit, which in this case is 1. So shifting the value of bval2 (11101000) by 2 bits gives the following:

11111010

This value is –6. Notice, that each signed right shift by 1 bit is equivalent to dividing the original value by 2.

Now consider the last assignment statement where the value of bval2 is shifted to the right by 2, but bit positions in the high order bit are filled with zeros. So shifting the value of bval2 (11101000) by 2 bits gives the following:

00111010

This value of bval3 is 58.

Another operator for integers is the modulus (%) operator. The modulus operator gives the remainder of a division operation. The following is the general syntax for using the modulus operand:

operand1 % operand2

operand1 is divided by *operand2*. The result is the remainder of the division.

Consider the following examples:

```
int  ival1 = 33;
int  ival2 = 5;
int  ival3;
ival3 = ival1 % 4;
ival3 = ival1 % ival2;
```

In the first assignment statement ival3 evaluates to the remainder of 1, and in the second assignment statement ival3 evaluates to the remainder of 3.

Examining the Floating Point Data Type

The floating point data type consists of two data types of different sizes and ranges (see fig. 3.7). The floating point data type float is 32-bits wide long, and the floating point data type double, as the name suggests has twice as many bits—64 bits. All floating point data types are represented by the IEEE (Institute of Electronic and Electrical Engineers) floating point standard—the IEEE 754–1975 standard.

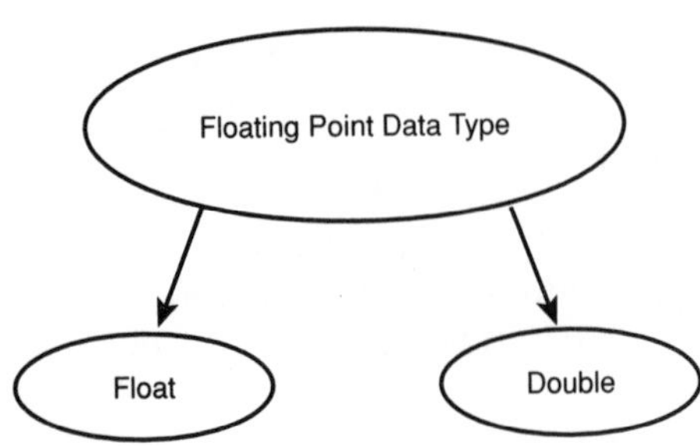

Figure 3.7
Floating point data types.

The reason for defining two floating point data types is to give the programmer flexibility in dealing with floating point values of varying ranges and memory requirements. Floating point numbers are used to represent fractional numbers. They can be used to represent the set of real numbers with a varying degree of precision. Figure 3.8 shows the set of real numbers on a real number line. Because of the finite size of the floating point size representation, the floating point number cannot model all points on the real number line. The actual points that are represented accurately are shown as notches on the real number line. The set of numbers that can be represented accurately are crowded around zero (0) on the real number line. As you go further away from the zero point on the real number line, the numbers that can be represented accurately are further spread apart.

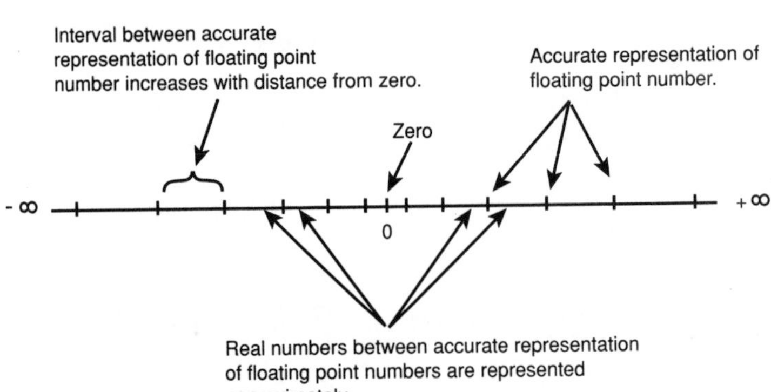

Figure 3.8
The real number line.

The difference between a number of float type and a double type is that the double type number has twice as many bits, and therefore twice as much precision. If the float and double numbers were represented on the real number line, the numbers with double will have more numbers that can be represented accurately (see fig. 3.9). The smallest non-zero and maximum floating point representations for float and double values are the following:

Float MIN_VALUE = 1.4013e–045

MAX_VALUE = 3.40282e+038

Double MIN_VALUE = 2.22507e–308

MAX_VALUE = 1.79769e+308

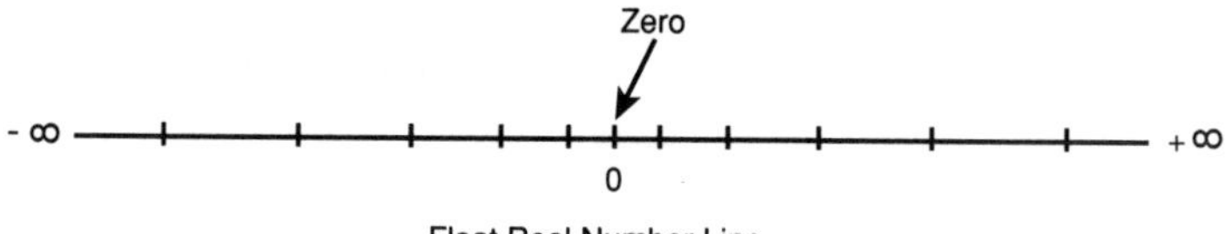

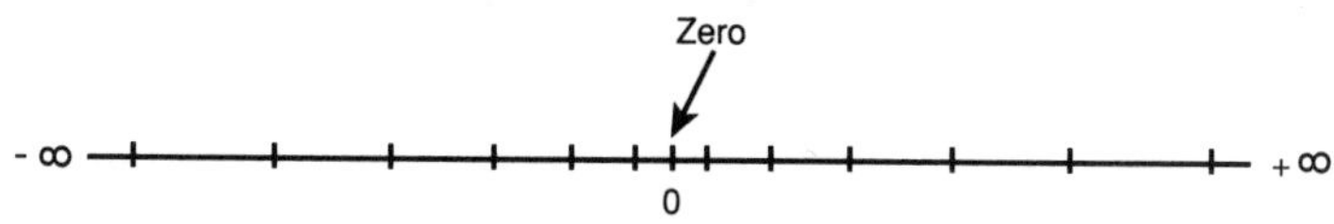

Figure 3.9
Float and double number types on the real number line.

What if the result of a floating point number calculation results in a number that is not accurately represented? Conceptually, such a number would fall between two numbers that can be represented accurately. In this case, the math routines used by the Java language will round to the nearest accurate number. As you can see, for a large number of complex calculations, such errors can lead to some uncertainty in the accuracy of results. The use of a larger precision such as double can help in reducing this uncertainty.

Floating point literals are written as a sequence of decimal digits with an optional decimal point, optionally followed by an exponent. The exponent values are to the base 10, and are written as the letter e or E, followed by the exponent value. The exponent notation is also called the scientific notation for representing floating point numbers. Here are some examples of floating point numbers:

333. 3.33e2 33.3E1 .333e3 0.333E3

These numbers denote the same floating point value of 333.0. Floating point numbers such as those just described are automatically of type double, unless they have a trailing f or F. Similarly, a trailing d or D can be explicitly used to specify a double floating point literal. The following are examples of the number 333.0 as float literals:

333.f 3.33e2F 33.3E1f .333e3f 0.333E3F

A zero value in floating point representation can be a positive 0.0 or a negative –0.0. The actual sign often depends on the sign of the overall expression that may evaluate to zero. In terms of numerical values, a positive zero or a negative zero are equal, but they can produce slightly different results in computations. Division by zero for floating point numbers, for example, is defined as Inf (infinity). Division by positive zero or negative zero will produce different results. For example, 1d/0d is +Inf, whereas 1d/–0d is –Inf.

Arithmetic operations involving a double floating point number will produce a double result. A double floating point number cannot be assigned to a float variable, even if the double value is within the precision of a float variable. The double result can be explicitly converted to a floating point by using a cast before it can be assigned to a float.

Java defines another representation of a floating point number to describe those cases where the floating point number is not a number. The symbol NaN means "not a number." The NaN value can be produced as a result of calculations that result in meaningless values. An example of this is if you divide Inf by Inf, which produces a NaN result. Any comparison involving NaN will yield a false value, except for the not equal operator (!=) comparison, which will always yield a true value.

On the CD 

Consider some examples of defining floating point variables that are in the FloatEval.java file on the CD-ROM. This program is reproduced in listing 3.2.

Listing 3.2

```
Line=================Java Source=================
/**
 * FloatEval: Test program to examine
 * syntax errors for floating point
 * evaluation.
 *
 * Author: Karanjit S.G.S. Siyan
 */
class FloatEval
{
    public static void main(String args[])
    {
            float   f1 = 12.0;
            float   f2 = 24f;
            float   f3;
            float   f4;
            float   f5;
```

```
        float   f6;
        float   f7;

        // Example 1
        f3 = f1/f2;
        System.out.println("f3 = "+f3);

        // Example 2
        f1 = 0D;
        f4 = f3/f1;
        System.out.println("f4 = "+f4);

        // Example 3
        f5 = 2.0 * f3;
        System.out.println("f5 = "+f5);

        // Example 4
        f6 = 1/0f;
        f6 = f6/f4;
        System.out.println("f6 = "+f6);

        double d1 = 1;
        double d2 = 3.0f;

        // Example 5
        f6 = d1;

        // Example 6
        d1 = d1/d2;
        System.out.println("d1 = "+d1);

        // Example 7
        f1 = f3/d2;
        System.out.println("f1 = "+f1);


    } // end main

} // end FloatEval
```

Lines 12–18 define floating point variables. Lines 12 and 13 additionally assign an initial value to the floating point variable. The definition of variable f1 on line 12 in listing 3.2 will produce a compiler error message. Can you tell why?

```
float f1 = 12.0;
```

The reason for the error is that the number 12.0 is treated as a double type, and you cannot assign a double to a float. The definition and initialization of float variable f2 is correct because the initialization value has been explicitly defined as a float number:

```
float f2 = 24f;
```

Next, examine lines 20–22 in Example 1 in listing 3.2. Line 21 performs a division of two float variables. The result is a float number and can be assigned to a float variable. From the given initial values of f1 and f2, the value of f3 should be 0.5.

```
// Example 1
f3 = f1/f2;
System.out.println("f3 = "+f3);
```

Next, examine lines 24–27 in Example 2 in listing 3.2. Line 25 performs an assignment of a double zero to a float variable. This will produce a compiler error message because even though the value zero can be assigned to a float variable, in this case, it is double zero, and a double cannot be assigned to a float. The division on line 26 will produce a result that is Inf.

```
// Example 2
f1 = 0D;
f4 = f3/f1;
System.out.println("f4 = "+f4);
```

Next, examine lines 29–31 in Example 3 in listing 3.2. Line 30 performs an arithmetic multiplication and an assignment to a float variable. At first sight this may appear to be correct, but on closer examination you will notice that 2.0 is a double. When a double is involved in an arithmetic expression, the result is a double, and this cannot be assigned to a float variable.

```
// Example 3
f5 = 2.0 * f3;
System.out.println("f5 = "+f5);
```

Next, examine lines 33–36 in Example 4 in listing 3.2. Line 34 performs an arithmetic division by a float 0. The result is the value Inf and is assigned to f6. In line 35, f6 is divided by f4, whose value is also Inf (see Example 2). The result of the division is a NaN value, and this is assigned to f6.

```
// Example 4
f6 = 1/0f;
f6 = f6/f4;
System.out.println("f6 = "+f6);
```

Next, examine lines 41–42 in Example 5 in listing 3.2. Line 42 assigns a double variable to a float variable. This will produce a compiler error, even though the double value is in the range of the float variable.

```
// Example 5
f6 = d1;
```

Next, examine lines 44–46 in Example 6 in listing 3.2. Line 45 assigns the result of a division of two double variables to a double variable. This statement is correct, and will produce a value of 0.333333.

```
// Example 6
d1 = d1/d2;
System.out.println("d1 = "+d1);
```

Next, examine lines 48–50 in Example 7 in listing 3.2. Line 49 divides a float variable with a double variable. The result is a double, and cannot be assigned to a float variable. The compiler therefore produces an error message.

```
// Example 7
f1 = f3/d2;
System.out.println("f1 = "+f1);
```

Notice that there are five compiler error messages that are produced, and this is consistent with the previous discussion. These error messages are listed here for your reference.

```
floateval.java(12): Incompatible type for declaration. Explicit cast needed to
convert double to float.
          float   f1 = 12.0;
                       ^
floateval.java(25): Incompatible type for =. Explicit cast needed to convert
double to float.
          f1 = 0D;
             ^
floateval.java(30): Incompatible type for =. Explicit cast needed to convert
double to float.
```

```
            f5 = 2.0 * f3;
                 ^
floateval.java(42): Incompatible type for =. Explicit cast needed to convert
double to float.
            f6 = d1;
                 ^
floateval.java(49): Incompatible type for =. Explicit cast needed to convert
double to float.
            f1 = f3/d2;
                 ^
5 errors
```

To eliminate the errors in listing 3.2, you must explicitly define the floating point numbers as float or double, or make use of the cast operator to perform the conversion. To cast an expression from *type1* to *type2*, use the following syntax:

(type2) type1_expr

Listing 3.3 shows the corrected version of FloatEval.java. The source code for this listing is in file FloatEval2.java on the CD-ROM at the back of this book. Compare this listing with that in listing 3.2 to see the corrections that have been made.

Listing 3.3

```
Line==================Java Source==================
/**
 * FloatEval2: Test program that contains the
 * corrected syntax errors of FloatEval.java.
 *
 * Author: Karanjit S.G.S. Siyan
 */
class FloatEval2
{
      public static void main(String args[])
      {
            float   f1 = 12.0f;
            float   f2 = 24f;
            float   f3;
            float   f4;
            float   f5;
            float   f6;
```

```
        float   f7;

        // Example 1
        f3 = f1/f2;
        System.out.println("f3 = "+f3);

        // Example 2
        f1 = 0F;
        f4 = f3/f1;
        System.out.println("f4 = "+f4);

        // Example 3
        f5 = 2.0f * f3;
        System.out.println("f5 = "+f5);

        // Example 4
        f6 = 1/0f;
        f6 = f6/f4;
        System.out.println("f6 = "+f6);

        double d1 = 1;
        double d2 = 3.0f;

        // Example 5
        f6 = (float) d1;

        // Example 6
        d1 = d1/d2;
        System.out.println("d1 = "+d1);

        // Example 7
        f1 = (float) (f3/d2);
        System.out.println("f1 = "+f1);


    } // end main

} // end FloatEval2
```

Figure 3.10 shows the results of executing the corrected FloatEval2 program in a command prompt window.

Figure 3.10

Output of FloatEval2 program.

Notice that the output of this program is consistent with the previous discussion. In particular, note that the Inf value is reported as a number followed by INF, and the NaN value is reported as a number followed by IND.

As expected, all the standard arithmetic operators such as *, +, / work with floating point numbers, in addition to the modulus (%) operator. The shift operators (<<, >>, >>>) and the bitwise operators (|, &, ^, ~) do not work on floating point numbers. You can always convert floating point numbers to integer value and perform the operation on the integer value in case you need to perform these operations on floating point numbers.

Examining the Character Data Type and String Literals

Java makes a distinction between a character type and a sequence of characters represented as a string literal. The character type holds a single character value. Character values are unicode values that use 16 bits to represent a character. Internally, the compiler treats the 16-bit unicode character as a 16-bit unsigned number. This enables the Java language to handle the symbols used for non-English languages and leads to internationalization of the language.

A character type is represented by using the reserved word `char`. The following is an example of character variable definitions.

```
char m;
char n, p, q;
char r = 'a';
```

The previous statements define character variables. In the last definition of character variable r, an initial value of `'a'` is also assigned. Character literals are enclosed in single quotes, such as the example of `'a'`. A character variable can be assigned literal values, using statements such as the following:

```
m = 'I';
n = 'T';
p = 'h';
q = 'I';
```

What if you wanted to assign a character such as the linefeed or carriage return to a character variable. These characters are not visible in a text editor, and attempting to type these characters causes the text editor to insert a new line. To solve this problem, *escape sequences* can be used to represent non-visible character values in a program.

Table 3.4 shows the common escape code sequences used in Java. The numbers in parentheses represent the unicode values for the escape codes.

TABLE 3.4
Escape Code Sequences for Character Literals

Escape Code	Description
\n	newline (\u000A)
\r	carriage return (\u000D)
\t	tab (\u0009)
\b	backspace (\u0008)
\f	form feed (\u000C)
\\	backslash (\u005C)
\'	single quote(\u0027)
\"	double quote(\u0022)
\ddd	octal code for character, with each d as an octal digit
\u*dddd*	A unicode character, with each digit as a hexadecimal digit

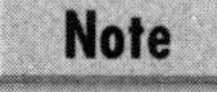

If you are a C/C++ programmer, note that Java does not define escape codes for vertical tab (\v) and the bell (\a) character.

String literals are represented as a sequence of characters in double quotes. All the escape codes that can be used for characters can be used in strings. The following are examples of string literals:

"blue"

"violet"

"Om!"

"Where I stand there is Morya!\nAnd in"

"I am embedding a tab \t here."

"Java\u2122"

Note that if you want to embed a non-visible character such as a linefeed or a tab in a string, you must use its escape code. Notice that the unicode character \u2122 in the last example evaluates to the trademark symbol. If your display type does not support the display of a unicode character, the corresponding symbol will not be displayed. You must, therefore, configure your operating system and display driver software for the appropriate unicode set to display the unicode characters.

Java does not have a basic data type for strings; however, a String class is defined in the language. The String class is used to define String objects. An advantage of defining the string type as a class is that the language predefines a set of useful methods to perform operations on strings at a high level. You have, for example, already seen the example of the string concatenation operator "+" used as the argument to the `System.out.println()` method in listings 3.2 and 3.3.

When string literals are used in a Java program, the compiler automatically constructs a String object, whose value is set to the string literal. This behavior is unusual because for all other classes, one must explicitly construct the object of the class type.

Examining the Boolean Data Type

A Boolean data type can hold only two values—true and false. This data type is used to model states of behavior, such as an on or off value for a switch. The keyword Boolean is used to describe this data type. The following are examples of Boolean variables definitions:

```
boolean        cond1
boolean    switch, state;
boolean    endOfList = false;
```

A Boolean variable is set by assigning the literal values true or false. For example:

```
switch = true;
state = false;
```

You cannot perform arithmetic operations on Boolean data types, but you can perform logical operations on Boolean data values. Consider the following example:

```
boolean    bval1 = true;
boolean    bval2 = false;
boolean    bval3;
int            x = 3;
int            y = 9;
bval3 = bval1 && bval2;
bval3 = bval1 || bval2;
bval3 = !bval3;
```

The symbols &&, ||, ! stand for *logical and, logical or,* and *logical not,* respectively. If you are not familiar with these Boolean operators, tables 3.5–3.7 will explain the behavior of these Boolean operators. In these tables, the last column represents the result of applying the operator on the preceding columns. By using these tables, you can verify that the value of bval3 in the first assignment statement is false; the value of bval3 in the second assignment statement is true; and the value of bval3 in the last assignment statement is false.

TABLE 3.5
Boolean And (&&) Operator

Operand1	Operand2	Result
false	false	false
false	true	false
true	false	false
true	true	true

Table 3.6
Boolean Or (||) Operator

Operand1	Operand2	Result
false	false	false
false	true	true
true	false	true
true	true	true

Table 3.7
Boolean Not (!) Operator

Operand	Result
false	true
true	false

Boolean values can also result from the evaluation of a relational operator. In Java, the relational operators are equals to (==), *less than* (<), *greater than* (>), *less than or equal to* (<=), *greater than or equal to* (>=), and *not equal to* (!=).

Using the examples of Boolean variables defined previously, consider the following statements:

```
bval1 = x == y;
bval1 = x < y;
bval1 = x > y;
bval1 = x != y;
bval1 = x*3 == y;
```

The first assignment statement is comparing x with y to see if they are equal. Clearly, they are not, because x is 3 and y is 9. Therefore, bval1 is set to the value of false. Similarly, the values of bval1 in the second, third, and fourth assignment statements are true, false, and true respectively. In the last assignment statement, the arithmetic expression x*3 is compared with y. Because these expressions each evaluate to 9, they are equal, and bval1 is set to true.

When a Boolean expression is evaluated, the expression is evaluated only until its value can be determined. Any remaining part of the expression that does not contribute to the evaluation of the expression is ignored. This type of evaluation is called the short-circuit evaluation and can result in an efficient evaluation of the code.

Consider the following example:

```
int             x1 = 10;
int             x2 = 20;
int             x3 = 30;
boolean       b1, b2;
b1 = x1 > 9 || x2 < 25;
b2 = x2 < 10 && x3 > 10;
b3 = x2 < 25 && x3 > 10;
```

In the first assignment statement, the expression x1 > 9 evaluates to true. Because the Boolean OR is used, regardless of the value the second expression x2 < 25 evaluates to, the result will be true. Therefore, the second expression is not evaluated, and b1 is set to true.

In the second assignment statement, the expression x2 < 10 evaluates to false. Because the Boolean AND is used, regardless of the value the second expression x3 > 10 evaluates to, the result will be false. Therefore, the second expression is not evaluated, and b2 is set to false.

In the third assignment statement, the expression x2 < 25 evaluates to true. Because the Boolean AND is used, you cannot at this point determine the overall value of the expression. In fact, the overall value will depend on the second expression x3 > 10, which must be evaluated. This evaluates to a true, therefore, b2 is set to true.

Notice that in the first and second assignment statements, the short circuit evaluation method could be used by discarding the evaluation of the remaining expression. In the third assignment statement, however, the complete expression had to be evaluated.

Listing 3.4 shows a Java program that illustrates the behavior of Boolean expressions.

Listing 3.4

```
Line=================Java Source=================
/**
 * BoolEval: Test program showing how boolean
 * expressions are evaluated.
 *
 * Author: Karanjit S. G. S. Siyan
```

continues

Listing 3.4, Continued

```
*
*/
class BoolEval
{

    public static void main(String args[])
    {

          boolean b1;
          boolean b2;
          boolean b3;

          short  x1 = 100;
          short  x2 = 200;
          short  x3 = 300;

          // Example 1
          b1 = x1*2 == x2;
          System.out.println("b1 = "+b1);

          // Example 2
          b2 = x1+x2 != 3*x1;
          System.out.println("b2 = "+b2);


          // Example 3
          b3 = (x3 - 2*x2 < 0) || ((x3 = 400) < 2*x2);
           System.out.println("b3 = "+b3+"\t x3 ="+x3);


          // Example 4
          b3 = (x3 - 2*x2 > 0) || ((x3 = 400) < 2*x2);
          System.out.println("b3 = "+b3+"\t x3 ="+x3);

          double   d1 = 0D;
          double   d2, d3, d4;
          boolean      b4, b5;

```

```
44              // Example 5
45              d2 = 2.0/d1;
46              d3 = 3.0/d1;
47              System.out.println("d2 = "+d2+"\t d3 ="+d3);
48              b4 = (d2 == d3);
49              System.out.println("b4 = "+b4);
50
51              // Example 6
52              d4 = d2/d3;
53              b5 = d4 != 100000000.0;
54              System.out.println("d4 = "+d4+"\t b5 ="+b5);
55
56
57       }  // end main
58
59
60  }  // end BoolEval
```

Consider the Example 1 on lines 22–24 in listing 3.4. In line 23 the expression x1*2 evaluates to 200, and x2 has a value of 200. Because the test is one of inequality, b1 evaluates to true.

```
// Example 1
b1 = x1*2 == x2;
System.out.println("b1 = "+b1);
```

Consider the Example 2 on lines 26–28 in listing 3.4. In line 27 the expression x1+x2 evaluates to 300, and 3*x1 evaluates to 300. Because the test is one of inequality, b2 evaluates to false.

```
// Example 2
b2 = x1+x2 != 3*x1;
System.out.println("b2 = "+b2);
```

Consider the Example 3 on lines 31–33 in listing 3.4. In line 32 the expression (x3–2*x2 < 0) is evaluated first. Because x3 –2*x2 is –100, this expression evaluates to true. This is where the short-circuit behavior of Boolean expression evaluation is seen. The overall expression is going to be true, regardless of the value of the second expression (x3 = 400) < 2*x2. Therefore, the second expression is not evaluated, and the overall expression is true. Another interesting item to note in the second expression is the use of the assignment operator (=) in x3 = 400. x3 is assigned a value of 400, and this is compared to 2*x2. Because the second expression evaluation is skipped, the value of x3 is never set to 400 as it may first appear on examining the expression.

```
// Example 3
b3 = (x3 - 2*x2 < 0) || ((x3 = 400) < 2*x2);
System.out.println("b3 = "+b3+"\t x3 ="+x3);
```

Consider the Example 4 on lines 36–38 in listing 3.4. In line 37 the expression (x3 –2*x2 > 0) is evaluated first. Because x3 –2*x2 is –100, this expression evaluates to false. The overall expression will now be determined by the value of the second expression (x3 = 400) < 2*x2. Therefore, the second expression is evaluated. Because of the assignment operator in x3 = 400, x3 is assigned a value of 400, and this is compared to see if it is less than 2*x2. 2*x2 evaluates to 400 also, and, therefore, the overall expression and b3 evaluates to false.

```
// Example 4
b3 = (x3 -2*x2 > 0) || ((x3 = 400) < 2*x2);
System.out.println("b3 = "+b3+"\t x3 ="+x3);
```

When comparing Examples 3 and 4, notice that in one case the second expression is skipped, and, in the other case, it is evaluated. Evaluation of the second expression has the side-effect of changing the value of x3.

Consider Example 5 on lines 40–49 in listing 3.4. The double variables d2 and d3 are set to an expression that involves division by zero, and they are therefore both set to Inf. A comparison check of equality (==) on the two Inf values will show that the result is true.

```
double   d1 = 0D;
double   d2, d3, d4;
boolean       b4, b5;

// Example 5
d2 = 2.0/d1;
d3 = 3.0/d1;
System.out.println("d2 = "+d2+"\t d3 ="+d3);
b4 = (d2 == d3);
System.out.println("b4 = "+b4);
```

Consider Example 6 on lines 51–54 in listing 3.4. The double variable d4 involves division of two double numbers whose value is Inf. Therefore, d4 is set to a NaN (Not a Number) value. When a NaN != *anynumber* is evaluated, it always returns true. Therefore, the value of b5 should be set to true.

```
// Example 6
d4 = d2/d3;
b5 = d4 != 100000000.0;
System.out.println("d4 = "+d4+"\t b5 ="+b5);
```

You can load the program BoolEval.java, which can be found in the CD-ROM at the back of this book, and compile and run it. Figures 3.11 and 3.12 show the results of compilation and execution with javac. The output values of this program have been discussed in the previous paragraphs.

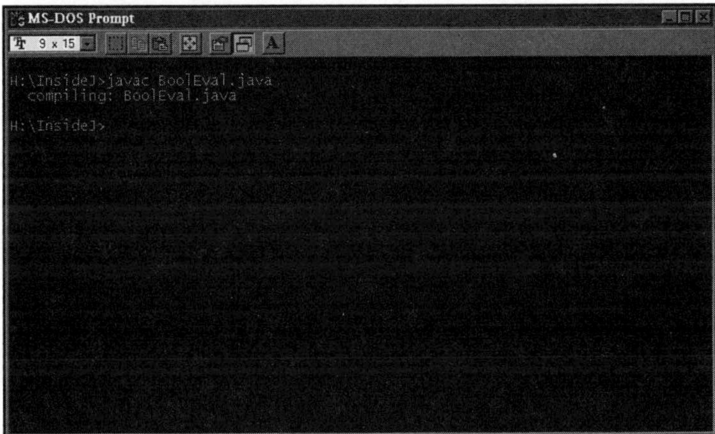

Figure 3.11

Compiling BoolEval with javac.

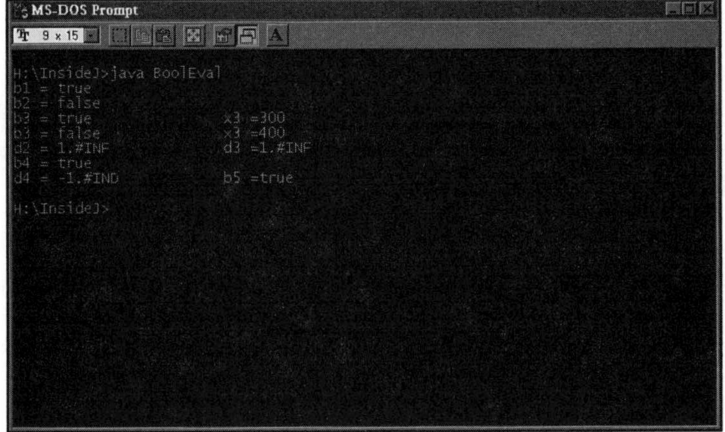

Figure 3.12

Output of the BoolEval program.

Understanding Expression Evaluation

In the examples that have been discussed in this chapter you saw several examples of arithmetic and Boolean expressions. The Java language defines the order in which operators must be evaluated in case of expressions consisting of several operators. In the expression x * y + z, for example, should you multiply x with y first and then add z; or should you add y and z first, and then multiply the result by x? Most of you would select the first order of evaluation because these are the rules of algebra. The Java language contains rules on which operators must be evaluated. These rules are described by *operator precedence.*

Understanding Operator Precedence

Table 3.8 shows the operator precedence order. The operators that are described at the top of the table earlier have a higher precedence than those at the bottom. Operators at the same entry in the table have the same precedence. The general evaluation order for operators in an expression that has the same precedence is from left to right, with the exception of the assignment operator that evaluates from right to left. Operators that evaluate from left to right are called *left associative,* and operators that evaluate from right to left are called *right associative.* As an example of the left associative rule consider the following expression:

```
x + y + z + 1
```

The Java compiler will evaluate this expression starting with the leftmost "+" operator and then the next one on the left, and so on. Therefore, the previous expression is equivalent to the following:

```
((x + y) + z) + 1
```

In the example of BoolEval program in listing 3.4, you noticed that an assignment statement in Java can be treated as an expression. The following is an example of the use of several assignment operators in an expression:

```
x = y = z = 1;
```

The meaning of this assignment statement is that 1 is assigned to z, then z is assigned to y, and finally y is assigned to x. The value of the expression is the value of x.

If the left associative rule is used to evaluate this expression, the expression would have to be evaluated as the following:

```
((x = y) = z) = 1;
```

The problem with the previous expression is how should y be assigned to x, when the value of y is not known, as yet? Therefore, for assignment statements it makes sense that the order of evaluation of the assignment operator (=) should be with the rightmost. That is, the previous assignment statement should be evaluated as the following:

```
x = (y = (z = 1));
```

TABLE 3.8
Operator Precedence

Level	Operator Type	Operator
1	Parenthesis	()
2	Postfix operators	[] . (*params*) *expr*++ *expr*--
3	Prefix unary operators	+*expr* -*expr* ~*expr* !*expr* ++*expr* --*expr*
4	Creation or cast	new (*type*) *expr*
5	Multiplicative	* / %
6	Additive	+ -
7	Shift	<< >> >>>
8	Relational	< > >= <= instanceof
9	Equality	== !=
10	Bitwise AND	&
11	Bitwise XOR	^
12	Bitwise OR	|
13	Logical AND	&&
14	Logical OR	||
15	Conditional	?:
16	Assignment	= += -= *= /= %= >>= <<= <<<= &= ^= |=

The conditional operator ?: evaluates an expression based upon the value of a Boolean expression. This is a ternary operator, as it involves three operands whose general syntax is as follows:

BooleanExpr ? *TrueExpr* : *FalseExpr*

If the *BooleanExpr* evaluates to true, *TrueExpr* will be evaluated, and it will become the value of the overall expression. If the *BooleanExpr* evaluates to false, *FalseExpr* will be evaluated, and it will become the value of the overall expression.

Here is an example of the use of the conditional operator:

```
long   a;
long   b;
long   max, min;

max = (a > b) ? a : b;
min = (a > b) ? b : a;
```

In the first assignment statement, if a > b the value of the expression is a; otherwise it is b. Notice that the conditional operator is used here to find the maximum value of two numbers. Similarly, in the second assignment statement, if a > b the value of the expression is b; otherwise it is a. In this case, the conditional operator is used to find the minimum value of two numbers.

Mixing Data Types in Expressions

From the examples that have been presented in the book so far, you saw numerous instances of when different types of data types could be combined in an expression. Table 3.9 gives a more complete definition of what happens when different data types are combined in an arithmetic expression.

Table 3.9
Result of Mixing Data Types in Expressions

Operands	byte	short	int	long	char	float	double
byte	int	int	int	long	int	float	double
short	int	int	int	long	int	float	double
int	int	int	int	long	int	float	double

Operands	byte	short	int	long	char	float	double
long	long	long	long	long	long	float	double
char	int	int	int	long	int	float	double
float	float	float	float	float	float	float	double
double	double	double	double	double	double	double	double

Performing Math Calculations

In many languages, mathematical calculations involving trigonometric and other mathematical functions are carried out by library routines that are either defined in the language or have to be written separately. In Java, all the standard mathematical functions are static methods in the Math class. So these can be called directly by using a suitable syntax for calling a static method of a class.

The Math class is in the package java.lang. You will learn more about packages in later chapters, but for now a brief introduction to packages will be helpful. A *package* is a collection of Java classes. You have learned about Java classes in Chapter 2, "Getting Started with Java." They are essentially the syntax used in Java to describe the type of an object that consists of data and methods that operate upon the data. When you write large Java programs, you can define your own classes and put them inside packages for ease of managing classes that perform similar or related functions. Java comes with its own predefined classes that are defined in packages. These packages have standard names. One of these packages is the java.lang package. Normally, to use a package in your Java program, you have to use the import statement, as shown in the following example:

```
import java.lang.*;
class ImportExample
{
      // Contents of the class ImportExample
      //
      ...
} // end ImportExample
```

The use of the import statement with an asterisk (*) following the package name makes all classes defined in the package java.lang available for use in the class ImportExample. If you wanted to just access a specific class, such as the Math class, you would use the following import statement:

```
import      java.lang.Math;
```

By default, the Java compiler automatically includes the import java.lang.* statement, if one has not been explicitly provided by you. Therefore, the following definition of the ImportExample class is equivalent to the previous one because the java.lang package is *implicitly* imported.

```
class ImportExample
{
      // Contents of the class ImportExample
      //
      ...

} // end ImportExample
```

You can, therefore, access the method `abs()` in the Math package by using the following syntax:

```
int  x = -3;
int  y;
y = Math.abs(x);
```

Table 3.10 lists the static methods that are available in the Math class. You can use the javadoc to generate Java API documentation for all the standard Java methods and objects. Figure 3.13 shows an example of the page for the `rint()` function.

To create the Java API documentation for the Math class:

1. Open a command prompt window.
2. If you have not already done so, unzip the src.zip file located in the /java/src directory. This file contains all the source code for the standard java classes.
3. Change to the directory in which you unzipped the java source files.
4. Change to the /src/java/lang directory.
5. Type **javadoc java.lang.math**.
6. You can now load the java.lang.math.html file into your favorite HTML viewer.

Table 3.10
Methods in the java.lang.Math Class

Method Name	Argument Types	Result Type	Description
abs	int a	int	Absolute function
abs	long a	long	Absolute function
abs	float a	float	Absolute function
abs	double a	double	Absolute function
acos	double a	double	Arc cosine function
asin	double a	double	Arc sine function
atan	double a	double	Arc tangent function
atan2	double a, double b	double	Arc tangent of a/b
ceil	double a	double	Ceiling function
cos	double a	double	Cosine
exp	double a	double	Exponent using the Napierian constant *e*
floor	double a	double	Floor function
log	double a	double	Natural log function
max	int a, b	int	Maximum of a and b

continues

Table 3.10, Continued
Methods in the java.lang.Math Class

Method Name	Argument Types	Result Type	Description
max	long a, b	long	Maximum of a and b
max	float a, b	float	Maximum of a and b
max	double a, b	double	Maximum of a and b
min	int a, b	int	Maximum of a and b
min	long a, b	long	Minimum of a and b
min	float a, b	float	Minimum of a and b
min	double a, b	double	Minimum of a and b
pow	double a, double b	double	a to the power of b function
random	None	double	Random function
rint	double a	double	Rint function. (Returns closest double value to that is equal to a mathematical integer)
round	double a	double	Rounding function

Method Name	Argument Types	Result Type	Description
sin	double a	double	Sine function
sqrt	double a	double	Square root function
tan	double a	double	Tangent function

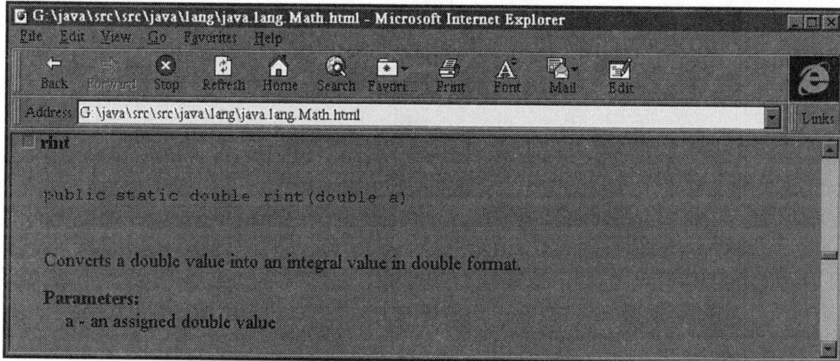

Figure 3.13

Viewing the Java.Lang.Math. rint() function.

As an example of how the Math class can be used, examine listing 3.5. This listing generates the dimensions of two of the sides of a right-angled triangle (see fig. 3.14) randomly using the `Math.random()` function listed in table 3.10. The sides of the triangle vsize and hsize in figure 3.14 are generated randomly. The `random()` function returns a value between 0 and 1. In the program listing, this value is scaled by a factor of 10, so that the maximum vertical and horizontal sides will be 10 units long.

The formulas for computing the dimensions of the triangle are also listed in figure 3.14. If you are familiar with a little trigonometry and geometry, you can readily verify these formulas. If not, don't worry—it will not detract from your understanding of the Java language.

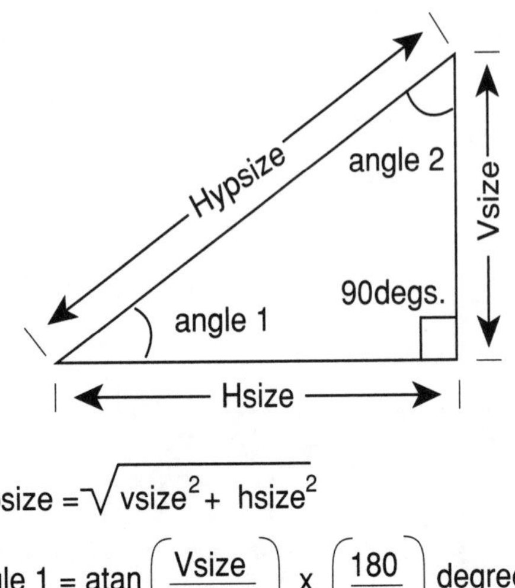

Figure 3.14
Random triangle generated by program MathEval.

$$hypsize = \sqrt{vsize^2 + hsize^2}$$

$$angle\ 1 = atan\left(\frac{Vsize}{Hsize}\right) \times \left(\frac{180}{\pi}\right) degrees$$

$$angle\ 2 = 180 - angle\ 1$$

$$area = \frac{1}{2} vsize * hsize$$

Listing 3.5

```
Line=================Java Source=================

/**
 * MathEval: Test program showinghow math
 * expressions are evaluated.
 *
 * Author: Karanjit S. G. S. Siyan
 *
 */
class MathEval
{

  public static void main(String args[])
  {
        double  vsize;  // Vertical side
        double  hsize;  // Horizontal side
        double  hypsize; // Hypotenuse of traingle
```

```

        double  angle1; // Angle 1
        double  angle2; // Angle 2
        double  area;   // Triangle area

        // Generate the triangle sides randomly
        vsize = 10.0 * Math.random();
        hsize = 10.0 * Math.random();

        // Compute the hypotenuse side
        hypsize = Math.sqrt(vsize*vsize + hsize*hsize);

        // Compute the angle
        angle1 = Math.atan2(vsize, hsize);

        // Now convert the radians into
        // degrees.
        angle1 = (180.0/Math.PI)*angle1;
        angle2 = 180.0 - angle1;

        // Compute the area of the triangle
        area = 0.5*vsize*hsize;

        // Now generate the report on the triangle.
        System.out.println("Dimensions of randomly generated triangle are:");
        System.out.println("\tVertical side = "+vsize);
        System.out.println("\tHorizontal side = "+hsize);
        System.out.println("\tHypotenuse = "+hypsize);
        System.out.println("\tAngle near horizontal side = "+angle1+" degs");
        System.out.println("\tAngle near vertical side = "+angle2+" degs");
        System.out.println("\tArea of triangle = "+area+" square units");

    } // end main

} // end MathEval
```

Figure 3.15 shows the results of executing the MathEval program. Depending on how the `random()` function is implemented, the results may be different each time you run it because of the random nature of the `random()` function.

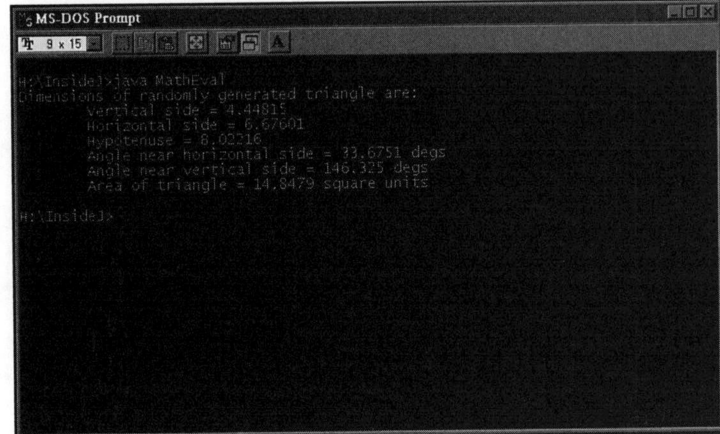

Figure 3.15
Output of the MathEval function.

Summary

In this chapter you were introduced to the concepts of types and variables, and you saw examples of how to use Java's basic types such as byte, short, int, float, double, char, Boolean, and string literals. You learned about the range of legal values that are permissible for each of the data types and how they are represented internally. You also learned about the operations that can be performed on the basic types. Several arithmetic operations that can be performed on integers such as shifts, bitwise operations, modulus, and so on, were discussed.

You learned about the unicode representation of characters in Java that enables it to support non-English languages. You were presented with examples of how you can mix and match data types and the type of the result that is generated. Many examples of the use of data types, and variables were presented.

CHAPTER 4

Java Flow Control

In the previous chapter, you learned about the different Java basic data types. You may have noticed that in all the examples in the previous chapters, only the assignment statement was discussed. Furthermore, in these examples, the statements were executed sequentially one after another. Programs that are used to model real-life systems are seldom that simple. You are often required to execute statements depending on a test condition.

Java provides many statements to affect the flow of logic within a program, so that depending upon a Boolean condition that is evaluated, a different part of the program is executed. In this chapter you learn to control the sequence of statements that are executed in a program. These statements are generically referred to as *control flow statements* and include statements such as the if-statement, while-statement, do-while statement, switch statement, and so on.

Understanding Types of Statements

For the sake of a better understanding, the different Java statements can be grouped into the following categories (see fig. 4.1):

- Assignment statement
- Expression statement
- Block statement
- Control flow statement

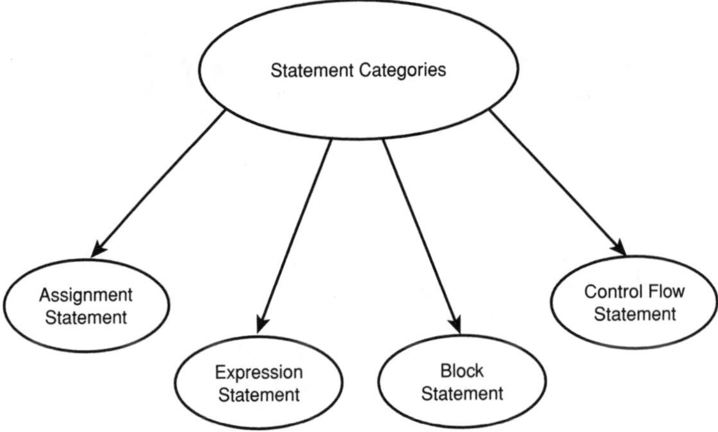

Figure 4.1
Categories of assignment statements.

Assignment Statement

You have seen mostly examples of assignment statements in previous chapters. Assignment statements have the following general syntax:

```
L-value = expression { = expression };
```

The *L-value* is any program item to which a value can be assigned. The most common examples of this are variables such as those discussed in Chapter 3, "Experimenting with Java Data Types and Variables." The *expression* could be an arithmetic expression or a Boolean expression consisting of Boolean operators and relational operators (< > == != <= >=). The value of *expression* is assigned to the *L-value.* The type of the *expression* must be consistent with the type of the *L-value.* You, for example, cannot assign a Boolean expression to an int type variable. Among integers and floating point types, you can perform an assignment with the general rule that the precision and range of the *expression* should not exceed that of the *L-value.* Between integer and floating point data types, you can force a conversion by using a *type cast.* You can, for example, force a conversion from a double floating point expression to a long type, but it will result in a loss of precision. Consider the following example:

```
long            circumference;
double          PI = 3.1415926536;
double          radius = 33.0;
circumference = (long) 2.0 * PI * radius;
```

The use of the cast specifier (long) for the double floating point expression converts it into a long type, but any fractional part in the numeric value is lost.

The use of the braces { } in the syntax of the assignment statement indicates that the contents within braces can occur zero or more times. The { } characters serve as meta-characters to describe the syntax of the assignment statement and are not part of the assignment statement. This form of assignment statement is convenient because it can be used to set several variables to the same value, as seen in the following fairly common example where several variables need to be set to the same value:

```
short  x, y, z;

x = y = z =  0;
```

Another form of assignment statement combines an arithmetic operator, shift, or bitwise operator with the assignment operator. The general syntax of this assignment operator is the following:

```
L-value op= expression;
```

The *L-value* and *expression* have the same meaning as discussed before, and *op* is any of the following operators:

+ – * / % >> << <<< & ^ |

The above assignment statement is equivalent to the following:

L-value = (L-value) op (expression);

Notice the parentheses around the expressions. Therefore, the following statement

a *= b–c;

is actually the following:

a = a * (b–c);

rather than

a = a*b–c;

Essentially, this type of statement is a shortcut expression. Here are some examples of this statement:

```
int  x = 1;
int  y = 7;

x += 1;       // x is now 2
y -= 3;       // y is now 4
x <<= 1;      // x is now 4
y >>= 1;      // y is now 2
y *= x + 1;   // y is now 10
y /= x -2;    // y is now 5
y %= 3;       // y is now 2
y ^= 3;       // y is now 1

x &= 2;       // x is now 0
y |= 3;       // y is now 3
```

Assignment operators of the type just described can be quite intuitive to understand. When, for example, you want to increase x by 4, you do not say "take x add 4, and then assign it to x." Instead, it is more natural to say "add 4 to x." This is exactly what is meant by the expression x += 4.

Note The *L-value op= expression* expression preserves compatibility with C and C++. Originally, this existed in the C language as an aid for compilers to perform optimization. In the case of +=, for example, the compilers could generate code that would evaluate the right-hand side and add it to the *L-value*.

Expression Statement

An expression statement is any expression that is on a line by itself and ends with a semicolon. In truth, the assignment statement is also an expression statement because the following construct is an expression:

L-value = expression

Therefore, any of the following are expressions:

```
x = 0
y = 3
```

Notice, that these expressions do not end in a semicolon. If they did, they would become an expression statement—also called an assignment statement, in this case, because of the use of the assignment (=) operator.

An expression statement is the expression followed by a statement. Consider the following:

```
long z = 11;

++z;
```

This expression statement has the result of incrementing the value of z by 1. It is equivalent to each of the following expression statements:

```
z += 1;
z = z + 1;
z++;
```

Similarly, the decrement operator can be used as an expression operator. Thus, the following statements are all equivalent:

```
--z;
z--;
z -= 1;
z = z-1;
```

Each of these expressions results in a change in value. If, however, you write the following statement in Java, it will not result in any change in value:

```
x + 3;
```

Although this statement compiles correctly, it is a useless statement because it does not cause any change in the program logic. The reason for this is because there is no L-value in the statement.

Block Statement

A block statement is a grouping of statements within { } brackets. Examine the method `main()` from the previous chapters. It has the following general syntax:

```
public static void main(String args[])
{
   // statements
}
```

The block statement is shown in bold, and it consists of statements. These statements can be definitions of Java basic types, assignment, control flow, or even another block statement. A block statement can occur wherever a statement can occur in a Java program. A block statement is also called a *compound statement.*

Consider the program listing 4.1 of a sample `main()` program:

Listing 4.1

```
Line==================Java Source=================
/**
 * BlockStmt: First attempt to write a block
 * statement. This produces a syntax error.
 *
 * Author: Karanjit S. G. S. Siyan
 */

class BlockStmt
{

     public static void main(String args[])
     {
         int x = 1;
         int y = 5;


             // Start a compound block
             {
                 int z = 21;

                 ++x;

                 System.out.println("Inside block x = "+x);
                 System.out.println("Inside block y = "+y);
                 System.out.println("Inside block z = "+z);

```

```
27              } // end compound block
28
29              System.out.println("Outside block x = "+x);
30              System.out.println("Outside block y = "+y);
31              System.out.println("Outside block z = "+z);
32
33      } // end main
34
35 } // end BlockStmt
```

In listing 4.1, x and y on lines 13 and 14 are defined and initialized at the start of the `main()` method. The variables, such as x, y, and z have a scope. The *scope* is the region of a program over which the variable can be referenced by its name. The scope of a variable is the region of program text from its of definition to the end of the enclosing block. Therefore, the point of x is from lines 13–33, and the scope of y is from lines 14–33.

Lines 18–27 define a block statement. Within this block statement is a declaration for z on line 19. The scope of z is therefore from line 19 to the end of the enclosing block on line 27. The variable z cannot be referenced outside this block. An attempt to reference z outside the block on line 31 will produce a syntax error. You can verify this by compiling this program contained in file BlockStmt.java on the CD-ROM that accompanies this book. Figure 4.2 shows the javac compiler error message that says that variable z is not defined (because it is referenced outside its scope).

Figure 4.2

Compiler error for referencing a variable outside its scope.

To fix the compiler error in listing 4.1, you must define a variable z, such as that shown on line 29 in listing 4.2. Figure 4.3 shows that this second variation of the

BlockStmt program compiles without error, and figure 4.4 shows the result of executing this program.

Figure 4.4 shows that the value of x that is incremented on line 21 in listing 4.2 is reported correctly inside the block statement and outside the block statement. The value of y is unchanged from its initial value of 5. The value of z is reported differently inside the block and ouside the block. Inside the block the value of z is 21, and outside the block the value of z is 66. The two zs on lines 19 and 29 are different; they have different scopes and are allocated memory in distinct memory locations.

Listing 4.2

```
Line=================Java Source=================
01 /**
02  * BlockStmt2: Second attempt to write a block
03  * statement. This fixes the syntax error in BlockStmt.
04  *
05  * Author: Karanjit S. G. S. Siyan
06  */
07
08 class BlockStmt2
09 {
10
11      public static void main(String args[])
12      {
13           int x = 1;
14           int y = 5;
15
16
17           // Start a compound block
18           {
19                int z = 21;
20
21                ++x;
22
23                System.out.println("Inside block x = "+x);
24                System.out.println("Inside block y = "+y);
25                System.out.println("Inside block z = "+z);
26
27           }  // end compound block
28
```

```
        int z = 66;

        System.out.println("Outside block x = "+x);
        System.out.println("Outside block y = "+y);
        System.out.println("Outside block z = "+z);

    }  // end main

}  // end BlockStmt2
```

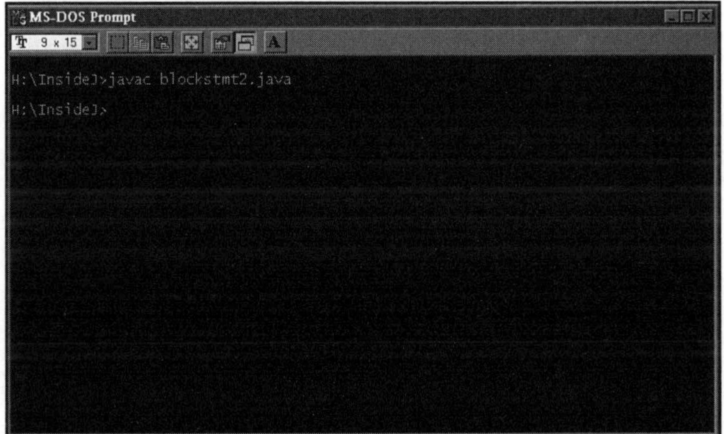

Figure 4.3

Successful compilation of BlockStmt2 program.

Figure 4.4

Output of theBlockStmt2 program.

The Control Flow Statements

The Java language defines several forms of control flow statements. These statements can be categorized as follows (see fig. 4.5):

- if statement
- switch statement
- while statement
- for statement
- do-while statement
- break statement
- continue statement
- return statement

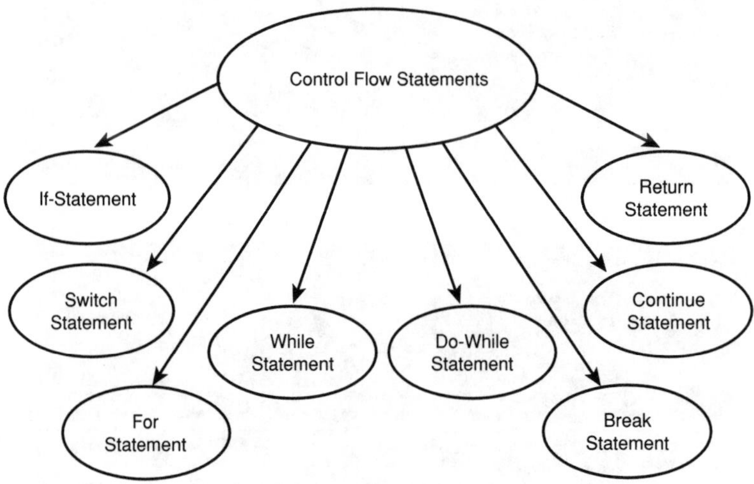

Figure 4.5
Java control flow statements.

These statements are discussed in the sections that follow.

The if Statement

The if statement is the most basic form of statement to execute statements based upon the evaluation of a conditional expression. In the if statement, a Boolean expression is evaluated. If the result of the Boolean expression is true, a certain group of statements is executed; if the result is false, another group of statements is executed.

The following example shows the general syntax of the if statement:

```
if (booleanExpression)

      statement-true

[else

      statement-false]
```

The *booleanExpression* is any of the Boolean expression types discussed in Chapter 3. The *statement-true* is any legal Java statement including the block statement, and it is executed if *booleanExpression* evaluates to true. Similarly, the *statement-false* is any legal Java statement including the block statement, and it is executed if *booleanExpression* evaluates to false. The *statement-true* is also called the *then-statement* and the *statement-false* is called the *else-statement.*

The brackets [ ] around the else part are meta-characters that indicate that the else part is optional. These meta-characters are not part of the syntax of the if statement. Figure 4.6 shows a logic flow diagram that shows the behavior of the if statement.

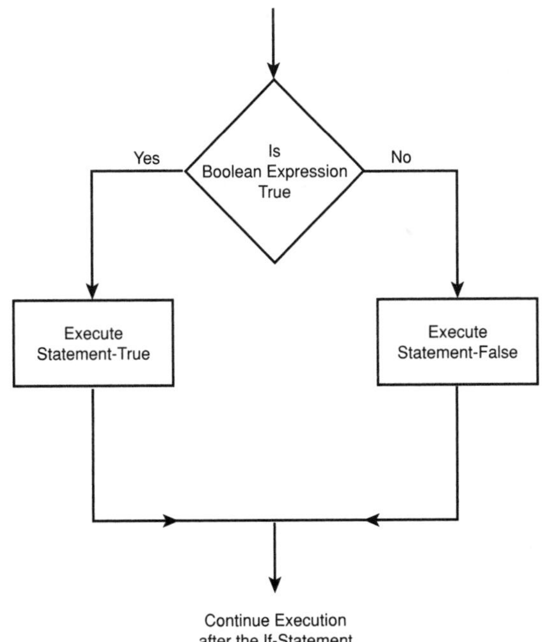

Figure 4.6

Logic flow diagram for if statements.

The following are examples of if statements:

```
int   x = 11;
int   y = 22;
int   z ;

// if1
if  (x > 0)
     z = 2;
```

In the preceding if statement, there is no else part. If the expression x > 0 evaluates to true, the statement `z = 2;` is executed.

Consider another example:

```
// if2
if (x <= y)
    z = 2;
else
    z = 111;
```

The preceding example has an else part with single statements that get executed depending on whether x <= y is true or false. Notice that you can use the conditional operator ?: to write this same logic in an alternate way. The preceding if statement, therefore, is equivalent to the following single assignment statement:

```
z = (x <= y) ? 2 : 11;
```

The next if statement uses a single block statement that is executed only if the expression y != 0 is true:

```
// if3
if (y != 0)
{
     y *= 10;
     x = 100-x;
}
```

Notice that the block statement must be used when you want to execute more than one statement in the if statement.

In the following example of an if statement, two block statements are used for each of the *statement-true* and *statement-false*.

```
// if4
if (y < 0)
{
    y = x-y;
    x = x + 20;
}
else
{
    x = x + y-20;
    y += 30;
}
```

In the following example, because there is only one statement in the *statement-true* part, a block statement is not used, but for the *statement-false* part, a block statement *is* used because it consists of more than one statement.

```
// if5
if (x-y > 3)
    y = -100;
else
{
    y = -300*x;
    x = -x;
}
```

The next example is similar to the preceding one. It has only one statement in the *statement-false* part, and so a block statement is not used. But in the *statement-true* part, a block statement is used because it consists of more than one statement.

```
// if6
if (x + y != 100)
{
    z = 100;
    x = z + y;
    y %= 3;
}
else
    z = -y;
```

As an issue of style, the author prefers to use compound blocks even if single statements are in the statement-true and statement-false. The reason for this is that there is less editing work to do in the code maintenance phase of the program if an additional statement needs to be added. Another reason is that such a convention makes the if statements look uniform, and this makes the program more readable. The use of compound blocks for single statements does not affect the code size in any way. The author, therefore, would prefer to code the example labeled "if2," as follows:

```
// if2
if (x <= y)
{
    z = 2;
}
else
{
    z = 111;
} // end if
```

Notice the use of the comment `// end if` on the closing brace (}) on the block statement aids in program readability as it tells you that this is the end of the if statement. This is particularly valuable in a program that has many nested statements and closing braces.

Suppose that if the Boolean expression in the if statement evaluates to false, you need to execute another if statement. You can code this type of if statement by using the else-if statement. Here is an example:

```
if (x == 10)
{
    --x;
}
else if (x == 20)
{
    ++x;
} // end if
```

In the preceding example, you want to execute different statements when the value of x is 10 or 20. In general, situations occur when you want to execute a multiway decision. The following is the general syntax of coding this multiway decision by using an if statement:

```
if  (booleanExpression1 )
      statement1
else if  (booleanExpression2 )
      statement2
else if  (booleanExpression3 )
      statement3
...
else if  (booleanExpressionN )
      statementN
[else
      statement-last]
```

The expressions *booleanExpression1*, *booleanExpression2*, and so on are evaluated in the order in which they occur in the if statement. If any of the Boolean expressions evaluates to true, the corresponding statement is executed, and then execution transfers to the end of the if statement and the remaining Boolean expressions and statements are not evaluated. The *statementN* can be any statement including the block statement.

The optional else part at the end of the multiway if is executed only if all other Boolean expressions evaluate to false. The else part, therefore, is used to handle the default code in *statement-last*, if no other conditions (Boolean expressions) are satisfied. If there is no default code, you can leave out the last else part.

Listing 4.3 shows a program that illustrates the use of the if statement to perform the following functions:

1. The program reads a character from the screen.
2. If the character that is read is a digit, a message `"A digit was entered"` is displayed.
3. If the character that is read is a *not* a digit, a message `"No valid digit was entered"` is displayed.

Listing 4.3

```
Line=================Java Source=================
/**
 * IfStmt: Illustrates the use of the if
 * statement.
 *
```

continues

Listing 4.3, Continued

```
 * Author: Karanjit S. G. S. Siyan
 */
import java.io.*;   // For exception handling
class IfStmt
{

   public static void main(String args[])
       throws IOException
   {
       boolean zeros = false;
       boolean ones  = false;
       boolean twos  = false;
       boolean threes = false;
       boolean fours = false;
       boolean fives = false;
       boolean sixes = false;
       boolean sevens = false;
       boolean eights = false;
       boolean nines  = false;

       char inpCh;

       System.out.println("Enter a digit:");
       inpCh = (char)System.in.read();

       if (inpCh == '0')
       {
           zeros = true;
       }
       else if (inpCh == '1')
       {
           ones = true;
       }
       else if (inpCh == '2')
       {
           twos = true;
       }
       else if (inpCh == '3')
```

```
        {
            threes = true;
        }
        else if (inpCh == '4')
        {
            fours = true;
        }
        else if (inpCh == '5')
        {
            fives = true;
        }
        else if (inpCh == '6')
        {
            sixes = true;
        }
        else if (inpCh == '7')
        {
            sevens = true;
        }
        else if (inpCh == '8')
        {
            eights = true;
        }
        else if (inpCh == '9')
        {
            nines = true;

        } // end if

        if (zeros  || ones  || twos  || threes ||
            fours  || fives  || sixes ||
            sevens || eights || nines )
        {
            System.out.println("A digit was entered");
        }
        else
        {
            System.out.println("No valid digit was entered");
```

continues

Listing 4.3, Continued

```
82          }  // end if
83
84     }  // end main
85
86 }  // end IfStmt
```

Lines 14–23 in listing 4.3 define a Boolean variable that is initally set to false. These Boolean variables are defined one for each digit, and are set to true, if the corresponding digit is entered.

Line 25 defines the character variable, `inpCh`, that holds the character that was entered. Line 27 displays a message prompting the user to enter a digit, and line 28 reads the digit by using the `System.in.read()` method. This method is similar to the `System.out.println()` method that has been used in many of the previous examples, except that it reads a byte value from the input stream. The `System.in.read()` method returns an int value, and this is converted to a character value by using the cast operation (char).

To support the `System.in.read()` method, notice the addition of the import statement in line 7:

```
import java.io.*;
```

This statement makes all the class definitions for package java.io available. In particular, it makes available the class IOException, which is needed in the invocation of the `System.in.read()` method. The call to this method can result in an error condition, which is handled in Java as an *exception.* An exception in Java signals an event, such as an error, or an abnormal condition. You can use the exception to transfer control to another point within the program that is better able to handle the error.

The specification of the `System.in.read()` method states that the exception IOException defined in the java.io package will be signalled or *raised,* and you must explicitly handle this. In this case, if an IO exception takes place in the reading of input, the exception IOException will be raised, and this will cause the termination of the program by causing the `main()` to throw the exception. Notice that in line 12, the clause throws IOException has been added to the `main()` declaration. This clause informs the Java compiler that it should not complain about an exception not being explicitly handled within the Java program, and it is the programmer's intention that the exception will be raised by the `main()` program and control be transferred to the caller of the `main()` program. This caller of the `main()` program in this case is the runtime environment that initiated the execution of the Java progam, and it will cause the termination of the Java program when it sees an exception. There are certainly more graceful ways to handle an exception, and you will learn about them in detail in Chapter 11, "Performing Java Input/Output."

Lines 30–70 contain the multiway if statement that sets the Boolean variable corresponding to the digit that was entered. Lines 72–82 contain the if statement that generates the display message, whether a digit or non-digit character was entered.

Figure 4.7 shows the ouput of this program by using javac when a digit or a non-digit is entered.

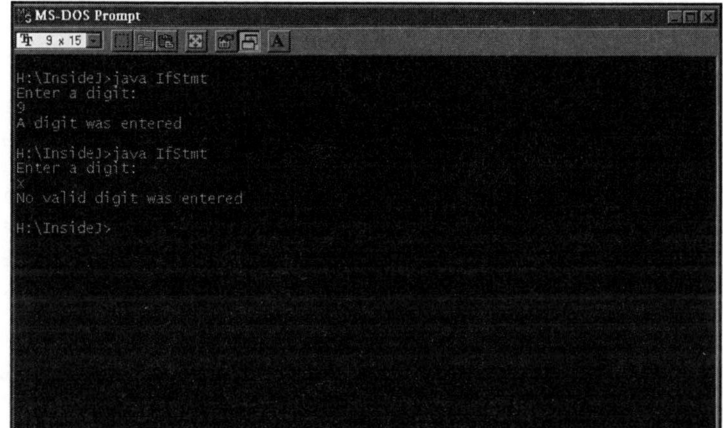

Figure 4.7

Output of IfStmt program.

The switch Statement

A switch statement is a special multiway decision statement. The switch statement evaluates an expression and executes a group of statements that are labeled by the expression value. The following example is the general form of a switch statement:

```
switch (expression)
      {
case const1:
      {statement;}

case const2:
      {statement;}

...

case constN:
      {statement;}
```

```
[default:
     {statement;}]
}
```

After *expression* is evaluated, it is checked to see if it matches any of the constant values *constN* on the case label. If the expression matches the constant case value, the group of statements listed under it as `{statement;}` are executed. The {} around statements are meant as meta-characters and indicate zero or more occurrences of a Java statement. These meta-characters should not be considered the characters for a block statement.

At the end of the execution of the last statement in the case statement group, execution continues on to the statements for the next case label, *unless* a break statement is encountered. When a break statement is encountered, execution of further statements in the switch statement is terminated, and the control is passed to the end of the switch statement. The break statement is used to exit to the end of the switch statement. Execution will *fall through* to the next case label, unless you have a break statement.

The default label and statements are optional. The statements under the default label are executed when the expression value does not match any of the case labels. It is good programming practice to always include the default label because it shows the reader of the program that you have considered all possible values of the expression. If there is no default action to perform, you do not have to enter any statements for the default label.

The case labels and default labels can occur in any order, but the case labels must all have different values.

The following is an example of a switch statement:

```
int  x;
int  y;
int  z;

// Statements initializing x, y, and z.

switch (x)
{
case 1:
   y++;
```

```
case 2:
   z++;
   break;

case 3:
   z -= x;
   break;

default:
   y = -9;
   break;

} // end switch
```

In this switch statement, if the value of x is –1, the following statements are executed:

```
y++;
z++;
```

Notice that the statement z++ is also executed because the execution *falls through* to the next case statement due to the absence of the break statement.

If the value of x is 2, the following statement is executed:

```
z++;
```

Notice that execution of further statements for values of x equal to 1 or 2 is terminated when the break statement is encountered.

If the value of x is set to 3, the following statement is executed:

```
z -= x;
```

For all other values of x that are not 1, 2, or 3, the following statement is executed:

```
y = -9;
```

Notice that there is a break statement after the last default statement in the switch, even though it is logically not necessary. This is done in case another case statement is added at the end of the default statement. The break statement prevents an inadvertent fall through to the next case statement.

Listing 4.4 shows a program listing of the same program in listing 4.3, but uses a switch statement for the multiway decision. Note that the multiway if statement has been replaced by a switch statement. You will find this program in the file SwitchStmt.java on the CD-ROM that accompanies this book.

Listing 4.4

```
Line=================Java Source=================
/**
 * SwitchStmt: Illustrates the use of the switch
 * statement.
 *
 * Author: Karanjit S. G. S. Siyan
 */
import java.io.*;   // For exception handling
class SwitchStmt
{

    public static void main(String args[])
        throws IOException
    {
        boolean zeros = false;
        boolean ones  = false;
        boolean twos  = false;
        boolean threes = false;
        boolean fours = false;
        boolean fives = false;
        boolean sixes = false;
        boolean sevens = false;
        boolean eights = false;
        boolean nines  = false;

        char inpCh;

        System.out.println("Enter a digit:");
        inpCh = (char)System.in.read();

        switch (inpCh)
        {
            case '0':
```

```
            zeros = true;
            break;

        case '1':
            ones = true;
            break;

        case '2':
            twos = true;
            break;

        case '3':
            threes = true;
            break;

        case '4':
            fours = true;
            break;

        case '5':
            fives = true;
            break;

        case '6':
            sixes = true;
            break;

        case '7':
            sevens = true;
            break;

        case '8':
            eights = true;
            break;

        case '9':
            nines = true;
            break;
```

continues

Listing 4.4, Continued

```

            default:
                break;

        } // end if

        if (zeros  || ones   || twos  || threes ||
            fours  || fives  || sixes ||
            sevens || eights || nines )
        {
            System.out.println("A digit was entered");
        }
        else
        {
            System.out.println("No valid digit was entered");

        } // end switch

    } // end main

} // end SwitchStmt
```

The output produced by this program is the same as that illustrated in figure 4.7.

The while Statement

The while statement is the basic statement that is used for creating a loop. Most programs need to perform some form of repeated action, and the while statement provides a nice solution for performing this repeated action.

The general syntax of the while statement is as follows:

```
while (booleanExpression)

      statement
```

The *booleanExpression* is evaluated at the beginning of each loop execution. If this expression evaluates to a true, the *statement* is executed. This *statement* is any Java statement including the block statement. At the end of the *statement* execution, control is transferred to the top of the loop where *booleanExpression* is evaluated again.

If the evaluation yields a true result, the *statement* is executed again. So as long as the *booleanExpression* evaluates to true, the *statement* is executed, and this implements a loop. The loop terminates only when *booleanExpression* evaluates to a false. When the loop terminates, control is transferred to the end of the while loop.

Figure 4.8 shows the logic diagram of a while statement.

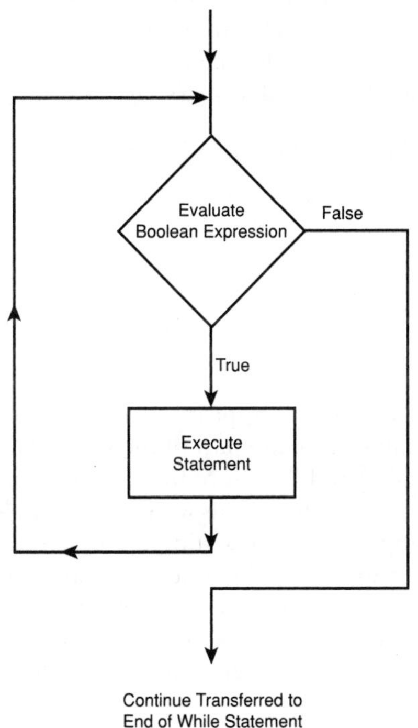

Figure 4.8

Logic flow diagram for a while statement.

Consider the following example of a while statement:

```
short    x = 0;
short    max = 40;
double   y = 100000000.0;
double   z = 2.0;

while (x++ < max)
{
      y = Math.sqrt(y);
      z = Math.exp((double)x);
```

```
        System.out.println("y = "+y);
        System.out.println("exp("+x+") = "+z);

} // end while
```

This while statement will execute until the expression x++ < max becomes false. This will happen when the value of x before the postfix increment is 40. Within the while loop, the value of x will range from 1 to 40. The loop will successively take the square root of a large number 100000000.0 and display the results. Additionally, the loop takes the exponent of values of variable x, and displays the results.

Consider another example of a while statement that is often useful:

```
while (true)
{
        // Statements

} // end while
```

At first sight, this type of while statement may appear strange because you are testing for the constant true in the Boolean expression part of the while statement. Clearly such a test will never evaluate to false, and therefore the loop will continue indefinitely. Actually, this is the precisely the point of this while statement—it sets up an indefinite loop. The indefinite loop is useful for setting up background processes and "server" processes that need to be running all the time. These processes could perform repeated polling action. An example of a server process would be a printer server process, running on a computer with several printers attached to the computer. This print server process would loop indefinitely listening for print requests from other computers.

There is actually even a better way of setting up an indefinite loop. You will learn more about this in the next section on for statements.

Listing 4.5 shows a program that uses a while statement to loop through a sequence of input characters and print a classification of the characters that were supplied on input, based on the following:

1. The number of total characters that were read from the input stream.
2. The number of digits.
3. The number of white space characters, such as blanks, newlines, and tabs.
4. The loop terminates on a non-digit or non-whitespace character. The character causing the loop termination is displayed.

Listing 4.5

```
Line=================Java Source=================
/**
 * WhileStmt: Illustrates the use of the while
 * statement.
 *
 * Author: Karanjit S. G. S. Siyan
 */
import java.io.*;   // For exception handling
class WhileStmt
{
   public static void main(String args[])
       throws IOException
   {
       int      nDigits;
       int      nWhiteSpaces;
       int      nTotal;
       boolean  endChar = false;
       char inpCh;
       char termCh = '\0';
       nDigits = nWhiteSpaces = nTotal = 0;
       System.out.println("To terminate enter non-digit or white space
➥character.");
       System.out.println("Enter a string of numbers or white spaces:");
       while (!endChar)
       {
           inpCh = (char)System.in.read();
           switch (inpCh)
           {
               case '0':
               case '1':
```

continues

Listing 4.5, Continued

```
                case '2':
                case '3':
                case '4':
                case '5':
                case '6':
                case '7':
                case '8':
                case '9':
                    nDigits++;
                    break;

                case ' ':
                case '\n':
                case '\t':
                    nWhiteSpaces++;
                    break;

                default:
                    endChar = true;
                    termCh = inpCh;
                    break;

            }  // end switch

            nTotal++;

        }  // end while

        System.out.println("\nReport on characters that were read");
        System.out.println("Total chars read = "+nTotal);
        System.out.println("Number of digits = "+nDigits);
        System.out.println("Number of white spaces = "+nWhiteSpaces);
        System.out.println("Terminating character = "+termCh);

    }  // end main

}  // end WhileStmt
```

The Boolean variable endChar is defined on line 18 and initialized to a value of false. This variable is checked in the while statement on line 28. The while statement exits when the endChar variable is set to true. On line 54, the endChar variable is set to true, when it encounters a non-digit or non-whitespace character, at which time the variable termCh is set to indicate the terminating character (see line 55). The switch statement is used to classify the input character. If it is a digit, the statement nDigits++ on line 44 keeps a tally of the number of digits encountered. If the input character is a whitespace (blank, tab, or newline), the statement nWhiteSpaces++ on line 50 keeps a tally of the whitespace characters.

On exiting the while statement, the statements on lines 64–68 print a report on the classification of the input characters. Figure 4.9 shows the output of executing the program in listing 4.5 by using the javac compiler. This program can be found on the CD-ROM that accompanies this book.

```
MS-DOS Prompt

H:\InsideJ>java WhileStmt
To terminate enter non-digit or white space character.
Enter a string of numbers or white spaces:
432534 435534 534 6546 576347 X

Report on characters that were read
Total chars read = 31
Number of digits = 25
Number of white spaces = 5
Terminating character = X

H:\InsideJ>java WhileStmt
To terminate enter non-digit or white space character.
Enter a string of numbers or white spaces:
34254 3456 547656 657 K

Report on characters that were read
Total chars read = 23
Number of digits = 18
Number of white spaces = 4
Terminating character = K

H:\InsideJ>
```

Figure 4.9

Output of the WhileStmt program.

The for Statement

The for statement also implements a loop, but unlike the while statement it contains specific constructs for a loop variable initilization, loop test condition, and loop variable change. The general syntax of the for statement is shown next:

```
for (initStmt  boolExpr; incrExpr)

        statement
```

Before the start of the loop the *initStmt* is executed. This inital statement could be any statement; it is typically an assignment statement that initializes the value of a loop variable that is used to control the execution of the loop. Here are some examples of these assignment statements.

```
x = 0;
y = 10;
z = MIN_VAL + 1;
```

In these examples the loop variables, x, y, and z, had to be defined earlier in the program. Because *initStmt* can also be a statement that defines a variable with an initial value, you can use the following forms of *initStmt*:

```
int   x = 0;
long  y = 10;
short z = MIN_VAL + 1;
```

The *initStmt* is evaluated just once, when the for loop is executed. After the *initStmt* is evaluated, the *boolExpr* is evaluated. If the evaluation yields a true value, the *statement* is executed; if it yields a false value, the for loop is terminated and execution proceeds with the next statement after the for loop. The *statement* can be any statement including a block statement. At the end of *statement* execution, the *incrExpr* is evaluated. The *incrExpr* is used typically to change the value of the loop variable that was set up in the *initStmt*. After the *incrExpr* has been evaluated, the control is transferred to the top of the loop, and *boolExpr* is evaluated again. It is important to realize that *initStmt* is outside the loop, just before the loop begins.

The for loop is actually equivalent to the following while statement:

```
{
        initStmt
        while (boolExpr)
        {
                statement
                incrExpr;
        }
}
```

In a later section (see section "The continue Statement"), you will learn about the continue statement that transfers control to the top of the loop and skips the remaining statements. If, however, a continue statement occurs as part of the statement, the incrExpr is always executed before transferring control to the top of the loop.

Figure 4.10 shows the logic flow diagram for a for statement.

Consider the following example of a for loop.

```
int  fiats;
int  sum;
int  MAX_FIATS = 18;

for (fiats = 0; fiats < MAX_FIATS; fiats++)
sum += fiats*9;
```

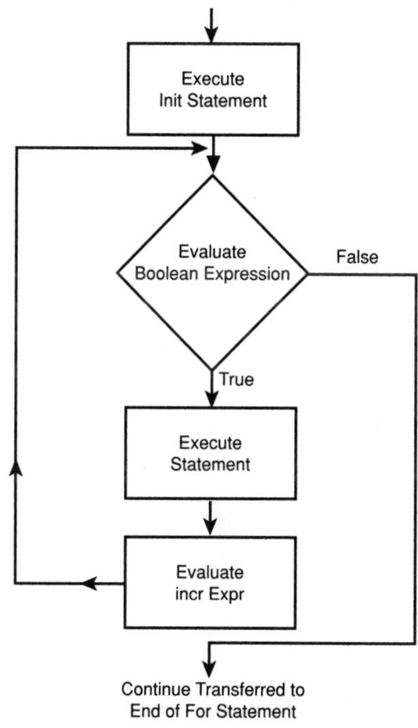

Figure 4.10

Logic flow diagram for a for statement.

In this for loop, *fiats* is the loop varaiable. The loop variable is also called the *iteration variable.* In this example, the *initStmt* is fiats = 0; the *boolExpr* is fiats < MAX_FIATS, and the *incrExpr* is fiats++. The *statement* is sum += fiats*9, and is executed 18 times.

The previous for loop is executed 18 times with the loop variable iterating through the values of 0 to 17. When the loop terminates, the loop variable, fiats, is set to 18.

Consider another example of a for loop:

```
int    sum = 0;
int    y = 100;

for (int x = 2; x <= 100;  x+=2)
{
       sum += x;
       y -= x;

} // end for
```

Notice that in the previous example, *statement* is a block statement. Any time you have to execute more than one statement in a loop, you must enclose it in a block statement.

You can also have lists of statements in the *initStmt* or a for loop, or a list of expressions in the *intExpr*. Each of these statements and expressions are evaluated in the order in which they are listed.

The following for loop is equivalent to the previous one.

```
for (int x = 2, y = 100, sum = 0; x <= 100;  x+=2)
{
       sum += x;
       y -= x;

} // end for
```

Notice that the *initStmt* actually consists of three statements. These statements define the variables x, y, and sum and also initialize their values.

Here is another example of a for statement that also has several expressions as part of the *incrExpr*.

```
int    sumx = 0;
int    sumy = 0;

for (int x = 0,y = 0; x != 100; x += 2,y += 3)
{
       sumx += x;
       sumy += y;

} // end for
```

The *initStmt, boolExpr,* and *incrExpr* in the for statement can be omitted. Here is an example of a for statement in which the *initStmt* has been omitted.

```
// Value of p was set earlier.
for (; p >= 100 && p <= 900; p++)
{
      // Statements

} // end for
```

Here is an example of a statement that sets up an infinite loop. Notice that all the *initStmt, boolExpr,* and *incrExpr* parts are missing:

```
// Infinite loop
for (;;)
{
      // Statements executed
      // forever.

} // end for
```

In this assignment statement, there are no statements or expressions to evaluate. A loop, however, is still set up, except that it is an infinite loop. This form of an infinite loop is superior to the while statement, which has a true constant in the Boolean expression:

```
// Infinite loop with a while statement
while (true)
{
      // Statements executed
      // forever.

} // end while
```

In the preceding infinite loop implemented with a while statement, the expression true has to be evaluated. A smart compiler will optimize this and eliminate the evaluation of the expression as it always returns a true value; however, this is not guaranteed, and in the worst case a few compute cycles will be wasted in checking the while expression.

Consider the progam in listing 4.6 that attempts to print the value of the loop variables x and y defined as part of the for statement on line 16. Figure 4.11 shows an attempt to compile this program with javac. Notice that the error message states that the variables x and y are not defined. Why?

Loop variables defined in the for statement have a scope that is within the for loop only. Remember that the for statement can be regarded as consisting of a while loop:

```
{
      initStmt
      while (boolExpr)
      {
         statement
         incrExpr;
      }
}
```

The for loop on lines 16–21 in listing 4.6, therefore, is equivalent to the following:

```
{
      int x= 0, y = 10; // intStmt

      while (x < 10 /* boolExpr */)
      {
         sumx += x;
         sumy += y;
         x++;    // incrExpr
         y++;    // incrExpr
      }

} // end of block statement
```

The loop variables x and y have a scope that ends with an enclosing block statement. Any attempt to reference x and y outside this block will produce a syntax error that the variable is undefined.

Listing 4.6

```
Line=================Java Source=================
01 /**
02  * ForStmt: Illustrates the scope of loop variables
03  * in a for statement.
04  *
05  * Author: Karanjit S. G. S. Siyan
06  */
07 class ForStmt
08 {
```

```

    public static void main(String args[])
     {

         int sumx = 0;
         int sumy = 0;

         for (int x = 0, y = 10; x < 10; x++, y++)
         {
             sumx += x;
             sumy += y;

         } // end for

         System.out.println("x = "+x);
         System.out.println("y = "+y);

     } // end main

} // end ForStmt
```

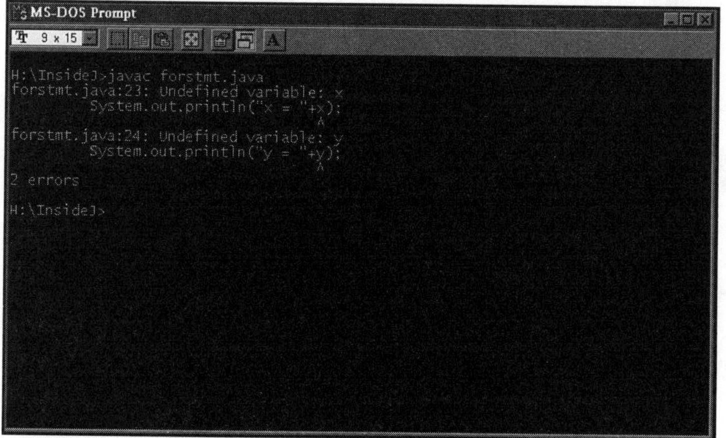

Figure 4.11

Compilation of ForStmt with javac.

In the example of listing 4.6, if you need access to the loop variables, you must define them outside the for loop. Listing 4.7 shows a correction to this program, where x and y are moved to an outer scope—the scope of the block statement of the `main()` method. Figure 4.12 shows the compilation of the program with javac without errors.

Listing 4.7

```
Line=================Java Source=================
/**
 * ForStmt2: Illustrates the scope of loop variables
 * in a for statement, and how to access them outside
 * the for statement.
 *
 * Author: Karanjit S. G. S. Siyan
 */
class ForStmt2
{

   public static void main(String args[])
   {
       int x;  // Loop variable
       int y;  // Loop variable

       int sumx = 0;
       int sumy = 0;


       for (x = 0, y = 10; x < 10; x++, y++)
       {
           sumx += x;
           sumy += y;

       }  // end for

       System.out.println("x = "+x);
       System.out.println("y = "+y);

   }  // end main

}  // end ForStmt2
```

Loops can be nested, and it is typical to use nested for loops with matrix type calculations. Matrices are a collection of cells where each cell can be identified by a row and a column. To represent matrices in Java, you need the concept of arrays with different dimensions. Arrays are covered in detail in a later chapter, so it is best not to use any array examples here. Instead, we will use a program example that prints out a table of products of odd numbers and demonstrates nesting of loops.

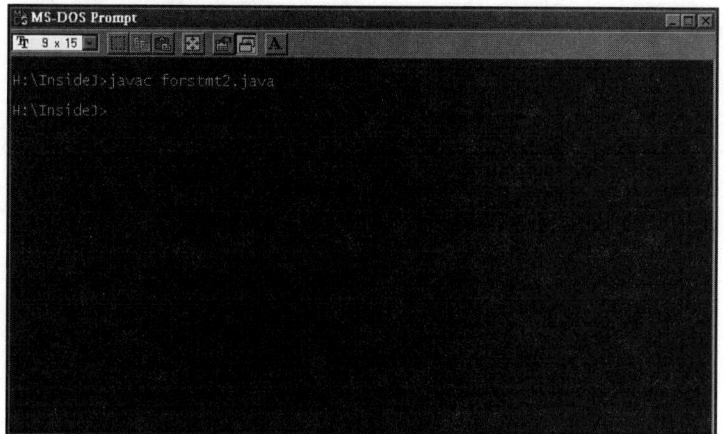

Figure 4.12

Compilation of corrected program ForStmt2.

Listing 4.8 shows such a program. This program in listing 4.8 is in the file ForNesting.java in the CD-ROM that accompanies this book. The first for loop from lines 18–22 prints out the column numbers. The many `System.out.println()` statements are for printing out the row, column labels, and the actual product.

The outermost for loop is from lines 29–53; the innermost for loop is from lines 42–49. For each value of y of the outermost loop, a complete run of the innermost loop is made.

Listing 4.8

```
Line=================Java Source=================
01 /**
02  * ForNested: Illustrates the nesting of
03  * for loops.
04  *
05  * Author: Karanjit S. G. S. Siyan
06  */
07 class ForNested
08 {
09
10   public static void main(String args[])
11     {
12          int x, y;   // Loop variables
13
```

continues

Listing 4.8, Continued

```
        int MAX = 15;

        // Print column numbers
        System.out.print("      ");
        for (x = 1; x <= MAX; x += 2)
        {
            System.out.print(x+"\t");

        } // end for

        // Flush out output buffer
        System.out.println("");
        System.out.println("------------------------------");


        for (y = 1; y <= MAX; y += 2)
        {

            if (y < 10)
            {
                System.out.print(y+ "  ¦ ");
            }
            else
            {
                System.out.print(y+ " ¦ ");

            }  // end if

            for (x = 1; x <= MAX; x += 2)
            {
                int z;

                z = x*y;
                System.out.print(z+"\t");

            }  // end for

```

```
                System.out.println("");

            }  // end for

        }  // end main

} // end ForNested
```

Figure 4.13 shows the output of the program in listing 4.8.

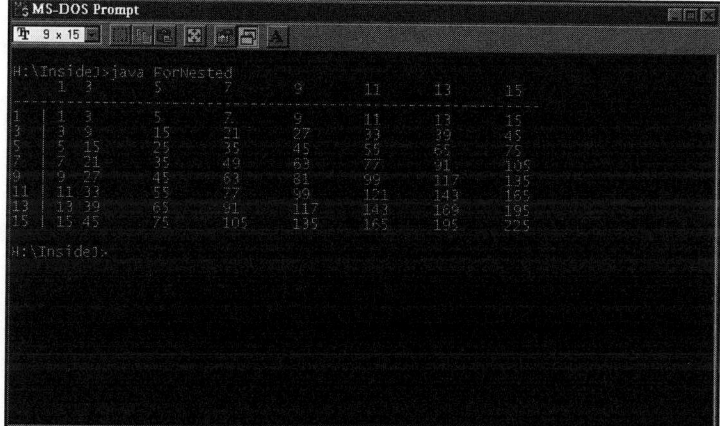

Figure 4.13
Output of ForNested.

The do-while Statement

The do-while statement is another type of loop statement. Recall that in the while and for statements, the Boolean test is performed at the top of the loop. In the do-while statement, the Boolean test is performed at the end of the loop. The general syntax of the do-while statement is shown next:

```
do
        statement
while  (boolExpr);
```

The *statement* can be any Java statement, including the block statement. The *boolExpr* is the test condition for the loop. The *statement* is executed first. Next, the Boolean expression, *boolExpr,* is evaluated. If this evaluates to true, control is transferred to the top of the loop. If the Boolean expression evaluates to false, the loop is terminated and control is transferred to the end of the loop.

Figure 4.14 shows the logic flow diagram of a do-while statement.

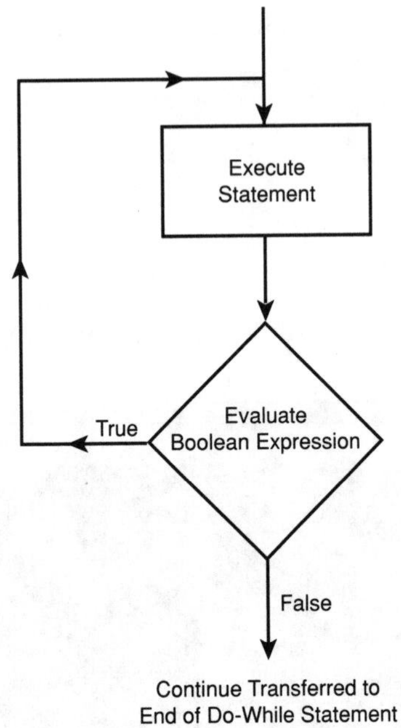

Figure 4.14
Logic flow diagram of a do-while statement.

The following example shows the use of a do-while statement:

```
int   x = 0;
int   xpoints;

// Value of xpoints is set through some
// calculations.
xpoints = 20;

System.out.println("Table of exponent values\n")
do
{
      y = Math.exp((double)x);
      System.out.println("texp("+x+") =\t"+y);

} while (x++ < points);
```

The do-while statement is used less frequently than the while and for loop statements. It is primarily useful in situations where the statement in the loop needs to be executed at least once, regardless of the Boolean test condition.

The break Statement

In the discussion on switch statements, you saw how the break statement can be used to exit out of a switch statement. The break statement can be used to exit any block, not just a switch statement. A break statement is typically used in a for, while, do-while loop to exit the innermost loop. Thus, if you have nested loops, a break statement in any loop will only exit the innermost loop in which the break statement occurs.

The following is the general syntax of the break statement:

```
break [label];
```

The label is optional. Without the label, the innermost enclosing block is exited. You can use the label to break out of several nested loops.

Consider the following example of using a break statement:

```
for (int x = 0; x < 1000; x++)
{
      y += x*2;
      if  (y % 500 == 333)
      break;

} // end for
```

The preceding for loop would normally exit when the value of x becomes 1000. A test condition, however, is performed in the if statement. If this condition is met, the break statement will be executed, and it will cause the premature termination of a for loop.

Consider another example of a labeled for loop:

```
outer:
for (int x = 0; x < 100; ++x)
{
      for (int y = 0; y < 100; ++y)
      {
         int   z = x*y;
         if (z == 6003)
            break outer;
         else if (z == 2475)
            break;
```

```
        } // end for

} // end for
```

The outermost loop is labeled with the label outer: In the innermost loop there are two break statements. The first break statement will be executed if the value of z becomes 6003, at which time the outermost, and hence also the innermost loop, will terminate. The second break statement does not have a label. It will be executed only when the value of z becomes 2475, at which time only the innermost loop will terminate; it will not affect the outer loop.

The continue Statement

The continue statement is used inside a loop to skip the remaining statements in the loop and to go to the top of the loop. At the top of the loop, the Boolean expressions, if any, are evaluated and the rest of the loop execution continues.

The continue statement is used to skip the current iteration of the loop and go on to the next iteration. If a continue statement is executed in a while statement, the Boolean expression at the top of the loop is evaluated next. If a continue statement is executed in a do-while statement, the Boolean expression at the bottom of the loop is evaluated next. And if a continue statement is executed inside a for loop, the control is transferred to the increment expression (*incrExpr*).

The syntax of the continue statement is the reserved word continue on a line by itself with an optional label:

```
continue [label];
```

When the *label* is used, the loop will continue to the loop that has the label. The inner loop will restart when it is executed again.

Consider the following example that uses a continue statement:

```
for (int x = 1; x < 999; x++)
{
      y += x*3;
      if  (x == 333)
              continue;


      y += 5;

} // end for
```

In the previous for loop when the value of x becomes 333, the statement that follows y += 5 is skipped, and the next value of x becomes 334, and the next iteration of the loop is executed with this value.

The return Statement

The return statement is used in methods to exit from the method. It is also used to return a value from the method that is supposed to return a value. The structure of methods will be discussed in later chapters, so in this section only the syntax of the return statement is presented for the sake of completion.

The following is the general syntax of the return statement:

```
return [°expression];
```

The *°expression* is in brackets, which indicates that the *expression* is optional.

Summary

In this chapter, you learned about the different statement types in Java. The different statement types enable you to code the logic of a program. The most fundamental statement types are the assignment and the block statement. If you want to write logic that depends on test conditions, you need to use control flow statements. You learned many different types of control flow statements in this chapter such as the if statement, while statement, do-while statement, switch statement, continue statement, and break and return statements.

CHAPTER 5

Using Java Objects and Arrays

So far you have learned about basic Java data types and control flow statements. Besides basic data types, Java contains many predefined classes. As you learned in Chapter 2, "Getting Started with Java," when you create an instance of a class, that instance is called an *object*. In this chapter, you will learn how to use those objects. Note that you have not yet learned to define a full blown class type, although you have learned to define a simple class to encapsulate the `main()` method. It is not necessary to know the full details of how a class is defined to use classes.

Sometimes one needs to access aggregates of a variable of the same type through some kind of indexing mechanism. Java provides the array mechanism to support indexing of aggregates of a data type. The use of arrays has become fundamental to modern programming languages. Any data structure that consists of cells of data is a good candidate for representation by arrays. The mathematical concept of matrix can be easily represented as an array.

This chapter also discusses how arrays are defined in Java. You learn how to define multidimensional arrays, how to initialize them properly, and how arrays are different from ordinary variables. In many languages the concept of strings of characters is represented as an array of characters. In Java the string data type is implemented by the class String. Internally, this String class uses an array of characters for representing the sequence of characters. By encapsulating the array of characters in a class, however, powerful string manipulation methods become available for operating on the string data. This chapter discusses how strings can be used in Java programs.

Using Java Objects

The types of Java data types that you examined in Chapter 3, "Experimenting with Java Data Types and Variables," have been simple "unadorned" data types such as integers, floating point data, Booleans, and characters. These basic data types are available in most languages. One of the things that distinguishes Java as a programming language is its object-oriented nature that enables the use of a higher level representation of data called an *object.* An object is a collection of data items along with the methods (programs or functions) that operate upon the data.

Creating Objects

For an object, the format of the data and the definitions of the methods that operate upon the data are described by a class. A class, in Java, is a template for how the object is to be constructed. Creating an object from the data template represented by the class is called creating an *instance* of the class. The object instance is assigned a name that is similar to the names used for variables of the basic Java data types. This name is called the *object name.*

The object name can be of any length. Some limitations exist on the characters you can use to create the object name. The object name, like a variable name in Java, must begin with a letter, followed by any combination of letters and digits. A letter is a *set* consisting of letters a–z, A–Z and the underscore (_) and dollar ($) characters.

Recall that if you needed to create a variable of a basic Java data type, you could use the type name followed by the variable names as shown in the following example:

```
int   aVarName;
float area;
char  inpCh;
```

If you need to create an object instance, the syntax is similar to creating a variable name. You, however, must also use a *constructor* for that object. What is a constructor?

A *constructor* is a special method that contains the program code to build the object. Building the object may involve initializing the data elements in the object. All classes must have this constructor method. If one has not been defined, the Java language supplies this default constructor. The name of the constructor method is the same as the name of the class. Consider a class called Aircraft:

```
class Aircraft
{
// Data elements describing the class

// Constructor method
Aircraft() {…}
}
```

Notice that the following line in the preceding class definition is the constructor method:

```
Aircraft() {…}
```

Notice that the name of the constructor method is the same as the class name—this is what is used to identify the constructor method.

The { … } contains the statements that implement the constructor method. The parentheses after Aircraft and before the { … } contain the arguments to the method. *Arguments* are data that is passed on to the method.

To create an object of this class—called instantiating the class—you can use the following syntax:

```
Aircraft     boeing_747 = new Aircraft();
```

The object name is boeing_747. The `= new Aircraft()` initializes the object with the object created by the constructor. Notice that the call to the `Aircraft()` constructor is preceded with `new`. Whenever you call a constructor to create an object you must precede it with the `new` keyword.

The object `boeing_747` could also have been created in two steps, as shown next:

```
Aircraft     boeing_747;
boeing_747 = new Aircraft();
```

The statement `Aircraft boeing_747;` just declares the variable; it does not define the variable. No object is associated with this variable; it is a reference to nothing. More specifically, the variable is set to the value of null. The reserved word null is used to indicate that no object is associated with the `boeing_747`. The second statement `boeing_747 = new Aircraft();` defines the value of the object.

Creating and Using Objects of the Date Class

Figure 5.1 shows the definition of the class Date defined in the package `java.util`, which uses javadoc and an HTML browser. From the discussion in Chapter 4, "Java Flow Control," recall that packages are collections of classes that have similar functions.

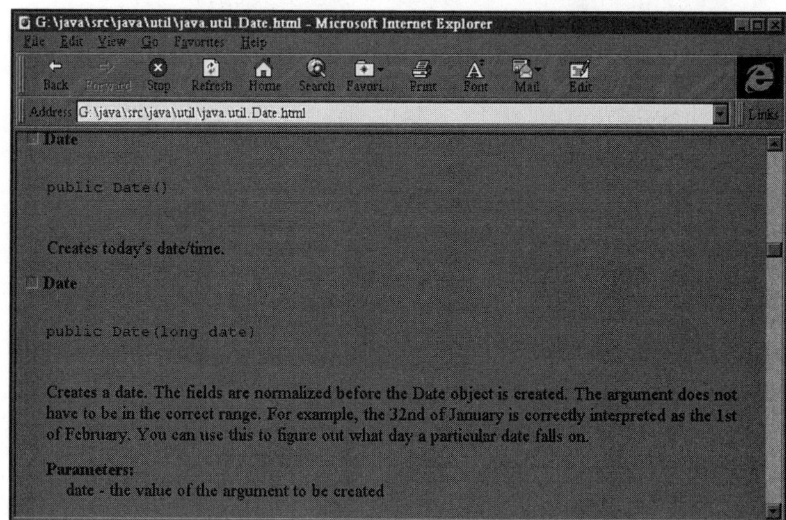

Figure 5.1
Date constructor definition.

On the CD

Listing 5.1 contains a program that uses the Date class, and figure 5.2 shows the output of this program by using the java interpreter. This program is in the file DateUse.java on the CD-ROM that accompanies this book.

Line 18 in listing 5.1 defines a simple use of the creation of the Date object, `todate`. The constructor `"Date()"` that is used to build the Date object does not have any arguments. This type of Date constructor returns the current date and time information. Line 19 contains a printout of the date value. From figure 5.2, you can see that the date is printed out as the following:

```
Fri Jul 19 11:49:05 Mountain Daylight Time 1996
```

Notice that the `System.out.println()` method, on line 19, is able to print out the date object. It can do this because all Java objects have a method called `toString()` that converts the object's value to a string representation. The Date class has an explicit method called `toString()` that converts the date object's value to a string representation. An *explicit method* is a method that is defined in the class itself, and it is different from an *implicit method* that is inherited from a parent class. You will learn about how methods can be inherited in later chapters.

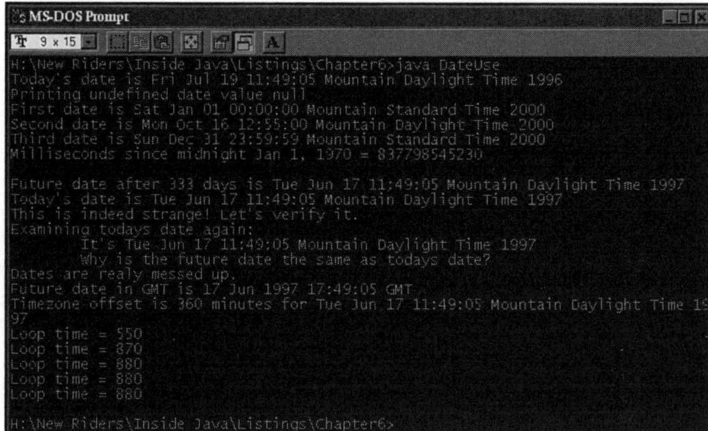

Figure 5.2
Output of DateUse program.

The `System.out.println()` method was used often in the previous chapters. You are in a better position to understand this method now that the use of objects has been formally introduced. Java has a class called System, defined in the package java.lang, that has only static variables and methods. Two of the very important static variables are in and out. The variables in and out define objects of the class InputStream and PrintStream, respectively. Because out is an instance of the class PrintStream, all the methods that are available for PrintStream can be invoked by using this notation:

```
Object.method();
```

In this example, *Object* is the object `System.out` and *method* is `println()`.

Lines 21–23 contain the definition of the objects `date1`, `date2`, and `date3`. Notice that in these definitions, the objects are initialized to a null value. On line 25, the value of the `date1` object is printed out. From figure 5.2, you can see that the value printed out is the string "null":

```
Printing undefined date value null
```

All the predefined Java classes are written with the consideration that if an attempt is made to access an undefined value, a value of null is set for the object.

Lines 27–29 initialize the date objects with values built by calling the constructors for date. Each of these lines represents a different constructor for the class Date. Note that the constructors have the same name Date, but different arguments, and this makes them different. In general, methods that have the same name but different arguments are distinct from each other. This capability to have several methods with the same name is called *method overloading*.

The Date constructor on line 27 is past arguments of *year, month,* and *date.* The year is the number of years since the year 1900; month is the month number—January is month number 0 and December is month number 11; date is the day of the month with values from 1 to 31. The object date's value is printed out by line 31:

```
First date is Sat Jan 01 00:00:00 Mountain Standard Time 2000
```

The Date constructor on line 28 is past arguments of *year, month, date, hours,* and *minutes.* The *year, month,* and *date* have the same values described for the previous date constructor, but *hours* and *minutes* have the expected value of the hour of the day, and minutes in the hour. The value of *hours* can be from 0 to 23, and *minutes* is from 0 to 59. The object date2's value is printed out by line 32:

```
Second date is Mon Oct 16 12:55:00 Mountain Daylight Time 2000
```

The Date constructor on line 29 is past arguments of *year, month, date, hours, minutes,* and *seconds.* The *year, month, date, hours,* and *minutes* have the same values described for the previous date constructor, but *seconds* has the expected value of the seconds in the next minute. The value of *seconds* can be from 0 to 59. The object date3's value is printed out by line 33:

```
Third date is Sun Dec 31 23:59:59 Mountain Standard Time 2000
```

Lines 35 and 37 show how you can get the number of milliseconds since midnight for a particular date object value. Line 35 defines the long variable m that will contain the number of milliseconds. Line 37 contains a call to the method `getTime()`. The method `getTime()` is defined for the class Date and returns the number of milliseconds since midnight. You can use the javadoc utility to get information on the method. Figure 5.3 shows the description of the `getTime()` method by using Internet Explorer after creating the HTML files with javadoc. How do you know what type of variable should be defined for holding the millisecond value? Examining figure 5.3, you can see the following definition of `getTime()`:

```
public long getTime()
```

The type of value returned is indicated by the data type that precedes the name of the method. In this example, the data type is long, and hence you must define the variable to receive the method value as being a long type. Line 38 prints out the value of the number of milliseconds since midnight Jan 1, 1970 GMT (Greenwich Mean Time):

```
Milliseconds since midnight Jan 1, 1970 = 837798545230
```

Lines 41–49 compute the date, which is 333 days from today's date. To do this, the number of milliseconds in a day is computed and stored in `msPerDay`. Line 46 sets the `futureDate` to `todate` by using an assignment statement, so the value of `futureDate` is the same as `todate`. Next, line 47 uses the method `setTime()` for class Date to change the date to a future date. Figure 5.4 shows the description of the `setTime()` method by using Internet Explorer and the HTML documents created by javadoc.

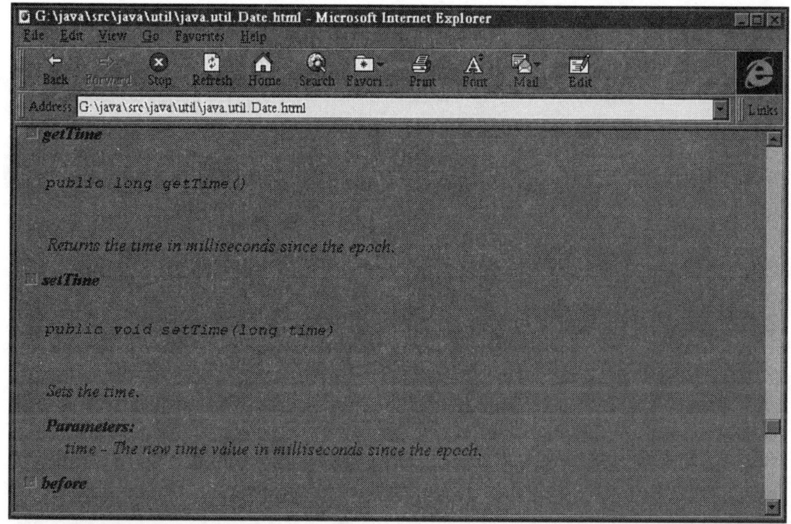

Figure 5.3
Definition of `Date.getTime()`.

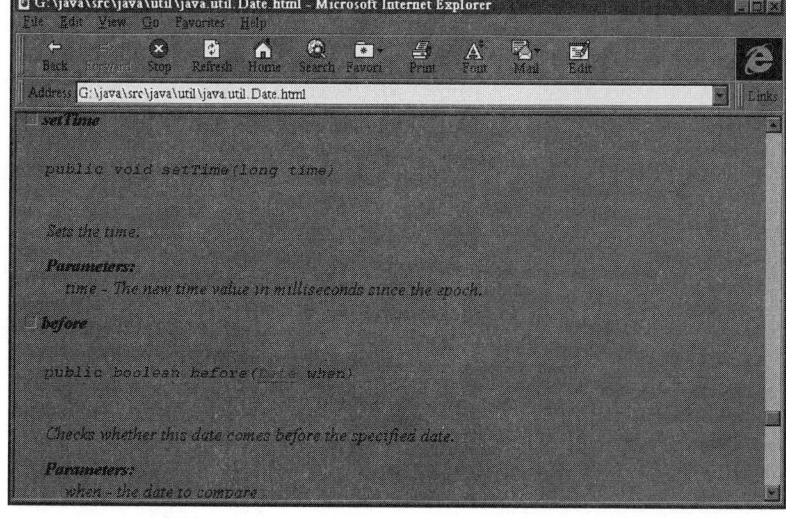

Figure 5.4
Definition of `Date.setTime()`.

Lines 49 and 50 print out the future date and today's date:

```
Future date after 333 days is Tue Jun 17 11:49:05 Mountain Daylight Time 1997
Today's date is Tue Jun 17 11:49:05 Mountain Daylight Time 1997
```

Lines 52–66 check the value of the future date to see if it is different from today's date as one would expect. The method used to perform this check is the `equals()` method. Again, you can use the documentation generated by javadoc to see the definition of this method (see fig. 5.5).

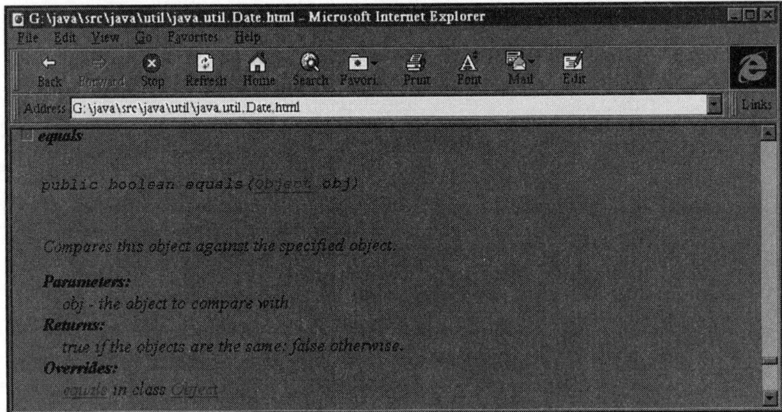

Figure 5.5
Definition of `Date.equals()`.

The output in figure 5.2 reveals that something strange has taken place—the value of the today's date was somehow changed to that of the future date:

```
Today's date is Tue Jun 17 11:49:05 Mountain Daylight Time 1997
This is indeed strange! Let's verify it.
Examining todays date again:
            It's Tue Jun 17 11:49:05 Mountain Daylight Time 1997
            Why is the future date the same as todays date?
```

As you examine the code from lines 44–50, apparently no change has been made to the future date. This mysterious change is due to a very important aspect of how object variable values are set in Java. Figure 5.6 shows the `futureDate` and `todate` variable values prior to making the assignment on line 46. Notice that although `todate` has a reference to the object that was created when the constructor was called on line 18, `futureDate` does not have any such reference. When an object is declared, as in line 44, and no constructor has been called to set its value, the object variable has a value of null. In line 46, the value of object variable `futureDate` is set to `todate`. The assignment statement does not create a copy of the value of `todate`; it sets `futureDate` to reference the same date object that is referenced by `todate` (see fig. 5.7). When `futureDate` is modified in line 47, by the call to method `setTime()`, the value of `todate` is also modified, because `futureDate` and `todate` are referencing the same date object (see fig. 5.8). You will learn to solve this type of problem in listing 5.2, which presents a variation of the program in listing 5.1. But before you examine listing 5.2, you should examine the remainder of the program in listing 5.1.

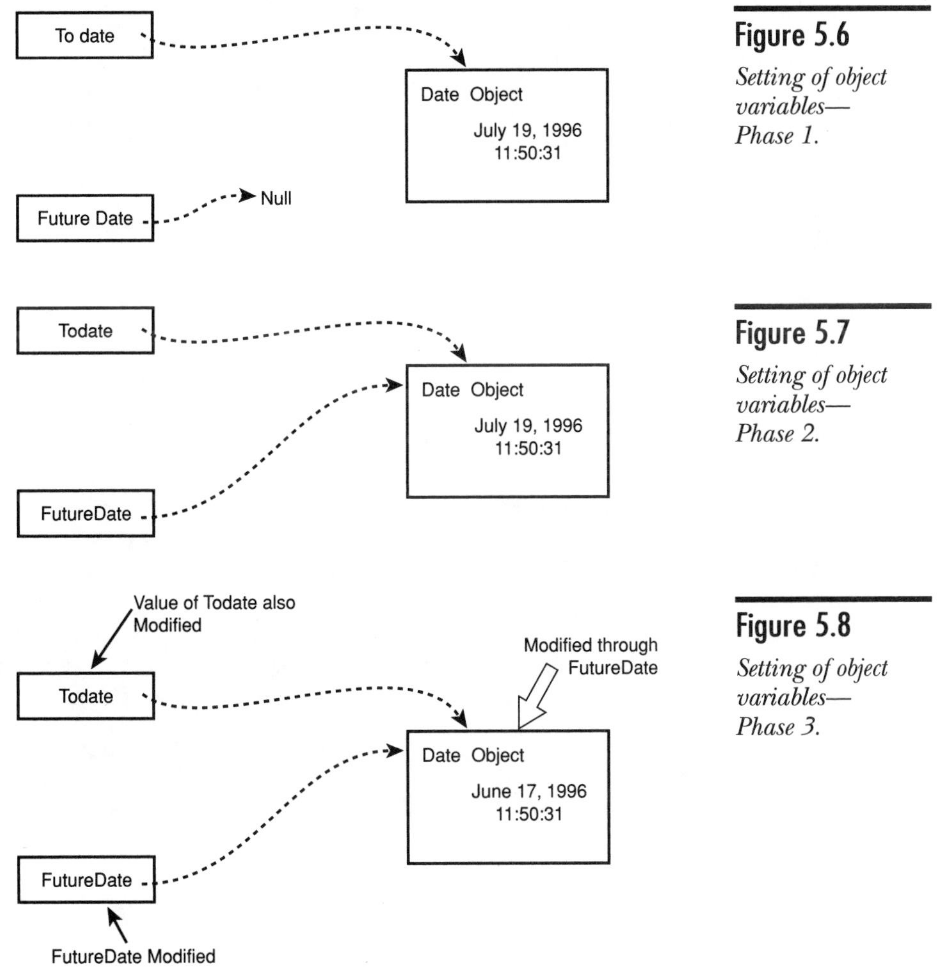

Figure 5.6
Setting of object variables— Phase 1.

Figure 5.7
Setting of object variables— Phase 2.

Figure 5.8
Setting of object variables— Phase 3.

Line 69 contains a display of the future date in terms of GMT. The method `toGMTString()` displays the GMT version of the date value:

```
Future date in GMT is 17 Jun 1997 17:49:05 GMT
```

The definition of method `toGMTString()` can be obtained by using javadoc and an HTML browser to view the generated files (see fig. 5.9).

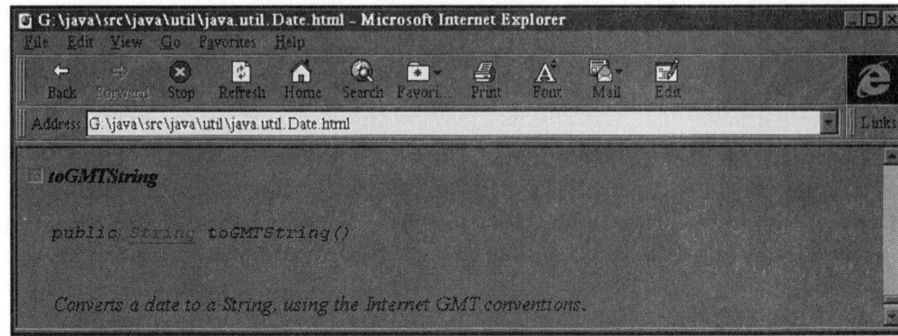

Figure 5.9
Definition of *`Date.toGMTString()`.*

Line 71 computes the time zone offset for `futureDate`, and line 72 displays this value:

```
Timezone offset is 360 minutes for Tue Jun 17 11:49:05 Mountain Daylight
Time 1997
```

The method `getTimezoneOffset()` displays the time zone offset in minutes from GMT. The definition of method `getTimezoneOffset()` can be obtained by using javadoc and an HTML browser to view the topic(see fig. 5.10).

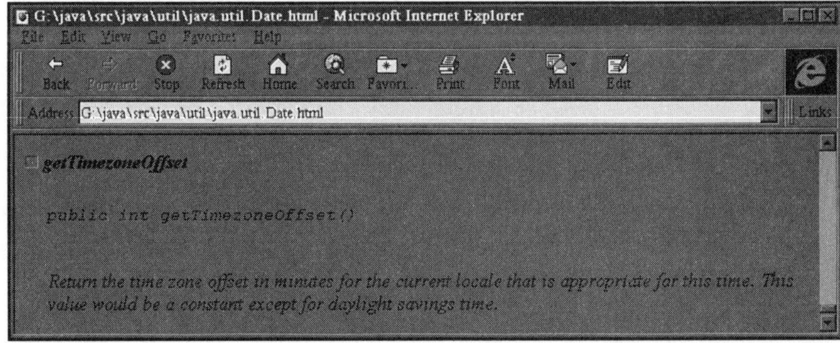

Figure 5.10
Definition of *`Date.getTimezoneOffset()`.*

Lines 77–100 show an example of how you can use the methods in the Date class to compute the amount of time taken for each execution of the loop.

Line 78 is used to get a timestamp in milliseconds since midnight Jan 1, 1970 GMT. Notice the slightly unusual way of calling the `getTime()` method when compared with how this method was called earlier in line 37:

```
ms = (new Date()).getTime();
```

The use of `new Date()` returns an object of class Date. Normally, you would assign this object to a Date object variable, and then you would invoke the methods for this object. If, however, you only need to call just once, only one of the methods of that Date object, the previous syntax is more compact. The compiler creates a temporary object variable to store the value returned by `new Date()`, but this is a temporary variable name that is internal to the Java compiler and not available to the programmer. Similarly, note that line 95 contains a similar statement to line 78, to get the timestamp at the end of the loop:

```
ms = (new Date()).getTime();
```

The variable `deltaT` is used to hold the time for each iteration of the outer `for` loop in milliseconds, and this time is displayed by line 97:

```
Loop time = 550
Loop time = 870
Loop time = 880
Loop time = 880
Loop time = 880
```

The inner `for` loop does mathematical calculations.

Note The timing values for the loop iterations involving Math class functions are different because they depend on the algorithm used to compute the Math functions. For certain values, the arithmetic series used to implement trigonometric functions converge rapidly, and take less time to compute. For values such as zero (0), many Math class functions are able to make a quick check and return almost immediately.

Listing 5.1

```
Line=================Java Source=================
001 /**
002  * DateUse: This demonstrates the use of objects using
003  * the predefined date class in package java.util.
004  *
005  * Author: Karanjit S. G. S. Siyan
006  *
007  */
008
009 import java.util.Date;
010
```

continues

Listing 5.1, Continued

```
class DateUse
{

    public static void main(String args[])
    {
        // Example 1

        Date    todate = new Date();
        System.out.println("Today's date is "+todate);

        Date    date1 = null;
        Date    date2 = null;
        Date    date3 = null;

        System.out.println("Printing undefined date value "+date1);

        date1 = new Date(100, 0, 1);
        date2 = new Date(100, 9, 16, 12, 55);
        date3 = new Date(100, 11, 31, 23, 59, 59);

        System.out.println("First date is "+date1);
        System.out.println("Second date is "+date2);
        System.out.println("Third date is "+date3);

        long    ms;

        ms = todate.getTime();
        System.out.println("Milliseconds since midnight Jan 1, 1970 = "+ms);


        long    days = 333L;
        long    msPerDay = 24*3600000L;

        Date    futureDate;

        futureDate = todate;
        futureDate.setTime(ms + days*msPerDay);

```

```
        System.out.println("\nFuture date after "+days+" days is
➥"+futureDate);
        System.out.println("Today's date is "+todate);
        if (futureDate.equals(todate))
        {
            System.out.println("This is indeed strange! Let's verify it.");
            System.out.println("Examining todays date again:\n\tIt's
➥"+todate);
            System.out.println("\tWhy is the future date the same as today's
➥date?");
        }
        else if (futureDate.after(todate))
        {
            System.out.println("Yes. As expected the future date is indeed
➥after today's date.");
        }
        else
        {
            System.out.println("Dates are realy messed up.");
        }  // end if
        System.out.println("Future date in GMT is
➥"+futureDate.toGMTString());
        int tzOffset = todate.getTimezoneOffset();
        System.out.println("Timezone offset is "+tzOffset+" minutes for
➥"+todate);
        // Example 2
        long    ns;
        ms = (new Date()).getTime();
        for (int i = 0; i < 5; i++)
        {
```

continues

Listing 5.1, Continued

```
      double  x = (double)i;
      double  y = 1;
      long    deltaT;

      for (int j = 0; j < 1000; j++)
      {
        y = Math.atan(x)*Math.sqrt(x)*Math.sin(x)*y;
        x += y;
        x = Math.abs(x);

      } // end for


      ns = (new Date()).getTime();
      deltaT = ns - ms;
      System.out.println("Loop time = "+deltaT);
      ms = ns;

    } // end for

  } // end main

} // end DateUse
```

So how do you fix the problem illustrated in figures 5.6 to 5.8 where the value of the `todate` variable changes unexpectedly? The solution is to make sure that each of the Date objects reference their own separate data objects. Some classes implement a method called `clone()`. When implemented, you can call this method by using the following method to obtain a copy of the object:

```
Object.clone();
```

The class Date, however, is not one of the classes that implements the clone method, so you must seek another type of solution. One way is to extend the class Date and create another class that supports the cloneable interface. To do this you need to understand how Java inheritance and interfaces work, and these are topics that deserve a separate treatment.

Consider the alternate following solution to create a separate `futureDate` object that has the same value as `todate`:

```
Date futureDate = new Date(todate.getTime());
```

In this solution, a different constructor for Date is being used, whose argument is the number of milliseconds since midnight Jan 1, 1970 GMT. The use of a constructor for `futureDate` ensures that the data for this object is distinct from any other Date object.

In listing 5.2, the assignment statement that created the problem of two references to the same object has been eliminated. The `futureDate` is created with its own constructor, as can be seen on line 46 in listing 5.2. Listing 5.2 contains the modified program and figure 5.11 shows the output of the program. Comparing figure 5.11 with the program in figure 5.2, you can observe that the problem with the date object value changing unexpectedly has been fixed. The modified program is in the file DateUse2.java on the CD-ROM that accompanies this book.

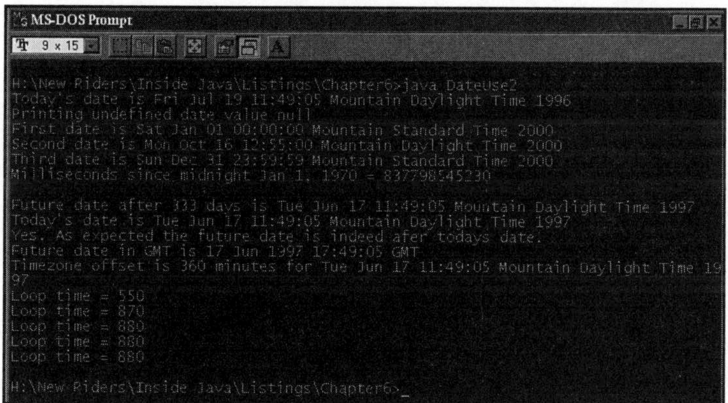

Figure 5.11

Output of modified program DateUse2.java.

Listing 5.2

```
Line=================Java Source=================
001 /**
002  * DateUse2: This demonstrates the use of objects using
003  * the predefined date class in package java.util. It
004  * fixes the object reference problem in the program in
005  * file DateUse.java
006  *
007  * Author: Karanjit S. G. S. Siyan
008  *
009  */
010
```

continues

Listing 5.2, Continued

```
import java.util.Date;

class DateUse2
{

    public static void main(String args[])
    {
        // Example 1

        Date    todate = new Date();
        System.out.println("Today's date is "+todate);

        Date    date1 = null;
        Date    date2 = null;
        Date    date3 = null;

        System.out.println("Printing undefined date value "+date1);

        date1 = new Date(100, 0, 1);
        date2 = new Date(100, 9, 16, 12, 55);
        date3 = new Date(100, 11, 31, 23, 59, 59);

        System.out.println("First date is "+date1);
        System.out.println("Second date is "+date2);
        System.out.println("Third date is "+date3);

        long    ms;

        ms = todate.getTime();
        System.out.println("Milliseconds since midnight Jan 1, 1970 = "+ms);


        long    days = 333L;
        long    msPerDay = 24*3600000L;

        Date    futureDate = new Date(ms);

```

```
        futureDate.setTime(ms + days*msPerDay);

        System.out.println("\nFuture date after "+days+" days is "+futureDate);
        System.out.println("Today's date is "+todate);

        if (futureDate.equals(todate))
        {
            System.out.println("This is indeed strange! Let's verify it.");
            System.out.println("Examining today's date again:\n\tIt's "+todate);
            System.out.println("\tWhy is the future date the same as today's date?");
        }
        else if (futureDate.after(todate))
        {
            System.out.println("Yes. As expected the future date is indeed afer today's date.");
        }
        else
        {
            System.out.println("Dates are realy messed up.");

        }  // end if


        System.out.println("Future date in GMT is "+futureDate.toGMTString());

        int tzOffset = todate.getTimezoneOffset();
        System.out.println("Timezone offset is "+tzOffset+" minutes for "+todate);


        // Example 2

        long    ns;
        ms = (new Date()).getTime();
```

continues

Listing 5.2, Continued

```
        for (int i = 0; i < 5; i++)
        {

            double  x = (double)i;
            double  y = 1;
            long    deltaT;

            for (int j = 0; j < 1000; j++)
            {
                y = Math.atan(x)*Math.sqrt(x)*Math.sin(x)*y;
                x += y;
                x = Math.abs(x);

            }  // end for


            ns = (new Date()).getTime();
            deltaT = ns - ms;
            System.out.println("Loop time = "+deltaT);
            ms = ns;

        }  // end for

    }  // end main

}  // end DateUse2
```

Using the Type Wrapper Classes

The type wrappers are Java classes that are used with Java basic data types such as the Boolean, character, int, long, double, and float to provide additional methods to perform operations upon these data types. The term *type wrapper* is used to describe these classes because these classes take a basic Java type and encapsulate them with methods.

Because type wrappers are classes, the methods defined in that class are available for use by any object of that class. You cannot perform arithmetic operations on the type wrapper classes directly. You must have access to the basic type values that are encapsulated in the type wrapper class before you can perform arithmetic operations on them. This means that the type wrapper class and its corresponding basic Java type are not interchangeable. The type wrapper classes often have the same or similar name as the Java basic types but are distinguished by beginning with a capital letter.

Note By convention all Java classes begin with a capital letter, and all object variables begin with a lowercase letter. Although this convention is not enforced by the Java language, you will find this convention universally used among all the Java built-in classes. For the sake of consistency, you may want to adopt this convention also.

The Java type wrapper classes, for example, have the following predefined names:

- Boolean
- Character
- Double
- Float
- Integer
- Long

Each of these class names has special methods that operate on the data type that it encapsulates. A great deal of commonality in the type and syntax of many of these methods exists. These common types, therefore, will be presented first.

Common Methods for Type Wrapper Classes

The common method types for each type wrapper class are the following:

- `public classtype(basictype)`
- `public basictype classtypeValue()`
- `public String toString()`
- `public boolean equals(Object obj)`
- `public int hashCode()`

The `classtype` is the name of the type wrapper classes such as Boolean, Character, Double, Float, Integer, Long; the `basictype` is the name of the corresponding basic type such as Boolean, character, double, float, int, long.

The first method type "`public classtype(basictype)`" is used as a constructor to build an object of the *classtype*. The following are examples of how this can be used:

```
Integer ic = new Integer(99);
Boolean btrue = new Boolean(true);
Character cc = new Character('K');
Float fc = new Float(3.14159F);
Double dc = new Double(1.414);
```

After the objects of the type wrapper class have been created, you can use the methods for that class on that object.

The second method type "`public basictype classtype Value()`" is used to extract the native Java basic data type value from the type wrapper class. Before performing any arithmetic or Boolean operations, you must extract the value of these basic types. The examples below extract the basic type values from each of the type wrapper classes defined in the previous example:

```
int iv = ic.intValue(); // Set to 99
boolean bv = btrue.booleanValue(); // Set to true
char cv = cc.charValue(); // Set to 'K'
float fv = fc.floatValue(); // Set to 3.14159F
double dv = dc.doubleValue(); // Set to 1.414
```

The third method type "`public String toString()`" is used to convert the value stored in the type wrapper class to an equivalent string representation. This method is primarily used for creating string representations of the Java data types for display or storing them into a text file. The examples below can be used to display the data types on the console.

```
System.out.println(ic.toString());
System.out.println(btrue.toString());
System.out.println(cc.toString());
System.out.println(fc.toString());
System.out.println(dc.toString());
```

The fourth method type "`public boolean equals(Object obj)`" is used to test if the value in one type wrapper object is the same as the one in another type wrapper object. This method is a convenient way to check the equality of values contained in the wrapper objects. Note that you cannot use the equals operator (==) to compare two class objects. The following example shows the use of this method.

```
Integer ic1 = new Integer(33);
Integer ic2 = new Integer(33);
Integer ic3 = new Integer(44);

if (ic1.equals(ic2))
{
System.out.println("ic1 equals ic2");
}
else
{
System.out.println("ic1 not equal to ic2");

} // end if

boolean test = ic2.equals(ic3);
System.out.println(test);
```

The output that will be displayed by running the preceding code fragment will be:

```
ic1 equals ic2
false
```

The fifth common method type `"public int hashCode()"` is used to return an internal integer value that contains a value that is a mathematical summation of the value that is encapsulated in the type wrapper class. The hash code is used for operations with the Hashtable class in package java.util.

The Boolean Type Wrapper Class

The Boolean type wrapper, because it encapsulates either a true or false value, does not implement any other methods besides the common methods discussed in the previous section. The Boolean class has two public static variables defined as follows within that class:

```
public static final boolean TRUE = new boolean(true);
public static final boolean FALSE = new boolean(false);
```

These statements define TRUE and FALSE as Boolean objects, containing the Boolean value TRUE and FALSE, respectively. The use of the reserved words public, static, and final as qualifiers for these types has an interesting meaning.

The use of the reserved word `public` before a method declaration or class variable definition, makes the method or variable accessible to programs outside that class. In this case, the objects TRUE and FALSE are available for use outside the Boolean class.

The use of the reserved word `static` for a class variable makes the variable available to all instances of that class. In other words, all object instances will share the same copy of the static object. Because the variable is not especially associated with any particular object instance, you can access the variable without defining an instance of this class. You could, for example, access these Boolean objects by using the following notation:

```
boolean.TRUE
boolean.FALSE
```

Notice that Boolean is the name of the class and not the name of an object instance of that class.

The use of the reserved word `final` for a class variable makes the variable constant. In other words, the value of the constant variable cannot be modified. Therefore, any attempts to modify the values of the Boolean objects TRUE and FALSE will be caught by the compiler and the runtime Java environment.

The Character Type Wrapper Class

Besides the common methods for type wrapper classes, the Character class provides additional methods that are all static. Because these methods are all static, they can be invoked without creating an object instance of the Character class, using the following syntax:

```
Character.method(args);
```

The following are the additional Character methods:

1. `public static boolean isLowerCase(char ch)`
2. `public static boolean isUpperCase(char ch)`
3. `public static int digit(char ch, int radix)`
4. `public static boolean isDigit(char ch)`
5. `public static char forDigit(char ch)`
6. `public static char toLowerCase(char ch)`
7. `public static char toUpperCase(char ch)`
8. `public static char isSpace(char ch)`

The descriptions of these methods are in table 5.1. Some examples of the use of these methods are the following:

```
Character chc1 = new Character('F');
Character chc2 = new Character('f');

if (Character.isLowerCase(chc1))
{
System.out.println("chc1 is lower case");
}
else if (Character.isUpperCase(chc1))
{
System.out.println("chc1 is upper case");

} // end if

if (Character.isLowerCase(chc2))
{
System.out.println("chc2 is lower case");
}
else if (Character.isUpperCase(chc2))
{
System.out.println("chc2 is upper case");

} // end if

Character cdgt1 = new Character('2');

if (Character.isDigit(cdgt1))
{
System.out.println("cdgt1 is a digit");
}
else
{
System.out.println("cdgt1 is not a digit");

} // end if

char d = chc1.charValue(); // Value of d is 'F'
int iv;
```

```
iv = Character.digit(d, 16); // Value of d is 'F' (hexadecimal 15)
System.out.println("iv = "+iv);

char ch1 = 'U';
char ch2 = 'u';

ch1 = Character.toLowerCase(ch1);
System.out.println("ch1 = "+ch1);

ch2 = Character.toUpperCase(ch2);
System.out.println("ch2 = "+ch2);

ival = 11;
ch = Character.forDigit(ival, 16); // ch = 'B';
System.out.println("ch = "+ch);
The output of the preceding code fragment would be the following:
chc1 is upper case
chc1 is lower case
cdgt1 is a digit
iv = 15
ch1 = u
ch2 = U
ch = B
```

Table 5.1
Character Type Wrapper Additional Methods

Method Name	Arguments	Return Type	Description
isLowerCase	char ch	Boolean	Returns a true if the character is a lowercase, and a false if it is not. The method is static, so you can use the method without creating an instance of the Character class.
isUpperCase	char ch	Boolean	Returns a true if the character is an uppercase, and a false if it is not. The method is static, so you can use the method without creating an instance of the Character class.

Method Name	Arguments	Return Type	Description
digit	char ch, int radix int		Returns the integer value of the int character ch. The radix is used to determine the base of the number that is returned. A radix value of 2, for example, is for binary numbers, 8 is for octal numbers, and 16 is for hexadecimal numbers. The method is static, so you can use the method without creating an instance of the Character class.
isDigit	char ch	Boolean	Returns a true if the character is a digit (0–9), and a false if it is not. The method is static, so you can use the method without creating an instance of the Character class.
forDigit	int digit, int radix char		Returns a character value for the integer digit specified in the radix base. This is the converse of the `digit()` method. The method is static, so you can use the method without creating an instance of the Character class.
toLowerCase	char ch	char	Returns the lowercase equivalent of the character ch. If the character is already in a lowercase form, it is returned unmodified. The method is static, so you can use the method without creating an instance of the Character class.
toUpperCase	char ch	char	Returns the uppercase equivalent of the character ch. If the character is already in its uppercase form, it is returned unmodified. The method is static, so you can use the method without creating an instance of the Character class.
isSpace	char ch	Boolean	Returns true if the character is one of the space characters, such as a newline, tab, linefeed, and so on.

The Integer, Long, Float, and Double Type Wrapper Classes

The Integer, Long, Float, and Double type wrapper classes deal with numeric values. Besides the common methods for type wrapper classes, the number type wrappers provide other common methods and definitions that are common to these classes:

```
public final static datatype MIN_VALUE;
public final static datatype MAX_VALUE;
public static classtype valueOf(String s);
```

The MIN_VALUE and MAX_VALUE are defined as constants that contain the minimum (closest to zero) and maximum values of the *datatype* (int, long, float, double).

Note Java does not have special type wrappers for byte. Short data types such as these can be handled by the Integer type wrapper, for the most part.

The `valueOf()` method is used to return a type wrapper class object for a given string numeric value. Note that the type returned is *classtype*, which is the type of the wrapper class. In addition, the Integer and Long classes have another variation of the `valueOf()` method that includes a second argument, which is the radix of the number contained in the string numeric value:

```
public static classtype valueOf(String s, int radix);
```

An example of the use of `valueOf` is when you have a string representation of a number, and you want to convert this to the type wrapper class:

```
Long xval = Long.valueOf("314159265");
```

Suppose that you want to convert the string representation of an int, you can use the following:

```
int  ival;
ival = Integer.valueOf("27283").intValue();
```

In the preceding statement the `Integer.valueOf("27283")` will result in the creation of a temporary Integer type wrapper class object. For this temporary Integer object, the method `intValue()` will be invoked, and this will result in the int value being returned.

The Float and Double type wrapper classes contain the following definitions that are particular to the floating point classes only:

```
public final static datatype NaN
public final static datatype NEGATIVE_INFINITY
public final static datatype POSTIVE_INFINITY
public boolean isInfinite()
public static boolean IsInfinite(datatype v);
public boolean isNaN()
public static boolean IsNaN(datatype v);
public int intValue();
public long longValue();
```

The NaN variable defined in `public final static` *`datatype`* `NaN` is the representation of the Not a Number value discussed in Chapter 3, "Experimenting with Java Data Types and Variables." The value of *datatype* can be either a float or double.

The NEGATIVE_INFINITY and POSITIVE_INFINITY contain the special values for minus infinity and plus infinity, respectively. See Chapter 3 for a discussion of these concepts.

The method `isInfinite()` is used to check if the value of the type wrapper object is infinite, and the `isNaN()` method is used to check if the value is NaN. Note that both static and non-static versions of these methods exist. For the non-static method you must invoke it for an instance of the object. These methods are therefore called *instance* methods.

Note In Java, static methods of a class are called *class wide methods*. Methods that are not static are called *instance methods* because they need to be invoked for each instance of the class object.

The `intValue()` and `longValue()` are also instance methods that can be used with a Float or Double object to convert its value into an equivalent int or long type.

The Double type wrapper has the following special methods:

```
public static long doubleToLongBits(double value)
public static double longBitsToDouble(long bits)
```

The `doubleToLongBits()` method enables you to get the exact representation of the double number as a long integer. After you have converted the number into a long integer, you can extract the individual bits by using shift and bitwise logical operations. The `longBitsToDouble()` enables you to convert the long bits to the double value.

Similarly, the Float type wrapper has the following special methods:

```
public static int floatToIntBits(float value)
public static double intBitsToFloat(int bits)
```

The `floatToIntBits()` method enables you to get the exact representation of the float number as an int integer. After you have converted the number into an int integer, you can extract the individual bits by using shift and bitwise logical operations. The `intBitsToFloat()` enables you to convert the int bits to the float value.

The Integer and Long type wrapper classes have the following similar methods:

Integer class:

```
public static Integer getInteger(String nm)
public static Integer getInteger(String nm, int val)
public static Integer getInteger(String nm, Integer val)
public static int parseInt(String s)
public static int parseInt(String s, int radix )
public float floatValue()
public double doubleValue()
```

Long class:

```
public static Long getLong(String nm)
public static Long getLong(String nm, long val)
public static Long getLong(String nm, Long val)
public static int parseLong(String s)
public static int parseLong(String s, int radix )
public float floatValue()
public double doubleValue()
```

The `getInteger()` and `getLong()` static methods are used to convert the string representation of a number to the equivalent type wrapper class object.

The `parseInt()` and `parseLong()` static methods are used to convert the string representation of these numbers to their internal numeric data types. An optional radix value can be passed to indicate the base for the string representation.

The `floatValue()` and `doubleValue()` instance methods are used to convert the integer types to their float and double values, respectively.

Listing 5.3 shows a sample program that uses type wrappers to test simple equality operation for integer and the `doubleValue()` method to convert the Integer value to double. This listing also shows the MIN_VALUE and MAX_VALUE for Integer, Long, Float, and Double classes. Additionally, it shows the bit representation of numbers –5.0 to +5.0 in their bit representation for float and double data types.

Lines 6 and 7 in listing 5.3 define Integer objects. Lines 10–12 contain the `System.out.println()` statement that checks the equality of these numbers and displays the result of this equality. Notice that the argument to `System.out.println()` is particularly clever:

```
ide.equals(inu) ?
            "ide equals inu" :
            "ide does not equal inu");
```

The argument contains the ternary operator ?. If the Boolean expression ide.equals(inu), which checks the equality of ide and inu evaluates to true, the argument is the string `"ide equals inu"` otherwise, the argument is the string `"ide does not equal inu."`

Lines 14–17 use the ide and inu values to compute the approximate value of the mathematical constant pi.

Lines 19–30 are used to print out the values of MIN_VALUE and MAX_VALUE for Integer, Long, Float, and Double.

Lines 33–43 contain a for loop that prints out the internal representations of numbers from –5.0 to +5.0 for float and double values.

Listing 5.3

```
Line=================Java Source=================
01 class TypeWrappers
02 {
03
04     public static void main(String args[])
05     {
06        Integer inu = new Integer(355);
07        Integer ide = new Integer(113);
08
09        // Example 1: equals operation; doubleValue()
10        System.out.println(ide.equals(inu) ?
11            "ide equals inu" :
12            "ide does not equal inu");
13
```

continues

Listing 5.3, Continued

```
        double pi;

        pi = inu.doubleValue()/ide.doubleValue();
        System.out.println("Approximate value of pi = "+pi);

        // Example 2: MIN_VALUE and MAX_VALUE
        System.out.println("\nInteger MIN_VALUE ="+Integer.MIN_VALUE+
                           "\tMAX_VALUE = "+Integer.MAX_VALUE);

        System.out.println("Long MIN_VALUE ="+Long.MIN_VALUE+
                           "\tMAX_VALUE = "+Long.MAX_VALUE);

        System.out.println("Float MIN_VALUE ="+Float.MIN_VALUE+
                           "\tMAX_VALUE = "+Float.MAX_VALUE);

        System.out.println("Double MIN_VALUE ="+Double.MIN_VALUE+
                           "\tMAX_VALUE = "+Double.MAX_VALUE);


        // Example 3: Internal representation
        System.out.println("");
        for (int i = -5; i <= 5; i++)
        {
            int ifv = Float.floatToIntBits((float)i);
            System.out.println("Float bit rep of
➥"+i+"\n\t"+Integer.toString(ifv, 2));

            long lfv = Double.doubleToLongBits((double)i);
            System.out.println("Double bit rep of
➥"+i+"\n\t"+Long.toString(lfv, 2));

        }  // end for

    }  // end main

}  // end TypeWrappers
```

The program in listing 5.3 is in the file TypeWrappers.java. After compiling it with javac, you can run it by using the command:

```
java TypeWrappers
```

The results scroll through more than one screen. So instead of giving you a picture of the screen output, the expected output is listed here:

```
ide does not equal inu
Approximate value of pi = 3.14159

Integer MIN_VALUE =-2147483648        MAX_VALUE = 2147483647
Long MIN_VALUE =-9223372036854775808 MAX_VALUE = 9223372036854775807
Float MIN_VALUE =1.4013e-045 MAX_VALUE = 3.40282e+038
Double MIN_VALUE =2.22507e-308        MAX_VALUE = 1.79769e+308

Float bit rep of -5
-111111011000000000000000000000
Double bit rep of -5
-11111111101100000000000000000000000000000000000000000000000000
Float bit rep of -4
-111111100000000000000000000000
Double bit rep of -4
-11111111110000000000000000000000000000000000000000000000000000
Float bit rep of -3
-111111110000000000000000000000
Double bit rep of -3
-11111111111000000000000000000000000000000000000000000000000000
Float bit rep of -2
-1000000000000000000000000000000
Double bit rep of -2
-100000000000000000000000000000000000000000000000000000000000000
Float bit rep of -1
-1000000100000000000000000000000
Double bit rep of -1
-100000000010000000000000000000000000000000000000000000000000000
Float bit rep of 0
0
Double bit rep of 0
0
```

```
Float bit rep of 1
111111100000000000000000000000
Double bit rep of 1
11111111110000000000000000000000000000000000000000000000000000
Float bit rep of 2
1000000000000000000000000000000
Double bit rep of 2
100000000000000000000000000000000000000000000000000000000000000
Float bit rep of 3
1000000010000000000000000000000
Double bit rep of 3
100000000001000000000000000000000000000000000000000000000000000
Float bit rep of 4
1000000100000000000000000000000
Double bit rep of 4
100000000010000000000000000000000000000000000000000000000000000
Float bit rep of 5
1000000101000000000000000000000
Double bit rep of 5
100000000010100000000000000000000000000000000000000000000000000
```

Using Basic I/O Classes

Java contains a very rich set of classes to perform input/output operations in a flexible manner. In this section, only two classes—the FileOutputStream and PrintStream classes are discussed. These classes are sufficient to perform basic input/output operations. All the Java input/output classes are in the package java.io.

You have used the static variables System.out and System.in in earlier examples to perform output and input operations. The System.out variable typically is used to print to the display device, but it is in no way restricted to output data to the display device only. You could send the output to a text file, for example. The static variables System.out and System.err are instances of the PrintStream class. The System.err class is used for sending error messages. By default, both the System.out and System.err static variables are connected to the display device.

The class FileOutputStream is used to write data to an arbitrary file. Suppose, for example, that you wanted to write data to a file, you would first have to create an instance of the class FileOutputStream:

```
FileOutputStream fos = new FileOutputStream("intdata.dat");
```

The object `fos` is built by using the FileOutputStream constructor that accepts the name of an external file to which data is to be output. Now that you have created an instance of the class, the following instance methods of the class become available:

```
public void close()   // Close print stream
public void flush()   // Flush any buffered output to the file
public void write(int b) // Write an int value
public void write(int b[]) // Write an array of bytes
public void write(byte b[], int off, int len) // Write len bytes starting
        // at offset off in the byte array b.
```

If, for example, you wanted to write a sequence of integer values to a file, you could use the following:

```
for (int x = 0; x < 100; x++)
{
fos.write(x);

} // end for
```

Note that the values that are written to the file are not text representations of the integer values, but binary representations. In the previous example, 100 integer values will have been written to the file intdata.dat. You would, for example, not be able to display the contents of this file by using a text editor or displaying the contents on the console screen by using an operating system command such as `TYPE`. To output the data in text format, you must use the PrintStream class.

The instance of the class FileOutputStream can also be used to build a PrintStream class, as shown in the following example:

```
FileOutputStream dfs = new FileOutputStream("application.log");

PrintStream logf = new PrintStream(dfs);

logf.println("This is application log data");
int x = 33;
logf.println("x = "+x);
logf.close();
```

The execution of the preceding lines of code will produce the following contents in the file application.log:

```
This is application log data
x = 33
```

Note that an instance of the PrintStream class requires that an instance of the FileOutputStream class be constructed beforehand. After you have an instance of the PrintStream class, such as logf in the previous example, you can use any of the methods associated with the PrintStream class. Some of the methods of the PrintStream class are the following:

```
public boolean checkError()  // Check for errors in print stream
public void close()  // Close print stream
public void flush()  // Flush any buffered output to the file
public void write(int b) // Write an int value
public void write(byte b[], int off, int len) // Write len bytes starting
        // at offset off in the byte array b.
public void print(Object obj) // Generic print for any object
public void println(Object obj) // Generic print for any object.
        // Terminate with a newline
// Now the other print functions
public void print(String s);
public void println(String s);
public void print(char s[]);
public void println(char s[]);
public void print(char c);
public void println(char c);
public void print(int x);
public void println(int x);
public void print(long l);
public void println(long l);
public void print(float f);
public void println(float f);
public void print(double d);
public void println(double d);
public void print(boolean b);
public void println(boolean b);
public void println();
```

Consider the example in listing 5.4, where you want to redirect the output of calls through System.out to a file instead of the display device. Figure 5.12 shows the default redirection of the System.in, System.out, and System.err variables, and figure 5.13 shows how they are redirected in the program in listing 5.4. This program is in the file IoUse.java on the CD-ROM that accompanies this book.

Line 8 in listing 5.4 imports the classes in the package java.io. Line 13 specifies that the IOException could be thrown. This exception needs to be specified because it could be thrown on line 16 when new `FileOutputStream()` is invoked to build the PrintStream object. Line 16 is interesting because it shows a constructor call within the constructor call. The call to the constructor `FileOutputStream()` returns an object of type `FileOutputStream`, which is then passed to the constructor PrintStream.

Line 18 saves the default value of System.out in the variable oldstream. Line 20 prints a message to the console. In line 23, the System.out variable is redirected to the print stream constructed on line 16. This print stream is connected to the file applic.log. Any output done through System.out is redirected to the file applic.log until line 32. On line 32, the default redirection is restored. Any output done through System.out after line 32, appears on the console.

The program in listing 5.4 is contained in the file IoUse.java and is featured on the CD-ROM that accompanies this book. Figure 5.14 shows the result of running this program. This figure also displays the contents of the file applic.log. Note that the lines appear to be skewed because the lines are terminated by a newline (ASCII code 10) character, and the end-of-line convention for DOS/Windows system is an extra carriage return along with the line feed character. In the absence of the carriage return, the lines will appear to be skewed.

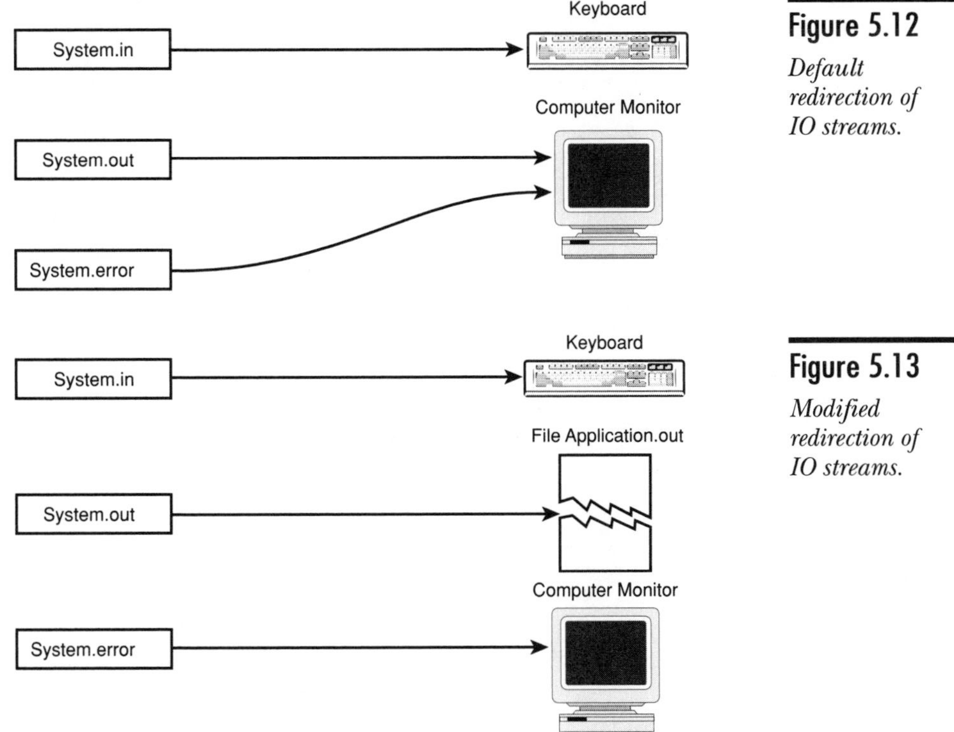

Figure 5.12

Default redirection of IO streams.

Figure 5.13

Modified redirection of IO streams.

Listing 5.4

```
Line==================Java Source=================
/**
 * IoUse: This is used to demonstrate the use
 * of IO redirection.
 *
 * Author: Karanjit S. G. S. Siyan
 *
 */
import java.io.*;
class IoUse
{

    public static void main(String args[])
        throws IOException
    {

        PrintStream pos = new PrintStream(new
➥FileOutputStream("applic.log"));

        PrintStream oldstream = System.out;

        System.out.println("Message 1 appears on console");

        // Redirection takes place here
        System.out = pos;

        System.out.println("Message 2 appears in file");

        System.out.println("Message 3 appears in file");

        System.out.println("Message 4 appears in file");

        // Restore the redirection to the default
        System.out = oldstream;

        System.out.println("Message 5 appears on console");

```

```
        System.out.println("Message 6 appears on console");

    } // end main

} // end IoUse
```

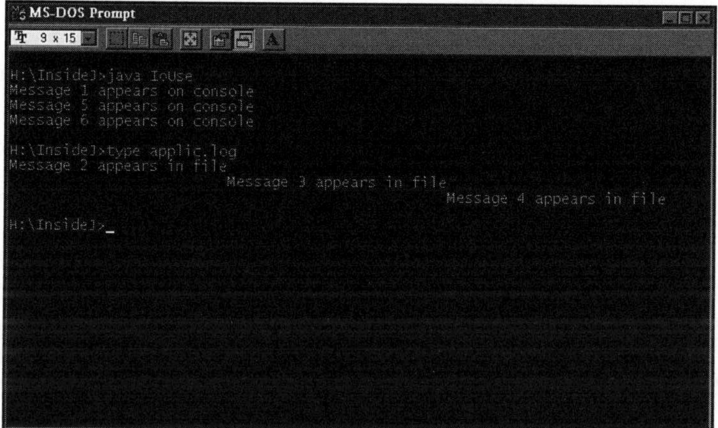

Figure 5.14
Output of program in IoUse.java.

Using Arrays in Java

Arrays are a collection of objects or data types that are stored in cells. Each object so stored is called an *element of the array* (see fig. 5.15). Each element of the array is of the same type. The cells in an array may be considered to be slots in which objects can be stored, or from which objects can be retrieved. The cells are numbered with the first element always numbered as zero. In the example of figure 5.15, there are 10 cells that are numbered from 0–9. Each of the array elements are accessed by using the cell number, also called the *index*.

In the array in figure 5.15, for example, the first element of the array is referenced by a[0], the second element by a[1], and the last element by a[9]. The number of elements in an array is called the *size* of the array. Therefore, if the size of the array is *N*, the index will be from the value of 0 to *N*–1, with index 0 referencing the first element and index *N*–1 referencing the last element. The index value of the array is checked at runtime, and if it is outside the valid range for the index, an exception called `IndexOutOfBoundsException` is generated. The automatic check of index ranges makes Java a more robust and secure language.

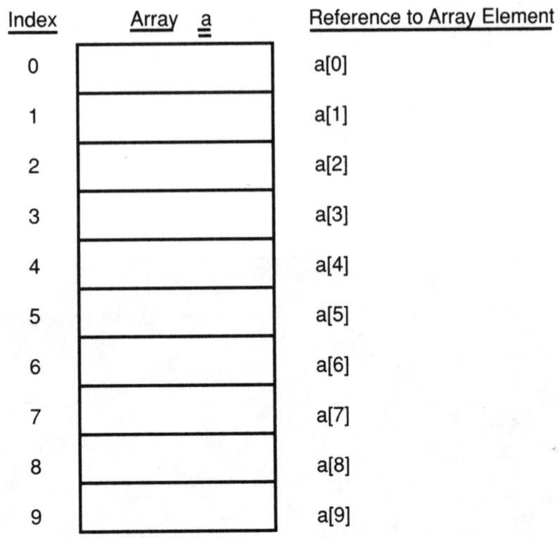

Figure 5.15

Array of size 10.

Index	Array a	Reference to Array Element
0		a[0]
1		a[1]
2		a[2]
3		a[3]
4		a[4]
5		a[5]
6		a[6]
7		a[7]
8		a[8]
9		a[9]

Creating Arrays

Arrays are created by using the following syntax:

```
type arrayname = new type[size];
```

or

```
type[] arrayname = new type[size];
```

The *type* is any of the data types or class names. The *arrayname* is the name of the array being defined, and the *size* is the size of the array being defined. The use of the new operator allocates space for the array.

Consider how you can use the previous syntax to define an array of integers such as that shown in figure 5.15.

```
int a[] = new int[10];
```

To declare an array of 100 float values, you could use the following syntax:

```
float fval[] = new float[100];
```

You can also use an alternative syntax for the array, and define these arrays as follows:

```
int[] a = new int[10];
float[] fval = new float[100];
```

The alternative syntax is identical to the earlier syntax for defining arrays; it is considered to be more intuitive in situations where an array of method types are being defined. Suppose that you want to define a function that returns an array of integers. If you use the first syntax to define this array named xtab, it would look like the following:

```
int xtab()[]
```

The juxtaposition of () with [] is confusing. The following alternative syntax is simpler:

```
int[] xtab()
```

In the preceding declaration, you can more easily see that the return type of the method xtab() is int[], an array of integers.

It is the use of the new operator, which actually allocates space. Without this operator, you are just declaring that a variable is an array. Consider the following example, where you want to declare an array of 50 elements, each of type char.

```
char[] b;
```

In the preceding statement, b is declared as an array, but you cannot access any element of this array unless you allocate space for the array. To complete the definition, you must have the following statement:

```
b = new char[50];
```

In this definition of the array of 50 characters, the declaration of the array and its allocation (constructing the array object) have been separated out. You can combine these two steps into a single step, as shown next:

```
char[] b = new char[50];
```

Initializing Arrays

Arrays can be used to hold large amounts of elements of the same data type in each of its cells. You can initialize the cells by reading data from a file or a network connection. If the array data is small and known at compile time, you can use the following syntax to initialize the array:

```
type arrayname[] = {e1, e2, … eN};
```

or

```
type[] arrayname = {e1, e2, … eN};
```

The preceding syntax defines an array with the name *arrayname* where each element is of type *type*, and the size of the array is determined by the number of elements listed in { }. Moreover, each of the array elements is initialized in order by the values listed in { }. This type of syntax takes care of declaring, instantiating, and initializing the array in a single statement. Notice also that there is no `new` used to specify the size of the array to be allocated because the size is determined by the number of elements in the initialization list { }.

The following are some examples of this type of syntax:

```
int[] xa = { 0, -1, 3, 4, 7, 10}; // defines and initializes an
          //  array of 6 elements.
char[] vowels = {'A', 'E', 'I', 'O', 'U'); // An initialized
     // char array of 5 elements.


double[] samples = {3.2, 56.2, 345.43};
// An initialized array of 3 doubles.
```

In all the examples considered so far, the size of the array was known at compile time. Java permits you to define dynamically sized arrays. As an example, consider the following:

```
int  size;
int[] points;

size = computeArraySize(); // Method that
        // computes array size.
points = new int[size];
```

In this example, the size of the array was not known at compile time. The method `computeArraySize()` was used to compute the size of the array, and this size was used in the last statement to compute the size.

Arrays of Objects

An array is an object within Java. Each element of the array can be a Java basic type or a classname. In the latter case, arrays can be used to store Java objects. The array then becomes a Java object that contains other Java objects.

All array objects have a variable length associated with them that can be used to determine the size (also called *length*) of the array. To get the length of the array, you can use the following syntax:

```
arrayname.length;
```

Consider the following sample program:

```
int[] xi = new int[50];
char[] xc = {'E', 'L', ' ', 'M', 'O', 'R', 'Y', 'A'};
float[] xf = {-3.0F, 2.0F, 9.7F, 9.02F, 344.23F};
short[] xs;

int xsLength;

xsLength = xc.length + xf.length;
xs = new short[xsLength];

System.out.println("xi length = "+xi.length);
System.out.println("xc length = "+xc.length);
System.out.println("xf length = "+xf.length);
System.out.println("xs length = "+xs.length);
The output of the preceding code fragment would be:
xi length = 50
xc length = 8
xf length = 5
xs length = 13
```

Consider another example, where you need to create an array of nine objects. Assume that the object is defined by the class Aircraft that has been defined elsewhere, and that this class has a single constructor with no arguments `Aircraft()`.

```
Aircraft[] flights = new Aircraft[9];
```

The preceding statement defines the array flights of nine elements. The array object is instantiated, and each element in the array is the type of the class Aircraft. At this point each element of the array is ready to hold an Aircraft object, but these objects must be instantiated in a separate step by calling the constructor for the class Aircraft. The following illustrates how this can be done:

```
for (int x = 0; x < 9; x++)
{
flights[x] = new Aircraft();

} // end for
```

This loop will instantiate each of the elements of the array and assign it to a cell in the array flights.

In preceding examples of array definitions where the element type of the array is a Java basic type, there was no need to call a constructor for each element. This is because Java basic types are instantiated by declaring them; that is, space for Java data types need not be defined in a separate step. Java objects behave differently from Java basic data types. For Java objects a constructor must be called to instantiate the object.

A question that you may ask is what is stored in each of the cells in the array when the following array is defined, but before each of the array objects is instantiated separately?

```
Aircraft[] flights = new Aircraft[9];
```

Figure 5.16 shows a graphical description of the array before each element object in the array is instantiated. Notice that each cell contains an object reference that has the value of null. Consider figure 5.17, which shows the appearance of the array after each element has been instantiated. In this case, each array element contains a reference to the instantiated object.

Note Java uses pointers (addresses) internally to store references to objects, and for elements of an array of objects. These pointers, however, are used internally in Java, and are not available for programmer use.

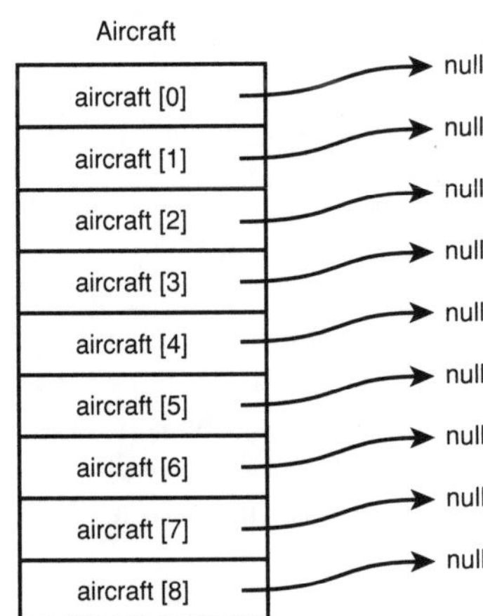

Figure 5.16

Array of objects before instantiating the element objects.

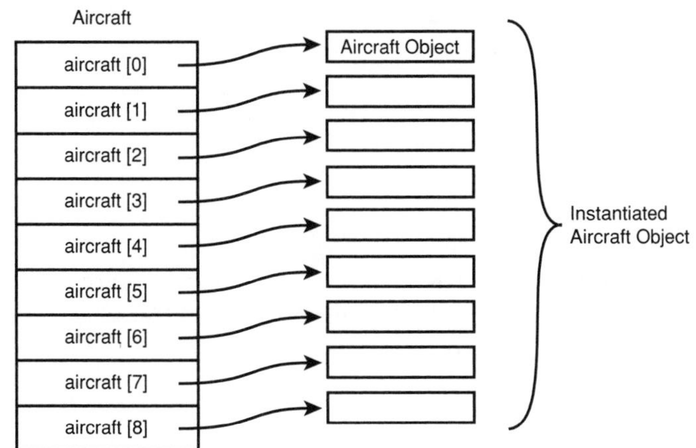

Figure 5.17

Array of objects after instantiating the element objects.

Defining Multidimensional Arrays

So far, all the examples of arrays use single-dimensional arrays. Many problems may require multidimensional arrays, such as matrix representation or representation of a simple spreadsheet. Another example would be if you wanted to store the best timings for a given number of athletes of swimmers for several competitive events. The idea of a two-dimensional array is shown in figure 5.18. There are two indexes, one that indexes the columns, and the other that indexes the rows. For the cell that has a row index of x, and a column index of y, the cell is referenced by

```
mat[x][y]
```

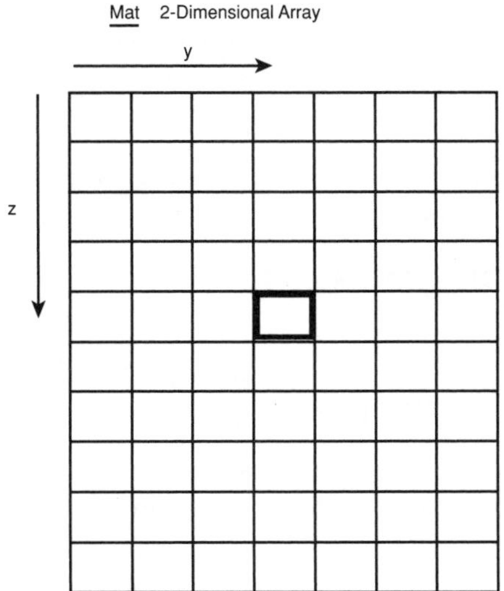

Figure 5.18

Two-dimensional array.

If this matrix has 10 rows and 12 columns, it is defined by using either of the following syntax:

```
int mat[][] = new int[10][12];
```

or

```
int[][] mat = new int[10][12];
```

The actual array that is created is an array of arrays as shown in figure 5.19. Each of the elements of the array `mat[0]` to `mat[9]` contains another array object that has 12 elements of type int.

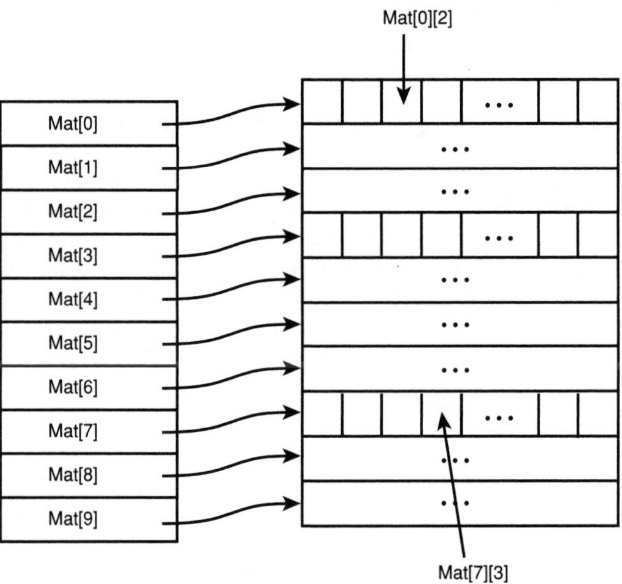

Figure 5.19

Array of array objects.

You can extend this idea to an array of any dimensions. An array of four dimensions, for example, could be defined as either of the following:

```
int matx[][][][] = new int[10][20][30][40];
```

or

```
int[][][][] matx = new int[10][20][30][40];
```

You can even define variable size arrays of arrays as long as the first dimension of the array has been specified beforehand. Consider the following example:

```
int xa[][] = new int[6][];
xa[0] = new int[10];
xa[1] = new int[12];
xa[2] = new int[5];
xa[3] = new int[4];
xa[4] = new int[6];
xa[5] = new int[5];
```

The declaration of int `xa[][] = new int[6][]` creates a 6 element array. Each element of the array is a reference to another array that has yet to be instantiated. These secondary arrays are instantiated in the separate assignment statements. Figure 5.20 shows a graphical representation of the variable sized array. You must be careful how you index this array. If you exceed the valid index range, an exception will be raised.

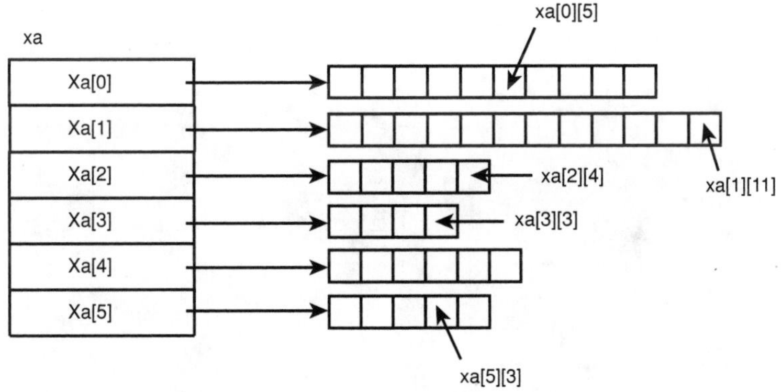

Figure 5.20

Variable sized array.

Using Arrays

On the CD

Listing 5.5 shows a program that sorts an array in either ascending or descending order. This program exists in the file ArraySort.java on the CD-ROM that accompanies this book. Figures 5.21 and 5.22 show the output of this program run, using the java interpreter. After you compile this program, you can run it by using either of the following command lines:

```
java ArraySort ascending
```

or

```
java ArraySort descending
```

This program expects a command line parameter (ascending or descending) to determine how to sort the array.

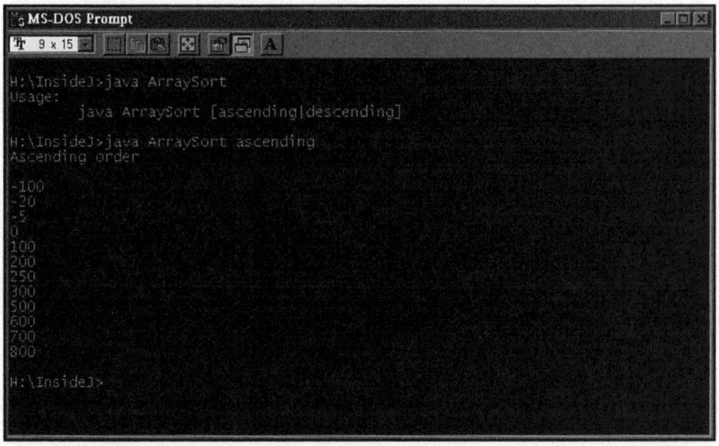

Figure 5.21

Ouput of ArraySort—screen 1.

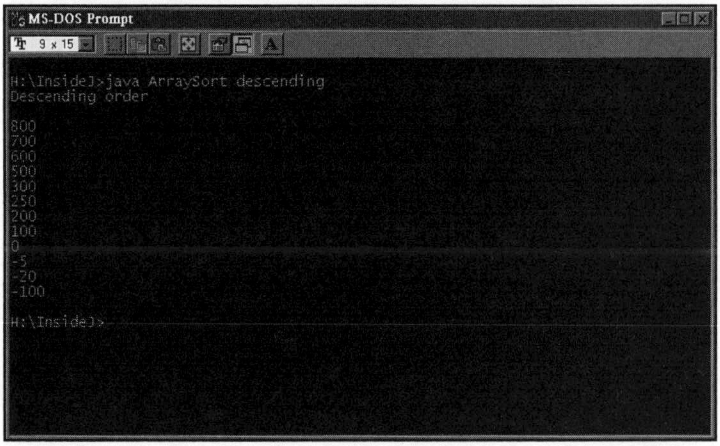

Figure 5.22

Ouput of ArraySort—screen 2.

The main progam on lines 10–51 examines the argument passed to it in the parameter `"String args[]"` to see if it contains the value ascending or descending. This value is used to determine if the array `xa[]` defined on lines 13 and 14 is to be sorted in an ascending or descending order.

Before invoking the `sort()` method defined on lines 61–89, a copy of the array is made on lines 43 and 44. Note that the `System.arraycopy()` method is used to make this copy. The `sort()` method implements a well known sorting algorithm called the *shell sort.* You can examine the method `sort()` to figure out how this algorithm works.

The method `print()` defined on lines 127–138 is used for printing the contents of the array.

The method `orderOK()` defined on lines 96–121 is used as a support function in the method `sort()` to determine if the order of the two elements being compared is correct.

Listing 5.5

```
Line=================Java Source=================
001 /**
002  * ArraySort: This sorts a collection of integer
003  * values represented by an array.
004  *
005  * Author: Karanjit S.G.S. Siyan
006  *
007  */
008 class ArraySort
009 {
010     public static void main(String[] args)
011     {
012         boolean sortAscending = true; // Controls type of sort.
013         int[] xa = { -20, 500, 200, 100, 300, -5,
014                       0, 800, 600, 250, 700, -100};
015
016         if (args.length != 1)
017         {
018             System.out.println("Usage:\n\tjava ArraySort
➥[ascending¦descending]");
019             System.exit(1);
020
021         }  // end if
022
023         if (args[0].equalsIgnoreCase("ascending"))
024         {
025             sortAscending = true;
026
027         }
028         else if (args[0].equalsIgnoreCase("descending"))
029         {
030             sortAscending = false;
031
```

continues

Listing 5.5, Continued

```
        }
        else
        {
            System.out.println("Illegal parameter to program.");
            System.exit(1);

        }  // end if

        // Make a copy of the array so that the original
        // is not modified.

        int[] ya = new int[xa.length];
        System.arraycopy(xa, 0, ya, 0, xa.length);
        sort(sortAscending, ya);
        print(sortAscending ?
                "Ascending order":
                "Descending order", ya);


    } // end main


    /*
     * sort: This is the sort procedure that sorts
     * the specified array in an ascending or
     * descending order. This procedure implements
     * the shell sort algorithm.
     *
     */
    static void sort(boolean sortAsc, int st[])
    {

        for (int gap = st.length/2; gap > 0; gap /= 2)
        {
            for (int x = gap; x < st.length; x++)
            {
                for (int y = x-gap; y >= 0; y-gap)
```

```
                {
                    int temp;

                    if (orderOK(sortAsc, st[y], st[y+gap]))
                    {
                        break;

                    }  // end if

                    // Exchange
                    temp = st[y];
                    st[y] = st[y+gap];
                    st[y+gap] = temp;

                }  // end for

            }  // end for

        } // end for

    }  // end sort

   /*
    * orderOK: This determines if the existing order of the
    * two elements in the array is OK.
    *
    */
    static boolean orderOK(boolean sortAsc, int xe, int ye)
    {
        boolean result = false;

        if (sortAsc)
        {
            if (xe <= ye)
            {
                result = true;

            } // end if
```

continues

Listing 5.5, Continued

```
        }
        else
        {

            if (xe > ye)
            {
                result = true;

            }  // end if

        }  // end if

        return result;

    }  // end orderOK

    /*
     * print: This is used to print the
     * values of the array.
     */
    static void print(String msg, int[] xa)
    {
        System.out.println(msg+"\n");

        for (int x = 0; x < xa.length; x++)
        {

            System.out.println(xa[x]);

        }  // end for

    }  // end print

}  // end ArraySort
```

Using Strings in Java

Strings are a sequence of characters and use many types of data, such as names of people, addresses, cities, and so on. In Java, the string data type is encapsulated in a special class called the String class. The String class is defined in the package java.lang. This package is imported by default in all Java programs.

The String class has several constructors and this provides many ways of creating strings. These constructors are listed next:

```
public String();
public String(String value);
public String(char[] value);
public String(char[] value, int offset, int count);
public String(char[] value);
public String(byte[] ascii, int hibyte, int offset, int count);
public String(byte[] ascii, int hibyte);
public String(StringBuffer buffer);
```

The value of hibyte in some of the constructors contains the upper 8 bits that are made the high byte of each character to transform it into a Unicode character.

Here are some common examples of creating String objects.

```
String name1 = new String("Saint Germain");
String name2 = "Saint Germain";
```

The first definition shows the conventional way of invoking a constructor to create an object. The second definition is a concise way of stating the constructor. On seeing a sequence of characters in quotes, the compiler instantiates the String object and initializes it to the quoted string. In the first definition, a temporary String object is instantiated whose value is initialized with "Saint Germain." Next, the temporary String object is used as an argument to the constructor String(String value), to create the string name1. Thus, the first definition leads to two instantiations, one of which is the instantiation of the temporary String object. Because the temporary String object has the same value as the name1 object, this is a little bit of a waste. For this reason, the second definition is preferred for string constants.

You can also use an array of characters or an array of bytes to instantiate a String object:

```
char[]        xc = {'K', 'R', 'I', 'S', 'H', 'N', 'A'};
String vishnu = new String(xc); // vishnu = "KRISHNA"

byte[] ba = {'1', 'A', 'C'};
String bs = new String(ba, 0, 1, 2); // bs = "AC"
```

After a String object has been created, it is treated as a constant, and you should not attempt to modify its value. If you want to define a String variable whose value can be modified, you must use the StringBuffer class.

Table 5.2 shows some of the methods for the String class.

Table 5.2
Some Methods for the String Class

Method Name	Arguments	Return Type	Description
charAt	int index	char	Returns the character in the string at the specified index.
compareTo	String anotherstr	int	Compares string to another string. A negative, zero, or positive value is returned if this string is less than, equal to, or greater than the specified string, anotherstr.
concat	String str	String	Concatenates the specified string to this string.
endsWith	String str	Boolean	Checks if the specified string is at the very end of this string.
equals	String str	Boolean	Checks if the specified string is equal to this string. The comparison is case-sensitive.
equalsIgnoreCase	String str	Boolean	Checks if the specified string is equal to this string. The comparison is case-insensitive.
getBytes	int srcBegin,	void	This is used to obtain a slice int srcEnd, of string values from a byte[] dst, specified location (srcBegin, int dstBegin srcEnd) in the string and place the result at a

Method Name	Arguments	Return Type	Description
			specified location (dst Begin) in the byte array.
getChars	int srcBegin, int srcEnd, char[] dst, int dstBegin	void	This is used to obtain a slice of string values from a specified location (srcBegin, srcEnd) in the string and place the result at a specified location (dstBegin) in the character array.
hashCode	none	int	Returns a mathematical hash value of the string. Used for storing string values in the java.util.Hashtable class.
indexOf	int ch/int ch, int fromIndex/ String str/ String str, int fromIndex	int	Returns the index into the string where the specified value first occurs. Index values start from 0. The different sets of arguments are shown with a / separator.
lastIndexOf	int ch/int ch, int fromIndex/ String str/ String str, int fromIndex	int	Returns the index into the string where the specified value last occurs.
intern	none	String	Returns a string that is equal to this string but is guaranteed to be from the unique string literal pool. A special internal hash table that is unique to this String object is used to store the string values.
length	none	int	Returns the length of the string.

continues

Table 5.2, Continued
Some Methods for the String Class

Method Name	Arguments	Return Type	Description
regionMatches	int toffset, String other, int ooffset, int len/ boolean ignore Case, int toffset, String other, int ooffset, int len	Boolean	Checks if a region of this string matches the region of the specified string. The boolean ignoreCase determines if the match is case-sensitive or not. The toffset is where to start looking in this string, and the ooffset is where to start looking in the other string; the len is the number of characters to compare.
replace	char oldChar	String	This replaces occurrences of the char /NewChar doldChar in the string with the newChar in the string. A new String value is returned with the replaced characters.
startsWith	String prefix, with the String prefix	Boolean int toffset/	Checks if the string starts specified string.
substring	int beginIndex/		String returns a slice of the string int beginIndex, starting from beginIndex to the int endIndex end of the string, or ending at endIndex.
toCharArray	none	char[]	Returns the string value as an array of characters.
toLowerCase	none	String	Converts the string to lowercase.
toUpperCase	none	String	Converts the string to uppercase.
trim	none	String	Removes leading and trailing white spaces in the string.

Method Name	Arguments	Return Type	Description
toString	none	String	Returns the string itself.
copyValueOf	char[] data, int offest, int count/char[] data		Returns a string that is equivalent to the specified value of the character array. The character array is copied internally to the new String object.
valueOf	Object obj/ char [] data/ char[] data, int offset, int count/ boolean b/char c /int I/long l/ float f/double d	String	This method accepts different types of arguments and is used to convert the given data type to a String object.

The following example shows some of the uses of the String methods of table 5.2.

```
String retreat = "Lake Banff and Louise";

System.out.println("Length of retreat = "+retreat.length());
// Previous statement should display a length of 21.

// The following creates another string with the same value
// as the string retreat.
String aname = new String(retreat);

boolean bx = retreat.equals(aname);
// Previous statement sets bx to true.

String lake1 = retreat.substring(0, 9);
String lake2 = retreat.substring(15);

bx = lake1.equals(lake2);
// Previous statement sets bx to false.

int ix = retreat.indexOf('e');
// Previous statement sets ix to 3
```

```
ix = retreat.lastIndexOf('e');
// Previous statement sets ix to 20

Lake2 = Lake2.concat(Lake2).concat(Lake2);
// Lake2 is set to "LouiseLouiseLouise"
```

Note that in the last statement, the value of Lake2 is actually modified even though it is of String type. So the String object is not as unchangeable as it was originally designed to be. Actually, the right-hand expression is internally converted to StringBuffer, and the resulting expression is converted to String.

The StringBuffer class is meant to be used as a string variable whose values can be changed. Table 5.3 shows the methods that are available for the StringBuffer class.

TABLE 5.3
Some Methods for the StringBuffer Class

Method Name	Arguments	Return Type	Description
charAt	int index	char	Returns the character in the StringBuffer at the specified index.
setCharAt	int index, char ch	void	Sets the character at the specified location(index) in the StringBuffer.
append	Object obj/ String str/ int offset, char[] str, int len/ boolean b/ char c/int I/ char[] str/ long l/float f /double d	StringBuffer	Appends the specified value to the StringBuffer.
getChars	int srcBegin, int srcEnd, char[] dst, int dstBegin	void	This is used to obtain a slice of string values from a specified location (srcBegin, srcEnd) in the string and to place the result at a specified location (dstBegin) in the character array dst.

Method Name	Arguments	Return Type	Description
hashCode	none	int	Returns a mathematical hash value of the string. Used for storing string values in the java.util.Hashtable class.
length	none	int	Returns the length of the string.
toString	none	String	Returns the String equivalent of the StringBuffer.
capacity	none	int	Returns the current capacity of the StringBuffer. StringBuffer capacity expands to accommodate growth in value of the string. This value may not be the same as the length.
ensureCapacity	int minimum Capacity	int	This allocates additional capacity, if necessary, so that the storage space is set to at least the specified minimum capacity.
setLength	int newLength	void	This sets the StringBuffer to the new length. If the new length is less than the current length, the StringBuffer value is truncated. If the length is extended, the value of the new character is set to 0.

The following example illustrates the use of the StringBuffer class.

```
StringBuffer svar = new StringBuffer("Darjeeling");

svar.append(", Palace of Light");
// svar is set to Darjeeling, Palace of Light

svar.insert(12, "Lake Mansa, ");
// svar is set to Darjeeling, Lake Mansa, Palace of Light
```

```
svar.setCharAt(20, 'a');
svar.setCharAt(21, 's');
// svar is set to Darjeeling, Lake Manas, Palace of Light

int len = svar.length();
// len is the number of characters in the string = 38

svar.setLength(32);
// svar is now set to Darjeeling, Lake Manas, Palace of

int cap = svar.capacity();
// Reflects amount of space allocated internally to svar.
// The StringBuffer capacity automatically expands on need.
```

Summary

In this chapter, you have learned to use Java objects. Java objects are instances of Java classes. You have learned how to access the methods of a class. Java methods can be static or non-static. Static methods are class wide, and non-static methods are associated with each object instance of a class.

You were presented with numerous example of how objects can be used. The examples were based on predefined Java classes, such as Date, PrintStream, and so on. Because of the way methods are exposed for use in Java classes, you can begin to use them without knowing the details of how the class is built.

This chapter also discussed arrays and how they can be used to represent an aggregate of values of the same data type. Array data types can be basic Java data types, as well as class types defined in Java. For arrays of Java objects, each of the object elements must be instantiated separately. At the end of the chapter, you learned how to create, access, and modify string values by using the String class and the StringBuffer class.

CHAPTER 6

Defining Java Classes

In the previous chapter, you learned how to use some of Java's predefined classes. These classes, however, were already available for use. When writing new programs and modeling concepts that are not covered in the predefined Java classes, you have to build your own classes.

This chapter will teach you how to write your own Java classes. To better appreciate how best to design and use classes, some principles of objected-oriented programming will be discussed, as well as a new Java feature called inner classes.

Inner Classes

Inner classes enable classes to be defined in any scope. Previously, Java supported only top-level classes, which had to be members of packages. Now the programmer can define inner classes as members of other classes, locally within a block of statements, or anonymously within an expression. The use of inner classes makes it easier for the Java programmer to connect objects together, because classes can be defined closer to the objects they need to manipulate, and can directly use the variables and methods that they need. With the removal of restrictions on the placement of classes, Java's scoping rules became more lenient, like those of classical block structured languages, such as Pascal.

Defining an Inner Class

When a class definition is local to a block, it may access any names that are local to that block, including variables defined by the block and parameters of the enclosing method. Here is an example of an inner class that makes use of both kinds of local variables. Keep in mind that the example is not so important for what it does, but rather for how it is done.

```
Enumeration myEnumeratedClass(Object array[])
   {
   int nIndex = 0;
   class EnumClass1 implements Enumeration
      {
      public boolean moreElements()
         {
         return nIndex < array.length;
         }
      public Object nextElement()
         {
         return array[nIndex++];
         }
      }
   return new EnumClass1();
   }
```

The inner class EnumClass1 is completely contained within the definition of the myEnumeratedClass. This avoids the clutter of class definitions that are used only once in isolated situations. An interesting note is that even after the method myEnumberatedClass returns, both array and nIndex may still be used by the inner object, EnumClass1. They are not allowed to be freed up until all the inner classes and methods are completely finished with them.

Notice that nIndex can be changed, and subsequent calls into the inner object will be able to use the changed value. If two instances of the inner class EnumClass1 were somehow produced by the method, they would both share a single occurrence of nIndex, this would produce synchronization issues. The variable would exist as long as either instance of the class also continued to exist.

Anonymous Inner Classes

A subset of inner classes are *anonymous classes.* These anonymous inner classes are an abbreviated notation for local objects, which makes it easy to introduce a chunk of code inline within any expression. Not every inner class should be anonymous, but very simple one-shot local classes are such a common case that they merit the use of anonymous classes.

Anonymous inner classes are useful for writing small encapsulated *callbacks,* such as enumerations or iterators. They are also helpful for adding behavior to objects that already have names, such as AWT components and threads.

In the previous example, the local class name EnumClass1 adds little or no clarity to the code. To make classes as concise as possible, Java 1.1 allows an abbreviated notation for local objects. A single expression syntax combines the definition of the anonymous class with the allocation of the instance.

```
Enumeration myEnumeratedClass(Object array[])
   {
   int nIndex = 0;
   return new Enumeration()
      {
      public boolean moreElements()
         {
         return nIndex < array.length;
         }
      public Object nextElement()
         {
         return array[nIndex++];
         }
      };
   }
```

As you can see in this example, no class name is defined for the new Enumeration class. It is not necessary because we only want to use it for a very short time to iterate through the array. This enables the code to be more compact and easy to follow.

Uses for Inner Classes

The inner class's name is not usable outside its scope, except in a qualified name. This helps in structuring the classes within a package. The code of an inner class can use simple names from enclosing scopes—including both class and instance members of enclosing classes—and local variables of enclosing blocks. Inner classes are also useful for adding behavior to objects that already have names and writing one-shot classes or encapsulated callbacks. This helps to clarify and maintain code.

The Class Structure

The class structure can be defined as follows:

```
class classname
{
        // class variable definitions


        // class methods


}
```

The class variable definitions can occur anywhere inside the class but must be outside the methods. Variables defined within the methods are called *local variables*, and these are distinct from class variables.

The class methods can occur anywhere inside the class. Class methods cannot be nested; that is, one class method cannot have the definition of another class method embedded in it.

Defining Class Instance Variables

As an example of class variable definitions, consider the following code fragment:

```
class Room
{
        int maxRooms;
        int entranceType;
        float area;
        boolean bathroom;
        // Other variables.
```

```
        // Other methods

}
```

The preceding definition of the class Room contains four variable definitions. These are called class variables, and they have the following meaning for a room in a hotel:

- maxRooms: Some rooms in hotels are suites of smaller rooms. This defines the maximum number of such rooms.
- entranceType: This is a code for the entrance type for the room. Different codes may be assigned to whether the entrance is near the elevator, has special facilities for physically challenged people, and so on.
- area: The area of the room. This is a measure of how big the rooms are.
- bathroom: A Boolean flag to indicate whether it has a bathroom (the bathroom could be a shared facility outside the room).

The scope of these class variables is from the point of definition to the end of that class. If you compare how the class variables are declared and defined with how the local variables are defined in a method, you will see no difference in their syntax. This is good because everything you learned in the previous chapters about declaring and defining variables applies to class variables.

A major difference between class variables and local variables is the location in which these variables are placed. Class variables are in the class definition, but outside the class methods. Local variables are defined inside the method (see fig. 6.1).

To declare an object of the class Room, you can use the following:

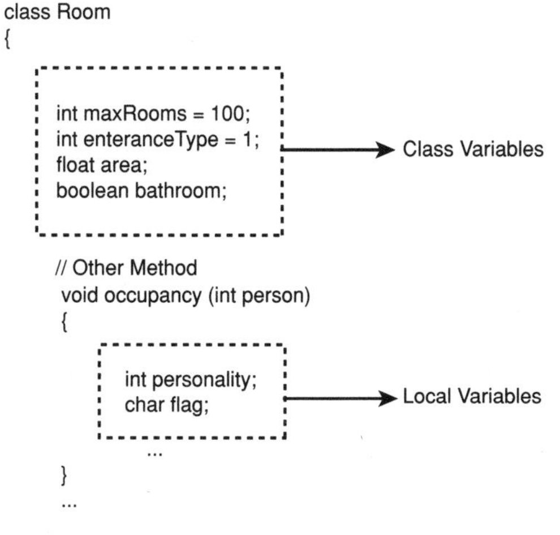

Figure 6.1

Class variables versus local variables.

```
Room      rm1;
Room      rm2;
```

These statements define two instances of the Room class. Each of the objects rm1 and rm2 are shown in figure 6.2. Each of the class variables are called instance variables. The class instance variables are referenced by using the following syntax:

instanceobject.variablename

The *instanceobject* is the name of the class object, such as rm1 or rm2. The *variablename* is the name of the class variable defined inside the class. The following are examples of referencing class instance variables:

```
rm1.maxRooms
rm2.maxRooms
rm1.area
rm2.area
```

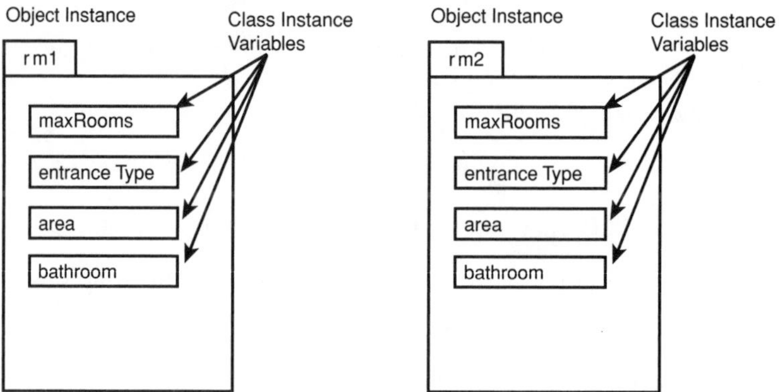

Figure 6.2
Instance objects and instance variables.

The class instance variables rm1.maxRooms and rm2.maxRooms have values that are specific to each object instance. The class instance variables occupy different memory and can have different values. For example, rm1.maxRooms can be set to a value of 1, and rm2.maxRooms can be set to a value of 3.

Defining Class Variables

As you learned in the previous section, class instance variables for separate objects have a separate existence. A class variable or a class wide variable, on the other hand, is common for all class instances. These class variables are preceded with the reserved word static:

```
static type variable = [initialize_value];
```

Suppose that you want to keep track of the number of times a room has been occupied, and also track the number of times repairs were done to the room. You cannot effectively use instance variables to keep track of these values because instance variables are defined for a particular class instance only, and you need global counters for all class instances.

Consider an extension to the class Room:

```
class Room
{
      // Class instance variables
      int maxRooms;
      int entranceType;
      float area;
      boolean bathroom;


      // Class variables
      static int nOccupancies;
      static int nRepairs = 0;

      // Other variables.

      // Other methods

}
```

The variables nOccupancies and nRepairs are class variables because they are preceded by the reserved word static. Both variables are of type int, but one of them (nRepairs) has an initial value of 0. The variable nOccupancies is used to keep track of the number of times the room has been occupied, and the variable nRepairs is used to keep track of the number of repairs to the room.

Consider the two instances rm1, rm2 of the previous class. How would you reference the variables nOccupancies and nRepairs? You cannot reference them by using the following syntax:

```
rm1.nOccupancies
rm2.nRepairs
```

This attempt to reference the class variables is incorrect, because the class variables are common to all instances of the class. Figure 6.3 shows the difference in storage space for class instance and class variables.

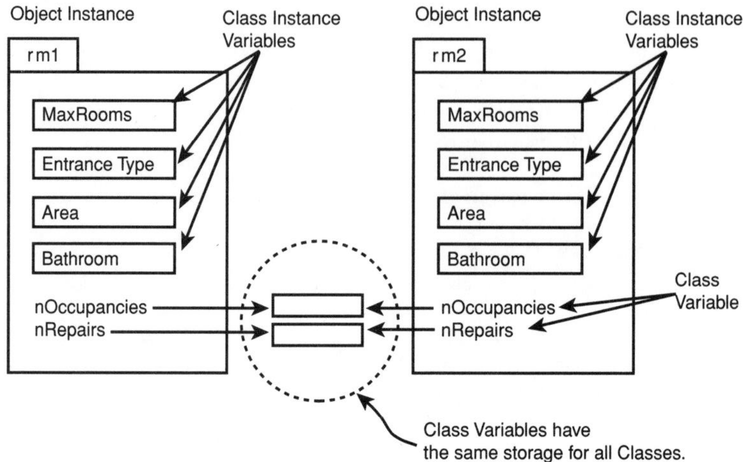

Figure 6.3
Class instance and class variables.

To correctly reference class variables, you must use the following syntax:

classname.variablename

Therefore to reference the class variable `nOccupancies` and `nRepairs`, you must use the following syntax:

```
Room.nOccupancies
Room.nRepairs
```

Because the data area storage for class variables is the same for all class instances, changing a class variable will change it for all class instances.

Class Constants

Suppose that you want to define an integer array of size 312. You can use a constant literal to specify the size of the array:

```
int[] xa = new int[312];
```

But this is not always good programming practice because the constant values (312 in the preceding example) appear to be like "magic numbers," and it is harder to figure out why a particular constant value is used. For this reason, a variable name that is to be treated as a constant is generally preferred. When defined within a class, these constants are called class constants. If, for example, the array size was defined by the constant `MAX_SIZE` with value 312, you could write the preceding array definition as the following:

```
int[] xa = new int[MAX_SIZE];
```

The preceding statement is not only more readable, but does not raise the question, as did the first version of this statement, as to why a value of 312 was used. You can more readily tell that the value 312 is the maximum size of the array.

You could define MAX_SIZE as follows:

```
int MAX_SIZE = 312;
```

In this definition, however, MAX_SIZE is a variable whose value can be accessed and changed within the program—it is not really a constant. Java enables you to define symbolic constants or named constants called *class constants*, which can be referred to by an identifier by using the following syntax:

```
final type variable = initialize_value;
```

The class constant definition is similar to a class variable definition with the exception of the reserved word final preceding the definition. The reserved word final indicates that the value assigned by *initialize_value* is the final value (constant value), and it cannot be changed. Any attempt to change the value of the class constant will generate a syntax error when the program is compiled. Thus, MAX_SIZE could be defined as follows:

```
final int MAX_SIZE = 312;
```

Here is an example of the use of class constants:

```
class ConstClass
{
      final int MAX_STUDENTS = 100;

      public void Ex1()
      {
         int[] grades = new int[MAX_STUDENTS];

         for (int x = 0; x < MAX_STUDENTS; x++)
      {
            grades[x] = 0;

         } // end for

         } // end Ex1

} // end ConstClass
```

Notice that the class constant MAX_STUDENTS was defined in the class and outside a method. Could you have placed the definition of MAX_STUDENTS inside the method Ex1? The answer is no. This is not a severe limitation, as it may first seem, because methods always occur inside classes, and a class constant defined in a class is accessible by all methods in the class (see fig. 6.4).

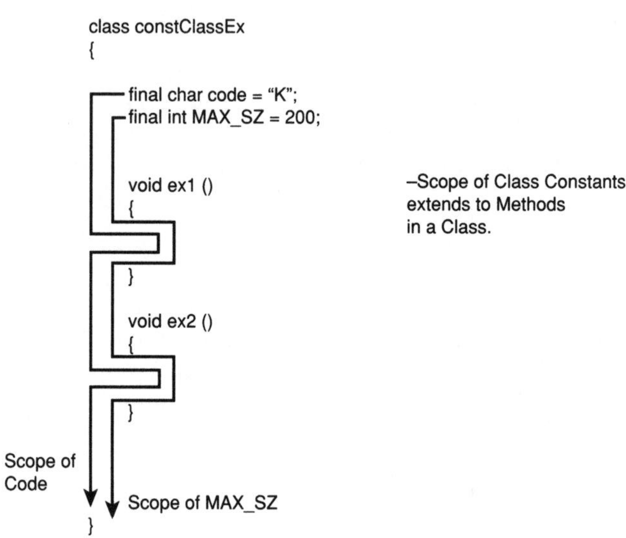

Figure 6.4
Scope of class constants.

Note Constants defined by using the final keyword can only occur in classes. They cannot be defined inside a method.

Implementing Class Methods

Most of the logic for classes is contained in the class methods. The class variables are also important to define because they describe the data structures that are used in the class methods, but the behavior of the class is contained in the class methods.

When you implement classes, you will spend most of the time defining the methods and implementing their logic. The following sections focus on different aspects of defining class methods.

Defining Class Methods

You have seen examples of several class methods already in this book. The most common example you have seen in the previous chapters has been the `main()` method, which must be defined for all Java applications that are to run stand-alone without the help of a Web browser.

All methods have the following components (see fig. 6.5):

- The name of the method
- The type of data returned by this method
- The parameter for the method
- The body of the method

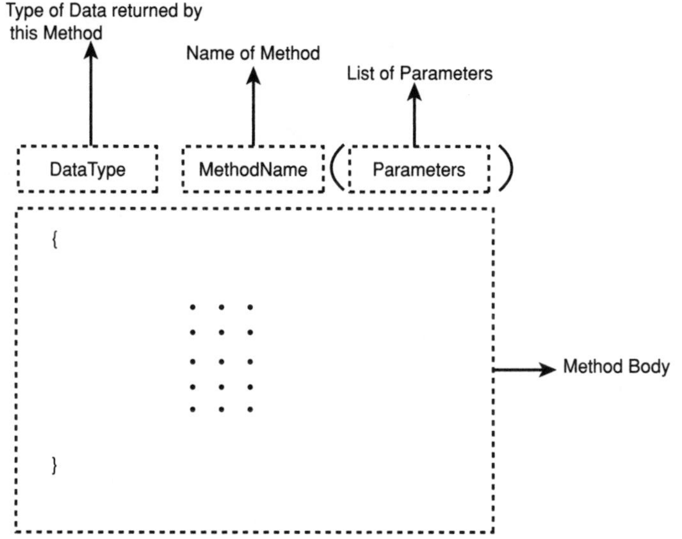

Figure 6.5
Method components.

The following is the general syntax of a method:

```
qualifiers return_type methodname( type1 param1, type2 param2, ... )
{
      ...

}
```

The *qualifiers* are reserved words such as public, static, and so on. The *qualifiers* are optional and control how the method is used or accessed by other Java program code.

The *return_type* is the data type of the value returned by the method. The *return_type* can be a Java basic type (such as int, char, float, and so on), or it can be a class name, or the reserved word void. If the reserved word void is used, it indicates that no value is returned by the method.

If the method has to return an array of values, such as an array of integers, it can be written in either of the following forms:

```
int[] methodname(parameters)
{
        ...
}
```

or

```
int methodname(parameters)[]
{
        ...
}
```

The first method is more intuitive and easier to understand, and for this reason it is the preferred form.

If a *return_type* is not void, you must have at least one return statement of the following type:

```
    return expression;
```

The data type of the return expression must match the *return_type* of the method. If the *return_type* is void, you do not have to use a return statement. The method will exit when its last statement is executed. If you need to terminate a void type method before its last statement, you can use the return statement without the expression:

```
    return;
```

The parameters are optional and are used to pass data to the method. If the method doesn't have any parameters, you write the method with an empty list of parentheses ():

```
void methodname()
{
        ...
}
```

The parameter list is a set of variable declarations separated by commas. Writing these parameters is similar to writing class variables or local variables, except that you must use commas to separate them, instead of semicolons. The parameters act as placeholders for the actual parameter value that is passed to the method. The parameters to the method are also called *arguments*. The parameters are also treated as local variables inside the body of the method.

The body of the method can contain any valid statement and expressions, such as variable and object definitions, assignment statements, and conditional statements, such as for, while, do-while, if, switch, and so on.

The *methodname* is the name of the method, and it is any valid Java identifier. An identifier in Java can be a sequence of unicode characters of *any* length. For practical reasons, you may not want to abuse this lack of limitation in the length of an identifier. Defining a method, for example, whose name is 500 characters will not only make the program difficult to create, but also create significant difficulties for anyone who is trying to understand and modify the program. The characters that you can use to create the identifier are limited. A Java identifier must begin with a letter, followed by any combination of letters and digits. A letter is a set consisting of letters a–z, A–Z, and the underscore (_) and dollar ($) characters.

Methods within a class can call each other by using the method name followed by a list of argument values that match the number and type of parameters for the method being called. Java code that is outside the class, in another method, must use an object name or class name reference for calling the method:

```
reference.methodname(parameters);
```

The *reference* is the object name or class name (for static methods). The *methodname* is the name of the method that is being called, and *parameters* is a list of argument values with which the method is being called.

The program in listing 6.1 shows an example of the use of calling method names from within a class and outside a class. This program is the SortArray program discussed in Chapter 5, "Using Java Objects and Arrays," but it is written as two separate classes instead of one single class. The program is in the file MethodCalls.java in the CD-ROM that accompanies this book. Figure 6.6 shows the classes and methods that you can use to quickly examine the structure of the program. From this figure, you can see that the program consists of two classes MethodCalls and ArraySort2. The MethodCalls class contains the method main(), and the ArraySort2 class contains the methods sort(), orderOK(), and print().

Lines 10–55 in listing 6.1 contain the MethodCalls class, and lines 57–146 contain the ArraySort2 class. Lines 47–50 contain the following statements:

```
ArraySort2.sort(sortAscending, ya);
        ArraySort2.print(sortAscending ?
                 "Ascending order":
                 "Descending order", ya);
```

Notice that the methods sort() and print() are static methods in an another class ArraySort2. To invoke these methods from the MethodCalls, you have to precede them with a reference to their class name, ArraySort2.

Within the method sort() in class ArraySort2, on line 78, a call is made to another method orderOK() in the same class. Because orderOK() is in the same class as the method that calls it, there is no need to precede this by the reference to the class name.

Figure 6.6
Class view.

MethodCalls classes
ArraySort2
orderOK()
print()
sort()
MethodCalls
main()

Listing 6.1

```
Line=================Java Source=================
/**
 * MethodCalls: This shows the manner in which methods
 * are called inside a class and outside a class.
 * The example used is that of an array sort.
 *
 * Author: Karanjit S.G.S. Siyan
 *
 */

class MethodCalls
{
    public static void main(String[] args)
    {
        boolean sortAscending = true; // Controls type of sort.
        int[] xa = { -20, 500, 200, 100, 300, -5,
                         0, 800, 600, 250, 700, -100};

        if (args.length != 1)
        {
            System.out.println("Usage:\n\trunvm ArraySort
            ➥[ascending¦descending]");
            System.exit(1);

        } // end if

        if (args[0].equalsIgnoreCase("ascending"))
        {
            sortAscending = true;

        }
```

```
        else if (args[0].equalsIgnoreCase("descending"))
        {
            sortAscending = false;

        }
        else
        {
            System.out.println("Illegal parameter to program.");
            System.exit(1);

        }  // end if

        // Make a copy of the array so that the original
        // is not modified.

        int[] ya = new int[xa.length];
        System.arraycopy(xa, 0, ya, 0, xa.length);
        ArraySort2.sort(sortAscending, ya);
        ArraySort2.print(sortAscending ?
                "Ascending order":
                "Descending order", ya);


    } // end main

} // end MethodCalls

class ArraySort2
{

   /*
    * sort: This is the sort procedure that sorts
    * the specified array in an ascending or
    * descending order. This procedure implements
    * the shell sort algorithm.
    *
    */
    static void sort(boolean sortAsc, int st[])
    {
```

continues

Listing 6.1, Continued

```

        for (int gap = st.length/2; gap > 0; gap /= 2)
        {
            for (int x = gap; x < st.length; x++)
            {
                for (int y = x - gap; y >= 0; y -= gap)
                {
                    int temp;

                    if (orderOK(sortAsc, st[y], st[y+gap]))
                    {
                        break;

                    }  // end if

                    // Exchange
                    temp = st[y];
                    st[y] = st[y+gap];
                    st[y+gap] = temp;

                }  // end for

            }  // end for

        } // end for

    }  // end sort

   /*
    * orderOK: This determines if the existing order of the
    * two elements in the array is OK.
    *
    */
    static boolean orderOK(boolean sortAsc, int xe, int ye)
    {
        boolean result = false;

        if (sortAsc)
        {
```

```
            if (xe <= ye)
            {
                result = true;

            } // end if
        }
        else
        {

            if (xe > ye)
            {
                result = true;

            } // end if

        } // end if

        return result;

    } // end orderOK

    /*
     * print: This is used to print the
     * values of the array.
     */
    static void print(String msg, int[] xa)
    {
        System.out.println(msg+"\n");

        for (int x = 0; x < xa.length; x++)
        {

            System.out.println(xa[x]);

        } // end for

    } // end print

} // end ArraySort2
```

Method Signatures and Method Overloading

The method name must have a unique *signature* within the class. The signature of the method consists of the name of the method and the number and type of its parameters. Consider, for example, the following class method definition with several methods all named sampleReadings:

```
class OverLoad
{
      int sampleReadings()
      {
         ...
      }

      int sampleReadings(int x)
      {
         ...
      }

      int sampleReadings(float x)
      {
         ...
      }

      int sampleReadings(int x, int y)
      {
         ...
      }

      int sampleReadings(int x, float y)
      {
         ...
      }

      int sampleReadings(float x, int y)
      {
         ...
      }

      int sampleReadings(float x, float y)
      {
```

```
            ...
        }
}
```

Each of the methods has an unique signature because even though the method name is the same, there is a difference between each method in the combination of the number of arguments and the types of arguments. When several methods with the same name but with unique signatures are used in a class, the method name is said to be *overloaded.*

The method signature does not include the return type. Consider the example program in listing 6.2 (file OverLoadedError.java on the CD-ROM accompanying this book). The class OverLoadedError contains four overloaded functions `factor()`. The methods on lines 18 and 25 differ only in their return types—one returns an `int` and the other returns a `float`:

```
int factor(int x, int y) { ... }

float factor(int x, int y) { ... }
```

If you compile this program, you will receive the following error message (see fig. 6.7) that the two methods differ only in their return type.

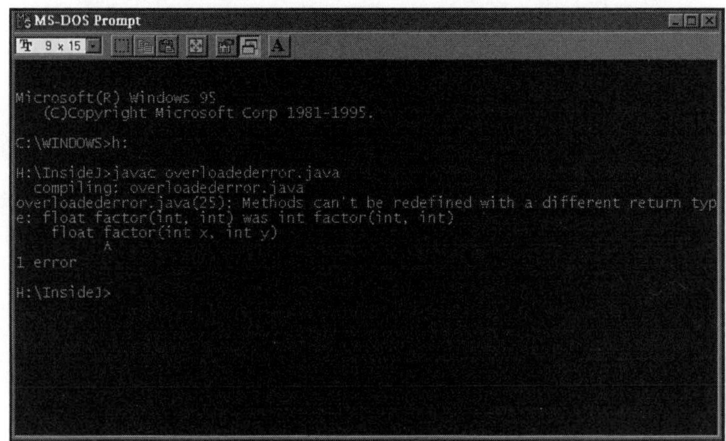

Figure 6.7

Compile error on overloading by return types.

Listing 6.2

```
Line==================Java Source==================
/**
 * OverLoadedError: This shows that you cannot
 * overload methods based upon differences in
 * return type.
 *
 * Author: Karanjit S.G.S. Siyan
 *
 */
class OverLoadedError
{
    int factor()
    {
        System.out.println("factor() called");
        return 1;

    }  // end factor

    int factor(int x, int y)
    {
        System.out.println("int factor(int, int) called");
        return 1;

    }  // end factor

    float factor(int x, int y)
    {
        System.out.println("float factor(int, int) called");
        return 1.0f;

    }  // end factor

    int factor(int x, float y)
    {
        System.out.println("int factor(int, float) called");
        return 1;

    }  // end factor
```

```
} // end OverLoadedError
```

Note You cannot overload class methods with differences only in their return type.

Understanding Parameter Passing in Methods

Parameter passing in Java is accomplished by a technique called *call by value.* It's called this because a copy of the value of the parameter, stored in separate memory from the original parameter value, is passed. When a method is executed, it works with copies of the parameter values. Any changes that the method makes are made to the copy of the parameter value only. These changes will not affect the original parameter value that was passed.

The program in listing 6.3 (file CallByValue.java in the CD-ROM accompanying this book) demonstrates the call by value nature of Java parameter passing. Figure 6.8 shows the output of this program. Before calling `multBy3()` on line 15, the value of `x` is printed out; it is 10. Within the method `multBy3()`, the value of `x` is printed out on entry to the method and after it is multiplied by 3—these values are 10 and 30, respectively. On line 17, the value of `x` is printed out after the call to `multBy3()`. Figure 6.8 shows that while the value of `x` was modified in `multBy3()`, there was no change in the value on return from `multBy3()`. This is because a copy of the value of `x` was passed to `multBy3()`. Changes to `x` inside `multBy3()` were done on this copy, and not the original value, so the value of `x` in line 17 is unchanged.

Figure 6.9 illustrates the call by value for the program in listing 6.2.

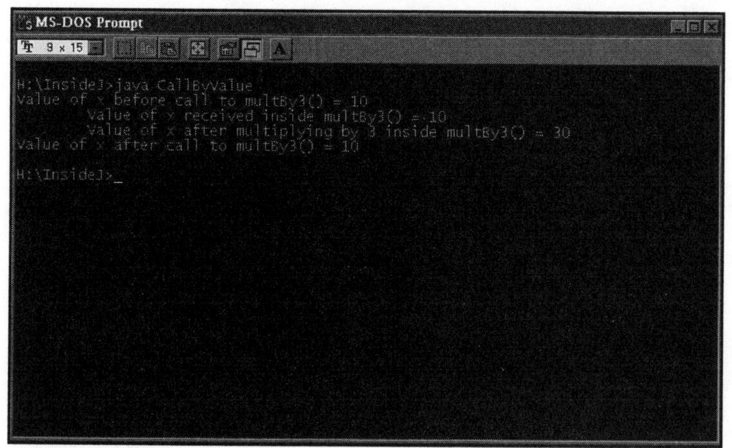

Figure 6.8

Output of CallByValue.

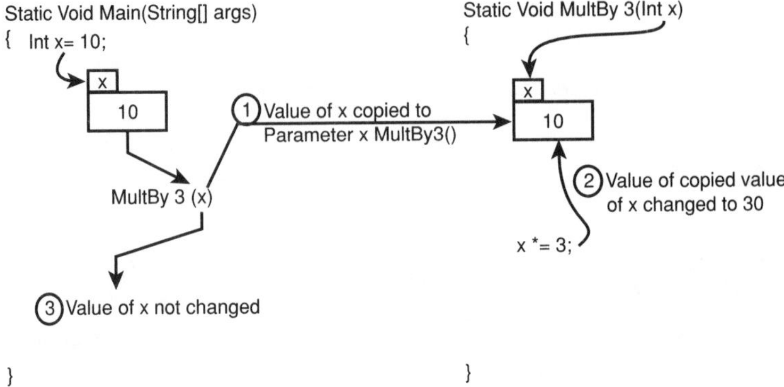

Figure 6.9 *Call by value illustrated.*

Listing 6.3

```
Line=================Java Source=================
/**
 * CallByValue: This shows how call by value works.
 *
 * Author: Karanjit S.G.S. Siyan
 *
 */
class CallByValue
{
    public static void main(String[] args)
    {
        int x = 10;

        System.out.println("Value of x before call to multBy3() = "+x);

        multBy3(x);

        System.out.println("Value of x after call to multBy3() = "+x);

    }  // end main

    static void multBy3(int x)
    {
        System.out.println("\tValue of x received inside multBy3() = "+x);

        x *= 3;

```

```
        System.out.println("\tValue of x after multiplying by 3 inside
➥multBy3() = "+x);

    } // end multBy3

} // end CallByValue
```

The example in listing 6.3 used a basic Java type passed as a parameter. If, however, Java objects such as arrays and class instances are passed as parameters, their reference values are passed by value. A reference value for a Java object is the internal address of the object. This internal address is not available to you, the programmer, for manipulation.

Consider the example of passing an object to a method shown by program in listing 6.4 (see file CallByValue2.java on the CD-ROM accompanying this book).

The output of this program CallByValue2 is shown in figure 6.10. This output shows that the color of the car object is modified after a call to the method.

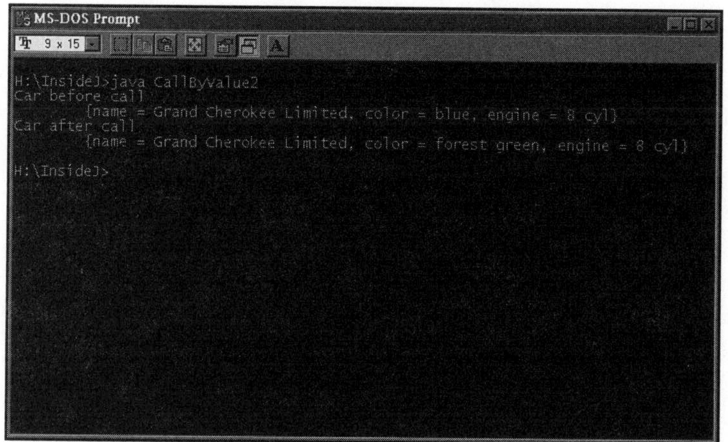

Figure 6.10

Output of call by value for Java objects.

Lines 9–41 contain the declaration of the CallByValue2 class and lines 44–71 contain the definition of the Car class. A good place to start understanding this program is to examine the Car class first, and then the CallByValue2 class that uses the Car class.

Lines 46–48 define class variables name, color, and nCylinders for holding the make of the car, the color of the car, and the number of cylinders in the car engine.

Lines 51–57 define a constructor for the car. Recall that a constructor builds the instance of the class. In the case of the constructor for Car, the name, color, and number of cylinders are passed as parameters to the constructor, and the class variables are set to these parameter values.

```
61      public String toString()
62      {
63          String descr = "{name = "+name+
64                          ", color = "+color+
65                          ", engine = "+nCylinders+" cyl}";
66
67          return descr;
68
69      } // end toString
```

Lines 61–69 contain the toString() method for class Car. The toString() method needs to be defined for every class that expects its value to be printed out by using the print() and println() methods defined for the PrintStream class. These print methods call the toString() method to generate a printable string value for all objects passed to them.

Next, examine the class CallByValue2. Line 18 instantiates the Car class and builds an object called car by calling the constructor for class Car.

```
Car car = new Car("Grand Cherokee Limited", "blue", 8);
```

Line 20 prints out the current value of the car object. The `println()` method uses the `toString()` method defined in class Car to print out the car object.

```
System.out.println("Car before call\n\t"+car);
```

Line 22 calls the `changeToGreen()` method defined in the class CallByValue2 to change the color of the car object passed to it to green.

```
changeToGreen(car);
```

When the car object is passed to this method, the reference (address) to the car object is passed by value. Figure 6.11 shows that there are two references to car object. One is the actual object car and the other is the parameter for the car object, autoRef, in the `changeToGreen()` method.

Step 1 in figure 6.11 shows that the reference value of car is passed by value to the autoRef parameter. At this point, both car and autoRef point to the same object (see step 2). In step 3, when the color value is modified by using autoRef, the actual color value of the object that was passed is modified. This is illustrated in the output in figure 6.10.

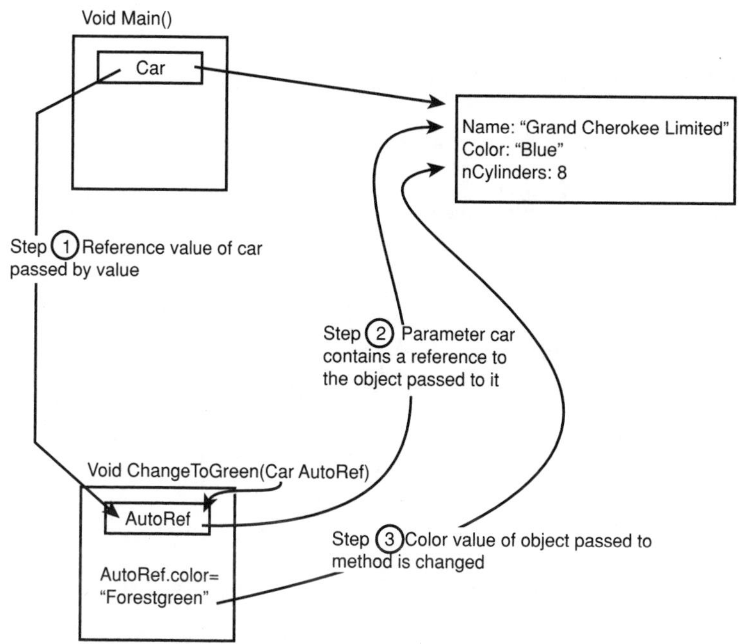

Figure 6.11

Two references to car object.

Listing 6.4

```
Line=================Java Source================
/**
 * CallByValue2: This shows how call by value works
 * for Java objects.
 *
 * Author: Karanjit S.G.S. Siyan
 *
 */

class CallByValue2
{
    /*
     * main: Main procedure that is called
     * by Java runtime.
     */
    public static void main(String[] args)
    {
        // Build a new car
```

continues

Listing 6.4, Continued

```
        Car car = new Car("Grand Cherokee Limited", "blue", 8);

        System.out.println("Car before call\n\t"+car);

        // Change color of car to green
        changeToGreen(car);

        // What do you think:
        //      Has the color changed?
        System.out.println("Car after call\n\t"+car);

    } // end main


   /*
    * changeToGreen: Selectively changes color of car
    */
    static void changeToGreen(Car autoRef)
    {
        autoRef.color = "forest green";

    } // end changeToGreen

} // end CallByValue2

// Car class definition
class Car
{
    String name = "no name";
    String color = "no color";
    int nCylinders;

    // Car constructor
    Car (String nam, String col, int nCyl)
    {
        name = nam;
        color = col;
        nCylinders = nCyl;

```

```
    } // end Car

    // toString: Needed by System.out.println
    // to print string value of car.
    public String toString()
    {
        String descr = "{name = "+name+
                       ", color = "+color+
                       ", engine = "+nCylinders+" cyl}";

        return descr;

    } // end toString

} // end Car
```

Passing object references by values avoids large copies of data structures that would become necessary if the entire object was passed by value. If, for example, you were passing a large object such as an int array of 1000 bytes to a method by value, instead of the array reference, the compiler would have to copy 4000 bytes of data. Obviously, this is very inefficient. Because the array reference is passed by value, only the size of the reference (address) value needs to be copied internally, and this amounts to just a few bytes (typically 4 bytes on a 32-bit processor).

Use of this

Java provides a reserved word called *this* to refer to an instance of the class object itself. When writing a method, you do not know ahead of time what the name of the object is. Use of *this* can, in many instances, simplify the writing of the class methods.

Consider the following example that defines two classes AnotherClass and Continent:

```
class AnotherClass
{
      void getArea(Continent cont)
      {
         // statements

      } // end getArea

      // Other methods
```

```
} // end AnotherClass

class Continent
{
      void drift()
      {
         AnotherClass uobj;

         uobj.getArea(this);


      } // end drift

      // Other methods
} // end Continent
```

In the getArea() method of the AnotherClass, an object of type Continent is passed. In the method `drift()` in the class Continent, the method `getArea()` needs to be called. `getArea()` needs to be called with an instance of the class Continent, and, in this case, the instance is the same object for which the method `drift()` was called. The problem here is that you do not know beforehand the name of the object instance. This is where this comes in handy! Notice that `getArea()` is called with this as a parameter:

```
uobj.getArea(this);
```

Actually, the use of this is implied for all references to the class variables within the class. Consider, for example, the following Java code fragment:

```
class ExThis
{
      float area = 10F;
      int       index = 0;
      char      ch;

      void method1()
      {
         int        x = 20;
         float      y = 40f;
         float      z = 1f;
```

```
            area = 20f;
            index = 20;
            ch = 'x';


        } // end method1
} // end ExThis
```

The preceding code fragment is equivalent to the following:

```
class ExThis
{
    float area = 10F;
    int     index = 0;
    char    ch;

    void method1()
    {
        int         x = 20;
        float       y = 40f;
        float       z = 1f;

        this.area = 20f;
        this.index = 20;
        this.ch = 'x';

    } // end method1

} // end ExThis
```

Notice that in the second version of the code fragment, the use of this is used to reference all class variables for the object for which the method was invoked. This illustrates the fact that the use of this is implied for all reference to class variables within the class itself. You can omit this for referencing class variables and reference them just by the name; the use of this, in this case is implicit.

You can also use this to distinguish between class variables and local variables. Consider the example of the constructor for Car in the listing 6.4.

```
class Car
{
        String name = "no name";
```

```
    String color = "no color";
    int nCylinders;

    // Car constructor
    Car (String nam, String col, int nCyl)
    {
        name = nam;
        color = col;
        nCylinders = nCyl;

    } // end Car

    // toString: Needed by System.out.println
    // to print string value of car.
    public String toString()
    {
        String descr = "{name = "+name+
                       ", color = "+color+
                       ", engine = "+nCylinders+" cyl}";

        return descr;

    } // end toString

} // end Car
```

Notice that the parameters for the constructor `Car()` were changed so as not to conflict with the class variable names. If you wanted to use the same names for both the class variables and parameters, you could use the following:

```
class Car
{
    String name = "no name";
    String color = "no color";
    int nCylinders;

    // Car constructor
    Car (String name, String color, int nCylinders)
    {
        this.name = name;
```

```
        this.color = color;
        this.nCylinders = nCylinders;

    }  // end Car

    // toString: Needed by System.out.println
    // to print string value of car.
    public String toString()
    {
        String descr = "{name = "+name+
           ", color = "+color+
           ", engine = "+nCylinders+" cyl}";

        return descr;

    }  // end toString

}  // end Car
```

The statements that have been changed are in bold so that you can more easily identify the changes. The this.name, this.color, and this.nCylinders refer to the class instance variables, and the name, color, and nCylinders refer to parameters.

One reason that you may want to use the same name for class variables, parameters, and locals is that the name you selected is a good one, and is descriptive of the actual usage of the variable.

Note that you could also have written the toString() method by using this, as shown next:

```
public String toString()
    {
        String descr = "{name = "+this.name+
           ", color = "+this.color+
           ", engine = "+this.nCylinders+" cyl}";

        return descr;

    }  // end toString
```

But use of this can be omitted in this code because it is implicit.

Scope of Class Variables and Local Variables

A scope is the region of program text over which a variable is considered to have existence. Earlier in this chapter, you learned that the scope of a class variable is from its point of declaration in the class to the end of that class. The scope of local variables in a method is from its point of definition in the method to the nearest enclosing block (see fig. 6.12).

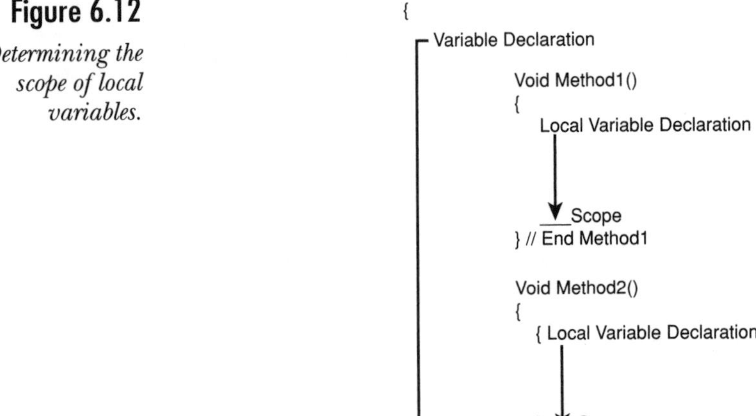

Figure 6.12

Determining the scope of local variables.

When a variable reference (local or class variable) occurs, the Java compiler checks to see if its declaration is in the current statement block. A statement block is statements defined in braces { }, and it defines a separate scope (see fig. 6.13). If the variable declaration is not in the current statement block, the next outermost scope is searched. If the search expands to outside the method, the variable is not a local variable—it is a class instance variable or a class wide variable. Classes in Java can have a super class from which this class has been derived. You will learn more about super classes in Chapter 7, "Object-Oriented Programming with Java." If the variable is not found in the current class, its super class is searched for the occurrence of the variable.

On the CD 

A variable in an inner scope can "hide" a variable in an outer scope, and this can lead to subtle errors in the program when this hiding is unintended. Listing 6.5 shows a program that illustrates these subtle effects (file VariableScope.java on the CD-ROM that accompanies this book).

Line 12 defines a class variable xvar whose value is set to 0. The scope of this variable is from line 12–59. Lines 16–18 of the main method calls the methods `print1()`, `print2()`, and `print3()` in succession. These methods print out the value of xvar. Some of these methods have local variables also defined by using the same name xvar as the class variable.

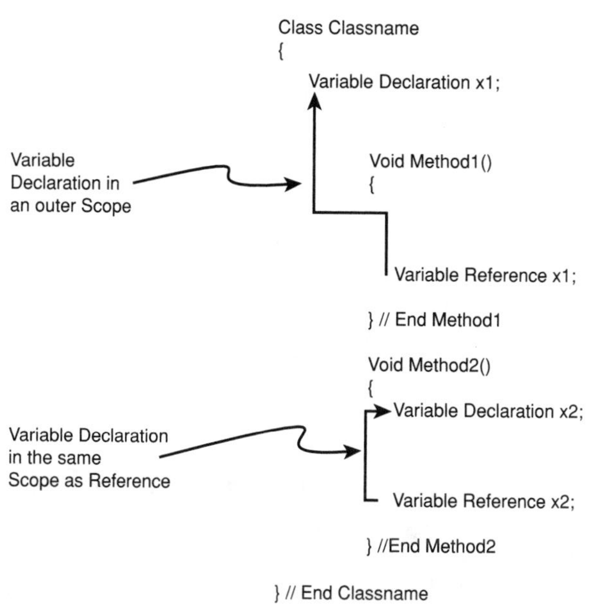

Figure 6.13

A statement block.

When `print1()` is called, it prints the value of xvar (line 25) and increments it (line 27) before exiting the method. The xvar referenced in print1() is the class variable xvar. Therefore, the value of xvar that is printed out is 0, and the value of class variable xvar is set to 1, just after the method `print1()` has been called.

Next, `print2()` is called. A local variable with the same name as the class variable xvar is defined on line 34, and its value is set to 2 on line 36. Line 37 prints the value of xvar, which is a reference to the local variable on line 34 and not the class variable. The value of xvar that is printed out is 2. On line 39 local variable xvar is incremented to 3, but when method print2() exists, this value is lost.

```
44      static void print3()
45      {
46          {
47              int xvar;
48
49              xvar = 3;
50              System.out.println("print3()inside block:xvar = "+xvar);
51
52              xvar++;
53          }
54
55         System.out.println("print3()outside block:xvar = "+xvar);
56
57      }  // end print3
```

Finally, `print3()` is called. This method defines a statement block on lines 46–53, and inside the block it defines a local variable xvar with the same name as the class variable. The scope of this local variable is from line 47 to the end of the statement block on line 53. Within the block statement, xvar is set to 3 (line 49), printed out (line 50), and incremented (line 52). The value of xvar that is printed out is 3, the value of the local variable xvar defined in line 47.

At the end of the block statement, the value of xvar is printed out again (line 55). This xvar is outside the scope of the block statement, and therefore is a reference to the xvar in the nearest enclosing block; that is, the class variable on line 12 whose value was set to 1 in line 25 when `print1()` was called.

Figure 6.14 shows the result of running the VariableScope program. You can see that the output is consistent with the previous discussion.

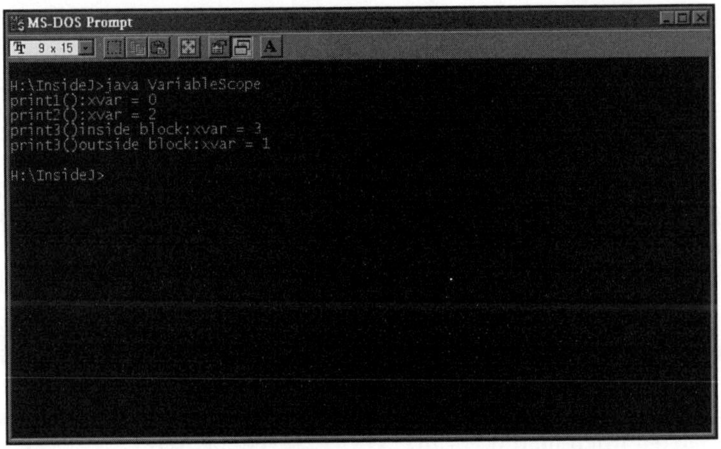

```
H:\InsideJ>java VariableScope
print1():xvar = 0
print2():xvar = 2
print3()inside block:xvar = 3
print3()outside block:xvar = 1

H:\InsideJ>
```

Figure 6.14

Output of VariableScope program.

Listing 6.5

```
Line=================Java Source=================
01 /**
02  * VariableScope: This shows the problem of
03  * information hiding of variables with the
04  * same name.
05  *
06  * Author: Karanjit S.G.S. Siyan
07  *
08  */
09
10 class VariableScope
```

```
{
    static int xvar = 0;

    public static void main(String[] args)
    {
        print1();
        print2();
        print3();

    } // end main

    static void print1()
    {

        System.out.println("print1():xvar = "+xvar);

        xvar++;

    } // end print1


    static void print2()
    {
        int xvar;

        xvar = 2;
        System.out.println("print2():xvar = "+xvar);

        xvar++;

    } // end print2


    static void print3()
    {
        {
            int xvar;

            xvar = 3;
```

continues

Listing 6.5, Continued

```
            System.out.println("print3()inside block:xvar = "+xvar);

            xvar++;
        }

        System.out.println("print3()outside block:xvar = "+xvar);

    } // end print3

} // end VariableScope
```

Constructor Methods

Constructors are special methods for classes whose primary purpose is to build an instance of the class. As part of the instantiation of a class, class instance variables and class variables may have to be initialized. The operator new is used to allocate space for the object being built. In many languages, objects that have been explicitly allocated space have to be explicitly freed up by the programmer. Not so in Java.

In Java you allocate space for an object by instantiating it, but you never explicitly reclaim the allocated space. The Java runtime automatically reclaims space for objects that are no longer in use. This process of reclaiming memory space is called *garbage collection*, and it is automatic in Java. By making garbage collection automatic, the programmer does not have to worry about a class of insidious bugs dealing with improper freeing up of memory, or the problem of forgetting to free up memory, which can result in “memory leakage”—memory that seems to have disappeared just when you need it!

The following shows the general syntax of a class constructor method:

```
qualifiers classname (parameters)
{

}
```

The name of the constructor is the same as the class name. The *parameters* are similar to that used for other methods and are optional. The *qualifiers* can control access to the constructor and are usually reserved words such as public or private. You will learn about the effect of these qualifiers in detail in Chapter 7. For now all that needs to be said about them is that public makes the constructor callable from any Java code outside the class. The use of private prohibits the call of the constructor, and hence the instantiation of the class, from outside the class.

An important difference that you may note between constructors and other class methods is the absence of the return type. You may think that because constructors do not have a return type, you can use a return type of void. But this is not allowed by the language.

Java constructor methods are always invoked with the use of the new operator:

```
new  classname(parameters);
```

The *parameters* must match, in number and type, one of the constructors defined for the class.

You can overload Java constructor methods. This means that you can define several constructor methods for a class that differ in the parameter number and type. In fact, it is typical to define several constructors for a method. Consider the following modified example of the class Car that was discussed in listing 6.4:

```
class Car
{
      String name = "no name";
      String color = "no color";
      int nCylinders;

      Car ()
      {
         this.name = "Ford";
         this.color = "yellow";
         this.nCylinders = 6;

      } // end Car

      // Car constructor
      Car (String name, String color, int nCylinders)
      {
         this.name = name;
         this.color = color;
         this.nCylinders = nCylinders;

      } // end Car

      // toString: Needed by System.out.println
      // to print string value of car.
```

```
    // toString: Needed by System.out.println
    // to print string value of car.
    public String toString()
    {
       String descr = "{name = "+name+
          ", color = "+color+
          ", engine = "+nCylinders+" cyl}";

       return descr;

    } // end toString

} // end Car
```

Notice the definition of a constructor `Car()` with no arguments. Calling this constructor defaults to a car object being created that is a Ford car, with yellow color, and a six-cylinder engine. You may also note that the code in the second constructor for Car (with parameters) is similar to the first constructor. You can simplify the code by having the first constructor call the second constructor:

```
Car ()
{
      Car("Ford", "yellow", 6);

} // end Car

// Car constructor
Car (String name, String color, int nCylinders)
{
      this.name = name;
      this.color = color;
      this.nCylinders = nCylinders;

} // end Car
```

Another interesting aspect of class constructors is the use of this within a constructor. In a class instance method, the use of this refers to the object for which the method was called. Inside a constructor method, this means the name of the class. So you could actually write the preceding code for the constructors as follows:

```
Car ()
{
      this("Ford", "yellow", 6);

}  // end Car

// Car constructor
Car (String name, String color, int nCylinders)
{
      this.name = name;
      this.color = color;
      this.nCylinders = nCylinders;

}  // end Car
```

Static Blocks

You have seen the use of static variables in a class definition. These variables are called class variables because they are defined for all instances of the class and they have a common data space.

Java permits the use of static initialization blocks that can perform a number of complex initializations before the main Java code is executed. The syntax of static initialization block is described next:

```
class classname
{

   static
   {

         // Static initialization code
   }


}
```

Consider a situation where you want to initialize an array of integers with numbers based on a certain algorithm or formula:

```
class Fibonacci
{
        static int[] series = new int[100];

        static
        {
           series[0] = series[1] = 1;
           for (int f = 2; f < 100; f++)
           {
              series[f] = series[f-1] + series[f-2];

           } // end for

        }

} // end Fibonacci
```

Note that the static initialization code does a fairly complex initialization of an array of 100 integers by using a for loop within the static initialization block.

The static initialization code is executed when the class is loaded. The static initialization code is executed left-to-right and top-to-bottom. In the previous example, this order of execution ensures that the array will have been defined before the static initialization code is executed.

It is possible for static initialization code in a class A to invoke a method in class B, which then invokes a method in class A. When the method in class A is invoked in this manner, it may access static fields in class A that have yet to be properly initialized because the static initialization for A has not been completed. Static fields that do not have their initializers executed are set to a default value, which is false for Booleans, 0 for numbers, null for object references, and '\u0000' for characters.

Building Modular Methods

Part of the process of creating an easy-to-understand yet powerful class is deciding on which methods you are going to define, what kind of parameters are going to be passed to the method, and how the methods are going to interact with each other. It is important to partition the functionality of methods in such a way that their use is intuitive.

The following steps are general guidelines that you can use for defining classes:

1. It is better to write several simple methods to accomplish a task rather than one super method that can handle different logic functions depending on the parameters passed to that function.

2. Try to restrict the size of a method to about three pages of text code (75 lines). In my opinion, this is the level of complexity that an average programmer can comprehend quickly.

3. Logic functions that are *orthogonal* should be in their own methods. Orthogonal functions are those that are logically quite different from each other, and have a high degree of independence between them.

4. If several methods in the class perform similar logic, you may want to define a separate "helper" method that is called by other methods. You may also want to restrict access to the helper method from outside the class.

Summary

In this chapter you learned the structure of Java classes and the new inner classes defined in Java 1.1. Java classes typically consist of class variables, class instance variables, and methods. You were presented with several examples that showed how classes can be defined. You learned about the issues of overloading Java methods and constructors, method signatures, the scope or class variables versus local variables, how parameters are passed to methods, and static initialization blocks for classes. Finally, you were presented with some useful guidelines for writing classes.

CHAPTER 7

Object-Oriented Programming with Java

In the previous chapter you learned how to define and structure classes. In this chapter you will learn to use an important technique of programming that is generally lumped into a category called object-oriented programming.

Java supports object-oriented programming by using an inheritance mechanism that enables a class to extend another class. In this chapter you will learn about superclasses and inheritance, and how these mechanisms enable you to reuse logic in existing classes.

Inheritance in Java

This section will explain the basic properties of inheritance in relationship to the Java language.

Understanding Inheritance Terminology

When a class E extends a class S, a relationship of the type shown in figure 7.1 is set up between them. The class S is called the *superclass*, and the class E is called the *subclass* or *extended class*. Other terms that also have been used to describe this relationship refer to S as the *parent class* and refer to E as the *derived class*, or *child class*. Class E is also said to *inherit* from class S.

In the inheritance relationship shown in figure 7.1, class E, as well as being able to access its own instance variables and methods, also can use the methods and instance variables that class S has made available for just such a purpose.

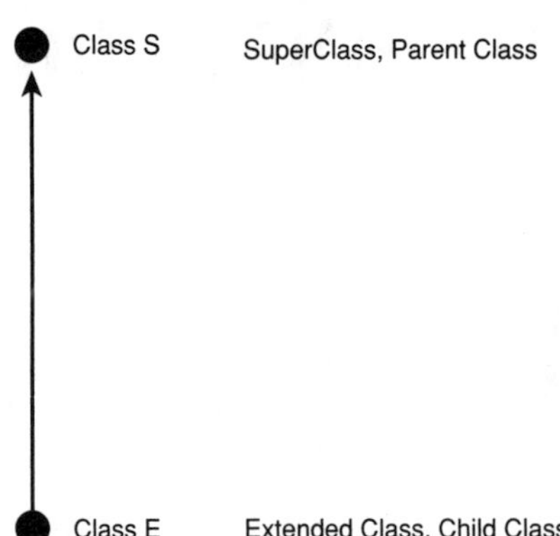

Figure 7.1
Inheritance relationship.

In Java syntax, the relationship of figure 7.1 is described as the following:

```
class E extends S
{
      // Definition for class E

} // end E
```

Notice that the use of the reserved word extends the definition of the superclass S.

Consider the following skeleton structure for the two classes:

```
class S
{
      // Declarations for instance variable sa, sb, sc.

      void s_method1()
      {
         ...
      } // end s_method1

      void s_method2()
      {
         ...

      } // end s_method2

      void s_method3()
      {
         ...

      } // end s_method3


} // end S


class E extends S
{
      // Declarations for instance variable ea, eb, ec.

      void e_method1()
      {
         ...
      } // end e_method1

      void e_method2()
      {
         ...

      } // end e_method2
```

```
        void e_method3()
        {
            ...

        } // end e_method3


} // end E
```

All the methods in E can use their class E's instance variables ea, eb, ec, and methods `e_method1()`, `e_method2`, `e_method3()`. In addition, these classes can also use the instance variables in class S, sa, sb, and sc. Additionally, the code in E can also use the methods in S; that is, `s_method1()`, `s_method2()`, and `s_method3()`.

The relationship between classes S and E is also shown in figure 7.2. The inherited class E (subclass) is shown as encapsulating the class S, to indicate that the methods and instance variables in S are available in class E.

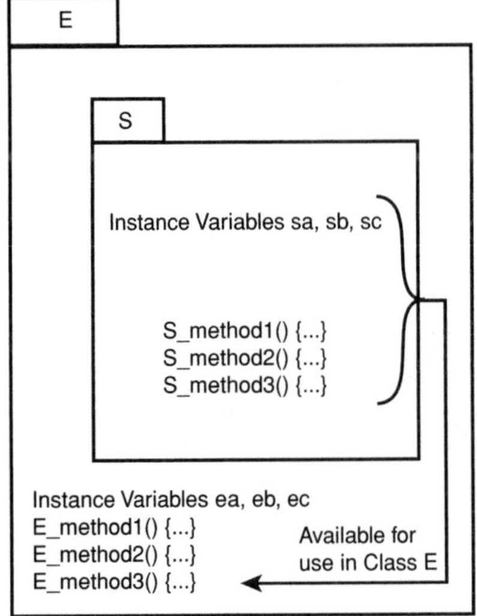

Figure 7.2

Class inheritance from E to S.

Building a Derivation Chain

You can also define other classes that can inherit from class E, even though class E inherits from another class S, as seen in the previous section. This type of inheritance relationship is shown in figure 7.3. The diagram of figure 7.3 is also called a *class hierarchy diagram.* Class hierarchies describe the relationship between Java classes. Java's predefined classes use class hierarchy diagrams.

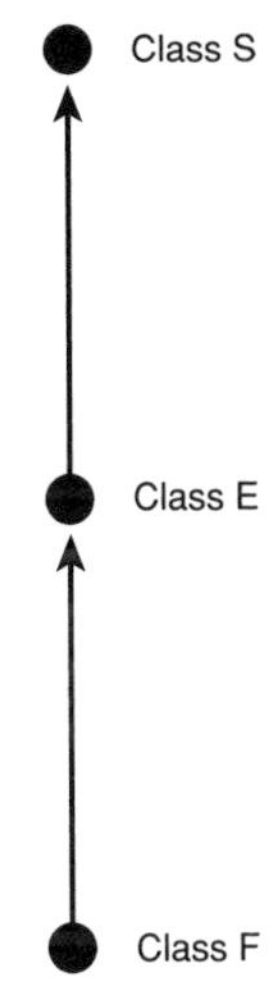

Figure 7.3

A three-level inheritance chain.

Consider another class F inherited from the class E, as shown in the following example:

```
class F extends E
{
      // Declarations for instance variable fa, fb, fc.

      void f_method1()
      {
         ...
      } // end f_method1

      void f_method2()
      {
```

```
        ...

    } // end f_method2

    void f_method3()
    {
        ...

    } // end f_method3


} // end F
```

All the methods in class F can, of course, use their instance variables fa, fb, fc, and methods `f_method1()`, `f_method2`, `f_method3()`. In addition, these classes can also use the instance variables in class E, ea, eb, and ec; and also instance variables in E's superclass sa, sb, and sc. Additionally, the code in F can also use the methods in class E and the superclass S; that is, `e_method1()`, `e_method2()`, `e_method3()`; and `s_method1()`, `s_method1()`, and `s_method3()`.

The relationship between classes S, E, and F is also shown in figure 7.4. The inherited class F is shown as encapsulating the class E, which is shown encapsulating S. This indicates that the methods and instance variables in E and S are available in class F.

Understanding Inheritance Rules in Java

Listing 7.1 shows a program (file InheritRules.java on the CD-ROM that accompanies this book) in which class E inherits from class S. Both classes, S and E, define instance variables and instance methods. Figure 7.5 shows at a quick glance the method and instance variables in the two classes.

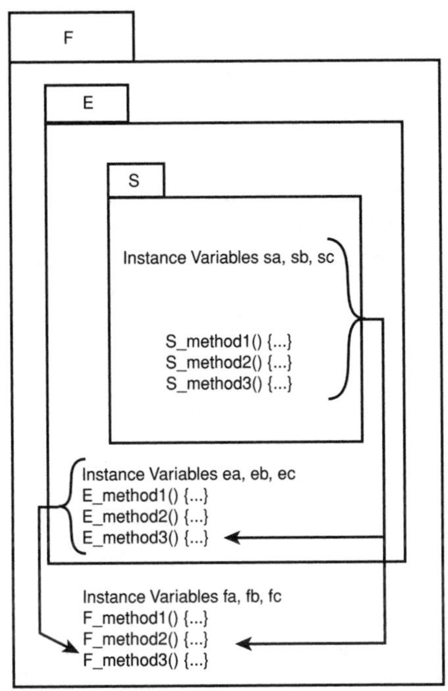

Figure 7.4

Class inheritance between F, E, and S.

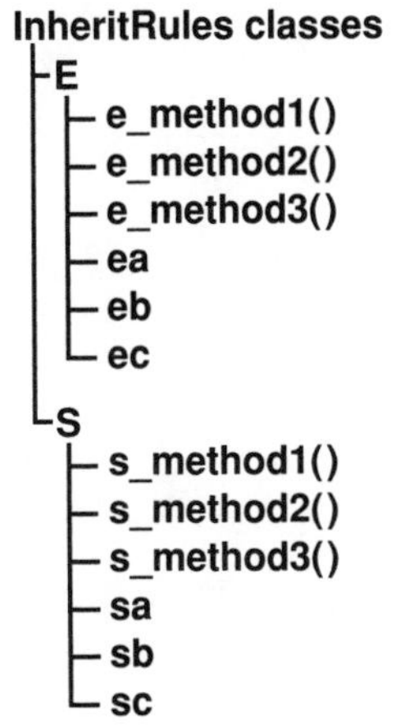

Figure 7.5

ClassView for InheritRules.java.

Listing 7.1

```
Line==================Java Source==================

/**
 * InheritRules: This demonstrates the use of object inheritance.
 *
 * Author: Karanjit S. G. S. Siyan
 *
 */

class S
{
    // Instance variables for class S.
    int sa;
    int sb;
    int sc;

    // Instance methods for class S
    void s_method1()
    {
        System.out.println("sa = "+sa);

        // Question 1: Can a method in class E be
        // invoked from class S?
        e_method1();


    }  // end s_method1

    void s_method2()
    {
        System.out.println("sb = "+sb);

        // Question 2: Can a method in classe S reference
        // an instance variable in class E?
        eb = 5;


    }  // end s_method2
```

```

    void s_method3()
    {
        System.out.println("sc = "+sc);

    }  // end s_method3

}  // end S


class E extends S
{
    // Instance variables for class E.
    int ea;
    int eb;
    int ec;

    // Instance methods for class E
    void e_method1()
    {
        System.out.println("ea = "+ea);

        // Question 3: Can a method in class E
        // invoke a method in class S?
        s_method1();

    }  // end e_method1

    void e_method2()
    {
        // Question 4: Can a method in class E
        // reference an instance variable in E?
        System.out.println("eb = "+eb);

    }  // end e_method2

    void e_method3()
    {
        System.out.println("ec = "+ec);
```

continues

Listing 7.1, Continued

```
77         // Question 5: Can a method in class E
78         // reference an instance variable in S?
79         sa = 10;
80
81
82     } // end e_method3
83
84 }  // end E
```

The comments in listing 7.1 have questions that are asked about the use of instance variables and instance methods. These questions are followed by a statement that attempts to perform the action described in the question. These questions are listed as follows:

Question 1: Can a method in class E be invoked from class S?

Question 2: Can a method in class S reference an instance variable in class E?

Question 3: Can a method in class E invoke a method in class S?

Question 4: Can a method in class E reference an instance variable in E?

Question 5: Can a method in class E reference an instance variable in S?

At this point, you may want to compile the file InheritRules.java by using the javac compiler to see if you can answer these questions. On compiling this program, you will find two errors on lines 23 and 34 respectively. Both of these errors are in class S. All other statements compile correctly. The lines in error deal with questions 1 and 2, and indicate that the answers to these questions is "No."

The following is a detailed analysis of the questions in listing 7.1:

Question 1: *Can a method in class E be invoked from class S?* No. Class S is a superclass for class E. Superclasses do not have access to the methods in subclasses. This is because a subclass, such as E, may extend the definition of class S by adding additional instance variables. Having an instance of class S does not guarantee that a subclass such as E has been instantiated, and its instance variables set up correctly.

Question 2: *Can a method in class S reference an instance variable in class E?* No—for reasons similar to the answer to question 1. Remember that class S is a superclass for class E. Superclasses do not have access to the internals (methods and instance variables) for subclasses. This is because creating an instance of class S does not guarantee that a subclass such as E has been instantiated, and its instance variables set up correctly.

***Question 3:** Can a method in class E invoke a method in class S?* Yes. Class E is a subclass of class S. A method subclass can invoke a method in its superclass.

***Question 4:** Can a method in class E reference an instance variable in E?* Yes. This is the normal behavior for all classes. Instance variables in a class are visible to all methods of that class.

***Question 5:** Can a method in class E reference an instance variable in S?* Yes. Class E is a subclass of class S. A subclass can access the instance variables in its superclass, unless such an access has been denied by making the superclass instance variable private. One of the reasons it may want to access an instance variable in the superclass is to perform additional logic for methods in the subclass.

Overriding Methods for Java Classes

Listing 7.2 shows a program (file OverrideMethod.java on the CD-ROM that accompanies the book) in which class E inherits from class S. Both classes, S and E, define instance variables and methods. Some of the instance methods in class E and S, however, are the same. Figure 7.6 shows the method and instance variables in the two classes. Notice that the method `size()` occurs in both class S and its subclass E. When a method with the same signature occurs in a subclass and its superclass, the method in the subclass is said to override the method of the superclass. The method `E.size()`, therefore, overrides the method `S.size()`, the method in the superclass. This means that if the method `size()` was invoked for an instance of class E, the method that would be invoked would be that of the corresponding class E.

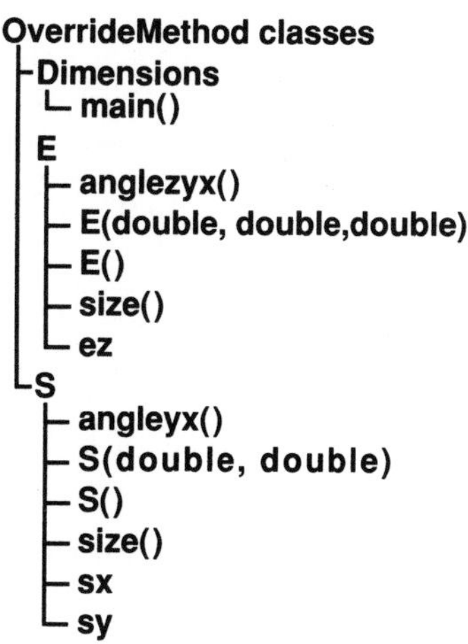

Figure 7.6

ClassView for OverrideMethod.java.

The set of methods that can be invoked for a class is called its *contract.* If a method invoked for a class is not found in the contract for the class, the superclass of the method is searched for that method. If the method is not found in the superclass, the search proceeds up the inheritance hierarchy. From listing 7.2, you can see that the contracts for class S and E are the following:

Contract for S:

```
S()
S(double sx, double sy)
double size()
double angleyx()
```

Contract for E:

```
E()
E(double x, double y, double z)
double size()
double anglezyx()
```

The *protocol* of a class is the set of methods that can be invoked for a class. This includes the methods in the contract for the class, plus the methods in the superclass minus the superclass methods that have been overridden. The following is an example of the protocol for the class E:

```
S()             // In class S
S(double sx, double sy) // In class S
double angleyx() // In class S
E()        // In class E
E(double x, double y, double z) // In class E
double size() // In class E
double anglezyx() // In class E
```

The method `size()` defined in class S is not listed in the protocol for class E because it is overridden.

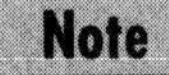

When a method with the same signature occurs in both the superclass and its subclass, the method in the subclass overrides the method in the superclass.

Lines 10–45 define the class Dimension with the method `main()` needed for the standalone program. The remaining lines in the program define the superclass S and its subclass E.

Lines 49–97 define the superclass S. The superclass S defines the class instance variables sx and sy on lines 52 and 53. These instance variables represent the coordinates of a point on the X–Y plane. The instance variable sx represents the x-coordinate and the instance variable the y-coordinate of the point. The point <sx, sy> is also considered to be a vector from the origin <0,0>, to the point <sx, sy> (see fig. 7.7).

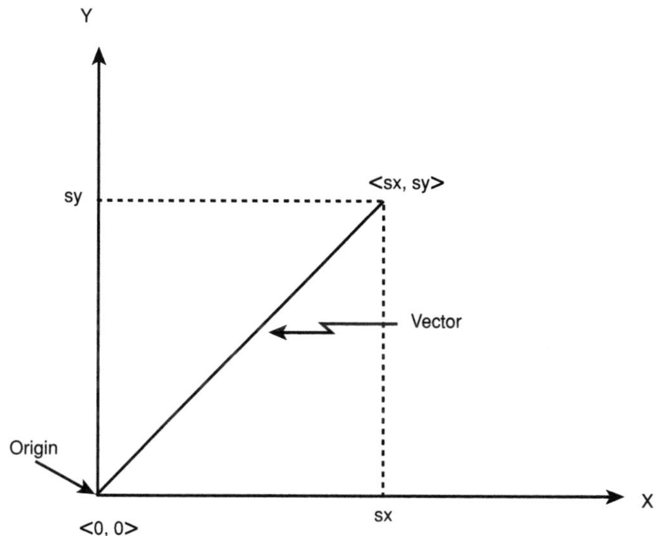

Figure 7.7

Point <sx, sy> as a vector.

Lines 57–61 define one of the constructors for class S. This constructor has no arguments, and it is also called the *default constructor*. This constructor sets the values of the instance variables to default values of 1.

Lines 63–68 define another constructor for class S. This constructor takes two arguments corresponding to the values to be assigned to the instance variables sx and sy. Notice that the following assignment statements are used to set the instance variables:

```
this.sx = sx;
this.sy = sy;
```

The left-hand side of the assignment statements uses the `this` qualifier to distinguish it from the parameters with the same name.

Note The *default constructor* is the class constructor with no arguments.

Lines 73–83 define the `size()` method. This method performs a mathematical calculation to determine the length of the line joining the point <sx, sy> to the origin represented by the point <0,0>. If you are not familiar with the mathematics of this calculation, do not worry—it is not important for understanding the Java elements of the program.

Lines 85–95 define the `angleyx()` method. This method computes the angle that the vector <sx, sy> makes with the X-axis (see fig. 7.8). The unit of measurement for the computed angle is degrees.

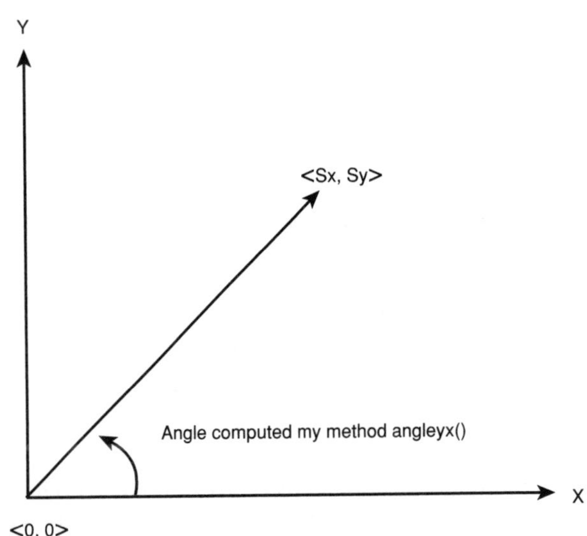

Figure 7.8
Angle computed by method `angleyx()`.

Lines 100–156 define the subclass E that is inherited from the superclass S. The purpose of class E is to use the definition of a two-dimensional point in class S and extend it to the definition of a three-dimensional point. This is done by defining the instance variable ez (line 103), representing the coordinate of the point in three-dimensional space (see fig. 7.9).

Lines 106–111 define the default constructor for class E. This constructor sets the values of the instance variables for class S and class E to default values of 1.

Lines 113–119 define another constructor for class E. This constructor takes three arguments corresponding to the values to be assigned to the instance variables sx and sy in class S, and instance variable ez in class E. Notice that there is no need to use the `this` qualifier because the parameter names are distinct from the names of the instance variables.

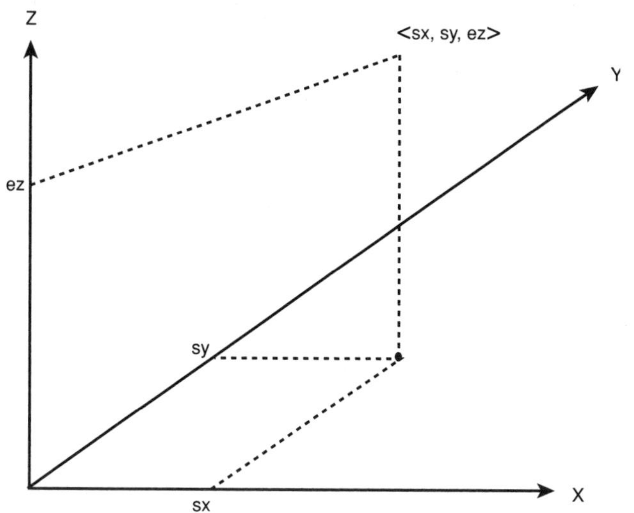

Figure 7.9

Three-dimensional point modeled by class E.

Lines 124–135 define the `size()` method. This method has the same signature as the `size()` method defined in class S (line 73), and therefore overrides the method in class S. The `size()` method performs a mathematical calculation to determine the length of the line joining the point <sx, sy, ez> to the origin represented by the point <0,0,0> (see fig. 7.10).

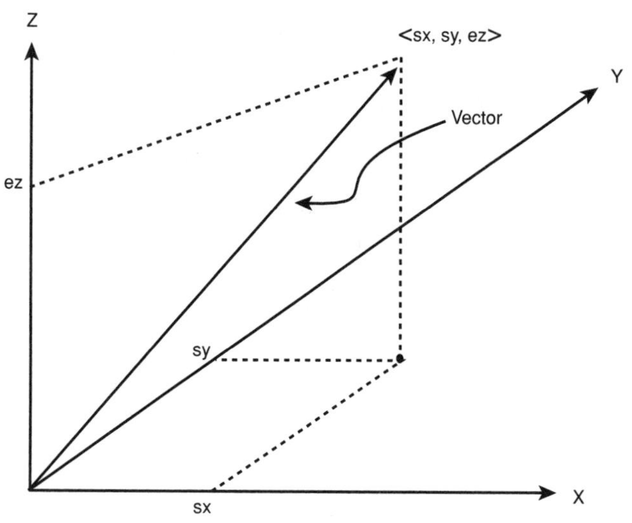

Figure 7.10

Vector <sx, sy, ez> defined by class E.

Lines 140–153 define the `anglezyx()` method. This method computes the angle that the vector <sx, sy, ez> makes with the X–Y plane (see fig. 7.11). The unit of measurement for the computed angle is degrees.

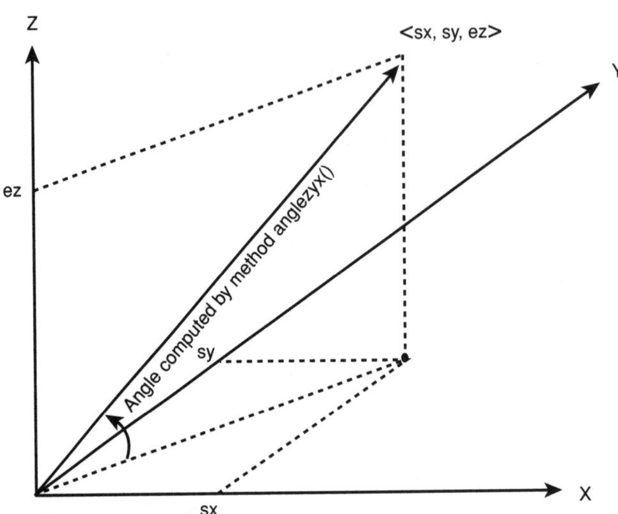

Figure 7.11
Angle computed by method `anglezyx()`.

The `main()` method instantiate two objects ptxy1 and ptxy2 (lines 14 and 15) of class S by using the two constructor methods for that class. Lines 20–27 print out the size and angle values of these two objects by using the methods `size()` and `angleyx()`.

Lines 30 and 31 instantiate two objects ptxyz1 and ptxyz2 of class E by using the two constructors for that class. Lines 32–41 print out the size and angle values of these two objects by using the methods `size()`, `angleyx()`, and `anglezyx()`. When the method `angleyx()` is invoked, the method is not found in the class E, so the method `angleyx()` in the superclass S is invoked instead.

Figure 7.12 shows the output of the program in listing 7.2, using the java interpreter. You can examine this output in conjunction with the previous discussion of the `main()` method to observe how the output is produced.

Listing 7.2

```
Line=================Java Source=================
001
002 /**
003  * OverrideMethod: This demonstrates the use of
004  * overriding object methods.
005  *
```

```
 * Author: Karanjit S. G. S. Siyan
 *
 */

class Dimensions
{
    public static void main(String[] args)
    {
        S  ptxy1 = new S();
        S  ptxy2 = new S(1.0, 2.0);

        double sz, angle;

        // Dimensions for ptxy1
        sz = ptxy1.size();
        angle = ptxy1.angleyx();
        System.out.println();

        // Dimensions for ptxy2
        sz = ptxy2.size();
        angle = ptxy2.angleyx();
        System.out.println();

        // Dimensions for ptxyz1
        E ptxyz1 = new E();
        E ptxyz2 = new E(1.0, 2.0, 3.0);
        sz = ptxyz1.size();
        angle = ptxyz1.angleyx();
        angle = ptxyz1.anglezyx();
        System.out.println();

        // Dimensions for ptxyz2
        sz = ptxyz2.size();
        angle = ptxyz2.angleyx();
        angle = ptxyz2.anglezyx();
        System.out.println();

    }  // end main

```

continues

Listing 7.2, Continued

```
} // end Dimensions
// Superclass S
class S
{
    // Instance variables for class S.
    double sx;      // X-axis coordinate
    double sy;      // Y-axis coordinate
    // Constructors of S
    S()
    {
        sx = sy = 1.0;
    } // end S
    S(double sx, double sy)
    {
        this.sx = sx;
        this.sy = sy;
    } // end S
    // Instance methods for class S
    double size()
    {
        double ret;
        ret = Math.sqrt(sx*sx + sy*sy);
        System.out.println("S.size() = "+ret+" units");
        return ret;
```

```
    } // end size

    double angleyx()
    {

        double ang;

        ang = Math.atan2(sy,sx) * 180.0/Math.PI;
        System.out.println("S.angleyx() = "+ang+" degs");

        return ang;

    } // end angleyx

} // end S

// Subclass S
class E extends S
{
    // Instance variables for class E.
    double  ez;     // Z-axis coordinate

    // Constructors for E
    E()
    {

        sx = sy = ez = 1.0;

    } // end E

    E(double x, double y, double z)
    {
        sx = x;
        sy = y;
        ez = z;

    } // end E

```

continues

Listing 7.2, Continued

```
    // Instance methods for class E

    // Compute the size of the vector E
    double size()
    {
        double  ret;

        ret = Math.sqrt(sx*sx + sy*sy +ez*ez);

        System.out.println("E.size() = "+ret+" units");

        return ret;


    }  // end size

    // Compute angle of point in 3 dimensional
    // space with reference to origin and x-y
    // plane
    double anglezyx()
    {

        double ang;
        double rxy;

        rxy = Math.sqrt(sx*sx + sy*sy);

        ang = Math.atan2(ez,rxy) * 180.0/Math.PI;
        System.out.println("E.anglezyx() = "+ang+" degs");

        return ang;

    }  // end anglezyx


} // end E
```

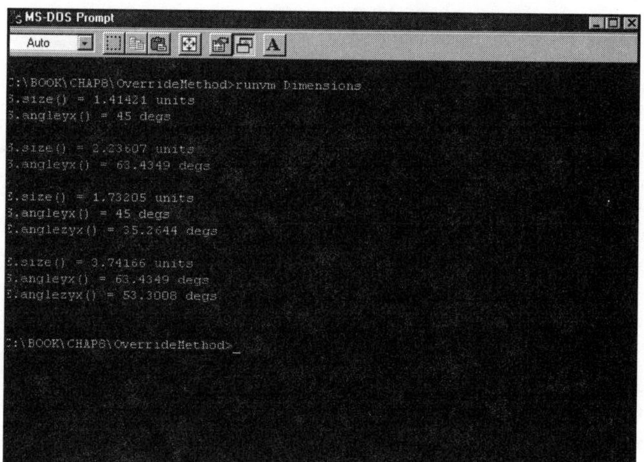

Figure 7.12

Output of OverrideMethod.java.

Overriding Methods Using super and this

You can use the reserved word `this` in constructor methods to indicate the name of the class itself. This is a convenient way of invoking another constructor defined in the class to implement a constructor. If, for example, you examine the constructor methods for class S in listing 7.2, you can see that the default constructor `S()` can be implemented by calling the constructor `S(double, double)` with the values of 1.0 and 1.0:

```
S()
      {
         this(1.0, 1.0);

      }  // end S

      S(double sx, double sy)
      {

         this.sx = sx;
         this.sy = sy;

      }  // end S
```

In the default constructor, `S()`, there is a call to the second constructor:

```
        this(1.0, 1.0);
```

The preceding statement is equivalent to the following:

```
        S(1.0, 1.0);
```

You can also use the reserved word super in class methods to indicate the name of the superclass. This is useful if you want to invoke a method in the superclass. If, for example, you want to call the default constructor in the superclass, you can use the following statement:

```
super();
```

You can invoke the superclass's constructor only from the constructor method in the subclass. When you've done so, the call to the superclass's constructor has to be the first statement in the subclass's constructor. Actually, every constructor must invoke its superclass's constructor in its first statement. If there is no invocation to the superclass's constructor, the Java language automatically inserts a constructor of the following type:

```
super();
```

If there is no default constructor—a constructor with no arguments defined—then this is a programming error. If a superclass does not have a default constructor, you must explicitly invoke the superclass constructor and pass it the required arguments:

```
super(arguments);
```

To invoke a method in the superclass from a method in the subclass, you can use the following:

```
super.methodname(parameters);
```

The *methodname* is the name of the method in the superclass, and *parameters* are the parameters to this method.

Note Every constructor must invoke its superclass's constructor in its first statement. If there is no invocation to the superclass's constructor in the first statement, the Java language automatically inserts a statement to call the superclass's default constructor.

An alternative way of implementing the default constructor for E in listing 7.2 is to invoke the constructor for the superclass, S:

```
E()
{
   super();
   ez = 1.0;
} // end E
```

In the preceding example, the call to the superclass constructor is, as expected, the first statement in the default constructor for E. This call to the superclass constructor has the effect of setting the superclass's instance variables sx and sy to 1.0. The statement that follows the `super()` statement sets the value of ez to 1.

The second constructor for class E in listing 7.2 can also be written as the following:

```
E(double x, double y, double z)
{
   super(x, y);
   ez = z;

} // end E
```

The statement `super(x, y)` results in the call to the `S(double, double)` constructor in class S. The statement that follows sets the instance variable ez in class E.

To see an example of invoking the superclass's methods from the subclass E in listing 7.2, consider alternate implementations of the methods `size()` and `anglezyx()` in class E. The method `size()` in class E can be implemented as follows:

```
double size()
{
   double  ret;
   double  rxy = super.size();

   ret = Math.sqrt(rxy*rxy +ez*ez);
   return ret;

} // end size
```

This method uses the call to `super.size()` to obtain the size of the two-dimensional vector in the X–Y plane. This value is then used to compute the size of the three-dimensional vector.

The following is another alternative implementation of `anglezyx()`:

```
double anglezyx()
{

    double ang;
    double rxy;

    rxy = super.size();

    ang = Math.atan2(ez,rxy) * 180.0/Math.PI;

    return ang;

} // end anglezyx
```

The call to `super.size()` computes the vector's projection on the X–Y plane, and the call to `atan2()` computes the angle to this plane (see fig. 7.13).

Listing 7.3 shows an alternate implementation of the class S and it subclass E (file OverrideMethod1.java on the CD-ROM accompanying this book). This listing shows the use of the reserved word this and super as described previously. This listing contains `println()` statements in the methods and constructors for the class S and class E so that you can follow the order in which these methods are executed when the program is run.

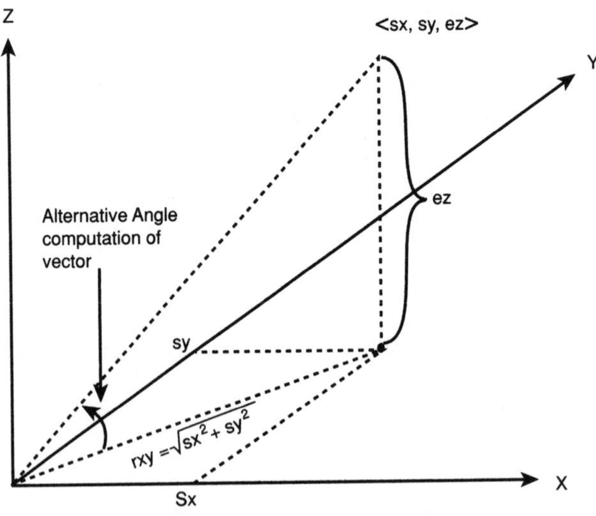

Figure 7.13
Angle computation of vector <sx, sy, ez>.

Listing 7.3

```
Line=================Java Source=================

/**
 * OverrideMethod1: This demonstrates the use of
 * using superclass methods to extend the functionality
 * of extended classes.
 *
 * Author: Karanjit S. G. S. Siyan
 *
 */

class Dimensions
{
    public static void main(String[] args)
    {
        S  ptxy1 = new S();
        S  ptxy2 = new S(1.0, 2.0);

        double sz, angle;
        System.out.println();


        // Dimensions for ptxy1
        sz = ptxy1.size();
        angle = ptxy1.angleyx();
        System.out.println();

        // Dimensions for ptxy2
        sz = ptxy2.size();
        angle = ptxy2.angleyx();
        System.out.println();

        // Dimensions for ptxyz1
        E ptxyz1 = new E();
        E ptxyz2 = new E(1.0, 2.0, 3.0);
        System.out.println();

```

continues

Listing 7.3, Continued

```
        sz = ptxyz1.size();
        angle = ptxyz1.angleyx();
        angle = ptxyz1.anglezyx();
        System.out.println();

        // Dimensions for ptxyz2
        sz = ptxyz2.size();
        angle = ptxyz2.angleyx();
        angle = ptxyz2.anglezyx();
        System.out.println();

        // Printing S and E objects
        String sprnt = ptxy1.toString();
        System.out.println("ptxy1 (string) = "+sprnt);
        System.out.println("ptxy1 (println) = "+ptxy1);

        String eprnt = ptxyz1.toString();
        System.out.println("ptxyz1 (string) = "+eprnt);
        System.out.println("ptxyz1 (println) = "+ptxyz1);




    } // end main

} // end Dimensions


// Superclass S
class S
{
    // Instance variables for class S.
    double sx;      // X-axis coordinate
    double sy;      // Y-axis coordinate


    // Constructors of S
    S()
```

```
{
    this(1.0, 1.0);
    System.out.println("Exiting constructor S()");


} // end S

S(double sx, double sy)
{

    System.out.println("Invoking constructor S(double, double)");

    this.sx = sx;
    this.sy = sy;

} // end S



// Instance methods for class S
double size()
{
    double ret;

    ret = Math.sqrt(sx*sx + sy*sy);

    System.out.println("S.size() = "+ret+" units");

    return ret;

} // end size

double angleyx()
{

    double ang;

    ang = Math.atan2(sy,sx) * 180.0/Math.PI;
    System.out.println("S.angleyx() = "+ang+" degs");
```

continues

Listing 7.3, Continued

```

        return ang;

    }  // end angleyx

}  // end S

// Subclass S
class E extends S
{
    // Instance variables for class E.
    double  ez;     // Z-axis coordinate

    // Constructors for E
    E()
    {
        super();
        ez = 1.0;
        System.out.println("Exiting constructor E()");

    }  // end E

    E(double x, double y, double z)
    {
        super(x, y);
        ez = z;
        System.out.println("Invoking constructor E(double, double,
➥double)");


    }  // end E

    // Instance methods for class E

    // Compute the size of the vector E
```

```
    double size()
    {
        double  ret;
        double  rxy = super.size();


        ret = Math.sqrt(rxy*rxy +ez*ez);

        System.out.println("E.size() = "+ret+" units");

        return ret;


    } // end size

    // Compute angle of point in three-dimensional
    // space with reference to origin and x-y
    // plane
    double anglezyx()
    {

        double ang;
        double rxy;

        rxy = super.size();

        ang = Math.atan2(ez,rxy) * 180.0/Math.PI;
        System.out.println("E.anglezyx() = "+ang+" degs");

        return ang;

    } // end anglezyx


} // end E
```

The output of the program in listing 7.3 is shown in figures 7.14 and 7.15. You can use the screen captures of the output, and the listing in 7.3 to see the order in which the constructors are invoked.

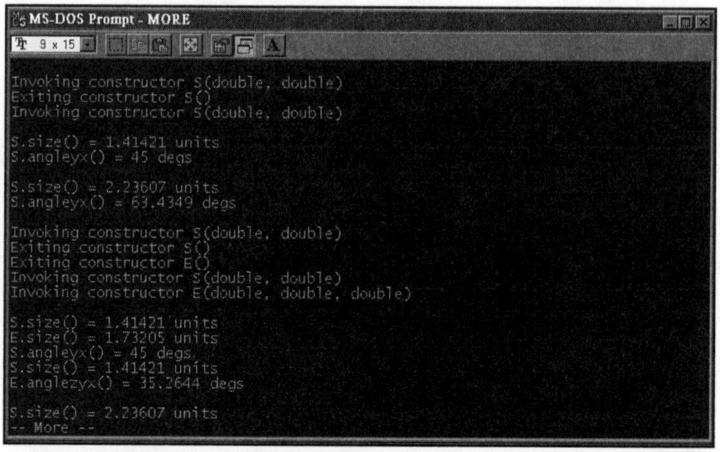

Figure 7.14

Output of OverrideMethod1. java by using java—Screen 1.

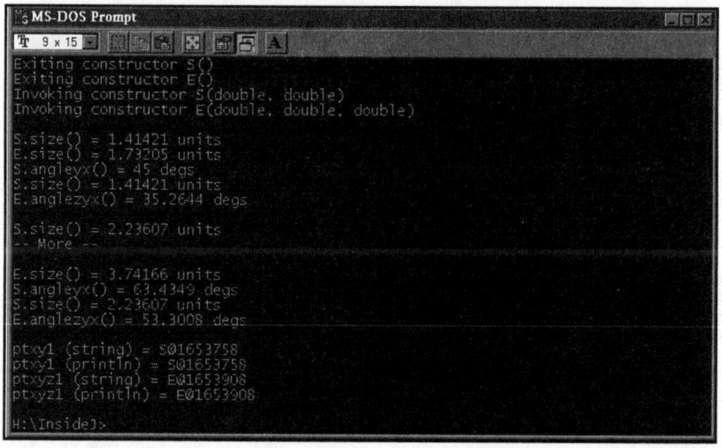

```
MS-DOS Prompt - MORE
Invoking constructor S(double, double)
Exiting constructor S()
Invoking constructor S(double, double)

S.size() = 1.41421 units
S.angleyx() = 45 degs

S.size() = 2.23607 units
S.angleyx() = 63.4349 degs

Invoking constructor S(double, double)
Exiting constructor S()
Exiting constructor E()
Invoking constructor S(double, double)
Invoking constructor E(double, double, double)

S.size() = 1.41421 units
E.size() = 1.73205 units
S.angleyx() = 45 degs
S.size() = 1.41421 units
E.anglezyx() = 35.2644 degs

S.size() = 2.23607 units
-- More --
```

Figure 7.15

Output of OverrideMethod1. java using java—Screen 2.

```
MS-DOS Prompt
Exiting constructor S()
Exiting constructor E()
Invoking constructor S(double, double)
Invoking constructor E(double, double, double)

S.size() = 1.41421 units
E.size() = 1.73205 units
S.angleyx() = 45 degs
S.size() = 1.41421 units
E.anglezyx() = 35.2644 degs

S.size() = 2.23607 units
-- More --

E.size() = 3.74166 units
S.angleyx() = 63.4349 degs
S.size() = 2.23607 units
E.anglezyx() = 53.3008 degs

ptxy1 (string) = S@1653758
ptxy1 (println) = S@1653758
ptxyz1 (string) = E@1653908
ptxyz1 (println) = E@1653908

H:\InsideJ>
```

Method overriding is different from method overloading. In method overloading, you are providing methods with the same name but more than one signature, such as methods with different arguments. All the overloaded methods exist simultaneously. When you override a method, you are providing a method with the same signature as a method in the superclass. The overriding method provides an alternative implementation to the overridden method. The overriding method may invoke the overridden method in the superclass by using the reserved word super to refer to an instance of the superclass.

Using Methods in the Root Object

Lines 49–55 in the `main()` method in listing 7.3 invoke the `toString()` method to get a string representation of the objects ptxy1 and ptxyz1. This string representation is then printed out. Lines 51 and 55 in listing 7.3 print these objects using the `println()` method. The `println()` method uses the `toString()` method to print the object.

Figures 7.14 and 7.15 show the output of the program in listing 7.3. In figure 7.15 you see displayed the results of the call to `toString()`. As you examine listing 7.3 you will notice that there is no `toString()` method defined in classes S and E. Yet the program compiles and executes to produce the display in figures in 7.14 and 7.15. So where is the `toString()` method defined? You can find the answer to this question by examing the inheritance hierarchy diagram of figure 7.16.

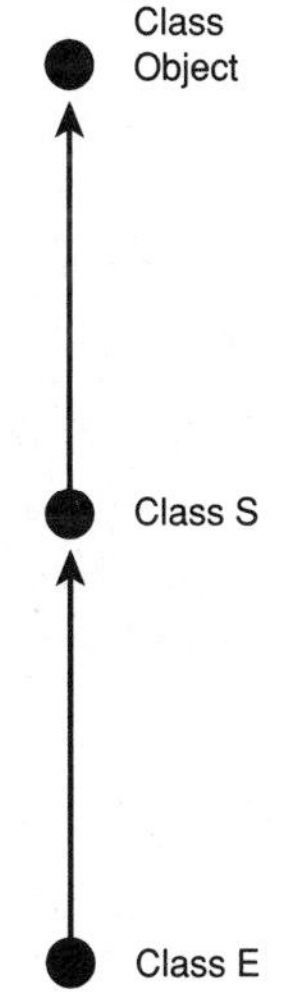

Figure 7.16

Inheritance hierarchy diagram for classes S and E.

In Java, the built-in class Object is the superclass of all objects. As you traverse up the inheritance chain to find the superclasses of an object, you will ultimately arrive at the point of the class called Object. The class `Object` is called the root class, and has predefined methods whose declarations are:

```
class Object
{
      public Object();        // Empty. Does nothing.
      public boolean equals(Object obj); // Tests if two objects have same
                                         value
      public final Class getClass(); // Returns Class object associated with
                                     Object
      public int hashCode(); // Mathematical hashcode value used with class
                             Hashtable
      public final void notify(); // Thread synchronization method
      public final void notifyAll(); // Thread synchronization method
      public final void wait(long timeout); // Thread synchronization method
      public final void wait(long timeout, int nanos); // Thread
                                                       synchronization method
      public final void wait(); // Thread synchronization method
      public String toString(); // Converts object to string representation
      public Object clone(); // Produces a separate copy of object
      public Object finalize(); // Releases resources no longer in use.
}
```

The class `Object` has a method called `toString()`. So when this method is invoked for the classes S and E, the `toString()` method for the class Object is called, and this produces a display of the object that is seen in figure 7.15.

The class S defined in listing 7.3 is implicitly inherited from the class Object. Thus, the following class definitions are equivalent:

```
class S
{
      ...
}

class S extends Object
{
      ...
}
```

As you can see from the preceding example, when the extends reserved word is left out in defining a class, the Java language automatically defaults to extending the class from the class Object.

Overriding the toString() Method

If you want to print out the value of an object using the `println()` method or use the + or += operators to concatenate the object with a string, the `toString()` method for the object is invoked. If you do not have a `toString()` method defined for the class, and you do not want to use the default `toString()` method defined for the `Object` class, you must implement the `toString()` method for the class. If you want classes S and E to be printed out, each of the classes S and E should define the `toString()` method with the following signature:

```
public String toString()
{
    // Implementation
    // details...

} // end toString
```

The qualifier `public` ensures that the method `toString()` can be invoked from classes that are not in the same file as the class S and class E.

The `toString()` method for class S is:

```
public String toString()
{

    String pstr = "<"+sx+", "+sy+">";
    return pstr;

}  // end toString
```

The preceding method prints the two-dimensional point in the following format:

```
<sx, sy>
```

The `toString()` method for class E is shown next:

```
public String toString()
{

    String pstr = super.toString();

    pstr = pstr.substring(0, pstr.lastIndexOf('>'))+", "+ez+">";
```

```
        return pstr;

    } // end toString
```

The preceding method prints the three-dimensional point in the following format:

```
    <sx, sy, ez>
```

The method `toString()` for class E uses the `toString()` method of the superclass in its implementation. It strips the trailing “>” character returned by `super.toString()` and appends the value of the instance variable ez. An alternative to this implementation is to not use the superclass's `toString()` method, but to create the string representation from scratch:

```
    public String toString()
    {

        String pstr = "<"+sx+", '+sy+", "+ez+">";

        return pstr;

    } // end toString
```

Listing 7.4 contains the complete program (file OverrideMethod2.java on the CD-ROM accompanying this book) that shows the modified program in listing 7.3. This program defines the `toString()` method in each of the classes S and E. The `toString()` method in class S overrides the same method in class Object, and the `toString()` method in class E overrides the method in class S.

Listing 7.4

```
Line=================Java Source=================

/**
 * OverrideMethod2: This demonstrates the use of
 * using superclass methods to extend the functionality
 * of extended classes. Shows how to override toString().
 *
 * Author: Karanjit S. G. S. Siyan
 *
 */
```

```
class Dimensions
{
    public static void main(String[] args)
    {
        S  ptxy1 = new S();
        S  ptxy2 = new S(1.0, 2.0);
        double sz, angle;
        System.out.println();
        // Dimensions for ptxy1
        sz = ptxy1.size();
        angle = ptxy1.angleyx();
        System.out.println();
        // Dimensions for ptxy2
        sz = ptxy2.size();
        angle = ptxy2.angleyx();
        System.out.println();
        // Dimensions for ptxyz1
        E ptxyz1 = new E();
        E ptxyz2 = new E(1.0, 2.0, 3.0);
        System.out.println();
        sz = ptxyz1.size();
        angle = ptxyz1.angleyx();
        angle = ptxyz1.anglezyx();
        System.out.println();
        // Dimensions for ptxyz2
        sz = ptxyz2.size();
        angle = ptxyz2.angleyx();
        angle = ptxyz2.anglezyx();
        System.out.println();
        // Printing S and E objects
```

continues

Listing 7.4, Continued

```
        String sprnt = ptxy1.toString();
        System.out.println("ptxy1 (string) = "+sprnt);
        System.out.println("ptxy1 (println) = "+ptxy1);

        String eprnt = ptxyz1.toString();
        System.out.println("ptxyz1 (string) = "+eprnt);
        System.out.println("ptxyz1 (println) = "+ptxyz1);


    }  // end main

}  // end Dimensions


// Superclass S
class S extends Object
{
    // Instance variables for class S.
    double sx;       // X-axis coordinate
    double sy;       // Y-axis coordinate

    // Constructors of S
    S()
    {
        this(1.0, 1.0);
        System.out.println("Exiting constructor S()");


    }  // end S

    S(double sx, double sy)
    {

        System.out.println("Invoking constructor S(double, double)");

        this.sx = sx;
        this.sy = sy;

```

```
    } // end S


    // Instance methods for class S
    double size()
    {
        double ret;

        ret = Math.sqrt(sx*sx + sy*sy);

        System.out.println("S.size() = "+ret+" units");

        return ret;

    } // end size

    double angleyx()
    {

        double ang;

        ang = Math.atan2(sy,sx) * 180.0/Math.PI;
        System.out.println("S.angleyx() = "+ang+" degs");

        return ang;

    } // end angleyx

    public String toString()
    {

        String pstr = "<"+sx+", "+sy+">";
        return pstr;

    } // end toString

} // end S

// Subclass S
```

continues

Listing 7.4, Continued

```
class E extends S
{
    // Instance variables for class E.
    double  ez;     // Z-axis coordinate

    // Constructors for E
    E()
    {
        super();
        ez = 1.0;
        System.out.println("Exiting constructor E()");

    } // end E

    E(double x, double y, double z)
    {
        super(x, y);
        ez = z;
        System.out.println("Invoking constructor E(double, double,
➥double)");


    } // end E

    // Instance methods for class E

    // Compute the size of the vector E
    double size()
    {
        double  ret;
        double  rxy = super.size();


        ret = Math.sqrt(rxy*rxy +ez*ez);

        System.out.println("E.size() = "+ret+" units");

```

```
        return ret;


    } // end size

    // Compute angle of point in three-dimensional
    // space with reference to origin and x-y
    // plane
    double anglezyx()
    {

        double ang;
        double rxy;

        rxy = super.size();

        ang = Math.atan2(ez,rxy) * 180.0/Math.PI;
        System.out.println("E.anglezyx() = "+ang+" degs");

        return ang;

    } // end anglezyx

    public String toString()
    {

        String pstr = super.toString();

        pstr = pstr.substring(0, pstr.lastIndexOf('>'))+", "+ez+">";

        return pstr;

    } // end toString


} // end E
```

Figure 7.17 shows the last screen of the output produced by the program in listing 7.4.

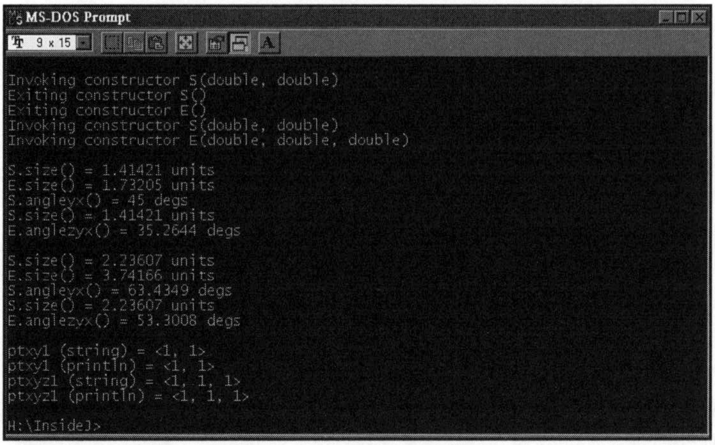

Figure 7.17

Output of program OverrideMethod 2.java.

```
Invoking constructor S(double, double)
Exiting constructor S()
Exiting constructor E()
Invoking constructor S(double, double)
Invoking constructor E(double, double, double)

S.size() = 1.41421 units
E.size() = 1.73205 units
S.angleyx() = 45 degs
S.size() = 1.41421 units
E.anglezyx() = 35.2644 degs

S.size() = 2.23607 units
E.size() = 3.74166 units
S.angleyx() = 63.4349 degs
S.size() = 2.23607 units
E.anglezyx() = 53.3008 degs

ptxy1 (string) = <1, 1>
ptxy1 (println) = <1, 1>
ptxyz1 (string) = <1, 1, 1>
ptxyz1 (println) = <1, 1, 1>

H:\InsideJ>
```

Controlling Access to Classes

In the examples of this chapter, the Java program code was contained in a single file. In general, when writing larger programs, you may want to split the Java code in separate files. The Java language has rules about which methods are accessible to other classes in the same file or a different file. These rules are discussed next.

Controlling Class Access Using Public, Protected, Private, or Friendly

The reserved words public, protected, and private can be used to control the level of visibility of a class method or variable.

When you precede a method definition or variable with the reserved word `public`, the method or variable can be accessed from any class in any package. This includes classes defined in the same file as the class with the public method/variable or a class defined in another file. Classes defined in other files are part of a named package. Recall that a package is a collection of classes grouped together based on their logic and function. In the program examples of listing 7.4, if you wanted other packages to use the class S and E, you should declare their constructors as public:

```
class S extends Object
{
      // Variable definitions

      public S()
```

```
    {
       this(1.0, 1.0);

    }  // end S

    public S(double sx, double sy)
    {

       this.sx = sx;
       this.sy = sy;

    }  // end S

// Other methods

} // end S

class E extends S
{
// Variable definitions

    public E()
    {
       super();
       ez = 1.0;

    }  // end E

    public E(double x, double y, double z)
    {
       super(x, y);
       ez = z;

} // end E

    // Other methods

} // end E
```

If you want to make a method/variable in a class available to any subclass inherited from it, you should declare the method/variable as protected. Protected methods/variables are accessible to any subclass of the declaring class or a class in the same package as a declaring class. The instance variables in class S, for example, sx and sy (listing 7.4) could be declared as protected. Then these instance variables would be accessible in class E, even if the class E was defined in another package:

```
class S extends Object
{
      protected double sx;
      protected double sy;

      public S()
      {
         this(1.0, 1.0);

      }  // end S

      public S(double sx, double sy)
      {

         this.sx = sx;
         this.sy = sy;

      }  // end S

// Other methods

} // end S

class E extends S
{
// Variable definitions

      public E()
      {
         super();
         ez = 1.0;

      }  // end E
```

```
      public E(double x, double y, double z)
      {
         super(x, y);
         ez = z;

} // end E

      // Other methods

} // end E
```

If you want to make a method/variable in a class inaccessible to any class, you should declare the method/variable as private. Private methods/variables are inaccessible to any other class, including the subclass of the declaring class or a class in the same package as a declaring class. The instance variable in class E, for example, ez (listing 7.4) could be declared as private, as there is no need for any outside class to access this variable:

```
class S extends Object
{
      protected double sx;
      protected double sy;

      public S()
      {
         this(1.0, 1.0);

      }  // end S

      public S(double sx, double sy)
      {

         this.sx = sx;
         this.sy = sy;

      }  // end S

// Other methods
```

```
} // end S

class E extends S
{
private double ez;

       public E()
       {
          super();
          ez = 1.0;

       } // end E

       public E(double x, double y, double z)
       {
          super(x, y);
          ez = z;

} // end E

       // Other methods

} // end E
```

If a method/variable is not preceded by any of the access modifiers such as public, private, or protected, then the method/variable is said to be *friendly.* Note that there is no reserved word called "friendly"; instead the absence of explicit access modifiers makes the method/variable friendly. A friendly method/variable can be accessed within the declaring class and any class or subclass in the same package. This access mode is also sometimes called the *default access mode.* Listing 7.3 shows a default mode being used for all method/variable declarations in the package. Even though there is no explicit package statement defined in this listing, the compiler treats the contents of the file as belonging to a package with "noname."

Another access mode called the "private protected" may be used to further restrict the behavior of the protected access mode. Recall that in the definition of the protected access mode, any class in the same package as the declaring class can access the method/variable. Suppose that you want to provide access to the method/variable to the subclasses only, and not other classes defined in the same package.

You can do this by defining the method/variable as being a private protected. In the earlier example of the protected class, any other class defined in the same package as class S could access the instance variables sx and sy by creating an instance of the class S:

```
class S extends Object
{
      protected double sx;
      protected double sy;

      public S()
      {
         this(1.0, 1.0);

      } // end S

      public S(double sx, double sy)
      {

         this.sx = sx;
         this.sy = sy;

      } // end S

// Other methods

} // end S

class E extends S
{
// Variable definitions

      public E()
      {
         super();
         ez = 1.0;

      } // end E
```

```
      public E(double x, double y, double z)
      {
         super(x, y);
         ez = z;

} // end E

      // Other methods

} // end E

class X
{

      void trouble()
      {
         S point = new S();

         // Unexpected modification of
         // instance variables
         point.sx = -99999.0;
         point.sy = 2345235.32;

      } // end trouble

} // end X
```

In the preceding example, class X defined in the same package as S, defines a method `trouble()` that has unexpected access to instance variables of S. To prevent the type of modifications by class X in the preceding example, you can declare sx and sy as being private protected:

```
class S extends Object
{
      private protected double sx;
      private protected double sy;

      public S()
```

```
      {
         this(1.0, 1.0);

      }  // end S

      public S(double sx, double sy)
      {

         this.sx = sx;
         this.sy = sy;

      }  // end S

      // Other methods

} // end S

class E extends S
{
      // Variable definitions

      public E()
      {
         super();
         ez = 1.0;

      }  // end E

      public E(double x, double y, double z)
      {
         super(x, y);
         ez = z;

      } // end E

      // Other methods

} // end E
```

Table 7.1 summarizes the behavior of the different access modes discussed in this section.

Table 7.1
Access Modes

Mode	Subclass in same package	Non-subclass in same package	Subclass in different package	Non-subclass different in package
public	Yes	Yes	Yes	Yes
protected	Yes	Yes	Yes	No
private	No	No	No	No
private protected	Yes	No	Yes	No
friendly (default)	Yes	Yes	No	No

Marking Methods and Classes as Final

In the examples that you have seen so far, you can see that you can extend a class by defining a new class that inherits from an existing class. But suppose that you want to prevent this type of inheritance. You may, for example, want to prevent anyone extending the definition of a class E to, let's say, create a four-dimensional point. You can do so by marking the class E as final:

```
final class E extends S
{
   // Class implementation

} // end E
```

The preceding code prevents another class from inheriting from class E. Therefore, the following definition of a class F will be caught by the Java compiler as an error:

```
class F extends E
      {
         ...

      } // end F
```

Note A class marked as final cannot be subclassed.

You can also mark a method as being final. A final method cannot be overridden. You may want to do so for security reasons, where you want to prevent another programmer from changing the definition of the method. In listing 7.4, for example, you may want to prevent a subclass of S from overriding the method `angleyx()` defined in S:

```
class S extends Object
{
   // Instance variables for class S.
  double sx;       // X-axis coordinate
  double sy;       // Y-axis coordinate

  // Constructors of S

  // Instance methods for class S

  final double angleyx()
  {

      double ang;

      ang = Math.atan2(sy,sx) * 180.0/Math.PI;
      System.out.println("S.angleyx() = "+ang+" degs");

      return ang;

   }  // end angleyx

}  // end S
```

The preceding code would prevent subclass E from overriding the method `angleyx()` in class S.

Finalizing a Class

You can define the `finalize()` method for a class that can perform important cleanup actions before memory for the object of that class is reclaimed. Java implements an automatic garbage collector that runs periodically to reclaim space occupied by unreferenced objects. You may, however, want your class to perform other actions, such as close network connections or file handles, before the space for the object is reclaimed. The garbage collector is not able to perform closing actions important for your program. The "last rites" for an object can be performed by the `finalize()` method. Typically, you implement the `finalize()` method by using the following:

```
protected void finalize() throws Throwable
{
   super.finalize();

   // Other cleanup code.

} // end finalize
```

The call to `super.finalize()`, although not required by the language, is a good programming practice. It ensures that the finalize code for instances of the superclass is executed and any cleanup actions needed to be performed by the superclass portion of the object is executed. Otherwise, only the finalize actions for the subclass extension of the object will be performed, and the superclass's `finalize()` method will not be called.

When an application terminates, the `finalize()` method of all the objects are run. Under severe error conditions, the Java runtime may not be able to execute the `finalize()` methods. If, for example, an "out of memory" error occurs, there may not be enough memory to execute the code to invoke the `finalize()` methods of the classes. Under normal operating conditions, you can expect the `finalize()` method to be executed any time before the application terminates.

Making Classes and Methods Abstract

Java permits you to define classes that provide the structure of how the methods should be designed, with the restriction that the class itself cannot be instantiated. These classes are called abstract classes. You can, however, subclass the abstract class, and create an instance of the class. The abstract class can also be used to provide a partial implementation of the class, and use extended classes to provide the remaining implementation. Abstract classes are useful for modeling the basic behavior of an object, while leaving the implementation details to programmers. Abstract classes can be used to create the protocol that will be used with the class.

Abstract classes can also be used to model the behavior of *abstract data types* (ADTs), used in object-oriented design. You can declare a class to be abstract by marking it with the reserved word abstract:

```
abstract class classname
{
    ...
}
```

Each method not specifically implemented in *classname* is marked as abstract. For greater clarity and readability, you can individually mark the methods in the class as being abstract. If any of the methods of a class is abstract, the entire class is marked implicitly as abstract. Therefore, the following class is also abstract:

```
class classname
{
    abstract datatype methodname(parameters);
    ...
}
```

As part of good programming practice, you should declare the entire class as being abstract so that you can readily identify the class as being abstract without having to scan all the methods to see if there is an abstract method that would make the class abstract.

Consider the following abstract class construction:

```
abstract class Connection
{
      // Returns a true if the connection is
      // successful; otherwise, a false is
      // returned.
      public abstract boolean makeConnection();

      public void tryConnection(int retrys)
      {
         for (int x = 0; x < retrys; x++)
         {
            if (makeConnection())
            {
                  return;

            } // end if
```

```
            } // end for

            System.out.println("Connection failure");

        } // end tryConnection
} // end Connection
```

The abstract class, Connection, defines an abstract method called `makeConnection()` that is used to make a logical connection between two computers on a network. Because `makeConnection()` is marked as abstract, there is no code provided for this method; the code will have to be provided by an extended class. Method `tryConnection()` invokes `makeConnection()` a certain number of times to ensure that the connection takes place.

To use the abstract class `Connection`, you will have to subclass it and provide the implementation of the abstract method:

```
class MoneyTransac extends Connection
{

        public boolean makeConnection()
        {
                // Code that returns a true
                // if the connection is
                // successful; otherwise, a false
                // is returned.

            } // end makeConnection

            // Method tryConnection()
            // is inherited.

} // end MoneyTransac
```

If a subclass of an abstract class fails to provide an implementation of an abstract method, it too is marked abstract. You can therefore have an inheritance chain where several classes that do not implement an abstract method are implicitly abstract.

Note Subclasses of an abstract class that do not provide an implementation of an abstract method are also abstract.

Summary

In this chapter you learned how to implement the inheritance mechanism of Java. The inheritance mechanism in Java is fundamental to support object-oriented programming in the Java language. In this chapter you learned about superclasses and subclasses. You were presented with a number of examples illustrating class inheritance. Creating a subclass of an existing class is also called extending the class. You can create restrictions on how the methods of a class are accessed by subclasses and other classes in the same package as the declaring class or another package. You can create alternative and more refined implementations of methods of a superclass by overriding the superclass methods.

CHAPTER 8

Creating Java Applets

In the previous chapters you learned a sufficient number of elements of the Java language to write stand-alone applications. You can also use Java to write applications that run from within a Web browser such as Nescape's Navigator or Microsoft's Internet Explorer. These special applications are called Java applets.

In this chapter you will learn about the basic structure of Java applets and how to write Java applets. As part of learning to write Java applets, you will also learn how to create a simple HTML file to run the applet and how to pass parameters to Java applets.

Understanding Applets

Java applets are run from inside a Web browser as opposed to running as a stand-alone programs. Alternatively, you can run the applet for debugging and testing purposes from within the Applet Viewer program. Both the Web browser and the Applet Viewer are GUI (Graphical User Interface) programs. To display or paint data within the display of these programs, the applet must use Java classes specifically designed for displaying information in a GUI environment. The Java GUI classes are contained in the package java.awt. The AWT classes are an Alternative Windowing Toolkit library of classes that provide the graphic elements (also called *widgets*) for writing GUI-enabled applications. To write sophisticated applets, you have to familiarize yourself with the classes in the AWT library.

The applet is a subclass of the class `Panel` in package `java.awt`; that is, the class `java.awt.Panel`. To facilitate the creation of applets, a collection of methods and constructors have been created in the class `Applet` in the package `java.applet`. Figure 8.1 shows the hierarchy diagram for the `Applet` class.

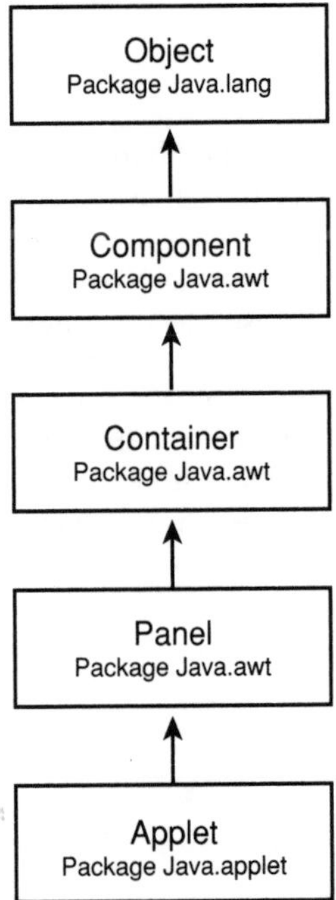

Figure 8.1
Hierarchy diagram for the Applet class.

Features of Applets

Applets were originally created for hand-held devices such as PDAs (Personal Digital Assistants). They were designed to run in an embedded environment; for example, an environment embedded within the hardware or software of the PDAs. This property of running applets in embedded environments has made it possible to adapt applets to run within the environment of a Web browser, and therefore the environment of the Internet.

The applet code is generally small (around a few kilobytes), and it can be downloaded relatively quickly through the Internet to run inside a Web browser (see fig. 8.2). The Web browser is Java-enabled and contains the Java runtime environment to execute the applet code. The location of the applet code is embedded in an HTML (HyperText Markup Language) file or document. HTML documents contain instructions that the Web browsers interpret to render the HTML document graphically inside the display of the Web browser.

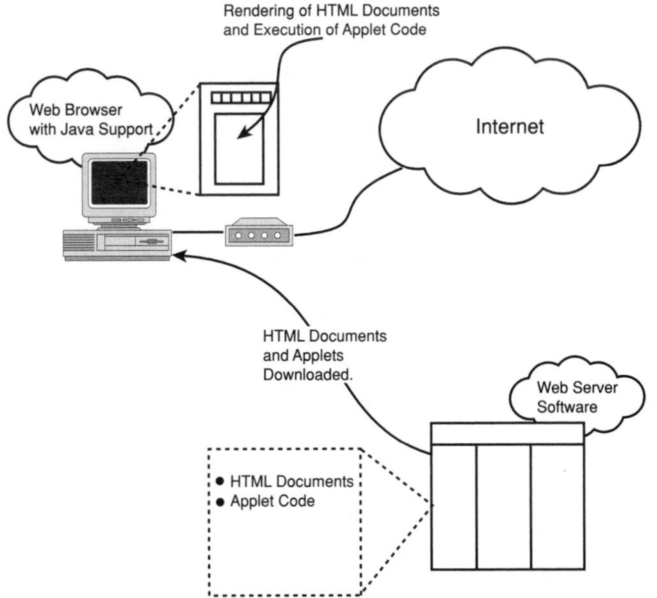

Figure 8.2

Running applets.

The applets can enhance the rendering of HTML documents in the Web browser by the following:

- ◆ Providing animation
- ◆ Accepting interactive input from the user

- Displaying sound (audio clips) with animated images
- Providing graphical elements such as scrolling bars, text area, buttons, and so on

The applets can take advantage of built-in features of the Web browser. Applets, for example, can use the Web browser's decoder programs for image files, such as GIF and JPEG files. By using the Web browser's methods to decode the images, the applet code is insulated against changes in the graphic image format.

Security Concerns for Applets

Because applets are executed from within another program, such as a Web browser, they are not full-featured applications. Applets rely on the Web browser to perform a number of functions, such as the decoding of images. In addition, because of security concerns about downloading executable programs, such as applets from an untrusted host, applets have limited file and network access.

As seen in figure 8.2, applet code is downloaded from a host on the Internet, and the precompiled byte code is executed within the Web browser running at the user's workstation. The byte code interpreter is hardware-platform and operating-system specific, but the byte code itself is platform independent. This means that the byte code does not have to change to accommodate the different hardware and operating specific platforms on the Internet.

To further increase the security of the Java byte code, a verification process is performed on the downloaded byte code before it can be run. As part of the verification, all methods and variables referenced in the program are checked to see that they do not violate any Java language conventions. Methods and variables, for example, in Java are referenced by names. The verification process ensures that this is indeed so, and that the program is not accessing memory areas that may contain other applications or operating system code.

Applets have limited access to the local file system of the workstation that they run on. Currently, applets are not permitted to save files locally, or to read files on the local disk. If applets were permitted to do this without any restrictions, a virus applet could alter your files, or even read sensitive information from files on your local disk and distribute them to unknown parties on the Internet. Applets cannot dynamically interact with libraries written for other languages. They cannot, for example, load C/C++ libraries in memory and dynamically link to them. Java has the capability to link class methods statically with other language libraries by declaring the method to be native. Because the code in other language libraries cannot be verified properly, native methods cannot be used in writing applets.

The Web browser may also place limitations on how an applet is run. The Web browser is regarded by the user as a trusted application, as it has access to the local file system. Applets that run in the browser are downloaded from untrusted hosts on the network, and are untrusted applications. In fact, the Web user may not make an explicit choice to run the applet; all that the user may have done is access a Web page, and the HTML document for the Web page that contains a reference to an applet will cause the applet to be automatically downloaded to the user's computer.

Applets are also restricted to making network connections to the host from which they are downloaded. They cannot establish new connections to other computers on the network. If an applet were able to do so, it could send information to other computers on the network and perform tasks such as impersonating a user by sending an e-mail on behalf of the user.

Building Applets

Figure 8.1 shows the inheritance hierarchy of the class Applet. The Applet class is inherited from the class Panel, which in turn is inherited from the class Container, which in turn is inherited from the class Component, and which in turn (finally!) is inherited from the class Object. Because of this long inheritance chain, the Applet class acquires features that are a composite of its superclasses. To create a new applet, you must extend the Applet class:

```
public class MyNewApplet extends java.applet.Applet
{
   ...

} // end MyNewApplet
```

As explained in Chapter 7, "Object-Oriented Programming with Java," the use of the reserved word `public` makes the class accessible from other packages. The class `MyNewApplet` is the new applet that you are defining, and as part of the definition, you are extending the class `Applet` defined in package `java.applet`.

Understanding the Applet Class

To best understand how an applet is written, it is worthwhile to examine which methods/variables are inherited by your new applet from the predefined class Applet. The following example shows the methods that are available to your new applet class from the superclass Applet:

```
public class Applet extends Panel
{
      public Applet(); // Default constructor

      // The following methods are empty. That is they have
      // no code. To provide their functionality, they must
      // be overridden.
      public void init(); // Performs initialization of the applet
      public void start(); // This starts the applet execution
      public void stop(); // This stops the applet execution
      public void destroy(); // Frees up resources that applet may be holding

      // The following methods have code in them. These
      //  inherited methods can be used to write applet code.
      public AppletContext getAppletContext(); // Get info on the applet
                                               // environment
      public String getAppletInfo(); // Returns text string on author of
                                     // applet,vers no,
              // copyright, etc.
      public AudioClip getAudioClip(URL url); // Obtain audio clip for playing
      public AudioClip getAudioClip(URL url, String name);
      public URL getCodeBase(); // Obtain URL of applet code
      public URL getDocumentBase(); // Obtain URL of HTML document
      public Image getImage(URL url); // Obtain image for the URL
      public String getParameter(String name); // Get parameter value
      public String[][] getParameterInfo(); // Get a table of parameter info.
      public boolean isActive(); // Is applet active
      public void play(URL url); // Play the audio clip
      public void play(URL url, String name); // Play the audio clip
      public void resize(int width, int height); // Changes the applet display
                                                 // area
      public void resize(Dimension d); // Changes the applet display area
      public final void setStub(AppletStub stub); // Sets applet stub
      public void showStatus(String msg); // Shows a message in browser status
                                          // area
} // end Applet
```

Because your applet extends the Applet class, all the public methods described in the Applet class are inherited and available for your use. Some of the Applet class methods are empty; that is, they do not have any code. These are the methods `init()`, `start()`, `stop()`, and `destroy()`. To use these methods, you must override them and define your own code.

Recall that for writing Java applications, you had to define the method `main()` with a specific signature. Control was transferred to the `main()` method, which then performed all the logic of the application.

For an applet, control is transferred to it by the Web browser when it finds an applet specified in the HTML document. This control is transferred to the applet by first loading the applet and calling specific methods for the applet.

Implementing Applets

Most of the functionality of applets is already contained in the Applet class. For you to perform functions specific to your class, you must extend the Applet class and override the methods `init()`, `start()`, `stop()`, and `destroy()`. You do not have to override the `destroy()` method if your applet does not have any resources that require special handling when the applet terminates. You must, however, at least provide code for the `init()`, `start()`, and `stop()` methods.

Figure 8.3 shows how the Web browser calls the Applet methods. This figure also shows a typical order of execution for the applet methods. First the method `init()` is called; next the method `start()` is called. The method `stop()` may be called to temporarily suspend the execution of the applet. The method `destroy()` is called when the applet is terminated.

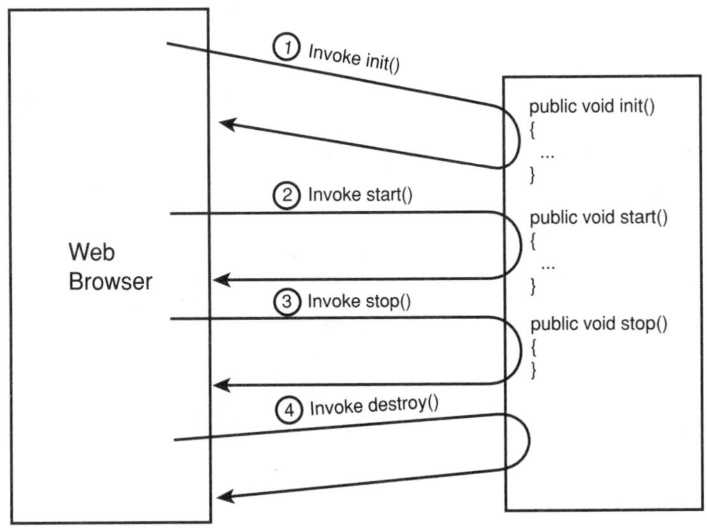

Figure 8.3

Web browser and applet interaction.

The init() method is called when the applet is first loaded. Its primary function is to initialize the applet. This may involve creating instances of classes, setting up initial values of applet data structures, setting parameters, loading images and fonts, and so on. You override the init() method in your applet class and add the necessary code:

```
public class MyNewApplet extends java.applet.Applet
{
        public void init()
       {
       // Your initialization code
       // goes here.

       } // end init

} // end MyNewApplet
```

After an applet has been initialized by the Web browser calling the init() method, the Web browser invokes the start() method. The start() method may be called several times to restart a suspended applet that may have been suspended by a call to the stop() method. Applet suspension can occur if the Web user leaves the Web page on which the applet is displayed by following a link. The applet will be restarted using the start() method when the user returns to the Web page. A major difference between init() and start() is that the init() method is called only once during an applet's lifetime, whereas the start() method may be called several times. Typically, the start() method contains code to display messages, send messages (method invocation) to other objects, create threads to perform parallel execution of applet code, and so on.

You override the start() method in your applet class and add the necessary code:

```
public class MyNewApplet extends java.applet.Applet
{
          public void init()
          {
          // Your initialization code
          // goes here.

          } // end init

       public void start()
       {
```

```
        // Your start up code
        // goes here.

    } // end start


} // end MyNewApplet
```

As mentioned earlier, if the Web user leaves the Web page on which the applet is displayed, the Web browser suspends the applet by calling the `stop()` method. If the `stop()` method is not called, the applet will consume CPU resources even though it is not displayed. This is clearly undesirable. So you must provide a `stop()` method for applet suspension. A suspended applet is restarted by the Web browser by sending the message `start()` to the applet. To implement `stop()`, you must define it to override the `stop()` method in the `Applet` class:

```
public class MyNewApplet extends java.applet.Applet
{
    public void init()
    {
        // Your initialization code
        // goes here.
    } // end init

    public void start()
    {
        // Your start up code
        // goes here.

    } // end start

    public void stop()
    {
        // Your stop code
        // goes here.

    } // end stop


} // end MyNewApplet
```

Normally, when an applet terminates, the resources used by the objects are reclaimed. If, however, you have started additional threads, or have opened files on the Web server, you must release these resources explicitly. This is where the `destroy()` method comes in handy. You use the `destroy()` method for general cleanup of the applet resources. The `destroy()` method that you define overrides the empty `destroy()` method in the class Applet:

```
public class MyNewApplet extends java.applet.Applet
{
      public void init()
      {
         // Your initialization code
         // goes here.

      } // end init

      public void start()
      {
      // Your start up code
      // goes here.

      } // end start

      public void stop()
      {
         // Your stop code
         // goes here.

      } // end stop

      public void destroy()
      {
         // Your cleanup code
         // goes here.

      } // end destroy

} // end MyNewApplet
```

Note The `destroy()` method is different from the `finalize()` method described in Chapter 7. The `finalize()` method is a general purpose method that can be used to reclaim resources for any Java class. The `destroy()` method has been specifically designed for Java applets. The `destroy()` method is called whenever the applet has finished execution—this can occur if the applet is reloaded or the browser is terminating. The `finalize()` method, on the other hand, may not always be executed, especially if a severe error condition occurs.

There is one additional method that you need to implement a useful Java applet. This method is the `paint()` method. The `paint()` method is called whenever there is a need for the browser to redraw the applet. This will occur at least once, after the applet has been initialized, and any time when the browser window is moved, resized, or uncovered after being covered over by another application (see fig. 8.4).

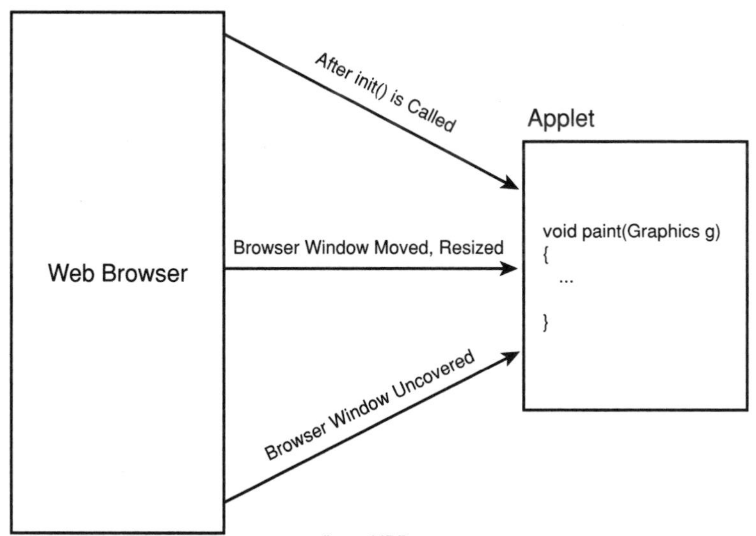

Figure 8.4

The `paint()` method.

If you examine the methods of the Applet class discussed in this section, you will not see any definition of the `paint()` method. The `paint()` method is actually defined in the abstract class Component, which is part of the hierarchy diagram for the Applet class (see fig. 8.1):

```
public void paint(Graphics g)
{
      // Empty body.
}
```

The paint() method in the Component class is empty; that is, it has no code. Therefore, to paint the applet, you must override the paint() method defined in the Component superclass. If you do not override the paint() method, your applet will not do much of anything as far as its display area of the applet is concerned. The argument to the method paint() is an instance of the class Graphics. This object defines the graphic context for modifying the display area of the applet. The Graphics class is instantiated by the browser, and this instance of the object is passed to the method paint(), so you do not have to create the object argument. The Graphics class is defined in the package java.awt, and defines among other things, methods for drawing lines, ellipses, circles, lines, squares, and so on.

The applet now has the following structure:

```
public class MyNewApplet extends java.applet.Applet
{
      public void init()
      {
         // Your initialization code
         // goes here.

      } // end init

      public void start()
      {
         // Your start up code
         // goes here.

      } // end start

      public void stop()
      {
         // Your stop code
         // goes here.

      } // end stop

      public void destroy()
      {
         // Your cleanup code
         // goes here.
```

```
    } // end destroy

    public void paint(Graphics g)
    {
        // Your paint code
        // goes here.

    } // end paint

} // end MyNewApplet
```

Writing the HelloWorld Applet

Now that you know the structure of applets, you are ready to write a simple Java applet. In fact, let us write an applet version of the HelloWorld program described in Chapter 2, "Getting Started with Java."

Listing 8.1 (file HelloAppletWorld.java on the CD-ROM accompanying this book) contains the applet version of the HelloWorld program. Line 9 defines an import statement to import the Graphics class. This import statement is necessary, as the Graphics class is needed in the `paint()` method. If you are performing several graphics related tasks and using a number of classes from the java.awt package, you could replace the import statement on line 9 with the following:

```
import java.awt.*;
```

The preceding statement imports all the classes defined in the package java.awt.

Lines 15–19 define the `init()` method to override the method in the class Applet. This method contains just one line to invoke the method `resize()`. The method `resize()` is defined in class Applet. For your reference, figure 8.5 shows its definition, created with the javadoc application. The applet size is resized to the specified dimensions (line 17) of 500 pixels of width and 300 pixels of height.

The methods `start()`, `stop()`, and `destroy()` are not defined in the class HelloWorld. Therefore, these methods are inherited from class Applet. As mentioned earlier, these methods do not contain any code and therefore do not provide any functionality. These methods are not needed because there is nothing to start, stop, or destroy in the applet. The `paint()` method (lines 23–28) is called whenever the browser window that displays the applet is moved, resized, or uncovered.

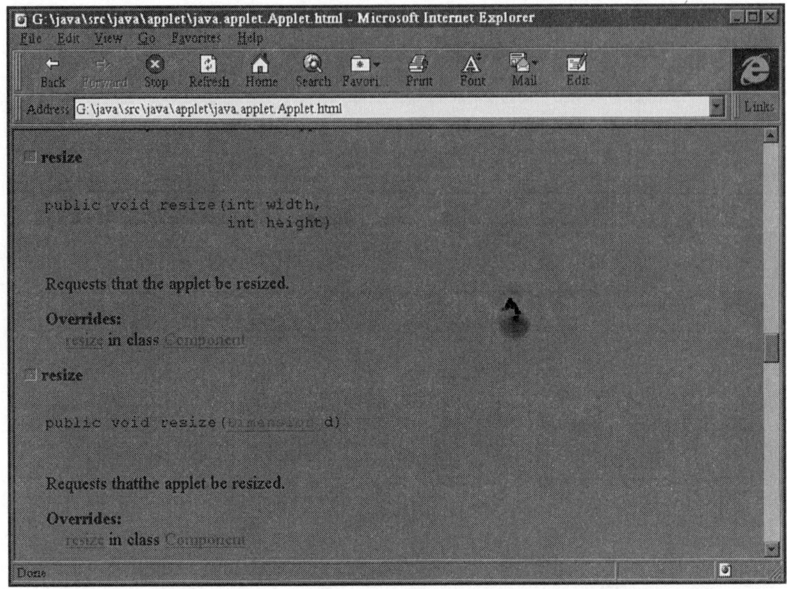

Figure 8.5

Method `resize()` definition using Java.

The `paint()` method contains just one call to the `drawString()` method of the Graphics object that was passed as a parameter to the `paint()` method. The `drawString()` method draws the string that is passed at the coordinates <10, 20>. The coordinates are measured in pixels. The origin is the top left-hand corner. The value of 10 is along the X-axis and the value of 20 is along the Y-axis (see fig. 8.6).

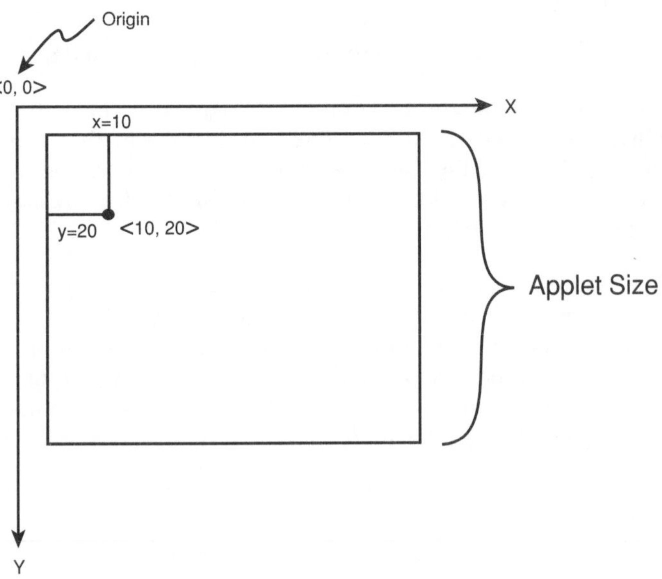

Figure 8.6

Coordinate for the positioning of the Applet.

Listing 8.1

```
Line=================Java Source=================
/**
 * HelloAppletWorld: Applet version of the HelloWorld
 * program.
 *
 * Author: Karanjit S. G. S. Siyan
 *
 */

import java.awt.Graphics;

public class HelloWorld extends java.applet.Applet
{

    // init: Override method in Applet
    public void init()
    {
        resize(500, 300);

    } // end init


    // paint: Override method in Component
    public void paint(Graphics g)
    {

        g.drawString("Hello World! This is a simple Java applet!", 10, 20);

    } // end paint

} // end HelloWorld
```

The next step is to run the applet. In earlier chapters, you ran Java applications by using the Java interpreter. To run applets in a simulated Internet environment, the Applet Viewer application is used. To run the applet in Applet Viewer, you must first define an HTML document that specifies the applet byte code location and any parameters that you want to send to the applet. You will learn to do this in the next section.

Defining HTML Documents to Run Applets

The subject of defining HTML documents can fill an entire book. The goal in this section is to present only sufficient elements of HTML to show how applet specifications can be embedded in an HTML document.

Listing 8.2 (file HelloAppletWorld.html on the CD-ROM accompanying this book) shows an example of an HTML document for running the HelloWorld program defined in the previous section. The line numbers in this listing are for reference purposes only, and are not part of the HTML document.

HTML documents consist of *tags* enclosed in angular brackets:

```
<tag>
```

A tag is used to specify the type of data that is encoded in the document. Most tags have an end-of-tag specifier that marks the end-of-tag definition. These end-of-tag specifiers have the following format:

```
</tag>
```

Spaces and lines outside a set of tag specifiers are usually not significant.

Lines 1 and 15 of listing 8.2 define the tags <HTML> and </HTML>, respectively. These tags specify that everything between these tag specifiers is part of an HTML document.

Lines 2 and 4 of listing 8.2 define tags <HEAD> and </HEAD>, respectively. These tags specify the head of the HTML document. Within this head specification is the <TITLE> and </TITLE> tags on line 3. Inside the <TITLE> specification is the string `"A simple HelloWorld Applet"`. This title will be displayed as the title of the HTML document in the Web browser.

Lines 6 and 14 of listing 8.2 define tags <BODY> and </BODY>, respectively. These tags specify the body of the HTML document that will be rendered as a graphics document in the Web browser.

On line 7 is the tag specifier <P> that defines a new paragraph. The end </P> tag specifying the end of the paragraph has been left out because it is optional.

The tag <BR> on line 8 causes a line break, and displays the contents that follow on a new line. Lines 10–13 define the applet. Note that these contain the <APPLET *attributes*> and the end of applet specification tag </APPLET>.

The *attributes* in the applet tag can contain a number of attribute specifications. In this example, only three attributes, CODE, WIDTH, and HEIGHT are defined.

A number of other attributes can also be specified. These are discussed in later examples in this chapter.

The CODE="*URL*" attribute specifies the URL location of the applet code. This URL location specifies the file that contains the applet class. Note that this file contains the byte code for the applet and must be specified by using the `.class` extension. In this case, the class file is in the same directory as the HTML file. If the class file is in a different directory than the HTML file, you can use the CODEBASE="*directory*" attribute to specify the different directory.

The WIDTH and HEIGHT specify in pixels the width and height of the bounding rectangle that contains the applet. It is used to specify how big a box to draw for the applet. You should specify appropriate sizes for the applet, taking into account how big a graphics object is painted by the applet. The `resize()` method can be called from within the applet code to resize these dimensions.

The text between the <APPLET *attributes*> and </APPLET> tags is optional. If specified, this text is displayed by non-Java-enabled browsers. In the example in listing 8.2, the following statement will appear in non-Java-enabled browsers, where the applet would normally be displayed:

You will not know what you are missing unless you upgrade your browser to a Java-enabled browser! You should display a similar message (probably a less obnoxious one!) to indicate the fact that the applet cannot be run in the user's browser.

Listing 8.2

```
Line==================HTML Source==================
<HTML>
<HEAD>
<TITLE>A simple HelloWorld Applet</TITLE>
</HEAD>

<BODY>
<P>My first applet says:
<BR>

<APPLET CODE="HelloWorld.class" WIDTH=300 HEIGHT=300>
You will not know what you are missing unless
you upgrade your browser to a Java enabled browser!
</APPLET>
</BODY>
</HTML>
```

Running Applets

You can use the Applet Viewer application included with the JDK or any Java-enabled browser to run the applet.

You can run the applet with Applet Viewer by using the following steps:

1. After you have copied the contents of the HelloAppletWorld directory from the CD-ROM (at the back of this book) to your local disk, you should build the .class file by running the Java compiler.
2. From the directory in which you copied the code, type **javac HelloAppletWorld.java**.
3. After the program compiles with no errors, type **appletviewer HelloAppletWorld.html**. The Applet Viewer should launch, and you will see the applet display as shown in figure 8.7.

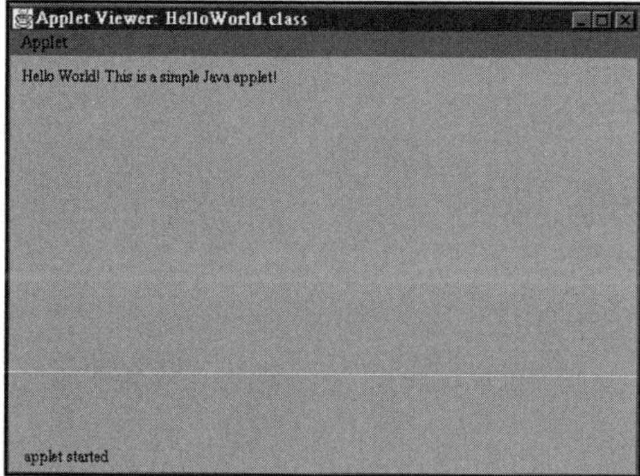

Figure 8.7

Running the HelloAppletWorld with the Applet Viewer.

You can also start the applet in a Web browser such as Internet Explorer. You can specify the name of the HTML file to load in the address field of the browser (see fig. 8.8).

Using Fonts and Colors in Applets

The Graphics class provides a number of classes that you can use to set the font and colors of any text or graphic elements that you draw in the applet. You can, for example, use the `setFont()` and `setColor()` method to draw strings with different fonts and colors.

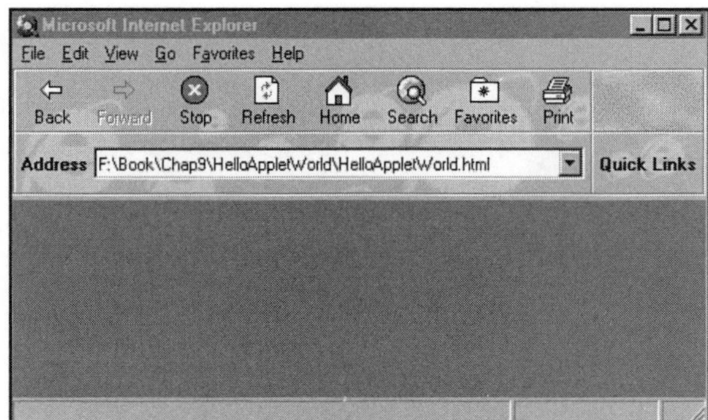

Figure 8.8

Specifying the HTML file in Internet Explorer.

For your reference, figures 8.9, 8.10, and 8.11 show the definition of the `setFont()`, `setColor()`, and `drawString()` methods for the `Graphics` class, using the documentation produced from the javadoc application. These methods are used in the modified version of the HelloWorld program shown in listing 8.3 (see file HelloAppletWorld1.java on the CD-ROM at the back of the book).

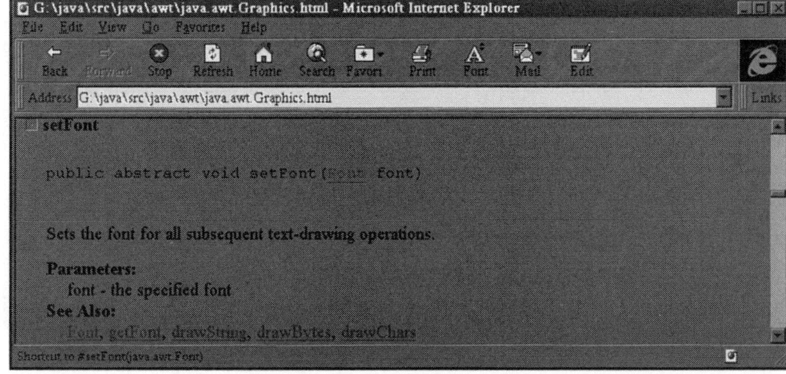

Figure 8.9

Definition of `setFont()` *method.*

Lines 9–11 of listing 8.3 contain the import statements. In addition to the class Graphics, the class Font and Color are imported from the package java.awt.

The `init()` method on lines 19–23 calls `resize()` to set the size of the applet.

Line 16 sets up a private instance variable of class Font: `private Font fnt = new Font("Times Roman", Font.ITALIC, 20);`

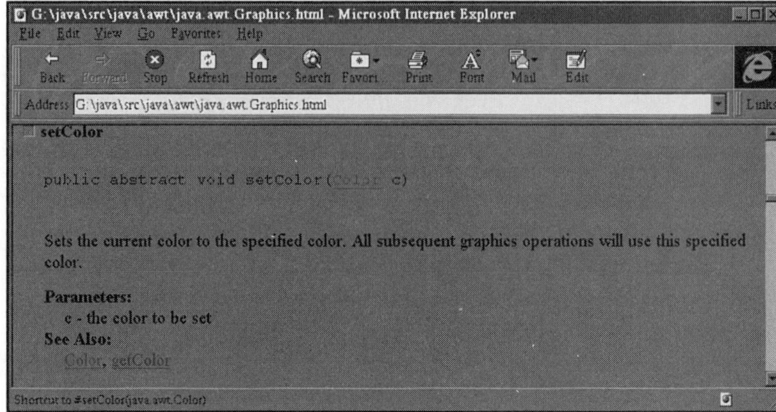

Figure 8.10 *Definition of* `setColor()` *method.*

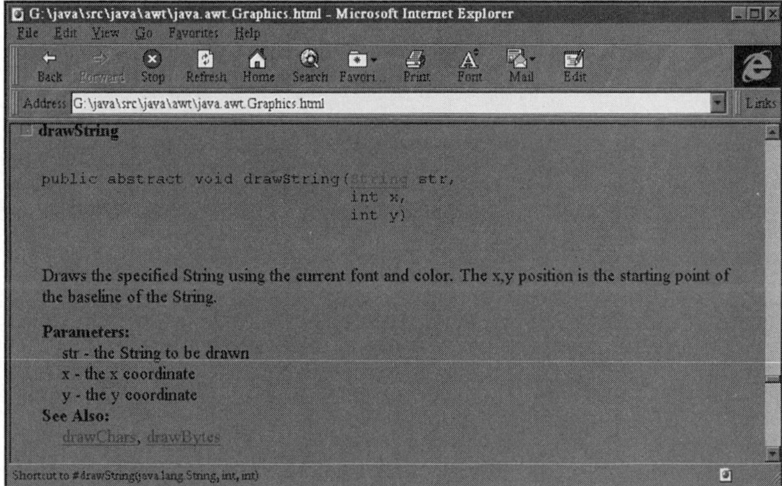

Figure 8.11 *Definition of* `drawString()` *method.*

The font variable, `fnt`, is needed as an argument to the method `setFont()`. On line 16, the constructor for class Font is called. For your reference the definition of this constructor is shown in figure 8.12. The first argument to the constructor is a text description of the font; the second argument is the style of the font; and the last argument is the size of the font. The style of the font can have the values Font.PLAIN, Font.ITALIC, and Font.BOLD. You can also combine them with the "+" operator to produce combination fonts:

```
Font.ITALIC + Font.BOLD   // Produces an italic bold.
```

The style values are integers so adding them is perfectly fine.

The `paint()` method sets the font on line 30 by using the `fnt` variable defined on line 16 and the `setFont()` method (see fig. 8.13).

Line 31 sets the color of all subsequent drawing operations, such as `drawString()` on line 32. The color is set to blue by invoking the `setColor()` method:

```
g.setColor(Color.blue);
```

For your reference, figure 8.14 shows the definition of `setColor()`. The color argument is an instance of class Color. For your convenience, the class Color contains the following class constants that can be used for standard colors:

```
public  final  class  java.awt.Color
      extends  java.lang.Object
{
      // Fields
      public final static Color black;
      public final static Color blue;
      public final static Color cyan;
      public final static Color gray;
      public final static Color darkGray;
      public final static Color lightGray;
      public final static Color green;
      public final static Color magenta;
      public final static Color orange;
      public final static Color pink;
      public final static Color red;
      public final static Color white;
      public final static Color yellow;

      // Other definitions
      ...

} // end Color
```

Each of these class constants can be references such as `Color.yellow`, `Color.black`, and so on.

Java uses a 24-bit color model with which you can create new colors by supplying the red, green, and blue values to a special Color constructor. Each of the color values can be a number from 0–255. Table 8.1 shows the RGB values of the standard colors.

Table 8.1
RGB Value of Standard Colors

Color	R,G,B Value
black	0,0,0
blue	0,255,0
cyan	0,255,255
gray	128,128,128
darkGray	64,64,64
lightGray	192,192,192
green	0,255,0
magenta	255,0,255
orange	255,200,0
pink	255,175,175
red	255,0,0
white	255,255,255
yellow	255,255,0

To create a color with an arbitary RGB value of 200, 134, 56, you can use the following:

```
Color color = new Color(200, 134, 56);
```

You can represent the values from 0–255 on a scale of 0 to 1.0. Therefore, you can also use the float point numbers as arguments to the Color constructor:

```
Color color = new Color(0.25, 0.75, 0.5);
```

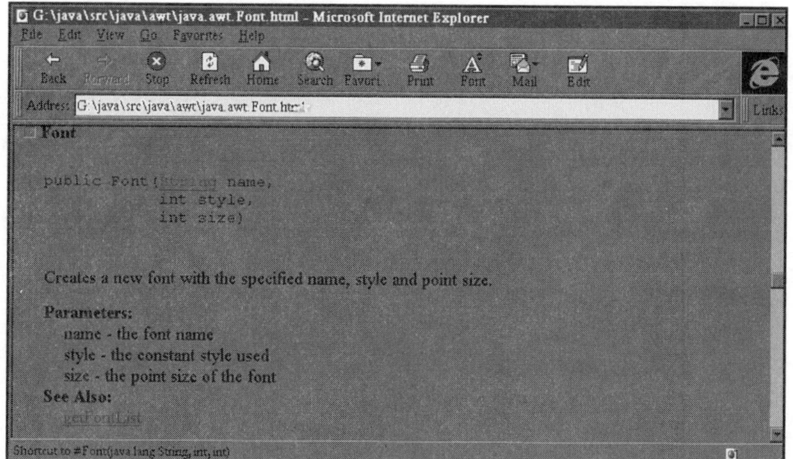

Figure 8.12

Definition of Font constructor.

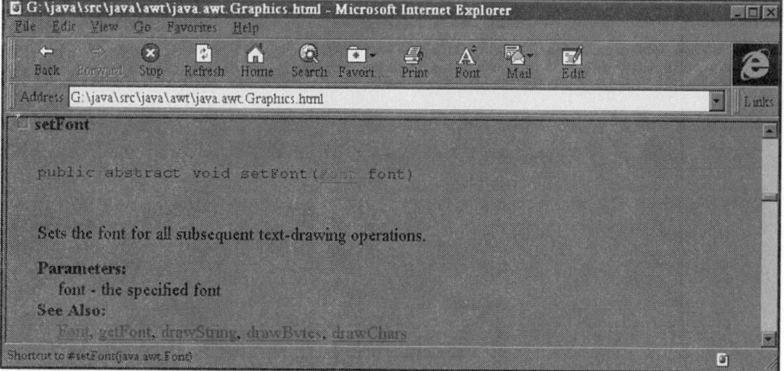

Figure 8.13

Definition of `setFont()` *method.*

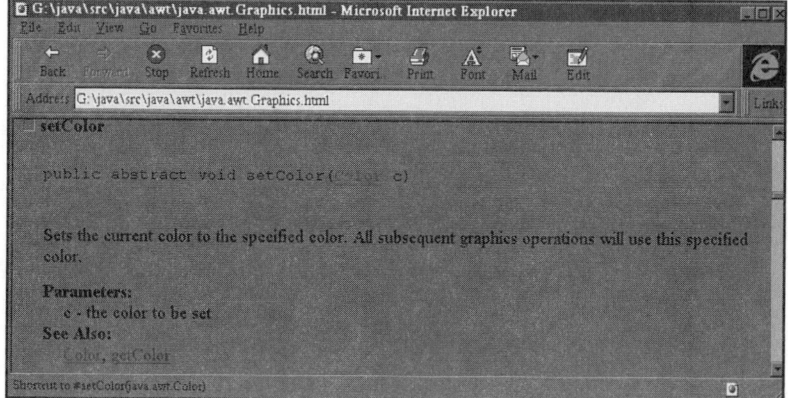

Figure 8.14

Definition of `setColor()` *method.*

Listing 8.3

```
Line==================Java Source==================
/**
 * HelloAppletWorld1: Applet version of the HelloWorld
 * program. Uses fonts and colors.
 *
 * Author: Karanjit S. G. S. Siyan
 *
 */

import java.awt.Graphics;
import java.awt.Font;
import java.awt.Color;

public class HelloWorld1 extends java.applet.Applet
{

    private Font fnt = new Font("Times Roman", Font.ITALIC, 20);

    // init: Override method in Applet
    public void init()
    {
        resize(600, 300);

    }  // end init


    // paint: Override method in Component
    public void paint(Graphics g)
    {

        g.setFont(fnt);
        g.setColor(Color.blue);
        g.drawString("Hello World! This is a simple Java applet!", 10, 40);

    }  // end paint

}  // end HelloWorld1
```

After compiling the program in listing 8.3, you must create an HTML file to run the program from a Web browser. Listing 8.4 contains a sample HTML file used for running the HelloAppletWorld1 applet, and figure 8.15 shows the output of this program.

Listing 8.4

```
Line==================HTML Source=================
<HTML>
<HEAD>
<TITLE>A simple HelloWorld Applet</TITLE>
</HEAD>

<BODY>
<APPLET CODE="HelloWorld1.class" WIDTH=600, HEIGHT=300>
You will not know what you are missing unless
you upgrade your browser to a Java enabled browser!
</APPLET>
</BODY>
</HTML>
```

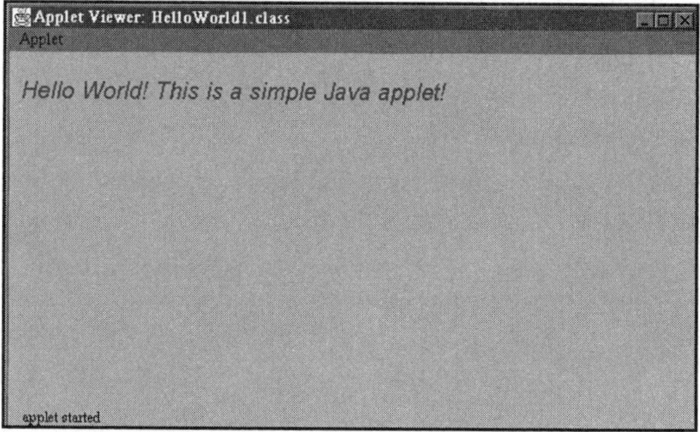

Figure 8.15

Output of HelloAppletWorld1.

Aligning Applets in the Web Browser

You can use the ALIGN attribute of the APPLET tag to align the applet with respect to the rest of the Web page. The following is the syntax of the ALIGN attribute:

```
<APPLET CODE="location" WIDTH=d HEIGHT=d ALIGN=alignvalue>
```

The *alignvalue* can have the values listed in table 8.2. When the LEFT or RIGHT value is used for alignment, the text will flow as indicated until a <BR CLEAR=*clearvalue*> tag is encountered. Recall that the <BR> tag causes a line break. The CLEAR is an attribute that can be specified to control the behavior of the line break. The *clearvalue* can be LEFT, RIGHT, or ALL. A *clearvalue* of LEFT will start the text to the next clear left margin; a *clearvalue* of RIGHT will start the text to the next clear right margin; a *clearvalue* of ALL will start the text on the next line whose left and right margins are both clear.

The align values of TOP, TEXTTOP, MIDDLE, ABSMIDDLE, ABSBOTTOM, BASELINE, BOTTOM are meant to be used for small applets that would be embedded in a single text line.

TABLE 8.2
Values for the ALIGN Attribute in the APPLET Tag

Alignvalue	Meaning
LEFT	The applet is placed at the left margin of the Web page, and all HTML text that follows the applet tag flows into the space that is to the right of the applet.
RIGHT	The applet is placed at the right margin of the Web page, and all HTML text that follows the applet tag flows into the space that is to the left of the applet.
TOP	Sets the applet with the topmost item in the line. The item could be text, applet, or image.
TEXTTOP	Sets the top of the applet with the top of the highest text in the line.
MIDDLE	Sets the middle of the applet with the middle of the line.
ABSMIDDLE	Sets the middle of the applet with the middle of the largest item in the line.
ABSBOTTOM	Sets the bottom of the applet with the lowest item in the line.
BASELINE	Sets the bottom of the applet to the baseline.
BOTTOM	Same as BASELINE.

You can also use the HSPACE and VSPACE attributes of the APPLET tag to control the amount of space between the applet and the surrounding text. An example of this is shown next:

```
<APPLET CODE="HelloAppletWorld1.class" WIDTH=600 HEIGHT=300 HSPACE=60
➥VSPACE=30>
</APPLET>
```

The values of HSPACE and VSPACE are measured in pixels. A value of 60 for HSPACE will set the space above and below the applet to 60 pixels. A value of 30 for VSPACE will set the space to the left and right of the applet to 30.

You can also use the <ALT=*alternate*> tag to specify an alternate image of text for Web browsers that are not Java-enabled. The *alternate* is replaced by the URL of the text or image.

Passing Parameters to Applets

When you write Java applications, you can pass parameters via the argument to the `main()` method. These parameters are specified on the command line (see the ArraySort program example in Chapter 5, "Using Java Objects and Arrays"), and they are usually designed to control the behavior of the program.

Suppose that you want to change the behavior of the applet by passing a parameter to the applet. How can you accomplish this task? You cannot pass parameters to the `main()` method because applets do not have a `main()` method. Instead, you pass parameter values through the HTML document that specifies the applet location. The parameter values to an applet are passed through the following special parameter tag:

```
<PARAM NAME=name VALUE=value>
```

The *name* is the name of the parameter, and *value* is its value. If, for example, you wanted to draw the string in the previous HelloAppletWorld1 example in a different color or size, you could define the following parameters:

```
<PARAM NAME=COLOR VALUE="Magenta">
<PARAM NAME=SIZE VALUE="36">
```

If you were animating an applet and wanted to control its speed, you could define the following value:

```
<PARAM NAME=speed VALUE="5">
```

Here the value of the speed parameter has a meaning that is internal to the applet program.

The parameters to the applet must be specified between the APPLET tag:

```
<APPLET CODE="location" WIDTH=400 HEIGHT=300 ALIGN=LEFT>
<PARAM NAME=COLOR VALUE="Red">
<PARAM NAME=SIZE VALUE="36">
</APPLET>
```

The next step is to obtain the parameter values from the HTML document into the applet code. This step is typically performed as part of the initialization of the applet in the method `init()`.

Remember that the definition of the Applet class includes a method called `getParameter()`. This method is inherited by the class that you extend from the Applet class. You can specify the parameter name as an argument to `getParameter()`, which will then return the value of the parameter as a string object. The parameter name must match exactly (including case) the parameter name specified in the <PARAM> tag, otherwise a value of `null` is returned.

To read the parameter values of COLOR and SIZE described previously, for example, you can use the following:

```
class MyApplet extends java.applet.Applet
{

      String color;
      String size;

      public void init()
      {
         color = getParameter("COLOR");
         size = getParameter("SIZE");

      } // end init

      // Other methods
} // end MyApplet
```

Listing 8.5 shows a program that takes parameters from the HTML document and displays a greeting whose color, style, and size are dependent on the passed parameters. Listing 8.6 shows the corresponding HTML document that was used for the applet.

Lines 16 and 17 of listing 8.5 define the instance variables that are needed by the applet class methods. Note that these class instance variables have a private access type to prevent another class from accessing these variables and potentially misusing them. These instance variables contain the font and color values needed in the method `paint()`.

The `init()` method obtains the parameter values of style, color, and size by calling the `getParameter()` method in lines 27–29. These parameter values are passed in lines 12–14 (see listing 8.6) by the <PARAM> tag.

Lines 33–51 contain a multiway if-statement to convert the string value of the parameter to an integer font style value that can be used in the applet. These types of conversions are typical, as the parameter values are passed as strings, and the applet may need the string values converted to different data or class types.

Lines 55–112 contain a long multiway if-statement to convert the string value of the color parameter to the class Color value that can be used in the applet.

Lines 116–125 contain an if-statement to convert the string size value to an equivalent integer value. The static public method `Integer.parseInt()` is used to make this conversion.

Line 127 constructs the font based on the parameter values:

```
fnt = new Font("Times Roman", styleVal, sizeVal);
```

Figure 8.16 shows the output of the applet in a Web browser.

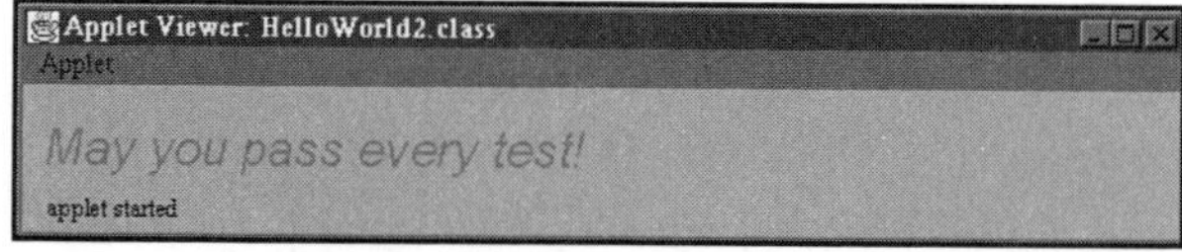

Figure 8.16

Output of program HelloAppletWorld2 in a Web browser.

Listing 8.5

```
Line=================Java Source================
001 /**
002  * HelloAppletWorld2: Applet version of the HelloWorld
003  * program. Shows parameter passing.
004  *
005  * Author: Karanjit S. G. S. Siyan
006  *
```

continues

Listing 8.5, Continued

```
 */

import java.awt.Graphics;
import java.awt.Font;
import java.awt.Color;

public class HelloWorld2 extends java.applet.Applet
{

    private Font fnt;        // Font of message
    private Color colorVal; // Color of message

    // init: Override method in Applet
    public void init()
    {
        String style; // style parameter
        String color; // color parameter
        String size;  // size parameter

        resize(600, 50);
        style = getParameter("style");
        color = getParameter("color");
        size = getParameter("size");

        // Convert style parameter to a style
        // value that can be used in the applet.
        int styleVal = 0;
        if (style == null)
        {
            // Not specified. Use default.
            styleVal = Font.BOLD;
        }
        else if (style.equalsIgnoreCase("bold"))
        {
            styleVal = Font.BOLD;
        }
        else if (style.equalsIgnoreCase("italic"))
        {
```

```
            styleVal = Font.ITALIC;
        }
        else if (style.equalsIgnoreCase("bold"))
        {
            styleVal = Font.PLAIN;

        }  // end if

        // Convert color parameter to a color
        // value that can be used in the applet.
        if (color == null)
        {
            // Not specified. Use default.
            colorVal = Color.blue;
        }
        else if (color.equalsIgnoreCase("black"))
        {
            colorVal = Color.black;
        }
        else if (color.equalsIgnoreCase("blue"))
        {
            colorVal = Color.blue;
        }
        else if (color.equalsIgnoreCase("cyan"))
        {
            colorVal = Color.cyan;
        }
        else if (color.equalsIgnoreCase("darkGray"))
        {
            colorVal = Color.darkGray;
        }
        else if (color.equalsIgnoreCase("gray"))
        {
            colorVal = Color.gray;
        }
        else if (color.equalsIgnoreCase("lightGray"))
        {
            colorVal = Color.lightGray;
```

continues

Listing 8.5, Continued

```
        }
        else if (color.equalsIgnoreCase("green"))
        {
            colorVal = Color.green;
        }
        else if (color.equalsIgnoreCase("magenta"))
        {
            colorVal = Color.magenta;
        }
        else if (color.equalsIgnoreCase("orange"))
        {
            colorVal = Color.orange;
        }
        else if (color.equalsIgnoreCase("pink"))
        {
            colorVal = Color.pink;
        }
        else if (color.equalsIgnoreCase("red"))
        {
            colorVal = Color.red;
        }
        else if (color.equalsIgnoreCase("white"))
        {
            colorVal = Color.white;
        }
        else if (color.equalsIgnoreCase("yellow"))
        {
            colorVal = Color.yellow;

        }  // end if

        // Convert size parameter to a size
        // value that can be used in the applet.
        int sizeVal;
        if (size == null)
        {
            sizeVal = 20;
        }
```

```
        else
        {
            sizeVal = Integer.parseInt(size);

        }  // end if

        fnt = new Font("Times Roman", styleVal, sizeVal);

    }  // end init


    // paint: Override method in Component
    public void paint(Graphics g)
    {

        g.setFont(fnt);
        g.setColor(colorVal);
        g.drawString("May you pass every test!", 10, 40);

    }  // end paint

}  // end HelloWorld2
```

Listing 8.6

```
Line=================HTML Source=================
<HTML>
<HEAD>
<TITLE>A simple HelloWorld Applet</TITLE>
</HEAD>

<BODY>
<P>My third applet says:
<BR>
<HR>

<APPLET CODE="HelloWorld2" WIDTH=600 HEIGHT=50 ALIGN=LEFT>
<PARAM NAME=style VALUE="italic">
<PARAM NAME=color VALUE="magenta">
```

continues

Listing 8.6, Continued

```
<PARAM NAME=size VALUE="25">
A Java applet greeting would appear here.
</APPLET>
<BR CLEAR=ALL>
<P>Other greetings could appear here.
</BODY>
</HTML>
```

Summary

In this chapter you learned the basic structure of Java applets and how to write Java applets. You saw several examples of writing a simple HelloWorld applet with various refinements such as changing the font, style, color of a string, and passing parameters to an applet. As part of learning to write Java applets, you also learned how to create a simple HTML file to run the applet and how to pass parameters to Java applets through the HTML file.

CHAPTER 9

Animating Applets with Java Graphics, Images, Colors, and Sound

In the previous chapter, you learned about the basic structure of an applet and how to write simple applets. However, because you had not yet learned about how to draw graphic elements, there was not much you could do with these applets.

In this chapter, you will learn the basics of using Java's built-in graphic primitives to produce lines, shapes, images, and sounds. You will use Java's graphic primitives to produce more interesting applets. You will also learn about multithreading and how this concept can be used in Java applets and applications. You will learn to produce applets that include sound, image animation, and interaction with the user.

Overview of the Graphics Class

Most of the drawing methods in Java are defined as methods in the Graphics class. The Graphics class is part of the package java.awt, and you can access it by importing this class:

```
import       java.awt.Graphics;
```

You can use these methods to draw lines, shapes, text strings, and images on the display area of your applet. You do not have to create an instance of the Graphics object within the applet code to have access to the drawing methods. Recall the definition of the `paint()` method that you wrote in the simple Java applets of the previous chapter:

```
public void paint(Graphics g)
{
        // Your code

} // end paint
```

The instance of the Graphics object is passed to you by the Web browser when it calls the `paint()` method. This Graphics object instance is created by the Web browser. Because it is passed to the applet through the `paint()` method, you do not have to create a separate instance of the Graphics class.

Understanding the Graphics Coordinates

Many of the methods in the Graphics class make use of a coordinate system to define the location of points, graphic elements, and so on. This coordinate system is the familiar X–Y plane used in geometry, except that the X-axis starts at the top-left-hand corner of the display area and with increasing values of X, proceeds to the top-right corner of the display area. The Y-axis also starts at the top-left-hand corner of the display area and with increasing values of Y, proceeds to the bottom-left corner of the display area (see fig. 9.1).

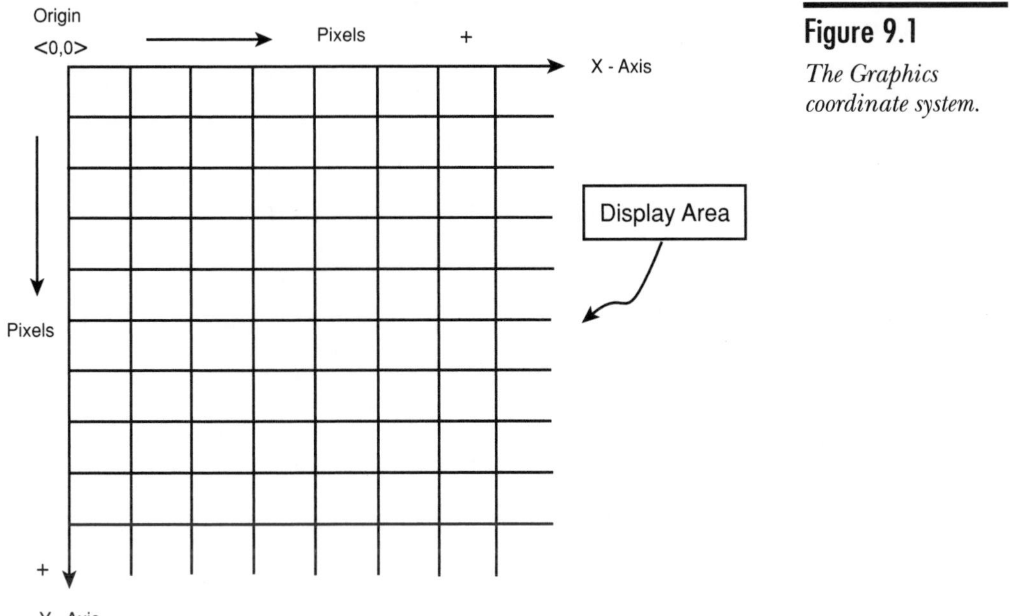

Figure 9.1
The Graphics coordinate system.

Examining the Graphics Class

The Graphics class is very extensive and provides a device-independent interface to the graphics capabilities in Java. It contains many methods to draw lines, images, copy areas, and so on. If you are going to be adding graphical appeal to your applets, chances are that you will end up using one of the methods in the Graphics class. You will have access to the Graphics methods in applets through the instance of the Graphics class that is passed as a parameter to the applet's `paint()` method.

Because the Graphics class is important for drawing applets, listing 9.1 is the skeleton of the Graphics class for your reference. The code in listing 9.1 looks like Java code, and it contains the description of all the methods and parameters needed to call a Graphic method. It is not really syntactically correct Java code because the body of the code for the methods has been omitted for reasons of space and because it is not important for learning to use the Graphics class. You should quickly review this description of the Graphics class (even though it is, unfortunately, several pages long!) to get an idea of the methods that are available for your use. You can come back and review these method definitions later in detail when writing the Graphics code. Note that you have already learned to use some of the Graphics methods such as `setColor()`, `setFont()`, and `drawString()` in Chapter 8, "Creating Java Applets."

Listing 9.1

```
Line=================Java Source================
public abstract class Graphics
{
/**
 * Note: In all the methods that follow the parameters
 * x, y, width, and height have the following meaning:
 * x = x coordinate
 * y = y coordinate
 * width = width of the area
 * height = height of the area
 */

 //
 // Constructs a new Graphics Object. Graphic contexts
 // cannot be created directly. They must be obtained
 // from another graphics
 // context or created by a Component.
 protected Graphics();

 //
 // Creates a new Graphics Object that is a copy of the
 // original Graphics Object.
 public abstract Graphics create();


 //
 // Creates a new Graphics Object with the specified
 // parameters, based on the original Graphics Object.
 // This method translates the specified parameters,
 // x and y, to the proper origin coordinates and then
 // clips the Graphics Object to the area.
 public Graphics create(int x, int y, int width,
   int height);

 //
 // Translates the specified parameters into the origin
 // of the graphics context. All subsequent operations
 // on this graphics context will be relative to this
```

```
// origin.
public abstract void translate(int x, int y);

//
// Gets the current color.
public abstract Color getColor();

//
// Sets the current color to the specified color. All
// subsequent graphics operations
// will use this specified color.
// c = color to be set
public abstract void setColor(Color c);

//
// Sets the paint mode to overwrite the destination with
// the current color.
public abstract void setPaintMode();

//
// Sets the paint mode to alternate between the current
// color and the new specified color.  When drawing
// operations are performed, pixels which are the current
// color will be changed to the specified color and
// vice versa.  Pixels of colors other than those two
// colors will be changed in an unpredictable, but
// reversible manner—if you draw the same figure twice
// then all pixels will be restored to their
// original values.
//
//  c1 = the second color
public abstract void setXORMode(Color c1);

//
// Gets the current font.
public abstract Font getFont();

//
// Sets the font for all subsequent text-drawing
```

continues

Listing 9.1, Continued

```
// operations.
// font = the specified font
public abstract void setFont(Font font);

//
// Gets the current font metrics.
public FontMetrics getFontMetrics();


//
// Gets the current font metrics for the
// specified font.
// f = the specified font
public abstract FontMetrics getFontMetrics(Font f);


//
// Returns the bounding rectangle of the current
// clipping area.
public abstract Rectangle getClipRect();

//
// Clips to a rectangle. The resulting clipping area
// is the intersection of the current clipping area
// and the specified rectangle. Graphic operations
// have no effect outside of the clipping area.
public abstract void clipRect(int x, int y,
 int width, int height);

//
// Copies an area of the screen.
//  dx = the horizontal distance
//  dy = the vertical distance
public abstract void copyArea(int x, int y,
 int width, int height, int dx, int dy);

//
// Draws a line between the coordinates (x1,y1)
```

```
// and (x2,y2).
// The line is drawn below and to the left of
// the logical coordinates.
//  x1 = the first point's x coordinate
//  y1 = the first point's y coordinate
//  x2 = the second point's x coordinate
//  y2 = the second point's y coordinate
public abstract void drawLine(int x1, int y1,
 int x2, int y2);

//
// Fills the specified rectangle with the current color.
public abstract void fillRect(int x, int y,
 int width, int height);

//
// Draws the outline of the specified rectangle using
// the current color.
// Use drawRect(x, y, width-1, height-1) to draw the
// outline inside the specified rectangle.
public void drawRect(int x, int y,
 int width, int height);


//
// Clears the specified rectangle by filling it with
// the current background color of the current
// drawing surface.
// Which drawing surface it selects depends on how
// the graphics context was created.
public abstract void clearRect(int x, int y, int width,
 int height);

//
// Draws an outlined rounded corner rectangle using
// the current color.
//  arcWidth = the horizontal diameter of the arc
//        at the four corners
//  arcHeight = the vertical diameter of the arc
```

continues

Listing 9.1, Continued

```
//                at the four corners
public abstract void drawRoundRect(int x, int y,
 int width, int height, int arcWidth, int arcHeight);

//
// Draws a rounded rectangle filled in with the
// current color.
//  arcWidth = the horizontal diameter of the arc at the
//                four corners
//  arcHeight = the vertical diameter of the arc at the
//                four corners
public abstract void fillRoundRect(int x, int y,
  int width, int height, int arcWidth, int arcHeight);

//
// Draws a highlighted 3D rectangle.
//  raised = a boolean that states whether the rectangle
//                is raised or not
public void draw3DRect(int x, int y, int width, int height,
  boolean raised);

//
// Paints a highlighted 3D rectangle using the
// current color.
//  raised = a boolean that states whether the rectangle
//                is raised or not
public void fill3DRect(int x, int y, int width, int height,
  boolean raised);

//
// Draws an oval inside the specified rectangle using the
// current color.
public abstract void drawOval(int x, int y,
  int width, int height);

//
// Fills an oval inside the specified rectangle using
// the current color.
```

```
public abstract void fillOval(int x, int y,
 int width, int height);

//
// Draws an arc bounded by the specified rectangle
// starting at startAngle, where 0 degrees is at the
// 3-o'clock position, and extending for arcAngle
// degrees. Positive values for arcAngle indicate
// counter-clockwise rotations, negative values
// indicate clockwise rotations.
//  startAngle = the beginning angle
//  arcAngle = the angle of the arc (relative to
//             startAngle).
public abstract void drawArc(int x, int y, int width,
  int height, int startAngle, int arcAngle);

//
// Fills an arc using the current color. This generates
// a pie shape. The extent of the arc is the same as is
// described for the drawArc method.
//  startAngle = the beginning angle
//  arcAngle = the angle of the arc (relative to
//             startAngle).
public abstract void fillArc(int x, int y,
  int width, int height, int startAngle, int arcAngle);

//
// Draws a polygon defined by an array of x points
// and y points.
//  xPoints = an array of x points
//  yPoints = an array of y points
//  nPoints = the total number of points
public abstract void drawPolygon(int xPoints[],
  int yPoints[],  int nPoints);

//
// Draws a polygon defined by the specified point.
//  p = the specified polygon
public void drawPolygon(Polygon p);
```

continues

Listing 9.1, Continued

```

//
// Draws the specified String using the current font
// and color. The x,y position is the starting point
// of the baseline of the String.
// str = the String to be drawn
public abstract void drawString(String str, int x, int y);

//
// Draws the specified characters using the current font
// and color.
//  data = the array of characters to be drawn
//  offset = the start offset in the data
//  length = the number of characters to be drawn
public void drawChars(char data[], int offset,
 int length, int x, int y);


//
// Draws the specified bytes using the current font
// and color.
// data = the data to be drawn
// offset = the start offset in the data
// length = the number of bytes that are drawn
public void drawBytes(byte data[], int offset, int length,
 int x, int y);


//
// Draws the specified image at the specified
// coordinate (x, y).
// If the image is incomplete the image observer
// will be notified later.
// img = the specified image to be drawn
// observer = notifies if the image is complete or not
public abstract boolean drawImage(Image img, int x, int y,
               ImageObserver observer);
```

```

//
// Draws the specified image inside the specified
// rectangle. The image is scaled if necessary. If
// the image is incomplete, the image observer will be
// notified later.
// img = the specified image to be drawn
// observer =  notifies if the image is complete or not
public abstract boolean drawImage(Image img, int x, int y,
 int width, int height, ImageObserver observer);

//
// Draws the specified image at the specified
// coordinate (x, y), with the given solid background
// Color.  If the image is incomplete the image observer
// will be notified later.
// img = the specified image to be drawn
public abstract boolean drawImage(Image img, int x, int y,
                     Color bgcolor,
                     ImageObserver observer);

//
// Draws the specified image inside the specified rectangle,
// with the given solid background Color. The image is
// scaled if necessary. If the image is incomplete the image
// observer will be notified later.
// img = the specified image to be drawn
// observer = notifies if the image is complete or not
public abstract boolean drawImage(Image img, int x, int y,
                     int width, int height,
                     Color bgcolor,
                     ImageObserver observer);

//
// Disposes of this graphics context.  The Graphics context
// cannot be used after being disposed of.
public abstract void dispose();

//
```

continues

Listing 9.1, Continued

```
307 // Disposes of this graphics context once it is no longer
308 // referenced.
309 public void finalize();
310
311 //
312 // Returns a String object representing this Graphic's value.
313 public String toString();
314
315
316 // Fills a polygon with the current color using an
317 // even-odd fill rule (otherwise known as an
318 // alternating rule).
319 //  xPoints = an array of x points
320 //  yPoints = an array of y points
321 //  nPoints = the total number of points
322 public abstract void fillPolygon(int xPoints[],
323  int yPoints[],  int nPoints);
324
325 //
326 // Fills the specified polygon with the current color
327 // using an even-odd fill rule (otherwise known as an
328 // alternating rule).
329 //  p = the polygon
330 public void fillPolygon(Polygon p);
331
332 } // end Graphics
```

Drawing Lines

The main method used to draw a line is the method `drawLine()` (see lines 114–123 in listing 9.1). This method takes parameters for the start of the line, and the end of the line. If, for example, you wanted to draw lines diagonally inside an applet region and the size is 200 pixels by 200 pixels (see fig. 9.2), you would use code similar to the following:

```
public void paint(Graphics g)
{
      g.drawLine(0, 0, 200, 200);
```

```
        g.drawLine(0, 200, 200, 0);

} // end paint
```

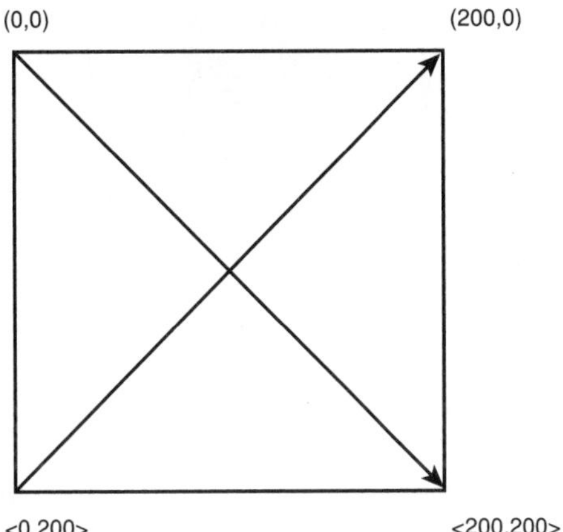

Figure 9.2

Diagonal lines in an applet.

The first two parameters are the <x,y> coordinates of the starting point from which the line is to be drawn, and the remaining two parameters are the end point of the line to be drawn.

Drawing Rectangles

The Graphics class has methods to draw rectangles with square corners, rectangles with rounded corners, and three-dimensional rectangles with shaded borders. For each of these rectangles, you have a choice of two methods:

- The method that has the "draw" prefix draws an outline form of the rectangle.
- The method that has the "fill" prefix draws the rectangle filled with color. The color value can be set by using the `setColor()` method.

Consider, for example, that you want to draw two rectangles: one filled and one that is in an outline form (see fig. 9.3). The inner rectangle is filled, so you will use the `fillRect()` method (see lines 126–128 of listing 9.1). The outer rectangle is in outline form, so you will use the `drawRect()` method (see lines 131–136 of listing 9.1). The arguments to these methods are the <x,y> coordinate of the top-left-hand corner, the width of the rectangle, and the height of the rectangle.

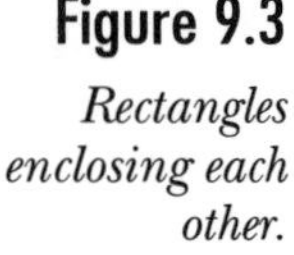

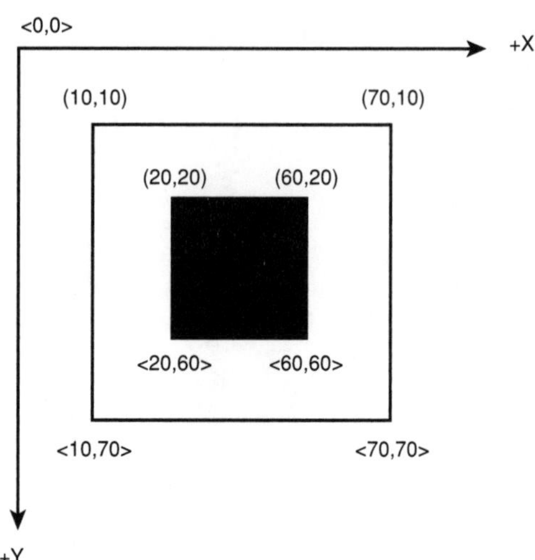

Figure 9.3
Rectangles enclosing each other.

The following is the `paint()` method that was used to draw figure 9.3:

```
public void paint(Graphics g)
{
      g.fillRect(20, 20, 40, 40);
      g.drawRect(10, 10, 60, 60);

} // end paint
```

The `fillRect()` will use the current color setting. To change this color setting, you must use the `setColor()` method (see lines 46–50 of listing 9.1).

Drawing Rounded Rectangles and Circles

The Graphics class has methods to draw rectangles with rounded corners. A circle is seen as an extreme case of a rounded rectangle.

Consider, for example, that you want to draw four rectangles: two that are filled with a color and two that are in an outline form (see fig. 9.4). To create the filled, rounded rectangles, you will use the `fillRoundRect()` method (see lines 159–166 of listing 9.1); to create the outline rounded rectangles you will use the `drawRoundRect()` method (see lines 149–156 of listing 9.1).

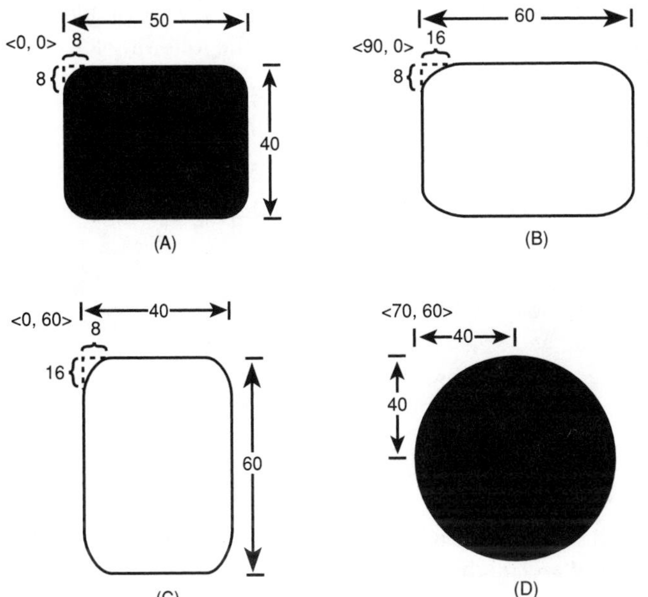

Figure 9.4

Example of rounded rectangles.

The arguments to these methods are the <x,y> coordinate of the top-left-hand corner, the width of the rectangle and the height of the rectangle, and two additional arguments. These two additional arguments define how far along the edges of the rectangle that the arc for the corner will start. The first of the two additional arguments is the arc width, and this is the diameter of the circle that will produce the horizontal arc (see fig. 9.5); the last argument is the arc height, and it is the diameter of the circle that will produce the vertical arc.

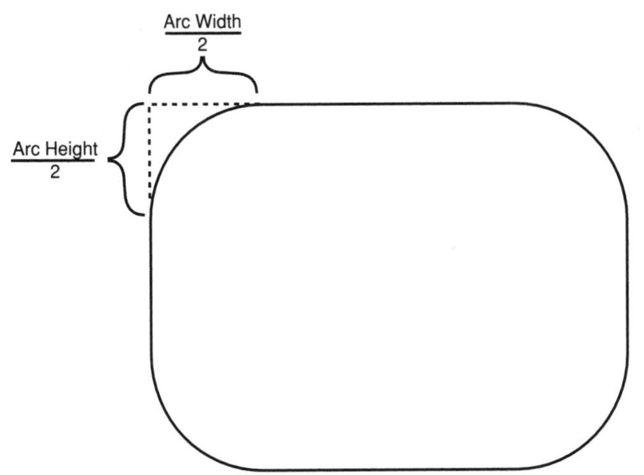

Figure 9.5

Arc Width and Arc Height of a rounded rectangle.

The following is the `paint()` method to draw the figures in 9.4. The top-left-hand corners of the rounded rectangles are assumed to start at the following locations:

```
 <0,0>
 <70, 0>
<0, 60>
<70, 60>
public void paint(Graphics g)
{
g.fillRoundRect( 0,  0, 50, 40, 16, 16);
g.drawRoundRect(70,  0, 60, 40, 32, 16);
g.drawRoundRect( 0, 60, 40, 60, 16, 32);
g.fillRoundRect(70, 60, 80, 80, 80, 80);

} // end paint
```

Note that a solid circle is drawn by the last statement. A circle is drawn when the width, height, arcWidth, and arcHeight are the same.

Drawing 3D Rectangles

You can use the Graphics class to simulate three-dimensional rectangles. These rectangles produce a shadow effect that make them appear three-dimensional.

What if, for example, you want to draw two rectangles: one that is filled with a color and looks like a raised 3D button and the other that is in an outline form but appears pressed. To create these 3D rectangles, you will use the `fill3DRect()` method (see lines 176–181 of listing 9.1) and the `draw3DRect()` method (see lines 169–173 of listing 9.1).

The arguments to these methods are the <x,y> coordinate of the top-left-hand corner, the width of the rectangle and the height of the rectangle, and a Boolean argument. If the Boolean argument is true, the rectangle is raised; otherwise, the rectangle is indented.

The following is the `paint()` method that produces a solid-raised rectangle and an outline-indented rectangle.

```
public void paint(Graphics g)
{
        g.fill3DRect(10, 10, 20, 20, true);
        g.draw3DRect(10, 50, 30, 15, false);

} // end paint
```

Drawing Ovals

You can use the Graphics class to draw ellipses and circles. You can also produce the same effect by using rounded rectangles, except that the use of the oval method is easier to use to produce ellipses and circles.

Consider, for example, that you want to draw two ovals, one that is a circle filled with a color, and the other that is an ellipse in an outline form (see fig. 9.6). To create these oval shapes, you will use the `fillOval()` method (see lines 190–193 of listing 9.1) and the `drawOval()` method (see lines 184–187 of listing 9.1).

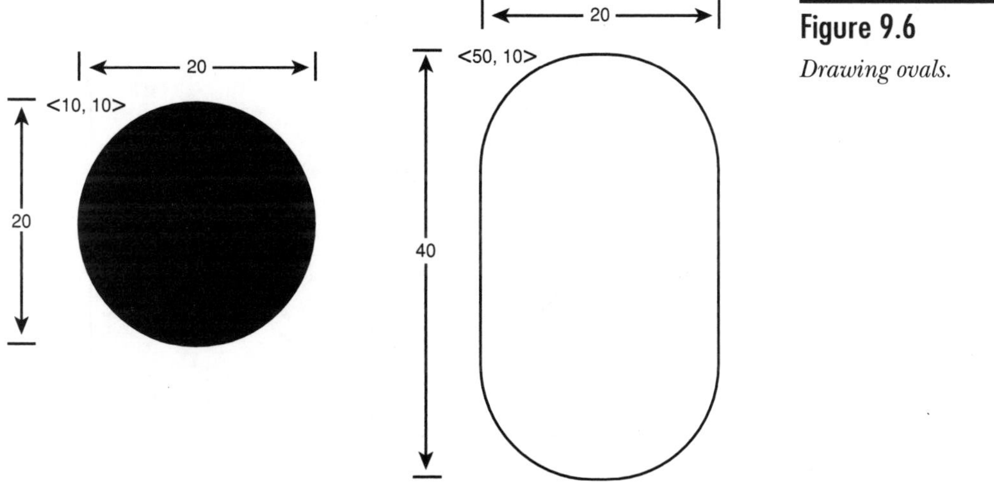

Figure 9.6
Drawing ovals.

The arguments to these methods are the <x,y> coordinate of the top-left-hand corner, the width of the oval, and the height of the oval. The following is the `paint()` method to produce the shapes in figure 9.6:

```
public void paint(Graphics g)
{
      g.fillOval(10, 10, 20, 20);
      g.drawOval(50, 10, 20, 40);

} // end paint
```

Drawing Arcs

Arcs are segments of the circumference of an oval. To define an arc, you must first see it as part of an oval (see fig. 9.7). The arc is only a portion of the oval.

The arc drawing methods are `drawArc()` (see lines 196–206 in listing 9.1) and `fillArc()` (see lines 209–216 in listing 9.1). The first four parameters for drawing an arc are the same as that of an imaginary oval of which the arc is part. The fifth parameter is the start angle of the arc. The start angle is measured with respect to the center of the circle. Zero degrees is at the 3 o'clock line; 90 degrees is at the 12 o'clock line; 180 degrees is at the 9 o'clock line; and 270 degrees is at the 6 o'clock line (see fig. 9.8). The sixth, and last parameter, is the arc angle, and it is the number of degrees that you must "sweep" from the start angle to create the arc. A positive value of the arc angle will result in a counter-clockwise motion, and a negative value will result in a clockwise motion.

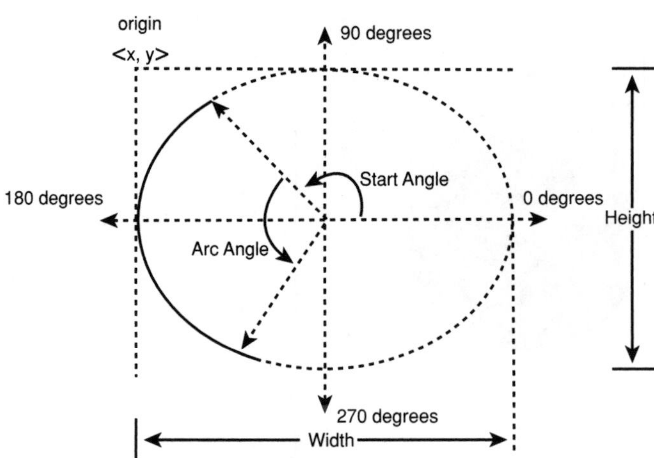

Figure 9.7
Defining an arc.

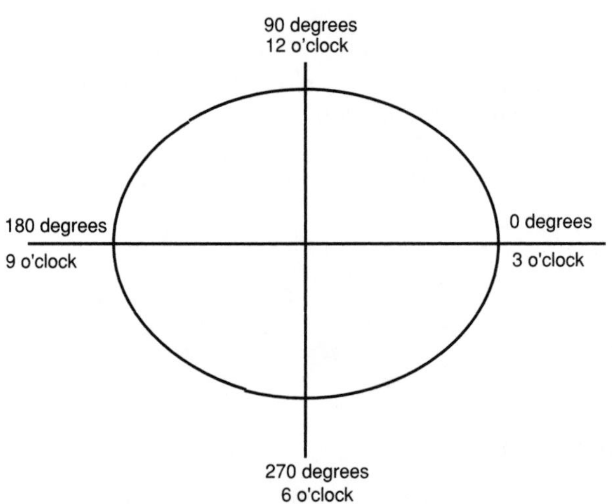

Figure 9.8
Measurement of angles for drawing arcs.

To draw the arc, for example, which is the top half of the circle (see fig. 9.9), you would use the following `paint()` method:

```
public void paint(Graphics g)
{
        g.drawArc(10, 10, 50, 50, 0, 180);

} // end paint
```

You can draw the arc from either end points of the arc. Therefore, the arc in figure 9.9 can also be drawn by starting from the opposite point as shown in the following `paint()` method:

```
public void paint(Graphics g)
{
        g.drawArc(10, 10, 50, 50, 180, -180);

} // end paint
```

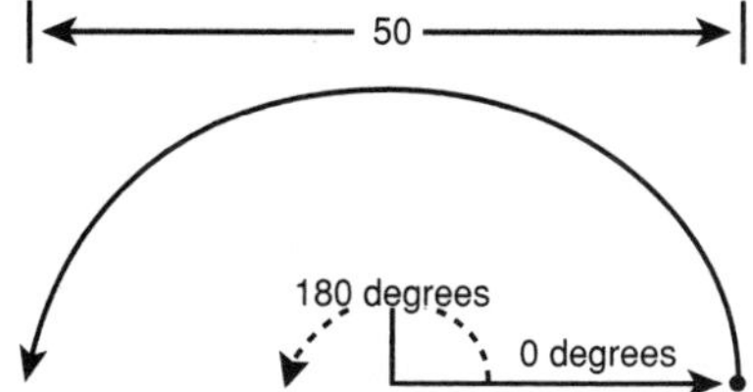

Figure 9.9
Arc to be drawn.

Notice that the start angle is 180 degrees, but the arc angle has a negative sweep to cause a motion in the clockwise direction.

You can also draw a filled arc by invoking the `fillArc()` method. To draw the filled elliptical arc, for example, shown in figure 9.10, you would use the following `paint()` method:

```
public void paint(Graphics g)
{
        g.fillArc(20, 20, 40, 30, 200, 30);

} // end paint
```

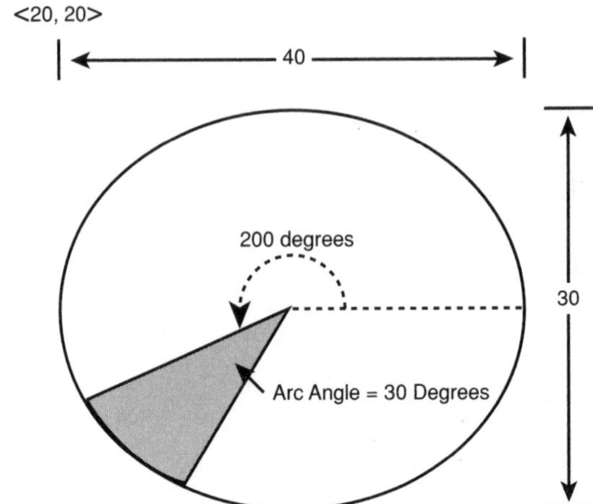

Figure 9.10
Filled arc to be drawn.

Drawing Polygons

Polygons are arbitrary shapes with many sides drawn by straight lines. Familiar figures, such as squares, rectangles, triangles, pentagons, and so on, are all examples of closed polygons. Polygons are closed because they bound a region of two-dimensional space.

Polygons are drawn by the methods `drawPolygon()` (see lines 219–230 in listing 9.1) and `fillPolygon()` (see lines 316–330 in listing 9.1). These methods accept two types of arguments—arrays of x- and y-coordinates or an instance of the Polygon class.

If you are using arrays, you must provide three arguments. The first argument is an array of x-coordinates; the second argument is an array of y-coordinates; the last argument is the number of elements in each of the two array arguments. The number of elements in each of the x- and y-coordinate array must be the same.

The polygon draw methods do not automatically close the shape. If you want a closed shape, the last point in the array must be the same as the start point in the array. If you draw a filled polygon, the method will join the start and end points.

The following is an example of a `paint()` method that draws the triangle of figure 9.11:

```
public void paint(Graphics g)
{
      int[] xa = {10, 40, 25, 10};
      int[] ya = {60, 60, 10, 60};
```

```
        g.drawPolygon(xa, ya, xa.length);

    } // end paint
```

You can pass a Polygon object to the `drawPolygon()` and `fillPolygon()` methods. This class is particularly useful if you want to dynamically add an additional point to the polygon to change its shape. This can be done by sending `addPoint()` to an instance of the Polygon class.

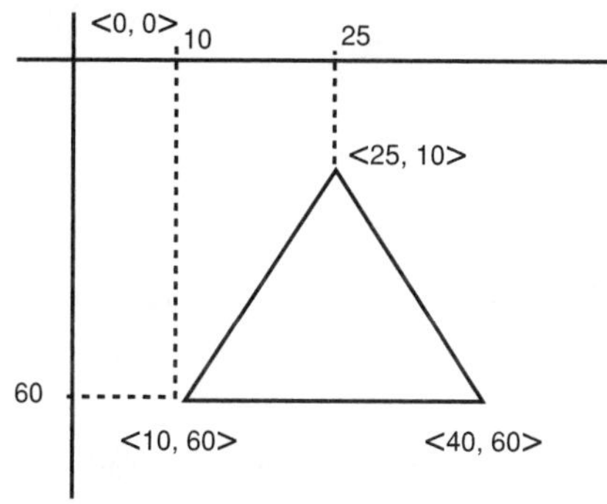

Figure 9.11

Triangle to be drawn with the polygon draw methods.

The following are examples of creating polygon objects.

```
Polygon mygon = new Polygon();
```

The preceding statement creates an empty polygon called mygon.

You can add points to the polygon by using `addPoint()`. Here is an example of adding five points:

```
mygon.addPoint(10, 60);
mygon.addPoint(40, 60);
mygon.addPoint(60, 30);
mygon.addPoint(25, 20);
```

To draw a filled polygon, you could then use the following statement:

```
g.fillPolygon(mygon);
```

Here `g` is the Graphics object instance passed to the `paint()` method.

You could rewrite the previous example of creating a triangle by using the following:

```
public void paint(Graphics g)
{
        int[] xa = {10, 40, 25, 10};
        int[] ya = {60, 60, 10, 60};

        Polygon triangle = new Polygon(xa, ya, xa.length);

        g.drawPolygon(triangle);

} // end paint
```

On the CD

Drawing an Applet

Listing 9.2 (file SunSet.java on the CD-ROM accompanying this book) shows an example of an applet method that uses some of the draw methods discussed previously to draw a picture of a setting sun.

Line 12 defines the instance variable `color`, which will be used for painting the sun. Line 13 defines the length of the sun's rays in pixels.

Lines 17–84 define a private helper method, `getColor()`, which converts the color string parameter value passed through the HTML file for the applet to a value used by the `setColor()` method.

Lines 88–98 define the `init()` method to obtain the color parameter value and call the `getColor()` helper method.

Lines 100–123 define the `paint()` method that draws the applet. Lines 103 and 104 paint a string message in the color parameter value. Lines 106–108 paint a rectangle block in blue to represent a sunset over the ocean. Lines 109 and 110 paint the sun by using the `fillArc()` method.

The for-loop on lines 112–124 draws the rays of the sun. Figure 9.12 shows a display of the applet.

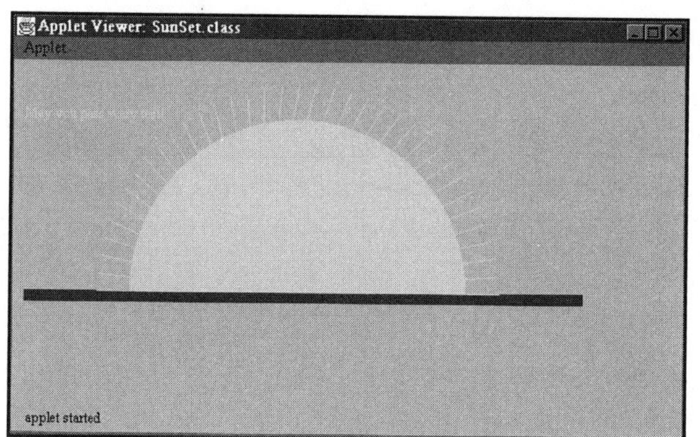

Figure 9.12

SunSet applet display.

Listing 9.2

```
Line==================Java Source=================
/**
* SunSet: Example of applet using string
* draw methods:
*
* Author: Karanjit S. G. S. Siyan
*
*/
import java.awt.Graphics;
import java.awt.Color;
public class SunSet extends java.applet.Applet
{
   private Color color; // Color of message
   private double rayLength = 180.0;

   // getColor: Helper method to convert
   // color string to a Color value.
   private Color getColor(String colorstr)
   {
      Color colorVal = null;

      // Convert color parameter to a color
      // value that can be used in the applet.
      if (colorstr == null)
      {
```

continues

Listing 9.2, Continued

```
            // Not specified. Use default.
            colorVal = Color.orange;
        }
        else if (colorstr.equalsIgnoreCase("black"))
        {
            colorVal = Color.black;
        }
        else if (colorstr.equalsIgnoreCase("blue"))
        {
            colorVal = Color.blue;
        }
        else if (colorstr.equalsIgnoreCase("cyan"))
        {
            colorVal = Color.cyan;
        }
        else if (colorstr.equalsIgnoreCase("darkGray"))
        {
            colorVal = Color.darkGray;
        }
        else if (colorstr.equalsIgnoreCase("gray"))
        {
            colorVal = Color.gray;
        }
        else if (colorstr.equalsIgnoreCase("lightGray"))
        {
            colorVal = Color.lightGray;
        }
        else if (colorstr.equalsIgnoreCase("green"))
        {
            colorVal = Color.green;
        }
        else if (colorstr.equalsIgnoreCase("magenta"))
        {
            colorVal = Color.magenta;
        }
        else if (colorstr.equalsIgnoreCase("orange"))
        {
```

```
        colorVal = Color.orange;
    }
    else if (colorstr.equalsIgnoreCase("pink"))
    {
        colorVal = Color.pink;
    }
    else if (colorstr.equalsIgnoreCase("red"))
    {
        colorVal = Color.red;
    }
    else if (colorstr.equalsIgnoreCase("white"))
    {
        colorVal = Color.white;
    }
    else if (colorstr.equalsIgnoreCase("yellow"))
    {
        colorVal = Color.yellow;

    }  // end if

        return colorVal;

    }  // end getColor


    // init: Override method in Applet
    public void init()
    {
        String colorstr; // color parameter

        resize(600,300);
        colorstr = getParameter("color");
        color = getColor(colorstr);

    }  // end init


    // paint: Override method in Component
    public void paint(Graphics g)
```

continues

Listing 9.2, Continued

```
        {

            g.setColor(color);
            g.drawString("May you pass every test!", 10, 50);

            g.setColor(Color.blue);
            g.fillRect(10, 200, 500, 10);

            g.setColor(color);
            g.fillArc(105, 50, 300, 300, 0, 180);

            for (int x = 0; x <= 180; x += 5)
            {
            int xend, yend;
            double angle;

            // Convert angle to radians
            angle = ((double)x)*Math.PI/180.0;
            xend = 255 + (int)(rayLength*Math.cos(angle));
            yend = 200 - (int)(rayLength*Math.sin(angle));

            g.drawLine(225, 200, xend, yend);

            }          // end for

      } // end paint

   } // end SunSet
```

Operations on the Graphics Area

The Graphics class has a number of operations that can be performed on the graphics area for the applet, such as making a copy of an area to another area of the screen, clearing an area of the screen, obtaining the dimensions of the applet, and so on.

To copy an area of a screen to another location you use the `copyArea()` method (lines 107–111 of listing 9.1). The area to be copied is enclosed in an imaginary rectangle. Therefore, the first four parameters of the `copyArea()` method are the same as for the `drawRect()` and `fillRect()` methods; that is, the first two parameters are the x- and y-coordinates of the top-left-hand corner of the rectangle, and the third and fourth parameters are the width and height of the imaginary rectangle. The last two parameters are the distance in the x- and y-axis to copy the area. Suppose that you want to copy the area in figure 9.13 to another area as shown in the figure. You can perform this by using the following:

```
public void paint(Graphics g)
{
      g.copyArea(10, 10, 50, 50, 90, 90);

} // end paint
```

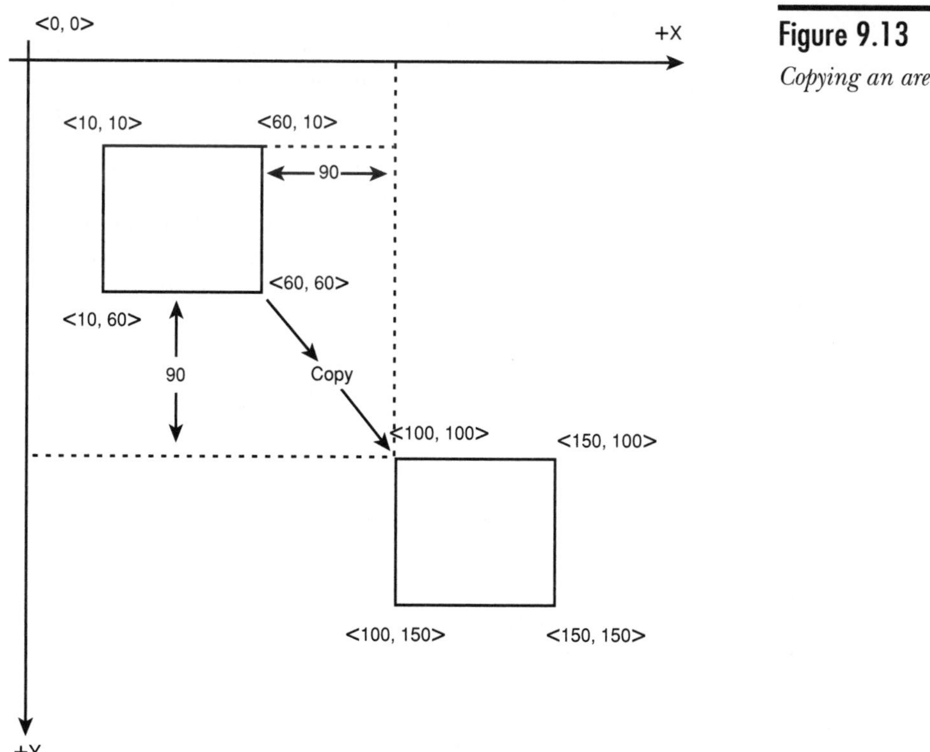

Figure 9.13

Copying an area.

To clear a specific area, you use the `clearRect()` method. This clears a rectangular area of the specified dimensions and fills it with the background color. The dimensions specified for `clearRect()` are the same as that specified for the `drawRect()` and `fillRect()` methods; that is, the first two parameters are the x- and y-coordinates of the top-left-hand corner of the rectangle, and the third and fourth parameters are the width and height of the rectangle area to be cleared.

If, for example, you want to create the effect of moving the area in figure 9.13, instead of copying it, you would have to clear the original area. You could do this by using the following:

```
public void paint(Graphics g)
{
      g.copyArea(10, 10, 50, 50, 90, 90);
      g.clearRect(10, 10, 50, 50);

} // end paint
```

If you need to clear the entire applet, first get the dimensions of the applet. You can get the dimensions by invoking the `size()` for the instance of the applet by using `this.size()`. The `size()` method is inherited by your applet from the Component class, and it returns an instance of the class Dimension. The Component class is one of the superclasses in the inheritance hierarchy chain for the Applet class.

The Dimension object is returned by a number of other methods in the java.awt package, and it is a convenient way of specifying dimensions such as a rectangular area as an object. The top-level specification of Dimension is included here to assist in understanding its behavior:

```
public class Dimension extends Object
{
      // Public constructors
      public Dimension();
      public Dimension(Dimension d);
      public Dimension(int width, int height);

      // Public instance variables
      public int height;
      public int width;

      // Public instance methods
      public String toString(); // Overrides Object.toString();

} // end Dimension
```

Therefore, to get the width and height of a class, you could use the following:

```
this.size().width                          // Gets the width
this.size().height                         // Gets the height
```

In the preceding statements `this.size()` returns a Dimension object, so you can access the public instance variables width and height of this object. The Dimension object is a temporary object and is created each time `this.size()` is called, which is a little inefficient. The following `paint()` method shows the applet area being cleared and filled with the background color, using only a single instance of the Dimension class:

```
public void paint(Graphics g)
{
      Dimension d = this.size();

      g.clearRect(0, 0, d.width, d.height);

} // end paint
```

Setting Background and Foreground Colors

When you clear a rectangle by using the `clearRect()` method, the cleared area is filled with the background color. By default, this color is a dark gray. If you want to use a different background color, you must use the `setBackground()` method. There is also a corresponding `setForeground()` method that sets the foreground color. Both of these methods are inherited by your applet from the Component class. They both take a single argument that is of instance Color. To change the background of the applet to a yellow color, for example, you would use the following:

```
setBackground(Color.yellow);
```

When you use `setForeground()`, you change the color of all text or graphic elements that have been drawn in a single stroke. To change the color of all graphic elements that have been drawn to pink without redrawing the applet, for example, you would use the following:

```
setForeground(Color.pink);
```

You have already seen the use of the `setColor()` method defined in the Graphics class (see lines 46–50 of listing 9.1) to set the color for all future drawing operations. You can also use the `getColor` method defined in the Graphics class (see lines 42–43 of listing 9.1) to obtain the current color setting. To change the foreground color of the applet to the current color setting, for example, you could use the following:

```
public void paint(Graphics g)
{

       // Other statements for setting
       // colors of the applet

       // Now change everything to the last
       // color setting.
       setForeground(g.getColor());

} // end paint
```

Getting Font Information

When you are writing text in an applet, you can set the font by using the call to the `setFont()` method that is inherited from the Component class. The `setFont()` method takes an instance of the Font object. In the program listings in Chapter 8, "Creating Java Applets," you saw examples of creating the Font object. You can query the Font object by calling its methods. A top-level description of these Font methods is shown next:

```
public class Font
{
 public static final int PLAIN        = 0;
 public static final int BOLD         = 1;
 public static final int ITALIC       = 2;

  //
  // The logical name of this font.
  protected String name;

  //
  // The style of the font. This is the sum of the
  // constants PLAIN, BOLD, or ITALIC.
  protected int style;

  //
  // The point size of this font.
```

```
protected int size;

//
// Creates a new font with the specified name, style
// and point size.
// name = the font name
// style = the constant style used
// size = the point size of the font
public Font(String name, int style, int size);

//
// Gets the platform specific family name of the font.
// Use getName to get the logical name of the font.
public String getFamily();


//
// Gets the logical name of the font.
public String getName();

//
// Gets the style of the font.
public int getStyle();

//
// Gets the point size of the font.
public int getSize();

//
// Returns true if the font is plain.
public boolean isPlain();

//
// Returns true if the font is bold.
public boolean isBold();

//
// Returns true if the font is italic.
```

```
public boolean isItalic();

//
// Gets a font from the system properties list.
// nm = the property name
public static Font getFont(String nm);

//
// Gets the specified font from the system properties list.
// nm = the property name
// font = a default font to return if property 'nm'
//    is not defined
public static Font getFont(String nm, Font font);

//
// Returns a hashcode for this font.
public int hashCode();

//
// Compares this object to the specifed object.
// obj = the object to compare with
// Returns true if the objects are the same; false otherwise.
public boolean equals(Object obj);

//
// Converts this object to a String representation.
public String toString();

} // end Font
```

If you need additional information on a font, you can create a FontMetrics object by a call to `getFontMetrics()` inherited from the Component class, and query this object with methods from the FontMetrics class. The following code fragment, for example, returns the number of pixels in a specified string for a specified font:

```
Font fnt = new Font("Times Roman",
        Font.BOLD+Font.ITALIC, 20);
FontMetrics fm = getFontMetrics(fnt);
String msg = "To Be or Not to Be!";
```

```
// Number of pixels in message.
int pixels = fm.stringWidth(msg);
```

A top-level description of the FontMetrics methods is shown next:

```
public abstract class FontMetrics
{
 protected Font font;
 protected FontMetrics(Font font);

 //
 // Gets the font.
 public Font getFont();

 //
 // Gets the standard leading, or line spacing, for the
 // font. This is the logical amount of space to be reserved
 // between the descent of one line of text and the ascent
 // of the next line. The height metric is calculated to
 // include this extra space.
 public int getLeading();

 //
 // Gets the font ascent. The font ascent is the distance
 // from the  base line to the top of most Alphanumeric
 // characters.  However, that some characters in the font
 // may extend above this height.
 public int getAscent();

 //
 // Gets the font descent. The font descent is the distance
 // from the  base line to the bottom of most Alphanumeric
 // characters.  However, that some characters in the font
 // may extend below this height.
 public int getDescent();

 //
 // Gets the standard height of a line of text in this font.
 // This is the distance between the baseline of adjacent
 // lines of text. It is the sum of the leading + ascent +
```

```
// descent.  There is no guarantee that lines of text spaced
// at this distance will be disjoint; such lines may overlap if
// some characters overshoot either the standard ascent or
// the standard descent metric.
public int getHeight();

//
// Gets the maximum ascent of all characters in this Font.
// No character will extend further above the baseline than
// this  distance.
public int getMaxAscent();

//
// Gets the maximum descent of all characters in this Font.
// No character will descend further below the baseline
// than this distance.
public int getMaxDescent();


//
// For backward compatibility only.
// same as getMaxDescent
public int getMaxDecent();

//
// Gets the maximum advance width of any character in
// this Font. The advance width is the amount by which
// the current point is moved from one character to the
// next in a line of text.
public int getMaxAdvance();


//
// Returns the advance width of the specified character in
// this Font. The advance width is the amount by which the
// current point is moved from one character to the next
// in a line of text.
// ch = the character to be measured
public int charWidth(int ch);
```

```
//
// Returns the advance width of the specified character in
// this Font. The advance width is the amount by which the
// current point is moved from one character to the next in
// a line of text.
// ch = the character to be measured
public int charWidth(char ch);



//
// Returns the total advance width for showing the
// specified String in this Font. The advance width is the
// amount by which the current point is moved from one
// character to the next in a line of text.
// str = the String to be measured
public int stringWidth(String str)


//
// Returns the total advance width for showing the
// specified array of characters in this Font.
// The advance width is the amount by which the current
// point is moved from one character to the next in a
// line of text.
// data = the array of characters to be measured
// off = the start offset of the characters in the array
// len = the number of characters to be measured from the array
public int charsWidth(char data[], int off, int len);

//
// Returns the total advance width for showing the specified
// array of bytes in this Font. Similar to charsWidth() except
// that it deals with an array of bytes.
// data = the array of bytes to be measured
// off = the start offset of the bytes in the array
// len = the number of bytes to be measured from the array
public int bytesWidth(byte data[], int off, int len);
```

```
//
// Gets the advance widths of the first 256 characters in the
// Font. The advance width is the amount by which the current
// point is moved from one character to the next in a line
// of text.
public int[] getWidths();


//
// Returns the String representation of this
// FontMetric's values.
public String toString();

} // end FontMetrics
```

Animating Applets

Now that you know how to use the graphic elements in Java, you will learn how to animate applets. Most applet animation involves the use of threads. A *thread* is the set of instructions executed in logical sequence within a program and represents a focus of control within the program. Using threads, you can execute parallel paths within your program simultaneously (see fig. 9.14).

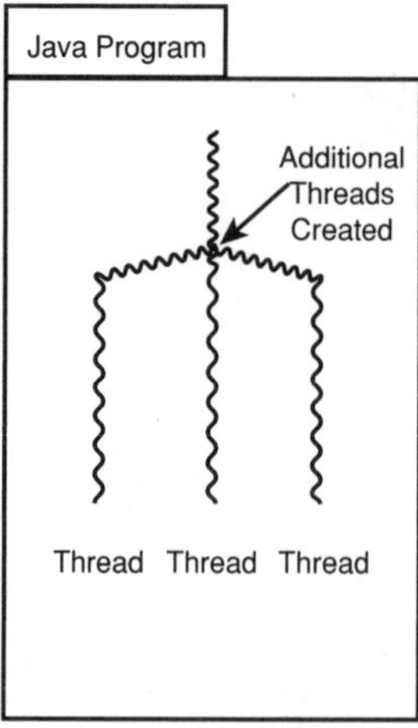

Figure 9.14
Multiple threads within a program.

If your computer has a single processor, simultaneous execution of the threads is not strictly possible. The threads share the same processor. At any time only one thread is running, but when the thread has executed for a time period it is suspended, and another thread is run. The thread scheduling algorithm that is used to schedule the threads to run on the processor is different for different operating systems and run-time environments such as the Java environment.

In applet animation, threads are typically assigned specific tasks, such as painting a specific area of the applet.

Creating Threads

There are two ways of using threads in Java. One way is to create a subclass of a predefined Java class called Thread, and the other way is to use the Java Runnable interface.

You will first examine thread creation by creating a subclass of the Thread class. The Thread class is in the package java.lang. When you extend the class, you inherit a number of thread methods such as `run()`, `start()`, and `stop()`:

```
class MyThreadClass extends Thread
{

      // Method run() inherited

      // Method start() inherited

      // Method stop() inherited but
      // is a final method so you
      // cannot override ***Insert Table

      // Other Thread methods inherited.


} // end MyThreadClass
```

To create a thread, you must first instantiate your extended class:

```
MyThreadClass thd;
```

Next, you must invoke the `start()` method for the instantiated class:

```
thd.start();
```

The preceding statement calls the `start()` method inherited from the Thread class. This results in a call to the `run()` method. The `run()` method, however, is also inherited, and therefore will not execute any code in your MyThreadClass. So for your class to perform anything useful, you must override the `run()` method and execute the logic that you want the thread to execute within the run method. Consider, therefore, the following modified version of the MyThreadClass program in listing 9.3. This program computes a series of numbers according to the algorithm in the method `run()`.

Lines 13 and 14 define private class variable instances to store the start of the series. Lines 18–23 define the constructor for the class that stores the start value of the series in instance variables `ax2` and `ax1`.

Lines 26–44 defines the `run()` method that gets called when the thread is started. The run method declares that it could throw an InterruptedException (see line 27 in listing 9.3). This is because the class `Thread` method `sleep()` is called on line 40 to delay the loop by 2000 milliseconds (2 seconds); otherwise, the output of the for loop flashes by you too rapidly.

The `run()` method computes the value of the next term in the series as the sum of the previous two values. For a start value of 1 and 1, this produces an arithmetic series called the Fibonacci series. Notice that an infinite loop is set up in the `run()` method. This is typical for most threads. When the `run()` method terminates, that thread ends, and, in due course, it will be terminated by the Java runtime environment.

On lines 50 and 51 of listing 9.3 in the `main()` method, two thread objects are created. These threads are started on lines 53 and 54. The first thread produces a positive number series, and the second thread produces a negative number series. Figure 9.15 shows the output of the two threads. Notice that the output shows that the positive and negative numbers occur consecutively, thus indicating that the two threads run one after another.

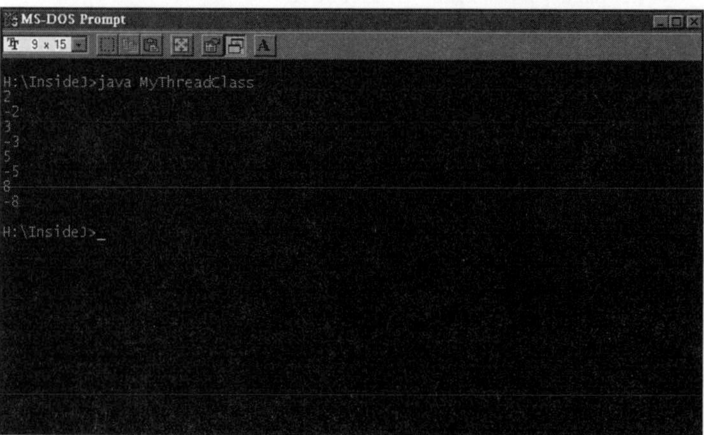

Figure 9.15
Output of MyThreadClass.

Listing 9.3

```
Line=================Java Source=================
/**
 * MyThreadClass: Demonstrates creation of
 * threads by subclassing Thread
 *
 * Author: Karanjit S. G. S. Siyan
 *
 */

class MyThreadClass extends Thread
{
 // Method start() inherited

 private int ax2; // First term in series.
 private int ax1; // Second term in series.

 // Constructor for class to initialize
 // start of series.
   public MyThreadClass(int ax2, int ax1)
   {
 this.ax2 = ax2;
 this.ax1 = ax1;

   } // end MyThreadClass

   // Overrides run() in Thread
 public void run()
 throws InterruptedException
   {
 // Loop forever!
          for(;;)
          {
           int ax;

           ax = ax1 + ax2;
           System.out.println(ax);

```

continues

Listing 9.3, Continued

```
// Get ready for the next iteration,
            ax2 = ax1;
            ax1 = ax;
sleep(2000);  // Sleep for 2 seconds

          } // end for

  } // end run

// main entry point
public static void main(String[] args)
{

MyThreadClass thd1 = new MyThreadClass(1,1);
MyThreadClass thd2 = new MyThreadClass(-1,-1);

thd1.start();  // Fibonacci series
thd2.start();  // Negative Fibonacci series

}  // end main

} // end MyThreadClass
```

Implementing Threads Using the Runnable Interface

What if you wanted to create threads within an applet? Can you extend the applet from the Thread class as discussed in the previous example? The answer is no. To understand why, consider the inheritance diagram in figure 9.16. This figure shows that you need to inherit the applet from the Applet class, but if you try to inherit from the Thread class also, you have a situation of multiple inheritance. For the sake of simplicity, the Java language does not support multiple inheritance. This means that you cannot simultaneously inherit from two classes.

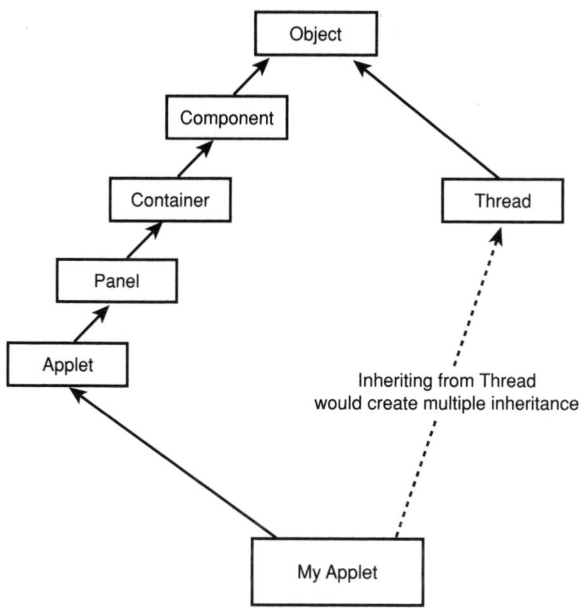

Figure 9.16

Problem of creating an applet by subclassing Thread.

To implement threads in an applet, you can use the Runnable interface. The Runnable interface has the following form:

```
public abstract interface Runnable
{
 //
  // The method that is executed when a
  // Runnable object is activated.
  // The run() method is the main
  // component of a Thread. It is in
  // this method that all the action
  // of a Thread takes place.
public abstract void run();

} // end Runnable
```

If an applet needs to implement threads, it needs to implement the Runnable interface. Specifically, this means that you must define your applet class as implementing the Runnable interface and then defining the method `run()` in the your applet class:

```
class MyApplet extends java.applet.Applet
         implements Runnable
{
      public void run()
      {
         // Thread logic.

      } // end run

} // end MyApplet
```

For applets, you must use the Runnable interface. For other types of classes, you can extend the Thread class as discussed in the previous section, or you can also implement the class by using the Runnable interface. You, for example, could implement the MyThreadClass discussed in the previous section as follows:

```
class MyThreadClass extends Object
         implements Runnable
{

      // Implement the run() method
      public void run()
      {
         // Thread logic

      } // end run

} // end MyThreadClass
```

To create the thread, you need to first instantiate the MyThreadClass and then pass the instance as an argument to the Thread constructor:

```
// Instantiate the class first.
MyThreadClass myc1 = new MyThreadClass();
MyThreadClass myc2 = new MyThreadClass();

// Create the threads
Thread thd1 = new Thread(myc1);
Thread thd2 = new Thread(myc2);
```

```
// Start the threads.
thd1.start();
thd2.start();
```

On the CD 

Listing 9.4 (file MyThreadClass1.java on the CD-ROM accompanying this book) shows an alternative way of implementing the Thread class example of listing 9.3 by using the Runnable interface. Most of the listing differences are on lines 9 and 10 for defining the class and in the `main()` method (lines 48–60). The nature of these differences has been discussed earlier in this section.

Listing 9.4

```
Line==================Java Source=================
01 /**
02  * MyThreadClass1: Demonstrates creation of
03  * threads by using the Runnable interface.
04  *
05  * Author: Karanjit S. G. S. Siyan
06  *
07  */
08
09 class MyThreadClass1 extends Object
10  implements Runnable
11 {
12       // Method start() inherited
13
14      private int ax2; // First term in series.
15      private int ax1; // Second term in series.
16
17      // Constructor for class to initialize
18      // start of series.
19      public MyThreadClass1(int ax2, int ax1)
20      {
21            this.ax2 = ax2;
22            this.ax1 = ax1;
23
24      } // end MyThreadClass1
25
26      // Overrides run() in Thread
27      public void run()
```

continues

Listing 9.4, Continued

```
throws InterruptedException
{
//Loop forever!
for(;;)
{
      int ax;

      ax = ax1 + ax2;
      System.out.println(ax);

      // Get ready for the next iteration,
      ax2 = ax1;
      ax1 = ax;
      Thread.sleep(2000);  // Sleep for 2 seconds

 } // end for

} // end run

// main entry point
public static void main(String[] args)
{

      MyThreadClass1 myc1 = new MyThreadClass1(1,1);
      MyThreadClass1 myc2 = new MyThreadClass1(-1,-1);

      Thread thd1 = new Thread(myc1);
      Thread thd2 = new Thread(myc2);

      thd1.start();  // Fibonacci series
      thd2.start();  // Negative Fibonacci series

}  // end main

} // end MyThreadClass1
```

Examining Thread Methods

Suppose that you want to create threads but define some threads with a higher priority than others. Threads with a higher priority are expected to run more often than threads with lower priorities. You can control the thread priority by using the `setPriority()` method and passing it an integer priority value. The integer priority value ranges from a value of Thread.MIN_PRIORITY to Thread.MAX_PRIORITY. The Thread class defines the following static class constants:

```
// The minimum priority that a Thread can have.
// The most minimal priority is currently defined as 1.
public final static int MIN_PRIORITY = 1;

// The default priority that is assigned to a Thread.
// The default priority is currently set to 5.
public final static int NORM_PRIORITY = 5;

// The maximum priority that a Thread can have.
// The maximal priority value a Thread
// is currently set to 10.
public final static int MAX_PRIORITY = 10;
```

To change the priority of a Thread object, `thd1`, to the maximum value, you can use the following:

```
thd1.setPriority(Thread.MAX_PRIORITY);
```

You can name threads at the time you create them by passing them string names:

```
MyThreadClass myc3 = new MyThreadClass();
MyThreadClass myc4 = new MyThreadClass();

// Create the named threads
Thread thd3 = new Thread(myc3, "I am thread 3");
Thread thd4 = new Thread(myc2, "I am thread 4");
```

You can get a thread's name by using `getName()`, and you can change a thread's name by using `setName()`:

```
// Change the thread's names
thd3.setName("Thread 3");
thd4.setName("Thread 4");
String thd3Name = thd3.getName(); // Returns "Thread 3"
String thd4Name = thd4.getName(); // Returns "Thread 4"
```

You can use the `sleep()` method and pass it the number of milliseconds or nanoseconds you would like the thread to be suspended. The definitions of these methods are shown here:

```
public static native void sleep(long millis)
        throws InterruptedException;

public static void sleep(long millis, int nanos)
         throws InterruptedException;
```

You can suspend a thread by calling `suspend()`, and continue again from where it left off, by calling `resume()`. These methods are marked as final so that you cannot override them and change their behavior:

```
public final void suspend();

public final void resume();
```

If you think that the currently executing thread is using up quite a few of the system resources, you can occasionally have it yield to other threads voluntarily by calling the method `yield()`. Other threads that are waiting to run will be scheduled to run next.

```
public static void yield();
```

To obtain the currently executing thread, you can call `currentThread()`:

```
public static Thread currentThread();
```

To check if a thread is alive (or terminated), you can call the `isAlive()` method for the thread. It will return a true if the thread is alive and a false otherwise. Note that this method is marked as final so that you cannot override and change it.

```
public final boolean isAlive();
```

Implementing Critical Regions

Because threads can be running simultaneously, they have access to the same global data such as class instance variables or static data. One of the sources of subtle errors that can occur is when threads try to modify the same data in such a way that the modification interferes with the logic of the thread. If, for example, one thread is trying to increment a variable, but gets preempted in the middle of the increment step, and a second thread runs and changes that variable, then when the first thread runs, it will wipe out any changes made by the second thread. These types of problems are called *race conditions.*

A simple way to help the Java compiler handle such variables is to specify the variable as being volatile. This tells the Java compiler not to make any assumptions about the value of that variable, and that it can be changed uncontrollably from external sources such as another running thread. Here is an example of an int variable declared as being volatile:

```
volatile int change;
```

If the variable is set to a constant such as 10:

```
change = 10;
```

and the compiler does not see a reference to directly change this variable, it may as part of its optimization, replace all references to `change` by 10. This would be erroneous if another thread is expecting to change the variable.

The use of the volatile does not avoid the race condition that may result because of simultaneous updates to a variable. You should use it when your program logic does work correctly in spite of simultaneous updates, or because you have another way to synchronize access.

A better way to synchronize simultaneous access to a section of Java code, so that two threads are not simultaneously executing within that region of code, is to use the synchronized qualifier. Consider the following method:

```
private synchronized void incr()
{
      ++p;
      System.out.println(p);

}
```

The use of the synchronized qualifier ensures that the method `incr()` will only be executed by one thread at a time. Another thread can only begin executing this thread if there is no other thread currently executing the method. If there is another thread currently executing the method, then the thread will have to wait until the currently executing thread exits from the method. The thread that has to wait becomes *blocked*. Blocked threads are put on a wait list of threads and do not actively consume system resources.

Note The Java compilers enable either of the following syntax to be used for synchronized:

```
public synchronized void method() {}

synchronized public void method() {}
```

The region of code protected by the synchronized qualifier is called a *critical region.* When the synchronized qualifier is used, a lock is associated with the critical region. This *lock* is an internal flag that is set to indicate if a thread is executing the critical region. Before executing a critical region, a thread checks the lock to see if a thread is already in the critical region. If the lock indicates that there is no other thread in the critical region, a thread can enter the critical region after setting the lock. When a thread exits the critical region, it unlocks it by setting an appropriate value for the lock variable.

The following is an example of class Score that contains a score variable that needs to be protected against unsynchronized access:

```
public class Score
{
    private int score;
    public Score(int score)
    {
       this.score = score;

    } // end Score

    public synchronized int setScore(int newScore)
    {
       score = newScore;

    } // end setScore

    public synchronized int addScore(int delta)
    {
       score += delta;

    } // end addScore

    public synchronized int getScore()
    {
       return score;

    } // end getScore

} // end Score
```

The constructor for `Score` is not synchronized because it is executed only when the object is instantiated, and this can occur only in one thread for an object that is being created. All the other methods that are reading or updating the value of Score are synchronized. The Score variable is declared as private, which means that it cannot be accessed directly outside the class—it can only be accessed by the accessor methods `setScore()`, `addScore()`, and `getScore()`.

In addition to making the code in a method a critical region, you can declare any statement in Java to be a critical region. The following is the general syntax of declaring a statement to be synchronized:

```
synchronized(expr)
    statement
```

The *statement* is any Java statement including a block statement. The *expr* must evaluate to an object to be locked; this is usually an object reference. A lock is associated with this object. Only when a lock is obtained on the object, the *statement* can be executed. The lock is released when the *statement* finishes executing. Here is an example of a synchronized block to reverse the elements of an array passed as a parameter to a method:

```
public synchronized void reverse(int[] xa)
{
        synchronized(xa)
        {
            int  midpt = xa.length/2;
            for (int x = 0; x < midpt; x++)
            {
            int temp = xa[x];
            int y = xa.length - x - 1;

            temp = xa[x];
            xa[x] = xa[y];
            xa[y] = temp;

            } // end for

        } // end synchronized

} // end reverse
```

In the method `reverse()`, the xa array is being modified. While the array is being modified, you do not want another thread to be accessing the elements of the array. You can prevent this by locking the array reference.

Animating a Line in an Applet

Listing 9.5 (program LineDraw.java on the CD-ROM accompanying this book) shows an applet animated by a thread. The applet draws a rotating line whose colors change randomly when the line rotates. Figure 9.17 shows a sample output of the display of this program by using AppletViewer. The rest of this section contains a detailed analysis on the workings of this applet.

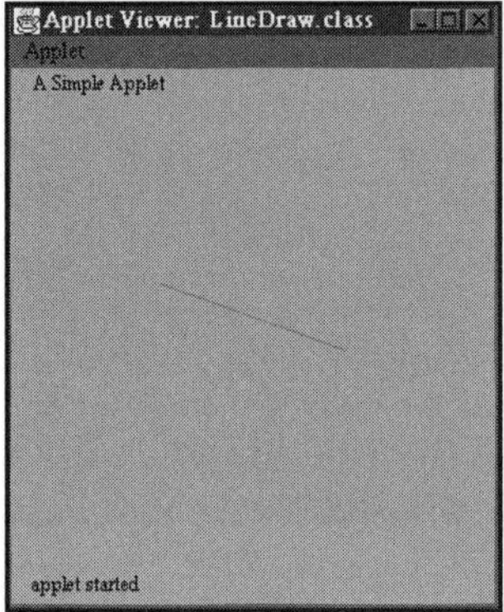

Figure 9.17

Output of LineDraw in AppletViewer.

Lines 11–94 contain the definition of two classes Angle and Line. The class *Angle* (lines 11–37) defines static methods `normalize()` and `radians()` for normalizing an angle and converting an angle from degrees to radians needed for the trigonometric functions.

The class *Line* (lines 60–71) defines a class to represent a line. The constructor for the line is called with the parameters xc and yc that define the point at which a line will be rotated within the applet, and a maximum size of the line maxsize. Within this constructor, a random function is used to draw a line of random length, which is between zero and maxsize pixels long. Other variables that are set in the constructor are for bookkeeping purposes. The method `rotate()` (lines 74–92) in the class Line rotates the line by the specified angle. The start and end of the rotated coordinates of the line are kept in the points <rotX[0], rotY[0]> and <rotX[1], rotY[1]>, respectively.

Lines 96–218 define the class *LineDraw* that is used to implement the applet. This class extends the Applet definition and implements the Runnable interface. Line 100 defines a label that is used to draw a label of text in the applet. You can paste text labels, buttons, menus, and other objects in an Applet. The dimX and dimY variables (see lines 103 and 104 in listing 9.5) are used for defining the size of the applet and determining the point in the applet at which the line will be rotated. Line 106 creates the line that will be rotated within the applet. Note that the parameters passed to it are the center of the applet. Line 109 defines the thread, paintThread, which will be used to paint the applet. Lines 111–126 define an array of colors that can be used to draw the line. This array is used in the private method `getColor()` that is defined on lines 184–197. The method `getColor()` returns a random color from the array of colors, ac.

When the applet is initially started, the method `init()` on lines 167 and 179 is run, just once. This method calls the superclass Applet's `int()` method to perform any initialization for the superclass. Currently, the class Applet's `init()` method is empty, but it is always a good idea to call this method in case it is no longer empty in future Java releases. Line 171 resizes the applet by calling the `resize()` method for the applet. Lines 173–177 add a label of text in the applet. When adding objects to a paint area such as an applet, you must set the layout manager to be used (see line 173 in listing 9.5). The layout manager is a Java class that is used to determine how the areas of a screen will be sectioned and how components added to the display screen will be placed. To define, for example, a flow layout in which the components will be added to the screen one at a time in a row, you would use the following:

```
this.setLayout ( new FlowLayout());
```

Note that `new FlowLayout()` is used to build an instance of the class FlowLayout. When the constructor is passed with no arguments, the components that are added are centered, and when a row gets full, the next row is automatically used. To create a layout where the alignment is to the left or right, instead of being centered, you would use the following:

```
this.setLayout ( new FlowLayout(FlowLayout.LEFT));
this.setLayout ( new FlowLayout(FlowLayout.RIGHT));
```

The Grid layout (class GridLayout) that divides the screen area into rows and columns, and each component that you add, is added to a cell within this grid. To create a grid that is 4 cells by 4 cells, for example, you would use the following:

```
this.setLayout(new GridLayout(4, 4));
```

If you want a 5-pixel horizontal gap and a 10-pixel vertical gap between these cells, you would use the following:

```
this.setLayout(new GridLayout(4,4,5,10));
```

The Border layout indicates where a component will be placed in terms of geographical directions of north, south, east, west, and center:

```
this.setLayout(new BorderLayout());
```

The components are added by using a special `add()` method in which the first argument is the geographic direction at which the component must be placed.

To add a label to the north and south of the display area, for example, you would use the following:

```
add("North", new Label("top label"));
add("South", new Label("bottom label"));
```

The card layout (class CardLayout) is used to add components to the screen that are not displayed at once. You select one of these components for display at any time. If you select the components in succession, you have a slide show effect with each frame of the slide being the selected component. The components that are added are other container components, such as the Panel class objects. Each of these individual components could use a different layout scheme. Here is an example of using a card layout:

```
setLayout(new CardLayout());
Panel slide1 = new Panel();
Panel slide2 = new Panel();
Panel slide3 = new Panel();
Panel slide4 = new Panel();
add("slide 1", slide1);
add("slide 2", slide2);
add("slide 3", slide3);
add("slide 4", slide4);
show(this, "slide 2");          // Show slide 2
show(this, "slide 4");          // and then slide 4.
```

Coming back to the example in listing 9.5, you will see that there is no layout manager being used as you are just adding a single object. So the argument to `setLayout()` is null.

Line 176 adds the label to the applet area, and line 177 positions the label at the point <1,1> and at a width of 100 and a height of 15 pixels.

After the `init()` method is called, the `start()` method is called (see lines 130–140). In this method a check is made to see if the thread has been instantiated by checking if the thread reference, `paintThread`, is null. If the thread reference is null, it means that the thread does not exist, in which case, a new thread is created with an argument, which is the instance of this applet:

```
paintThread = new Thread(this);
```

The instance of the applet class that you are defining is referenced by this. Next, line 135 starts the thread.

The corresponding `stop()` method (see lines 143–151) will get called if the user leaves the Web page on which the applet is running. This method checks to see if the thread reference is null. If it is null, the thread exists, and it is terminated by calling the thread's `stop()` method (line 147). After termination, line 148 sets the thread reference to null, thus making it available for garbage collection. If the user revisits the page on which the applet is created, the Web browser will call the `start()` method of the applet, and this will create a new thread.

The main logic of the thread is in the `run()` method (lines 154–164). This method is called soon after the thread is started in line 135. The run method sets up an infinite loop (see line 157 in listing 9.5). Within the loop, the method `repaint()` is called, and then the thread sleeps for 50 milliseconds, after which the actions in the loop are repeated.

The `repaint()` method is inherited from the Component class. When it is called, it results in a call to the `paint()` method for the applet. The `paint()` method is defined on lines 200–216. Lines 204–206 paint a light gray line to erase any previous line. Next, line 209 rotates the line. Line 212 sets a random color for the new line to be drawn. Lines 213 and 214 draw the new rotated line.

Listing 9.5

```
Line==================Java Source==================
001   /**
002   * LineDraw: Demonstrates how a thread can be
003   * used to animate a line.
004   *
005   * Author: Karanjit S. G. S. Siyan
006   *
007   */
008   import java.awt.*;
009   import java.applet.Applet;
010
011   class Angle
012      {
013
014      // Normalizes an angle and ensures that
015      // it is between 0 and 360 degrees.
016      public static int normalize(int degrees)
017      {
018
019         while (degrees < 360)
```

continues

Listing 9.5, Continued

```
        {
        degrees += 360;
        }

        return degrees ;

        }  // end normalize


        // Converts degrees to radians
         public static double radians(int degrees)
        {
           return ((double) degrees)* Math.PI/180.0;

        }  // end radians


   }  // end Angle

   class Line
 {
     // Line center
     int xc;
     int yc;

     double r; // Line radius from center

     // Initial coordinates
     int x[] = new int[2];
     int y[] = new int[2];

     // Rotated coordinates
     int rotX[] = new int[2];
     int rotY[] = new int[2];

  doublerotTheta;  // Last rotated angle

```

```
      int  maxsize; // Max size indicator

      // Constructor for creating Line
      public Line(int xc, int yc, int maxsize)
      {
         this.xc = xc;
         this.yc = yc;
         this.maxsize = maxsize;

         r = Math.random()*(double)(maxsize/2);
         rotTheta = 0.0F;
         x[0] = xc + (int)r;
         y[0] = yc;

      }  // end Line

      // Rotates the line by the specified degrees
      public void rotate(int degrees)
      {
         int projX;// Projection on X-axis
         int projY;// Projection on Y-axis

         degrees = Angle.normalize(degrees);

         rotTheta += Angle.radians(degrees);

         projX = (int)(r*Math.cos(rotTheta));
         projY = (int)(r*Math.sin(rotTheta));

         rotX[0] = xc - projX;
         rotX[1] = xc + projX;

         rotY[0] = yc + projY;
         rotY[1] = yc - projY;

      }  // end rotate

   }  // end Line

```

continues

Listing 9.5, Continued

```
public class LineDraw extends Applet
implements Runnable
{

   Label label; // Label for text

   // Resize values
   int dimX = 300;
   int dimY = 300;

   Line rotLine = new Line(dimX/2, dimY/2, 200);
   int rotDelta = 5;// rotation delta

   Thread paintThread = null;

   static Color[] ac =
   {
      Color.white,
      Color.black,
      Color.gray,
      Color.darkGray,
      Color.red,
      Color.green,
      Color.blue,
      Color.yellow,
      Color.magenta,
      Color.cyan,
      Color.pink,
      Color.orange

   }; // end ac


   // start method overrides method in Applet
   public void start()
   {
      if (paintThread == null)
      {
```

```
         paintThread = new Thread(this);
          paintThread.start();

         }  // end if


      }  // end start

      // stop method overrides method in Applet
      public void stop()
      {
         if (paintThread != null)
         {
             paintThread.stop();
             paintThread = null;
         }  // end if

      }  // end stop

      // run method implement the Runnable interface.
      public void run()
         throws InterruptedException
      {
         for(;;)
         {
             repaint();
             Thread.sleep(50);

         } // end for

      } // end run

      // init method overrides method in Applet
      public void init()
      {

         super.init();
         resize(dimX,dimY);

```

continues

Listing 9.5, Continued

```
        setLayout(null);

        label=new Label("A Simple Applet");
        add(label);
        label.reshape(1,1,100,15);

    }  // end init


    // gets random color, except the
    // background color lightGray
    private Color getColor()
    {
        int index;

        index = (int) (Math.random()*((double)ac.length));
        if (index == ac.length)
        {
            --index;

        }  // end if

        return ac[index];

    }  // end getColor

    // paint method overrides method in Component
    public void paint(Graphics g)
    {

        // Erase the previous line
        g.setColor(Color.lightGray);
        g.drawLine(rotLine.rotX[0], rotLine.rotY[0],
            rotLine.rotX[1], rotLine.rotY[1]);

```

```
        // Rotate the line
        rotLine.rotate(rotDelta);

        // Draw the rotated line
        g.setColor(getColor());
        g.drawLine(rotLine.rotX[0], rotLine.rotY[0],
           rotLine.rotX[1], rotLine.rotY[1]);

    } // end paint

} // end LineDraw
```

Reducing Animation Flicker

You may have noticed that the animation of Java applets creates an annoying flicker. The flicker is caused when each frame of the Java applet is repainted by a call to `repaint()`. In the discussion of the example in listing 9.5, it was explained that the call to `repaint()` results in a call to `paint()`. Actually, the sequence of actions that occur are the following:

1. The call to `repaint()` results in a call to `update()`, also inherited from the Component class:

```
public void update(Graphics g);
```

2. The `update()` method first clears the screen by filling it with the current background color, and then calls `paint()`:

```
public void paint(Graphics g);
```

3. The `paint()` method in your applet draws the frame.

The call to `update()` results in the animation flicker as it erases the previous contents of the frame. To prevent the animation flicker, you can use the following techniques:

- Override `update()`. Clear only parts of the screen that need to be redrawn, or do not clear the screen.
- Override `update()` and use double buffering:

The default version of `update()` defined in the Component class performs the following actions:

```
public void update(Graphics g)
{
       g.setColor(getBackground());
       g.fillRect(0, 0, width, height);
       g.setColor(getForeground());
       paint(g);

} // end update
```

From the preceding code, you can see that `update()` clears the screen by calling `fillRect()` with the width and height of the applet by using the background color. Next, it calls the `paint()` method.

Overriding Update Method to Reduce Flickering

You could fix the flicker of the LineDraw applet, in listing 9.5, by overriding the `update()` method, and have it call only `paint()`. Note that the `paint()` method in listing 9.5 already takes care of erasing the previous line:

A modified form of the LineDraw program is in the file LineDraw1.java on the CD-ROM at the back of the book. The only difference between this and the original LineDraw program is the inclusion of the following `update()` method:

```
// update method overrides method in Component
public void update(Graphics g)
{
  paint(g);

}  // end update
```

You can compile and test the LineDraw1 program by using javac and then compare it with the original LineDraw program.

You can also override `update()` and, rather than clearing the entire applet screen each time `update()` is called, just modify the section of the screen that needs modification. You can do this by using the `clipRect()` method of the Graphics class that was described earlier in this chapter (lines 99–104 of listing 9.1). Here is an example of using this in an `update()` method:

```
// update method overrides method in Component
public void update(Graphics g)
{
      // x, y, width, height must be set
```

```
        // according to applet logic.
        g.clipRect(x, y, width, height);
    paint(g);

    } // end update
```

Using Double Buffering to Reduce Flicker

In double buffering, an off-screen image is first drawn, and then this image is sent to the screen to be displayed. Here is an outline of the steps to be performed.

1. Create an off-screen image and a graphics context:

```
Image offScreenImage;
Graphics offScreenGraphics;
         Make these class instance variables in your applet class.
```

2. In the `init()` method of the applet, create object instances for the class instance variables of step 1.

```
public void init()
{
      super.init();
      Dimension d = this.size();

      offScreenImage = createImage(d.width, d.height);
      offScreenGraphics =
         offScreenImage.getGraphics();

      // Other logic
} // end init
```

3. Do all drawing of graphics in the `paint()` method to the off-screen graphics context. If, for example, you need to draw the image `flash`, do the following:

```
offScreenGraphics.drawImage(flash, x, y, this);
```

Here are examples of calling other methods for the off-screen graphics:

```
offScreenGraphics.setColor(Color.magenta);
offScreenGraphic.drawRect(10, 10, 50, 50);
offScreenGraphic.fillRect(80, 10, 50, 50);
```

4. Restore the off-screen graphic image to the real display screen by using the following:

```
g.drawImage(offScreenImage, 0, 0, this);
```

5. Override the `update()` method and include the following code:

```
public void update(Graphics g)
 {
  paint(g);

 }  // end update
```

Animating with Sound and Images

Java enables you to write applets that you can animate with images. Each image provides a frame of animation. By rapidly displaying the frames in succession, the illusion of continuous motion is maintained. The interval of time between successive frames can be controlled by delaying the thread that performs the animation for a period of time. The following sections present the classes that Java provides for dealing with images, sound, and interacting with the applet. Toward the end of the chapter, a complete listing of an applet that implements these features is discussed.

Using the Image Class

The Image class represents a displayable image and is defined in the java.awt package. You cannot instantiate the Image class by using a constructor. You must use either the `Applet.getImage()` or `Component.createImage()` methods. Within an applet, the most convenient way of creating an instance of this Image class is to call the `Applet.getImage()` method, which you inherit when you extend the Applet class.

The `Applet.getImage()`method has the following two forms:

```
public Image getImage(URL url);
public Image getImage(URL url, String pathname)
```

The first argument is the URL class. *URL* stands for *Uniform Resource Locator,* and it refers to the location of the server applet. The second form of `getImage()` has an additional argument for the pathname of the image file. The pathname of the file can also be combined as part of the URL—in fact, this is what needs to be done in the first form of `getImage()`—but by separating the hostname on which the applet resides with the pathname you'll have additional flexibility. In the second form of `getImage()`, for instance, if you have image files named `flame1.gif`, `flame2.gif`, `flame3.gif`, you can easily build the file names of the images in Java without having to modify the URL argument.

To build the URL argument, you can use the following two methods, also defined in the Applet class:

```
public URL getCodeBase();
public URL getDocumentBase();
```

The `getCodeBase()` gets an instance of the URL class that refers to the URL location of the directory in which the applet code resides. If, for example, the URL for your applet is `http://www.tsl.org/applet/flame.class`, then the call to `getCodeBase()` will return a URL containing the reference to `http://www.tsl.org/applet`.

Similarly, the `getDocumentBase()` gets an instance of the URL class that refers to the URL location of the directory in which the HTML file for the applet resides. If, for example, the URL for your applet's HTML file is `http://www.tsl.org/html/flame.html`, then the call to `getCodeBase()` will return a URL containing the reference to `http://www.tsl.org/html`.

You can use either `getDocumentBase()` or `getCodeBase()` to obtain the URL to be used in the `getImage()` method. Your choice will depend on whether your images are stored relative to your applet code directory or the HTML documents directory.

The following are some examples of calling `getImage()` within your applet to create an instance of the image:

```
// Uses first form of getImage()
Image img1 = getImage(
new URL("http://www.tsl.org/images/flame.gif"));

// Uses second form of getImage()
Image img2 = getImage(getCodeBase(), "flame.gif");
Image img3 = getImage(getDocumentBase(), "flame.gif");
```

If the images are stored in subdirectories relative to the applet code or HTML directory, you can enter the relative pathname to the file as the second argument:

```
// Uses second form of getImage() with pathname
Image img4 = getImage(getCodeBase(), "images/flame.gif");
Image img5 = getImage(getDocumentBase(), "images/flame.gif");
After you obtain the image, you can draw it within the applet's display
area using the drawImage() method defined in the Graphics class:
 //
 // Draws the specified image at the specified coordinate (x, y).
 // If the image is incomplete the image observer will be
```

```
// notified later.
// x = X-coordinate for drawing the image
// y = Y-coordinate for drawing the image
// img = the specified image to be drawn
// observer = notifies if the image is complete or not
public abstract boolean drawImage(Image img, int x, int y,
           ImageObserver observer);
```

The *ImageObserver* is an interface class, and refers to any class that implements the ImageObserver interface. One of the superclasses for the Applet class is the Component class and this implements the ImageObserver interface. So for the Image-Observer argument you will pass this, the instance of your applet class. Your applet can now receive information, asynchronously, about the status of loading the image.

You will typically use `drawImage()` in the `paint()` method, as shown next:

```
public void paint(Graphics g)
{
      // x and y should be set
      // before calling this method.
      g.drawImage(img, x, y, this);

} // end paint
```

Using the AudioClip Class

To play sound, you must first create an instance of the AudioClip class. This class contains a representation of the sound clip to be played. You create an instance of this class by calling the `getAudioClip()` method defined in the Applet class:

```
public AudioClip getAudioClip(URL url);
public AudioClip getAudioClip(URL url, String pathname)
```

Notice that the arguments to these methods are similar to the arguments for the `getImage()` method discussed in the previous section, so the same discussion applies to them. The following are examples of how to use these methods:

```
// Uses first form of getAudioClip()
AudioClip audio1 = getAudioClip(
new URL("http://www.tsl.org/audio/vflame.au"));
```

```
// Uses second form of getAudioClip()
AudioClip audio2 = getAudioClip(getCodeBase(), "bflame.au");
AudioClip audio3 = getAudioClip(getDocumentBase(), "bflame.gif");
AudioClip audio4 = getAudioClip(getCodeBase(),
        "audio/vflame.au");
AudioClip audio5 = getAudioClip(getDocumentBase(),
        "audio/vflame.au");
```

The audio files in these examples are SUN's au file format.

To play the audio clip once, you can send it the `play()` method:

```
audio1.play();
```

To play the audio clip continuously, send it the `loop()` method:

```
audio1.loop();
```

To stop the audio clip from playing at any time, send it the `stop()` method:

```
audio1.stop();
```

Typically, you can create an instance of the AudioClip in the `init()` method of your applet:

```
public void init()
{
      super.init();

      audio = getAudioClip(getCodeBase(),
          "audio/vflame.au");

      // Other initialization code.

} // end init
```

If you want the audio clip to play continuously, you can call its `loop()` method in the applet's `run()` method:

```
public void run()
{
      if (audio != null)
      {
          audio.loop();

      } // end if

      // Other thread logic.

} // end run
```

As seen in the preceding code fragment, you must always make sure that the audio clip instance is not null, before calling its method. If, for example, the audio clip file was not found in the call to the `getAudioClip()` method, a value of null will be returned. If you try to call any of the audio clip methods on a null instance, an exception will occur.

You can typically stop the audio clip in the applet's `stop()` method by using the following code:

```
public void stop()
{
      // thread =  instance of the animation thread.
      // audio =  instance of the AudioClip.
      if (thread != null)
      {
         if (audio != null)
         {
            audio.stop();

         } // end if

      thread.stop();
      thread = null;

      } // end if

} // end stop
```

Interacting with the Applet

You can interact with an applet by using an input device such as a mouse or keyboard. To handle mouse specific events, you can define any of the following methods in your applet class.

```
public boolean mouseDown(Event event, int x, int y);
public boolean mouseUp(Event event, int x, int y);
public boolean mouseDrag(Event event, int x, int y);
public boolean mouseMove(Event event, int x, int y);
public boolean mouseEnter(Event event, int x, int y);
public boolean mouseExit(Event event, int x, int y);
```

By defining these methods, you are overriding the method that would normally be inherited from the Component class.

The first argument is the event argument, and is generated by system specific events. The class Event describes such events. You can access variables and methods of the event object to find additional details on the event. The second and third arguments are the coordinates at which the event specified by the method name occurred.

The methods return a Boolean value. Your overriding method should return a true value if it has handled the event and does not need to pass the event to an enclosing component. A false value should be returned if an enclosing component needs to handle the event. The following is an example of the `mouseDown()` method:

```
public boolean mouseDown(Event e, int x, int y)
{
      System.out.println("Event at <"+x+","+y+">");

      return true;

} // end mouseDown
```

To capture a keyboard event, you override the `keyDown()` or `keyUp()` method in your applet class:

```
public boolean keyDown(Event event, int key);
public boolean keyUp(Event event, int key);
```

By defining these methods, you are overriding the method that would normally be inherited from the Component class. The second parameter is an integer representing the character codes for the key that was activated. To convert them to character values, you can cast it to a char value. The Event class also defines a set of values for the control keys. These values are passed to the method as the second argument. The following are these special value definitions taken from the Event class:

```
// Key modifiers
public static final int SHIFT_MASK;
public static final int CTRL_MASK;
public static final int META_MASK;
public static final int ALT_MASK;
// Special keys
public static final int HOME;
public static final int END;
public static final int PGUP;
public static final int PGDN;
public static final int UP;
public static final int DOWN;
public static final int LEFT;
public static final int RIGHT;
// Function keys
public static final int F1;
public static final int F2;
public static final int F3;
public static final int F4;
public static final int F5;
public static final int F6;
public static final int F7;
public static final int F8;
public static final int F9;
public static final int F10;
public static final int F11;
public static final int F12;
// Window events
public static final int WINDOW_DESTROY;
public static final int WINDOW_EXPOSE;
public static final int WINDOW_ICONIFY;
public static final int WINDOW_DEICONIFY;
public static final int WINDOW_MOVED;
// Key press events
public static final int KEY_PRESS;
public static final int KEY_RELEASE;
public static final int KEY_ACTION;
public static final int KEY_ACTION_RELEASE;
```

```
// Mouse events
public static final int MOUSE_DOWN;
public static final int MOUSE_UP;
public static final int MOUSE_MOVE;
public static final int MOUSE_ENTER;
public static final int MOUSE_EXIT;
public static final int MOUSE_DRAG;
// Line events
public static final int SCROLL_LINE_UP;
public static final int SCROLL_LINE_DOWN;
public static final int SCROLL_PAGE_UP;
public static final int SCROLL_PAGE_DOWN;
public static final int SCROLL_ABSOLUTE;
// List events
public static final int LIST_SELECT;
public static final int LIST_DESELECT;
// Action event
public static final int ACTION_EVENT;
// File events
public static final int LOAD_FILE;
public static final int SAVE_FILE;
public static final int GOT_FOCUS;
public static final int LOST_FOCUS;
```

The following is an example of the `keyDown()` method:

```
public void keyDown(Event event, int key)
{
      char charValue = (char) key;
      System.out.println("Char value = "+charValue);
      System.out.println("Int value = "+key);

      switch (key)
      {
         case Event.LEFT:
         System.out.println("Left key");
         break;
```

```
        case Event.RIGHT:
        System.out.println("Right key");
        break;

        case Event.UP:
        System.out.println("Up key");
        break;

        case Event.DOWN:
        System.out.println("Down key");
        break;

        default:
        System.out.println("Non arrow key");
        break;

    } // end switch

    return true;

} // end keyDown
```

The methods discussed in this section are called by the generic AWT event handler `handleEvent()` that is inherited from the Component class:

```
public boolean handleEvent(Event event);
```

To handle events other than the default events, you must override this handler and supply your own logic. The following is an example of an event handler:

```
public boolean handleEvent(Event e)
{

    if (e.id == Event.MOUSE_DOWN)
    {
        // Perform logic. In this case
        // a counter is decremented.
        -- counter;

        return true; // event handled.
    } // end if
```

```
        return super.handleEvent(e);

} // end handleEvent
```

In the last statement of this method, if the event is not a mouse down event, the superclass's `handlerEvent()` is called. This line of code ensures that the default handling for other types of events will be handled by the handler for the enclosing component.

Code-Walk of the Animation Applet

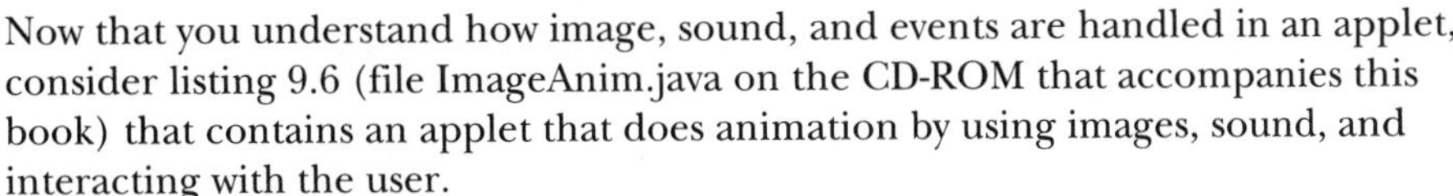

Now that you understand how image, sound, and events are handled in an applet, consider listing 9.6 (file ImageAnim.java on the CD-ROM that accompanies this book) that contains an applet that does animation by using images, sound, and interacting with the user.

The `init()` method defined on lines 184–256 performs the applet initialization. Lines 187 and 188 invoke the superclass's `init()` method and resize the applet dimensions. Line 190 sets the flow layout for laying the button components defined on lines 192 and 193. These button objects are declared as class instance objects on lines 76 and 77. Lines 194 and 195 add the buttons to the applet. Lines 202–233 obtain parameter values passed in the HTML file. A description of these parameter values is on lines 36–47. The `getParameter()` value is used to obtain a string representation of the parameter value. If the parameter value is not passed in the HTML file, a default value is assumed. Note the clever use of the ternary operator "?:" to do a concise assignment of the parameter values (lines 203, 207, 211, 215, 221, 226, 231, 233). Line 237 instantiates the array of images based on the `nimgs` parameter. Lines 239–243 load the file images into this array. Line 246 loads the audio clip. Lines 252–254 set up code to perform double buffering to reduce animation flicker.

The `start()` method defined on lines 91–100 performs the standard logic of creating a thread instance (line 95) and calling the start method for the thread (line 96).

After the thread is started, the `run()` method is called (see lines 128–151). On line 132, you can see a statement to reduce the thread's priority below the normal priority. This is not essential for the logic of the applet, but it is a nice gesture toward the applet user, to prevent this thread from impacting the user's computer system. Lines 134–138 start the audio clip for the thread. The audio clip is played continuously because the `loop()` method for the audio clip is called (see line 136). If the audio clip is not loaded, the instance variable audio will be set to null, and the if statement on line 134 will ensure that the `audio.loop()` will not be called. Lines 141–151 set up an infinite loop. Within this loop, the next image is extracted from the array of images, and the `repaint()` method is called. After the image is painted, the thread goes to sleep for delay milliseconds, and then the sequence of actions in the loop repeat.

The call to `repaint()` results in a call to `update()` (see lines 173–177), which then calls the `paint()` method (line 175). In the `paint()` method a check is made to see if the currImage that holds the image frame to be painted is not null. In line 162, the image is first drawn on the off-screen double buffer, and in line 163 this image is painted to the applet.

The `stop()` method on lines 107–119 stops the animation and the sound. If the thread is alive, it stops the audio (see lines 111–115), terminates the thread (line 116), and sets the thread object reference to null so it can be reclaimed by Java's automatic garbage collector.

The `handleEvent()` method on lines 258–281 checks whether the button labeled "Fast" or "Slow" is pressed by the user. If the Fast button is pressed, the delay interval between successive calls to `repaint()` is reduced by 10 milliseconds (line 263); and if the Slow button is pressed, this delay interval is increased by 10 milliseconds (line 274). The if-statement on lines 265–269 ensures that the delay does not drop below 0 seconds. The current delay value is displayed for the applet in the Web browsers status area by calling `showStatus()`. The `showStatus()` method is inherited from the Applet class. On line 279 the superclass's handler is called to handle all other events not handled by the overriding `handleEvent()` method.

Listing 9.6

```
Line=================Java Source=================
001 /**
002  *
003  *  Animator applet: Shows how to animate applets
004  *  using images.
005  *
006  *  Author: Karanjit S. G. S. Siyan
007  *
008  *
009  *This class is a basic extension of the Applet class.  It would generally be
010  *used as the main class with a Java browser or the AppletViewer.  But an
     instance
011  *can be added to a subclass of Container.  To use this applet with a
     browser or
012  *the AppletViewer, create an html file with the following code:
013  *
014  *<HTML>
015  *<HEAD>
016  *<TITLE> Three fold flame </TITLE>
```

```
 *</HEAD>
 *<BODY>
 *
 *<APPLET CODE="ImageAnim.class" WIDTH=332 HEIGHT=169>
 *<param name=imgdir value="images/flame">
 *<param name=imgfile value="flame">
 *<param name=imgtype value="gif">
 *<param name=audiopath value="audio/bgsound.au">
 *<param name=nimgs value=2>
 *<param name=delay value=250>
 *<param name=xpos value=20>
 *<param name=ypos value=20>
 *</APPLET>
 *
 *</BODY>
 *
 *</HTML>
 *
 *
 *LEGEND OF PARAMETERS USED FOR APPLET CLASS
 *imgdir  = Image directory
 *imgfile = Image file
 *imgtype = Image type (gif)
 *audiopath = Audio file path
 *nimgs= Number of image files.
 * Each file has the following template: flameX.gif
 * where X = 1, 2, 3, ...
 *
 *delay= Delay between each display of image in milliseconds
 *xpos = X-coordinate of applet
 *ypos = Y-coordinate of applet
 *
 *
 */

import java.awt.*;
import java.applet.*;

```

continues

Listing 9.6, Continued

```
public class ImageAnim extends Applet implements Runnable
{

    String  imgDir;// Image directory.
    String  imgFile;  // Image file.
    String  imgType;  // Image type.
    String  audioPath;// Audio file path.

    int  nimgs; // Number of images.
    int  delay; // Delay between consecutive images.
    int  xpos;  // X-coordinate to display the image.
    int  ypos;  // Y-coordinate to display the image.
    Imageimages[]; // Define the array that holds the images.
    ImagecurrImage;// Current image to be displayed.
    int  currIndex;// Current index into images array.

    AudioClipaudio;// Audio clip.

    Imageoimg;  // Off-screen image
    Graphics og;// Off-screen graphics context.

    Button  slow;  // Slow button
    Button  fast;  // Fast button

    /**
    * Initially, we are designing a single thread
    * to display all the images. So only a single
    * thread is being constructed.
    */
    Thread threadact = null;

   /**
    * start(): Called when the applet is visible.
    * It's primary function is to start the
    * threadact thread
    */
    public void start()
    {
```

```
        if (threadact == null)
        {
           threadact = new Thread(this, "threadact");
           threadact.start();

        } // end if

     } // end start

     /**
     * stop(): Called when the applet is no longer visible.
     * This stops the current thread by calling the thread's
     * stop method.
     */
     public void stop()
     {
        if (threadact != null && threadact.isAlive())
        {
           if (audio != null)
           {
           audio.stop();

        } // end if
        threadact.stop();
        threadact = null;

     } // end if


     } // end stop


    /**
     * run(): This implements the run method for the Runnable interface.
     */
     public void run()
     throws InterruptedException
     {
     // Diminish the thread's priority.
```

continues

Listing 9.6, Continued

```
    Thread.currentThread().setPriority(Thread.NORM_PRIORITY-1);

    if (audio != null)
    {
       audio.loop();

    } // end if

    // Set up the classical infinite loop for daemons.
    for (;;)
    {
       currImage = images[currIndex];
       currIndex = (++currIndex) % nimgs;

       repaint();
       Thread.sleep(delay);

    } // end for

   } // end run


    /**
    * paint(): Overrides the paint method defined in the
    * component class.
    */
    public void paint(Graphics g)
    {
       if (currImage != null)
       {
          og.drawImage(currImage, xpos, ypos, this);
          g.drawImage(oimg, 0, 0, this);

    } // end if

    } // end paint

```

```
    /**
    * update(): Overrides the update method defined in the
    * component class.
    */
    public void update(Graphics g)
    {
       paint(g);

    } // end update


    /**
    * init(): Standard init method that needs to be overriden
    * for the applet class.
    */
    public void init()
    {

       super.init();
       resize(230,190);

       setLayout(new FlowLayout(FlowLayout.RIGHT));

       slow = new Button("Slow");
       fast = new Button("Fast");
       add(slow);
       add(fast);

       // Initialize parameters passed through
       // the param values in the HTML file
       //

       // Define the image directory
       String param = getParameter("imgdir");
       imgDir = (param != null) ? param : "images/flame";

       // Define the image file name
       param = getParameter("imgfile");
       imgFile = (param != null) ? param : "flame";
```

continues

Listing 9.6, Continued

```

        // Define the image type
        param = getParameter("imgtype");
        imgType = (param != null) ? param : "gif";

        // Define the audio path
        param = getParameter("audiopath");
        audioPath = (param != null) ? param : "audio/bgsound.au";


        // Define the number of images.
        // Note, modify the default value of number of images.
        param = getParameter("nimgs");
        nimgs = (param != null) ? Integer.valueOf(param).intValue() : 2;

        // Define the time delay between image displays.
        // Unit is in milliseconds.
        param = getParameter("delay");
        delay = (param != null) ? Integer.valueOf(param).intValue() : 333;

        // Define the coordinates (xpos, ypos) at which to
        // display the image.
        param = getParameter("xpos");
        xpos = (param != null) ? Integer.valueOf(param).intValue() : 10;
        param = getParameter("ypos");
        ypos = (param != null) ? Integer.valueOf(param).intValue() : 10;


        // Next, load the images in the image array.
        images = new Image[nimgs];
        int  i, j; // Loop indexes
        for (i = 0, j = 1; i < nimgs; i++, j++)
        {
           images[i] = getImage(getCodeBase(), imgDir+"/
➥"+imgFile+j+"."+imgType);

        }  // end for

```

```
        // Get the audio clip.
        audio = getAudioClip(getCodeBase(), audioPath);

        // Set the current image index to 0.
        currIndex = 0;

        // Set up double buffering.
        Dimensioned = this.size();
        oimg = createImage(d.width, d.height);
        og = oimg.getGraphics();

    } // end init

    public boolean handleEvent(Event event)
    {

        if (event.target == fast)
        {
            delay - = 10;

        if (delay < 0)
        {
            delay = 0;

        } // end if

        }
        else if (event.target == slow)
        {
        delay += 10;

        } // end if

        showStatus("delay = "+delay+" ms");
        return super.handleEvent(event);

    } // end handleEvent

} // end ImageAnim
```

Summary

In this chapter, you learned the basics of using Java's built-in graphics primitives to produce lines, shapes, images, and sounds. You were presented with several examples of code that used the graphics method. When writing applets to display graphics, there are two main methods for creating the graphics: one method is to use the methods provided by the Graphics class, and the other is to use prebuilt images that you load from a file. You can, of course, use a combination of these techniques.

In this chapter, you learned about the basics of thread creation and activation. Thread creation is needed to produce applets with animation. The logic of painting or changing the applet display area is done by a thread specifically designed for this purpose.

You also learned how to load images and sound clips in your applet, and how to activate these images with a minimum of screen flicker by overriding the `update()` method and by using the double buffering technique.

CHAPTER 10

Implementing Java Exception Handling

Java provides a robust method for handling error conditions by providing a language construct for handling these errors. This language construct is the exceptional handling capability that was mentioned in earlier chapters.

This chapter discusses exceptional handling in greater detail. You learn how exceptions are defined and activated—a process called throwing an exception. Exceptions that are thrown must be caught or they will result in the termination of the program. You will learn how to catch these exceptions and process them. You will learn about the prebuilt exceptions in the Java language and how to define your own exceptions.

Understanding Exceptions

As part of executing a program, any number of error conditions may be encountered. Some of these errors may be expected, such as the potential for an end-of-file error when reading a file; although others may be totally unexpected, such as an arithmetic error resulting from dividing an integer by zero.

In many languages, an attempt is made to anticipate the error conditions by checking the status of status variables for these error conditions. The problem with this approach is that most programmers are not disciplined enough to check for every error condition, or they are so rushed for time that they skip the error checking in favor of getting a working version of the program. They may have every good intention of returning to the program to add the code to check for errors, but, alas, this seldom seems to happen. So the program is full of potential errors that are just waiting to happen, or it is filled with error-checking code for every conceivable error condition. The latter approach, although resulting in programs that have fewer bugs, also leads to somewhat unreadable programs because of all the error-checking code.

Languages such as Java provide a cleaner method of handling exceptions. When writing a new method, a Java programmer can identify all the potential error conditions that the caller should be able to handle. The method should try to handle as many error conditions as it can within the logic of the method, but there are certain situations, such as the "end-of-file" condition, that a caller should handle. These potential error conditions are called exceptions. All such potential error conditions are made part of the definition of the method, and they become an important part of the method's contract. Anyone who calls the method must handle these error conditions—this is enforced by the Java compiler.

Within the method, a programmer codes the logic so that when an exceptional condition is encountered, an exception is *thrown* or *raised.* A thrown exception must be *caught* at the point of the method invocation. If there is no explicit mechanism to catch the thrown exception, the exception is propagated up the chain of methods that resulted in the call to the method that raised the exception. If the exception is not explicitly caught, a default handler is invoked. This default handler usually prints some useful information about the exception and terminates the program.

The Exception Class

All exceptions defined in Java must extend either to the Throwable class or the Exception class. Figure 10.1 shows the relationship between the major exception classes. Throwable is subclassed from the Object class, and Exception is subclassed from the Throwable class. The Exception class acts as a superclass of all the major exception classes. The Throwable class defines a user-specified string and contains private instance variables that keep track of the runtime stack trace. Typically, new exception classes that you will create will extend the Exception class.

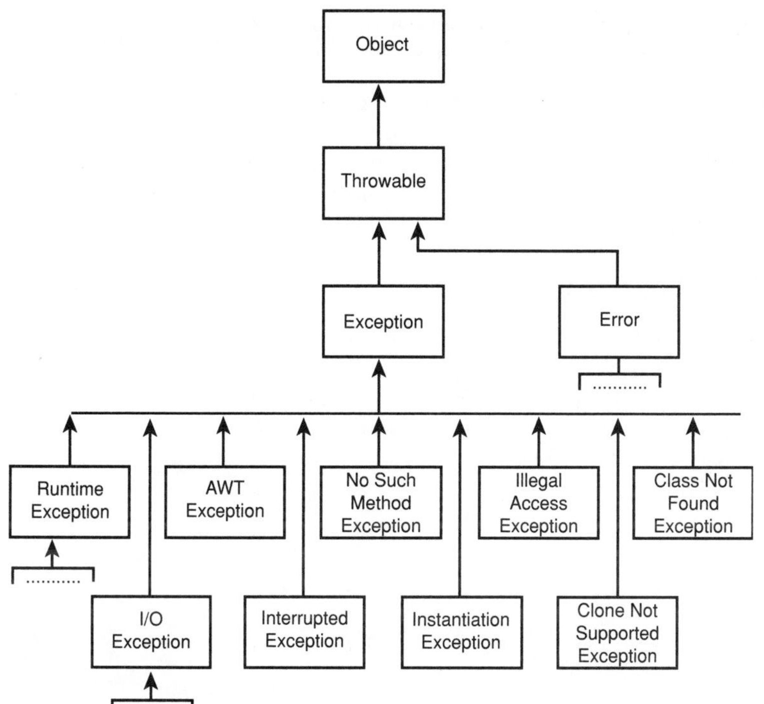

Figure 10.1
The exception classes' inheritance hierarchy diagram.

Checked and Unchecked Exceptions

Java exceptions can be classified into two major types of exceptions:

- Checked exceptions
- Unchecked exceptions

Checked exceptions are those that are checked by the Java compiler. As part of this checking, the Java compiler verifies that you can only throw exceptions in a method that you have defined in the method declaration. Exceptions that are defined by subclassing the Exception class exhibit this behavior.

Exceptions that are defined by subclassing the Error class or the Runtime class are not checked by the Java compiler. Such exceptions are called *unchecked exceptions.* These exceptions can occur anywhere within the program. If the rules of checked exceptions were strictly enforced for runtime exceptions and error conditions, every method would have to define a long chain of exception classes that could potentially be thrown.

Java Language Constructs for Exceptions

When defining a new exception type within your program, you must define a class that extends on one of the exception classes in figure 10.1. Next, you must use this exception class in a method to raise an exception. When the exception is thrown, it must be caught; so you must define an exception handler to catch this exception.

Defining an Exception

Typically, you will be extending the Exception class this way:

```
public class MyNewException extends Exception
{
      // Constructor
         public MyNewException()
         {
      super();

      } // end MyNewException

} // end MyNewException
```

The Exception class exists in the package java.lang. In the previous example, you are creating a new class that is subclassed from Exception, but you are not adding any new capability in the exception. In fact, in the constructor for the new exception class MyNewException, you are calling the default constructor for the superclass Exception. The Exception class has the following definition:

```
class Exception extends Throwable
{
     // Constructs an Exception with no specified
     // detail message.
    public Exception()
    {
   super();

    } // end Exception

    //
    // Constructs an Exception with the specified
    // detail message. A detail message is a
```

```
    // String that describes this particular exception.
    //
    // s = the detail message
    public Exception(String s)
    {
       super(s);

    } // end Exception

} // end Exception
```

As you can see from this definition of Exception, there are two constructors for Exception: a default constructor with no message and a constructor with a message. It is best to define a constructor for an exception class with a message that is descriptive of the error condition that is being handled. The following is an example of the modified form of MyNewException.

```
public class MyNewException extends Exception
{
      // Constructor
      public MyNewException(String msg)
      {
         super(msg);

      } // end MyNewException

} // end MyNewException
```

To create an instance of the error class, you would use the following:

```
MyNewException prob1 = new MyNewException("Out of widgets");
```

Your new exception class inherits the following methods from the class Throwable:

```
// Obtains the message associated with the exception
public String getMessage();
// Returns a short description of the exception
public String toString();

// Prints the Throwable and the Throwable's stack trace.
// The trace is printed on the System.err stream.
public void printStackTrace();
```

```
// Prints the Throwable and the Throwable's stack trace.
// The trace is printed on the specified print stream.
public void printStackTrace(java.io.PrintStream s);
```

You could, therefore, use any of the previous methods on the instance of your new exception class:

```
String excepMsg = prob1.getMessage();
String execpPrint = prob1.toString();
System.out.println(prob1); // Uses toString() to print
prob1.printStackTrace();
```

Throwing an Exception

Here is an example of how you would use your new exception within a method:

```
public void checkValue(String name)
      throws MyNewException
{
      if (name == null)
      {
         throw new MyNewException("null value!");

         } // end if

         // Other logic

} // end checkValue
```

This is a simple method that throws an exception if a null string value is passed to the method. The exception that is thrown is an instance of an exception class; that is, an exception object. The following expression calls the constructor for MyNewException and creates the exception object:

```
new MyNewException("null value!");
```

The throw statement throws the exception object to the caller of the method.

Another point to note is the use of the throws clause in the method declaration where the exception is being thrown:

```
public void checkValue(String name)
      throws MyNewException;
```

Because MyNewException was subclassed from Exception, it is a checked exception. The language rules require that all the checked exceptions thrown in the method must be declared in the method declaration as a comma-separated list of exception classes:

```
(qualifiers returntype method(parameters)
      throws excep1, excep2, excep3
{


} // end method
```

The preceding method defines a generic method that can throw three exceptions:

```
excep1, excep2, excep3
```

These three exceptions must be defined as exception classes.

You can throw exceptions that are extensions of the classes defined in the exception class. This is because you can use classes anywhere that its superclass is expected. Therefore, it is possible to write the following code:

```
public void checkValue(String name)
      throws Exception
{
      if (name == null)
      {
         throw new MyNewException("null value!");

      } // end if

      // Other logic

} // end checkValue
```

When a programmer examines the method declaration, he or she sees the following:

```
public void checkValue(String name)
      throws Exception
```

This tells the programmer that an object of class Exception is thrown by the method, but does not tell the programmer the actual name of the subclassed exception. You are therefore hiding useful information from the programmer because the programmer does not know which of the subclassed exception classes could be thrown. The following is even a worse, although legal, abuse of the language:

```
public void checkValue(String name)
      throws Object
{
      if (name == null)
      {
         throw new MyNewException("null value!");

      } // end if

      // Other logic

} // end checkValue
```

In this preceding example, the throws clause is devoid of any useful information as to the nature of the exception that is thrown by the method because it says that the exception that is thrown is of class Object. The class Object is a placeholder for any Java object. Recall that all Java classes ultimately are extensions of the root superclass Object.

Note In the throws clause, you should list the actual class of the exception that could be thrown by the method, and not the name of the superclass of the exception.

The standard runtime exceptions in Java include the following: Arithmetic Exception, NullPointerException, IndexOutOfBoundsException, ArrayStore-Exception, ClassCastException, IllegalArgumentException, IllegalMonitorState-Exception, IllegalThreadStateException, NegativeArraySizeException, NumberFormat Exception, SecurityException. These exceptions are extensions of the class RuntimeException and can occur anywhere in the program, and therefore do not have to be declared in the throws clause.

Extensions of the Error class also do not have to be declared in the throws clause. Error classes indicate more serious errors and include the following predefined error classes: AbstractMethodError, ClassFormatError, LinkageError, IllegalAccesError, IncompatibleClassChangeError, InstantiationError, Internal-Error, UnknownError, NoClassDefFoundError, NoSuchFieldError, NoSuchMethod-Error, OutOfMemoryError, StackOverflowError, ThreadDeath, UnsatisfiedLinkError, VerifyError, VirtualMachineError. An Error class signals a non-recoverable error, so there is no sense in attempting to catch it. It usually results in an error message being displayed. The ThreadDeath exception is an exception to this rule, and will not generate an error message. It causes the thread in which it is thrown to terminate.

An exception can be thrown inside the body of any method, including a constructor. A checked exception, however, cannot be thrown in initializers and static initialization code. The reason for this is that this type of code is executed during object construction, and there is no user code that can catch these exceptions.

Catching an Exception

When a checked exception is thrown, it should be caught. The catching of the exception is done by using the catch statement:

```
try
      trystatement
catch(exception_class identifier)
      block
catch(exception_class identifier)
      block
    .....
finally
      block
```

First, the try *trystatement* is executed, and if no exception is encountered in the execution of this statement, the finally block statement is executed, after which execution continues with the code after the try-statement The *trystatement* can be any Java statement including a block statement.

If an exception is encountered in the execution of the *trystatement,* further execution of any statements in the *trystatement* is halted, and control is transferred to the first `catch` clause. If the thrown exception is an instance of the class *exception_class,* the *identifier* value is set to the exception object that was thrown, and the corresponding block statement is executed. If there is no match with the *exception_class,* the catch clauses are tried in the order in which they were listed. At the end, the finally block is executed. The finally block is always executed last, regardless of whether an exception was thrown or not. Even if a `break` statement or return statement is used to exit the `try` statement, the finally block is always executed.

If there is no match with the catch clause of the `try` statement, the exception exits the `try` statement into an outer try statement that may be enclosing this `try` statement. This continues until there is a match with a catch clause. There can be any number of catch clauses in a try statement, including none. If there is no match with a catch clause in the method, exception is thrown to the statement that called this method.

It is important to list the catch statements in the order in which you want them to be tried. Consider the following example:

```
try
{
      anExceptionalMethod();


}
catch (IndexOutOfBounds ie)
{
      // exception code goes here
}
catch (IllegalArgumentException ae)
{
      // exception code goes here
}
catch(RuntimeException re)
{
      // exception code goes here
}
catch (IOException ioe)
{
      // exception code goes here
}
catch(MyNewException me)
{
      // exception code goes here
}
catch(Exception ex)
{
      // exception code goes here
}
catch(Throwable te)
{
      // exception code goes here

}   // end try
```

In this code, the first two catch clauses, IndexOutOfBounds and IllegalArgument-Exception, are subclasses of the RuntimeException class. If the thrown exception is a runtime exception and it does not match the first two exceptions, it will match the third catch clause, as this is the RuntimeException class. If there is no match with the RuntimeException class, then a check will be made to see if the exception type is IOException and MyNewException. If there is still no match, the Exception and Throwable class will be matched. A match should definitely occur here because all exceptions are subclasses of at least either the Exception or Throwable class. What if the previous catch statement was rewritten as the following:

```
try
{
      anExceptionalMethod();
}
catch(Throwable te)
{
      // exception code goes here
}
catch(Exception ex)
{
      // exception code goes here

}
catch (IndexOutOfBounds ie)
{
      // exception code goes here
}
catch (IllegalArgumentException ae)
{
      // exception code goes here
}
catch(RuntimeException re)
{
      // exception code goes here
}
catch (IOException ioe)
{
      // exception code goes here
}
catch(MyNewException me)
{
      // exception code goes here

}  // end try
```

Do you see a problem with this try statement? Because the first catch statement will try to match with the Throwable class, a match will always take place. Therefore, none of the other catch statements will be executed.

Note In the catch clauses of the try statement, always list the subclass exceptions before their superclass exceptions.

Code-Walk of an Exceptions Example

Listing 10.1 (file ThrowExceptions.java on the CD-ROM) shows an example of a program that illustrates the features of Java exceptions. This program prints the square root of an integer value between 0 and 1000, as long as the number is not an odd number, and it is a perfect square. A perfect square is a number that is the square of another number. Examples are 64 (square of 8), 100 (square of 10), 144 (square of 12), and so on.

Lines 10–28 define an IntException class subclassed from the Exception class. This class defines two constructors for building this class: one with an argument and one without.

Lines 31–60 define an IntSubException class subclassed from the IntException class. This class defines two constructors for building this class: one with an argument and one without. Additionally, the exception message is stored in a protected class instance variable.

Lines 63–81 define an IntLargeException class subclassed from the Exception class. This class defines two constructors for building this class: one with an argument and one without.

Figure 10.2 shows the class hierarchy diagram for the new exception classes.

Lines 84–205 define the ThrowExceptions class, which uses the three exception classes. The `try` statement (lines 92–111) calls `Integer.parseInt()` on the argument to `main()`. If no argument is passed, the reference to args[0] will result in the Array-IndexOutOfBoundsException exception. The catch clause on line 96 checks if this exception is raised. If it is, the statements in the catch clause (lines 99–101) are executed. These statements print out an error message and a message on how to invoke the program correctly.

If an attempt is made to pass a non-integer value, the exception NumberFormat-Exception will be thrown when `Integer.parseInt()` is called on line 94. This exception will be caught by the `catch` clause on line 104. If the NumberFormatException is thrown, the statements in the corresponding catch clause (lines 106–109) are executed. These statements print out an error message and a message on how to invoke the program correctly.

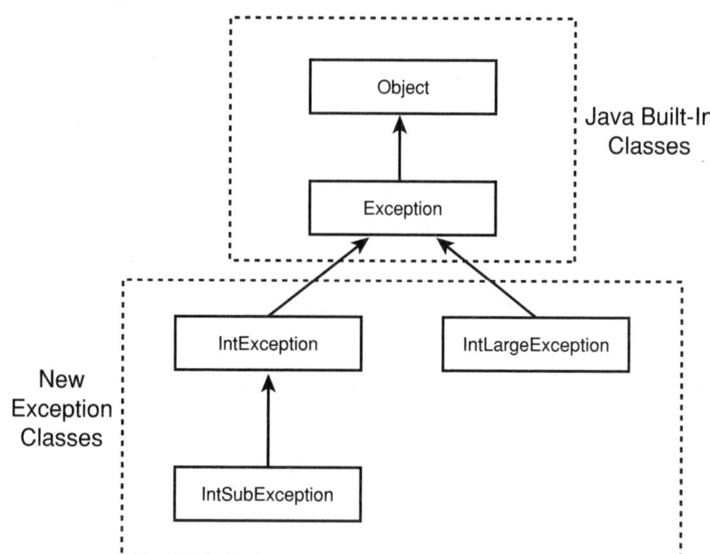

Figure 10.2

Class hierarchy diagram for exception classes in listing 10.1.

If an exception is thrown by calling `Integer.parseInt()`, the return statements on lines 101 and 109 will result in the termination of the `main()` method. If no exception is thrown, the `takeSqrt()` method on line 114 is executed.

In the `takeSqrt()` method (lines 120–160), the argument is first checked by calling `chkIntVal()` in a try statement (lines 124–154). On examining the throws clause for the `chkIntVal()` method (lines 164 and 165), you will notice that the checked exceptions IntException, IntLargeException, and IntSubException can be thrown. Consequently, you must make arrangements to catch these exceptions. If you do not have catch clauses to catch these exceptions, you must declare these exceptions in the throws clause of the `takeSqrt()` method. The catch clause on line 128 catches the IntException. This catch clause will catch both the IntException and its subclass, the IntSubException. The if-statement on line 130 uses the instanceof operator to distinguish between the two exception types. Alternatively, you could have separate catch clauses for both these subclasses as shown, next:

```
try
{
      chkIntVal(ival);
}
catch (IntSubException)
{
      // Code
}
```

```
catch (IntException)
{
        // Code
}
```

Using a superclass exception to catch all the subclass exceptions is useful if much of the exception handling code is the same. You can use the instanceof operator to distinguish between the subclasses.

Lines 132 and 136 print out a message on the exception that was thrown. Lines 140–143 are common to both the IntException and IntSubException exception. These lines print out the exception message by using `toString()` and `println()`. Line 142 prints out the exception stack.

If the IntLargeException is thrown, it is caught on line 146. The message for the exception is printed out (line 148). The output of `toString()` and `println()` is also printed out (lines 149 and 150). Line 151 prints out the exception stack for the thrown exception.

Line 156 prints the result of taking the square root of the integer.

Line 163–203 defines the `chkIntVal()`, which checks the integer value passed to it and throws an exception if it is not the expected value. Lines 164 and 165 shows the throws clause that enumerates the exceptions that can be thrown. Lines 168–170 define a local array of integers that are used to test if the value is a perfect square.

The if-statement on lines 172–181 throws an IntException exception (line 174) if the value is negative, and a IntLargeException exception (line 179) if the value is greater than 1000.

The if-statement on lines 184–188 throws an `IntSubException` exception if the integer value is odd.

The for-statement on lines 191–199 checks if the integer value is a perfect square. If not, the IntSubException is thrown on line 201.

Figures 10.3 and 10.4 show the output of the ThrowExceptions program under various input values.

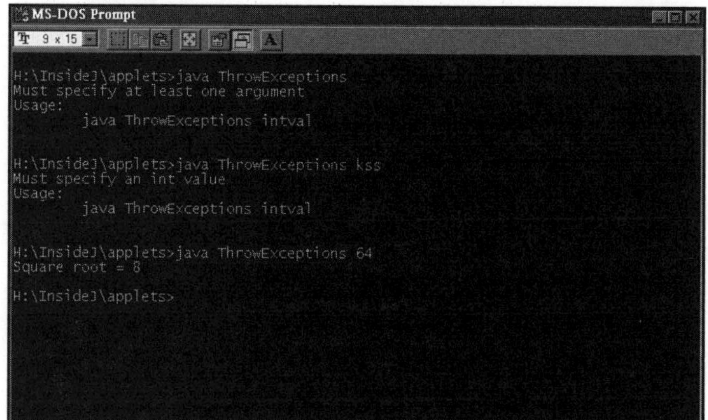

Figure 10.3

Output of ThrowExceptions—Screen 1.

Figure 10.4

Output of ThrowExceptions—Screen 2.

Listing 10.1

```
Line=================Java Source=================
/**
 * ThrowExceptions: Demonstrates the use of
 * exceptions:
 *
 * Author: Karanjit S. G. S. Siyan
 *
 */
```

continues

Listing 10.1, Continued

```

// IntException class
class IntException extends Exception
{

    // Constructor with one arg
    IntException(String msg)
    {
        super(msg);

    }  // end IntException

    // Constructor with no args
    // Default constructor
    IntException()
    {
        super();

    }  // end IntException

}  // end IntException

// A subclass of the IntException class
class IntSubException extends IntException
{

    protected String excepMsg;

    // Constructor with one arg
    IntSubException(String msg)
    {
        super(msg);
        excepMsg = msg;

    }  // end IntSubException

    // Constructor with no args
    // Default constructor
```

```
    IntSubException()
    {
        super();
        excepMsg = "thrown without message";

    }  // end IntSubException

    // Overriding toString() in Throwable
    public String toString()
    {
        return "{IntSubException: "+excepMsg+"}";

    }  // end toString

}  // end IntSubException

// Another exception class
class IntLargeException extends Exception
{

    // Constructor with one arg
    IntLargeException(String msg)
    {
        super(msg);

    }  // end IntLargeException

    // Constructor with no args
    // Default constructor
    IntLargeException()
    {
        super();

    }  // end IntLargeException

}  // end IntLargeException


```

continues

Listing 10.1, Continued

```
public class ThrowExceptions
{

    public static void main(String[] args)
    {
        int     iarg;           // Integer arg

        // Parse the passed parameter
        try
        {
            iarg = Integer.parseInt(args[0]);
        }
        catch (ArrayIndexOutOfBoundsException ae)
        {
            // Arg not supplied
            System.out.println("Must specify at least one argument");
            System.out.println("Usage:\n\tjava ThrowExceptions intval\n");
            return;

        }
        catch (NumberFormatException ne)
        {
            // Expecting an integer
            System.out.println("Must specify an int value");
            System.out.println("Usage:\n\tjava ThrowExceptions intval\n");
            return;

        }  // end try

        // Print the square root.
        takeSqrt(iarg);

    }  // end main

    // Prints square root if number is
    // not odd and a perfect square.
    public static void takeSqrt(int ival)
    {
```

```

        // First check the integer value
        try
        {
            chkIntVal(ival);
        }
        catch (IntException ie)
        {
            if (ie instanceof IntSubException)
            {
                System.out.println("IntSubException thrown");
            }
            else
            {
                System.out.println("IntException thrown");

            }  // end if

            System.out.println("\ttoString()="+ie.toString());
            System.out.println("\tprintln()="+ie);
            ie.printStackTrace();
            return;

        }
        catch  (IntLargeException ie)
        {
            System.out.println("IntException thrown");
            System.out.println("\ttoString()="+ie.toString());
            System.out.println("\tprintln()="+ie);
            ie.printStackTrace();
            return;

        }  // end try

        // Prints the square root.
        System.out.println("Square root = "+
            (int)Math.sqrt((double)ival));

```

continues

Listing 10.1, Continued

```
    }  // end takeSqrt

    // Checks the integer value.
    private static void chkIntVal(int ival)
        throws IntException, IntLargeException,
               IntSubException
    {

        int[] perfectSqs = {0, 4, 16, 36,  64, 100,
                            144, 196, 256, 324, 400,
                            484, 576, 676, 784, 900};

        if (ival < 0)
        {
            throw new IntException("Negative value for sqrt!");

        }
        else if (ival > 1000)
        {
            throw new IntLargeException("Number greater than 1000");

        }  // end if


        if (ival  == 1)
        {
            throw new IntSubException("Odd number");

        }  // end if


        for (int x = 0; x < perfectSqs.length; x++)
        {
            if (perfectSqs[x] == ival)
            {
                return;

            } // end if
```

```

        } // end for

        throw new IntSubException(ival+" not a perfect square");

    }  // end chkIntVal

}  // end ThrowExceptions
```

Summary

Java provides a robust method for handling error conditions by providing language constructs for handling errors as exceptions. You can define your own exceptions by extending the Throwable or Exception class already provided as part of the java.lang package.

In this chapter, you learned how exceptions are defined and how they are thrown. You learned how to use the catch statement to catch exceptions and the difference between checked and unchecked exceptions. Most exceptions that you define in your program will be checked exceptions. Unchecked exceptions are usually runtime exceptions or severe errors and can occur anywhere within a program.

CHAPTER 11

Performing Java Input/Output

In many languages the input/output mechanism is implemented by external libraries that are not part of the language. This approach gives flexibility to the user to define his/her own input/output mechanism but also results in non-portable code because the libraries are not standardized.

Java provides a built-in mechanism for defining input/output by using predefined classes that you can instantiate or extend to provide additional functionality. This chapter will give you a guided tour of the more important of these input/output classes.

Understanding Java Input/Output

Java input/output is provided by *streams.* Streams are an ordered sequence of data items. Typically, one thinks of files as being an ordered sequence of bytes or records with their own internal structure. In Java, these files can be considered streams.

You can have two types of streams: an *input stream* and an *output stream,* also called the *source stream* and the *destination stream.* You read data from the input stream, and you write data to the output stream. The input stream and output streams are modeled in Java as abstract classes of type InputStream and OutputStream (see fig. 11.1). Consequently, all input streams and output streams in Java either inherit the methods defined in the InputStream and OutputStream class, or must override these methods:

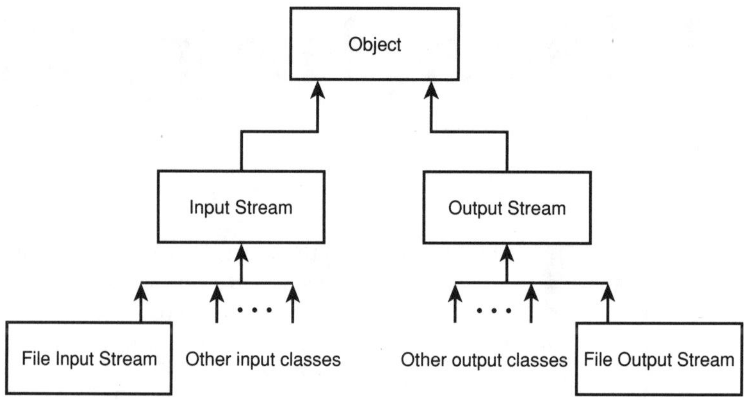

Figure 11.1
InputStream and OutputStream.

The InputStream and OutputStream classes are considered in more detail in the following sections because their methods are used or extended by all other input/output classes.

The InputStream Class

The following is a description of the InputStream class. This class serves as the base class for a number of input classes. This class is abstract, and therefore you cannot create instances of this class. Instead, you must use the subclasses that inherit from this class. Note that many of the input methods throw the IOException, so if you call these methods, your program must deal with them.

```
public abstract class InputStream
{
    // Public methods //
```

```
// (-------------) //

// This method reads a byte of data. It will
// block if no input is available. It returns the
// the byte that is read, or -1 if the end of the
// stream is encountered.
public abstract int read() throws IOException;

// This method reads into an array of bytes. It
// will block if no input is available. It returns
// the actual number of bytes that are read, or
// -1 if the end of the stream is encountered.
public int read(byte b[]) throws IOException;


// This method reads into an array of bytes. It
// will block if no input is available. It returns
// the actual number of bytes that are read, or
// -1 if the end of the stream is encountered.
// The off parameter indicates the offset into
// the byte array where data is read.
// The len parameter indicates the maximum
// number of bytes to be read.
public int read(byte b[], int off, int len)
           throws IOException;



// This method skips the specified number of
// bytes of input. It returns the actual number of
// bytes that are skipped. The method actually
// returns the value of a call to read()
// with a byte array equal to the size of the
// number of bytes to be skipped. It returns the
// result of this read(). If an end of stream
// is encountered, a value of -1 will be returned.
public long skip(long n) throws IOException;
```

```
    // This method returns the number of bytes that
    // can be read without blocking.
    public int available() throws IOException;


    // This method closes the input stream. It must
    // be called to release any resources associated
    // with the stream.
    public void close() throws IOException;

    // This method marks the current position in the
    // input stream. A call to reset() will
    // reposition the stream to the last marked
    // position so that subsequent reads will reread
    // the same bytes as long as no more than
    // readlimit bytes have been read since the call to
    // mark() and the call to reset().
    public synchronized void mark(int readlimit);


    // This method repositions the stream to the last
    // marked position. If the stream has not been
    // marked, or if the mark has been invalidated,
    // an IOException is thrown.
    public synchronized void reset()
     throws IOException;

    // This method returns a boolean indicating
    // whether or not this stream type supports
    // mark()/reset().
    // You should use this method to determine
    // if mark()/reset() is supported, otherwise
    // an I/O exception will be raised if you
    // attempt to use reset() and it is not supported.
    public boolean markSupported();

} // end InputStream
```

Because the InputStream is an abstract class, you cannot create direct instances of InputStream. You can, however, take instances of subclasses of InputStream. Consider the following example:

```
InputStream is = new FileInputStream("testfile.dat");


for(;;)
{
        int     ich;

        try
        {
            ich = is.read();
        }
        catch (IOException e)
        {
        System.out.println(e);

        } // end try

        if (ich == -1) break;

} // end for
```

The FileInputStream class is a subclass of the InputStream class. This class is used for performing file input operations. The following line creates an instance of the FileInputStream and assigns it to the is object:

```
InputStream is = new FileInputStream("testfile.dat");
```

Within the for loop, a call to the `read()` method for the input stream returns a byte from the input stream. The `read()` method can throw an IOException, so this must be caught or declared in the throws clause of the enclosing method. As you can see from the definition of `read()` in the class InputStream, a value of –1 returned from the `read()` indicates the end of file on that stream. The for loop is exited when a value of –1 is returned by `read()`.

Listing 11.1 shows a complete program that uses the `read()` method just discussed to perform a character analysis of the program. Figure 11.2 shows the output of this program by using the java interpreter.

Listing 11.1

```
Line=================Java Source=================
/**
 * ReadInputStream: Illustrates using the input
 * stream.
 *
 * Author: Karanjit S. G. S. Siyan
 *
 */

import java.io.*;

class ReadInputStream
{

    public static void main(String[] args)
    {

        InputStream  is = null;

        if (args.length == 0)
        {
            is = System.in;
        }
        else if (args.length == 1)
        {
            try
            {
                is = new FileInputStream(args[0]);
            }
            catch (FileNotFoundException e)
            {
                System.out.println("File "+args[0]+" not found");
                System.exit(0);
            }
            catch (IOException e)
            {
                System.out.println(e);

```

```
            }  // end try

        }  // end if

        try
        {
            readInput(is);
        }
        catch (IOException e)
        {
             System.out.println(e);

        }  // end try


    }  // end main


    public static void readInput(InputStream is)
        throws IOException
    {
        int ich;
        int count;
        int spaces = 0;
        int digits = 0;
        int lowers = 0;
        int uppers = 0;

        for (count = 0; (ich = is.read()) != -1; count++)
        {
            char ch = (char)ich;

            if (Character.isSpace(ch))
            {
                spaces++;
            }
            else if (Character.isDigit(ch))
            {
                digits++;
```

continues

Listing 11.1, Continued

```
            }
            else if (Character.isLowerCase(ch))
            {
                lowers++;
            }
            else if (Character.isUpperCase(ch))
            {
                uppers++;

            } // end if


        }  // end for

        System.out.println("Total chars "+count+
            "\n\tspaces = "+spaces+
            "\n\tdigits = "+digits+
            "\n\tlowers = "+lowers+
            "\n\tuppers = "+uppers);

        double density;

        density = ((double)spaces)/((double)count);
        System.out.println("\n\twhite space ratio = "+density);

    }  // end readInput

} // end ReadInputStream
```

If you want to read the contents of the input stream into a byte array, you can use the following read method:

```
public int read(byte b[]) throws IOException;
```

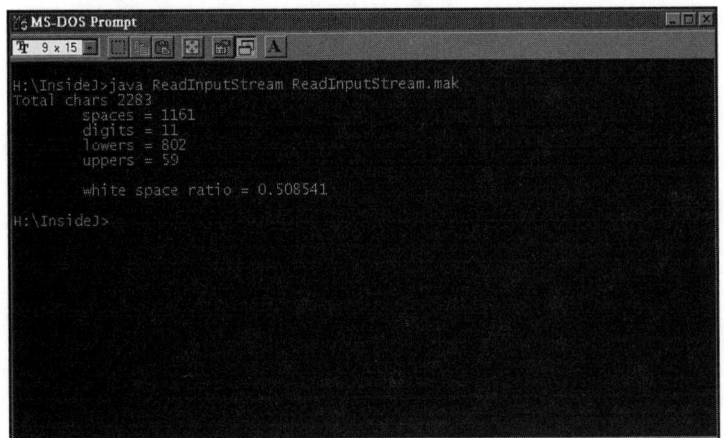

Figure 11.2
Output of ReadInput-Stream.

Consider the following code fragment that illustrates the use of this `read()` method:

```
InputStream is = new FileInputStream("testfile.dat");
byte[] buff = new byte[2048];

int bytesRead;
bytesRead = is.read();
if (bytesRead == -1)
{
      System.out.println("End of File");

}
else
{
      System.out.println("Bytes read = "+bytesRead);
      if (bytesRead < buff.length)
      {
         System.out.println("Buffer not full");
      }
      else
      {
         System.out.println("Buffer full");

      } // end if

} // end if
```

You can also read a specified number of bytes from the input stream into a slice of the byte array, starting from a specific location in the byte array:

```
public int read(byte b[], int off, int len)
            throws IOException;
```

Here is an example of using the preceding read:

```
try
{
    // Read 500 bytes starting at offset 10
    is.read(buff, 10, 500);
}
catch (IOException e)
{
    System.out.println(e);
}
```

If you would like to skip a certain number of bytes, you can use the `skip()` method:

```
public long skip(long n) throws IOException;
```

This method returns the number of actual bytes skipped. Here is an example of skipping the next 300 bytes from the input stream:

```
try
{
    // Skip 300 bytes
    bytesSkipped = is.skip(300);
}
catch (IOException e)
{
    System.out.println(e);
}

if (bytesSkipped != 300)
{
    System.out.println("Skipped fewer bytes");

} // end if
```

To find out how many bytes are available on the input stream, you can use the following method:

```
public int available() throws IOException;
```

This method returns the number of bytes that can be read from the input stream without blocking. Here is an example:

```
if (is.available() < 100)
{
      System.out.println("Nearing the end of the stream");

} // end if
```

Streams that model network connections or other abstract streams may not always return the correct number of bytes until the end of the stream. On a network connection, for example, the number of bytes waiting to be read may return zero, even though there is more data to be read. If you want a better answer, you will have to subclass the stream and define your own overriding `available()` method.

You can also mark a stream and then later reset the stream to the marked position by using the following methods:

```
public synchronized void mark(int readlimit);
public synchronized void reset()
     throws IOException;
```

The readlimit parameter to the `mark()` method specifies the number of bytes that you intend to allow to be read/skipped before you intend to reset to the marked position. This limit is used so that the stream can remember the bytes that may be skipped. If you read beyond this number and then attempt to reset to the marked position, the mark is no longer valid, and an exception will be thrown. The mark/reset is useful if you need to do an analysis of the data on the input stream up to a particular number of bytes to determine what type of data is being read, and then invoke a suitable parser to handle the data.

Before attempting to use `mark()` and `reset()`, you must use the `markSupported()` method to determine if the mark/reset option is supported for the input stream; otherwise, an exception will be thrown.

```
public boolean markSupported();
```

Here is an example of some sample code that uses the `mark()`, `reset()`, and `markSupported()` methods:

```
InputStream is = new FileInputStream("testdata.txt");
if (is.markSupported())
{
      is.mark(3000); // readlimit to 3000 bytes

      // Do processing

      is.reset(); // reset to the mark point

      // Now reread from the marked point

} // end if
```

After you are done reading the data, you should close the stream to release the resources associated with reading the stream:

```
public void close() throws IOException;
```

Here is a sample code fragment that illustrates the use of `close()`:

```
InputStream is = new FileInputStream("testfile.dat");
byte[] buff = new byte[2048];

try
{

      is.read(buff);
}
catch (IOException e)
{
      System.println(e)
}
finally
{
      is.close();

} // end try
```

The finally clause will always be executed, whether an exception occurs or not, and this will close the file.

The OutputStream Class

You have examined the basics of the InputStream class in the previous section. In this section, you will examine the basics of performing operations on output streams.

The OutputStream class is an abstract superclass for output streams, and it defines the basic output methods for all output streams. Because it is an abstract class you cannot instantiate it. There are several standard subclasses of the OutputStream that you can use for performing output operations.

The following is an overview of the methods in the OutputStream class.

```
public abstract class OutputStream
{

    // Public methods //
    // (--------------) //

    // This method writes a byte, b, to the output
    // stream. It will block until the byte is
    // actually written.
    public abstract void write(int b)
                    throws IOException;


    // This method writes an array of bytes, b,
    // to the output stream. It will block until
    // the byte is actually written.
    public void write(byte b[]) throws IOException;

    // This method writes a sub array of bytes, b,
    // to the output stream. It will block until
    // the byte is actually written. The sub array
    // is len bytes long and begins at off.
    public void write(byte b[], int off, int len)
                throws IOException;


    // This method flushes the output stream.
    // Flushing the stream will write any buffered
    // output bytes.
```

```
    public void flush() throws IOException;

    // This method closes the stream and releases
    // any resources associated with the stream.
    public void close() throws IOException;


} // end OutputStream
```

Because the OutputStream is an abstract class, you cannot create direct instances of InputStream. You can, however, take instances of subclasses of OutputStream. Consider the following example that writes 100 integers into the output stream.

```
OutputStream os = new FileOutputStream("testfile.dat");

for(int x = 1; x <= 100; x++)
{

      try
      {
         os.write(x);
      }
      catch (IOException e)
      {
         System.out.println(e);

      } // end try

} // end for
```

The FileOutputStream class is a subclass of the OutputStream class. This class is used for performing file output operations. The following line creates an instance of the FileOutputStream and assigns it to the os object:

```
OutputStream os = new FileInputStream("testfile.dat");
```

Within the for loop, a call to the `write()` method for the output stream writes the byte value of the integer to the output stream. The `write()` method can throw an IOException, so this must be caught or declared in the throws clause of the enclosing method.

Listing 11.2 shows a complete program that uses the `read()` and `write()` methods to copy a file.

Listing 11.2

```
Line==================Java Source=================
/**
 * CopyStreams: Illustrates using the input
 * and output streams. Copies input stream
 * to output stream.
 *
 * Author: Karanjit S. G. S. Siyan
 *
 */

import java.io.*;

class CopyStreams
{

    public static void main(String[] args)
    {

        InputStream  is = null;
        OutputStream os = null;

        if (args.length == 2)
        {
             try
             {
                 is = new FileInputStream(args[0]);
             }
             catch (FileNotFoundException e)
             {
                 System.out.println("File "+args[0]+" not found");
                 System.exit(0);
             }
             catch (IOException e)
             {
```

continues

Listing 11.2, Continued

```
                System.out.println(e);

            }  // end try


            try
            {
                os = new FileOutputStream(args[1]);

            }
            catch (IOException e)
            {
                System.out.println(e);

            }  // end try

        }
        else
        {
            System.out.println("Usage:\n\t"+
                "java CopyStreams inputfile outputfile");

        }  // end if

        try
        {
            copyStream(is, os);
        }
        catch (IOException e)
        {
             System.out.println(e);

        }  // end try

    }  // end main

    // Copies is stream to os stream.
    public static void copyStream(InputStream is,
```

```
                                          OutputStream os)
        throws IOException
    {
        int count;

        for (count = 0;;count++)
        {
            int ch = is.read();

            if (ch == -1)
            {
                break;

            } // end if

            os.write(ch);

        } // end for

        System.out.println("Total bytes copied "+count);

    } // end copyStream

} // end CopyStreams
```

If you want to write the contents of a byte array to an output stream, you can use the following read method:

```
public void write(byte b[])
      throws IOException;
```

Consider the following code fragment that illustrates the use of this `write()` method:

```
OutputStream os = new FileOutputStream("testfile.dat");
byte[] buff = new byte[2048];

// Code to fill the buff array

try
{
```

```
        os.write(b);
}
catch (IOException e)
{
        System.out.println(e);

} // end try
```

You can also write a specified number of bytes from a slice of the byte array, starting from a specific location to the output stream:

```
public void write(byte b[], int off, int len)
            throws IOException;
```

Here is an example of using the preceding `write()` method:

```
try
{
        // Write 500 bytes starting at offset 10
        os.write(buff, 10, 500);
}
catch (IOException e)
{
        System.out.println(e);

} // end try
```

When you write to the output stream, your data may be temporarily cached in internal buffers before being written out to the actual destination. If you want to ensure that all data cached in internal buffers is flushed out to the destination, you can use the `flush()` method:

```
public void flush() throws IOException;
```

The `flush()` method for OutputStream is empty. Subclasses of OutputStream that implement buffering are expected to override the `flush()` method with logic that will perform the flushing action on the internal buffers. The output stream classes BufferedOutputStream and PrintStream implement buffering.

Here is an example of the use of the `flush()` method:

```
// Output stream, os, constructed
// that uses buffering.

byte[] buff = new byte[2048];

// Code to fill the buff array

try
{
      os.write(b);
      os.flush();
}
catch (IOException e)
{
      System.out.println(e);

} // end try
```

After you are done writing the data, you should close the stream to release the resources associated with writing the stream:

```
public void close() throws IOException;
```

Here is a sample code fragment that illustrates the use of `close()`:

```
OutputStream os = new FileOutputStream("testfile.dat");
byte[] buff = new byte[2048];

// Code to fill the byte array buff.

try
{

      os.write(buff);
}
catch (IOException e)
{
      System.println(e)
}
finally
```

```
{
      os.close();

} // end try
```

The finally clause will always be executed, whether an exception occurs or not, and this will close the file.

Other Classes for Input/Output

So far you have examined the basic operations that are available for input and output streams. Java provides a number of additional classes that you can use to enhance these basic operations. These classes include the following:

- File
- ByteArrayInputStream and ByteArrayOutputStream
- StringBufferInputStream
- FilterInputStream and FilterOutputStream
- BufferedInputStream and BufferedOutputStream
- DataInputStream and DataOutputStream
- PipedInputStream and PipedOutputStream
- SequenceInputStream
- LineNumberInputStream
- PushbackInputStream
- PrintStream
- RandomAccessFile

Using the File Class

The File class provides a way of describing files and directories. After you build an instance of the file class, you can query the file object for information about the file or directory.

The class includes several different types of constructors for convenience in building the File object:

```
File fo1 = new File("testfile.dat");
File fo2 = new File("/docs", "file.dat");
```

You can then use test methods such as `canRead()`, `isFile()`, and so on, to test the properties of files and directories. Many of these tests are implemented internally by calling native methods for the underlying operating system and platform on which the Java environment is hosted.

Here is a detailed description of the File class methods:

```
public class File
{
    // Public constants //
    // ---------------- //

    // The system dependent file separator String
    // such as a forward slash (/) or backslash (\).
    public static final String separator;

    // The system dependent file separator character
    // such as a forward slash (/) or backslash (\)
    public static final char separatorChar;


    // The system dependent path separator String
    // such as a forward slash (/) or backslash (\).
    // Usually the same as the fileSepartor but
    // could be different.
    public static final String pathSeparator;



    // The system dependent path separator String
    // such as a forward slash (/) or backslash (\).
    // Usually the same as the fileSepartor but
    // could be different.
    public static final char pathSeparatorChar;
```

```
// Constructors

// Constructor 1:
// Build a File class given path name of file
public File(String path);

// Constructor 2:
// Creates a File object given the directory path
// of the file object and the file name.
// Concatenates path and name using separator
// variable to form the path name and calls
// constructor 1.
public File(String path, String name);


// Constructor 3:
// Creates a File object given the directory name
// and the file name.
// Obtains path of the directory, and calls
// constructor 2.
public File(File dir, String name);

// Public Methods //
// -------------- //

// Returns the name of the file without the
// directory prefix.
public String getName();

// Returns the path of the file that was
// built when the constructor was called.
public String getPath();

// Returns the complete path name of the file.
// If the path that was specified when the
// File constructor was called was a relative
// path name, it prepends the current directory
// to build the complete path name.
```

```
public String getAbsolutePath();


// Returns the parent directory. It returns if
// the path that was specified in the constructor
// for File was specified without a directory.
public String getParent();

// Returns a boolean indicating whether or not a
// file exists.
public boolean exists();

// Returns a boolean indicating whether or not
// a writable file exists.
public boolean canWrite();


// Returns a boolean indicating whether or not
// a readable file exists.

// Returns a boolean indicating whether or not
// a normal file exists.
public boolean isFile();


// Returns a boolean indicating whether or not
// a directory file exists.
public boolean isDirectory();

// Returns a boolean indicating whether the
// file name is absolute.
public native boolean isAbsolute();
// Returns the last modification time.
// The return value should only be used to
// compare modification dates. Its absolute
// value does not have any official meaning.
public long lastModified();
```

```
// Returns the length of the file in bytes.
public long length();


// Creates a directory and returns a boolean
// indicating the success of the creation.
public boolean mkdir();

// Renames a file and returns a boolean indicating
// whether or not the rename operation was
// successful.

public boolean renameTo(File dest);

// Creates all directories that are part of the
// path used to build the File object. It returns
// true if all directories in this path are
// created.

public boolean mkdirs();

// Lists the files in a directory. Works only on
// directories. The list will include all files
// that match the * wildcard, except the
// equivalent of "." (current directory) and
// ".." (parent directory).

public String[] list();

// Uses the specified filter to list files
// in a directory.
public String[] list(FilenameFilter filter);


// Deletes the specified file. Returns true
// if the delete operation was successful.
public boolean delete();
```

```
    // This computes a hashcode for the file.
    // This method overrides the Object.hashcode().
    // The current hashcode returns the exclusive OR
    // of the Object.hashcode() and
    // the constant 1234321.
    public int hashCode();

    // This compares this object against the
    // specified object.
    public boolean equals(Object obj);


    // Returns a String object representing
    // the File object's path. Is the same as
    // a call to getPath().
    public String toString();

} // end File
```

Using ByteArrayInputStream and ByteArrayOutputStream

Just as you can read data from a file or write data to a file, you may at times need to read data from a sequence of memory locations, or write data to these locations by using input and output stream methods.

If, for example, you need to read memory data as a stream, you can use the ByteArrayInputStream.

```
// Define a byte array
byte[] buff = new byte[100];

// Fill the byte array
for (int x = 0; x < buff.length; x++)
{
      buff[x] = x;

} // end for
```

```
// Create an instance of the ByteArrayInputStream
InputStream is = new ByteArrayInputStream(buff);

byte[] obuff = new byte[100];

// Reads input stream into obuff
is.read(obuff)
```

The use of the `available()` method returns the number of bytes in the array of bytes that have not been read. If you use `available()` on the input stream before any bytes have been read, it will always return the length of the array. If you call `reset()` on the ByteArrayInputStream, the stream will be reset to the beginning of the buffer, regardless of where the `mark()` method was called.

You can also create an instance of the ByteArrayInputStream by using a slice of a byte array.

```
// Input stream set to bytes 10 to 69 of the array.
InputStream is1 = new ByteArrayInputStream(buff, 10, 50);
```

You can similarly use ByteArrayOutputStream to redirect the output stream to an array of bytes:

```
// Create an instance of the ByteArrayOutputStream
OutputStream os = new ByteArrayInputStream();

for (int x = 0; x < 1000; x++)
{
      os.write(x);

} // end for
```

In the preceding code fragment, the size of the internal array for os will expand to any length to accommodate new data that is written. If you want to provide an initial capacity for the output stream array, you can pass the size of this array as an argument to the constructor forByteArrayOutputStream:

```
// Set the initial size of internal array to 1024 bytes
OutputStream os1 = new ByteArrayOutputStream(1024);
```

You can write the array to another stream by using the `writeTo()` method:

```
public synchronized void writeTo(OutputStream out)
      throws IOException;
```

To extract the internal array to a byte array, use the `toByteArray()` method:

```
public synchronized byte[] toByteArray();
```

To convert the internal array to a string, you can use the `toString()` method:

```
public String toString();
public String toString(int hibyte);
```

To get the size of the internal array, use the `size()` method:

```
public int size();
```

To reset the internal array so that old data is discarded and new data will be written from the beginning of the array, use the `reset()` method:

```
public synchronized void reset();
```

Here are example of using these methods:

```
// Extract to an array of bytes
byte[] extractArray = os.toByteArray();

// Convert to a string
String stringEquivalent = os.toString();

// Convert to a Unicode string using a value of 24 for
// the high byte.
String stringUnicodeEquivalent = os.toString(24);

// Get size of internal buffer.
int sz = os.size();

// Reset internal buffer
os.reset();
```

Using StringBufferInputStream

The StringBufferInputStream class is similar to the ByteArrayInputStream class. The difference is that input data is read from a String object instead of an array of bytes.

This class subclasses the InputStream class, defines the abstract method `read()`, and overrides the methods `available()`, `read(byte[] b, int off, int len)`, `reset()`, and `skip()`.

```
public class StringBufferInputStream
    extends InputStream
{

    // Protected variables //
    // ------------------- //

    // The String object in which the string is
    // placed.
    protected String buffer;

    // The position in the buffer for input
    // operations.
    protected int pos;

    // The number of characters to use in the buffer.
    // This is set to the length of the String.
    protected int count;


    // Public methods //
    // -------------- //

    // This constructor method creates a
    // StringBufferInputStream from the specified
    // String object.
    public StringBufferInputStream(String s);


    // This method reads a byte of data and returns
    // the byte read, or -1 if the end of the stream
    // is encounterd.
    // This method defines InputStream.read().
    public synchronized int read();
```

```
    // This method reads into an array of bytes, b.
    // The off parameter is the startof offset
    // into the data array.
    // The len parameter is the maximum number of
    // bytes read.
    // A value of -1 is returned when the end of the
    // stream is encountered.
    // This method overrides InputStream.read().
    public synchronized int read(byte b[], int off,
                                 int len);


    // This method skips the specified bytes of input.
    // It returns the actual number of bytes skipped.
    // This method overrides InputStream.skip().
    public synchronized long skip(long n);


    // This method returns the number of available
    // bytes in the buffer.
    // This method overrides InputStream.available().
    public synchronized int available();


    // This method resets the buffer to the beginning
    // of the byte array.
    public synchronized void reset();

} // end StringBufferInputStream

Here is an example of using the StringBufferInputStream:

String str = "An example string of data";
InputStream is = new StringBufferInputStream(str);

char ch = (char)is.read(); // Retuns 'A'
ch = (char)is.read(); // Returns 'n'
```

Using FilterInputStream and FilterOutputStream

The filter input/output classes are used to build a chain of filters. A filter reads data from an input stream, does some optional processing in the data, and sends it to an out stream, which is potentially read as an input stream by another filter or program (see fig. 11.3).

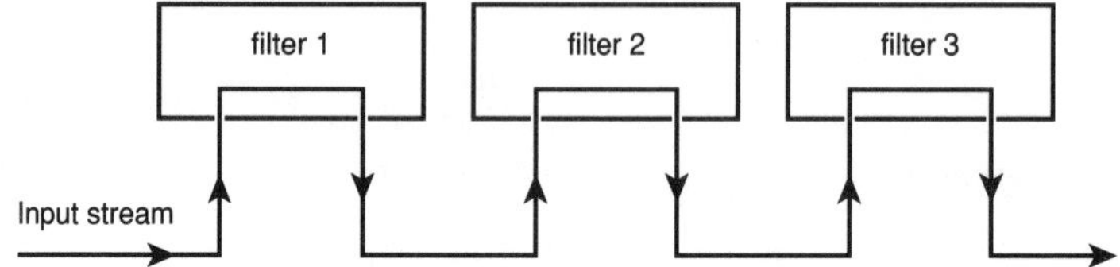

Figure 11.3
The concept of a filter.

The FilterInputStream class stores another input stream as part of its class definition. All method calls sent to the FilterInputStream are forwarded to this internal input stream. The FilterInputStream is constructed by passing it an instance of an input stream that will be stored internally. Consider the following chain of input filters:

```
InputStream is = new FileInputStream("test.dat");
FilterInputStream fis1 = new FilterInputStream(is);
FilterInputStream fis2 = new FilterInputStream(fis1);
FilterInputStream fis3 = new FilterInputStream(fis2);
FilterInputStream fis4 = new FilterInputStream(fis4);
```

Now consider the `read()` method sent to `fis4`:

```
fis4.read();
```

This will result in fis4 forwarding the `read()` method to fis3, which will then forward it to fis2, which will then forward it to fis1, which will finally forward it to stream `is` (see fig. 11.4).

The FilterInputStream class, in itself, does not do any processing but instead forwards the methods to its internal input stream. If you want useful processing to be done, you must subclass the FilterInputClass and provide the necessary processing. Examples of the standard subclasses of FilterInputStream are the following:

- BufferedInputStream
- DataInputStream
- LineNumberInputStream
- PushbackInputStream

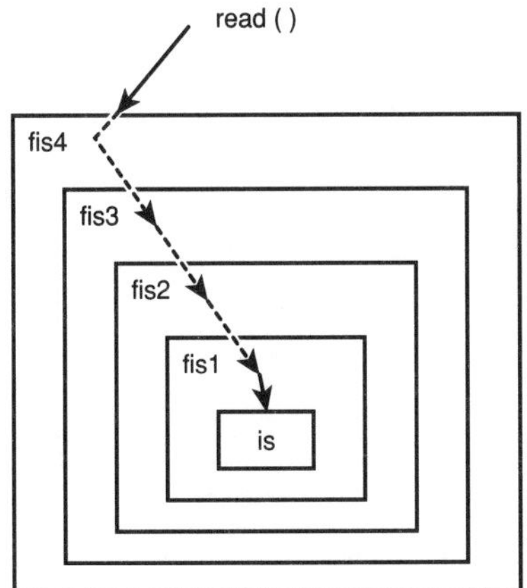

Figure 11.4
Method forwarding for the FilterInputStream class.

The FilterOutputStream is used to set up an output filter. The FilterOutputStream class stores another output stream as part of its class definition. All method calls sent to the FilterOutputStream are forwarded to this internal output stream. The FilterOutputStream is constructed by passing it an instance of an output stream that will be stored internally. Consider the following chain of output filters:

```
OutputStream os = new FileOutputStream("test.dat");
FilterOutputStream fos1 = new FilterOutputStream(os);
FilterOutputStream fos2 = new FilterOutputStream(fos1);
FilterOutputStream fos3 = new FilterOutputStream(fos2);
FilterOutputStream fos4 = new FilterOutputStream(fos4);
```

Now consider the `write()` method sent to fos4:

```
fos4.write();
```

This will result in fos4 forwarding the `write()` method to fos3, which will then forward it to fos2, which will then forward it to fos1, which will finally forward it to stream `os` (see fig. 11.5).

The FilterOutputStream class, in itself, does not do any processing but forwards the methods to its internal output stream. If you want useful processing to be done, you must subclass the FilterOutputClass and provide the necessary processing. Examples of the standard subclasses of FilterOutputStream are the following:

- ◆ BufferedOutputStream
- ◆ DataOutputStream
- ◆ PrintStream

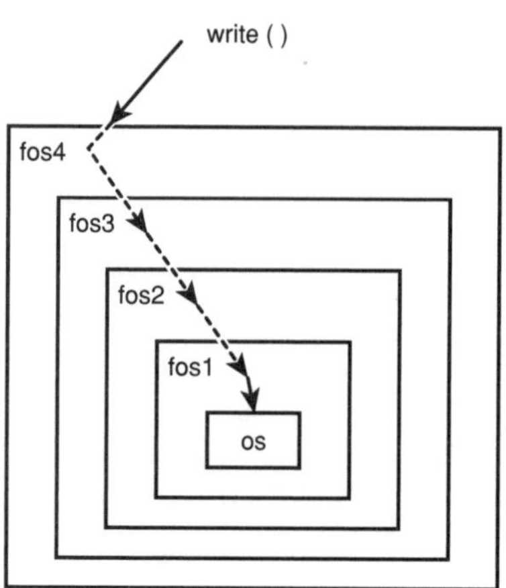

Figure 11.5
Method forwarding for the FilterOutputStream class.

Both FilterInputStream and FilterOutputStream override the methods of their respective superclasses: InputStream and OutputStream.

Using BufferedInputStream and BufferedOutputStream

The BufferedInputStream class overrides the methods of its superclass FilterInputStream to provide an internal buffering action that enables large amounts of data to be read internally within its buffer. Even though the FilterInputStream methods are overridden, the filter mechanism is retained. By using internal buffering, actual data is read in large pieces, such as the size of a disk block. Subsequent requests for reading are satisfied from the internal buffer and appear to be faster than disk access.

You can create BufferedInputStream objects by using any of the following constructors:

```
public BufferedInputStream(InputStream in);
public BufferedInputStream(InputStream in, int size);
```

The first form uses a default buffer size, and the second form uses a user specified buffer size as the second argument to the constructor. The default buffer size in current implementations of Java is 2048 bytes.

Earlier, you saw several examples of how to use the FileInputStream. This class does not implement buffering. To create a buffered version of an input stream class that performs file operations, you can do the following:

```
InputStream is = new BufferedInputStream(
        new FileInputStream("large.dat"), 4096);
```

The preceding statement input file stream class uses a buffer of 4096 bytes.

The BufferedOutputStream class overrides the methods of its superclass FilterOutputStream to provide an internal buffering action that enables large amounts of data that are written first internally within its buffer, and when the buffer is full to the actual output stream. Even though the FilterOutputStream methods are overridden, the filter mechanism is retained. By using internal buffering, actual data is written to internal memory, which appears to be faster than writes to the actual output stream.

You can create BufferedOutputStream objects by using any of the following constructors:

```
public BufferedOutputStream(OutputStream out);
public BufferedOutputStream(OutputStream out, int size);
```

The first form uses a default buffer size, and the second form uses a user specified buffer size as the second argument to the constructor. The default buffer size in current implementations of Java is 512 bytes.

Earlier, you saw several examples of how to use the FileOutputStream. This class does not implement buffering. To create a buffered version of an output stream class that performs file output operations, you can do the following:

```
OutputStream os = new BufferedOutputStream(
        new FileOutputStream("out.dat"), 1024);
```

The preceding statement output file stream class uses a buffer of 1024 bytes.

Using DataInputStream and DataOutputStream

The input/output stream classes you have seen so far process data as a stream of bytes. There are many applications where there is a need to process the data as one of the Java fundamental types, such as Booleans, bytes, integers, and floating point numbers. This is where the DataInputStream and DataOutputStream classes come in handy. By using these classes, you can write or read a stream of the Java fundamental data types.

The DataInputStream class extends the FilterInputStream class and implements the DataInput interface:

```
public class DataInputStream extends FilterInputStream
      implements DataInput
{
      ...
}
```

The methods of the DataInput interface are described next. The DataInputInterface is required to implement these methods:

```
public interface DataInput
{
    // Reads into byte array and blocks until
    // all bytes are read.
    void readFully(byte b[]) throws IOException;

    // Reads into byte subarray and blocks until all
    // bytes are read.
    void readFully(byte b[], int off, int len)
         throws IOException;

    // Skips bytes and blocks until all bytes are
    // skipped.
    int skipBytes(int n) throws IOException;

    // Reads in a boolean.
    boolean readBoolean() throws IOException;

    // Reads an 8 bit byte.
    byte readByte() throws IOException;

    // Reads an unsigned 8 bit byte.
    int readUnsignedByte() throws IOException;

    // Reads a 16 bit short.
    short readShort() throws IOException;

    // Reads an unsigned 16 bit short.
    int readUnsignedShort() throws IOException;

    // Reads a 16 bit char.
```

```
    char readChar() throws IOException;

    // Reads a 32 bit int.
    int readInt() throws IOException;

    // Reads a 64 bit long.
    long readLong() throws IOException;

    // Reads a 32 bit float.
    float readFloat() throws IOException;

    // Reads a 64 bit double.
    double readDouble() throws IOException;

    // Reads a line until the end of line or end of file.
    String readLine() throws IOException;

    // Reads Unicode text in UTF-8 format.
    String readUTF() throws IOException;

} // end DataInput
```

You build an instance of the DataInputStream by using the following constructor:

```
public DataInputStream(InputStream in);
```

Here is an example of using the DataInputStream:

```
DataInputStream dis = new DataInputStream(
         new FileInputStream("records.dat"));

// Now you can read the data in file "records.dat"
// as a stream of Java data types.

for(;;)
{
      // Assume record consists of int, long, double
      int fld1;
      long fld2;
      double fld3;
```

```
        try
        {
           fld1 = dis.readInt();
           fld2 = dis.readLong();
           fld3 = dis.readDouble();
        }
        catch(EOFException e)
        {
           break;
        }
        catch(IOException e)
        {
           System.out.println(e);
           break;

        } // end try

        // Code to process fld1, fld2, fld3.

} //end for
```

Within the for loop, a record is read that consists of an int, long, and double. When an IOException such as the EOFException is found, the for loop is exited. The preceding code also demonstrates the usefulness of the EOFException to sense the end of file. The EOFException is a subclass of IOException. You do not have to test for the –1 status code of the `read()` methods of the InputStream.

The DataOutputStream class performs data output of fundamental Java data types on output streams. The DataOutputStream class extends the FilterOutputStream class and implements the DataOutput interface:

```
public class DataOutputStream extends FilterOutputStream
        implements DataOutput
{
        …
}
```

The methods of the DataOutput interface are described next. The DataOutputInterface is required to implement these methods:

```
public interface DataOutput
{
    // This writes a byte, b. It will block until
    // the byte is actually written.
    void write(int b) throws IOException;

    // This method writes an array of bytes, b,
    // to the output stream. It will block until
    // the byte is actually written.
    void write(byte b[]) throws IOException;


    // This method writes a sub array of bytes, b,
    // to the output stream. It will block until
    // the byte is actually written. The sub array
    // is len bytes long and begins at off.
    void write(byte b[], int off, int len)
         throws IOException;


    // This method writes a boolean.
    void writeBoolean(boolean v) throws IOException;

    // This method writes an 8 bit byte.
    void writeByte(int v) throws IOException;

    // This method writes a 16 bit short.
    void writeShort(int v) throws IOException;

    // This method writes a 16 bit char.
    void writeChar(int v) throws IOException;

    // This method writes a 32 bit int.
    void writeInt(int v) throws IOException;

    // This method writes a 64 bit long.
    void writeLong(long v) throws IOException;

    // This method writes a 32 bit float.
```

```
    void writeFloat(float v) throws IOException;

    // This method writes a 64 bit double.
    void writeDouble(double v) throws IOException;

    // This method writes a String as a sequence
    // of bytes.
    void writeBytes(String s) throws IOException;

    // This method writes a String as a sequence
    // of chars.
    void writeChars(String s) throws IOException;

    // This method writes a String in UTF format.
    void writeUTF(String str) throws IOException;

} // end DataOutput
```

You build an instance of the DataOutputStream by using the following constructor:

```
public DataOutputStream(OutputStream out);
```

Here is an example of using the DataOutputStream:

```
DataOutputStream dos = new DataOutputStream(
        new FileOutputStream("records.dat"));

// Now you can write the data in file "records.dat"
// as a stream of Java data types.

for(int x = 1; x <= 100; x++)
{
      // Assume record consists of int, long, double
      int fld1;
      long fld2;
      double fld3;

      fld1 = x + 5;
      fld2 = x*5;
      fld3 = x*25;
```

```
    try
    {
       dos.writeInt(fld1);
       dos.writeLong(fld2);
       dos.writeDouble(fld3);
    }
    catch(IOException e)
    {
       System.out.println(e);
       break;

    } // end try

} //end for
```

Using LineNumberInputStream

The LineNumberInputStream is used to keep track of line numbers in the input stream. The line numbers are renumbered during the mark/reset operations. You can use the `getLineNumber()` to get the current line number and `setLineNumber()` to set the line number of the current line. If a line number is changed, subsequent lines are renumbered starting with the new line number. LineNumberInputStream is a subclass of the FilterInputStream.

Here is an example of how you can read data from a file as a stream of Java fundamental data types, and also buffer the data.

```
LineNumberInputStream lis =
    new LineNumberInputStream(
       new BufferedInputStream(
          new FileInputStream("rec.dat")));

DataInpuStream dis = new DataInputStream(lis);

String str1;

while ((str1 = dis.readLine()) != null)
{
    System.out.println("Read line "+lis.getLineNumber());
```

```
        // Process the string str1.

    } // end while
```

Note that this example uses a filter chain. The FileInputStream reads the data in the file. This data is buffered by using the BufferedInputStream filter, and later numbered by using the LineNumberInputStream filter. Finally, the input stream is interpreted as a stream of Java fundamental data types.

It is important to construct the filter chain in the order in which you expect to use the data in the stream. In the previous example, the DataInputStream had to be the outermost filter, as you were expecting to read Java data types. The inner filters should be nested in the order of their desired operation. If, for example, you are buffering the data, you must use BufferedInputStream as close to the data source as possible, as seen in the previous example.

Using the PipedInputStream and PipedOutputStream

The PipedInputStream and PipedOutputStream classes are used to build UNIX-like pipe streams. The PipedInputStream implements the input end of the pipe and the PipedOutputStream implements the output end of the pipe.

The PipedInputStream class is used to read data from the pipe that was written by using the PipedOutputStream class. Therefore, before using this class, you must connect it to the PipedOutputStream class. You can do this at the time you instantiate this class or by a call to the `connect()` method. The PipedInputStream contains very low-level methods for reading the data. A FilterInputStream may be used to provide a higher level of interface for reading data from the PipedInputStream class.

The PipedInputStream class subclasses the InputStream class, defines the abstract method `read()`, and overrides the methods `read(byte[] b, int off, int len)` and `close()`. The size of the pipe buffer in the current implementation is 1024 bytes. The methods for PipedInputStream are described next:

```
public class PipedInputStream
        extends InputStream
{

    // Public methods //
    // -------------- //

    // Constructor to create an input file connected
```

```
// to the specified PipedOutputStream.
public PipedInputStream (PipedOutputStream src)
  throws IOException;


// Constructor to create the object. But no
// connection is done as yet. You must
// connect it to a PipedOutputStream first.
// One reason for doing the connection
// later is that you may want to do some
// computation before deciding which
// PipedOutputStream to which to connect.
public PipedInputStream ();


// This method connects this input stream to
// the specified sender PipedOutputStream
// object.
public void connect(PipedOutputStream src)
       throws IOException;


// This method reads a byte of data. It will block
// if no input is available, and return a -1 if
// end of stream is encountered.
// This method defines InputStream.read().
public synchronized int read()
       throws IOException;

// This method reads into an array of bytes, b.
// The off parameter is the start of offset
// into the data array.
// The len parameter is the maximum number of
// bytes read.
// A value of -1 is returned when the end of the
// stream is encountered.
// This method overrides InputStream.read().
public synchronized int read(byte b[], int off,
       int len)  throws IOException;
```

```
    // This method closes the input stream. It must be
    // called to release any resources associated with
    // the stream.
    // This method overrides InputStream.close().
    public void close()  throws IOException;

} // end PipedInputStream
```

The PipedOutputStream class contains very low-level methods for writing the data. A FilterOutputStream may be used to provide a higher level of interface for writing data to the PipedOutputStream class. The methods for PipedOutputStream are described next:

```
public class PipedOutputStream extends OutputStream
{

    // Public methods //
    // -------------- //

    // Constructs the class using an output file
    // connected to the specified PipedInputStream.
    public PipedOutputStream(PipedInputStream snk);


    // This constructs the class that isn't connected
    // to anything yet. It must be connected before
    // being used.
    public PipedOutputStream();

    // This method connects this output stream to
    // a receive PipedInputStream.
    public void connect(PipedInputStream snk)
            throws IOException;


    // This writes a byte. This method will block
    // until the byte is actually written. Overrides
    // OutputStream.write().
```

```
    public void write(int b)  throws IOException;


    // This method writes a sub array of bytes, b,
    // to the output stream. It will block until
    // the byte is actually written. The sub array
    // is len bytes long and begins at off. Overrides
    // OutputStream.write().
    public void write(byte b[], int off, int len)
          throws IOException;


    // This closes the stream and releases
    // resources for the stream.
    public void close() throws IOException;

} // end PipedOutputStream
```

The following shows an example of using the piped stream:

```
PipedInputStream pis = PipedInputStream();
PipedOutputStream pos = PipedOutputStream(pis);
// A producer thread writes to pis.
for(;;)
{
      int x;

      // compute x
      pos.write(x);

} // end for
// The corresponding consumer thread reads from pis.
for(;;)
{
      int x;
      x = pis.read();

      // Process x

} // end for
```

Using SequenceInputStream

The SequenceInputStream class is a subclass of InputStream. You can use this class to combine two separate streams into one logical stream.

Data is read from the combined stream in the order in which the separate streams are specified. When the end of one stream is reached, data is read from the second stream in a seamless fashion.

```
public class SequenceInputStream extends InputStream
{

    // This constructs a new SequenceInputStream
    // initialized to the specified list e.
    public SequenceInputStream(Enumeration e);

    // This constructs a new SequenceInputStream
    // initialized to the two specified input streams.
    public SequenceInputStream(InputStream s1,
                               InputStream s2);

    // This continues reading in the next stream
    // if an EOF is reached.
    final void nextStream() throws IOException;


    // Reads a stream, and upon reaching an EOF,
    // starts to read from the next stream.
    // Returns -1 when all streams are read.
    public int read() throws IOException;


    // Reads data into a subarray of bytes, and upon
    // reaching an EOF it starts to read from the next
    // stream.

    // Closes the logical input stream. It starts
    // to read from the next stream, if an EOF
    // is reached. This method must be called to
    // release any resources associated with the
    // stream.
```

```
    public void close() throws IOException;

} // end SequenceInputStream
```

Here is an example of using the SequenceInputStream:

```
InputStream is1 = new FileInputStream("file1.dat");
InputStream is2 = new FileInputStream("file2.dat");

// Now combine these streams
SequenceInputStream sis = new SequenceInputStream(is1, is2);

for(;;)
{
      int data = sis.read();
      if (data == -1) break;

} // end for
```

Using PushbackInputStream

The PushbackInputStream class is used to implement a 1-byte push to the input stream by using the `unread()` method. The character that is pushed back into the InputStream is read by the next call to the `read()` method. This class could be used to implement a "lookahead" function, which returns the next character that would be read. This capability is useful in writing programs for parsing input. This class subclasses the FilterInputStream class.

```
public class PushbackInputStream
       extends FilterInputStream
{

    // Protected variables //
    // ------------------- //

    // The pushback character.
    protected int pushBack;

    // Public methods //
    // -------------- //
```

```
    // Builds the PushBackInputStream class from the
    // specified input stream.
    public PushbackInputStream(InputStream in);

    // This method reads a byte of data. It will block
    // if no input is available, and return a -1 if
    // end of stream is encountered.
    // This method overrides FilterInputStream.read().
    public int read() throws IOException;


    // This method reads into an array of bytes, b.
    // The off parameter is the start of offset
    // into the data array.
    // The len parameter is the maximum number of
    // bytes read.
    // A value of -1 is returned when the end of the
    // stream is encountered.
    // This method overrides FilterInputStream.read().
    public int read(byte bytes[], int offset,
                    int length) throws IOException;


    // This method pushes back a character to the
    // Input Stream. If an attempt is made to push
    // back more than one character, an I/O exception
    // is thrown.
    public void unread(int ch) throws IOException;

    // This returns the number of bytes that can be
    // read without blocking.
    public int available() throws IOException;

    // This returns true if this stream type supports
    // mark/reset.
    public boolean markSupported();

} // end PushbackInputStream
```

Here is an example of a code fragment that checks if the next byte from the file is a newline character. If it is not a newline character, the character is put back into the input stream and will be read on the next read:

```
FileInputStream fis = new FileInputStream("unknown.dat");
PushbackInputStream pis = new PushbackInputStream(fis);

// Code to process data in stream pis.

byte data = (byte) pis.read();
if (data != '\n')
{
      pis.unread(data);

} // end if
```

Using PrintStream

The PrintStream class is used primarily for displaying strings and Java data types in a human recognizable format. Therefore, this class is used for displaying messages on consoles or writing text data to files. The class defines several print() methods for different Java data types. As a convenience, a special version of the print method called `println()` is used to terminate the displayed value with a newline character. Using the `println()` version flushes the data in the output stream. All the data types that are converted to the String data type and this value are then displayed. This is different from the DataOutputStream, which outputs the binary representation of the value. This class does not display Unicode characters. The upper 8-bits of the 16-bit Unicode character are stripped, which results in the Latin-1 (ISO 8859-1) characters.

The System.out and System.err variables are both instances of the PrintStream class and are defined in the class System.

```
public class PrintStream extends FilterOutputStream
{

    // Public methods //
    // -------------- //

    // This constructs a new PrintStream.
    public PrintStream(OutputStream out);
```

```
// This constructs a new PrintStream, with
// or without auto flushing.
public PrintStream(OutputStream out,
                   boolean autoflush);

// This writes a byte. This method will block
// until the byte is actually written. Overrides
// FilterOuputStream.write().
public void write(int b);

// This writes a sub array of bytes starting
// at off and len bytes long.  Overrides
// FilterOuputStream.write().


// This flushes the stream which writes any
// buffered output bytes.
public void flush();


// This closes the stream and releases
// resources for the stream.
public void close();
// This flushes the print stream and returns
// whether or not there was an error on the
// output stream.  Errors are cumulative which
// means that after the print stream encounters
// an error this method will continue to
// return true on all successive calls.
public boolean checkError();


// This prints an object. It displays
// the String.valueOf(obj) as a string.
public void print(Object obj);


// This prints a String. Null strings
```

```
// are printed as "null".
synchronized public void print(String s);

// This prints an array of characters.
synchronized public void print(char s[]);


// This prints the specified character.
public void print(char c);


// This prints an integer.
public void print(int I);

// This prints a long.
public void print(long l);

// This prints a float.
public void print(float f);


// This prints a double.
public void print(double d);

// This prints a boolean as a
// "true" or "false" value.
public void print(boolean b);


// This prints a newline.
public void println();


// This prints an object followed by a newline.
synchronized public void println(Object obj);

// This prints a string followed by a newline.
synchronized public void println(String s);
```

```
    // This prints an array of characters followed
    // by a newline.
    synchronized public void println(char s[]);


    // This prints a character followed by a newline.
    synchronized public void println(char c);


    // This prints an integer followed by a newline.
    synchronized public void println(int I);


    // This prints a long followed by a newline.
    synchronized public void println(long l);


    // This prints a float followed by a newline.
    synchronized public void println(float f);


    // This prints a double followed by a newline.
    synchronized public void println(double d);

    // This prints a boolean followed by a newline.
    synchronized public void println(boolean b);

} // end PrintStream
```

Throughout this book, you have seen many example of the use of the PrintStream class, such as the operations of `println()` and `print()` for the system variable System.out. Here is an example of a print stream that automatically flushes:

```
// Passing a true value as a second argument to the
// PrintStream constructor automatically causes the
// print stream to flush.
PrintStream ps = new PrintStream(
        new FileOutputStream("debug.log"), true);
```

```
ps.println("Debug log file\n==============");

int x = 33;
float f = 3.14159;

// Print debug values of variables to debug file
ps.print("x = "+x"\tf = "+f);
```

Using RandomAccessFile

The RandomAccessFile class enables you to read and write bytes, text and Java data types to any location in a file. You must have appropriate access permissions to the file. For example, for read operations you must have at least read permissions; and for general update you must have read and write permissions.

Because the RandomAccessFile class is neither a pure input or output stream it does not subclass either InputStream or OutputStream. Note that Java does not support multiple inheritance so you cannot subclass two classes simultaneously. Instead, the RandomAccessFile class subclasses the Object class directly and implements the DataInput and DataOutput interfaces. This forces the RandomAccessFile class to implement the methods described in these two interfaces.

```
public class RandomAccessFile
      implements DataOutput, DataInput
{

   // Public methods //
   // -------------- //

   // This constructor creates a RandomAccessFile
   // with the specified file name and mode.
   // The mode "r" is for read-only and "rw"
   // for read and write.
   public RandomAccessFile(String name, String mode)
         throws IOException;
   // This constructor creates a RandomAccessFile
   // from a specified File object.
   // The mode "r" is for read-only and "rw"
   // for read and write.
   public RandomAccessFile(File file, String mode)
```

```
        throws IOException;


// This method returns the file descriptor
// object.
public final FileDescriptor getFD()
        throws IOException;


// Read methods //
// ------------ //

// This method reads a byte of data. This method
// will block if no input is available.
public native int read() throws IOException;


// This method reads into a sub array, b, as
// a sequence of bytes. The data is read at
// byte offset off and is len bytes long.
public int read(byte b[], int off, int len)
        throws IOException;
// This method reads data into an array of bytes.
// This method blocks until some input is
// available.
public int read(byte b[]) throws IOException;


// This method reads bytes into array b,
// and blocks until all bytes are read.
public final void readFully(byte b[])
        throws IOException;

// This method reads len bytes into the specified
// subarray at offset off and blocks until all
// bytes are read.
public final void readFully(byte b[], int off,
        int len) throws IOException;
```

```
// This method skips n bytes of the file.
public int skipBytes(int n) throws IOException;


// Write methods //
// ----------- //

// This method writes a byte of data. This method
// will block until the byte is actually written.
public native void write(int b)
       throws IOException;

// This method writes the array, b.
public void write(byte b[]) throws IOException;


// This method writes len bytes of a subarray,
// b, starting from offset off.
public void write(byte b[], int off, int len)
       throws IOException;



// This returns the current location of the file
// pointer.
public native long getFilePointer()
       throws IOException;

// This method sets the file pointer to the
// specified absolute position.
public native void seek(long pos)
       throws IOException;

// This method returns the length of the file.
public native long length() throws IOException;

// This method closes the file.
public native void close() throws IOException;
```

```
// Reads a boolean.
public final boolean readBoolean()
       throws IOException;


// Reads an 8 bit byte.
public final byte readByte() throws IOException;

// Reads an unsigned 8 bit byte.
public final int readUnsignedByte()
             throws IOException;

// Reads a 16 bit short.
public final short readShort() throws IOException;

// Reads 16 bit short.
public final int readUnsignedShort()
             throws IOException;


// Reads a 16 bit char.
public final char readChar() throws IOException;


// Reads a 32 bit int.
public final int readInt() throws IOException;


// Reads a 64 bit long.
public final long readLong() throws IOException;


// Reads a 32 bit float.
public final float readFloat() throws IOException;
```

```
// Reads a 64 bit double.
public final double readDouble()
            throws IOException;


// Reads in a line that has been terminated by
// a \n, \r, \r\n or EOF.
public final String readLine()
            throws IOException;


// Reads a UTF format String.
public final String readUTF() throws IOException;


// Reads a UTF format String from the given input
// stream. Note the use of the static qualifier
// that makes this a class method as opposed
// to the previous methods that apply to an
// object instance(instance methods).
public final static String readUTF(DataInput in)
            throws IOException;



// This writes a byte, b. It will block until
// the byte is actually written. Overrides
// OutputStream.write().
public synchronized void write(int b)
      throws IOException;

// This method writes a subarray of bytes, b,
// to the output stream. It will block until
// the byte is actually written. The subarray
// is len bytes long and begins at off. Overrides
// OutputStream.write().
public synchronized void write(byte b[], int off,
      int len) throws IOException;
```

```
// This method flushes the stream. This will
// write any buffered output bytes. Overrides
// OutputStream.flush().
public void flush() throws IOException;


// This writes a boolean. A true value is
// written as a an integer of value 1, and
// a false value is written as a value of 0.
public final void writeBoolean(boolean v)
       throws IOException;


// This writes an 8 bit byte.
public final void writeByte(int v)
       throws IOException;


// This writes a 16 bit short.
public final void writeShort(int v)
       throws IOException;

// This writes a 16 bit char.
public final void writeChar(int v)
       throws IOException;


// This writes a 32 bit int.
public final void writeInt(int v)
       throws IOException;

// This writes a 64 bit long.
public final void writeLong(long v)
       throws IOException;

// This writes a 32 bit float.
```

```
    public final void writeFloat(float v)
           throws IOException;


    // This writes a 64 bit double.
    public final void writeDouble(double v)
           throws IOException;


    // This writes a String as a sequence of bytes.
    public final void writeBytes(String s)
           throws IOException;


    // This writes a String as a sequence of chars.
    public final void writeChars(String s)
           throws IOException;

    // This writes a String in UTF format.
    public final void writeUTF(String str)
           throws IOException;


} // end RandomAccessFile
```

Here is an example of using the RandomAccessFile:

```
// Create a stream instance using read/write mode.
RandomAccessFile raf = new RandomAccessFile("file.dat", "rw");
byte[] buff = new byte[100];

// Read 100 bytes
raf.read(buff);

// Position to the 1000 byte location
raf.seek(1000);

// Write the first 100 bytes starting from the new location.
raf.write(buff);
```

Summary

Java provides a built-in mechanism for defining input/output by using predefined classes that you can instantiate or extend to provide additional functionality. In this chapter you learned the basic methods provided by the InputStream class and the OutputStream class. These classes serve as the parent superclass of the classes defined in the package java.io that are used for performing input/output. You were presented with a guided tour and examples of using the different input and output stream classes that are subclassed from InputStream and OutputStream.

CHAPTER 12

Networking with Java

Java provides a powerful set of classes in the package java.net that can be used for building useful applications that can perform network oriented tasks. Such tasks could include providing servers for other applications, building clients to access services on the Internet, or automating tasks such as file transfer or login to services on the Internet.

Overview of Networking Concepts

The primary communication protocol used on the Internet is TCP/IP (Transmission Control Protocol/Internet Protocol). The TCP/IP protocol is used by application services such as Telnet, FTP (File Transfer Protocol), and HTTP (HyperText Transfer Protocol) to provide services that are of interest to many users.

For the purpose of understanding how to write Java programs that use network services, the concepts are reviewed in the following sections.

Using IP Addresses

Every computer on a network has at least one network card. For a local area network (LAN), this is typically an Ethernet, Token Ring, or FDDI (Fiber Distributed Data Interface) network card. If you are a mobile user, you probably use a modem to make a connection to the network. Figure 12.1 illustrates some of these possibilities.

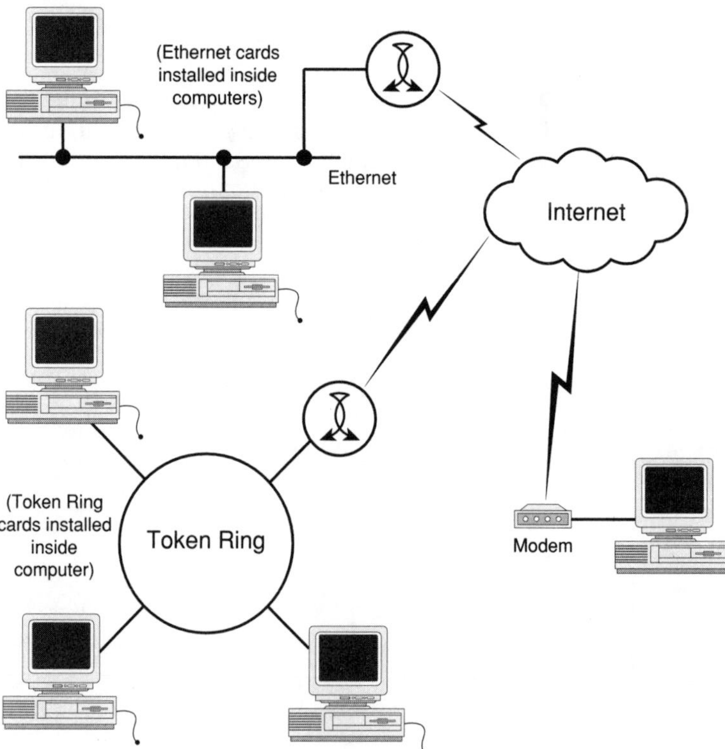

Figure 12.1
Network card for joining the network.

For a TCP/IP based network, every network connection, whether it be an Ethernet, Token Ring, FDDI, or modem link, is identified by an unique 32-bit number called the IP address. This number is typically written as a group of four numbers separated by periods. Here is an example:

```
200.12.34.171
```

Each of the numbers represents the decimal value of the four bytes comprising the IP address.

As mentioned earlier, every network connection must have this unique IP address. If you have two or more network connections, each network connection must have a unique IP address assigned to that connection (see fig. 12.2). Computers with more than one IP address are called *multihomed* hosts.

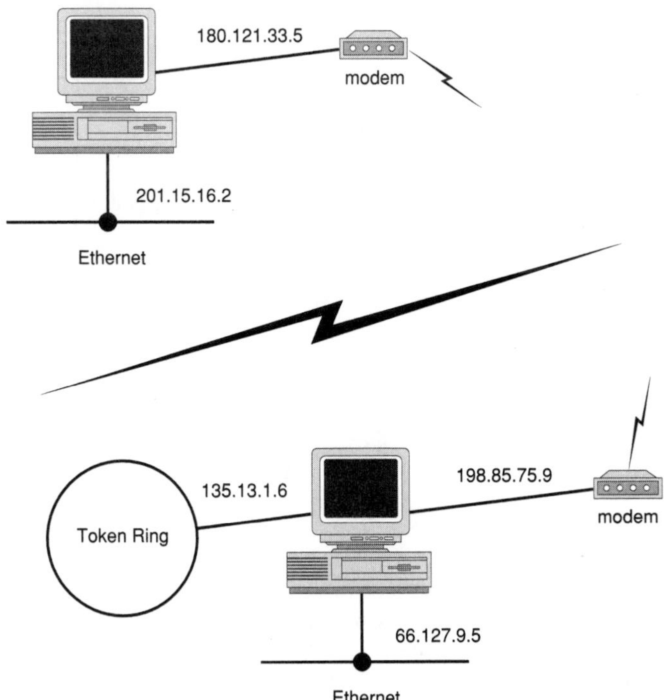

Figure 12.2
Multiple network connections.

In Java, the IP address is modeled by a special class called InetAddress. This class does not have a public constructor method, but provides three static methods to get an instance of the InetAddress class. The `getLocalHost()` returns an InetAddress for the local host. The `getByName()` returns an InetAddress of the specified host. If a host has several IP addresses (multihomed host), you can use the `getAllByName()` to return an array of IP addresses. You can use `getAddress()` on an InetAddress instance to get the

IP address as an array of bytes. If you want to get the host name corresponding to an IP address (also called an inverse query), you can use the `getAddress()` method on an InetAddress instance. The following are the declarations for the methods in InetAddress:

```
public final class InetAddress extends Object
{
   public static synchronized InetAddress getByName(String host)
   throws UnknownHostException;

   public static synchronized InetAddress[] getAllByName(String host)
   throws UnknownHostException;

   public static InetAddress getLocalHost()
   throws UnknownHostException;

   public boolean equals(Object obj);

   public String getHostName();

   public byte[] getAddress();

   public String toString();

   public int hashCode();

} // end InetAddress
```

Using Port Numbers

When your application makes a connection to a computer on a network using the TCP/IP protocol, it does not just connect to the IP address but to something called a port on that computer. This port is not a physical port, but a logical port specified by a 16-bit number. The port number is part of the TCP protocol, and it uniquely identifies an application service running on that computer (see fig. 12.3).

Common applications such as FTP, Telnet, and Web services have standard values for port numbers assigned to them. These standard ports are well known port numbers. Typically, port numbers 0–1,024 are already assigned. So if you are building a new application you should not reserve a port number in this range for your application.

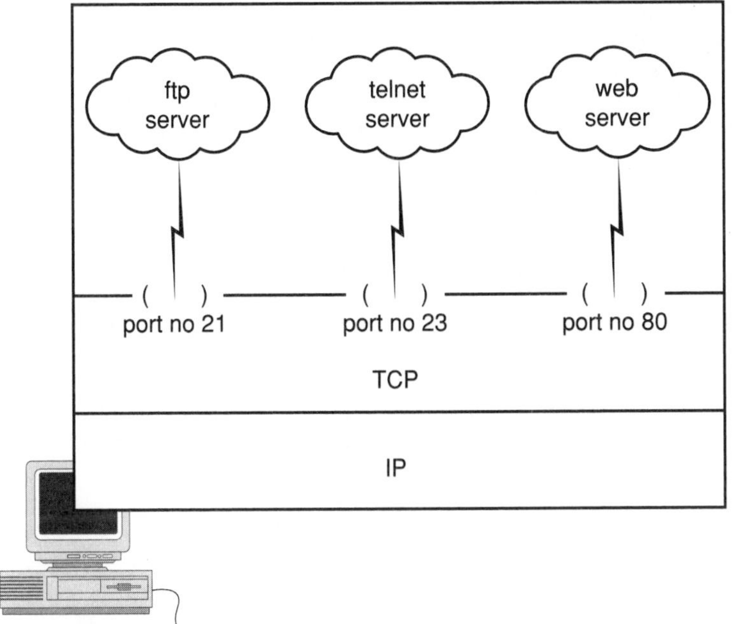

Figure 12.3
TCP port numbers.

Understanding Sockets

When TCP/IP was implemented on BSD UNIX, a low-level programming mechanism called sockets was created for writing programs to use the TCP/IP protocol. The sockets mechanism was modeled after the file input/output mechanism. To create a socket and connect to it, you use a set of system calls. After this point, you can use the socket as if it were a file. You can read from the socket or write to the socket.

In providing communication methods for accessing the TCP/IP protocol, the Java designers used the TCP/IP sockets mechanism to begin. There are a set of Java classes that model the sockets concept. These classes can be found in the java.net package and include the Socket and ServerSocket classes.

Implementing Clients and Servers on the Network

A *server* is a process that runs on a computer and provides services that are used by other processes, called *clients*, running on a computer. The server and client processes can be running on the same computer or different computers on a network (see fig. 12.4).

With JDK 1.1, several improvements were made to the java.net classes that enable sockets (Socket/ServerSocket) to be nonfinal and extendible classes. The goal is to enable extended sockets to be used wherever a base class Socket is used, without the need to rewrite application code. The one caveat to the modifications is that subclasses do not have direct access to the underlying SocketImpl in the bases classes.

The following is a concise list of the changes made to the Socket and ServerSocket classes:

- Remove the final modifier from the Socket and ServerSocket classes.
- Reattach the final modifier to only those methods where it is needed to avoid bypassing calls to the security manager.
- Define a new method in ServerSocket with signature: protected final void implAccept (Socket client) to use when initializing a newly accepted socket.
- Expose a default Socket constructor so that Socket subclasses could initialize their superclass without doing an actual connection in the superclass. This is also required so that a ServerSocket subclass can return the correct Socket subclass from `accept()`.

Figure 12.4
Client/server processes.

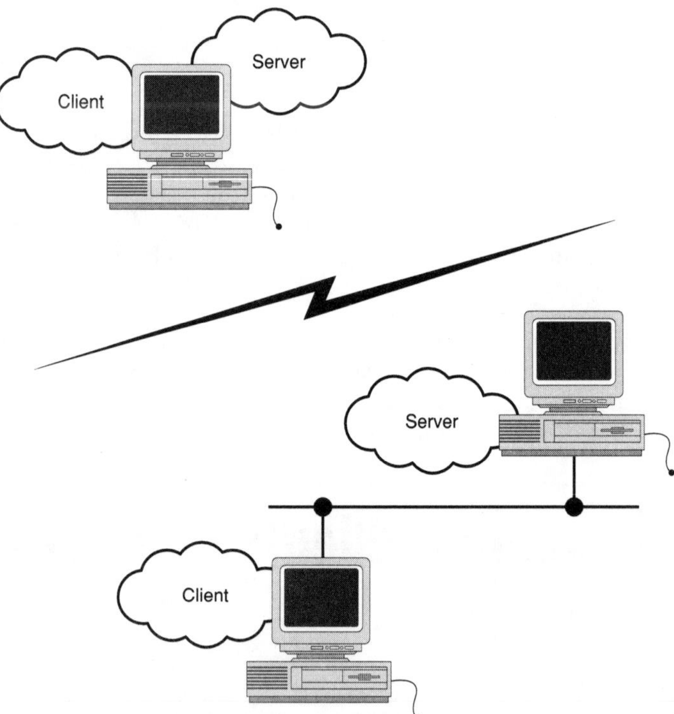

The following sections describe how a server and a client can be written in Java.

A Model for Writing a Server Application in Java

Figure 12.5 illustrates the model that can be used to write a server application.

Java provides the class ServerSocket to model the process of listening on a port for a connection (see fig. 12.5).

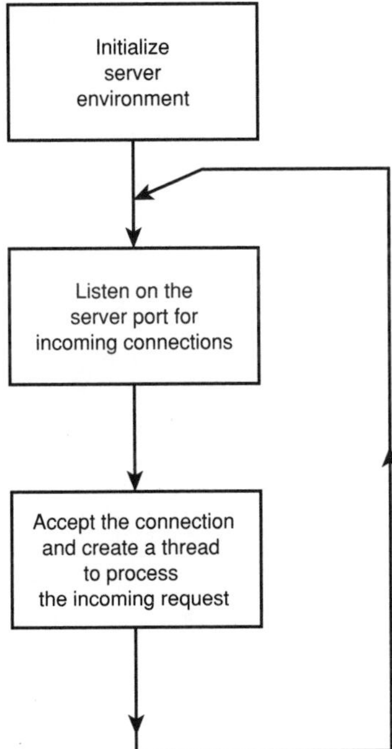

Figure 12.5
Model for writing a server.

The ServerSocket Class

You create the ServerSocket by passing to its constructor the port number on which the server should listen. When a connection request occurs, you can invoke the `getNetAddress()` instance method to get the InetAddress of the connecting client. The `accept()` instance method accepts the incoming connection and returns an instance of class Socket to handle future communication with the client. The method declarations for the ServerSocket are presented next.

Previously, all network errors in Java raised a SocketException, which didn't provide enough information to decipher what went wrong. JDK 1.1 adds three new classes that provide a finer granularity of reported errors. The one that deals with server-side errors will be introduced next. The other two deal with client-side errors and will be introduced in the next section.

The java.net.BindException is derived from SocketException. It is raised when the local port is in use, or when the requested bind address cannot be assigned locally.

```
public class ServerSocket extends Object
{

   protected final void implAccept(Socket client) throws IOExcpetion;
   public ServerSocket(int port) throws IOException;

   public ServerSocket(int port, int backlogQueueSize)
   throws IOException;

   public static synchronized void  setSocketFactory (SocketImplFact fac)
   throws IOException, SocketException;

   public Socket accept() throws IOException;

   public void close() throws IOException;
   public InetAddress getInetAddress();

   public int getLocalPort();

   public String toString();

} // end ServerSocket
```

The Socket Class

The Socket class is used for interprocess communications over a network. By calling the Socket class constructor method, you create a connection to the specified host and port number that is passed to the constructor. You can also specify if the communication through the socket should be a connection-oriented stream-based protocol such as TCP, or a connectionless protocol, such as UDP (User Datagram Protocol). UDP is a simpler form of transport protocol that does not guarantee the delivery that TCP does.

After creating the socket, you can use the `getInputStream()` and `getOutputStream()` instance methods to return an instance of the InputStream and OutputStream classes. With these classes you can perform any of the input/output methods discussed in Chapter 11, "Performing Java Input/Output." You can use `getInetAddress()` and `getPort()` to return the IP address and the port number to which you were connected. The instance method `getLocalPort()` returns the local port number that you are using. The method declarations for the Socket are presented next.

JDK 1.1 introduces two new exceptions to help refine the type of error that has occurred. Both exceptions are derived from SocketException.

The first is java.net.ConnectException, as is raised when a connection is refused at the remote host, implying that there is no process listening on that port. The second exception is java.net.NoRouteToHostException. This is raised when the connect attempt timed out, or the remote host is otherwise unreachable.

JDK 1.1 now provides a type safe way to set Socket options. Each socket class has a get/set method for each option it supports, taking and returning the appropriate type.

For the Socket and SocketServer classes these new methods are:

- TCP_NODELAY— Disable Nagle's algorithm.
- SO_LINGER— Specify a linger-on-close timeout.
- SO_TIMEOUT—Specify a timeout on blocking socket operations. (Caution: Never block forever!!!)

```
public class Socket extends Object
{

    public Socket(String host, int port)
    throws UnknownHostException, IOException;

    public Socket(String host, int port, boolean stream)
    throws IOException;

    public Socket(InetAddress address, int port)
    throws IOException;

    public Socket(InetAddress address, int port, boolean stream)
    throws IOException;

    public static synchronized void  setSocketImplFactory (SocketImplFact fac)
    throws IOException, SocketException;
```

```
    public void close() throws IOException;

    public InetAddress getInetAddress();

    public InputStream getInputStream();

    public OutputStream getOutputStream();

    public int getPort();

    public int getLocalPort();

    public String toString();

} // end Socket
```

Writing a Server Application in Java

The first step in writing the server is to initialize the server environment. But before you do this, you must define a class to represent the server program:

```
public class MyServer extends Thread
{

      // Constructor for MyServer
      public MyServer(int port)
      {
         // Code to initialize the server
         // environment.

      } // end MyServer

} // end MyServer
```

The server would be started with the following statement:

```
MyServer ms = new MyServer(portNumber);
```

The argument to the constructor is the port number on which the server is to wait and listen for a connection. The following is an example of how the MyServer constructors that initialize the server environment can be written:

```
public class MyServer extends Thread
{
      int   port;
      public final static int DEFAULT_SERVER_PORT = 4000;
      ServerSocket srvSock;

      // Constructor for MyServer
      public MyServer(int port)
      {
         // Code to initialize the server
         // environment.
         this.port = port;

         try
         {
            srvSock = new ServerSocket(port);
         }
         catch (BindException e) {
            System.out.println(e);
            System.exit(1);
         } catch (SocketException e) {
            System.out.println(e);
            System.exit(1);
         } // end try

         System.out.println("MyServer: Listening on port"+
port);

         start();

      } // end MyServer

      // Default constructor method
      public MyServer()
      {
         this(DEFAULT_SERVER_PORT);

      } // end MyServer

} // end MyServer
```

Within the MyServer constructor, the port number that is passed is recorded in the class instance variable port. An instance of the ServerSocket is created, and this is set to the class instance variable srvSock. The code in the constructor handles exceptions and prints messages. A default constructor is provided that creates a server socket with a default port number (4000).

At the end of the constructor a call is made to the `start()` method. Because MyServer is a subclass of Thread, the call to `start()` will result in a call to the `run()` method.

The `run()` method must be implemented in MyServer to implement the main thread logic. Here is an example of the `run()` method:

```
public void run()
{
    Socket clientSock;

    for(;;)
    {
        try
        {
            clientSock = srvSock.accept();
        }
        catch (UnknownHostException e) {
           System.out.println(e);
           System.exit(1);
        } catch (ConnectException e) {
           System.out.println(e);
           System.exit(1);
        } catch (NoRouteToHostException e) {
           System.out.println(e);
           System.exit(1);
        } catch IOException e) {
           System.out.println(e);
           System.exit(1);
        } // end try

        // Now process the connection request.
        ServerLogic srvLogic = new ServerLogic(clientSock);

    } // end for

} // end run
```

In the `run()` method, you set up an infinite loop. Within this loop, you call `accept()` on the server class instance, srvSock. This call will be blocked unless there is a connection request that is received.

When a connection request is received, you will return with an instance of class Socket. You pass this socket instance to a server logic thread that will deal with that connection. In the method `run()`, the class ServerLogic implements the server logic thread. An outline of this class is shown next:

```
class ServerLogic extends Thread
{
    protected Socket clientSock;
    protected InputStream is;
    protected DataInputStream dis;
    protected OutputStream os;
    protected PrintStream pos;

    public ServerLogic(Socket clientSock)
    {
        this.clientSock = clientSock;
        try
        {
            is = clientSock.getInputStream();
            dis = new DataInputStream(is);

            os = clientSock.getOutputStream();
            pos = new PrintStream(pos);

        }
        catch (IOException e)
        {
            System.out.println("IOException on getting streams for socket");
            try
            {
                clientSock.close();
            }
            catch (IOException ie)
            {
                System.out.println("IOException on closing socket");

            } // end try
```

```
            return;

        } // end try

        // Start the thread.
        start();

    } // end ServerLogic

    // Logic to handle client connection.
    public void run()
    {
        // Server logic to handle connection
        // goes here.

    } // end run

} // end ServerLogic
```

The ServerLogic constructor records the client socket in its instance variable. Next it performs `getInputStream()` and `getOutputStream()` on the client socket instance to get an instance of the input and output streams. The input stream instance is used to create an instance of DataInputStream so that incoming data from the client can be more easily handled. The output stream instance is used to create an instance of PrintStream so that printable string data can be sent to the client. The server logic thread is started by a call to `start()`. This calls the `run()` method. The `run()` method should handle the connection request and exit, at which the server logic thread will terminate.

The class instance variables for ServerLogic have protected access so that they can be inherited by another class that wants to subclass the ServerLogic and override the `run()` method:

```
public class MySpecialServerLogic
      extends ServerLogic
{

      public MySpecialServerLogic()
      {
```

```
         super();

      } // end MySpecialServerLogic

      public void run()
      {
         // Special logic

      } // end run

} // end MySpecialServerLogic
```

On the CD

Listing 12.1 shows a complete server implementation (file MyServer.java on the CD-ROM) that reads an input line sent by the client and returns the number of characters in that line. The logic of this program has already been presented in this section. The logic of handling the client message is in the `ServerLogic.run()` method on lines 153–176. The `main()` method to start this program is on lines 19–45. To run this program, you should make sure that you have a network connection, and that the TCP/IP stack is correctly loaded on your machine.

You could modify this program to do something more useful.

Listing 12.1

```
Line=================Java Source=================
001 /**
002  * MyServer: Demonstrates how a server can
003  * be written in Java.
004  *
005  * Author: Karanjit S. G. S. Siyan
006  *
007  */
008
009 import java.net.*;
010 import java.io.*;
011
012 public class MyServer extends Thread
013 {
014  private int port;
015  private final static int DEFAULT_SERVER_PORT = 4000;
```

continues

Listing 12.1, Continued

```
private ServerSocket srvSock;

    // main method to start the program.
    public static void main(String[] args)
    {
        int port;

        if (args.length == 1)
        {
            try
            {
                port = Integer.parseInt(args[0]);
            }
            catch (NumberFormatException e)
            {

                System.out.println("Expecting a numeric argument");
                System.exit(1);

            }  // end if

            new MyServer(port);
        }
        else
        {
            new MyServer();

        }  // end if

    }  // end main

    // Constructor for MyServer
    public MyServer(int port)
    {
         // Code to initialize the server
         // environment.
         this.port = port;

```

```
        try
        {
              srvSock = new ServerSocket(port);
        }
        catch (BindException e) {
           System.out.println(e);
           System.exit(1);
        } catch (SocketException e) {
           System.out.println(e);
           System.exit(1);
        } // end try
        System.out.println("MyServer: Listening on port"+
              port);

       // Start the thread.
       start();

  } // end MyServer

  // Default constructor method
  public MyServer()
  {
       this(DEFAULT_SERVER_PORT);

  } // end MyServer

  // run method overrides method in Thread.
  public void run()
  {
     Socket clientSock;

     for(;;)
     {
        try
        {
           clientSock = srvSock.accept();
        }
        catch (IOException e)
```

continues

Listing 12.1, Continued

```
            {
                System.out.println("IOException on accept");
                System.exit(1);

            }  // end try

            // Now process the connection request.
            ServerLogic srvLogic = new ServerLogic(clientSock);

            srvLogic = null; // Mark it for garbage collection

        }  // end for

    }  // end run

} // end MyServer

// Class ServerLogic to handle connection request.
class ServerLogic extends Thread
{
    protected Socket clientSock;
    protected InputStream is;
    protected DataInputStream dis;
    protected OutputStream os;
    protected PrintStream pos;

    public ServerLogic(Socket clientSock)
    {
        this.clientSock = clientSock;
        try
        {
            is = clientSock.getInputStream();
            dis = new DataInputStream(is);

            os = clientSock.getOutputStream();
            pos = new PrintStream(pos);

```

```
        }
        catch (IOException e)
        {
            System.out.println("IOException on getting streams for
➥socket");
            try
            {
                clientSock.close();
            }
            catch (IOException ie)
            {
                System.out.println("IOException on closing socket");

            }  // end try

            return;

        }  // end try

        // Start the thread.
        start();

    }  // end ServerLogic

    // Logic to handle client connection.
    public void run()
    {
        // Server logic to handle connection
        // goes here.

        String clientMsg;

        try
        {
            clientMsg = dis.readLine();
        }
        catch (IOException e)
        {
```

continues

Listing 12.1, Continued

```
            System.out.println("IOException reading line:\n"+e);
            return;

        }  // end try

        int msgLen = clientMsg.length();
        pos.println("Client message had "+msgLen+" characters.");

        // Thread terminates at this point.

    }  // end run

}  // end ServerLogic
```

Writing a Client Application in Java

Writing a client application in Java is simpler than writing a server application. There are usually no threads to create because the client is dedicated to making requests only and dealing with the response.

Listing 12.2 shows a sample client program (file MyClient.java on the CD-ROM) that could be used with the MyServer program of listing 12.1. The client program expects to be invoked as follows:

```
java MyClient host [port]
```

If a port number is not specified, a default port number is used to make the connection to the host. The client program reads input from the user from the console, sends it to the server, reads the output from the server, and prints the output on the console. If the user enters an empty line, or an error occurs in the input/output operations, the client terminates.

Note If the MyClient.java program after compiling with javac goes into a loop when an IOException is raised, your version of javac is generating incorrect bytecode. You can verify this by compiling the program with a competing vendor's Java compiler. The CD-ROM that is included with this book contains a version of MyClass.class that was compiled by using the Symantec Cafe compiler, and works correctly when exceptions are raised.

Listing 12.2

```
Line=================Java Source=================
/**
 * MyClient: Demonstrates how a client can
 * be written in Java.
 *
 * Author: Karanjit S. G. S. Siyan
 *
 */

import java.net.*;
import java.io.*;

public class MyClient extends Object
{
    private int  port;
    private final static int DEFAULT_PORT = 4000;
    private ServerSocket srvSock;
    private static String promptStr = "#";

    // main method to start the program.
    public static void main(String[] args)
    {
        int port = 0;

        if (args.length != 1 && args.length != 2)
        {
            printUsage();
            System.exit(0);

        } // end if

        if (args.length == 1)
        {
            // Port not specified
            port = DEFAULT_PORT;

```

continues

Listing 12.2, Continued

```
        }
        else
        {
            try
            {
                port = Integer.parseInt(args[1]);

            }
            catch (NumberFormatException e)
            {
                System.out.println("Must use a number for the port value");
                printUsage();
                System.exit(1);

            } // end try

        }  // end if

        // Invoke the client
        client(args[0], port);

    }  // end main

    // printUsage: Inform user on correct syntax
    private static void printUsage()
    {
        System.out.println("Usage:\n\tjava MyClient host [port]");

    } // end printUsage

    // client logic
    private static void client(String host, int port)
    {
        Socket clientSock;

        try
        {
            clientSock = new Socket(host, port);
```

```
        }
        catch (UnknownHostException e) {
           System.out.println(e);
           System.exit(1);
        } catch (ConnectException e) {
           System.out.println(e);
           System.exit(1);
        } catch (NoRouteToHostException e) {
           System.out.println(e);
           System.exit(1);
        } catch IOException e) {
           System.out.println(e);
           System.exit(1);
        } // end try
        // Connection created at this point.
        System.out.println("Connected to the host "+
            host+"("+clientSock.getInetAddress()+")"+
            " at port "+clientSock.getPort());
        // Create streams for performing I/O.
        InputStream is = null;
        OutputStream os = null;
        DataInputStream dis;
        PrintStream ps;
        try
        {
            is = clientSock.getInputStream();
        }
        catch (IOException e)
        {
            System.out.println("IOException on getting input stream");
```

continues

Listing 12.2, Continued

```
        }  // end try


        try
        {
            os = clientSock.getOutputStream();
        }
        catch (IOException e)
        {
            System.out.println("IOException on getting output stream");

        }  // end try

        dis = new DataInputStream(is);
        ps = new PrintStream(os);

        // Now encapsulate System.in so
        // you can read lines from the console

        DataInputStream cis = new DataInputStream(System.in);

        // Prompt for input
        // Send it through the socket
        // Read input and display it
        // Terminate on an empty line.
        String buff;
        for(;;)
        {
            System.out.print(promptStr);
            System.out.flush();

            // Read a line from console
            try
            {
                buff = cis.readLine();
            }
            catch (IOException e)
            {
```

```
                System.out.println("IOException reading from console");
                break;

            }  // end try

            // If input is null exit loop
            if (buff == null)
            {
                break;

            }  // end if

            // Send the line read to the server
            ps.println(buff);

            // Now read the server output.
            try
            {
                buff = dis.readLine();
            }
            catch (IOException e)
            {
                System.out.println("IOException reading from socket");
                break;

            }  // end try

            if (buff == null)
            {
                // Nothing read. Server connection
                // probably closed, so exit loop.
                break;


            }  // end if

            // Display the result from the server on console
            System.out.println(buff);
```

continues

Listing 12.2, Continued

```

        }  // end for

    }  // end client

} // end MyClient
```

Using Datagram Services

The example of the client/server application that was given in listings 12.1 and 12.2 used the TCP/IP connection-oriented protocol. The TCP/IP protocol provides a reliable guaranteed delivery, but has additional overhead in terms of the connection being maintained for the duration of the session. Where the underlying network is reliable enough, such as in a local area network, you may use the UDP protocol that does not guarantee delivery. Because you expect the underlying network to be reliable enough, it is sufficient to use UDP for some applications. UDP is called a connectionless transport protocol because there are no connections preestablished prior to sending data. UDP, although less reliable than TCP, has the advantage of being a faster protocol.

JDK 1.1 now provides a type safe way to set Socket options. Each socket class has a get/set method for each option it supports, taking and returning the appropriate type.

For the DatagramSocket class there is one new option:

- SO_TIMEOUT—Specify a timeout on blocking socket operations. (Caution: Never block forever!!!)

Using the DatagramPacket and DatagramSocket Classes

To write programs that use UDP datagrams, you can use the Java classes DatagramPacket and DatagramSocket. The DatagramPacket class is used to create the data packet that is to be sent, or a datagram packet that is to be received. The DatagramSocket class contains the methods `send()` and `receive()` to send and receive packets. You use this class to send and receive the data.

The following shows the declarations for the DatagramPacket and DatagramSocket:

```
public final class DatagramPacket
{

    //
    // This constructor is used to create a DatagramPacket object used
    // for receiving datagrams.
    // ibuf = where packet data is to be received.
    // ilength = the number of bytes to be received.
    public DatagramPacket(byte ibuf[], int ilength);

    //
    // This constructor is used construct the DatagramPacket to be sent.
    // ibuf = contains the packet data.
    // ilength = contains the packet length
    // iaddr and iport = destination ip addr and port number.
    public DatagramPacket(byte ibuf[], int ilength,
    InetAddress iaddr, int iport);

    //
    // Returns the address specified in the send constructor
    public InetAddress getAddress();

    //
    // Returns the port number specified in the send constructor
    public int getPort();

    //
    // Returns the byte array where the packet is stored.
    public byte[] getData();

    //
    // Returns the length of the packet
    public int getLength();


} // end DatagramPacket
```

```
public class DatagramSocket
{

    //
    // Creates a datagram socket.
    // Binds the udp socket to any local available port.
    public DatagramSocket() throws SocketException;


    //
    // Creates a datagram socket
    // port = local port to use
    public DatagramSocket(int port) throws SocketException;


    //
    // Sends datagram packet to the destination address
    // p = DatagramPacket to be sent. The DatagramPacket
    // contains the buffer of bytes, length,
    // destination InetAddress and port.
    public void send(DatagramPacket p) throws IOException;


    //
    // Receives datagram packet.
    // p = DatagramPacket to be received.
    // On return, the DatagramPacket contains the buffer in
    // which the data is received, packet length,
    // sender's address and sender's port
    // number. This method blocks until some input is available.
    public synchronized void receive(DatagramPacket p) throws IOException;


    //
    // Returns the local port to which this socket is bound.
    public int getLocalPort();

    //
    // Close the datagram socket.
    public synchronized void close();
```

```
  //
    // Ensures that the datagram socket gets closed.
    protected synchronized void finalize();


} // end DatagramSocket
```

Sending a Datagram Packet

Listing 12.3 contains a program (file SendDatagram.java on the CD-ROM) that sends a datagram to a specified host and port number. The following is the syntax for invoking this program:

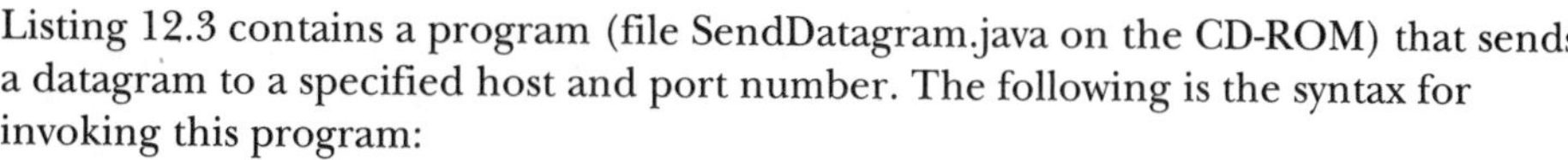

```
java SendDatagram hostname port message
```

or

```
java SendDatagram hostname message
```

In the second form, a default port number of 4000 is used to send the datagram. The message for this sample program is restricted to not containing blanks.

Most of the logic in the `main()` method (lines 16–74) is for parsing the arguments. The actual sending of the datagram is performed by the method `sendPacket()` on lines 86–113.

The DatagramPacket object is created on line 88, and the DatagramSocket object is created on line 93. On line 104, the `send()` method on the DatagramSocket object sends the packet.

Listing 12.3

```
Line=================Java Source=================
001 /**
002  * SendDatagram: Demonstrates how to send
003  * datagrams.
004  *
005  * Author: Karanjit S. G. S. Siyan
006  */
007
008 import java.net.*;
009 import java.io.*;
010
```

continues

Listing 12.3, Continued

```
class SendDatagram extends Object
{
    private static final int DEFAULT_PORT = 4000;

    // main method
  public static void main(String[] args)
    {
        InetAddress host = null;
        int port = 0;
        String msgStr = null;

        if (args.length != 2 && args.length != 3)
        {
            printUsage();
            System.exit(0);

        }  // end if

        if (args.length == 2)
        {
            // Port not specified
            port = DEFAULT_PORT;
            msgStr = args[1];

        }
        else
        {
            try
            {
                port = Integer.parseInt(args[1]);

            }
            catch (NumberFormatException e)
            {
                System.out.println("Must use a number for the port value");
                printUsage();
                System.exit(1);
```

```

            } // end try

            msgStr = args[2];

        }  // end if

        // Convert message to byte array
        int msgLen = msgStr.length();
        byte[] msg = new byte[msgLen];
        msgStr.getBytes(0, msgLen, msg, 0);

        // Get the host address
        try
        {
            host = InetAddress.getByName(args[0]);
        }
        catch (UnknownHostException e)
        {
            System.out.println("Host "+args[0]+" unknown.");
            System.exit(1);

        }  // end try

        sendPacket(host, port, msg);

    }  // end main

    // printUsage: prints the usage command.
    public static void printUsage()
    {
        System.out.println("Usage:\n\tjava SendDatagram hostname port
➥message\nor\n\t"+
             "java SendDatagram hostname message");


    }  // end printUsage

```

continues

Listing 12.3, Continued

```
    // sends the packet
    public static void sendPacket(InetAddress host, int port, byte[] msg)
    {
        DatagramPacket packet = new DatagramPacket(msg, msg.length, host,
➥port);
        DatagramSocket socket = null;

        try
        {
            socket = new DatagramSocket();
        }
        catch (SocketException e)
        {
            System.out.println("SocketException thrown:\n"+e);
            System.exit(1);

        }  // end try

        try
        {
            socket.send(packet);
        }
        catch (IOException e)
        {
            System.out.println("IOException thrown:\n"+e);
            System.exit(1);

        } // end try

    }  // end sendPacket

} // end SendDatagram
```

On the CD

Receiving a Datagram Packet

Listing 12.4 contains a program (file ReceiveDatagram.java on the CD-ROM) that receives datagrams on a specified port number on the host on which the program is run. The following is the syntax for invoking this program:

```
java ReceiveDatagram port
```

or

```
java SendDatagram hostname
```

In the second form, a default port number of 4000 is used to receive datagrams.

Most of the logic in the `main()` method (lines 16–53) is for parsing the arguments. The actual sending of the datagram is performed by the method `receivePacket()` on lines 65–113.

The DatagramPacket object is created on line 70. Because the DatagramSocket is a receive socket, no host address and port number are specified. The DatagramSocket object is created on line 77 with the port number to listen to specified as an argument to the constructor.

An infinite for loop is set up to receive datagrams. On line 94, the `receive()` method on the DatagramSocket object receives the packet. Assuming that the contents of the packet are displayable, they are converted to a string and printed out on the console (lines 105–108).

Listing 12.4

```
Line=================Java Source=================
001 /**
002  * ReceiveDatagram: Demonstrates how to receive
003  * datagrams.
004  *
005  * Author: Karanjit S. G. S. Siyan
006  */
007
008 import java.net.*;
009 import java.io.*;
010
011 class ReceiveDatagram extends Object
012 {
013     private static final int DEFAULT_PORT = 4000;
014
015     // main method
016  public static void main(String[] args)
017     {
018         int port = 0;
```

continues

Listing 12.4, Continued

```

        if (args.length != 0 && args.length != 1)
        {
            printUsage();
            System.exit(0);

        }  // end if

        if (args.length == 0)
        {
            // Port not specified
            port = DEFAULT_PORT;

        }
        else
        {
            try
            {
                port = Integer.parseInt(args[0]);

            }
            catch (NumberFormatException e)
            {
                System.out.println("Must use a number for the port value");
                printUsage();
                System.exit(1);

            } // end try

        }  // end if


        receivePacket(port);

    }  // end main

    // printUsage: prints the usage command.
```

```
    public static void printUsage()
    {
        System.out.println("Usage:\n\tjava ReceiveDatagram port\nor\n\t"+
            "java ReceiveDatagram");


    } // end printUsage

    // sends the packet
    public static void receivePacket(int port)
    {
        byte[] buff = new byte[16384];

        // Received datagram packet
        DatagramPacket packet = new DatagramPacket(buff, buff.length);

        // Listen datagram socket.
        DatagramSocket socket = null;

        try
        {
            socket = new DatagramSocket(port);
        }
        catch (SocketException e)
        {
            System.out.println("SocketException thrown in creating
➥DatagramSocket:\n"+e);
            System.exit(1);

        } // end try

        System.out.println("Listening for UDP datagrams on port "+port);

        for(;;)
        {
            String msg;

            try
```

continues

Listing 12.4, Continued

```
            {
                socket.receive(packet);

            }
            catch (IOException e)
            {
                System.out.println("IOException thrown on receive:\n"+e);
                System.exit(1);

            } // end try

            // Assume data is displayable
            msg = new String(buff, 0, 0, packet.getLength());
            System.out.println("Received packet from "+
                packet.getAddress()+", port = "+packet.getPort());
            System.out.println(msg);


        }  // end for

    }  // end sendPacket

}  // end ReceiveDatagram
```

Accessing WWW Resources

Java provides a flexible URL and URLConnection class to obtain information from resources on the network that have a URL address. You can create a URL class instance for a WWW address and then use the `getContent()` method for the URL class to download the content. The `getContent()` relies on content handlers that understand the format of the downloaded content and can convert it to an appropriate object. Currently, Java supports only the "text/plain," "image/gif," and "image/jpeg" data types. You can define your own content handler to understand other data types. This is done by many commercial Web browsers. It is not always necessary to define your own content handler. Instead, you can write your own application-specific program to parse the downloaded data.

Using URL and URLConnection

You can create URLs by specifying a single string value for the entire URL address, or separate values for the protocol (http, ftp, and so on), host name, port number, and file path. You can also create a URL by specifying a string value and a URL address relative to the string value. Creating a URL class instance can throw the MalformedURLException, so you must write code to handle this exception.

Here is a code fragment for getting the content of a URL:

```
// Create the URL instance. Enclosing
// code must handle MalformedURLException
String urlStr = "http://www.tsl.org";
URL url  = new URL(urlStr);

// Get the content of the URL
Object content = url.getContent();
String text;
Image img;

if (content instanceof String)
{
      text = (String)content;
}
else if (content instanceof Image)
{
      img = (Image)content;

} // end if
```

Besides using `getContent()`, you can also obtain the content of a URL address by using the URLConnection class. The URLConnection class is created by calling the `getConnection()` method of the URL class:

```
// Create the URL instance. Enclosing
// code must handle MalformedURLException
String urlStr = "http://www.tsl.org";
URL url  = new URL(urlStr);

URLConnection urlConn = url.openConnection();

// Gets MIME content type
```

```
String contType = urlConn.getContentType();

// Gets content length in bytes
int contLen = urlConn.getContentLength();
// Gets time last modified
// Milliseconds since epoch (Jan 1, 1970, midnight)
long lastMod = urlConn.getLastModified();

// Expiration time of the URL resource
// Milliseconds since epoch (Jan 1, 1970, midnight)
long expiration = urlConn.getExpiration();

// Get the content encoding of the URL
String contEncode = urlConn.getContentEncoding();

// Print out messages about the URL type
System.out.println("Content Type: "+contType);
System.out.println("Content Length: "+contLen);
System.out.println("Last Modified: "+ new Date(lastMod));
System.out.println("Expiration: "+ new Date(lastMod));
System.out.println("Content Encoding: "+ new Date(lastMod));
```

Alternatively, you can use the `openStream()` method of a URL class and get an instance of the InputStream class, which you can then read as an ordinary input stream:

```
// Create the URL instance. Enclosing
// code must handle MalformedURLException
String urlStr = "http://www.tsl.org";
URL url  = new URL(urlStr);

// Get the InputStream instance
InputStream is = url.openStream();

// Filter the input stream using DataInputStream
DataInputStream dis = new DataInputStream(is);

// Read the first 7 lines.
String line;
for (int x = 0; x < 7; x++)
{
```

```
        line = dis.getLine();

} // end for
```

Using WWW Resources from Applets

You can use the URL and URLConnection classes to obtain the contents of the URL and display them in any way you want within an applet. Alternatively, if you are running the applet from within the browser, you can pass the URL to the Web browser and have it display the content for you. This method passes the responsibility for displaying the contents to the Web browser, which has a greater understanding of how to handle and display different content types. You do this by getting the applets context first and then invoking the `showDocument()`method for this context.

One of the methods that is defined in the Applet class, the class all applets extend, is the `getAppletContext()`:

```
public AppletContext getAppletContext().
```

This method returns the AppletContext, which is the context in which the applet runs. This is usually the Web browser. The AppletContext is defined in Java as an interface class:

```
public abstract interface AppletContext
{
        public abstract Applet getApplet(String name);
        public abstract Enumeration getApplets();
        public abstract AudioClip getAudioClip(URL url);
        public abstract Image getImage(URL url);
        public abstract void showDocument(URL url);
        public abstract void showDocument(URL url, String target);
        public abstract void showStatus(String status);

} // end AppletContext
```

The `showDocument()` method for the AppletContext is used to pass the URL to the applet's context (the Web browser). Here is an example of a code fragment that can be part of an applet:

```
URL url = new URL("http://www.tsl.org");

if (url != null)
{
```

```
        getAppletContext().showDocument(url);

} // end if
```

The showDocument() method has a second form with a second argument that is a target string. The target string parameters has the following values:

"_self"	show in the current frame
"_parent"	show in the parent frame
"_top"	show in the top-most frame
"_blank"	show in a new unnamed top-level window
name	show in a new top-level window named *name*

The applet code in listing 12.5 (file AppletShowDocument.java) shows an example of using the showDocument() method within an applet. This applet reads the parameters in the HTML file shown in listing 12.6 to build a list of displayable buttons. When a button corresponding to a parameter value in the HTML file is selected, the corresponding URL address is passed to the Web browser.

The applet does not implement the paint() or update() methods, because all the logic is implemented in init() and there is no painting required. As the URLs are read from the HTML file, an array of class URLInfo is built. The URLInfo class is on lines 121– 155. The URLInfo class has two data items, which are the buttons corresponding to the URL and an instance of the URL class for the URL address value. The methods getURL() (lines 143–147) and getButton() (lines 149–153) are used to return the values of these two components.

The handleEvent() (lines) contains logic to find the button that was pressed. When the button has been identified, its corresponding URL is passed to the Web browser on line 105 by using the call to showDocument().

Listing 12.5

```
Line=================Java Source=================
001 /**
002  * AppletShowDocument: This demonstrates the use
003  * of the showDocument() method for
004  * passing the URL to the Web browser.
005  *
006  * Author: Karanjit S. G. S. Siyan
```

```
 *
 */
import java.awt.*;
import java.net.*;

public class AppletShowDocument extends java.applet.Applet
{
    protected int nurls;

    // Array of URLs
    URLInfo[] urla;

   /**
    * init(): Standard init method that needs to be overridden
    * for the applet class.
    */
    public void init()
    {

        super.init();
        System.out.println("init called");

        // Initialize parameters passed through
        // the param values in the HTML file
        //

        // Get the number of URLs
        String param = getParameter("nurls");
        if (param == null)
        {
            showStatus("No URLs specified in the HTML file");
            return;

        } // end if

        nurls = Integer.valueOf(param).intValue();

        urla = new URLInfo[nurls];
```

continues

Listing 12.5, Continued

```
        setLayout(new FlowLayout());


        for (int x = 1; x <= nurls; x++)
        {

            String urlStr = "URL"+x;
            param = getParameter(urlStr);
            if (param == null)
            {
                System.out.println("Incorrect or missing "+urlStr);
                return;

            }  // end if

            int posMark = param.indexOf('¦');
            if (posMark == -1)
            {
                showStatus("Incorrect url parameter"+x);
                return;

            }  // end if

            System.out.println("nurls="+nurls);

            String name = param.substring(0, posMark);
            Button b = new Button(name);
            add(b);
            urla[x-1] = new URLInfo(b, param.substring(posMark+1));

        }  // end for

    }  // end init

    // handleEvent for user interaction events
    public boolean handleEvent(Event event)
    {

```

```
        if (event.target instanceof Button)
        {

            for (int x = 0; x < urla.length; x++)
            {
                if (urla[x] == null)
                {
                    System.out.println("urla["+x+"] is null");
                    continue;

                }  // end if

                if (event.target == urla[x].getButton())
                {
                    URL url = urla[x].getURL();

                    if (url != null)
                    {
                        showStatus(urla[x].getButton().getLabel()+
                            " "+url.toExternalForm());

                        // Pass the URL to the Web browser
                        getAppletContext().showDocument(url);

                    } // end if

                }  // end if

            }  // end for

        }  // end if

        return super.handleEvent(event);

    } // end handleEvent

}  // end AppletShowDocument

```

continues

Listing 12.5, Continued

```
class URLInfo extends Object
{
    private Button button;
    private URL    url;

    URLInfo(Button button, String urlStr)
    {
        this.button = button;
        try
        {
            url = new URL(urlStr);
        }
        catch (MalformedURLException e)
        {
            System.out.println("Malformed URL: "
                +urlStr+"\n\t"+e);
            url = null;

        }  // end try

    } // end URLInfo

    Button getButton()
    {
        return button;

    }  // end getButton

    URL getURL()
    {
        return url;

    }  // end getURL

}  // end URLInfo
```

Listing 12.6

```
Line==================HTML Source=================
<HTML>
<HEAD>
<TITLE>Passing URL to Web browser</TITLE>
</HEAD>
<BODY>
<HR>
<APPLET CODE="AppletShowDocument.class" WIDTH=200 HEIGHT=190>
<param name=nurls value=10>
<param name=URL1 value=IBM¦http://www.ibm.com>
<param name=URL2 value=Hp¦http://www.hp.com>
<param name=URL3 value=Apple¦http://www.apple.com>
<param name=URL4 value=Cisco¦http://www.cisco.com>
<param name=URL5 value=Baynet¦http://www.baynet.com>
<param name=URL6 value=BSDI¦http://www.bsdi.com>
<param name=URL7 value=DEC¦http://www.dec.com>
<param name=URL8 value=ATT¦http://www.att.com>
<param name=URL9 value=Shiva¦http://www.shiva.com>
<param name=URL10 value=Xircom¦http://www.xircom.com>
</APPLET>
<HR>
</BODY>

</HTML>
```

Summary

Java provides a powerful set of classes in the package java.net that can be used for building useful applications that can perform network oriented tasks. You learned to use the classes Socket and ServerSocket to build a client/server program that uses the TCP/IP protocol. You also saw examples of using DatagramPacket and DatagramSocket for sending and receiving UDP datagrams. The URL and URLConnection classes can be used to access Web resources in Java applications and applets. You also learned how a Java applet can interact with the Web browser and pass URL information to the Web browser for rendering.

CHAPTER 13

The New, Improved AWT: GUI Components, Containers, and Layout Managers

Previous chapters detailed how to use Java's built-in graphic primitives to produce lines, shapes, images, and sounds. These primitives are included in the Java AWT (Abstract Window Toolkit, known as the Alternate Windowing Toolkit or Another Window Toolkit).

The Java AWT is a toolkit used to build applications. It is called abstract because the Java AWT enables the developer to write code to the AWT standard, and it is implemented by the underlying *windowing system* of the execution platform. A windowing system is the part of a platform's operating system that manages windows, GUI components, and events—like mouse-button clicks.

In this chapter and in Chapter 14, "The New, Improved AWT: Menus, Events, and More New Features," you will learn how to use the AWT to build Java programs that have GUI (Graphical User Interface) components such as buttons, menus, and text fields. Version 1.1 of the JDK

(Java Development Kit), developed by Sun, introduced many additions and changes to the AWT from version 1.0.2. For this reason, these chapters will focus more on the additions and changes than those features that remain constant. The JDK contains tools and Java class libraries for developing Java applets and applications.

This chapter covers the following basic building blocks of the Java AWT:

- Components, such as buttons and check boxes
- Containers, which contain the components on the screen
- Layout managers, which organize the layout of components within a container

Using AWT Components

AWT components are GUI elements (buttons, menus, and text fields for example) and can be used in any Java applet or application. All components are part of the java.awt package and are derived from the java.awt.Component class. Figure 13.1 illustrates the hierarchy of classes derived from the Component class. Take some time to examine this figure, because it will be referred to throughout this chapter.

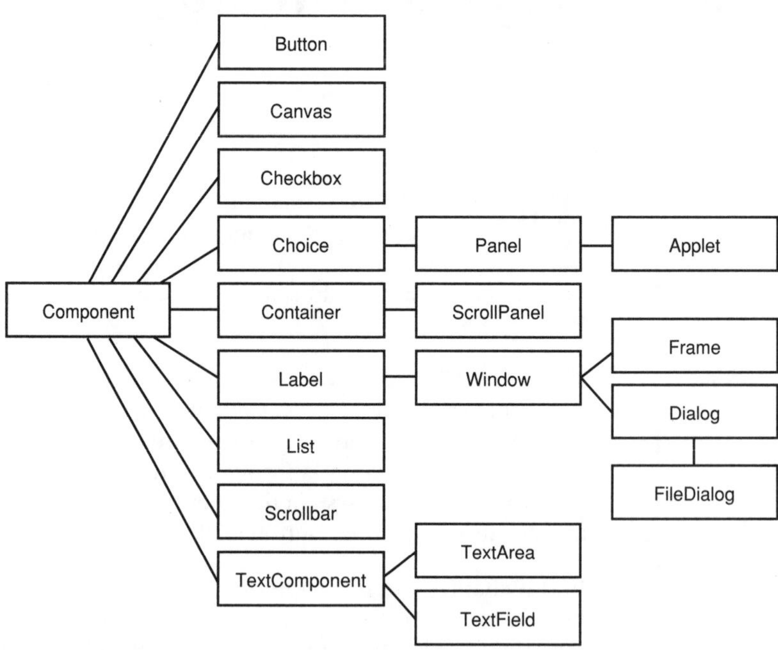

Figure 13.1
java.awt.Component class hierarchy.

In this hierarchy, the Component class contains by far the most methods. As with any class hierarchy, these methods are inherited by the derived classes. The `setEnable()` method, for example, (which is defined in the Component class) lets you either enable or disable a button, or any other GUI component in the hierarchy. The following section details the use of GUI elements in a simple Java program.

The HelloGuiWorld Applet

Listing 13.1, which is the program HelloGuiWorld.java on the CD-ROM accompanying this book, depicts an applet that serves as a simple example of how you can use GUI components in a Java program. Figure 13.2 displays this applet's user interface, which consists of a button and a label. When you click the button, the label displays "Hello GUI World!"; when you click the button again, the label displays "Goodbye!".

Listing 13.1

```
Line=================Java Source=================
//////////
// HelloGuiWorld.java  Example of using GUI components
// in a Java applet
//
// Author: James L. Weaver  JDK 1.1 beta1
//////////
import java.awt.*;
import java.applet.*;
import java.awt.event.*;

public class HelloGuiWorld extends Applet
                           implements ActionListener{

    // Declare a Button and a Label.
    Button pushButton;
    Label greetingLabel;

    String helloString = new String("Hello GUI World!");
    String goodbyeString = new String("Goodbye!");

    public void init() {

        // Create an instance of a Button that says
        // "Push" and add it to the applet.
```

continues

Listing 13.1, Continued

```
        pushButton = new Button("Push");
        add(pushButton);

        // Add an event "listener" for when an action
        // event happens to this button. The
        // actionPerformed method of the listener will
        // be called.
        pushButton.addActionListener(this);

        // Create an instance of a Label and add it to
        // the applet as well.
        greetingLabel = new Label(helloString);
        add(greetingLabel);
    }

    // This method is called when the Button is clicked.
    public void actionPerformed(ActionEvent e) {
        if (greetingLabel.getText().equals(helloString)) {
            greetingLabel.setText(goodbyeString);
        }
        else {
            greetingLabel.setText(helloString);
        }
        // Take next line out when bug in JDK 1.1 beta is fixed.
        greetingLabel.repaint();
    }
}
```

You can use the following HTML to run the applet in the Applet Viewer from Sun, or in a Java-enabled browser.

```
<HTML>
<HEAD>
<TITLE> Hello GUI World </TITLE>
</HEAD>
<BODY>
<APPLET CODE="HelloGuiWorld.class" WIDTH=300 HEIGHT=100></APPLET>
</BODY>
</HTML>
```

Lines 15 and 16 in listing 13.1 declare references to the objects of type Button and Label, which are named `pushButton` and `greetingLabel`, respectively. These instance variables manipulate the button and label GUI components that appear in the applet.

Line 25 creates the object to which `pushButton` refers. This form of the Button constructor takes one parameter—in this case the String "Push"—that appears on the face of the Button.

Similarly, line 36 creates the object to which `greetingLabel` refers. This form of the Label constructor takes one parameter as well, which is the text that appears on the label. The `add()` method in lines 26 and 37 adds the GUI components to the applet's display.

Note If you have written Java programs prior to JDK 1.1, you may be unfamiliar with the `addActionListener()` method in line 32 and the `actionPerformed()` method in line 41. These methods are part of a new event model, known as the Delegation Event Model, which is the preferred way of handling events. Using the `addActionListener()` method, the button registers an event "listener." When the event that is listened for occurs, the appropriate method in the listener is called—in this case, the `actionPerformed()` method. Chapter 14 will discuss the Delegation Event Model in more detail.

The `getText()` method in line 42 returns a String that contains the text currently displayed on the label. The `setText()` methods in lines 43 and 46 take a String as a parameter holding the text to be displayed in the label.

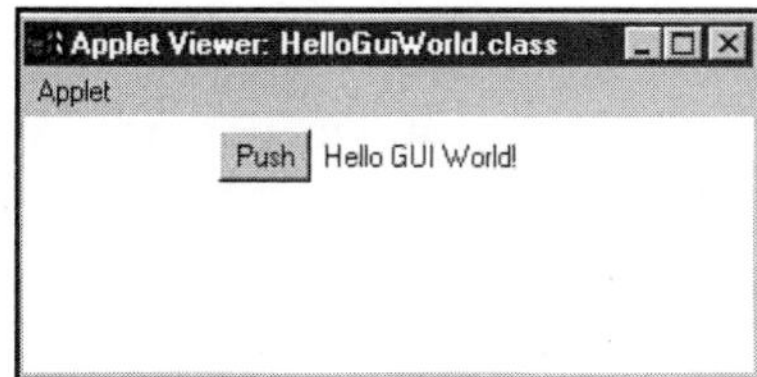

Figure 13.2
HelloGuiWorld applet display.

Table 13.1 lists some common methods used with Button. For a complete list, refer to the following Web page:

```
http://java.sun.com/products/JDK/1.1/docs/api/java.awt.Button.html
```

Table 13.1
Commonly Used Constructors and Methods in the Button Class

Constructor/Method	Description
Button(String)	Creates a Button with a specified label
String getLabel()	Returns the label that appears on the face of the Button
void setLabel(String)	Sets the Button label to the specified String
void addActionListener (ActionListener)	Registers an event listener to receive action events

Table 13.2 lists some commonly used Label methods. For a complete list, refer to the following Web page:

```
http://java.sun.com/products/JDK/1.1/docs/api/java.awt.Label.html
```

Table 13.2
Commonly Used Constructors and Methods in the Label Class

Constructor/Method	Description
Label(String)	Creates a Label with the specified String
String getText()	Returns the Label text
void setText(String)	Sets the Label to the specified String

The HelloGuiWorld applet described the basics of GUI programming in Java and illustrated how to manipulate the Button and Label classes. The following sections will detail other useful GUI components:

- Checkbox
- CheckboxGroup
- List
- Choice
- TextField

- TextArea
- ScrollBar
- Canvas

Checkbox and CheckboxGroup

Check boxes are useful GUI elements when you want to present the user with a true or false choice. You could use a check box, for example, in a "Find" dialog box to ask the user if the text to be found must match the case of the entered text. Check boxes can be grouped together into a CheckboxGroup, which presents a set of mutually exclusive choices to the user. When used in this way, check boxes look and behave like what are commonly referred to as radio buttons.

The following example creates three check boxes, labeled "Coffee," "Tea," and "Milk:"

```
Checkbox cb1 = new Checkbox("Coffee");
Checkbox cb2 = new Checkbox("Tea");
Checkbox cb3 = new Checkbox("Milk");
add(cb1);
add(cb2);
add(cb3);
```

The following code builds on the preceding example by creating three mutually exclusive check boxes (also known as radio buttons), with the last check box checked. Note that the constructor used in this example was added in JDK 1.1; the similar constructor that appeared in JDK 1.0.2 has been deprecated.

Note This is only one of the many constructors and methods new to JDK 1.1. Some of the new constructors and methods provide totally new functionality, and some replace older, *deprecated* constructors and methods. Deprecated, as referred to in the JDK documentation, means that a constructor or method has been replaced, and will be phased out in a future version of the JDK.

```
CheckboxGroup grp = new CheckboxGroup();
Checkbox cb1 = new Checkbox("Coffee", false, grp);
Checkbox cb2 = new Checkbox("Tea", false, grp);
Checkbox cb3 = new Checkbox("Milk", true, grp);
add(cb1);
add(cb2);
add(cb3);
```

Table 13.3 lists some common methods used with Checkbox. For a complete list, refer to the following Web page:

```
http://java.sun.com/products/JDK/1.1/docs/api/java.awt.Checkbox.html
```

Table 13.3
Commonly Used Constructors and Methods in the Checkbox Class

Constructor/Method	Description
Checkbox(String)	Creates a Checkbox with a specified label
Checkbox(String, Boolean)	Creates a Checkbox with a specified label and initial state
Checkbox(String, Boolean, CheckboxGroup)	Creates a Checkbox with a specified label, state, and CheckboxGroup
String getLabel()	Returns the displayed text label
void setLabel(String)	Sets the text label to be displayed
Boolean getState()	Returns the Checkbox state (true if checked)
void setState(Boolean)	Sets the Checkbox state (true if checked)
void addItemListener(ItemListener)	Registers an event listener to receive item events
void processEvent(AwtEvent)	Override to catch events in a subclass of a Checkbox
Object[] getSelectedObjects()	Exists as part of the new ItemSelectable interface that Checkbox implements

Table 13.4 lists some common methods used with CheckboxGroup. For a complete list, refer to the following Web page:

```
http://java.sun.com/products/JDK/1.1/docs/api/java.awt.CheckboxGroup.html
```

TABLE 13.4
Commonly Used Constructors and Methods in the CheckboxGroup Class

Constructor/Method	Description
CheckboxGroup()	Creates a new CheckboxGroup
Checkbox getSelectedCheckbox()	Returns the Checkbox currently selected (note that `getCurrent()` has been deprecated)
void setSelectedCheckbox(Checkbox)	Sets the given Checkbox to checked (note that `setCurrent()` has been deprecated)

As you are aware, the Checkbox component may be configured to restrict the user to a single, mutually exclusive choice, or it can be configured to enable multiple selections. Similarly, the List component also allows for single or multiple selection, as the following section details.

List Components

A List—commonly referred to as a list box—displays a scrolling list of choices to the user. A list box can be configured to accept either multiple selections or one selection, with one selection being the default. The following example creates a mutually exclusive list box with four entries and three visible lines. A scrollbar is automatically displayed for scrolling through the entire list:

```
List suits = new List(3);
suits.add("Clubs");
suits.add("Hearts");
suits.add("Spades");
suits.add("Diamonds");
add(suits);
```

Figure 13.3 shows the List component produced by this example.

Table 13.5 lists some commonly used List methods. For a complete list, refer to the following Web page:

```
http://java.sun.com/products/JDK/1.1/docs/api/java.awt.List.html
```

Table 13.5
Commonly Used Constructors and Methods in the List Class

Constructor/Method	Description
List(int)	Creates a new List with a specified number of visible rows.
List(int, boolean)	Creates a new List with a specified number of visible rows. This constructor also indicates whether or not multiple selections are allowed.
int getItemCount()	Returns number of items in the List. (Note that `countItems()` has been deprecated.)
String getItem(int)	Returns the String at the specified row. This argument is zero-based.
String[] getItems()	Returns a String array of the selected items.
add(String)	Adds an item to the end of the list. (Note that `addItem()` has been deprecated.)
void removeAll()	Removes all items from the list. (Note that `clear()` has been deprecated.)
void remove(int)	Removes the item from the specified row. (Note that `delItem()` has been deprecated.)
int getSelectedIndex()	Returns either the row index selected by the user or –1 if exactly one row isn't selected.
String getSelectedItem()	Returns either a String that contains the item selected by the user, or null if exactly one item isn't selected.
void select(int)	Selects the specified row.
void addItemListener (ItemListener)	Registers an event listener to receive item events.
void addActionListener (ActionListener)	Registers an event listener to receive action events.
Object[] getSelectedObjects()	Exists as part of the new ItemSelectable interface that List implements.

As you have seen, the List component displays a list of choices to the user. Another component, called the Choice component, also presents a set of choices, although in a slightly different manner, as the following section details.

Choice Components

A Choice—commonly referred to as a drop-down list—is similar to a List, except that the Choice component is displayed as only one line of text. When the user clicks this component, the list of choices drops down. Unlike a List, a Choice can accept only one selection at a time. The following example creates a Choice with the days of the week:

```
Choice days = new Choice();
days.add("Sunday");
days.add("Monday");
days.add("Tuesday");
days.add("Wednesday");
days.add("Thursday");
days.add("Friday");
days.add("Saturday");
add(days);
```

Figure 13.3 shows the Choice component produced by this example.

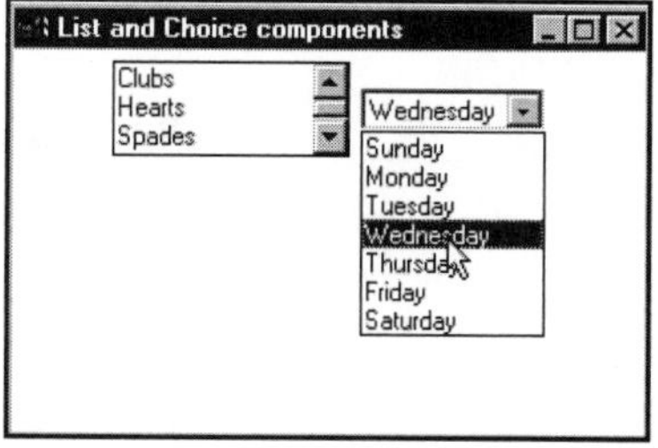

Figure 13.3
List and Choice components.

Table 13.6 lists some Choice methods. (This table also indicates the previous methods that they replace.) For a complete list, refer to the following Web page:

```
http://java.sun.com/products/JDK/1.1/docs/api/java.awt.Choice.html
```

TABLE 13.6
Commonly Used Constructors and Methods in the Choice Class

Constructor/Method	Description
Choice()	Creates a new Choice.
int getItemCount()	Returns number of items in the Choice. (Note that `countItems()` has been deprecated.)
String getItem(int)	Returns the String at the specified row. (This argument is zero-based.)
add(String)	Adds an item to the end. (Note that `addItem()` has been deprecated.)
void removeAll()	Removes all items. (Note that `clear()` has been deprecated.)
void remove(int)	Removes the item from the specified row. (Note that `delItem()` has been deprecated.)
int getSelectedIndex()	Returns the row index selected by the user.
String getSelectedItem()	Returns a String that contains the item selected by the user.
void select(int)	Selects the specified row.
void addItemListener (ItemListener)	Registers an event listener to receive item events.
Object[] getSelectedObjects()	Exists as part of the new ItemSelectable interface that Choice implements.

The components that you've seen so far are typically operated upon by clicking the mouse and making choices. The next two components enable the user to input text and numbers into your applications.

TextField and TextArea Components

The TextField and TextArea classes are used to display and receive text input from the user. The main difference between the two is that a TextField has one line of text, whereas TextArea can have multiple lines. As shown earlier in this chapter in figure 13.1, both classes are derived from the TextComponent class and share many of the same methods. The following example creates a TextField that is 20 columns wide and contains the words "Change me!". This example also creates an empty TextArea that is 20 columns wide and four rows high.

```
TextField tf = new TextField("Change me!", 20);
TextArea ta = new TextArea(null, 4, 20);
add(tf);
add(ta);
```

Because the TextField and TextArea classes are derived from the TextComponent class, some methods used with the TextField and TextArea components are defined there. Table 13.7 lists some commonly used methods defined in the TextComponent class. For a complete list, refer to the following Web page:

```
http://java.sun.com/products/JDK/1.1/docs/api/java.awt.TextComponent.html
```

TABLE 13.7
Commonly Used Methods in the TextComponent Class

Constructor/Method	Description
String getText()	Returns the text contained in this text component
void setText(String)	Sets the text to the specified String
String getSelectedText()	Returns the user-selected text in this text component
void selectAll()	Selects all text

Table 13.8 lists some commonly used TextField methods. For a complete list, refer to the following Web page:

```
http://java.sun.com/products/JDK/1.1/docs/api/java.awt.TextField.html
```

Table 13.8
Commonly Used Constructors and Methods in the TextField Class

Constructor/Method	Description
TextField(String, int)	Creates a TextField with the specified text and number of columns.
void setEchoChar(char)	Sets the character to be echoed. Usually facilitates password entry. (Note that `setEchoCharacter()` has been deprecated.)
void addActionListener (ActionListener)	Registers an event listener to receive action events.

Finally, table 13.9 lists some commonly used TextArea methods. For a complete list, refer to the following Web page:

```
http://java.sun.com/products/JDK/1.1/docs/api/java.awt.TextArea.html
```

Table 13.9
Commonly Used Constructors and Methods in the TextArea Class

Constructor/Method	Description
TextArea(String, int, int)	Creates a TextArea with the specified text, number of rows, and number of columns.
append(String)	Appends the text to the end of the text already in the TextArea.

This section discussed the text-oriented components. The following section explores another important component: the Scrollbar.

The ScrollBar Component

Scrollbars usually are used in conjunction with an area to be scrolled. Sometimes, however, a scrollbar can be used as a "slider" to enable the user to input a value. As figure 13.4 illustrates, scrollbars can be horizontal or vertical. This figure also shows some properties associated with scrollbars.

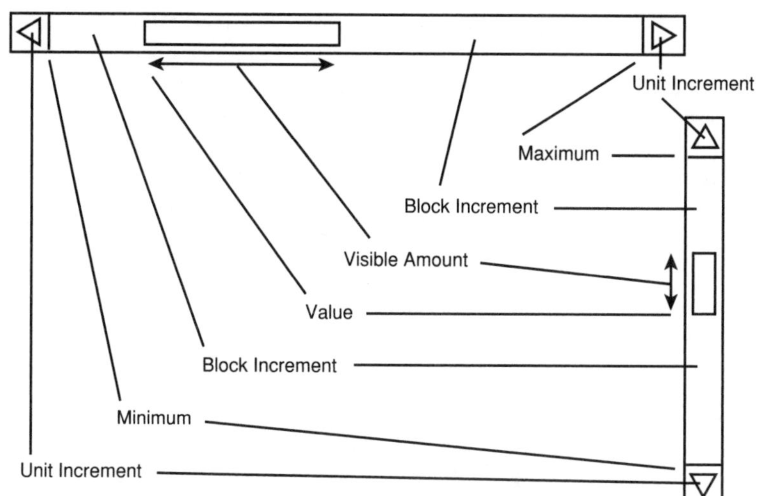

Figure 13.4
Scrollbar elements and properties.

A scrollbar has the following properties:

- Orientation: A scrollbar can be either horizontal or vertical.
- Maximum: This property represents the highest value that the scrollbar can represent.
- Minimum: This property represents the lowest value that the scrollbar can represent.
- Value: This property is the current value represented by the scrollbar.
- Visible Amount: When used in conjunction with an area to be scrolled, the size of the bubble in the scrollbar should be proportional to the visible area of the document being scrolled.
- Unit Increment: This property refers to the amount that the value will be increased when the user clicks the right or top arrow.
- Block Increment: This property refers to the amount that the value will be increased when the user clicks the area between the bubble and the right or top arrow.

You can get and set these properties by using the get and set methods associated with each property. Use the `setVisibleAmount()` method, for example, to set the visible amount. The adjustable interface, which the Scrollbar class implements, defines all these methods.

Listing 13.2, which is the program ScrollbarSlider.java on the CD-ROM accompanying this book, depicts an applet that serves as an example of how you can use a Scrollbar as a "slider" for user input. Figure 13.5 displays this applet's user interface. As you interact with the scrollbar by sliding the bubble, clicking the arrows, or clicking between the bubble and an arrow, the value of the scrollbar changes. The new value is then reflected in the text field.

Listing 13.2

```
Line=================Java Source================
//////////
// ScrollbarSlider.java  Example of using a Scrollbar
// as a "slider" for the user to set a value
//
// Author: James L. Weaver  JDK 1.1 beta1
//////////
import java.awt.*;
import java.applet.*;
import java.awt.event.*;

public class ScrollbarSlider extends Applet
                           implements AdjustmentListener{

    // Declare a Scrollbar and a TextField
    Scrollbar slider;
    TextField value;

    public void init() {

        // Set the layout to BorderLayout
        setLayout(new BorderLayout());

        // Create a Horizontal Scrollbar with an initial
        // value of 100, a visible amount of 1, a minimum
        // value of 0, and a maximum value of 200.
        slider = new Scrollbar(Scrollbar.HORIZONTAL,
                                 100, 1, 0, 200);

```

```
            // Set the Unit Increment value to 1, and the
            // Block Increment value to 25
            slider.setUnitIncrement(1);
            slider.setBlockIncrement(25);

            // Place the slider at the bottom of the
            // applet
            add("South", slider);

            // Create a TextField that initially contains "100"
            value = new TextField("100", 5);

            // Create a Panel to put inside the center
            // region of the applet, so that the
            // value TextField may be added to it.
            Panel p = new Panel();
            add("Center", p);
            p.add(value);

            // Add an event "listener" for when an adjustment
            // event happens to this Scrollbar. The
            // adjustmentValueChanged method of the listener will
            // be called.
            slider.addAdjustmentListener(this);

        }

        // This method is called when the Scrollbar is adjusted
        public void adjustmentValueChanged(AdjustmentEvent e) {
    if (e.getAdjustable() == slider) {
        // Put the value from the event into the TextField
        value.setText(new Integer(e.getValue()).toString());
    }
        }
    }
```

Here is the associated HTML:

```
<HTML>
<HEAD>
<TITLE> Scrollbar Slider </TITLE>
</HEAD>
<BODY>
<APPLET CODE="ScrollbarSlider.class" WIDTH=300 HEIGHT=100></APPLET>
</BODY>
</HTML>
```

Let's examine some of the more interesting points in this applet:

Line 21 sets the layout manager of the applet to BorderLayout. Layout managers are essentially classes that assist you in arranging AWT components on the screen. The next section discusses layout managers in more detail.

Lines 26 and 27 construct a horizontal scrollbar. This form of the ScrollBar constructor takes five parameters: Orientation, Value, Visible Amount, Minimum, and Maximum.

- Orientation: In this case, the final static variable Scrollbar.HORIZONTAL is passed, which produces a horizontal scrollbar. The other possibility is Scrollbar.VERTICAL.
- Value: The initial value is set to 100, which is halfway between the minimum and maximum values for this scrollbar. Using this value places the bubble's initial position at approximately the middle of the scrollbar.
- Visible Amount: Because this scrollbar represents only a value (and because it is not being used in conjunction with a scrolling area), the size of the bubble should be as small as possible. Therefore, a value of one is used for this parameter. You can set this value at any number greater than zero if you want to implement "proportional" scrollbars. The size of the bubble on a proportional scrollbar represents the visible amount of the document being scrolled. The horizontal scrollbar in figure 13.4, for example, has a bubble that is approximately 40 percent of the length of the scrollbar. This means that approximately 40 percent of the document's width is currently visible in the scrolling area.
- Minimum: In this case, the lowest value that this scrollbar can represent is set to zero.
- Maximum: In this case, the highest value that this scrollbar can represent is set to 200.

Line 31 determines the increment by which the value will be increased when the user clicks the left or right arrows on the scrollbar. From a usability standpoint, it is important to choose a reasonable value for Unit Increment. In this case, the value is set to one.

Line 32 determines the increment by which the value will be increased when the user clicks between the bubble and one of the arrows on the scrollbar. As with the Unit Increment, it is important to choose a reasonable value for Block Increment.

Line 36 causes the scrollbar to appear at the bottom of the applet's display, stretched to the full width of the applet.

Lines 39–46 create a text field in which to display the scrollbar's value. These lines also cause the text field to be centered above the scrollbar.

Line 52 identifies an "adjustment listener." This listener is called when the scrollbar emits an adjustment event, such as when the user drags the bubble. As mentioned previously, these concepts belong to the Delegation Event Model, which will be covered in Chapter 14, "The New, Improved AWT: Menus, Events, and More New Features."

Lines 57–62 contain the body of the adjustment listener, which obtains the current value of the scrollbar, converts it to a String, and adds it to the text box.

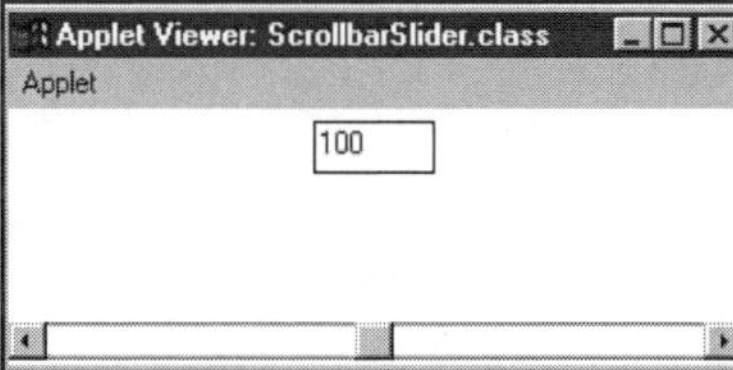

Figure 13.5
ScrollbarSlider applet display.

Table 13.10 lists some commonly used methods in the Scrollbar class. For a complete list, refer to the following Web page:

```
http://java.sun.com/products/JDK/1.1/docs/api/java.awt.Scrollbar.html
```

TABLE 13.10
Commonly Used Constructors and Methods in the Scrollbar Class

Constructor/Method	Description
Scrollbar(int)	Creates a Scrollbar with the specified orientation.
Scrollbar(int, int, int, int, int)	Creates a Scrollbar with the specified orientation, initial value, amount visible, minimum value, and maximum value.
int getValue()	Returns the current value represented by the Scrollbar.

continues

Table 13.10, Continued
Commonly Used Constructors and Methods in the Scrollbar Class

Constructor/Method	Description
void setValue(int)	Sets the value of the Scrollbar.
int getMinimum()	Gets the minimum value that can be represented by this Scrollbar.
void setMinimum(int)	Sets the minimum value that can be represented by this Scrollbar.
int getMaximum()	Gets the maximum value that can be represented by this Scrollbar.
void setMaximum(int)	Sets the maximum value that can be represented by this Scrollbar.
int getVisibleAmount()	Returns the visible amount, which is represented by the size of the scrollbar's bubble. (Note that `getVisible()` has been deprecated.)
void setVisibleAmount(int)	Sets the visible amount, which is represented by the size of the scrollbar's bubble.
int getUnitIncrement()	Returns the unit increment for this scrollbar. (Note that `getLineIncrement()` has been deprecated.)
void setUnitIncrement(int)	Sets the unit increment for this scrollbar. (Note that `setLineIncrement()` has been deprecated.)
int getBlockIncrement()	Returns the block increment for this scrollbar. (Note that `getPageIncrement()` has been deprecated.)
void setBlockIncrement(int)	Sets the block increment for this scrollbar. (Note that `setPageIncrement()` has been deprecated.)
void addAdjustmentListener (AdjustmentListener)	Registers an event listener to receive adjustment events.

Later in this chapter, you'll see another class called ScrollPane, which is new in JDK 1.1. ScrollPane works in conjunction with the Scrollbar class to make it much easier to implement a scrolling area associated with scrollbars.

So far, you've learned to use several Java GUI components. One more component will be explored in this section—the Canvas component.

The Canvas Component

The Canvas component is the simplest of all the components. This component is essentially a blank rectangular area in which the application can draw lines and shapes or display images. All the Graphics methods that you learned in Chapter 9, "Animating Applets with Java Graphics, Images, Colors, and Sound," can be used with the Canvas class. Because the Canvas class is derived from the Component class, it contains all the inherited capabilities, including appearance management and event-trapping.

To construct a new Canvas, use a no-argument constructor, as shown here:

```
Canvas c = new Canvas();
```

For more information on the Canvas class, refer to the following Web page:

```
http://java.sun.com/products/JDK/1.1/docs/api/java.awt.Canvas.html
```

You also can subclass the Canvas class to create your own custom components. You will learn how to create custom components in Chapter 15, "Java Beans: Java's Component Architecture."

Interesting Component Class Methods

Several methods are common to all the classes that you've seen so far in this chapter. The similarities exist because these classes are derived from the Component class. Table 13.11 lists some commonly used methods with GUI components. For a complete list, refer to the following Web page:

```
http://java.sun.com/products/JDK/1.1/docs/api/java.awt.Component.html
```

Table 13.11
Commonly Used/Interesting Methods in the Component Class

Constructor/Method	Description
String getName()	Returns the name of the component. (Introduced in JDK 1.1.)
void setName(String)	Enables you to name this component. Naming a component is useful for identifying the component that caused an event. (Introduced in JDK 1.1.)
Container getParent()	Returns the parent container of this component.
void setVisible(boolean)	Makes the component visible or invisible. (Note that `show()` and `hide()` have been deprecated.)
boolean isVisible()	Returns true if the component is visible.
void setEnabled(boolean)	Enables or disables this component. (Note that `enable()` and `disable()` have been deprecated.)
boolean isEnabled()	Returns true if this component is enabled.
void setLocation(int, int) void setLocation(Point)	Moves this component to the specified coordinates in the parent container. (Note that `move()` has been deprecated.)
Point getLocation()	Returns the current location of this component within its parent container. (Note that `location()` has been deprecated.)
void setSize(int, int) void setSize(Dimension)	Resizes the component to the specified dimension. (Note that `resize()` has been deprecated.)
Dimension getSize()	Returns the current size of the component. (Note that `size()` has been deprecated.)
void setBounds(Rectangle r) void setBounds(int, int, int, int)	Moves and resizes this component to the specified location and size within the parent container. (Note that `reshape()` has been deprecated.)
Rectangle getBounds()	Returns a Rectangle that represents the location and size of this component within the parent container. (Note that `bounds()` has been deprecated.)

Constructor/Method	Description
void setCursor(Cursor)	Sets the cursor image to the one specified. (Introduced in JDK 1.1 to provide the capability to have a cursor associated with each component.)
Cursor getCursor()	Returns the cursor associated with this component. (Introduced in JDK 1.1.)
Dimension getPreferredSize()	Returns the preferred size of this component. (Note that `preferredSize()` has been deprecated.)
void setFont(Font)	Sets the Font for this component.
Font getFont()	Returns the current Font associated with this component.
boolean isFocusTraversable()	Returns whether this component can receive focus when the user presses the Tab or Shift + Tab keys.

You have now seen all the components in the Abstract Window Toolkit. As shown in the HelloGuiWorld and ScrollbarSlider programs, these components must be placed in containers before they can be used.

Using AWT Containers

An AWT container is a specialized component that contains other components. Figure 13.1 shows that the Container class is derived from the Component class. Several types of containers are derived from the Container class—Panel, Applet, ScrollPane, Window, Frame, Dialog, and FileDialog.

Each container has a specialized purpose. A Dialog, for example, appears on the screen to display and gather input from the user. A ScrollPane is used to manage a scrolling area, and a Panel is used solely to organize other components. All share a common function, however—they contain and organize other components. These components are usually organized with the help of layout managers, which this chapter will discuss in later sections.

Table 13.12 lists some frequently used Container methods. Because Container is an abstract class, always use a derived class, such as Panel or Dialog, to contain other components. These methods are inherited by the derived classes. For a complete list, refer to the following Web page:

```
http://java.sun.com/products/JDK/1.1/docs/api/java.awt.Container.html
```

Table 13.12
Commonly Used Methods in the Container Class

Constructor/Method	Description
add(Component) add(Component, int) add(String, Component)	Adds the specified component to this Container. The component is positioned according to the rules of the layout manager, if one has been set.
int getComponentCount()	Returns the number of components in this container. (Note that `countComponents()` has been deprecated.)
Component[] getComponents()	Returns an array of components that are in this container.
Insets getInsets()	Returns an Insets that describes the non-usable border area of the Container. (Note that `insets()` has been deprecated.)
void setLayout(LayoutManager)	Sets the layout manager to the one specified.
void validate()	Forces the container and its components to be laid out according to the current layout manager. (Usually called after adding or resizing a component.)
Dimension getPreferredSize()	Returns the preferred size of this container. (Note that `preferredSize()` has been deprecated.)

Now that you are familiar with a container and some of its methods, let's discuss each of the containers individually.

Panel Class

The Panel class is the simplest of the Container classes. This class usually is used inside another container to sub-organize components. The ScrollbarSlider example (illustrated earlier in this chapter) used a Panel in this manner. Lines 39–46 of listing 13.2 depict a Panel that is created to hold a text field component. Because of the way the BorderLayout layout manager works, adding the text field directly to the applet would cause the text field to expand and fill most of the applet's display area. Instead, an instance of a Panel is added to the applet, and the text field is then added to the Panel. The default layout manager for a Panel is FlowLayout, so the text field is placed accordingly—at the top, center of the panel. Later sections in this chapter will discuss FlowLayout in more detail.

For more information on the Panel class, refer to the following Web page:

```
http://java.sun.com/products/JDK/1.1/docs/api/java.awt.Panel.html
```

Figure 13.1 illustrates that the Applet class is derived from the Panel class. The Applet class is the base class for all applets. Chapter 8, "Creating Java Applets," discusses the Applet class in more detail. For more information on the Applet class, refer to the following Web page:

```
http://java.sun.com/products/JDK/1.1/docs/api/java.applet.Applet.html
```

Now that we have examined the simplest container, let's explore the ScrollPane class.

ScrollPane Class

Prior to Java 1.1, users writing a program that contained scrolling areas associated with scrollbars had to manage the scrolling of these areas themselves. This new ScrollPane class, however, handles much of the work for you.

n the D

Listing 13.3, which is the program NoScrollPain.java on the CD-ROM accompanying this book, depicts an applet that serves as an example of how you can use the ScrollPane class. Figure 13.7 displays this applet's user interface. As you operate the scrollbars, the street map scrolls within the viewing area. Figure 13.6 diagrams the behind-the-scenes information—or, behind-the-Viewport information, to be more precise.

Listing 13.3

```
Line=================Java Source=================
//////////
// NoScrollPain.java  Example of using a ScrollPane
// to easily implement scrolling.
//
// Author: James L. Weaver  JDK 1.1 beta1
//////////
import java.awt.*;
import java.applet.*;
import java.awt.event.*;

public class NoScrollPain extends Applet {

    // Declare a ScrollPane
```

continues

Listing 13.3, Continued

```
    ScrollPane viewer;

    // Declare a component to scroll within the ScrollPane
    Map map;

    public void init() {

        // Construct the viewer
        viewer = new ScrollPane(ScrollPane.SCROLLBARS_AS_NEEDED);

        // Set the Unit Increment of the horizontal
        // scrollbar to 5, and the Block Increment to 50
        viewer.getHAdjustable().setUnitIncrement(5);
        viewer.getHAdjustable().setBlockIncrement(50);

        // Set the Unit Increment of the vertical
        // scrollbar to 5, and the Block Increment to 50
        viewer.getVAdjustable().setUnitIncrement(5);
        viewer.getVAdjustable().setBlockIncrement(50);

        // Set the layout to BorderLayout
        setLayout(new BorderLayout());

        // Place the viewer in the "Center" region of
        // the BorderLayout
        add("Center", viewer);

        map = new Map();
        viewer.add(map);
    }
}

class Map extends Canvas
{
    Map() {
        setSize(300, 200);
    }

```

```
52        public void paint(Graphics g) {
53            g.setColor(Color.white);
54            g.fillRect(0, 0, 300, 200);
55            g.setColor(Color.red);
56            g.drawLine(0, 100, 100, 100);
57            g.drawLine(100, 100, 100, 0);
58            g.drawLine(125, 0, 125, 100);
59            g.drawLine(125, 100, 300, 100);
60            g.drawLine(0, 125, 200, 125);
61            g.drawLine(200, 125, 200, 200);
62            g.drawLine(225, 200, 225, 125);
63            g.drawLine(225, 125, 300, 125);
64            g.drawString("Main street", 100, 120);
65        }
66    }
```

This is the associated HTML:

```
<HTML>
<HEAD>
<TITLE> NoScrollPain </TITLE>
</HEAD>
<BODY>
<APPLET CODE="NoScrollPain.class" WIDTH=100 HEIGHT=100></APPLET>
</BODY>
</HTML>
```

Before diving into the listing, take a look at figure 13.6, which illustrates both a viewport in which the street map can be viewed and a child component that contains the street map. Different sections of the child component appear within the viewport, depending on the positions of the scrollbars.

Line 14 in listing 13.3 declares a ScrollPane, which encapsulates the viewport and scrollbars depicted in the diagram.

Line 17 declares the child component to be viewed. In this case, the child component is a subclass of Canvas, named Map. (This class is defined in lines 46–66.) Note that in the Map constructor (line 49), the size of the child component is set to 300 pixels wide and 200 pixels high. Notice also that the Map class can draw a map on itself, as seen in the `paint()` method in lines 52–65.

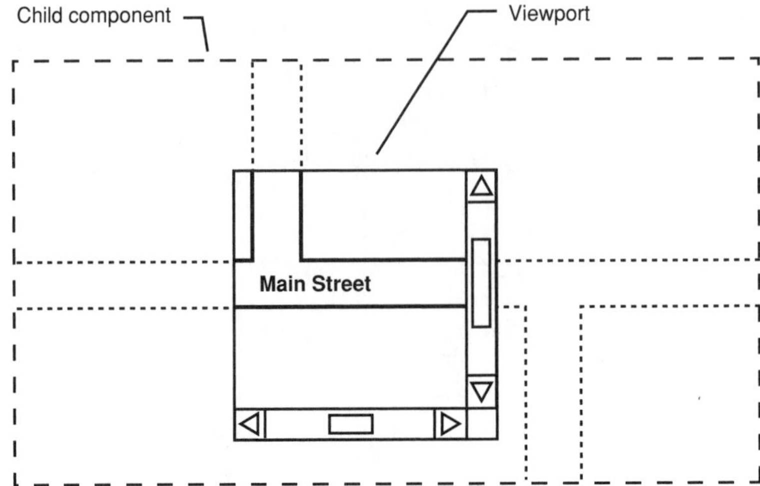

Figure 13.6

Behind the scenes of NoScrollPain.

The `init()` method of the applet (line 22) constructs the viewer. This version of the ScrollPane constructor takes an int as a parameter, which can be any one of the following final static variables:

- SCROLLBARS_ALWAYS—This variable places horizontal and vertical scrollbars in the ScrollPane, regardless of whether the child component is larger than the viewport.

- SCROLLBARS_AS_NEEDED—This variable places a scrollbar in the ScrollPane only when a dimension of the child component is larger than the viewport. If, for example, the dimensions of the viewport are 200 pixels wide by 300 pixels high and the child component is 150 pixels wide by 600 pixels high, then only the vertical scrollbar would appear in the ScrollPane.

- SCROLLBARS_NEVER—Scrollbars will not appear in the ScrollPane. In this case, the only way to scroll is from the program, by using the `setScrollPosition()` method.

In the NoScrollPain example, scrollbars will only appear when needed—which is always, because both dimensions of the child component are larger than the corresponding viewport dimensions.

Next, in lines 26–32, the unit increment and block increment values are set for the horizontal and vertical scrollbars. Because the scrollbars are encapsulated within the ScrollPane, methods of the ScrollPane class must be called to obtain a reference to them. The `getHAdjustable()` method returns a reference to the horizontal scrollbar, and the `getVAdjustable()` method returns a reference to the vertical scrollbar. As you recall from previous sections in this chapter, scrollbars implement the adjustable interface—hence the `getHAdjustable()` and `getVAdjustable()` method names.

In lines 35 and 39, the `BorderLayout` is used so that the viewer (an instance of ScrollPane) occupies the entire applet display area, as shown in figure 13.7.

Line 41 creates a new instance of the Map, named map, and line 42 adds map to the viewer (the child component to the ScrollPane). Internally, the ScrollPane now can ask the child component for its size and can display its scrollbars appropriately, with proper bubble sizes.

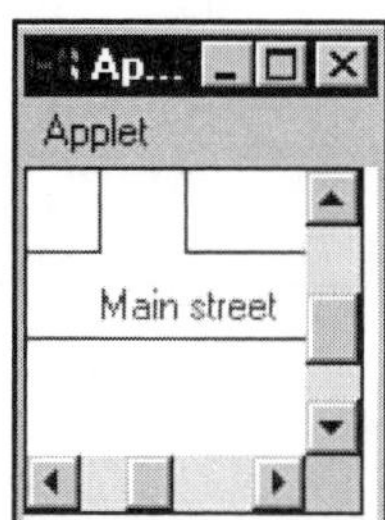

Figure 13.7
NoScrollPain applet display.

Table 13.13 lists some frequently used ScrollPane methods. For a complete list, refer to the following Web page:

```
http://java.sun.com/products/JDK/1.1/docs/api/java.awt.ScrollPane.html
```

TABLE 13.13
Commonly Used Methods in the ScrollPane Class

Constructor/Method	Description
ScrollPane(int) ScrollPane()	Creates a ScrollPane with the specified scrollbar display. (The default policy is `SCROLLBARS_AS_NEEDED`.)
Component add(Component)	Adds the child component to theScrollPane. If a child component is already present, it will be replaced because only one is allowed.
Dimension getViewportSize()	Returns the dimensions of the viewport.
Adjustable getVAdjustable()	Returns a reference to an adjustable object that represents the vertical scrollbar.
Adjustable getHAdjustable()	Returns a reference to an adjustable object that represents the horizontal scrollbar.

continues

Table 13.13, Continued
Commonly Used Methods in the ScrollPane Class

Constructor/Method	Description
void setScrollPosition(Point) void setScrollPosition(int, int)	Scrolls the child component to put the specified coordinates in the upper-left corner of the viewport. This is used to programmatically scroll the child component.
Point getScrollPosition()	Returns the coordinates of the child component that is displayed in the upper-left corner of the viewport.

As you can see, the ScrollPane class makes it very easy to implement scrolling areas.

The containers discussed thus far are displayed within other containers. The rest of the containers appear in their own window, and consequently are inherited from the Window class (see fig. 13.1). The Dialog class is the first class to be explored.

Dialog Class

Dialogs, commonly referred to as dialog boxes, generally are used to display and gather information from the user. Dialog boxes can be used in many different ways:

- Message boxes
- Property sheets
- General user input dialog boxes
- FileDialog, and other common dialog boxes

The following sections discuss each one in more detail.

Message Boxes

Message boxes are special purpose dialog boxes that give the user some information and then wait until the user responds to the information. When, for example, you try to exit a program without saving your work, a message box may ask, "Exit without saving?". Three buttons appear on the message box with choices such as "Yes, "No," and "Cancel." Message boxes usually are modal, which means that you must respond to them before you can interact with the rest of the application.

The following code fragment builds the user interface of the message box described above:

```
Dialog msgDialog = new Dialog(this, "My Application", true);
Panel messagePanel = new Panel();
messagePanel.add(new Label("Exit without saving?"));
msgDialog.add("Center", messagePanel);
Panel buttonPanel = new Panel();
buttonPanel.add(new Button("Yes"));
buttonPanel.add(new Button("No"));
buttonPanel.add(new Button("Cancel"));
msgDialog.add("South", buttonPanel);
msgDialog.setSize(300, 150);
msgDialog.show();
```

The following steps detail the creation of this message box.

1. Create the Dialog:

   ```
   Dialog msgDialog = new Dialog(this, "My Application", true);
   ```

   This first line creates the Dialog, passing it three parameters:

   - **The Frame that owns the dialog box.** All dialog boxes are owned by a Frame, which is usually the main Frame of the application.
   - **A String for the title bar of the dialog box.** Frequently, developers put the name of the application in the title bar, so that when the message box appears, the user knows from which application it came.
   - **The desired modality.** If true, the dialog box blocks the user from interacting with the rest of the application until the user has dealt with it.

2. Create a Panel in which to put the "Exit without saving?" message, add the message to the Panel, and then add the Panel to the "Center" area of the Dialog:

   ```
   Panel messagePanel = new Panel();
   messagePanel.add(new Label("Exit without saving?"));
   msgDialog.add("Center", messagePanel);
   ```

Note The default layout manager for a Dialog is the `BorderLayout`, which will be covered later in this chapter.

3. Now look at the next five lines:

```
Panel buttonPanel = new Panel();
buttonPanel.add(new Button("Yes"));
buttonPanel.add(new Button("No"));
buttonPanel.add(new Button("Cancel"));
msgDialog.add("South", buttonPanel);
```

   This section creates a Panel in which to put the three buttons. The code then adds the buttons to the Panel, and adds the Panel to the bottom area of the Dialog. Recall that the default layout manager for Panel is FlowLayout.

4. In the last two lines, the size of the dialog box is set to 300 pixels wide and 150 pixels high, and then the dialog box is made visible. This is necessary because Dialogs are invisible by default.

```
msgDialog.setSize(300, 150);
msgDialog.show();
```

Property Sheets

Property sheets are another kind of Dialog in which the properties of a given application element (for example, a cell in a spreadsheet, or a selection of text) are displayed and manipulated. Property sheets are becoming commonplace in applications. See figure 13.8 for an example of a property sheet.

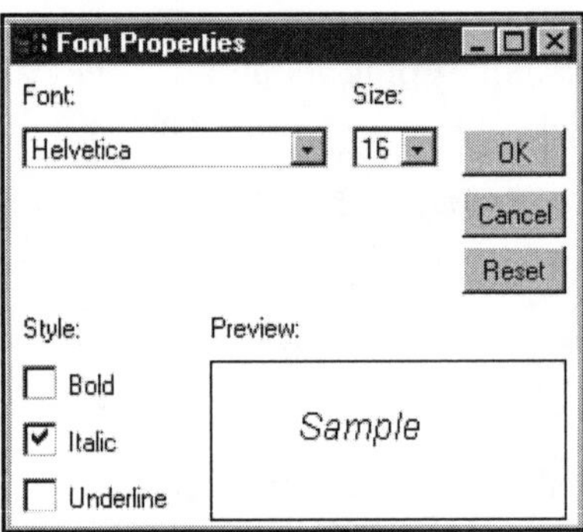

Figure 13.8
A sample property sheet.

Property sheets generally consist of the following:

- GUI components that display and enable the user to change properties. In figure 13.8, these components include TextField, CheckBox, Choice, and List.

- Notebook-style tabs. If too many properties exist, they sometimes are organized with the use of "tabbed components," which are components that resemble notebook tabs. When the user clicks on a tab, the information on that page is displayed.

Note Please note that the Java AWT does not have the tabbed components, but that they are available from Java component vendors.

- Two or more buttons. Property sheets almost always have an OK button and a Cancel button. Some sheets may have an Apply button for applying changes without closing the dialog box, and a Reset button for resetting the properties to their original state.
- A preview area in which a visual indication of the property changes can be seen before the user commits to the selection. The example in figure 13.8 has a preview area that illustrates the effects on the font changes. A Canvas component is well suited for the preview area.

Message boxes and property sheets are not supplied with the JDK, but as you have seen, you can certainly build them for use within your applications by using the Dialog class with other AWT components.

FileDialog and Other Common Dialog Boxes

Certain dialog boxes are implemented in different ways depending on the platform, but have a common function. These dialog boxes have a common look, however, among applications on the same platform. The FileDialog is an example of such a dialog box. You can use the FileDialog class within your application to enable the user to choose either a file to load or a file in which to save their information. Figure 13.9 illustrates the FileDialog prompting the user for a file to load.

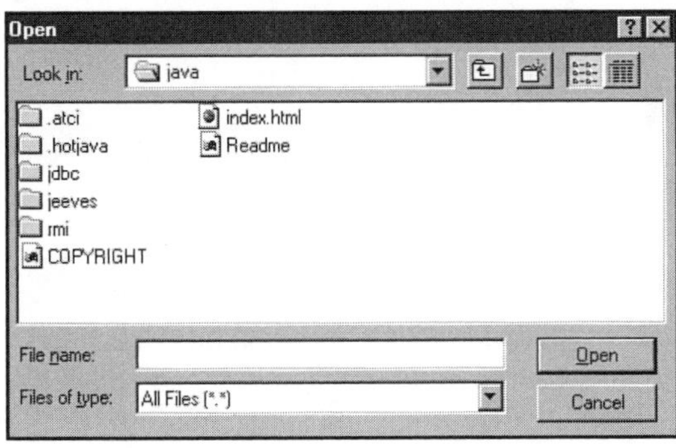

Figure 13.9

Example of a common FileDialog.

The following code fragment is used to create the FileDialog in figure 13.9:

```
FileDialog fd = new FileDialog(this, "Open", FileDialog.LOAD);
fd.setDirectory("c:\\java");
fd.show();
```

The first line creates a FileDialog, named fd, and passes it three parameters:

- A frame that owns the FileDialog
- A String to be displayed on the title bar of the FileDialog
- An indication of whether this is a load FileDialog or a save FileDialog

Table 13.14 lists some frequently used FileDialog methods. For a complete list, refer to the following Web page:

```
http://java.sun.com/products/JDK/1.1/docs/api/java.awt.FileDialog.html
```

Table 13.14
Commonly Used Methods in the FileDialog Class

Constructor/Method	Description
FileDialog(Frame, String, int) FileDialog(Frame, String)	Creates a FileDialog with the specified owner Frame, title, and load/save mode.
String getDirectory()	Gets the directory that is currently being referenced by the FileDialog.
void setDirectory(String)	Sets the directory of the FileDialog to the specified directory.
String getFile()	Gets the file name that is currently being referenced by the FileDialog.
void setFile(String file)	Sets the file name of the FileDialog to the specified file.
void setFilenameFilter (FilenameFilter)	Sets the FilenameFilter of the FileDialog. (FilenameFilter is an interface that can be implemented to filter the files shown by FileDialog.)

Other common dialog boxes exist on most platforms for setting fonts, setting colors, and printing. The only other common dialog box that Java currently implements (besides FileDialog) is one that obtains information from the user about a print job. Chapter 14, "The New, Improved AWT: Menus, Events, and More New Features," examines printing and this Print dialog box in more detail.

General User Input Dialog Boxes

Some dialog boxes are simply used in an application when the application requires input from the user. These dialog boxes have very general uses and have no typical case. Developers are on their own when designing them, but some good GUI style guides on the market can help. A good source for design ideas is to examine the design of dialog boxes in world-class applications.

Commonly Used Dialog Methods

Table 13.15 lists some frequently used Dialog methods. For a complete list, refer to the following Web page:

```
http://java.sun.com/products/JDK/1.1/docs/api/java.awt.Dialog.html
```

Table 13.15
Commonly Used Methods in the Dialog Class

Constructor/Method	Description
Dialog(Frame, String, boolean)	Creates a Dialog with the specified owner Frame, title, and modality.
void setModal(boolean)	Sets the modality of the dialog box. If "true," the Dialog blocks the application while shown. (Introduced in JDK 1.1.)
boolean isModal()	Returns "true" if this Dialog is modal; returns "false" if not modal.
void setTitle(String)	Sets the Dialog title bar to the specified String.
String getTitle()	Gets the title of the Dialog.
void setResizable(boolean)	Sets the resizability of this Dialog. (The user can't resize if this is set to false.)

continues

TABLE 13.15, CONTINUED
Commonly Used Methods in the Dialog Class

Constructor/Method	Description
void show()	Shows the dialog box. If the dialog box is modal, this will block user input to the rest of the program.
void processEvent(AWTEvent)	Can be overriden to catch events. (Note that `handleEvent()` has been deprecated.)
void addWindowListener (WindowListener)	Registers an event listener to receive window events.

The preceding examples and tables assume that a Frame reference exists to pass to the Dialog and FileDialog constructors. The following section deals with the use of the Dialog class in applets that don't use Frames.

Using Dialogs with Applets

Dialogs always require a Frame to own them, so how can you implement dialog boxes with applets that don't have Frames? One option is to cheat a little by using a Frame instead of a Dialog. The drawback to this, however, is that Frames can't be modal, so you lose the capability to make the user respond before continuing. In addition, the applet sometimes can obscure the Frame.

To solve this problem, get a reference to the Frame within which the applet itself is running. Whether the applet runs in Applet Viewer or a browser, a call to `getParent()` from within the applet should return a reference to a Frame. You then can pass this reference when creating the Dialog.

This section has discussed the different types of Dialogs and how to use them. The following section covers the last type of container, Frame.

Frame Class

A Frame is similar to a Dialog, and both are derived from the Window class. As with the Dialog, a Frame has a title, a border, and sometimes a menu. Unlike the Dialog, however, a Frame cannot be modal and is not owned by another AWT component. Essentially, a Frame is a top-level window.

Frames are commonly employed as the main window for an application. In this role, they often have a menu, a toolbar, and a status bar. Unfortunately, the AWT does not provide the latter two, so you must either obtain them from a Java component vendor or build them yourself.

In a document-centric application, the Frame is often where the document is displayed and operated upon. In a word processing application, for example, your document usually appears in the main window, which is where you make changes to it. Your document is the main focus of the application, and all GUI components that you interact with (such as dialog boxes, toolbar buttons, and menus) exist for the purpose of manipulating your document. Sometimes multiple documents are associated with an application, so there may be one Frame for each active document.

Note The use of the term "document" in this context can apply to any data, such as a spreadsheet, a picture, your schedule, or your checkbook register.

Frames can be created by an applet, but as stated earlier in this chapter, dialog boxes usually provide a better choice because of modality. Java stand-alone applications that have a GUI, however, must have a Frame as the top-level window.

The following line creates a new Frame with title "Example Frame."

```
Frame exampleFrame = new Frame("Example Frame");
```

Although you certainly can create an instance of a Frame, frames typically are subclassed to override and add methods, as in the following example:

```
public class MyFrame extends Frame{
    public MyFrame(String title) {
        super(title);
    }
}
```

As Chapter 7, "Object-Oriented Programming with Java" discussed, the `super()` method in the third line calls the constructor of the superclass, which in this case is Frame. This causes the title to appear in the title bar of the frame.

The following code creates an instance of `MyFrame` and displays it. The call to `setVisible()` is necessary because frames are initially invisible by default:

```
MyFrame frm = new MyFrame("My Frame");
frm.setSize(200, 200);
frm.setVisible(true);
```

Table 13.16 contains some frequently used Frame methods. For a complete list, refer to the following Web page:

```
http://java.sun.com/products/JDK/1.1/docs/api/java.awt.Frame.html
```

Table 13.16
Commonly Used Methods in the Frame Class

Constructor/Method	Description
Frame(String) Frame()	Creates a Frame with the specified String displayed in the title bar.
void setTitle(String)	Sets the title to the specified String.
String getTitle()	Returns the title from the title bar.
setMenuBar(MenuBar)	Associates a menu bar with this Frame.
MenuBar getMenuBar()	Returns the menu bar associated with this Frame.
void setResizable(boolean)	Sets the resizability of this Frame.
void dispose()	Disposes the Frame and releases any associated resources.
void processEvent(AWTEvent)	Can be overriden to catch events. (Note that `handleEvent()` has been deprecated.)
void addWindowListener (WindowListener)	Registers an event listener to receive window events.

At this point, we have discussed all AWT components and containers. The following section introduces layout managers and how to use them to organize the GUI portion of your Java programs.

Using Layout Managers

Java applets and applications can run on virtually any platform. A Java applet, for example, can run in any Java-enabled Web browser, and on any operating system in which the Java VM has been ported. This is one of the exciting and attractive features of Java. It is important, however, that your application's GUI looks good and functions well on any platform on which it is executed.

One of the difficulties in achieving this goal is that GUI components are not the same size on all supported platforms. For this reason, absolute positioning of GUI components is not recommended. This is one of the major reasons that the Java AWT has a feature known as layout managers. Layout managers help you position components within containers, such as panels, frames, and dialog boxes, without having to make assumptions about component and container sizes.

The Java AWT has five layout managers, each of which can implement the LayoutManager interface. The following list organizes these layout managers from simplest to most complex:

- FlowLayout
- BorderLayout
- CardLayout
- GridLayout
- GridBagLayout

Other layout managers are available from Java component vendors and Java Web sites. You also can create your own layout managers.

One or more layout managers can be used to lay out a container. This is because containers can hold other containers, and each of these containers can have a different layout manager. Table 13.17 describes some characteristics of each AWT layout manager.

TABLE 13.17
Characteristics of the Layout Managers

Layout Manager	Characteristics
FlowLayout	Easy to use. Adds new components from left to right within the container. Sometimes used to lay out a row of components in a Panel that is contained by a larger container.
BorderLayout	Easy to use. Has five areas in which to place components: North, South, East, West, and Center. Good for laying out dialog boxes that have buttons across the bottom. In this case, the Center area usually contains a Panel with another layout manager. Also good for "quick and dirty" applets.
CardLayout	A little harder than the previous two. One "card" (which can contain a component or container) is shown at a time. Can be used for implementing notebook-style (tabbed pages) functionality.

continues

Table 13.17, Continued
Characteristics of the Layout Managers

Layout Manager	Characteristics
GridLayout	Also a little harder to use than the first two. Divides the container into a matrix of rows and columns, with each cell identical in size. Great for implementing metaphors that look like grids, such as a calendar page, a battleship game, or a touch-tone pad. Too restrictive to lay out a complex container, but good for laying out a sub-container, such as a column of buttons on the East side of a BorderLayout.
GridBagLayout	The mother of all AWT layout managers. Can be a little difficult to use initially. Divides the container into a grid of cells that don't have to be the same size. Also, components can span cells. Uses GridBagConstraints associated with each component to specify how it is to be laid out. Good for laying out complex containers, often with the help of FlowLayout and GridLayout for sub-containers.

Now that we introduced the Java AWT layout managers, let's examine each one in more detail.

FlowLayout

Some examples that you have already seen in this chapter use FlowLayout to lay out components. Take another look at listing 13.1 (the HelloGuiWorld applet) and the associated display in figure 13.2. This applet creates a button and a label, and adds them to the applet's display. Recall that the Applet class is derived from the Panel class; the default layout manager for a Panel is FlowLayout. Therefore, because no layout manager is specified for the HelloGuiWorld applet, the default is FlowLayout.

Recapping listing 13.1, the button is created and added to the applet in lines 25 and 26:

```
25          pushButton = new Button("Push");
26          add(pushButton);
```

Lines 36 and 37 create and add the label to the applet:

```
        greetingLabel = new Label(helloString);
        add(greetingLabel);
```

As you can see, you simply call the `add()` method of the container to which you are adding the component. Because the FlowLayout layout manager has been (implicitly) set, it takes over the job of laying out the components. To explicitly set the layout manager of a container to FlowLayout, use the `setLayout()` method of the container with one of the following forms of the FlowLayout constructor:

```
setLayout(new FlowLayout(int align, int hgap, int vgap));
setLayout(new FlowLayout(int align));
setLayout(new FlowLayout());
```

The first form of the constructor takes three parameters:

- Alignment (can be LEFT, RIGHT, or CENTER). This controls where components will be added. If the components added exceed the width of the container, they will be added below the first row, using the specified alignment.
- Horizontal gap between components in pixels.
- Vertical gap between components in pixels.

The second form takes only the alignment parameter and defaults to horizontal and vertical gaps of five pixels.

The third form defaults to CENTER alignment and gaps of five pixels.

BorderLayout

For a good example of BorderLayout, look at listing 13.2 (the ScrollbarSlider applet) and the associated display in figure 13.5. BorderLayout is used in line 36 to stretch a Scrollbar (instance variable named slider) across the bottom of the applet:

```
36          add("South", slider);
```

In lines 44–46, a Panel is added to the center area of the applet so that a TextField (instance variable named value) can be added to the Panel and displayed:

```
44          Panel p = new Panel();
45          add("Center", p);
46          p.add(value);
```

If the text field had been added directly to the container in line 45, it would have stretched to fit the entire center area. The diagram in figure 13.10 shows the areas to which components can be added.

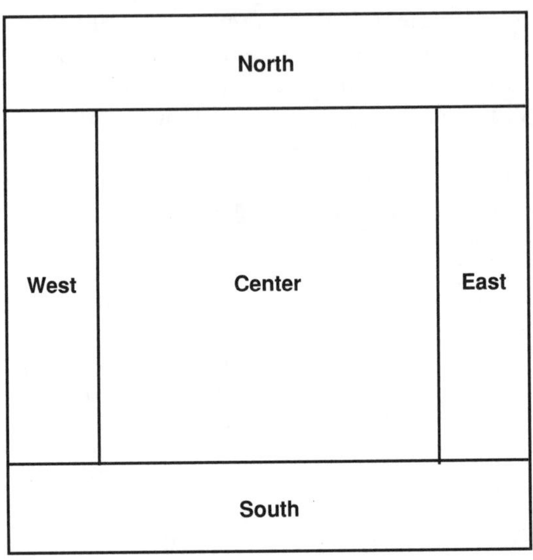

Figure 13.10
Diagram of BorderLayout areas.

To add a component to a container that is governed by a BorderLayout, use the following form of the container's `add()` method:

```
add(String name, Component comp)
```

The String in this case is either "North," "South," "East," "West," or "Center." The Component is the component that you want to add to the container. The component will be stretched horizontally if added to the North or South, or vertically if added to the East or West. The component will be stretched both horizontally and vertically to fill the remaining space if added to the Center area.

To set the layout of a container to BorderLayout, use the `setLayout()` method of the container with one of the following forms of the BorderLayout constructor:

```
setLayout(new BorderLayout(int hgap, int vgap));
setLayout(new BorderLayout());
```

The first form of the constructor takes two parameters: the horizontal gap and the vertical gap (in pixels) that will be placed between components.

The second form uses default values of zero for these gaps.

CardLayout

The CardLayout shows one "card" at a time in a set of cards. Each card can be a component, or a container of other components.

Listing 13.4 is an applet named CardDeck, which is an example of using the CardLayout layout manager. Figure 13.11 illustrates the CardDeck applet's user interface. When the user clicks one of the buttons at the bottom, the proper playing card appears. These buttons correspond to some of the CardLayout's methods for causing certain cards to appear.

Listing 13.4

```
Line=================Java Source=================
//////////
// CardDeck java  Demonstrates the use of the CardLayout
// layout manager.
//
// Author: James L. Weaver  JDK 1.1 beta1
//////////
import java.awt.*;
import java.applet.*;

public class CardDeck extends Applet {

Button firstButton,
       lastButton,
       prevButton,
       nextButton,
       queenButton;
CardLayout cardlayout;
Panel cards;

    public void init() {
        // Create a BorderLayout to have a
        // control panel area at the bottom, and the
        // rest of the applet display to show the cards.
        setLayout(new BorderLayout());
        Panel controls = new Panel();

```

continues

Listing 13.4, Continued

```
        // Create and add the controls to the panel, and
        // add the control panel to the "South" area of
        // the applet.
        firstButton = new Button("First");
        lastButton = new Button("Last");
        prevButton = new Button("Prev");
        nextButton = new Button("Next");
        queenButton = new Button("Queen");
        controls.add(firstButton);
        controls.add(lastButton);
        controls.add(prevButton);
        controls.add(nextButton);
        controls.add(queenButton);
        add("South", controls);

        // Create a panel to show the cards, and set the
        // layout to CardLayout so they will appear one
        // at a time.
        cards = new Panel();
        cardlayout = new CardLayout();
        cards.setLayout(cardlayout);

        // Add the playing cards to the cards panel
        cards.add("Ace", new Button("Ace of Hearts"));
        cards.add("Deuce", new Button("Two of Hearts"));
        cards.add("Three", new Button("Three of Hearts"));
        cards.add("Four", new Button("Four of Hearts"));
        cards.add("Five", new Button("Five of Hearts"));
        cards.add("Six", new Button("Six of Hearts"));
        cards.add("Seven", new Button("Seven of Hearts"));
        cards.add("Eight", new Button("Eight of Hearts"));
        cards.add("Nine", new Button("Nine of Hearts"));
        cards.add("Ten", new Button("Ten of Hearts"));
        cards.add("Jack", new Button("Jack of Hearts"));
        cards.add("Queen", new Button("Queen of Hearts"));
        cards.add("King", new Button("King of Hearts"));

        // Finally, add the cards Panel to the applet display.
        add("Center", cards);
```

```
    }

    // The JDK 1.0 event model may be used with 1.1
    // but may not be used in the same component with
    // the new event model.
    public boolean handleEvent(Event event) {
      if (event.id == Event.ACTION_EVENT &&
                      event.target == firstButton) {
          // Show the first card
          cardlayout.first(cards);
          return true;
      }
      if (event.id == Event.ACTION_EVENT &&
                      event.target == lastButton) {
          cardlayout.last(cards);
          // Show the last card
          return true;
      }
      if (event.id == Event.ACTION_EVENT &&
                      event.target == prevButton) {
          // Show the previous card
          cardlayout.previous(cards);
          return true;
      }
      if (event.id == Event.ACTION_EVENT &&
                      event.target == nextButton) {
          // Show the next card
          cardlayout.next(cards);
          return true;
      }
      if (event.id == Event.ACTION_EVENT &&
                      event.target == queenButton) {
          // Show the card with the name of "Queen"
          cardlayout.show(cards, "Queen");
          return true;
      }
        return super.handleEvent(event);
    }
}
```

This is the associated HTML:

```
<HTML>
<HEAD>
<TITLE> Card Deck </TITLE>
</HEAD>
<BODY>
<APPLET CODE="CardDeck.class" WIDTH=300 HEIGHT=300></APPLET>
</BODY>
</HTML>
```

The following steps walk you through some of the highlights of this example:

1. Declare some instance variables that will be used in more than one method of the CardDeck class.

   Lines 12–18 declare these instance variables.

2. Create a BorderLayout to segment the applet's display.

   In lines 24 and 25, a BorderLayout is created so that the applet's display can be divided into two different areas, which are a control panel along the bottom that contains buttons, and an area in which the playing cards are displayed.

3. Create and add the controls to the panel.

   Lines 30–40 create the buttons and add them to the control panel. These lines also add the control panel to the "South" area of the applet's display.

4. Create a panel to show the cards, and set the layout to CardLayout so they will appear one at a time.

   Lines 45–47 create a new Panel in which the playing cards are displayed, and the layout manager is set to CardLayout. Notice in line 46 that a reference is kept to the new instance of CardLayout. This is because methods of the CardLayout class will be called later in the program. When constructing the other AWT layout managers, it is generally not necessary to keep a reference, because you don't usually need to call the layout manager's methods directly.

5. Add the playing cards to the cards panel.

   Lines 50–62 add the 13 playing cards to the container. The `add()` method of the container takes two parameters:

   - A String that names the card so it can be referred to later
   - The component or container to be added to this container

6. Add the cards Panel to the applet display.

   Line 65 adds the container to the "Center" of the applet's display, which fills up all the area not used by the control panel in the "South" area.

7. Create the event handling code.

Note Note that this example uses the JDK 1.0 event-handling methods. This is permissible as long as the 1.1 event handling methods aren't used for the same component.

Lines 71–103 contain the event handling code. When the Button labeled "First" is clicked, the `first()` method in line 75 is called:

```
075            cardlayout.first(cards);
```

Notice that the `first()` method is a method of the CardLayout class. The parameter is the Container that holds the cards. When this method is called, the first card added to the container is displayed, as shown in figure 13.11.

Similarly, when the Button labeled "Last" is clicked, the `last()` method in line 80 is called:

```
080            cardlayout.last(cards);
```

When this method is called, the last card added to the container is displayed.

When the "Previous" button is clicked, the `previous()` method in line 87 is called:

```
087            cardlayout.previous(cards);
```

This causes the card that was added before the one currently being shown to be displayed.

Similarly, when the "Next" button is clicked, the `next()` method in line 93 is called:

```
093            cardlayout.next(cards);
```

This causes the card that was added after the one currently being shown to be displayed.

Finally, when the "Queen" button is clicked, the `show()` method in line 99 is called:

```
099            cardlayout.show(cards, "Queen");
```

The show method of the CardLayout class takes two parameters:

- The container that holds the cards
- The name that you gave the component in the `add()` method

This causes the card with the specified name to be displayed.

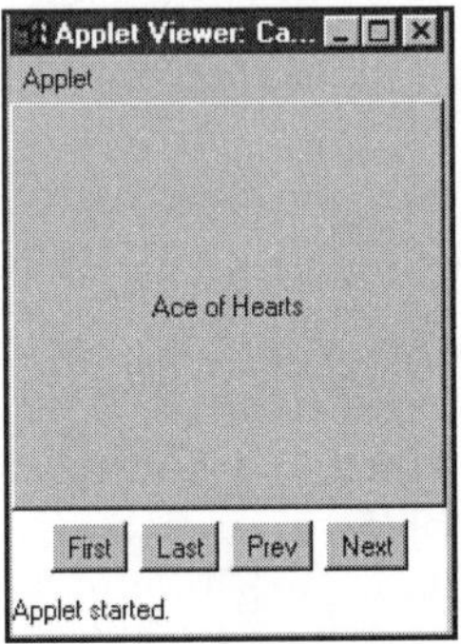

Figure 13.11
CardDeck applet display.

CardLayout can be used to implement a tabbed notebook metaphor, or to show one record at a time of a small table or result set. You probably can see how useful it is to combine layout managers in the same window. The final two layout managers, aptly named GridLayout and GridBagLayout, organize a container into rows and columns of cells.

GridLayout

The GridLayout layout manager divides a container into a grid of equally sized cells. You must specify the number of rows and columns desired when creating the layout. Each cell must have a component or container associated with it, because the cells are populated starting from the top, going left to right and top to bottom. Each component is resized to the size of the cell. The `add()` method is used to populate the container.

Listing 13.5 is an applet named JuneGrid that displays a month calendar view of June in the last year of the second millennium. Figure 13.12 shows the JuneGrid applet's display.

Listing 13.5

```
Line=================Java Source=================
//////////
// JuneGrid.java  Demonstrates the use of the GridLayout
// layout manager.
//
// Author: James L. Weaver  JDK 1.1 beta1
//////////
import java.awt.*;
import java.applet.*;

public class JuneGrid extends Applet {

    public void init() {
        // Use BorderLayout for dividing the applet display
        // into a header for month/year and a body for days
        // of the week and dates.
        setLayout(new BorderLayout());

        // Put month and year at top of applet
        Panel header = new Panel();
        header.add(new Label("June 2000"));
        add("North", header);

        // Create a Panel with a GridLayout for putting
        // the days and dates of the month in.
        Panel body = new Panel();
        body.setLayout(new GridLayout(6, 7));

        // Put the day of the week headers at the top
        String days = new String("SuMoTuWeThFrSa");
        for (int i=0; i<14; i+=2) {
            body.add(new Label(days.substring(i, i+2)));
        }

        // Make blank cells for Sunday - Wednesday
        for (int i=0; i<4; i++) {
            body.add(new Label());
```

continues

Listing 13.5, Continued

```
37            }
38
39            // Put the dates in
40            for (int i=1; i<=30; i++) {
41                // Convert integers to strings
42                body.add(new Button(new Integer(i).toString()));
43            }
44
45            add("Center", body);
46        }
47    }
```

As in other examples, BorderLayout is employed in line 16 to divide the container into different areas. In this case, we want an area in the "North" in which to put the month and year, and the "Center" area in which to put the grid of cells that hold days and dates.

Lines 19 and 21 center "June 2000" at the top of the applet's display.

Lines 25 and 26 create a Panel in which the GridLayout is set. The GridLayout in this case manages a grid with five rows and seven columns in which to place components.

The first entries in the grid are the abbreviated days of the week. These are added to the grid in lines 29–32. The simplest form of the `add()` method is used in line 31 to add the components.

In lines 35–37, four blank Labels are added because the first of June falls on a Thursday. A cell cannot be skipped, but you can use this technique to make a blank cell.

Lines 40–43 add buttons representing the dates from 1–30 to the grid as shown in figure 13.12. It is necessary in line 42 to convert the integers into strings, because this form of the Button constructor takes a String.

Finally, line 45 adds the Panel containing the days and dates to the "Center" area of the applet's display.

The final AWT layout manager is called the GridBagLayout. This is the most powerful of the AWT layout managers, but it also has a reputation of being difficult to use. The next section will de-mystify the GridBagLayout so that you can use it effectively.

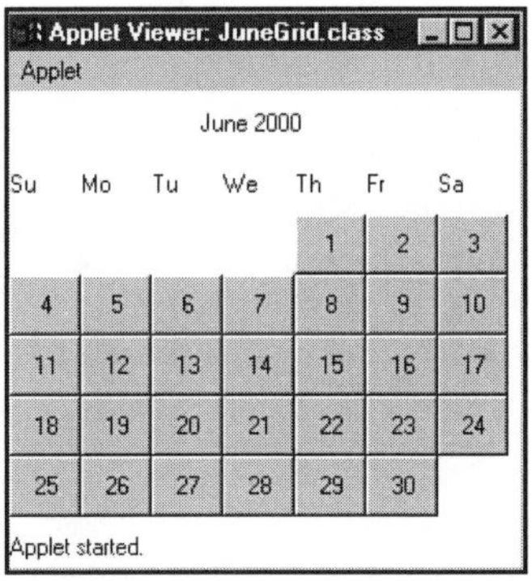

Figure 13.12

JuneGrid applet display.

GridBagLayout

GridBagLayout gives you more control over the layout of components in a container than GridLayout, for the following reasons:

- Unlike GridLayout, which makes all cells the same size, GridBagLayout enables you to influence row and column sizes, which then changes the cell sizes.
- Components placed in a GridLayout are resized to the size of the cell, but components placed in a GridBagLayout can retain their size and can be placed in one of several locations within a cell.
- The number of rows and columns in a GridLayout must be specified when the GridLayout is constructed, but this number is dynamically computed based upon placement of components in GridBagLayout.
- Components must be added left to right and top to bottom in a GridLayout, but components can be placed in a cell at a given row and column in GridBagLayout.
- Unlike GridLayout, components managed by a GridBagLayout can span two or more cells.

A *display area* is the cell or cells in which a component is placed. Each component in a GridBagLayout is associated with an instance of GridBagConstraints, which controls how the component will be laid out within its display area. Collectively, these constraints, along with component sizes, affect how the GridBagLayout layout manager arranges the components within the container.

The following constraints are specified in the GridBagConstraints class:

- gridx and gridy
- gridwidth and gridheight
- anchor
- fill
- weightx and weighty
- insets, ipadx, and ipady

Listing 13.6, which is the program PropertySheet.java on the CD-ROM accompanying this book, depicts an application that serves as an example of how you can use these GridBagConstraints constraints in conjunction with GridBagLayout to create a property sheet. It does not, however, have any code that affects the properties themselves, such as font size.

Figure 13.8 displays the output of this application, which is the user interface of the property sheet described earlier in this chapter. Please refer to the diagram in figure 13.13 during the discussion of this listing.

Listing 13.6

```
Line=================Java Source=================
//////////
// PropertySheet.java  Example of using GridBagLayout
// to position components within a container
//
// Author: James L. Weaver  JDK 1.1 beta1
//////////
import java.awt.*;

public class PropertySheet extends Frame{

    public PropertySheet() {
        super("Font Properties");

        GridBagLayout gridbag = new GridBagLayout();
        GridBagConstraints c = new GridBagConstraints();
        setLayout(gridbag);
```

```
        c.insets = new Insets(2,5,2,5);

        // Font Label
        c.gridx = 1;
        c.gridy = 1;
        c.gridwidth = 1;
        c.gridheight = 1;
        c.anchor = GridBagConstraints.SOUTHWEST;
        c.fill = GridBagConstraints.HORIZONTAL;
        c.weightx = 1.0;
        c.weighty = 0.0;
        Label fontLabel = new Label("Font:");
        gridbag.setConstraints(fontLabel, c);
        add(fontLabel);

        // Font Choice
        c.gridx = 1;
        c.gridy = 2;
        c.gridwidth = 2;
        c.gridheight = 1;
        c.anchor = GridBagConstraints.NORTHWEST;
        c.fill = GridBagConstraints.HORIZONTAL;
        c.weightx = 1.0;
        c.weighty = 0.0;
        Choice fontChoice = new Choice();
        fontChoice.addItem("Helvetica");
        fontChoice.addItem("TimesRoman");
        fontChoice.addItem("Courier");
        gridbag.setConstraints(fontChoice, c);
        add(fontChoice);

        // Size Label
        c.gridx = 3;
        c.gridy = 1;
        c.gridwidth = 1;
        c.gridheight = 1;
        c.anchor = GridBagConstraints.SOUTHWEST;
        c.fill = GridBagConstraints.HORIZONTAL;
        c.weightx = 1.0;
```

continues

Listing 13.6, Continued

```
        c.weighty = 0.0;
        Label sizeLabel = new Label("Size:");
        gridbag.setConstraints(sizeLabel, c);
        add(sizeLabel);

        // Size Choice
        c.gridx = 3;
        c.gridy = 2;
        c.gridwidth = 1;
        c.gridheight = 1;
        c.anchor = GridBagConstraints.NORTHWEST;
        c.fill = GridBagConstraints.HORIZONTAL;
        c.weightx = 1.0;
        c.weighty = 0.0;
        Choice sizeChoice = new Choice();
        sizeChoice.addItem("16");
        sizeChoice.addItem("18");
        sizeChoice.addItem("20");
        gridbag.setConstraints(sizeChoice, c);
        add(sizeChoice);

        // OK Button
        c.gridx = 4;
        c.gridy = 2;
        c.gridwidth = 1;
        c.gridheight = 1;
        c.anchor = GridBagConstraints.CENTER;
        c.fill = GridBagConstraints.HORIZONTAL;
        c.weightx = 1.0;
        c.weighty = 0.0;
        Button okButton = new Button("OK");
        gridbag.setConstraints(okButton, c);
        add(okButton);

        // Cancel Button
        c.gridx = 4;
        c.gridy = 3;
```

```
        c.gridwidth = 1;
        c.gridheight = 1;
        c.anchor = GridBagConstraints.CENTER;
        c.fill = GridBagConstraints.HORIZONTAL;
        c.weightx = 1.0;
        c.weighty = 0.0;
        Button cancelButton = new Button("Cancel");
        gridbag.setConstraints(cancelButton, c);
        add(cancelButton);

        // Reset Button
        c.gridx = 4;
        c.gridy = 4;
        c.gridwidth = 1;
        c.gridheight = 1;
        c.anchor = GridBagConstraints.CENTER;
        c.fill = GridBagConstraints.HORIZONTAL;
        c.weightx = 1.0;
        c.weighty = 0.0;
        Button resetButton = new Button("Reset");
        gridbag.setConstraints(resetButton, c);
        add(resetButton);

        // Style Label
        c.gridx = 1;
        c.gridy = 5;
        c.gridwidth = 1;
        c.gridheight = 1;
        c.anchor = GridBagConstraints.SOUTHWEST;
        c.fill = GridBagConstraints.HORIZONTAL;
        c.weightx = 1.0;
        c.weighty = 0.0;
        Label styleLabel = new Label("Style:");
        gridbag.setConstraints(styleLabel, c);
        add(styleLabel);

        // Bold Checkbox
        c.gridx = 1;
        c.gridy = 6;
```

continues

Listing 13.6, Continued

```
        c.gridwidth = 1;
        c.gridheight = 1;
        c.anchor = GridBagConstraints.WEST;
        c.fill = GridBagConstraints.HORIZONTAL;
        c.weightx = 1.0;
        c.weighty = 1.0;
        Checkbox boldCheckbox = new Checkbox("Bold");
        gridbag.setConstraints(boldCheckbox, c);
        add(boldCheckbox);

        // Italic Checkbox
        c.gridx = 1;
        c.gridy = 7;
        c.gridwidth = 1;
        c.gridheight = 1;
        c.anchor = GridBagConstraints.WEST;
        c.fill = GridBagConstraints.HORIZONTAL;
        c.weightx = 1.0;
        c.weighty = 1.0;
        Checkbox italicCheckbox = new Checkbox("Italic", null, true);
        gridbag.setConstraints(italicCheckbox, c);
        add(italicCheckbox);

        // Underline Checkbox
        c.gridx = 1;
        c.gridy = 8;
        c.gridwidth = 1;
        c.gridheight = 1;
        c.anchor = GridBagConstraints.WEST;
        c.fill = GridBagConstraints.HORIZONTAL;
        c.weightx = 1.0;
        c.weighty = 1.0;
        Checkbox underCheckbox = new Checkbox("Underline");
        gridbag.setConstraints(underCheckbox, c);
        add(underCheckbox);

        // Preview Label
```

```
        c.gridx = 2;
        c.gridy = 5;
        c.gridwidth = 1;
        c.gridheight = 1;
        c.anchor = GridBagConstraints.SOUTHWEST;
        c.fill = GridBagConstraints.HORIZONTAL;
        c.weightx = 1.0;
        c.weighty = 0.0;
        Label previewLabel = new Label("Preview:");
        gridbag.setConstraints(previewLabel, c);
        add(previewLabel);

        // Preview Canvas
        c.gridx = 2;
        c.gridy = 6;
        c.gridwidth = 3;
        c.gridheight = 3;
        c.anchor = GridBagConstraints.CENTER;
        c.fill = GridBagConstraints.BOTH;
        c.weightx = 1.0;
        c.weighty = 1.0;
        Preview preview = new Preview();
        gridbag.setConstraints(preview, c);
        add(preview);
    }

    public static void main(String args[]) {
        PropertySheet psFrame = new PropertySheet();
        // Before showing the frame, make the size
        // be dependent upon the sizes of the components.
        psFrame.pack();
        psFrame.setVisible(true);
        return;
    }

    // The JDK 1.0 event model can be used with 1.1
    // but it is not recommended, and it cannot be
    // mixed in the same component with the new event model.
    public boolean handleEvent(Event event) {
```

continues

Listing 13.6, Continued

```
208   if (event.id == Event.WINDOW_DESTROY) {
209       setVisible(false);
210       dispose();
211       System.exit(0);
212       return true;
213   }
214   return super.handleEvent(event);
215       }
216   }
217
218   // This class draws a preview of the selected font, style, and size
219   class Preview extends Canvas
220   {
221       Preview() {
222           setFont(new Font("Helvetica", Font.ITALIC, 16));
223       }
224       public void paint(Graphics g) {
225           int w = this.getSize().width;
226           int h = this.getSize().height;
227           g.clearRect(0, 0, w - 1, h - 1);
228           g.drawRect(0, 0, w - 1, h - 1);
229           g.drawString("Sample", w / 4, h / 2);
230       }
231   }
```

Line 14 creates an instance of GridBagLayout, and line 15 creates an instance of GridBagConstraints. As mentioned previously, an instance of GridBagConstraints will be associated with each added component, but because we will reuse the same instance, it is only necessary to have one instance.

Line 16 sets the layout manager of this Frame to GridBagLayout.

Line 199 causes the Frame to be resized as required by the components managed by the GridBagLayout.

Beginning with line 19, 13 sections of code exist. Each section is separated by a blank line, and does the following:

- Specifies constraints
- Creates one of the 13 components
- Places the component in the Frame

Lines 19–30, for example, deal with the Font label: Constraints such as gridx and gridy are set in lines 20–27, the Label is created in line 28, the constraints are associated with the Label in line 29, and the Label is added to the Frame in line 30. The following sections explain each of the constraints.

gridx and gridy

Lines 20 and 21 set the gridx and gridy constraints in the GridBagConstraints instance. This positions the Label component in the first column (gridx) and the first row (gridy). Please examine the other lines that set gridx and gridy (such as lines 33 and 34), and also study the corresponding components in figure 13.13.

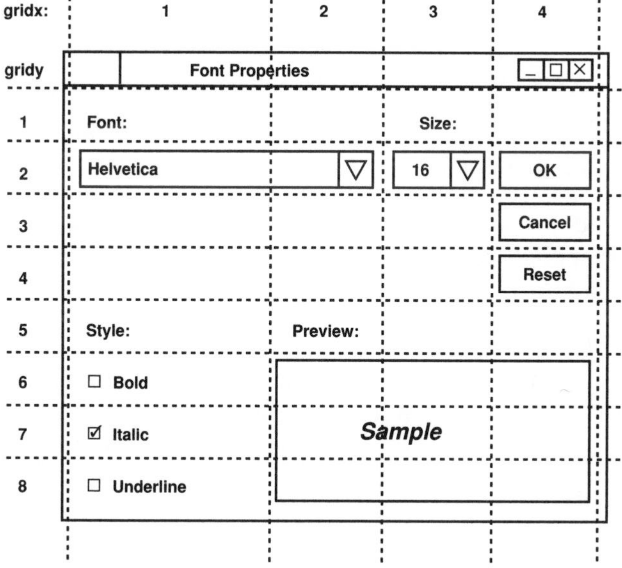

Figure 13.13

GridBagLayout diagram.

Another value for gridx and gridy is RELATIVE. This causes the component to be added directly below (for gridy) or to the right of the component that was most recently added (for gridx).

Note Note that the top row is row 1 in this case. This row also could have been referred to as 0 with the same results. Because no rows are referred to as 0, GridBagLayout puts row 1 at the top. The same holds true for other rows and columns. If, for example, column 7 has no components added to it, GridBagLayout will not provide any space for that column.

gridwidth and gridheight

Gridwidth specifies the number of cells in a row that the component's display area will occupy.

Lines 22 and 23 set the gridwidth and gridheight to one column and one row (which is the default). Note that in this example, most of the constraints are set for each component, so it's easy to tell which constraint values are being set.

Line 35 sets gridwidth to two, which causes the display area to take up two cells in the row. Examine the corresponding Choice component in figure 13.13.

Lines 184 and 185 set both gridwidth and gridheight of the preview component to three (see lines 218–231 for the Preview class.) Again, look at figure 13.13 to see the effect of this.

Two other possible values exist for gridwidth and gridheight:

- REMAINDER specifies that this component will be the last one in its row or column, respectively, so it will use the rest of the cells for its display area.
- RELATIVE specifies that this component will be the second to the last one in its row or column, respectively.

anchor

When the component is smaller than the display area, the value of the anchor constraint controls where the component should appear. The following list outlines the available choices:

- NORTH
- EAST
- SOUTH
- WEST
- NORTHEAST
- NORTHWEST
- SOUTHEAST
- SOUTHWEST
- CENTER (the default)

Line 24 sets the anchor of the Font Label to SOUTHWEST, and line 37 sets the anchor of the Font Choice to NORTHWEST. This is done to align both components to the left, and to make them as close as possible to each other vertically.

fill

The fill constraint enables you to control whether a component will be expanded to fill the display area. The following choices exist:

- HORIZONTAL: Expands the component's width to fill the display area, but not height.
- VERTICAL: Expands the component's height to fill the display area, but not width.
- BOTH: Expands both the component's width and height to fill the display area.
- NONE: The component is not expanded (the default).

Most fill constraints of the components in this example are set to HORIZONTAL for consistency of width and visual alignment. Line 187 causes the Preview component to be expanded both ways so that the component fills all the cells in its display area.

weightx and weighty

The highest weightx value in a given column influences the width of that column when there is extra horizontal space in the container. If, for example, all weightx values in a column are zero, then the column will not expand any wider than the widest component in the column. If there is a non-zero weightx value in the column, then the column will expand in proportion to the highest weightx value in each of the other columns.

The highest weighty value in a given row influences the height of that row when there is extra vertical space in the container. If, for example, all weighty values in a row are zero, then the row will not expand any taller than the tallest component in the row. If there is a non-zero weighty value in the row, then the row will expand in proportion to the highest weighty value in each of the other rows.

If you run the PropertySheet application and expand the Frame vertically, you will notice that the components in the top part of the Frame remain stationary. The components in the bottom part, however, increase in vertical separation, and the preview component expands. This is due to the weighty values associated with each component.

The components in the upper section have a weighty value of 0, so none of the rows expand (see lines 27, 40, 56, 69, 85, 98, 111, and 124.) At least one of the components in each of the lower four rows must have a weighty value of 1, to ensure they expand proportionately to each other (see lines 137, 150, 163 and 189).

Weightx and weighty can be any double precision value; the default is 0.

insets, ipadx, and ipady

Insets control the minimum amount of space that the component is to be inset from the edges of the display area. This causes the components not to be able to touch each other. Line 17 sets this value, which remains constant for all `setConstraints()` calls.

ipadx and ipady specify the amount of space to add to the minimum width and height of the component, respectively. These values default to zero and are not used in the example.

To continue gaining experience with GridBagLayout and the associated GridBagConstraints, you may want to test the effects of changing some of the constraints in this example.

Summary

This chapter detailed how to use components, containers, and layout managers in Java programs, as well as pointing out some features new to JDK 1.1. Among these features, the chapter discussed the Delegation Event Model, many new or deprecated methods, and the ScrollPane class.

The next chapter, "The New, Improved AWT: Menus, Events, and More New Features," focuses on more new JDK 1.1 features, including menus, the new PopupMenu class, and the capability to assign shortcut keys. The chapter also will examine the Delegation Event Model more closely, discuss how to access the colors used in the desktop environment, and will cover printing from a Java program. Finally, the clipboard will be discussed in connection with the underlying data transfer API.

CHAPTER 14

The New, Improved AWT: Menus, Events, and More New Features

The last chapter explored the use of components, containers, and layout managers in Java programs. Chapter 13, "The New, Improved AWT: GUI Components, Containers, and Layout Managers," discussed many new JDK 1.1 features, such as the Delegation Event Model, new and deprecated methods, and the ScrollPane class.

This chapter examines more new JDK 1.1 features. In the process of examining menus, you learn how to create pop-up menus and assign shortcut keys. The new Delegation Event Model, which has performance and scaleability advantages over the 1.0 event model, will be examined more closely. To round out the chapter, more new AWT-related features, such as focus transversal (which enables the user to tab between fields), accessing desktop colors, printing, and clipboard programming will be discussed.

Understanding AWT Menus

Two types of AWT menus exist:

- Menu bar menus reside in the menu bar of a frame.
- Pop-up menus, sometimes referred to as context menus, which were introduced in JDK 1.1.

An application usually has only one menu bar menu that generally appears in the main frame of the application. Because a menu bar requires a frame, an applet can't have this kind of menu unless it creates a frame with which the menu can be associated. Figure 14.2 shows an example of a menu bar menu.

Pop-up menus are becoming very standard. Users now expect that a pop-up menu will appear when they point at a user interface element and click the correct mouse button. This menu contains menu items pertinent to the element at which they are pointing. A pop-up menu associated with a selection of text in a word processor, for example, may have a menu item that opens a font selection dialog box. Figure 14.4 shows an example of a pop-up menu.

The classes that implement menus are all part of the java.awt package, and are derived from the java.awt.MenuComponent class. Figure 14.1 shows the hierarchy of classes derived from the Component class.

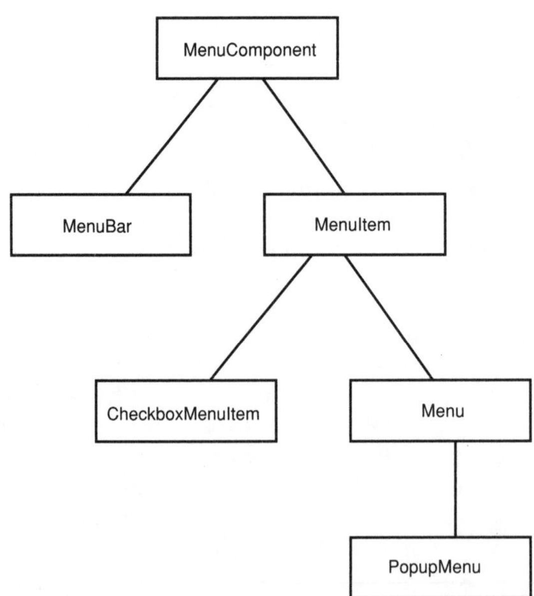

Figure 14.1
The java.awt. MenuComponent class hierarchy.

Each of the classes in this hierarchy are discussed in the following sections. These classes will be presented by loosely following the class hierarchy, but we will deviate slightly so that things appearing on menus (MenuItem and CheckboxMenuItem) are discussed after the menus themselves (Menu and PopupMenu).

The MenuComponent Class

All menu-related classes are derived from the MenuComponent class, which contains methods common to all menu-related classes. One such method is `setFont()`, which applies to any menu component.

The MenuBar Class

The MenuBar class contains methods that manage the menu bar. The `add()` method, for example, adds a menu to the menu bar, and the `getMenuCount()` method returns the number of top-level menus that a menu bar has. Table 14.1 shows some of the constructors and methods of the MenuBar class. For a complete list, see the following Web page:

```
http://java.sun.com/products/JDK/1.1/docs/api/java.awt.MenuBar.html
```

TABLE 14.1
Some Constructors and Methods in the MenuBar Class

Constructor/Method	Description
MenuBar()	Creates a new MenuBar.
void setHelpMenu(Menu)	Causes the specified menu to be the help menu, which has platform-specific locations.
menu add(Menu)	Adds the specified menu to the menu bar.
void remove(int)	Removes the menu at the specified index from the menu bar.
void remove(MenuComponent)	Removes the specified menu from the menu bar.
int getMenuCount()	Returns the number of menus in this menu bar. (Note that `countMenus()` has been deprecated.)
Menu getMenu(int)	Return the menu at the specified index.
Enumeration shortcuts()	Returns an Enumeration of the shortcuts on this menu bar.

A MenuBar contains menus, which are managed by the Menu class.

The Menu Class

The Menu class has methods that manage a particular menu. This menu could be a top-level menu on the menu bar, a submenu that appears within another menu, or a pop-up menu. The `remove()` method, which removes a particular menu item from the menu, is one such method. Table 14.2 shows some of the constructors and methods of the Menu class. For a complete list, refer to the following Web page:

```
http://java.sun.com/products/JDK/1.1/docs/api/java.awt.Menu.html
```

Table 14.2
Some Constructors and Methods in the Menu Class

Constructor/Method	Description
Menu(String)	Creates a new menu with the specified label.
int getItemCount()	Returns the number of items in this menu. (Note that `countItems()` has been deprecated.)
MenuItem getItem(int)	Returns the menu item at the specified index.
MenuItem add(MenuItem)	Adds the specified menu item to this menu.
void insert(MenuItem, int)	Inserts the specified menu item at the specified index.
void addSeparator()	Adds a separator line to this menu.
void insertSeparator(int)	Inserts a separator line to this menu at the specified index.
void remove(int)	Removes the item from this menu at the specified index.
void remove(MenuComponent)	Removes the specified menu item from this menu.
void removeAll()	Removes all items from this menu.

The pop-up menu is a type of menu new to JDK 1.1.

The PopupMenu Class

The PopupMenu is a specialization of the Menu class. Pop-up menus are used to supply context-sensitive menus within an applet or application. The PopupMenu menu class contains the `show()` method because a pop-up menu is not visible until the user requests it. For a complete list of constructors and methods in the PopupMenu class, refer to the following Web page:

```
http://java.sun.com/products/JDK/1.1/docs/api/java.awt.PopupMenu.html
```

The MenuItem Class

The MenuItem class contains methods that manage a particular menu item. The `setLabel()` method, for example, specifies the String to be displayed in the menu item, and the `setEnable()` method enables and disables a menu item. Notice that the Menu class is derived from the MenuItem class: This is because a menu within a containing menu is also a menu item of the containing menu. Table 14.3 shows some of the constructors and methods of the MenuItem class. For a complete list, refer to the following Web page:

```
http://java.sun.com/products/JDK/1.1/docs/api/java.awt.MenuItem.html
```

Table 14.3
Some Constructors and Methods in the MenuItem Class

Constructor/Method	Description
MenuItem(String)	Creates a new menu item with the specified label.
MenuItem(String, MenuShortcut)	Creates a new menu item with the specified shortcut.
String getLabel()	Returns the label for this menu item.
void setLabel(String)	Sets this menu item's label to the specified label.
boolean isEnabled()	Returns whether the menu item is enabled.
void setEnabled(boolean)	Enables the menu item so that the user can select it. (Note that `enable()` and `disable()` have been deprecated.)
MenuShortcut getShortcut()	Returns the shortcut associated with this menu item.

continues

Table 14.3, Continued
Some Constructors and Methods in the MenuItem Class

Constructor/Method	Description
void setShortcut(MenuShortcut)	Associates the specified menu shortcut to this menu item.
void deleteShortcut()	Removes the menu shortcut from this menu item.
void setActionCommand(String)	Sets the action command string to the specified string. This is embedded into the ActionEvent when an ActionEvent is fired.
void addActionListener (ActionListener)	Registers an event listener to receive action events.

Next, we will discuss the CheckboxMenuItem. A CheckboxMenuItem works like a check box, in that it stores a true or false state.

The CheckboxMenuItem Class

The CheckboxMenuItem class is a specialization of the MenuItem class that represents a menu item, which toggles between true and false when selected by the user. An example of a CheckboxMenuItem method is `getState()`, which returns the current true or false state of the item. Listing 14.1 creates a CheckboxMenuItem.

Menu Bar Menus

Listing 14.1 (program MenuDemo.java on the CD-ROM accompanying this book) shows an application that serves as nothing more than a simple example of how you can create menu bar menus and pop-up menus in a Java program. Figures 14.2, 14.3, and 14.4 display this application's user interface, which consists of a frame containing two buttons. When you click on the menu titles in the menu bar, the menu items appear. When you click the appropriate mouse button on the button labeled "Pops," a pop-up menu appears that contains varieties of "pops" (cola, soda, and root beer.) When you click the appropriate mouse button on the button labeled "Popups," or anywhere else in the frame, a different pop-up menu appears that contains things that "pop up" (pop tarts, weasels, clowns, and daisies.) This example also demonstrates how to assign shortcut keys to menu items. The sections following the listing will cover these topics in more detail.

Listing 14.1

```
Line=================Java Source=================
//////////
// MenuDemo.java  Demonstrates how to code menus
// that use shortcut keys, and pop-up menus.
//
// Author: James L. Weaver  JDK 1.1 beta3
//////////
package chapter14.code.menudemo;

import java.awt.*;
import java.awt.event.*;

public class MenuDemo extends Frame
                    implements ActionListener {

    public PopupMenu popMenu1, popMenu2;
    Button btn1, btn2;

    public MenuDemo() {
        super("Java Menu Demonstration");

        // Create and assign a listener to catch mouse events
        addMouseListener(new Madapt(this));
        addWindowListener(new Wadapt());
        setSize(300, 200);
        setLayout(new FlowLayout());

        btn1 = new Button("Popups");
        btn1.addMouseListener(new Madapt(this));
        add(btn1);
        btn2 = new Button("Pops");
        btn2.addMouseListener(new Madapt(this));
        add(btn2);

        buildMenu();
        buildPopup1();
        buildPopup2();
```

continues

Listing 14.1, Continued

```
        setVisible(true);
        btn1.requestFocus();
    }

    private void buildMenu() {
        // Create a menu bar and set in the frame.
        MenuBar mb = new MenuBar();
        setMenuBar(mb);

        // Create and populate a File menu.
        Menu fileMenu = new Menu("File");
        mb.add(fileMenu);

        MenuItem miNew = new MenuItem("New");
        miNew.addActionListener(this);
        fileMenu.add(miNew);

        MenuItem miOpen = new MenuItem("Open");
        miOpen.addActionListener(this);
        fileMenu.add(miOpen);

        MenuItem miSave = new MenuItem("Save");
        miSave.addActionListener(this);
        fileMenu.add(miSave);

        fileMenu.addSeparator();

        MenuItem miExit = new MenuItem("Exit");
        miExit.addActionListener(this);
        fileMenu.add(miExit);

        // Create and populate an Options menu
        // that contains three checkable items,
        // a separator, and a submenu.
        Menu optionsMenu = new Menu("Options");
        mb.add(optionsMenu);

```

```
        CheckboxMenuItem miBold =
                new CheckboxMenuItem("Bold", true);
        // Assign the Ctrl+b shortcut key.
        miBold.setShortcut(new MenuShortcut('b'));
        miBold.addActionListener(this);
        optionsMenu.add(miBold);

        CheckboxMenuItem miItalics =
                new CheckboxMenuItem("Italics", false);
        // Assign the Ctrl+i shortcut key.
        miItalics.setShortcut(new MenuShortcut('i'));
        miItalics.addActionListener(this);
        optionsMenu.add(miItalics);

        // Assign the Ctrl+u shortcut key.
        CheckboxMenuItem miUnder =
                new CheckboxMenuItem("Under", false);
        miUnder.setShortcut(new MenuShortcut('u'));
        miUnder.addActionListener(this);
        optionsMenu.add(miUnder);

        optionsMenu.addSeparator();

        // Create and populate a submenu to the Options menu.
        Menu suboptMenu = new Menu("Submenu");
        optionsMenu.add(suboptMenu);

        MenuItem miSubitem1 = new MenuItem("Sub Item 1");
        miSubitem1.addActionListener(this);
        suboptMenu.add(miSubitem1);

        MenuItem miSubitem2 = new MenuItem("Sub Item 2");
        miSubitem2.addActionListener(this);
        suboptMenu.add(miSubitem2);

        // Create and populate a Help menu.
        Menu helpMenu = new Menu("Help");
        mb.add(helpMenu);
        mb.setHelpMenu(helpMenu);
```

continues

Listing 14.1, Continued

```

        // Assign the Ctrl+a shortcut key.
        MenuItem miAbout = new MenuItem("About…",
                                new MenuShortcut('a'));
        miAbout.addActionListener(this);
        helpMenu.add(miAbout);

        // Assign the Shift+c shortcut key.
        MenuItem miContents = new MenuItem("Contents",
                                new MenuShortcut('c', true));
        miContents.addActionListener(this);
        helpMenu.add(miContents);
    }

    private void buildPopup1() {
        // Create a pop-up menu and attach it to this frame.
        popMenu1 = new PopupMenu();
        add(popMenu1);

        MenuItem miTarts = new MenuItem("Tarts");
        miTarts.addActionListener(this);
        popMenu1.add(miTarts);

        MenuItem miWeasels = new MenuItem("Weasels");
        miWeasels.addActionListener(this);
        popMenu1.add(miWeasels);

        MenuItem miClowns = new MenuItem("Clowns");
        miClowns.addActionListener(this);
        popMenu1.add(miClowns);

        MenuItem miDaisies = new MenuItem("Daisies");
        miDaisies.addActionListener(this);
        popMenu1.add(miDaisies);
    }

    private void buildPopup2() {
```

```
        // Create a pop-up menu and attach it to a button.
        popMenu2 = new PopupMenu();
        btn2.add(popMenu2);

        MenuItem miCola = new MenuItem("Cola");
        miCola.addActionListener(this);
        popMenu2.add(miCola);

        MenuItem miSoda = new MenuItem("Soda");
        miSoda.addActionListener(this);
        popMenu2.add(miSoda);

        MenuItem miRoot = new MenuItem("Root Beer");
        miRoot.addActionListener(this);
        popMenu2.add(miRoot);
    }

    public void actionPerformed(ActionEvent evt) {
        System.out.println(((MenuItem)evt.getSource()).getLabel());
    }

    public static void main(String args[]) {
        MenuDemo menuFrame = new MenuDemo();
        return;
    }
}

class Madapt extends MouseAdapter
{
    MenuDemo md;

    public Madapt(MenuDemo md) {
        // Save a reference to the MenuDemo instance
        // to access the pop-up menus.
        this.md = md;
    }

    public void mouseReleased(MouseEvent evt) {
        Component comp = (Component)evt.getSource();
```

continues

Listing 14.1, Continued

```
189            // Find out if the mouse event was a pop-up menu request.
190            if (evt.isPopupTrigger()) {
191                if (evt.getSource() == md.btn2)
192                    md.popMenu2.show(comp, evt.getX(), evt.getY());
193                else
194                    md.popMenu1.show(comp, evt.getX(), evt.getY());
195            }
196        }
197    }
198
199    class Wadapt extends WindowAdapter
200    {
201        public void windowClosing(WindowEvent evt) {
202            Frame frm = (Frame)evt.getSource();
203            frm.setVisible(false);
204            frm.dispose();
205            System.exit(0);
206        }
207    }
```

Before examining the steps to creating a menu, briefly examine the listing:

Lines 12–39 define the MenuDemo class, which is a Frame that will contain a menu bar with menus. Each menu will contain menu items.

Line 34 calls the `buildMenu()` method, which builds the application menu. Lines 41–125 hold the code for this method.

Lines 35 and 36 call `buildPopup1()` and `buildPopup2()`, which build certain pop-up menus that will be explained shortly. The code for these methods lie in lines 127–165, which you can ignore for now.

Figure 14.2 shows the two buttons in the user interface for this applet, along with the menu bar menu.

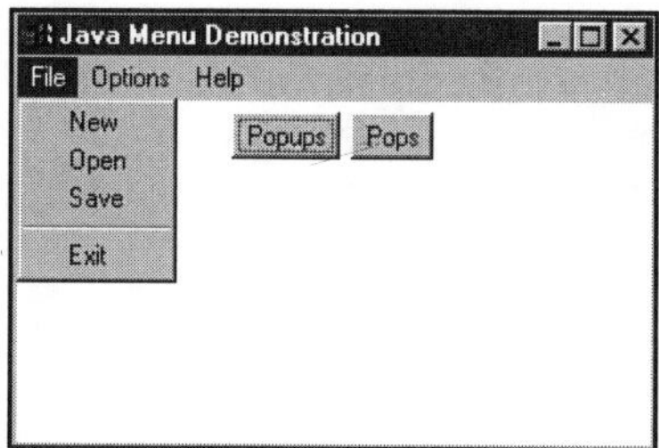

Figure 14.2

MenuDemo application display showing menu bar menu.

Steps for Creating a Menu Bar Menu

To build a menu that resides in the menu bar of a frame, follow these steps. The corresponding lines of code from listing 14.1 are provided to illustrate each step.

1. Create a menu bar. This is accomplished by creating an instance of MenuBar:

```
MenuBar mb = new MenuBar();
```

2. Set the menu bar into the Frame. Use the `setMenuBar()` method of the Frame class to accomplish this:

```
setMenuBar(mb);
```

3. Create one or more top-level menus. Each menu is an instance of Menu. You can pass a String to the constructor containing the menu's label, which by convention should not contain spaces:

```
Menu fileMenu = new Menu("File");
```

Tip Individual menu item labels can contain spaces, but menu labels should not.

4. Add the menu to the menu bar, using the `add()` method of the MenuBar class:

```
mb.add(fileMenu);
```

5. Create one or more menu items to put in each of the menus. Each menu item is an instance of MenuItem. You can pass a String containing the menu item's label into the constructor:

```
MenuItem miNew = new MenuItem("New");
```

6. You may want to associate an event listener to the menu item so that when the menu item is selected, a method of the listener will be called. This example adds an ActionListener, which handles "action" events, such as button clicks and menu selections. This chapter covers event handling in later sections.

```
miNew.addActionListener(this);
```

7. Add the menu item to the menu using the `add()` method of the Menu class:

```
fileMenu.add(miNew);
```

Although all the steps (except as noted in step six) are required in creating menus, they don't have to be performed in the order shown here—it is up to the developer's discretion. The previous example serves merely as an illustration of the process.

Creating Checkbox Menu Items

Lines 74–79 show an example of creating a checkbox menu item and adding it to a menu.

```
074    CheckboxMenuItem miBold =
075          new CheckboxMenuItem("Bold", true);
076    // Assign the Ctrl+b shortcut key.
077    miBold.setShortcut(new MenuShortcut('b'));
078    miBold.addActionListener(this);
079    optionsMenu.add(miBold);
```

In line 75, a version of the CheckboxMenuItem constructor is used to create a new CheckboxMenuItem instance with a label containing the String "Bold" and a true state. This means that the menu item will be checked by default.

Line 77 assigns this menu item a shortcut key, which will be discussed shortly. Line 79 adds the new checkbox menu item to the "Options" menu.

Table 14.4 shows some of the constructors and methods of the CheckboxMenuItem class. For a complete list, refer to the following Web page:

```
http://java.sun.com/products/JDK/1.1/docs/api/
java.awt.CheckboxMenuItem.html
```

TABLE 14.4
Some Constructors and Methods in the CheckboxMenuItem Class

Constructor/Method	Description
CheckboxMenuItem(String)	Creates a CheckboxMenuItem with the specified label. State defaults to false.
CheckboxMenuItem(String, boolean)	Creates a CheckboxMenuItem with the specified label and state.
boolean getState()	Returns the state of this CheckboxMenuItem.
void setState(boolean)	Sets the state of this CheckboxMenuItem.
void setLabel(String)	Sets the MenuItem label to the specified String.
void addItemListener(ItemListener)	Registers an event listener to receive item events.

Now that you know how to create regular menu items and checkbox menu items, we must cover two additional elements associated with menu items: the menu item separator and the submenu, which is a menu item that is also a menu.

Creating Menu Item Separators

A horizontal line is sometimes used to provide separation between menu items in the same menu. This is accomplished through the `addSeparator()` method of the Menu class:

```
        fileMenu.addSeparator();
```

Creating Submenus

As mentioned before, a menu can contain another menu, which is typically called a submenu, or cascading menu. The submenu adds an extra level to the menu structure, and is useful for organizing menu choices hierarchically. This keeps the user from being inundated with too many menu choices at one time. The theory behind submenus follows the GUI design principle of "progressive disclosure"—showing the user only what they need to see at a given time. Figure 14.3 shows the submenu in the MenuDemo example. Generally, it is not advisable to make the user navigate menus more than three or four levels deep. To create submenus, consider the following in listing 14.1:

Lines 71 and 72 create and add a menu labeled "Options" to the menu bar.

```
071          Menu optionsMenu = new Menu("Options");
072          mb.add(optionsMenu);
```

Lines 98–107 create and add a menu labeled "Submenu" to the "Options" menu. Menu items then are added to the submenu, as depicted in figure 14.3.

```
098          Menu suboptMenu = new Menu("Submenu");
099          optionsMenu.add(suboptMenu);
100
101          MenuItem miSubitem1 = new MenuItem("Sub Item 1");
102          miSubitem1.addActionListener(this);
103          suboptMenu.add(miSubitem1);
104
105          MenuItem miSubitem2 = new MenuItem("Sub Item 2");
106          miSubitem2.addActionListener(this);
107          suboptMenu.add(miSubitem2);
```

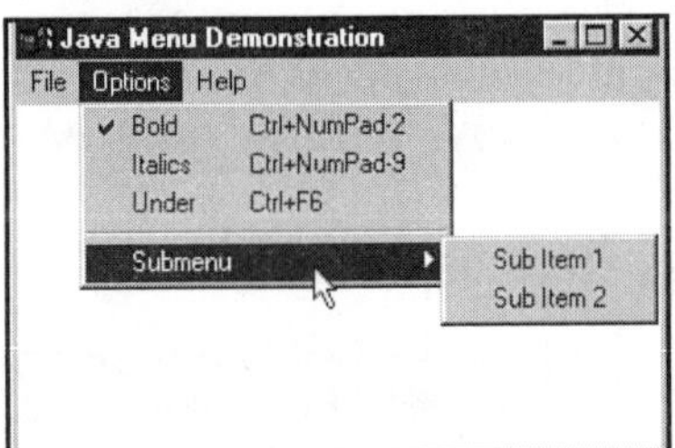

Figure 14.3
MenuDemo application display showing a submenu.

You now know how to create menus that reside on the menu bar. In the following section, you learn how to create pop-up menus.

Pop-Up Menus

Creating a pop-up menu is similar to creating a menu bar menu with one important difference. Instead of having a menu bar as its parent, a pop-up menu's parent is a GUI component. Two pop-up menus, for example, exist in the MenuDemo application—popMenu1 and popMenu2. The main frame owns popMenu1, while popMenu2 is owned by the btn2 button, which is labeled "Pops." These pop-up menus are depicted in figure 14.4.

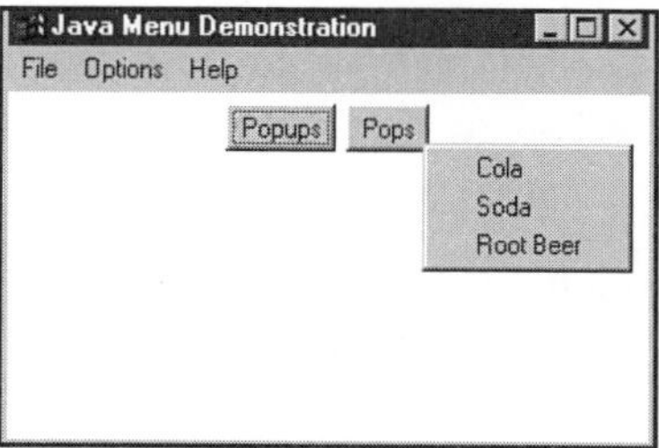

Figure 14.4

MenuDemo application display showing a pop-up menu.

Creating Pop-Up Menus

To build a pop-up menu, you can follow these steps. The steps do not necessarily have to be performed in this order. The corresponding lines of code from listing 14.1 are provided to illustrate each step.

1. Create an instance of PopupMenu.

   Line 129 of listing 14.1 shows popMenu1 being created. This action is similar to step 3 in the previous section, "Steps for Creating a Menu Bar Menu."

```
129            popMenu1 = new PopupMenu();
```

2. Add the pop-up menu to its parent component.

   Line 130 adds popMenu1 to the main frame of the application.

```
130            add(popMenu1);
```

   This action is similar to step 4 in the previous section, "Steps for Creating a Menu Bar Menu." The main frame is now the pop-up menu's parent, so the pop-up menu lies within the main frame's containment hierarchy.

   The process for adding a menu item to a pop-up menu is identical to the process for adding a menu item to a menu bar menu. Consider the similarity between steps 3, 4, and 5 in this section to steps 5, 6, and 7 in the previous section, "Steps for Creating a Menu Bar Menu."

3. Create one or more menu items to put in the pop-up menu.

```
132            MenuItem miTarts = new MenuItem("Tarts");
```

4. Optionally associate an event listener to the menu item.

```
133            miTarts.addActionListener(this);
```

5. Add the menu item to the menu using the `add()` method of the PopupMenu class.

```
        popMenu1.add(miTarts);
```

You also can add separators and submenus to a pop-up menu in the same manner that you would add them to a menu bar menu, as previously described.

Activating Pop-Up Menus

For the pop-up menu to be activated by a mouse event, the event must be trapped. In this example, line 22 adds a mouse event listener to the main frame.

```
022         addMouseListener(new Madapt(this));
```

Whenever the user presses and releases the mouse, the `mouseReleased()` method in lines 187–196 is called.

```
187     public void mouseReleased(MouseEvent evt) {
188         Component comp = (Component)evt.getSource();
189         // Find out if the mouse event was a pop-up menu request.
190         if (evt.isPopupTrigger()) {
191             if (evt.getSource() == md.btn2)
192                 md.popMenu2.show(comp, evt.getX(), evt.getY());
193             else
194                 md.popMenu1.show(comp, evt.getX(), evt.getY());
195         }
196     }
```

Line 190 calls the `isPopupTrigger()` method of the MouseEvent to find out if this event was caused by a pop-up menu request. A pop-up menu request is a platform-dependent mouse click (such as button 2 on MS-Windows, and button 3 on Sun Solaris.)

Line 188 identifies the component that fired the event, which in this case is the component that the user clicked. This is necessary because the PopupMenu `show()` method (in lines 192 and 194) shows the pop-up menu at a position relative to this component. The `show()` method of the Popup class is defined as follows:

```
public void show(Component origin, int x, int y)
```

Note that the user can cause btn1 (labeled Popups) to trigger popMenu1, even though the main frame, not btn1, owns popMenu1. This is because btn1 rests in the containment hierarchy of the main frame. A pop-up menu can be triggered from any component in the containment hierarchy of the pop-up menu's owner.

Now that you know how to create menu bar menus and pop-up menus, the next section presents shortcut keys, a menu feature new to JDK 1.1.

Assigning Shortcut Keys

Shortcut keys, also known as *keyboard equivalents* or *accelerator keys,* enable the user to make menu choices from the keyboard. Users who are experienced with an application often appreciate shortcut keys because they help the user to navigate the application more quickly. Shortcut keys also reduce the need for the use of a mouse for people who either prefer not to or can't use one.

The Ctrl key (or Command key on Macintosh) is used in conjunction with an alphanumeric key to produce a shortcut key. The Shift key also can be used in addition to the other two keys. Therefore, Ctrl+s, Ctrl+Shift+q, and Ctrl+3 are all valid shortcut keys, but Shift+z is not.

Lines 115 and 116 offer an example of how to create a menu item that also can be invoked with a shortcut key.

```
115         MenuItem miAbout = new MenuItem("About…",
116                                         new MenuShortcut('a'));
```

As a result, a platform-specific label appears beside the menu item (for example "Ctrl+a" on MS-Windows), and the menu item can be invoked by pressing Ctrl+a on the keyboard. This is depicted in figure 14.3, but due to a bug in JDK 1.1 beta 3, the labels aren't quite correct.

The new class java.awt.MenuShortcut has been added in JDK 1.1 to enable you to create shortcut keys. Table 14.5 shows some of the constructors and methods of the MenuShortcut class, which is derived from an event class. For a complete list, refer to the following Web page:

```
http://java.sun.com/products/JDK/1.1/docs/api/java.awt.MenuShortcut.html
```

The form of the MenuShortcut class constructor used in line 116 takes one parameter, which is the alphanumeric key used in the key combination that makes up this shortcut. The MenuShortcut instance is passed as the second parameter to a MenuItem constructor that is new to JDK 1.1, which creates the menu item with the specified shortcut key.

Table 14.5
Some Constructors and Methods in the MenuShortcut Class

Constructor/Method	Description
MenuShortcut(int)	Creates a menu shortcut with the specified key.
MenuShortcut(int, boolean)	Creates a menu shortcut with the specified key. If the second parameter is true, the Shift key must be used as well.
int getKey()	Returns the key associated with this menu shortcut.
boolean usesShiftModifier()	Returns whether the shortcut includes a Shift key.

Another way to assign a shortcut key to a menu item is to call the `setShortcut()` method of the desired menu item. Line 77, for example, assigns the Ctrl+b menu shortcut to the "Bold" menu item:

```
074         CheckboxMenuItem miBold =
075                 new CheckboxMenuItem("Bold", true);
076         // Assign the Ctrl+b shortcut key.
077         miBold.setShortcut(new MenuShortcut('b'));
```

For this example application to respond to menu shortcuts, one of the components in the frame must have *keyboard focus*. To achieve this, line 38 requests focus for the "Popups" button:

```
038         btn1.requestFocus();
```

When a component has keyboard focus, any keys pressed are delivered to the component. For example, if a text field has keyboard focus, when alphanumeric keys are pressed they appear in the text field. Pressing the Tab key moves keyboard focus from one component to another one.

This section has explained how to create two different kinds of menus: menu bar menus and pop-up menus. You have seen the classes that implement menus in Java, and you have learned to create menu shortcuts that grant the user keyboard access to menu items.

In the next section, you will learn about the Java event models that are new to JDK 1.1. Although the JDK 1.0 event model will work with JDK 1.1, JavaSoft suggests that new applications be developed using the JDK 1.1 event models.

Understanding the Java Event Models

Event handling is a mechanism by which events such as button clicks, key presses, and scrollbar adjustments can be fired, caught, and received by the code that is created to handle the events. JDK 1.1 introduced the following new models associated with event handling:

- The Delegation Event Model
- The Extended Component Event Model

These models were introduced to correct some of the deficiencies in the JDK 1.0 model, to increase performance, and to support Java Beans (which Chapter 15, "Java Beans: Java's Component Architecture," will cover).

The *Delegation Event Model* is the name used by JavaSoft for the new JDK 1.1 event model. The *Extended Component Event Model* is a name introduced by this book. It identifies a way of using the mechanisms defined in the *Delegation Event Model* to handle events in extended components.

Overview of Delegation Event Model

If you've examined the examples in Chapter 13, "The New, Improved AWT: GUI Components, Containers, and Layout Managers," and the example earlier in this chapter, you are already somewhat familiar with the Delegation Event Model. Look at the MenuDemo application in listing 14.1 again, this time to examine a simple example of the Delegation Event Model.

Lines 50–52 create and add a menu item with the label "New" to the "File" menu. During this process, line 51 assigns an *action listener* to this menu item, which causes any *action events* fired by this menu item to be delegated to the specified action listener.

```
050         MenuItem miNew = new MenuItem("New");
051         miNew.addActionListener(this);
052         fileMenu.add(miNew);
```

A *listener* is a class that implements a given interface, depending on the type of listener it is. In this case, the listener is an action listener, which implements the ActionListener interface. The ActionListener interface in turn defines the `actionPerformed()` method. In this simple example, line 51 specifies that the current object is the action listener.

Lines 12 and 13 declare that this class implements the ActionListener interface:

```
012  public class MenuDemo extends Frame
013                      implements ActionListener {
```

Lines 167–169 implement the ActionListener interface and are executed when the "New" menu item fires an action event.

```
167      public void actionPerformed(ActionEvent evt) {
168          System.out.println(((MenuItem)evt.getSource()).getLabel());
169      }
```

Line 168 calls the `getSource()` method of the event object that was passed. This returns a reference to the event source, which in this case is the MenuItem instance named miNew. The reference is cast to a MenuItem, and then the `getLabel()` method is called to return the label on the menu item, which is then printed. As a result, the string "New" prints to the system output when the user chooses the "New" menu item.

Figure 14.5 depicts the relationships between:

- The event source, which in this case is the miNew menu item.
- The event, which in this case is an ActionEvent.
- The event listener, which in this case is an ActionListener.

These three items (*event source, event,* and *event listener*) define the Delegation Event Model. When an *event* is emitted by an *event source,* the *event* is delegated to the *event listener,* which is responsible for carrying out the appropriate response.

When the `addActionListener()` method of miNew is called, a reference to the ActionListener is created and stored within miNew. This process is known as registering a listener. When the user chooses the miNew menu item, an ActionEvent is fired and passed to the `actionPerformed()` method of each registered ActionListener.

ActionListener is only one of several event listeners defined by the JDK. The next section explores each of these listeners, including ActionListener.

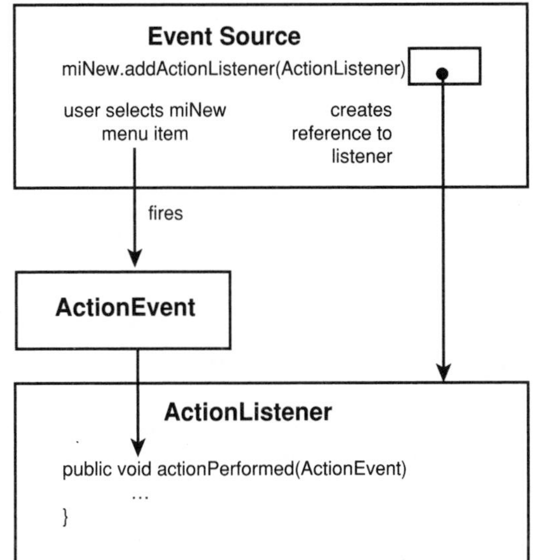

Figure 14.5
MenuDemo example of the Delegation Event Model.

Event Listeners

The JDK defines a total of nine listeners, and each listener has one or more types of events for which it listens. These listeners can be divided into two categories:

- Listeners that listen for low-level events
- Listeners that listen for semantic events

Low-Level Versus Semantic Events

Low-level events represent traditional events that can happen to a GUI element in a windowing system. These include event types such as MOUSE_CLICKED, FOCUS_LOST, and KEY_PRESSED.

Semantic events represent higher-level events that a user can perform. These events are associated here with Java AWT components, but you could create custom components that fire these events as well. Three semantic event types exist:

- The ACTION_PERFORMED event type is fired when the user chooses a MenuItem, clicks a Button, double-clicks a List, or presses the Enter key when a TextField has focus. This event type has a semantic meaning of "perform a command."

- The ADJUSTMENT_VALUE_CHANGED event type is fired when the value of a Scrollbar is adjusted, whether by dragging the bubble, clicking an arrow, or pressing the Page Up key. This event type has a semantic meaning of "an adjustable value changed."

- The ITEM_STATE_CHANGED event type is fired when the user selects or deselects an item in a List, Choice, Checkbox, or CheckboxMenuItem. This event type has a semantic meaning of "the state of an item has changed."

Note The difference between low-level events and semantic events can be confusing. The basic difference is that low-level events have no semantic meaning associated with them, and semantic events have a semantic meaning associated with them. For example, when you click a check box with a mouse, several events are emitted. Two of these events are MouseEvent.MOUSE_CLICKED which is a low-level event, and ItemEvent.ITEM_STATE_CHANGED which is a semantic event. The MouseEvent.MOUSE_CLICKED event is a specific event that happens to a GUI component, but has no semantic meaning associated with it. The ItemEvent.ITEM_STATE_CHANGED event has a semantic meaning associated with it: "the state of an item has changed." It is not tied to a specific low-level user interface event, rather it can be triggered by a clicking the check box or pressing the space bar when the check box has keyboard focus. Semantic events are useful because you don't have to be concerned with all of the low-level events that can produce the higher-level, semantic event.

Low-level and semantic events are grouped and organized into a hierarchy of event classes, which this chapter will discuss after examining the event listener classes.

The Event Listener Interfaces

Nine event listener interfaces exist: Three listen for semantic events and six listen for low-level events. The java.awt.event package includes each of these listener interfaces, which are derived from the java.util.EventListener interface.

The three semantic event listeners are:

- ActionListener

- AdjustmentListener

- ItemListener

The six low-level event listeners are:

- ComponentListener
- FocusListener
- KeyListener
- MouseListener
- MouseMotionListener
- WindowListener

Let's examine these event listeners one at a time:

ActionListener

An ActionListener listens for the ACTION_PERFORMED event type described previously. This event listener has one method, which is called when an event source registered with this listener fires an ACTION_PERFORMED event type. This method is the `actionPerformed(ActionEvent)`.

Notice the similarity between the event type "ACTION_PERFORMED" (which is actually the name of the constant that the ActionEvent class uses to identify this event type) and the method name "actionPerformed." This similarity is repeated for all event types with corresponding event listener methods.

The argument passed to all the event listener methods is an instance of the event class that contains the event type that was fired. The listener method can call methods of this object to gain more information about the event. For example, the `getSource()` method returns the *event source,* which is the component that fired the event.

The previous MenuDemo example demonstrates the use of ActionListener. For more information on ActionListener, refer to the following Web page:

```
http://java.sun.com/products/JDK/1.1/docs/api/
java.awt.event.ActionListener.html
```

AdjustmentListener

An AdjustmentListener listens for the ADJUSTMENT_VALUE_CHANGED event type described earlier. This event has one method, which is called when an event source registered with this listener fires an ADJUSTMENT_VALUE_CHANGED event type. This method is the `adjustmentValueChanged(AdjustmentEvent)`.

Look at the ScrollbarSlider example in Chapter 13 for an example of how to use AdjustmentListener. For more information on AdjustmentListener, refer to the following Web page:

```
http://java.sun.com/products/JDK/1.1/docs/api/
java.awt.event.AdjustmentListener.html
```

ItemListener

An ItemListener listens for the ITEM_STATE_CHANGED event type described earlier. This event listener has one method, which is called when an event source registered with this listener fires an ITEM_STATE_CHANGED event type. This method is the `itemStateChanged(ItemEvent)`.

For more information on ItemListener, refer to the following Web page:

```
http://java.sun.com/products/JDK/1.1/docs/api/
java.awt.event.ItemListener.html
```

ComponentListener

A ComponentListener listens for event types contained in the ComponentEvent class. This event listener has four methods, each of which correspond to an event type in the ComponentEvent class. These methods are:

- `componentHidden(ComponentEvent)`
- `componentMoved(ComponentEvent)`
- `componentResized(ComponentEvent)`
- `componentShown(ComponentEvent)`

The event types to which they correspond are COMPONENT_HIDDEN, COMPONENT_MOVED, COMPONENT_RESIZED, and COMPONENT_SHOWN.

Although the AWT automatically handles moving, resizing, showing, and hiding components, you can override these methods to notify you as these events occur. For more information on ComponentListener, refer to the following Web page:

```
http://java.sun.com/products/JDK/1.1/docs/api/
java.awt.event.ComponentListener.html
```

FocusListener

A FocusListener listens for event types contained in the FocusEvent class. This event listener has two methods, each of which correspond to an event type in the FocusEvent class. These methods are:

- `focusGained(FocusEvent)`
- `focusLost(FocusEvent)`

You could use these methods to perform edit checks on a text field when the user tabs away from it, for example. For more information on FocusListener, refer to the following Web page:

```
http://java.sun.com/products/JDK/1.1/docs/api/
java.awt.event.FocusListener.html
```

KeyListener

A KeyListener listens for event types contained in the KeyEvent class. This event listener has three methods, each of which correspond to an event type in the KeyEvent class. These methods are:

- `keyPressed(KeyEvent)`
- `keyReleased(KeyEvent)`
- `keyTyped(KeyEvent)`

You could use these methods to do your own text field formatting, for example. For more information on KeyListener, refer to the following Web page:

```
http://java.sun.com/products/JDK/1.1/docs/api/
java.awt.event.KeyListener.html
```

MouseListener

A MouseListener listens for some of event types contained in the MouseEvent class. This event listener has five methods, each of which correspond to an event type in the MouseEvent class. These methods are:

- `mouseClicked(MouseEvent)`
- `mouseEntered(MouseEvent)`

- `mouseExited(MouseEvent)`
- `mousePressed(MouseEvent)`
- `mouseReleased(MouseEvent)`

Lines 187–196 in listing 14.1 demonstrate how to use a MouseListener to know when to make a pop-up menu appear:

```
187         public void mouseReleased(MouseEvent evt) {
188             Component comp = (Component)evt.getSource();
189             // Find out if the mouse event was a popup menu request
190             if (evt.isPopupTrigger()) {
191                 if (evt.getSource() == md.btn2)
192                     md.popMenu2.show(comp, evt.getX(), evt.getY());
193                 else
194                     md.popMenu1.show(comp, evt.getX(), evt.getY());
195             }
196         }
```

For more information on MouseListener, refer to the following Web page:

```
http://java.sun.com/products/JDK/1.1/docs/api/
java.awt.event.MouseListener.html
```

MouseMotionListener

A MouseMotionListener listens for the motion-oriented event types contained in the MouseEvent class. This event listener has two methods, each of which correspond to an event type in the MouseEvent class. These methods are:

- `mouseDragged(MouseEvent)`
- `mouseMoved(MouseEvent)`

You could use these methods to implement a drawing pad within an application, for example. For more information on MouseMotionListener, refer to the following Web page:

```
http://java.sun.com/products/JDK/1.1/docs/api/
java.awt.event.MouseMotionListener.html
```

WindowListener

A WindowListener listens for event types contained in the WindowEvent class. This event listener has five methods, each of which correspond to an event type in the WindowEvent class. These methods are:

- `windowClosed(WindowEvent)`
- `windowClosing(WindowEvent)`
- `windowDeiconified(WindowEvent)`
- `windowIconified(WindowEvent)`
- `windowOpened(WindowEvent)`

Lines 201–206 in listing 14.1 demonstrate the use of a WindowListener to trap the WINDOW_CLOSING event type, which occurs when the user tries to close a window.

```
201     public void windowClosing(WindowEvent evt) {
202         Frame frm = (Frame)evt.getSource();
203         frm.setVisible(false);
204         frm.dispose();
205         System.exit(0);
206     }
```

For more information on WindowListener, refer to the following Web page:

```
http://java.sun.com/products/JDK/1.1/docs/api/
java.awt.event.WindowListener.html
```

The java.awt.event package contains some convenience classes that make it easier to implement the low-level event listeners described above. These sometimes are referred to as *event adapter convenience classes.*

Event Adapter Convenience Classes

To implement an interface in a class, you must put each method defined by the interface in that same class. This can be a tedious process, especially if you are only interested in certain methods of the interface.

Of the nine event listener interfaces described above, six have more than one method defined. These six are the low-level event listener interfaces. Typically, you will be interested in implementing only one or two of these methods in a given class, but as just mentioned, you must define them all.

To alleviate this problem, six classes correspond to the six low-level event listener interfaces and sometimes are referred to as event adapter convenience classes. These classes implement a corresponding event listener interface and have an empty method for each of the methods defined by that listener interface. The event adapter convenience classes are:

- ComponentAdapter
- FocusAdapter
- KeyAdapter
- MouseAdapter
- MouseMotionAdapter
- WindowAdapter

The MenuDemo application (listing 14.1) demonstrates the use of two of these classes: WindowAdapter and MouseAdapter. Consider the use of the WindowAdapter class in lines 199–207.

```
199   class Wadapt extends WindowAdapter
200   {
201       public void windowClosing(WindowEvent evt) {
202           Frame frm = (Frame)evt.getSource();
203           frm.setVisible(false);
204           frm.dispose();
205           System.exit(0);
206       }
207   }
```

This class is defined as a WindowListener for the main frame of the application in line 23:

```
023           addWindowListener(new Wadapt());
```

As mentioned earlier in the chapter, the `windowClosing()` method of the event listener is invoked when the user tries to close the main window of the application. In this case, the event listener is an instance of Wadapt, which is derived from the WindowAdapter class. Because the WindowAdapter class defines all the methods in the WindowListener interface, it is only necessary to override the method in which we're interested—in this case, the `windowClosing()` method.

Up to this point in the discussion of the Delegation Event Model, we have focused on event listeners. The next section will discuss the events themselves.

The Event Class Hierarchy

All the event types that the event listeners listen for are organized into classes, which are arranged in a class hierarchy. Although the java.awt.event package contains these classes, they are all directly or indirectly derived from the java.awt.AWTEvent class, which is derived from java.util.EventObject. Figure 14.6 shows this class hierarchy. (The classes marked by an asterisk are passed into one or more of the AWT event listener methods.)

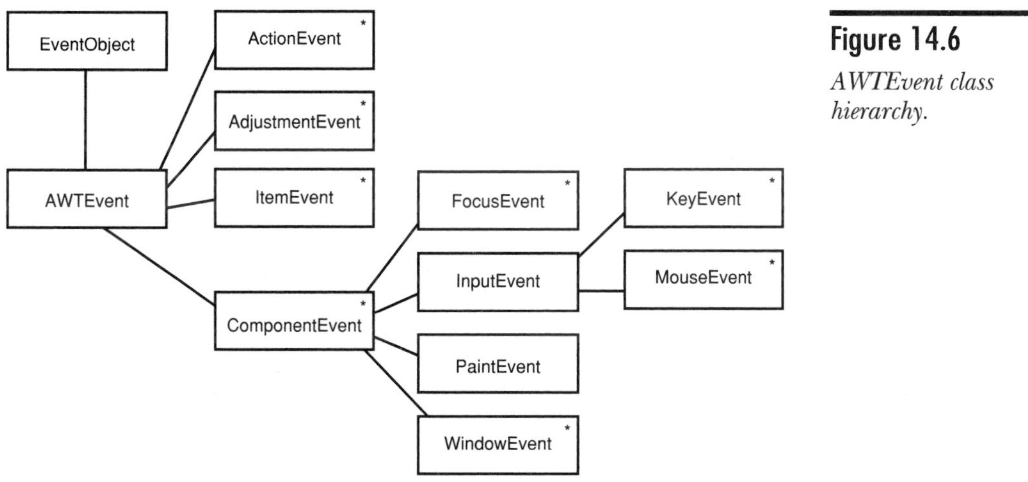

Figure 14.6

AWTEvent class hierarchy.

The following information will help you use each of these classes. Because the PaintEvent class is not used with the Delegation Event Model, it will not be covered.

EventObject Class

As shown in the diagram, the EventObject class sits at the top of the event class hierarchy. The EventObject class contains a method named `getSource()`—you can call this method on any event class in the hierarchy to determine which object fired the event. Recall that the `getSource()` method is used in the MenuDemo example:

```
System.out.println(((MenuItem)evt.getSource()).getLabel());
```

Line 168 uses the `getSource()` method to obtain a reference to the MenuItem object that fired the event so that a method of the MenuItem object can be called. For more information on the EventObject class, refer to the following Web page:

```
http://java.sun.com/products/JDK/1.1/docs/api/java.util.EventObject.html
```

AWTEvent Class

The AWTEvent class is the top-level class for all AWT-related event classes. Because most subclasses of AWTEvent contain multiple event types, the AWTEvent class contains a method named `getId()`. You can call the `getId()` method on any subclass in the hierarchy to determine which event type was fired. This is more useful in the "Extended Component Event Model," described later in this chapter. In the following lines of code, for example, taken from the WishList applet (listing 14.2) you'll see later on, `getId()` is used to find out which mouse event type was fired.

```
    protected boolean processMouseEvent(MouseEvent e) {
        if (e.getId() == MouseEvent.MOUSE_ENTERED) {
```

The AWTEvent class also contains some masks for use with the Extended Component Event Model. A *mask* in this case is a bit-mapped constant that can be compared to the bits in a given event in order to ascertain what kind of event it is. These masks are used to identify to the system which events should be delivered to a component's event processing methods. Although they are not used in conjunction with event listeners, one mask for each AWT event listener is defined in the "Delegation Event Model":

- ACTION_EVENT_MASK
- ADJUSTMENT_EVENT_MASK
- ITEM_EVENT_MASK
- COMPONENT_EVENT_MASK
- FOCUS_EVENT_MASK
- KEY_EVENT_MASK
- MOUSE_EVENT_MASK
- MOUSE_MOTION_EVENT_MASK
- WINDOW_EVENT_MASK

You will see these in use in the WishList applet, when the Extended Component Event Model is discussed later in this chapter. For more information on the AWTEvent class, see the following Web page:

```
http://java.sun.com/products/JDK/1.1/docs/api/java.awt.AWTEvent.html
```

ActionEvent Class

The ActionEvent class contains the event type ACTION_PERFORMED, which is the first semantic event type discussed earlier. An ActionEvent can be fired by:

- Clicking a button
- Double-clicking a list
- Choosing a MenuItem
- Pressing the Enter key when in a TextField

An *action command* is associated with the ActionEvent. An action command is a String that represents the name of the action to be performed. You can use the `setActionCommand()` method of the event source to assign an action command name to it. Consider the following code in the MenuDemo example (listing 14.1):

```
050           MenuItem miNew = new MenuItem("New");
051           miNew.addActionListener(this);
052           fileMenu.add(miNew);
```

```
167       public void actionPerformed(ActionEvent evt) {
168           System.out.println(((MenuItem)evt.getSource()).getLabel());
169       }
```

In line 168, the event listener obtains a reference to the menu item that fired the ActionEvent and then determines the label of the menu item. The listener could make decisions based upon either the menu item reference or the menu item label. This is not usually good practice for anything but the smallest of applications, however, because it ties the GUI very tightly to the application logic.

For a better approach, associate command names to the ActionEvent-oriented user-interface components. You could use the following code to associate the command name "New drawing" with the menu item:

```
miNew.setActionCommand("New drawing");
```

To determine the command name of the element that fired the event, call the `getActionCommand()` method of the ActionEvent object:

```
String command = evt.getActionCommand()
```

To determine whether a modifier key was being held down when the ActionEvent was fired, you can use the `getModifiers()` method. The return value of this method can be compared to the modifier constants supplied with the ActionEvent class. These constants are:

- ALT_MASK
- CTRL_MASK
- META_MASK
- SHIFT_MASK

For more information on the ActionEvent class, refer to the following Web page:

```
http://java.sun.com/products/JDK/1.1/docs/api/
java.awt.event.ActionEvent.html
```

AdjustmentEvent Class

The AdjustmentEvent class contains the event type ADJUSTMENT_VALUE_CHANGED, which is the second semantic event type discussed earlier. An AdjustmentEvent can be fired by:

- Manipulating a scrollbar.
- Manipulating a custom component, such as a slider. As you'll see in Chapter 15, "Java Beans: Java's Component Architecture," custom components (Beans) can fire any of the events in the AWT.

For an example of using the AdjustmentEvent class, see the ScrollbarSlider example in Chapter 13. This example uses the `getValue()` method of the AdjustmentEvent class to return the current value of the scroll bar.

The `getAdjustable()` method returns a reference to the component that fired the AdjustmentEvent. This reference is of type Adjustable, because all components that fire this event must implement the Adjustable interface. Note that this method returns the same reference as `getSource()` does, except that it is of type Adjustable, which means that you don't have to cast it. (Chapter 13, "The New, Improved AWT: GUI Components, Containers, and Layout Managers," discusses the Adjustable interface.)

If you need to know what type of adjustment caused the AdjustmentEvent to fire, call the `getAdjustmentType()` method. This returns one of the following values defined in the AdjustmentEvent class, which indicates the user action that fired the event:

- BLOCK_DECREMENT
- BLOCK_INCREMENT
- TRACK
- UNIT_DECREMENT
- UNIT_INCREMENT

For more information on the AdjustmentEvent class, refer to the following Web page:

```
http://java.sun.com/products/JDK/1.1/docs/api/
java.awt.event.AdjustmentEvent.html
```

ItemEvent Class

The ItemEvent class contains the event type ITEM_STATE_CHANGED, which is the third semantic event type discussed earlier. An ItemEvent can be fired by selecting or deselecting an item in a

- List
- Choice
- Checkbox
- CheckboxMenuItem
- Custom component (Java Bean)

To determine which type of state change caused the ItemEvent to fire, you can call the `getStateChange()` method. This returns one of the following values defined in the ItemEvent class, which indicates whether the user selected or deselected the item:

- SELECTED
- DESELECTED

The WishList applet (listing 14.2) uses `getStateChange()` (in line 59) to determine whether the affected item is currently selected.

```
057            // Find out if this event was caused by the user
058            // selecting the item (as opposed to deselecting it)
059            if (e.getStateChange() == ItemEvent.SELECTED) {
060                // Convert the selected item to lower case
061                int sel = ((Integer)(e.getItem())).intValue();
062                replaceItem(getItem(sel).toLowerCase(), sel);
063                // The replaceItem disturbs the selection
064                select(sel);
065            }
```

The ItemEvent class also contains the `getItemSelectable()` method, which returns a reference to the component that fired the ItemEvent. This reference is of type ItemSelectable, because all components that fire this event must implement the ItemSelectable interface. This method returns the same reference as `getSource()` does, except that it is of type ItemSelectable.

The `getItem()` method of the ItemEvent class returns an object that identifies the item that was changed. In the case of a List, for example, `getItem()` returns an Integer instance that contains an index of the item that incurred the state change. The WishList applet uses the `getItem()` method of the ItemEvent class in line 61 to determine which item in the list was newly selected.

```
061                int sel = ((Integer)(e.getItem())).intValue();
```

Note the distinction between this `getItem()` and the List class method named `getItem()` used in line 62:

```
062                replaceItem(getItem(sel).toLowerCase(), sel);
```

For more information on the ItemEvent class, refer to the following Web page:

```
http://java.sun.com/products/JDK/1.1/docs/api/
java.awt.event.ItemEvent.html
```

ComponentEvent Class

The ComponentEvent class is the root class for all low-level event classes. This class introduces a method named `getComponent()`, which can be used on any of its subclasses to return a Component reference to the component that fired the event. This returns the same reference as the `getSource()` method of the EventObject class, except that it is a Component reference, not an Object reference.

You can use the inherited `getId()` method to determine which event type was fired. These event types correspond to the ComponentListener methods, so it is not necessary to check for event type when you are in one of these methods. The `getId()` method is useful, however, when using the Extended Component Event Model, which is discussed later in this chapter. The ComponentEvent event types are:

- COMPONENT_HIDDEN
- COMPONENT_MOVED
- COMPONENT_RESIZED
- COMPONENT_SHOWN

Any component in the Component hierarchy can fire a ComponentEvent. For more information on the ComponentEvent class, refer to the following Web page:

```
http://java.sun.com/products/JDK/1.1/docs/api/
java.awt.event.ComponentEvent.html
```

FocusEvent Class

The FocusEvent class contains the following event types, which correspond to the methods in the FocusListener class:

- FOCUS_GAINED
- FOCUS_LOST

As with any other subclass of AWTEvent, you can use `getId()` to determine which of these event types was fired.

Any component in the Component hierarchy can receive a FocusEvent. For more information on the FocusEvent class, refer to the following Web page:

```
http://java.sun.com/products/JDK/1.1/docs/api/
java.awt.event.FocusEvent.html
```

InputEvent Class

The event listeners do not use InputEvent class—this is the root class for all input events. Figure 14.6 shows that InputEvent acts as the parent class of KeyEvent and MouseEvent, both of which are discussed next.

The InputEvent class contains some methods that you can use to determine which modifier keys and mouse buttons were pressed at the time of the event. The following three methods deal only with modifier keys and return whether a given modifier key was pressed:

- `isAltDown()`
- `isControlDown()`
- `isMetaDown()`
- `isShiftDown()`

The `getModifiers()` method returns an integer in which some of the bits represent the keys or mouse buttons that were down. This integer can be compared to the following constants defined by the InputEvent class:

- ALT_MASK
- CTRL_MASK
- META_MASK
- SHIFT_MASK
- BUTTON1_MASK
- BUTTON2_MASK
- BUTTON3_MASK

The InputEvent class introduces one more method, the `getWhen()` method, which returns a timestamp of when the event happened.

For more information on the InputEvent class, refer to the following Web page:

```
http://java.sun.com/products/JDK/1.1/docs/api/
java.awt.event.InputEvent.html
```

KeyEvent Class

The KeyEvent class contains the following event types, which correspond to the methods in the KeyListener class:

- KEY_PRESSED
- KEY_RELEASED
- KEY_TYPED

As with any other subclass of AWTEvent, you can use `getId()` to determine which of these event types was fired.

To determine which key fired the event, you can call the `getKeyCode()` method. This method returns an integer that is the key code of the key associated with the event. If the key is an action key, this integer will match one of the action key constants defined in the KeyEvent class. Some example action key constants are VK_F1, VK_HOME, and VK_PAGE_UP. The `isActionKey()` method returns whether or not the key is an action key.

You also can call the `getKeyChar()` method, which returns the character associated with the key that fired the event.

To determine whether any modifier keys were down at the time of the event, use the methods inherited from the InputEvent class.

Any component in the Component hierarchy that can accept keyboard focus can receive a KeyEvent. For more information on the KeyEvent class, refer to the following Web page:

```
http://java.sun.com/products/JDK/1.1/docs/api/java.awt.event.KeyEvent.html
```

MouseEvent Class

The MouseEvent class contains the following event types, which correspond to the methods in the MouseListener and MouseMotionListener classes:

- MOUSE_CLICKED
- MOUSE_ENTERED
- MOUSE_EXITED
- MOUSE_PRESSED
- MOUSE_RELEASED
- MOUSE_DRAGGED
- MOUSE_MOVED

Use the `getId()` method inherited from AWTEvent to determine which of these event types was fired.

To determine where the mouse cursor was when the event happened, you can call either the `getPoint()` method or the `getX()` and `getY()` methods. The MenuDemo application (listing 14.1) uses the latter methods to decide where to show the pop-up menu:

```
                    md.popMenu2.show(comp, evt.getX(), evt.getY());
```

The `getClickCount()` method returns the number of mouse clicks associated with the event.

To determine whether any modifier keys were down at the time of the event, use the methods inherited from the InputEvent class.

Any component in the Component hierarchy can receive a MouseEvent. For more information on the MouseEvent class, refer to the following Web page:

```
http://java.sun.com/products/JDK/1.1/docs/api/
java.awt.event.MouseEvent.html
```

WindowEvent Class

The WindowEvent class contains the following event types, which correspond to the methods in the WindowListener class:

- WINDOW_CLOSED
- WINDOW_CLOSING
- WINDOW_DEICONIFIED
- WINDOW_ICONIFIED
- WINDOW_OPENED

You can use the inherited `getId()` method to determine which of these event types was fired.

The WindowEvent class introduces a method named `getWindow()` that can be used to return a Window reference to the window that received the event. This returns the same reference as the `getSource()` method of the EventObject class, except that it is a Window reference, not an Object reference. Consider the `windowClosing()` method of the MenuDemo application (listing 14.1):

```
    public void windowClosing(WindowEvent evt) {
        Frame frm = (Frame)evt.getSource();
        frm.setVisible(false);
        frm.dispose();
        System.exit(0);
    }
```

Line 202 could be changed to the following, which would make the cast to Frame unnecessary:

```
Window frm = evt.getWindow();
```

This is true because:

- `getWindow()` returns a Window.
- `setVisible()` and `dispose()` are introduced higher in the Component hierarchy than Frame. The Window class is the most specific reference required for these method calls.

Any subclass of Window can receive a WindowEvent. For more information on the WindowEvent class, refer to the following Web page:

```
http://java.sun.com/products/JDK/1.1/docs/api/
java.awt.event.WindowEvent.html
```

Summary of the Delegation Event Model

Table 14.6 summarizes the AWT event listeners, associated event classes/types, and associate event sources.

Table 14.6
Summary of AWT Event Listeners, Event Classes, and Event Sources

Event Listener/Methods	Event Class/Types	Event Sources
ActionListener actionPerformed	ActionEvent ACTION_PERFORMED	Button, List, MenuItem, TextField
AdjustmentListener adjustmentValueChanged	AdjustmentEvent ADJUSTMENT_VALUE_CHANGED	Scrollbar
ItemListener itemStateChanged	ItemEvent ITEM_STATE_CHANGED	List, Choice, Checkbox, CheckboxMenuItem
ComponentListener componentHidden componentMoved	ComponentEvent COMPONENT_HIDDEN COMPONENT_MOVED	Any AWT component

continues

Table 14.6, Continued
Summary of AWT Event Listeners, Event Classes, and Event Sources

Event Listener/Methods	Event Class/Types	Event Sources
componentResized componentShown	COMPONENT_RESIZED COMPONENT_SHOWN	
FocusListener focusGained focusLost	FocusEvent FOCUS_GAINED FOCUS_LOST	Any AWT component
KeyListener keyPressed keyReleased keyTyped	KeyEvent KEY_PRESSED KEY_RELEASED KEY_TYPED	Any AWT component that can accept keyboard focus
MouseListener mouseClicked mouseEntered mouseExited mousePressed mouseReleased	MouseEvent MOUSE_CLICKED MOUSE_ENTERED MOUSE_EXITED MOUSE_PRESSED MOUSE_RELEASED	Any AWT component
MouseMotionListener mouseDragged mouseMoved	MouseEvent MOUSE_DRAGGED MOUSE_MOVED	Any AWT component
WindowListener windowClosed windowClosing windowDeiconified windowIconified windowOpened	WindowEvent WINDOW_CLOSED WINDOW_CLOSING WINDOW_DEICONIFIED WINDOW_ICONIFIED WINDOW_OPENED	Any subclass of the AWT Window class

The Delegation Event Model offers several advantages over the JDK 1.0 event model:

- Supports a GUI component architecture: The main reason for introducing the Delegation Event Model is to support the Java Beans component architecture, which is covered in the next chapter.
- Increases performance: The only events that your code has to handle are the events for which it explicitly listens.
- Separates application code from GUI code: Using this model facilitates this separation, especially with the action commands discussed earlier.

- Does not require sub-classing components: It is not necessary to sub-class and override an event handler to tie application code to a given event.
- Organizes an event class hierarchy: The event classes are organized into a hierarchy instead of one all-purpose event class.

It is not recommended to write Java programs that use both the Delegation Event Model and the JDK 1.0 event model.

The next section covers another new event model, sometimes referred to as the *Extended Component Event Model.*

The Extended Component Event Model

The *Extended Component Event Model* offers a way of handling events from classes that you extend from AWT components. This model takes advantage of the default event handling methods in the Delegation Event Model.

As an example, figure 14.7 shows the default handling methods that are invoked to call the `mouseEntered()` method of a registered MouseListener.

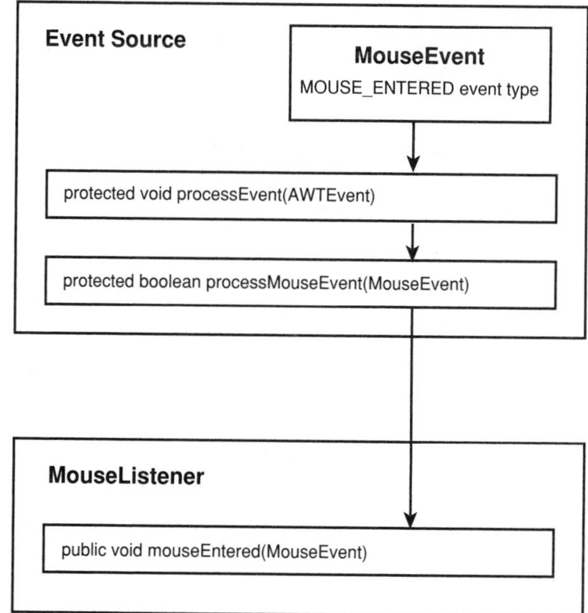

Figure 14.7
Flow of MouseEvent through default event handling methods.

The following depicts the path that the MouseEvent takes:

1. Because at least one MouseListener has been registered, the MouseEvent is passed to the component's `processEvent()` method.

2. Because this particular MouseEvent event type (MOUSE_ENTERED) is associated with the MouseListener interface, the `processEvent()` method passes the MouseEvent to the component's `processMouseEvent()` method. Note that if this had been a MOUSE_DRAGGED event type (and if a MouseMotionListener was registered), the `processMouseMotionEvent()` would have been called. This is because, as explained in the event listener section, the MOUSE_DRAGGED event type is associated with the MouseMotionListener interface. A `process<ListenerType>Event()` handler method exists for every *<ListenerType>*Listener associated with a given AWT component.

3. The `processMouseEvent()` passes the MouseEvent to the `mouseEntered()` method of any registered MouseListener.

Following is a complete list of the `process<ListenerType>Event()` handler methods mentioned in step two:

- `protected void processActionEvent(ActionEvent)`
- `protected void processAdjustmentEvent(AdjustmentEvent)`
- `protected void processItemEvent(ItemEvent)`
- `protected void processComponentEvent(ComponentEvent)`
- `protected void processFocusEvent(FocusEvent)`
- `protected void processKeyEvent(KeyEvent)`
- `protected void processMouseEvent(MouseEvent)`
- `protected void processMouseMotionEvent(MouseEvent)`
- `protected void processWindowEvent(WindowEvent)`

You can take advantage of these methods and the `processEvent()` method by overriding them in the components that you extend from AWT components. This eliminates the need for an event listener.

Of course, this presents a question: If a given event is not passed to `processEvent()` unless a corresponding event listener is registered, then how will the event be passed?

The answer: The `enableEvents()` method, defined in the AWT Component class, enables events to be passed to the `processEvent()` method. As explained in the

AWTEvent class section, the AWTEvent class defines nine constants, each of which corresponds to an event listener class:

- ACTION_EVENT_MASK
- ADJUSTMENT_EVENT_MASK
- ITEM_EVENT_MASK
- COMPONENT_EVENT_MASK
- FOCUS_EVENT_MASK
- KEY_EVENT_MASK
- MOUSE_EVENT_MASK
- MOUSE_MOTION_EVENT_MASK
- WINDOW_EVENT_MASK

By calling the component's `enableEvents()` method with one or more of these masks, the associated event types can be passed to the `processEvent()` method.

The WishList Applet

Listing 14.2 (program WishList.java on the CD-ROM accompanying this book) shows an application that serves as a simple example of how you can use the Extended Component Event Model to handle events in sub-classed components. It demonstrates handling three varieties of events: ItemEvent, ActionEvent, and MouseEvent.

Note This example application is called "WishList" because it contains a list of desirable qualities. This list is commonly known as the "fruit of the Spirit."

Figure 14.8 displays this applet's user interface, which consists of two list boxes that have the following behavior:

- When the mouse cursor enters either list box, all the items in that list box convert to uppercase letters.
- When an item is clicked, the letters in that item convert to lowercase.
- When an item is double-clicked, it is removed from the list box and added to the other one in lowercase letters.
- When the mouse cursor exits the list box, all the items in that list box convert to lowercase letters.

Listing 14.2

```
Line==================Java Source==================
//////////
// WishList.java  Example of using the Extended
// Component Event Model, and item events.
//
// Author: James L. Weaver   JDK version: 1.1 beta3
//////////
package chapter14.code.wishlist;

import java.awt.*;
import java.applet.*;
import java.awt.event.*;

public class WishList extends Applet {

    ExchangeList listA, listB;

    public void init() {
        listA = new ExchangeList(9);
        listB = new ExchangeList(9);

        listA.setMate(listB);
        listB.setMate(listA);

        listA.add("love");
        listA.add("joy");
        listA.add("peace");
        listA.add("patience");
        listA.add("kindness");
        listA.add("goodness");
        listA.add("faithfulness");
        listA.add("gentleness");
        listA.add("self-control");

        add(listA);
        add(listB);
    }
```

```
}

class ExchangeList extends List
{
    // Declare reference to the other ExchangeList
    ExchangeList mate;

    public ExchangeList(int lines) {
        super(lines);
        enableEvents(AWTEvent.ITEM_EVENT_MASK ¦
                     AWTEvent.ACTION_EVENT_MASK ¦
                     AWTEvent.MOUSE_EVENT_MASK);
    }

    public void setMate(ExchangeList mate) {
        this.mate = mate;
    }

    // This is called when an item is selected
    protected void processItemEvent(ItemEvent e) {
        // Find out if this event was caused by the user
        // selecting the item (as opposed to deselecting it)
        if (e.getStateChange() == ItemEvent.SELECTED) {
            // Convert the selected item to lower case
            int sel = ((Integer)(e.getItem())).intValue();
            replaceItem(getItem(sel).toLowerCase(), sel);
            // The replaceItem disturbs the selection
            select(sel);
        }
        // Always call the super class of a component's event
        // processing methods.
        super.processItemEvent(e);
    }

    // This is called when an element of the ExchangeList
    // is double-clicked
    protected void processActionEvent(ActionEvent e) {
        int sel = getSelectedIndex();
        if (sel > -1) {
```

continues

Listing 14.2, Continued

```
076               // Add the selected item to the other list
077               mate.add(getItem(sel));
078               remove(sel);
079           }
080           // Always call the super class of a component's event
081           // processing methods.
082           super.processActionEvent(e);
083       }
084
085       // This is called when a mouse event happens over
086       // the ExchangeList
087       protected void processMouseEvent(MouseEvent e) {
088           if (e.getId() == MouseEvent.MOUSE_ENTERED) {
089               // Convert all items in the list to upper case
090               for (int i=0; i<getItemCount(); i++) {
091                   replaceItem(getItem(i).toUpperCase(), i);
092               }
093           }
094           else if (e.getId() == MouseEvent.MOUSE_EXITED) {
095               // Convert all items in the list to lowercase
096               for (int i=0; i<getItemCount(); i++) {
097                   replaceItem(getItem(i).toLowerCase(), i);
098               }
099           }
100           // Always call the super class of a component's event
101           // processing methods.
102           super.processMouseEvent(e);
103       }
104   }
```

Line 15 declares two ExchangeList references, and lines 18 and 19 create two instances of this class.

Lines 39–104 define the ExchangeList class, which is extended from the List class. Each ExchangeList instance is given a reference to the other via the `setMate()` method in lines 51–53. This way, each one can add an item to the other when double-clicked.

You'll notice that no event listeners are registered, but in lines 46–48, a call to `enableEvents()` enables certain events to be processed:

```
046         enableEvents(AWTEvent.ITEM_EVENT_MASK |
047                      AWTEvent.ACTION_EVENT_MASK |
048                      AWTEvent.MOUSE_EVENT_MASK);
```

When the associated events are fired, they are sent to the `processEvent()` method, which is not overridden in this example. The default behavior of `processEvent()` sends these events to the proper `process<ListenerType>Event()` handler methods. In this case, these handler methods are:

- `processItemEvent()`
- `processActionEvent()`
- `processMouseEvent()`

When the mouse cursor enters either one of the ExchangeList list boxes shown in figure 14.8, a MouseEvent is fired and passed to `processEvent()`, which in turn passes it to `processMouseEvent()` in line 87.

```
087     protected void processMouseEvent(MouseEvent e) {
```

To determine which type of mouse event the MouseEvent represents, lines 88 and 94 call the inherited `getId()` method of the MouseEvent instance.

```
088         if (e.getId() == MouseEvent.MOUSE_ENTERED) {
```

```
094         else if (e.getId() == MouseEvent.MOUSE_EXITED) {
```

Line 102 calls the `processMouseEvent()` method of the superclass. This is very important because these event handler methods play a critical role in AWT event processing. Whenever you override `processEvent()` or `process<ListenerType>Event()`, always call that method in the superclass.

```
102         super.processMouseEvent(e);
```

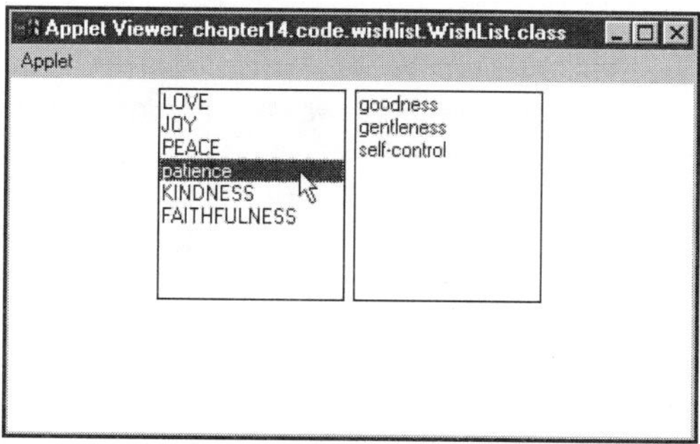

Figure 14.8

WishList applet display.

Deciding Which Event Model to Use

When deciding whether to use event listeners (in the Delegation Event Model) versus overriding event processing methods (in the Extended Component Event Model), consider the following points:

- Using event listeners is preferred because it is more scaleable, less prone to mistakes, and is conducive to separation of GUI and application logic.
- Extending a component should be reserved for cases where you actually extend the component's look or behavior. Making use of the event processing methods shouldn't be the only reason to extend a particular component.
- Using event listeners and overriden event processing methods in the same program is acceptable, even in the same component. If you use both in the same component, the events passed to `processEvent()` are those for which an event listener is registered, plus the ones that were enabled in the call to `enableEvents()`.

If you are familiar with the JDK 1.0 event model, you might have noticed that the Extended Component Event Model in JDK 1.1 is similar to it—both have event handling methods that can be overridden. The 1.1 Extended Component Event Model, however, is different in several respects:

- Combined with the `enableEvents()` method, this model enables you to choose the events delivered to the event handling methods. The default is that no events are delivered, which improves performance.
- The 1.1 version has a richer and better organized set of event processing methods.
- The most recent model uses the new 1.1 event class hierarchy.
- Events in the JDK 1.1 beta 1 release are not automatically propagated up the containment hierarchy, as they are in JDK 1.0.

Using the 1.0 and 1.1 event models in the same program is not recommended, because unpredictable results could occur. New Java programs written for 1.1 should take advantage of the new model.

Now that you have seen the new JDK 1.1 event models, this chapter will cover four more new AWT features.

Moving On to More New JDK 1.1

This section explores some additional JDK 1.1 features related to the AWT; focus traversal, accessing desktop colors, and how to use the clipboard and print from a java program are all discussed here. The first feature presented, focus traversal, enables the user to tab between fields. This feature was sorely missed by application developers using JDK 1.0.

Enabling the User to Tab Between Fields (Focus Traversal)

Users of most windowing systems expect to be able to use the Tab and Shift+Tab keys to move focus from component to component in a window (frame or dialog). With data entry and other applications, it is very handy to be able to use the Tab key to move from field to field. As in the case of shortcut keys, this reduces the need for the use of a mouse for people who either prefer not to or can't use a mouse. Java has begun implementing this feature in JDK 1.1.

Under most circumstances, you need not be concerned with the details of implementing this feature, because it works by default. AWT components, such as buttons and text boxes, that can accept focus automatically do so. Components, such as labels, that shouldn't accept are automatically skipped when tabbing. You must, however, be concerned with the tab order, or the order in which focus is received. In JDK 1.1, the tab order is the same order as the components contained in the containers. This is usually the same order in which the components were added to the containers.

A Simple Example of Focus Traversal

Consider the case of a dialog box that has a text field (for entering the user's first name) and two buttons (OK and Cancel.) The dialog box could be coded as follows:

```
Dialog nameDialog = new Dialog(this, "Enter First Name", true);
Panel buttonPanel = new Panel();
Panel entryPanel = new Panel();
buttonPanel.add(new Button("OK"));
buttonPanel.add(new Button("Cancel"));
entryPanel.add(new Label("First Name:"));
entryPanel.add(new TextField(null, 10));
nameDialog.add("Center", entryPanel);
nameDialog.add("South", buttonPanel);
nameDialog.setSize(300, 150);
nameDialog.setVisible(true);
```

When the focus is on the text field and Tab is pressed, the focus moves to the OK button, followed by the Cancel button, and back to the text field. This is because the components in the dialog box are `entryPanel` and `buttonPanel`, in that order. Within `entryPanel`, the component order is label and text field, but a label doesn't accept focus. Within `buttonPanel`, the component order is OK button and Cancel button.

Javasoft has stated that in a future version of the JDK, a better scheme will improve the process of setting the tab order. Until then, however, the current process remains workable.

How Java Implements Focus Traversal

The way that Java implements focus traversal is actually very simple. A private FocusManager object registered on the Window handles the focus traversal based upon both the order of components (as described above) and whether a component will accept keyboard focus when tabbing. The FocusManager determines this by making a call to the component's `isFocusTraversable()` method. If it returns true, the component receives focus, but if it returns false, the component won't receive focus.

Considerations for Custom Components (Java Beans)

When designing a custom component, keep the following points in mind, regarding focus traversal and keyboard focus.

- For the user to be able to tab to your custom component, the component's `isFocusTraversable()` must return true. If, for example, the custom component is derived from the Canvas class, the `isFocusTraversable()` must be overriden, because the Canvas class returns false by default.
- If you want your custom component to accept keyboard focus when the user clicks on it, you must catch the mouse-down event and call `requestFocus()`.
- You should provide some sort of visual feedback to the user that your component has received focus. Some components use a bounding box to indicate that they have keyboard focus. Text entry-oriented components indicate this with the presence of the carat.

Chapter 15, "Java Beans: Java's Component Architecture," examines these custom components in more detail. Many JDK 1.1 features were added, at least in part, to support Java Beans (the Java component architecture). The next feature, Desktop Colors, is no exception.

Accessing Desktop Colors

Sometimes, it is useful to know the details of the desktop color scheme, especially when you are designing custom components. If, for example, the user configures his desktop color scheme to make the background color for components bright red, you probably want your custom component to have that same background color. This enables your component to blend in with the user interface rather than always being the arbitrary colors that you chose when you designed it.

You can determine what the current desktop colors are by checking certain final static variables in the java.awt.SystemColor class. SystemColor.menu, for example, holds an instance of Color that represents the current background color of the menu. Table 14.7 contains a list of the desktop attributes and the associated SystemColor static variables.

Table 14.7
Desktop Attributes and Their Associated java.awt.SystemColor Variables

Desktop Attribute	SystemColor Variable
Background color of desktop	SystemColor.desktop
Background color for captions	SystemColor.activeCaption
Text color for captions	SystemColor.activeCaptionText
Border color for caption text	SystemColor.activeCaptionBorder
Background color for inactive captions	SystemColor.inactiveCaption
Text color for inactive captions	SystemColor.inactiveCaptionText
Border color for inactive captions	SystemColor.inactiveCaptionBorder
Background for windows	SystemColor.window
Color of window border frame	SystemColor.windowBorder
Text color inside windows	SystemColor.windowText
Background for menus	SystemColor.menu
Text color for menus	SystemColor.menuText

continues

Table 14.7, Continued
Desktop Attributes and Their Associated java.awt.SystemColor Variables

Desktop Attribute	SystemColor Variable
Color for highlight	SystemColor.highlight
Color for highlighted text	SystemColor.highlightText
Background color for controls	SystemColor.control
Text color for controls	SystemColor.controlText
Light highlight color for controls	SystemColor.controlLtHighlight
Highlight color for controls	SystemColor.controlHighlight
Shadow color for controls	SystemColor.controlShadow
Dark shadow color for controls	SystemColor.controlDkShadow
Text color for inactive controls	SystemColor.inactiveControlText
Background color for scrollbars	SystemColor.scrollbar
Background color for spot-help text	SystemColor.info
Text color for spot-help text	SystemColor.infoText

Java AWT components automatically check these variables before they are displayed. Incidentally, custom components aren't the only instance in which you would want to know the desktop colors. You may want to choose colors for drawing, for example, based upon the current desktop color scheme.

The next section explains how to print from Java programs—a much needed feature new to JDK 1.1.

Printing from a Java Program

New to JDK 1.1 is the capability to output information to a printer. This enables you to produce printed output, such as a report, and to print components of the graphical user interface.

Overview of Java Printing

Printing is implemented by Java primarily with a new class named PrintJob, which is located in the java.awt package. PrintJob represents a particular print job and contains methods that enable you to find information such as page size and page resolution. A method also exists in PrintJob that returns a graphics context (Graphics instance) in which you can draw the output for a given page.

To start a print job, call the new `getPrintJob()` method of the java.awt.Toolkit class. This method displays a Print dialog box where the user makes choices regarding printing. This dialog box is the common Print dialog box for a given platform and enables the user to choose a printer, the order in which to print pages, and other print options.

The following section demonstrates the use of the PrintJob class and the `getPrintJob()` method to print the proverbial "Hello World!".

An Example of Printing: The HelloPrint Application

On the CD

Listing 14.3 (program HelloPrint.java on the CD-ROM accompanying this book) is an example of how you can print from a Java application. When you click the button labeled "Hello," the words "Hello World!" are printed in the center of the page in 48 point type.

Listing 14.3

```
Line=================Java Source=================
//////////
// HelloPrint.java  Demonstrates how to print from
// a Java application.
//
// Author: James L. Weaver  JDK 1.1 beta1
//////////
package chapter14.code.helloprint;

import java.awt.*;
import java.awt.event.*;

public class HelloPrint extends Frame
                      implements ActionListener {

    Button printBtn;
```

continues

Listing 14.3, Continued

```

    public HelloPrint() {
        super("Hello World");

        addWindowListener(new Wadapt());
        setSize(300, 200);
        setLayout(new FlowLayout());

        printBtn = new Button("Hello");
        printBtn.addActionListener(this);
        add(printBtn);

        setVisible(true);
        printBtn.requestFocus();
    }

    private void printHello() {
        Graphics pg;
        String hello = new String("Hello World!");

        // Display a Print dialog box, and get a reference
        // to a PrintJob object
        PrintJob pj = getToolkit().getPrintJob(this, "HelloPrint",
➥null);

        if (pj != null) {
            int w = pj.getPageDimension().width;
            int h = pj.getPageDimension().height;

            // Ask the PrintJob instance for a graphics context in
            // which to draw
            pg = pj.getGraphics();
            if (pg != null) {
                pg.setFont(new Font("Helvetica", Font.BOLD, 48));

```

```
50                  int sw = pg.getFontMetrics().stringWidth(hello);
51                  int sh = pg.getFontMetrics().getHeight();
52                  pg.drawString(hello, (w - sw) / 2, (h + sh) / 2);
53
54                  // Flush the page to the printer
55                  pg.dispose();
56              }
57              // End the print job and do housekeeping
58              pj.end();
59          }
60      }
61
62      public void actionPerformed(ActionEvent evt) {
63          printHello();
64      }
65
66      public static void main(String args[]) {
67          HelloPrint printFrame = new HelloPrint();
68          return;
69      }
70  }
71
72  class Wadapt extends WindowAdapter
73  {
74      public void windowClosing(WindowEvent evt) {
75          Frame frm = (Frame)evt.getSource();
76          frm.setVisible(false);
77          frm.dispose();
78          System.exit(0);
79      }
80  }
```

When the Hello button is clicked, line 63 calls the `printHello()` method contained in lines 32–60.

Line 34 creates the String that will eventually be printed on the printer.

Line 38 gets a reference to the Toolkit object to call the `getPrintJob()` method. The `getPrintJob()` method takes three parameters:

- An instance of Frame.
- The name of the print job.
- A Properties object that may be used to supply platform-dependent information to the Print dialog box. It may also be used to find out what options the user chose in the Print dialog box because this method alters the Properties object passed to it.

The `getPrintJob()` method displays the Print dialog box to the user. If the user cancels the print job, this method returns null. Otherwise the `getPrintJob()` method returns a PrintJob object that represents the print job. Line 40 checks to see whether or not the user cancelled the print job.

Lines 41 and 42 call the `getPageDimension()` of the PrintJob object to find out the dimensions (in pixels) of a page.

Line 46 calls the `getGraphics()` method of the PrintJob object to get a Graphics object on which to draw. That object will eventually be printed. Each time `getGraphics()` is called, the graphics context for a new page is returned. Calling `getGraphics()` repeatedly results in multiple page printing.

The Graphics object that the `getGraphics()` method returns also implements an interface named PrintGraphics. The PrintGraphics interface contains the `getPrintJob()` method. This interface and method will be utilized in the following example.

Line 47 makes sure a graphics context is actually returned.

Line 48 sets the printer font to 48 point bold Helvetica.

Lines 50 and 51 calculate the width and height (in pixels) of the "Hello World!" string in the current font characteristics.

Line 52 prints "Hello World!" after calculating the characteristics needed to print in the center of the page.

Line 55 causes the page to be sent to the printer. In a multiple page scenario you would call the `dispose()` method for every page.

Line 58 ends the print job and performs any necessary housekeeping functions.

Figure 14.9 shows the HelloPrint application's display.

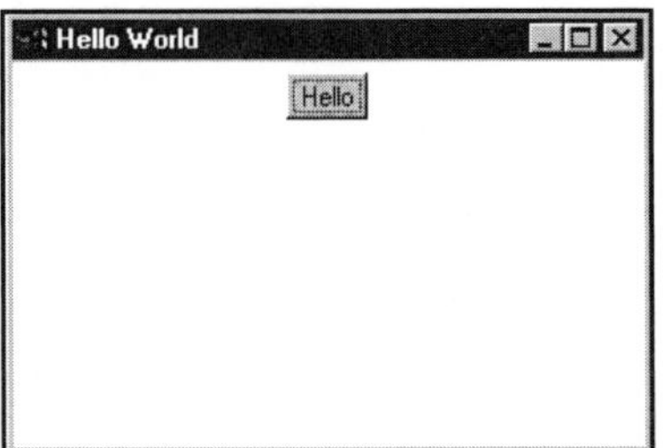

Figure 14.9
HelloPrint application display.

Printing the Graphical User Interface

To print a component, pass the graphics context of the printer page to the `print()` method of the component. Recall that the graphics context is returned from the `getGraphics()` method of the PrintJob object. The default implementation of the `print()` method is to call the `paint()` method, so the component's `paint()` method will be called with the graphics context as the argument. This causes the component to be rendered to the printer page.

An Example of Printing a Component: The HelloPrint2 Application

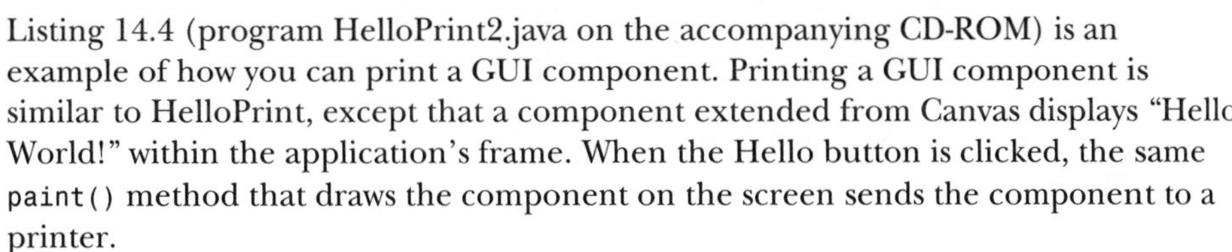

Listing 14.4 (program HelloPrint2.java on the accompanying CD-ROM) is an example of how you can print a GUI component. Printing a GUI component is similar to HelloPrint, except that a component extended from Canvas displays "Hello World!" within the application's frame. When the Hello button is clicked, the same `paint()` method that draws the component on the screen sends the component to a printer.

Listing 14.4

```
Line==================Java Source==================
//////////
// HelloPrint2.java  Demonstrates how to print a
// component from a Java application.
//
// Author: James L. Weaver  JDK 1.1 beta1
//////////
package chapter14.code.helloprint2;

import java.awt.*;
import java.awt.event.*;

public class HelloPrint2 extends Frame
```

continues

Listing 14.4, Continued

```
                        implements ActionListener {

    Button printBtn;
    HelloCanvas hc;

    public HelloPrint2() {
        super("Hello World");

        addWindowListener(new Wadapt());
        setSize(300, 200);
        setLayout(new BorderLayout());

        Panel p = new Panel();
        add("North", p);

        printBtn = new Button("Hello");
        printBtn.addActionListener(this);
        p.add(printBtn);

        hc = new HelloCanvas();
        add("Center", hc);

        setVisible(true);
        printBtn.requestFocus();
    }

    private void printHello() {
        Graphics pg;

        // Display a print dialog box, and get a reference
        // to a PrintJob object.
        PrintJob pj = getToolkit().getPrintJob(this, "HelloPrint2",
➥null);

        if (pj != null) {
            // Ask the PrintJob instance for a graphics context in
            // which to draw.
```

```
                pg = pj.getGraphics();
                if (pg != null) {

                    hc.print(pg);

                    // Flush the page to the printer
                    pg.dispose();
                }
                // End the print job and do housekeeping
                pj.end();
            }
        }

        public void actionPerformed(ActionEvent evt) {
            printHello();
        }

        public static void main(String args[]) {
            HelloPrint2 printFrame = new HelloPrint2();
            return;
        }
    }

    class HelloCanvas extends Canvas {
        protected String hello;

        public HelloCanvas() {
            hello = new String("Hello World!");
        }

        public void paint(Graphics pg) {
            int w, h;
            if (pg instanceof PrintGraphics) {
                w = ((PrintGraphics)pg).getPrintJob()
➥.getPageDimension().width;
                h = ((PrintGraphics)pg).getPrintJob()
➥.getPageDimension().height;
            }
            else {
```

continues

Listing 14.4, Continued

```
086                 w = this.getSize().width;
087                 h = this.getSize().height;
088             }
089             pg.setFont(new Font("Helvetica", Font.BOLD, 48));
090
091             int sw = pg.getFontMetrics().stringWidth(hello);
092             int sh = pg.getFontMetrics().getHeight();
093             pg.drawString(hello, (w - sw) / 2, (h + sh) / 2);
094         }
095     }
096
097     class Wadapt extends WindowAdapter
098     {
099         public void windowClosing(WindowEvent evt) {
100             Frame frm = (Frame)evt.getSource();
101             frm.setVisible(false);
102             frm.dispose();
103             System.exit(0);
104         }
105     }
```

In the HelloPrint2 constructor (lines 18–37), the HelloCanvas component is placed in the "Center" area of a BorderLayout, and the Hello button is placed in the "North."

The `printHello()` method in lines 39–60 gets the PrintJob and Graphics instances like in the original HelloPrint application. Line 52, however, is different. It calls the `print()` method of the HelloCanvas object, which calls the `paint()` method of the same object. Because the Graphics object passed is a printer page, the component will be drawn on that page.

Lines 79–94 contain the `paint()` method of the component being displayed and printed. Line 81 determines whether this component should be drawn to the printer or the screen. It does this by checking whether the Graphics instance passed into the `paint()` method implements the PrintGraphics interface. This is the case if `paint()` was called from line 52, because the `getGraphics()` method in line 49 returns a Graphics object that implements the PrintGraphics interface.

Lines 82 and 83 get the width and height (in pixels) of the printer page by using the `getPrintJob()` method of the PrintGraphics object to get the PrintJob object, and then calling the appropriate methods of the PrintJob object.

Lines 86 and 87 get the width and height of the HelloCanvas component.

Lines 89–93 do the same calculations and drawing as the original HelloPrint. The "Hello World!" string is centered both horizontally and vertically regardless of whether it is being displayed on the screen or printer.

Line 55 causes the page to be printed and line 58 ends the print job, just like the `printHello()` method of the original HelloPrint application.

An entire containment hierarchy of components can be printed by calling the `printAll()` method of the top-level component, passing the graphics context of the printer page.

Figure 14.10 shows the HelloPrint2 application's display.

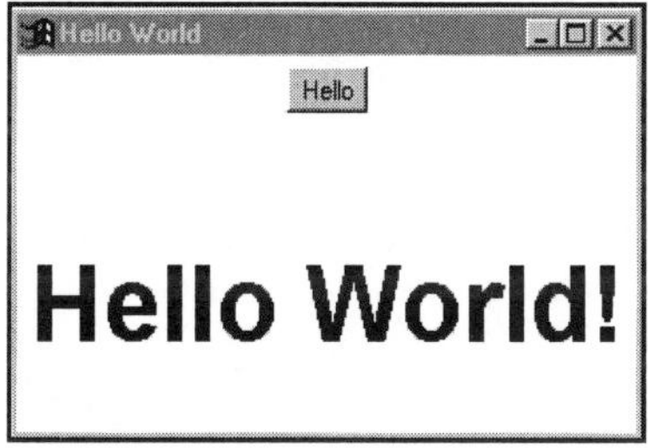

Figure 14.10
HelloPrint2 application display.

This section explained how to output information and GUI components to a printer, primarily by using the PrintJob class. For more information on this class, refer to the following Web page:

```
http://java.sun.com/products/JDK/1.1/docs/api/java.awt.PrintJob.html
```

The next section discusses how to use another new feature of the JDK 1.1—the clipboard.

Using the Clipboard from a Java Program

Users have come to expect the capability to cut, copy, and paste information within and across applications. Because Java uses the GUI components of the host windowing system, cut, copy, and paste are already available to a limited degree. New to JDK 1.1, however, is the capability to manipulate the clipboard from within your program.

Overview of Clipboard Programming

The new Java classes, interfaces, and exceptions involved in the clipboard scenario are:

- Clipboard class: Class representing a clipboard, which is either the native system clipboard or one created by your program.
- StringSelection class: Convenience class representing String data to be placed on the clipboard. Other convenience classes are created to handle transferring other data types.
- DataFlavor class: Class representing a format in which data is transferred. Data, for example, represented by the StringSelection class is transferred as a String or as characters in an InputStream.
- Transferable interface: Objects placed on the clipboard or retrieved from the clipboard must implement the Transferable interface.
- ClipboardOwner interface: Contains one method that is called when the ClipboardOwner object no longer owns the data on the clipboard.
- UnsupportedFlavorException exception: Implemented when a Transferable object doesn't support the transfer of its data in the requested format, or "data flavor."

These Java classes, interfaces, and exceptions are located in the new java.awt.datatransfer package. Figure 14.11 shows a common scenario for manipulating the clipboard. Figure 14.12 depicts the ClipboardDemo application described in the following section.

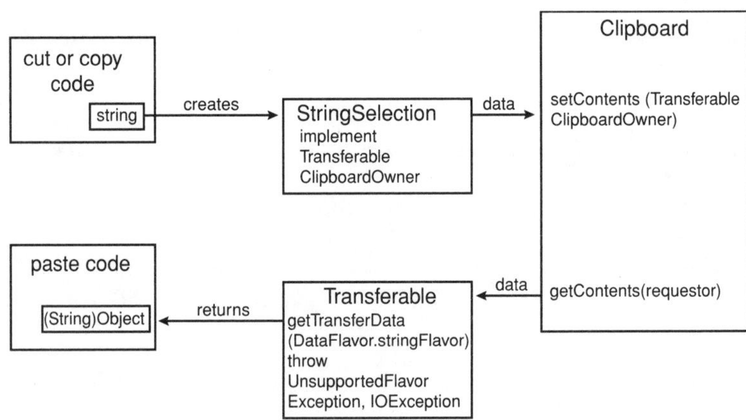

Figure 14.11
Common clipboard scenario.

The ClipboardDemo Application

On the CD 

Listing 14.5 (program ClipboardDemo.java on the accompanying CD-ROM) is an example of how you can manipulate the clipboard programmatically. Traditional cut, copy, and paste functionality is available in the two text fields by using the menu items in the Edit menu. Figure 14.12 shows the ClipboardDemo application's display.

Listing 14.5

```
Line==================Java Source=================
//////////
// ClipboardDemo.java  Demonstrates how to
// use the clipboard from a Java program.
//
// Author: James L. Weaver  JDK 1.1 beta1
//////////
package chapter14.code.clipboarddemo;

import java.awt.*;
import java.awt.event.*;
import java.util.*;
import java.awt.datatransfer.*;

public class ClipboardDemo extends Frame
                    implements ActionListener {

    TextField tf1, tf2;
    Menu editMenu;
    MenuItem miCut;
    MenuItem miCopy;
    MenuItem miPaste;
    Clipboard clip;

    public ClipboardDemo() {
        super("Java Clipboard Demonstration");

        // Get a reference to the native clipboard
        clip = getToolkit().getSystemClipboard();

        addWindowListener(new Wadapt());
```

continues

Listing 14.5, Continued

```
        setSize(300, 200);
        setLayout(new FlowLayout());

        // Create two text fields to cut, copy, and paste in
        tf1 = new TextField(null, 10);
        tf2 = new TextField(null, 10);
        add(tf1);
        add(tf2);

        buildMenu();
        setVisible(true);
        tf1.requestFocus();
    }

    private void buildMenu() {
        // Create a menu bar and set in in the frame
        MenuBar mb = new MenuBar();
        setMenuBar(mb);

        // Create and populate an Edit menu
        editMenu = new Menu("Edit");
        mb.add(editMenu);

        miCut = new MenuItem("Cut");
        miCut.setActionCommand("Cut");
        miCut.addActionListener(this);
        editMenu.add(miCut);

        miCopy = new MenuItem("Copy");
        miCopy.setActionCommand("Copy");
        miCopy.addActionListener(this);
        editMenu.add(miCopy);

        miPaste = new MenuItem("Paste");
        miPaste.setActionCommand("Paste");
        miPaste.addActionListener(this);
        editMenu.add(miPaste);
    }
```

```

    public void actionPerformed(ActionEvent evt) {
        TextField tf;
        String str;
        int caret;

        // If Cut or Copy is chosen, get the selected text of the
        // text field that has focus and put it on the clipboard.
        if (evt.getActionCommand().startsWith("C")) {
            if (getFocusOwner() instanceof TextField) {
                tf = (TextField)getFocusOwner();
                str = tf.getText();
                StringSelection cbdata =
                        new StringSelection(tf.getSelectedText());
                clip.setContents(cbdata, cbdata);

                // If Cut is chosen, cut out the selected text by
                // concatenating what was before the selection with
                // what was after the selection, and placing it in
                // the text field.
                if (evt.getActionCommand().equals("Cut")) {
                    caret = tf.getSelectionStart();
                    str = str.substring(0, tf.getSelectionStart())
                        + str.substring(tf.getSelectionEnd());
                    tf.setText(str);
                    tf.setCaretPosition(caret);
                }
            }
        }
        else if (evt.getActionCommand().equals("Paste")) {
            // Get the contents of the clipboard and verify that
            // the component that has focus is a text field.
            Transferable cbdata = clip.getContents(this);
            if (getFocusOwner() instanceof TextField) {
                tf = (TextField)getFocusOwner();
                if (cbdata != null) {
                    try {
                        // Try to get data from the clipboard as
                        // a String.
```

continues

Listing 14.5, Continued

```
                        String data = (String)cbdata.
➥getTransferData(
                                DataFlavor.stringFlavor);
                        // Insert the string at the cursor, deleting
                        // any selected text.
                        caret = tf.getSelectionStart();
                        str = tf.getText();
                        str = str.substring(0, tf.
➥getSelectionStart())
                            + data
                            + str.substring(tf.getSelectionEnd());
                        tf.setText(str);
                        tf.setCaretPosition(caret + data.length());
                    }
                    catch (Exception e) {
                        System.out.println("Data not string flavor");
                    }
                }
            }
        }
    }

    public static void main(String args[]) {
        ClipboardDemo cdFrame = new ClipboardDemo();
        return;
    }
}

class Wadapt extends WindowAdapter
{
    public void windowClosing(WindowEvent evt) {
        Frame frm = (Frame)evt.getSource();
        frm.setVisible(false);
        frm.dispose();
        System.exit(0);
    }
}
```

The steps that you can take to put a String on the clipboard are as follows:

1. Get a reference to the native system clipboard.

   Line 28 calls the `getSystemClipboard()` method of the Toolkit class to get the necessary reference.

2. Create a StringSelection object that contains the String to be placed on the clipboard.

   In lines 81 and 82 a StringSelection object is created using the selected text in the active text field as the constructor. Line 79 returned the active text field by calling the `getFocusOwner()` method of the frame.

   The StringSelection class is a convenience class for transferring strings to and from the clipboard. This class implements the two interfaces listed previously; Transferable and ClipboardOwner.

3. Place the String on the clipboard.

   Line 83 calls the `setContents()` method of the Clipboard class to accomplish this. The parameters of the `setContents()` method are:

   - A Transferable object that contains the data being placed on the clipboard. The Transferable object in this case is cbdata, an instance of StringSelection.

   - A ClipboardOwner object, which has a method named lostOwnership() that is called when the object no longer owns the data on the clipboard. This is usually a result of another object placing data on the clipboard.

The object that implements the Transferable interface must contain the data being transferred. The object that implements the ClipboardOwner interface, however, can be any object, not always the one that contains the data as is the case here. The StringSelection class implements the ClipboardOwner interface out of convenience, because you will not usually care when the clipboard changes ownership.

The steps that you can take to retrieve a String from the clipboard are as follows:

1. Get a reference to the native system clipboard.

   As pointed out before, this is taken care of in line 28.

2. Get the Transferable object from the clipboard (if one exists).

Line 101 calls the `getContents()` method of the Clipboard class that returns a reference to the Transferable object on the clipboard. The argument to this method is a reference to the requesting object.

3. Get the data from the Transferable object in the desired format or "data flavor."

Lines 108 and 109 call the `getTransferData()` method of the Transferable object with an argument that describes the desired "data flavor," in this case String. The `getTransferData()` method returns an Object that must be cast into the desired type. This method throws an UnsupportedFlavorException if the data is not available in the requested flavor.

In addition to the `getTransferData()` method, the Transferable interface defines two methods that enable you to find out which data flavors are available:

- DataFlavor[] `getTransferDataFlavors()`—Returns an array of available data flavors.
- Boolean isDataFlavorSupported(DataFlavor)—Returns true if the given data flavor is supported.

Finally, lines 112–118 update the text field that is the target of the paste operation.

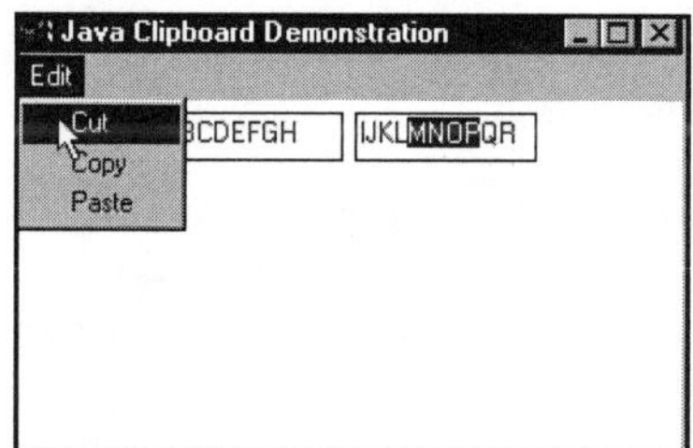

Figure 14.12
ClipboardDemo application display.

Summary

In this chapter, you learned how to create menu bar menus, pop-up menus, and how to assign shortcut keys to them. You also learned about the new JDK 1.1 Delegation Event Model, the associated event listeners, and the new event class hierarchy. The chapter also presented the Extended Component Event Model as a way to make use of the Delegation Event Model mechanisms in sub-classed components by overriding the event processing methods. Lastly, this chapter covered focus traversal, accessing desktop colors, printing, and clipboard programming.

The next chapter focuses on the Java component architecture known as Java Beans. You also learn about two more AWT features new to JDK 1.1: printing from a Java program and using the clipboard.

CHAPTER 15

Java Beans: Java's Component Architecture

This chapter focuses on the new Java component architecture known as Java Beans. The following sections define Java Beans, discuss its associated properties, methods, and events, and provides examples of Beans and their usage. Many new JDK 1.1 features were added primarily for the sake of supporting Java Beans; this chapter mentions some of these features, such as introspection, serialization, and JAR files, that haven't been covered in previous chapters.

Understanding Java Beans

Java Beans is JavaSoft's name for the Java component architecture. In this context, a component is a reusable software-building block (or "Bean" to perpetuate the coffee metaphor). The purpose of a component architecture is to enable the building of applications by assembling preexisting components.

Java Beans Defined

According to JavaSoft, "A Java Bean is a reusable software component that can be manipulated visually in a builder tool."

In this definition, a builder tool is typically an integrated application development environment, but other possibilities do exist. A builder tool, for example, could be a Web page authoring tool, where Beans could be dragged and dropped onto a page. Another builder tool is the beanbox test container, which is included in the BDK (Beans Development Kit) that JavaSoft has made available for developers to test their Java Beans.

Note BDK 1.1 beta 2 was used to test and display the example Beans in this chapter. To download the BDK, access the following Web page and follow the download instructions.

```
http://splash.javasoft.com/beans/
```

Instructions on how to use the BDK, as well as lots of Java Beans documentation are included as a part of the BDK.

In JavaSoft's definition of Java Beans, "manipulated visually" means that the developer can change the Bean's appearance and behavior by using the builder tool's graphical user interface.

Five attributes are common to Java Beans:

- Properties: A Bean has properties that can be manipulated from both a program and a builder tool.
- Customization: Some Beans have properties whose type is unknown to a builder tool. In this case, the builder tool has no standard way of enabling the developer to visually edit the property. When this happens, the Bean should provide its own *property editor*. Also, some Beans are too complex to be edited by the builder tool's default mechanisms. In this case, the Bean should provide its own *customizer* with which the developer can visually edit the Bean's properties. Property editors will be covered later in this chapter.

- Persistence: Beans often are distributed in a serialized form, which means that a builder tool or application can load the Bean and restore the state of its properties. A Bean must, therefore, be serializable. Serialization is covered in more detail in Chapter 16, "Remote Method Invocation and Object Serialization."

- Events: A Bean typically emits and/or receives events. Beans use the Delegation Event Model, which is discussed in Chapter 14, "The New, Improved AWT: Menus, Events, and More New Features."

- Introspection: A Bean is constructed in a such manner that a builder tool can find out about such elements as a Bean's properties and events. Introspection will be covered later in this chapter.

It is important to understand that Beans can execute in two environments:

- The design environment: This is often a builder tool, as described previously. In the *design environment,* the Bean must supply information about itself. This information is often contained in classes that are separate from the classes that define the Bean's runtime behavior.

- The runtime environment: This is any application in which the Bean is used, including applications developed in a scripting language. No need exists to supply the extra information to the typical application in which a Bean runs, so only the classes that define a Bean's runtime behavior are needed.

Reasons for Beans

The software industry has always championed the concept of reuse. Over the years, the scope, or granularity, of reuse has increased, which has produced an accompanying increase in productivity. Four levels of granularity exist:

- Since programming began, sections of source code were made available to, and reused by, other developers.

- When structured programming came in vogue in the 1970s, function libraries were shared.

- As object-oriented programming matured in the 1980s, class libraries were shared by developers and sold by third parties.

- As GUI development has exploded in the 1990s, third-party components have become instrumental in enabling developers to build reliable applications quickly. VBX and OCX components, for example, have become popular tools for building Visual Basic applications.

Java Beans belong to the last level of reuse granularity. An increasing number of Java Beans are becoming available from software component developers. Integrated Java development environments typically come with several Beans that developers can use.

Some of the more popular Beans are those that function as higher-level GUI widgets, such as multicolumn list boxes and toolbar managers. Beans also can be small applications, such as a drawing program, that can be embedded in a compound document. Beans also can be non-visual software components: A timer widget, for example, emits a "tick" event at a predetermined interval.

Now that you have an idea of Beans and their uses, consider the following example of a simple Bean.

An Example Bean: Scope

Listing 15.1 depicts a Java class named Scope, which serves as a simple example of a Java Bean. The Scope Bean is similar to an electronic scope in that it contains graduated marks in the horizontal and vertical axes. When the user moves the mouse cursor over the Bean, crosshairs appear whose intersection occurs at the hotspot of the cursor. Listing 15.2, later in this chapter, displays the Bean in an application window. Figure 15.2 shows the application's display, which is essentially the Scope Bean filling up the entire application window.

Listing 15.1

```
Line=================Java Source=================
//////////
// Scope.java  A very simple Java Bean.
//
// Author: James L. Weaver  JDK 1.1 beta1
//////////
package chapter15.code.scope;

import java.awt.*;
import java.awt.event.*;
import java.io.Serializable;

public class Scope extends Canvas implements Serializable
{
    protected int xCoord = 0,
                  yCoord = 0,
                  ticks = 8;
```

```
    protected String coordString = "0,0";

    public Scope() {
        // Enable mouse and mouse motion events to be processed
        enableEvents(AWTEvent.MOUSE_MOTION_EVENT_MASK ¦
                     AWTEvent.MOUSE_EVENT_MASK);
        setSize(200, 200);
    }

    // The presence of both a setTick and getTick cause the
    // Introspector to assume there is a "tick" property
    public void setTicks(int ticks) {
        this.ticks = ticks;
    }

    public int getTicks() {
        return ticks;
    }

    public void paint(Graphics g) {
        int tickSize = 5;
        int xMax = getSize().width -1;
        int yMax = getSize().height -1;
        int xRes = xMax/ticks;
        int yRes = yMax/ticks;

        // Draw the crosshairs
        g.setColor(Color.red);
        g.drawRect(0, 0, xMax, yMax);
        g.drawLine(xCoord, 0, xCoord, yMax);
        g.drawLine(0, yCoord, xMax, yCoord);

        // Build and draw the coordinate string
        coordString = new Integer(xCoord) + "," +
                      new Integer(yCoord);
        g.drawString(coordString, tickSize, yMax - tickSize);

        // Draw the tick marks
        for (int i=0,x=0; i<ticks; i++,x+=xRes) {
```

continues

Listing 15.1, Continued

```
56              g.drawLine(x, 0, x, tickSize);
57              g.drawLine(x, yMax - tickSize, x, yMax);
58          }
59          for (int i=0,y=0; i<ticks; i++,y+=yRes) {
60              g.drawLine(0, y, tickSize, y);
61              g.drawLine(xMax - tickSize, y, xMax, y);
62          }
63      }
64
65      // When the mouse moves, update the display
66      protected boolean processMouseMotionEvent(MouseEvent e) {
67          if (e.getId() == MouseEvent.MOUSE_MOVED) {
68              xCoord = e.getX();
69              yCoord = e.getY();
70              repaint();
71          }
72          super.processMouseMotionEvent(e);
73          return false;
74      }
75
76      // When the mouse exits the Scope bean area,
77      // set coordinates to 0,0
78      protected Boolean processMouseEvent(MouseEvent e) {
79          if (e.getId() == MouseEvent.MOUSE_EXITED) {
80              xCoord = 0;
81              yCoord = 0;
82              repaint();
83          }
84          super.processMouseEvent(e);
85          return false;
86      }
87  }
```

As mentioned earlier in the "Java Beans Defined" section, a Bean must be persistent, which means that it must know how to store itself to a stream and then restore itself from a stream. For this reason, the Scope Bean implements the Serializable interface in line 12 of listing 15.1.

```
12   public class Scope extends Canvas implements Serializable
```

Also in line 12, you'll notice that this class extends Canvas. You choose the class that you want the Bean to extend, based upon the functionality that you want to use. This particular Bean draws a lot, so Canvas is a good choice for the superclass.

Lines 14–17 declare four different fields of this class, but only one represents a property of the Scope Bean. (This will be explained in a moment.)

```
14       protected int xCoord = 0,
15                     yCoord = 0,
16                     ticks = 8;
17       protected String coordString = "0,0";
```

In the constructor, the enableEvents() method in lines 21 and 22 should look familiar, because it was covered in a previous chapter. In this case, we want all mouse events to be sent to processEvent() so that they can be handled by the event processing methods of this subclass.

```
21           enableEvents(AWTEvent.MOUSE_MOTION_EVENT_MASK |
22                        AWTEvent.MOUSE_EVENT_MASK);
```

Lines 28–34 define two methods of this Bean. Because a setTicks() method exists for a corresponding getTicks() method, this Bean defines a read/write property named "ticks." In general, whenever a public set<PropertyName>() method co-exists with a corresponding public get<PropertyName>() method, a read/write "propertyName" property is defined. In this Bean, the "ticks" field is used to store the value of the "ticks" property, but the field could have been named anything.

```
28       public void setTicks(int ticks) {
29           this.ticks = ticks;
30       }
31
32       public int getTicks() {
33           return ticks;
34       }
```

The define properties discussed in the preceding paragraph are useful in builder tools. When a builder tool loads a Bean, it undergoes some of the following steps:

1. When a Bean is loaded into a builder tool it goes through a process known as *introspection,* which analyzes the Bean.

2. During part of the introspection process, the properties of the Bean are analyzed. In this case, the introspection would see the matching `setTicks()` and `getTicks()` methods, and then define a property named "ticks." This `set<PropertyName>() get<PropertyName>()` rule is called a *design pattern*, which is one of many design patterns used in the introspection process to analyze a Bean.

3. The introspection process defines the "ticks" property as an integer because `getTicks()` returns an integer and `setTicks()` takes an integer argument.

4. Because of the introspection process, when the builder tool displays a property sheet for editing the properties of the Scope Bean, the property sheet contains an input field for the "ticks" property. Figure 15.1 shows the Scope Bean property sheet generated by the BDK beanbox.

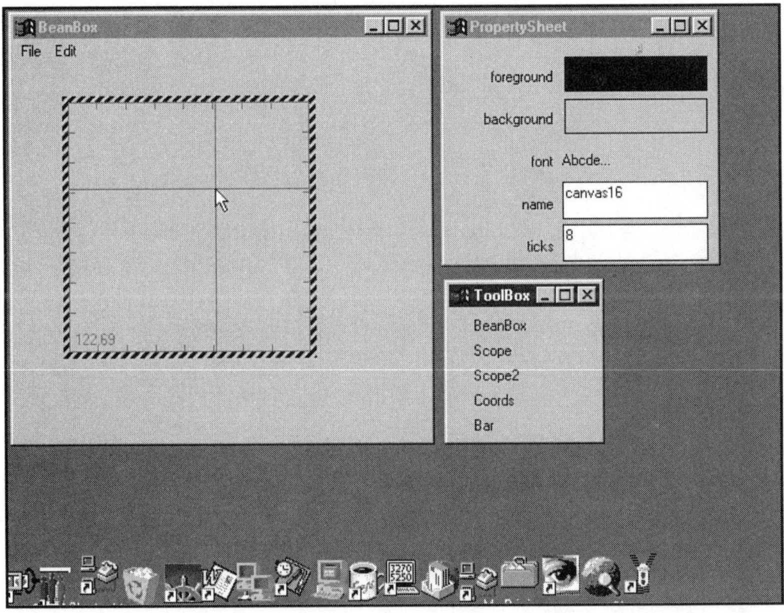

Figure 15.1

The Scope Bean and PropertySheet in the BDK BeanBox.

Lines 36–63 initiate the overridden `paint()` method, which draws the visual aspects of the Bean.

Lines 38–41 calculate how far apart the tick marks should be on each axis, based upon the dimensions of the Bean and the value of the ticks property. Because this Bean can be resized, the calculation is performed whenever the `paint()` method is invoked.

```
38          int xMax = getSize().width -1;
39          int yMax = getSize().height -1;
40          int xRes = xMax/ticks;
41          int yRes = yMax/ticks;
```

Lines 44–47 draw a rectangle around the Bean and the crosshairs that track with the mouse cursor. The *xCoord* and *yCoord* variables are changed by the mouse event handling methods further down in the program.

```
44          g.setColor(Color.red);
45          g.drawRect(0, 0, xMax, yMax);
46          g.drawLine(xCoord, 0, xCoord, yMax);
47          g.drawLine(0, yCoord, xMax, yCoord);
```

Lines 50–52 construct and draw a string that contains the current coordinates of the mouse cursor, separated by a comma.

```
50          coordString = new Integer(xCoord) + "," +
51                        new Integer(yCoord);
52          g.drawString(coordString, tickSize, yMax - tickSize);
```

Lines 55–62 draw the graduated tick marks in both dimensions, based upon the previous calculations.

```
55          for (int i=0,x=0; i<ticks; i++,x+=xRes) {
56              g.drawLine(x, 0, x, tickSize);
57              g.drawLine(x, yMax-tickSize, x, yMax);
58          }
59          for (int i=0,y=0; i<ticks; i++,y+=yRes) {
60              g.drawLine(0, y, tickSize, y);
61              g.drawLine(xMax - tickSize, y, xMax, y);
62          }
```

Lines 66–74 contain the overridden mouse motion handling method. The only mouse motion of interest to this Bean is the MOUSE_MOVED event type. When the mouse moves over the Bean's display area, the x and y coordinates are retrieved from the MouseEvent instance, and the Bean's display is repainted.

```
66      protected boolean processMouseMotionEvent(MouseEvent e) {
67          if (e.getId() == MouseEvent.MOUSE_MOVED) {
68              xCoord = e.getX();
69              yCoord = e.getY();
70              repaint();
```

```
71          }
72          super.processMouseMotionEvent(e);
73          return false;
74      }
```

When the user moves the mouse outside the Bean's display area, the crosshairs must disappear. Lines 78–86 handle this event:

```
78      protected boolean processMouseEvent(MouseEvent e) {
79          if (e.getId() == MouseEvent.MOUSE_EXITED) {
80              xCoord = 0;
81              yCoord = 0;
82              repaint();
83          }
84          super.processMouseEvent(e);
85          return false;
86      }
```

Of course, the user must be able to see the Bean. In listing 15.2, the ScopeFrame application creates an application window, initiates an instance of the Bean, and displays the Bean in the application window.

Listing 15.2

```
Line=================Java Source=================
//////////
// ScopeFrame.java  Frame in which to run the Scope
// Java Bean.
//
// Author: James L. Weaver  JDK 1.1 beta1
//////////
package chapter15.code.scope;

import java.awt.*;
import java.awt.event.*;

public class ScopeFrame extends Frame {

    Scope scope;

```

```
    public ScopeFrame() {
        super("Scope Java Bean Demo");

        setLayout(new BorderLayout());
        addWindowListener(new Wadapt());
        setSize(300, 300);

        scope = new Scope();

        // Set the "ticks" property of the Scope Bean
        scope.setTicks(8);

        // The Scope Bean will fill the entire Frame
        add("Center", scope);

        setVisible(true);
    }

    public static void main(String args[]) {
        ScopeFrame menuFrame = new ScopeFrame();
        return;
    }
}

class Wadapt extends WindowAdapter
{
    public void windowClosing(WindowEvent evt) {
        evt.getWindow().setVisible(false);
        evt.getWindow().dispose();
        System.exit(0);
    }
}
```

The ScopeFrame class in listing 15.2 contains an application that was developed to display the Bean so that the user can interact with it. ScopeFrame is not a builder tool, so it doesn't do any introspection or display property sheets. This application is, however, an example of how easy it can be to work with Java Beans inside an application.

Line 23 creates an instance of the Scope Bean:

```
23          scope = new Scope();
```

In line 26, the ticks property is set to eight, which causes eight tick marks to be displayed in each dimension:

```
26          scope.setTicks(8);
```

In line 19, the layout is set to BorderLayout so that in line 29 the Bean fills the entire frame. When the frame is resized, the Scope Bean is also.

```
19          setLayout(new BorderLayout());
```

```
29          add("Center", scope);
```

Figure 15.2 shows the Scope Bean running in an application.

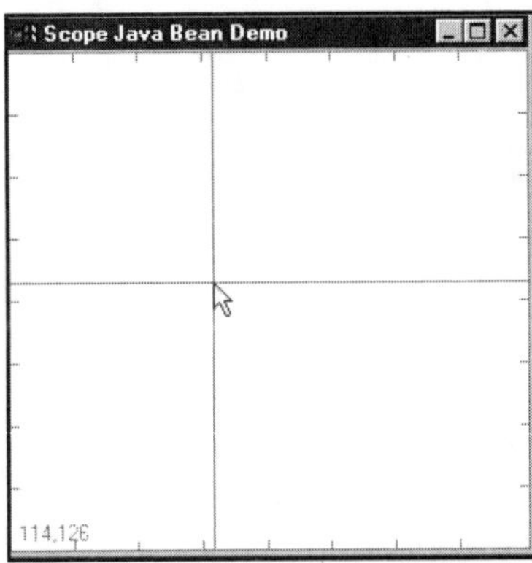

Figure 15.2
The Scope Bean running in an application.

Now that you have seen a simple example of a Java Bean, it is time to take a closer look at the three most important features contained in Java Beans: properties, methods, and events.

Properties in Java Beans

Properties are the attributes of a Bean that can be accessed by a builder tool or application. Properties are always accessed via accessor methods, which are methods with which a property can be examined and modified. Properties should not be confused with the fields of a class. In the Scope Bean, four fields exist in the Scope subclass, but only one represents a property, because only one has associated accessor methods.

Properties affect either a Bean's appearance or its behavior. In the Scope example, setting the ticks property caused the appropriate number of tick marks to be displayed.

Java Beans have four kinds of properties:

- Simple properties
- Indexed properties
- Bound properties
- Constrained properties

Not all properties are mutually exclusive. A property is always either simple or indexed. A property also can be bound, constrained, both bound and constrained, or neither bound nor constrained. Bound and constrained properties will be covered in the "Bound and Constrained Properties" section of this chapter.

Simple properties represent one value, and indexed properties represent an array of values. The next sections cover both simple and indexed properties.

Simple Properties

The ticks property in the Scope example is a simple property, because it has only one value associated with it. The accessor methods for the ticks property are setTicks() and getTicks(). Note that the "T" is capitalized in the accessor method but is converted to lowercase in the property name. The introspection process always initiates this action unless the *<PropertyName>* portion of the accessor method starts with more than one capital letter. The property name for setUPPER(), for example, is UPPER.

Accessor methods for simple properties usually take these forms:

- public void set<PropertyName>(PropertyType)
- public PropertyType get<PropertyName>()

These act as the design patterns for accessor methods of simple properties. If only the get<PropertyName> is present, a read-only property named propertyName is defined. If only the set<PropertyName> is present, a write-only property is defined.

If the property type is Boolean, an accessor method could take the form of this design pattern:

- public boolean is<PropertyName>()

Accessor methods for a property don't have to follow the design patterns, but this is encouraged for readability and consistency. If the accessor methods don't follow the design patterns, the properties must be exposed to the builder tool in a different way. This is done via the BeanInfo interface, which will be discussed in the "Java Bean Introspection" section of this chapter.

Indexed Properties

Sometimes it is desirable for a property to be an array of values. These properties are called indexed properties, and their accessor methods usually take these forms:

- public void `set<PropertyName>(PropertyElement[])`
- public *PropertyElement*[] `get<PropertyName>()`
- public void `set<PropertyName>(int, PropertyElement)`
- public PropertyElement `get<PropertyName>(int)`

The first two methods set and get the entire indexed property, which is represented by an array. The latter two methods set and get one element of the indexed property, specified by the integer argument. If methods matching either of the first two design patterns are found, then an indexed property named *`propertyElement[]`* is defined. The builder tool assumes that either of the latter two methods can be used to get and set individual elements of the indexed property.

Properties in Superclasses

Notice that the property sheet in figure 15.1 contains more than just the ticks property. It also has the background, foreground, name, and font properties. This is because one superclass of Scope, which in this case is the Component class, contains the `setBackground()` and `getBackground()` methods. The introspection process follows the derivation chain and looks for design patterns in the superclasses as well.

Methods in Java Beans

The builder tool considers all public methods in the class to be the methods of the Bean, unless the Bean's methods are explicitly identified by using the BeanInfo interface.

Because a Bean can find itself in a multithreaded environment, it is a good idea to make all the Bean's methods thread-safe by using a synchronized modifier. The synchronized modifier prevents more than one thread from calling an object's methods at a given time.

Events in Java Beans

Java Beans use the Delegation Event Model covered in Chapter 14 to communicate with each other. In fact, this model was introduced into Java mainly to support Java Beans.

When designing a Bean, you must decide which events it will emit to registered listeners external to the Bean. Two possibilities are:

- Your Bean can emit native Java events, which are covered in Chapter 14.
- You can create your own event classes and listeners.

The next section explores these possibilities.

Emitting Native Java Events from a Bean

By default, a Bean can emit any events supported by its parent class. Because the Scope Bean in listing 15.1 is derived from the Canvas class (which is derived from the Component class), it can emit a ComponentEvent, FocusEvent, KeyEvent, and MouseEvent to the appropriate registered listeners.

Let's consider, however, what happens in a Bean that has subcomponents if an event occurs on one of its subcomponents. The Calendar1 Bean, for example, which follows, is derived from the Panel class and contains a Button instance for each day of the month. When the user clicks one of these buttons, the event source is the button, not the Calendar1 Bean. Thus, the Calendar1 Bean follows this set of steps to solve the problem:

1. Intercept the event that occured on the subcomponent.
2. Create a new event. In the Calendar1 Bean, for demonstration purposes, the newly created event is not the same type of event as the one that was intercepted.
3. Post the new event to the system-event queue in such a manner that any of the Bean's registered listeners (of that event type) will receive it.

Let's examine the Calendar1 Bean to see how this solution is implemented.

Note JDK 1.1 beta 1 did not support the notion of events automatically sent up the containment hierarchy if not handled by a subcomponent. (For example, if a button doesn't handle an event, the containing frame receives the event.) JavaSoft has stated that this must be supported, but the details were not available at the time this was written. These specifics could provide an additional solution to the scenario described above.

On the CD

The Calendar1 Bean

Listing 15.3 depicts a Java Bean named Calendar1, which enables the user to navigate to any month and year, and then select a date within that month. This Bean performs the following actions:

- Serves as an example of the event solution just described.
- Offers an example of a more sophisticated and useful Bean than Scope.
- Demonstrates some methods in the new Calendar and GregorianCalendar classes.
- Illustrates the use of the synchronized modifier to make the Bean thread-safe.

Listing 15.4 depicts a very simple Bean named Listener1 that listens for the fabricated mouse events emitted by Calendar1. The Bean uses accessor methods to obtain the date and then display the date. Listing 15.5 depicts the CalendarFrame1 application, which displays these Beans and registers the Listener1 Bean with the Calendar1 Bean.

Listing 15.3

```
Line=================Java Source=================
//////////
// Calendar1.java  An example Java Bean that demonstrates
// one approach to emitting events.
//
// Author: James L. Weaver  JDK 1.1 beta1
//////////
package chapter15.code.calendar1;

import java.awt.*;
import java.awt.event.*;
import java.beans.*;
import java.io.Serializable;
import java.util.*;

public class Calendar1 extends Panel
                implements Serializable, ActionListener
{
    protected Date date;
    protected GregorianCalendar calendar;
    protected Panel header = null;
```

```
    protected Panel body = null;
    protected Button prevMonth, nextMonth;
    protected Label monthLabel;

    protected String days = new String("SunMonTueWedThuFriSat");
    protected String months =
            new String("JanFebMarAprMayJunJulAugSepOctNovDec");

    public Calendar1() {
        // Get current date and time info
        calendar = new GregorianCalendar();

        setSize(200, 200);
        setLayout(new BorderLayout());

        // Put month and year at top of applet,
        // as well as next and previous buttons.
        header = new Panel();
        prevMonth = new Button("<<");
        prevMonth.addActionListener(this);
        nextMonth = new Button(">>");
        nextMonth.addActionListener(this);
        header.add(prevMonth);
        monthLabel = new Label(null, Label.CENTER);
        header.add(monthLabel);
        header.add(nextMonth);
        add("North", header);

        // Create a Panel with a GridLayout for putting
        // the days and dates of the month in.
        body = new Panel();
        body.setLayout(new GridLayout(0, 7));

        // Put the day of the week headers at the top
        for (int i=0; i<21; i+=3) {
            body.add(new Label(days.substring(i, i+3), Label.CENTER));
        }
        add("Center", body);

```

continues

Listing 15.3, Continued

```
        // Create and display the date buttons
        displayCalendar();
    }

    // The "date" property accessor methods
    public synchronized Date getDate() {
        return calendar.getTime();
    }

    public synchronized void setDate(Date date) {
        calendar.setTime(date);
        displayCalendar();
    }

    protected synchronized void displayCalendar() {
        // Save the current values
        int yearNum = calendar.get(Calendar.YEAR);
        int monthNum = calendar.get(Calendar.MONTH);
        int dayNum = calendar.get(Calendar.DATE);

        // Build a string containing month and year
        // to display at the top between the buttons
        String monthStr = months.substring(monthNum * 3,
                                           monthNum * 3 + 3);
        monthLabel.setText(monthStr + " " + yearNum);
        monthLabel.repaint();

        // Remove all the grid cells except day names
        while (body.getComponentCount() > 7)
            body.remove(7);

        // Calendar day of week method is not working in
        // JDK 1.1 beta 1 so use date method to find
        // out which day the 1st of the month falls on
        calendar.set(Calendar.DATE, 1);
        date = calendar.getTime();
        int day = date.getDay();

```

```
        // Make blank cells until 1st of month
        for (int i=0; i<day; i++) {
            body.add(new Label());
        }

        // Put the date buttons in
        Button dayBtn;
        for (int i=1; i<=32; i++) {
            // Convert integers to strings
            dayBtn = new Button(new Integer(i).toString());
            dayBtn.addActionListener(this);
            body.add(dayBtn);

            // Increment the date
            calendar.add(Calendar.DATE, 1);

            // Make the currently selected date receive focus
            if (i == dayNum)
                dayBtn.requestFocus();

            // Stop adding buttons when a new month is reached
            if (calendar.get(Calendar.DATE) <= 1)
                break;
        }
        // Restore the current values
        calendar.set(yearNum, monthNum, dayNum);
        body.validate();
    }

    public synchronized void actionPerformed(ActionEvent e) {
        if (e.getSource() == prevMonth || e.getSource() == nextMonth) {
            // The previous or next month button was clicked, so
            // set the day of the month to 1, and go to the
            // proper month
            calendar.set(Calendar.DATE, 1);
            calendar.add(Calendar.MONTH,
                         e.getSource() == prevMonth ? -1 : 1);
            displayCalendar();
         }
```

continues

Listing 15.3, Continued

```
137             else {
138                 // One of the day buttons was clicked, so set the
139                 // calendar object to that date
140                 calendar.set(Calendar.DATE, Integer.parseInt(
141                             ((Button)e.getSource()).getLabel()));
142            }
143            // Create and post a mouse event that simulates a mouse
144            // click directly on the top of the containment hierarchy.
145            // By doing this, the instance of the Bean can be
146            // accessed by the mouse listener.
147            EventQueue.getEventQueue().postEvent(new MouseEvent(this,
148                               MouseEvent.MOUSE_CLICKED, 0,0,0,0,1));
149        }
150    }
```

In listing 15.3, lines 15 and 16 extend the Calendar1 Bean from the Panel class. Most of the functionality of the Bean happens when the date buttons or previous month/next month buttons are pressed, so all that these buttons require is a container in which to live. For this reason, the Panel—the simplest of all container subclasses—is chosen.

```
015    public class Calendar1 extends Panel
016                    implements Serializable, ActionListener
```

Line 31 uses the new GregorianCalendar class, which is a subclass of the new, very powerful Calendar class (not to be confused with the Calendar1 class that you are now reviewing). This version of the GregorianCalendar constructor creates an instance with the current date and time.

```
031            calendar = new GregorianCalendar();
```

Many Date class methods have been replaced by Calendar class methods because of internationalization issues.

The Calendar1 constructor in lines 29–62 sets the layout to BorderLayout. Buttons for displaying the previous and next month, as well as a label that will contain the selected month and year, are placed in the "North" (top) area. Both of these buttons have an action listener registered. A GridLayout-controlled panel seven columns wide fills the "Center" (middle) area of the Bean and contains day labels. As soon as `displayCalendar()` is called, the panel also contains one button for each day of the month.

The last line of the constructor calls the protected method named `displayCalendar()`, which is contained in lines 74–125. This method contains the logic necessary to accomplish the following actions:

- Places the correct month and year in the label
- Removes all existing buttons that represent days of the month
- Ascertains which day of the week begins the month
- Adds a button for each day of the selected month

Lines 76–78 in the `displayCalendar()` method store the currently held year, month, and day values because this calendar instance will be altered later in the method. The Calendar `get()` method takes an integer argument that represents the attribute of the calendar to be returned. This replaces the corresponding `getYear()`, `getMonth()`, and `getDate()` methods in the Date class. Note that the method in line 76 returns a four-digit year, not a two-digit year as returned by `getDate()`.

```
076              int yearNum = calendar.get(Calendar.YEAR);
077              int monthNum = calendar.get(Calendar.MONTH);
078              int dayNum = calendar.get(Calendar.DATE);
```

Lines 88 and 89 remove all the components in the GridLayout-controlled panel, except for the seven day labels.

```
088              while (body.getComponentCount() > 7)
089                  body.remove(7);
```

To set an element of the date or time in a Calendar or GregorianCalendar instance, use the set method shown in line 94:

```
094              calendar.set(Calendar.DATE, 1);
095              date = calendar.getTime();
096              int day = date.getDay();
```

Instead of using the Date class in lines 95 and 96 to obtain the day of the week, use a method of the Calendar class:

```
int day = calendar.get(Calendar.DAY_OF_WEEK);
```

The JDK 1.1 beta 1 implementation, however, didn't always return the correct result (as beta software is prone to do).

Lines 104–121 contain the loop that populates the GridLayout-controlled panel with "day of the month" buttons. Each button has an action listener registered to it. In each iteration, line 112 advances the date by using the `add()` method of the Calendar class. In this case, one day is added, but any number of days, months, years, hours, minutes, or seconds can be added or subtracted.

```
112                 calendar.add(Calendar.DATE, 1);
```

To indicate the currently selected day, keyboard focus is requested for the corresponding button when that day is reached in the loop.

```
115                 if (i == dayNum)
116                     dayBtn.requestFocus();
```

To determine when to stop adding date buttons, the Calendar class `get()` method is called. The day of the month rolling over to 1 indicates that the next month has been reached. When the iterations are complete, the current year, month, and date values are restored by using a form of the Calendar `set()` method. The Panel is then validated so that the buttons will be laid out again:

```
123             calendar.set(yearNum, monthNum, dayNum);
124             body.validate();
```

Lines 127–149 contain the action event listener for all the buttons in the Calendar1 Bean.

If the next or previous buttons were chosen, the day of the month is first set to 1, a month is then added or subtracted, and the calendar is updated:

```
132                 calendar.set(Calendar.DATE, 1);
133                 calendar.add(Calendar.MONTH,
134                              e.getSource() == prevMonth ? -1 : 1);
135                 displayCalendar();
```

If a day of the month button is clicked, then the date is set to the selected date, which is ascertained by reading the button's label:

```
140               calendar.set(Calendar.DATE, Integer.parseInt(
141                              ((Button)e.getSource()).getLabel()));
```

Then, in lines 147 and 148 a MouseEvent is created with the following arguments:

- This instance of the Bean as the source
- The MOUSE_CLICKED event type

- A value of zero for the time-date stamp argument, key modifiers argument, and x, y coordinate arguments, because the listener doesn't need any of this information
- A single click, as opposed to a double-click

The fabricated mouse event then is posted to the system event queue. A reference to this queue can be obtained by calling the static `getEventQueue()` method of the new EventQueue class.

```
        EventQueue.getEventQueue().postEvent(new MouseEvent(this,
                                  MouseEvent.MOUSE_CLICKED, 0,0,0,0,1));
```

The event is delivered to any registered listeners by using the built-in `processEvent()` and `processMouseEvent()` methods of the Panel class from which the Bean is derived.

Lines 65–72 are the accessor methods for the "date" property:

```
065     public synchronized Date getDate() {
066         return calendar.getTime();
067     }
068
069     public synchronized void setDate(Date date) {
070         calendar.setTime(date);
071         displayCalendar();
072     }
```

The `getDate()` accessor method returns the value of the Calendar `getTime()` method. This `getTime()` method returns a Date object that represents the date/time information held by the Calendar instance; in this case, the information is the currently selected date.

The `setDate()` accessor method calls the `setTime()` method of the Calendar object. This `setTime()` method takes a Date argument and causes the Calendar object to represent the given date and time. The `setDate()` accessor method then calls the `displayCalendar()` method, which, as described above, updates the face of the Calendar1 Bean with the proper "day of the month" buttons. This means that an application using the Calendar1 Bean simply can call the `setDate()` accessor method, and not only will the internal state of the Bean change, but Calendar1 also will turn to the given month. The same behavior happens in a builder tool as well: When the developer changes the date property in the property sheet, the Bean automatically displays the entered month. One stipulation exists, however: The builder tool must know how to present the Date type in the property sheet for editing. In the "Developing Property Editors" section of this chapter, a Date property editor is built for use with the Calendar1 and Calendar2 (shown later) Beans.

Now it's time to examine listing 15.4 that, as mentioned earlier, uses a simple Bean called Listener1.

Listing 15.4

```
Line=================Java Source=================
//////////
// Listener1.java  Listens for mouse clicks
// on the Calendar1 Bean.
//
// Author: James L. Weaver  JDK 1.1 beta1
//////////
package chapter15.code.calendar1;

import java.awt.*;
import java.awt.event.*;
import java.text.*;
import java.util.*;
import java.io.Serializable;

public class Listener1 extends TextField
                        implements Serializable, MouseListener
{
    public Listener1() {
        super("?????????", 15);
        setEditable(false);
    }

    // Required by MouseListener interface
    public void mousePressed(MouseEvent evt) {}
    public void mouseReleased(MouseEvent evt) {}
    public void mouseEntered(MouseEvent evt) {}
    public void mouseExited(MouseEvent evt) {}

    public synchronized void mouseClicked(MouseEvent evt) {
        // Get a reference to the Calendar1 Bean
        Calendar1 src = (Calendar1)evt.getComponent();

        // Set the "date" property of the Calendar1 Bean
        // and display it in the text field
```

```
35          Date date = src.getDate();
36          SimpleDateFormat df = new SimpleDateFormat("MM/dd/yyyy");
37          setText(df.format(date));
38      }
39  }
```

The Listener1 Bean depicted in listing 15.4 listens for mouse events from the Calendar1 Bean and then displays the selected date as a text string. For this reason, the Listener1 Bean extends the TextField class, although any subclass capable of displaying text could have been chosen.

Because Java doesn't support multiple class inheritance, the Listener1 class can't extend the MouseAdapter convenience class (which, as you recall, implements an empty method for each method in the MouseListener interface). For this reason, these methods are explicitly defined in lines 24–29.

In the `mouseClicked()` method (lines 29–38), a reference to the Calendar1 Bean is retrieved from the event, and the `getDate()` accessor method then is called to get the selected date. To display the date, another new class related to internationalization, named SimpleDateFormat, is used. This class enables you to display date and time information in a flexible manner.

It is now necessary to create the frame in which to run the Calendar1 and Listener1 Beans.

Listing 15.5

```
Line=================Java Source=================
//////////
// CalendarFrame1.java  Frame in which to run the Calendar1
// Java Bean.
//
// Author: James L. Weaver  JDK 1.1 beta1
//////////
package chapter15.code.calendar1;

import java.awt.*;
import java.awt.event.*;
import java.util.*;

public class CalendarFrame1 extends Frame {

```

continues

Listing 15.5, Continued

```
    Calendar1 cal;
    Listener1 listener;

    public CalendarFrame1() {
        super("Calendar1 Java Bean Demo");

        setLayout(new BorderLayout());
        addWindowListener(new Wadapt());
        setSize(300, 300);

        cal = new Calendar1();
        add("Center", cal);

        Panel p = new Panel();
        add("North", p);
        listener = new Listener1();
        p.add(listener);

        // Wire the Beans together by adding the Listener1 Bean
        // as a mouse event listener to the Calendar1 Bean
        cal.addMouseListener(listener);
        setVisible(true);

        // Set the "date" property of the Scope Bean to today
        cal.setDate(new Date());
    }

    public static void main(String args[]) {
        CalendarFrame1 calFrame = new CalendarFrame1();
        return;
    }
}

class Wadapt extends WindowAdapter
{
    public void windowClosing(WindowEvent evt) {
        evt.getWindow().setVisible(false);
```

```
52             evt.getWindow().dispose();
53             System.exit(0);
54         }
55     }
```

The CalendarFrame1 application depicted in listing 15.5 creates a Calendar1 Bean and a Listener1 Bean and then places them in the application window.

Line 35 registers the Listener1 Bean as a mouse event listener of the Calendar1 Bean. This enables the MOUSE_CLICKED event type to be delivered, which in this case means that a new date is selected in the Calendar1 Bean.

Line 39 sets the date property of the Calendar1 Bean to today's date, which causes the current month to be displayed on the Bean.

Figures 15.3 and 15.4 show the outcome of the code we have created. Figure 15.3 illustrates the Calendar1 and Listener1 Beans running in an application.

Figure 15.3

The Calendar1 and Listener1 Beans running in an application.

Figure 15.4 shows the Calendar1 Bean and PropertySheet in the BDK BeanBox.

This Calendar1 Bean is one example of how native Java events can be emitted from a Bean. The Calendar2 Bean in the next section offers an example of creating your own event classes, types, and listeners.

Creating Your Own Events and Listeners

For some Beans, it is better to create a specialized event class than to use a native Java event class. In the Calendar1 example, the MouseEvent is used to communicate that the selected date changed. It might be more natural to create a specialized DateEvent class that contains a "date changed" event type. This event could be fired each time the selected date changes, and a method of the event object could be called by the listener to determine the newly selected date.

Figure 15.4

The Calendar1 Bean and PropertySheet in the BDK BeanBox.

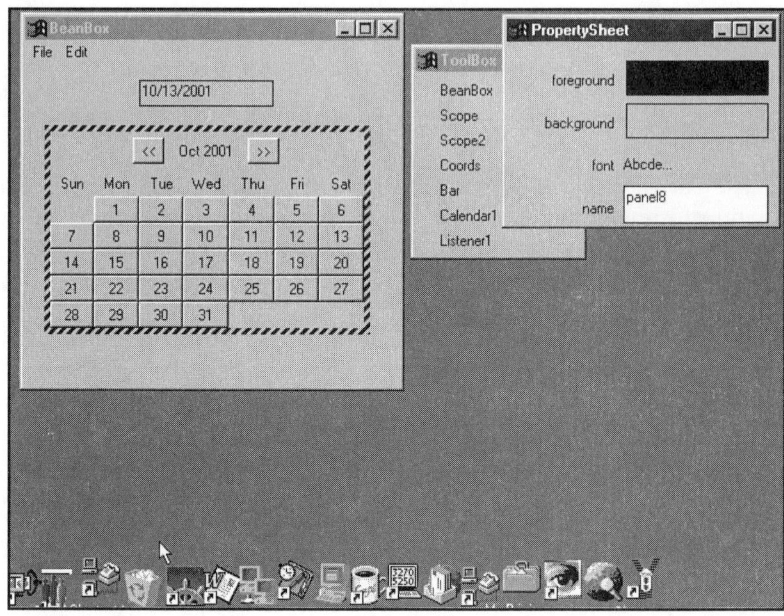

On the CD

The Calendar2 Bean

Listing 15.6 depicts a Java Bean named Calendar2 that emits a specialized event class named DateEvent to its listeners whenever the selected date changes. Listing 15.7 is the DateEvent class; listing 15.8 is the DateEventListener interface that listeners of the DateEvent class must implement. Listing 15.9 is a Bean named Listener2 that implements the DateEventListener interface. Listing 15.10 is the CalendarFrame2 application that creates, displays, and wires up the Beans to each other by registering the Listener2 Bean as a DateEventListener. The application's appearance is identical to Calendar1, which was shown in figures 15.3 and 15.4.

Note Two more classes, which will be covered in the advanced section of this chapter, are associated with the Calendar2 Bean, and are contained in listings 15.15 and 15.17. Listing 15.15 (Calendar2BeanInfo.java) depicts how you can use the BeanInfo interface to provide explicit data to the introspection process; in this case, the data provides information about the icons associated with a Bean. Listing 15.17 (DateEditor.java) is a property editor that can be used with a builder tool to enable the user to edit a property that is represented by a Date instance.

Listing 15.6

```
Line=================Java Source=================
//////////
// Calendar2.java  An example Java Bean that demonstrates
// emitting a custom made event type (named DateEvent).
//
// Author: James L. Weaver  JDK 1.1 beta1
//////////
package chapter15.code.calendar2;

import java.awt.*;
import java.awt.event.*;
import java.io.Serializable;
import java.util.*;

public class Calendar2 extends Panel
             implements Serializable, ActionListener
{
    protected Date date;
    protected GregorianCalendar calendar;
    protected Panel header = null;
    protected Panel body = null;
    protected Button prevMonth, nextMonth;
    protected Label monthLabel;

    protected String days = new String("SunMonTueWedThuFriSat");
    protected String months =
              new String("JanFebMarAprMayJunJulAugSepOctNovDec");

    // Create a Vector to hold DateListeners
    protected Vector dateListeners = new Vector();

    public Calendar2() {
        // Get current date and time info
        calendar = new GregorianCalendar();

        setSize(200, 200);
        setLayout(new BorderLayout());
```

continues

Listing 15.6, Continued

```

        // Put month and year at top of applet,
        // as well as next and previous buttons.
        header = new Panel();
        prevMonth = new Button("<<");
        prevMonth.addActionListener(this);
        nextMonth = new Button(">>");
        nextMonth.addActionListener(this);
        header.add(prevMonth);
        monthLabel = new Label(null, Label.CENTER);
        header.add(monthLabel);
        header.add(nextMonth);
        add("North", header);

        // Create a Panel with a GridLayout for putting in
        // the days and dates of the month.
        body = new Panel();
        body.setLayout(new GridLayout(0, 7));

        // Put the day of the week headers at the top
        for (int i=0; i<21; i+=3) {
            body.add(new Label(days.substring(i, i+3), Label.CENTER));
        }
        add("Center", body);

        // Create and display the date buttons
        displayCalendar();
    }

    // The "date" property accessor methods
    public synchronized Date getDate() {
        return calendar.getTime();
    }

    public synchronized void setDate(Date date) {
        calendar.setTime(date);
        displayCalendar();
        // Call the DateEvent processing method so that each
```

```
        // DateListener is notified of the change
        processDateEvent(new DateEvent(this, calendar.getTime()));
    }

    protected synchronized void displayCalendar() {
        // Save the current values
        int yearNum = calendar.get(Calendar.YEAR);
        int monthNum = calendar.get(Calendar.MONTH);
        int dayNum = calendar.get(Calendar.DATE);

        // Build a string containing month and year
        // to display at the top between the buttons
        String monthStr = months.substring(monthNum * 3,
                                           monthNum * 3 + 3);
        monthLabel.setText(monthStr + " " + yearNum);
        monthLabel.repaint();

        // Remove all the grid cells except day names
        while (body.getComponentCount() > 7)
            body.remove(7);

        // Calendar day of week method is not working in
        // JDK 1.1 beta 1, so use date method to find
        // out which day the 1st of the month falls on
        calendar.set(Calendar.DATE, 1);
        date = calendar.getTime();
        int day = date.getDay();

        // Make blank cells until 1st of month
        for (int i=0; i<day; i++) {
            body.add(new Label());
        }

        // Put the date buttons in
        Button dayBtn;
        for (int i=1; i<=32; i++) {
            // Convert integers to strings
            dayBtn = new Button(new Integer(i).toString());
            dayBtn.addActionListener(this);
```

continues

Listing 15.6, Continued

```
                body.add(dayBtn);

                // Increment the date
                calendar.add(Calendar.DATE, 1);

                // Make the currently selected date receive focus.
                if (i == dayNum)
                    dayBtn.requestFocus();

                // Stop adding buttons when a new month is reached.
                if (calendar.get(Calendar.DATE) <= 1)
                    break;
            }
            // Restore the current values
            calendar.set(yearNum, monthNum, dayNum);
            body.validate();
        }

        public synchronized void actionPerformed(ActionEvent e) {
            if (e.getSource() == prevMonth || e.getSource() == nextMonth) {
                // The previous or next month button was clicked, so
                // set the day of the month to 1, and go to the
                // proper month.
                calendar.set(Calendar.DATE, 1);
                calendar.add(Calendar.MONTH,
                             e.getSource() == prevMonth ? -1 : 1);
                displayCalendar();
            }
            else {
              // One of the day buttons was clicked, so set the
              // calendar object to that date.
              calendar.set(Calendar.DATE, Integer.parseInt(
                             ((Button)e.getSource()).getLabel()));
            }
            // Call the DateEvent processing method so that each
            // DateListener is notified of the change.
            processDateEvent(new DateEvent(this, calendar.getTime()));
        }
```

```

    // The application that uses this Bean will call this method
    // to register the Bean with a DateListener.
    public synchronized void addDateListener(DateListener dl) {
        dateListeners.addElement(dl);
    }

    // The application that uses this Bean will call this method
    // to deregister the Bean from DateListener.
    public synchronized void removeDateListener(DateListener dl) {
        dateListeners.removeElement(dl);
    }

    // This should be called from within the Bean whenever the
    // selected date changes so that each DateListener is notified.
    protected void processDateEvent(DateEvent evt) {
        Vector list;

        // Make a copy of the listeners vector, in case listeners are
        // added or removed while events are being delivered.
        synchronized(this) {
            list = (Vector)dateListeners.clone();
        }
        for (int i=0; i<list.size(); i++) {
            ((DateListener)list.elementAt(i)).dateChanged(evt);
        }
    }
}
```

The DateEvent class in listing 15.7 defines the event that is fired when the date selected in the Calendar2 Bean changes.

Listing 15.7

```
Line==================Java Source=================
//////////
// DateEvent.java  Example of an event created for
// enabling the Calendar2 Bean to communicate with listeners
//
// Author: James L. Weaver  JDK 1.1 beta1
```

continues

Listing 15.7, Continued

```
//////////
package chapter15.code.calendar2;

import java.util.*;

public class DateEvent extends EventObject
{
    protected Date date;

    public DateEvent(Object obj, Date date) {
        super(obj);
        this.date = date;
    }

    public Date getDate() {
        return date;
    }
}
```

As noted earlier, listing 15.8 creates the DateEventListener interface implemented by listeners of the DateEvent class.

Listing 15.8

```
Line=================Java Source=================
//////////
// DateEventListener.java  Listener interface created
// for the DateEvent class
//
// Author: James L. Weaver  JDK 1.1 beta1
//////////
package chapter15.code.calendar2;

import java.util.*;

public interface DateListener extends EventListener
{
    public void dateChanged(DateEvent evt);
}
```

In listing 15.9, a Bean named Listener2 is created that implements the DateEventListener interface.

Listing 15.9

```
Line=================Java Source=================
//////////
// Listener2.java  Listens for date changes
// on the Calendar2 Bean.
//
// Author: James L. Weaver  JDK 1.1 beta1
//////////
package chapter15.code.calendar2;

import java.awt.*;
import java.awt.event.*;
import java.text.*;
import java.util.*;
import java.io.Serializable;

public class Listener2 extends TextField
                        implements Serializable, DateListener
{
    public Listener2() {
        super("?????????", 15);
        setEditable(false);
    }

    public synchronized void dateChanged(DateEvent evt) {
        // Get the "date" property of the DateEvent
        // and display it in the text field
        Date date = evt.getDate();
        SimpleDateFormat df = new SimpleDateFormat("MM/dd/yyyy");
        setText(df.format(date));
    }
}
```

In listing 15.10, the CalendarFrame2 application creates, displays, and wires the Beans to each other by registering the Listener2 Bean as a DateEventListener.

Listing 15.10

```
Line==================Java Source==================
//////////
// CalendarFrame2.java  Frame in which to run the Calendar2
// Java Bean.
//
// Author: James L. Weaver  JDK 1.1 beta1
//////////
package chapter15.code.calendar2;

import java.awt.*;
import java.awt.event.*;
import java.util.*;

public class CalendarFrame2 extends Frame {

    Calendar2 cal;
    Listener2 listener;

    public CalendarFrame2() {
        super("Calendar2 Java Bean Demo");

        setLayout(new BorderLayout());
        addWindowListener(new Wadapt());
        setSize(300, 300);

        cal = new Calendar2();
        add("Center", cal);

        Panel p = new Panel();
        add("North", p);
        listener = new Listener2();
        p.add(listener);

        // Wire the Beans together by adding the Listener2 Bean
        // as a mouse event listener to the Calendar2 Bean.
        cal.addDateListener(listener);
        setVisible(true);

```

```
            // Set the "date" property of the Scope Bean to today.
            cal.setDate(new Date());
        }

        public static void main(String args[]) {
            CalendarFrame2 calFrame = new CalendarFrame2();
            return;
        }
    }

    class Wadapt extends WindowAdapter
    {
        public void windowClosing(WindowEvent evt) {
            evt.getWindow().setVisible(false);
            evt.getWindow().dispose();
            System.exit(0);
        }
    }
```

Steps for Creating and Using New Events in a Bean

You can use the following steps to create your own event class and listener interface, and incorporate them into your Bean:

1. Design the new event.

   Examine the DateEvent class in listing 15.7. Line 11 derives this class from the EventObject class, which is a typical case.

   ```
   11  public class DateEvent extends EventObject
   ```

   In the DateEvent constructor in line 15, the first argument is a reference to the event source; the second argument is a Date instance that represents the current value of the date property. Storing this value in the event enables the listener to obtain the value from the event instance itself rather than having to get a reference to the event source.

   ```
   15      public DateEvent(Object obj, Date date) {
   16          super(obj);
   17          this.date = date;
   18      }
   ```

For the listener to obtain the Date value that is stored in the event instance, the DateEvent class supplies a method named `getDate()`, which is defined in lines 20–22.

```
20        public Date getDate() {
21            return date;
22        }
```

The DateEvent class is associated with only one event type, "date changed." Therefore, it is not necessary to embed the type within the event. If more than one event type existed, then it would be necessary to implement a scheme similar to the `getId()` method in the AWTEvent class, which provides a way to retrieve the event type.

For more ideas regarding event class design, revisit some of the EventObject subclasses covered in Chapter 14.

2. Design a listener interface for the event.

   Now take a look at the DateEventListener interface in listing 15.8. This interface extends the EventListener interface, which is also a typical case. One method is defined and serves as the one and only event type associated with this event class. You can define as many listener methods as needed. Notice that the DateEvent instance is the only argument passed to the listener—this is consistent with all the JDK 1.1 event listeners.

```
public interface DateListener extends EventListener
{
    public void dateChanged(DateEvent evt);
}
```

3. Create the event listener registry and associated methods in the Bean.

   In the Calendar2 Bean in listing 15.6, lines 155–157 define the `addDateListener()` method, and lines 161–163 define the removeDateListener method.

```
155        public synchronized void addDateListener(DateListener dl) {
156            dateListeners.addElement(dl);
157        }
```

```
161        public synchronized void removeDateListener
➥(DateListener dl) {
162            dateListeners.removeElement(dl);
163        }
```

These methods add and remove references to listeners that implement the DateListener interface. These references are held in a Vector defined in line 29, which serves as the DateListener registry.

```
29    protected Vector dateListeners = new Vector();
```

Following are the design patterns for events:

- public void add<EventListenerType>(EventListenerType)
- public void remove<EventListenerType>(EventListenerType)

When the introspection process discovers these patterns, it assumes that an <EventListenerType> interface exists in which listener methods can be discovered. It is important to either stay consistent with this design pattern or explicitly define these methods using the BeanInfo interface.

4. Create an event processor method for the new event listener type.

   As explained in Chapter 14, an associated process<ListenerType>Event method exists for each event listener in JDK 1.1. The MouseListener, for example, has an associated processMouseEvent() method. This method is responsible for delivering the event to the correct method in the registered event listeners.

   For consistency, the Calendar2 Bean contains a method named processDateEvent() that is responsible for delivering DateEvent instances to registered DateListener event listeners. Lines 167–178 of the Calendar2 Bean (listing 15.6) contain the processDateEvent() method.

```
167      protected void processDateEvent(DateEvent evt) {
168          Vector list;
169
170          // Make a copy of the listeners vector, in case
➥listeners are
171          // added or removed while events are being delivered.
172          synchronized(this) {
173              list = (Vector)dateListeners.clone();
174          }
175          for (int i=0; i<list.size(); i++) {
176              ((DateListener)list.elementAt(i)).dateChanged(evt);
177          }
178      }
```

Lines 172–174 create a copy of the Vector (which was created in step 3) that stores the listener references. The reason for copying this Vector is so that it can't change while the events are being delivered in lines 175–177. This also could have been achieved by making the `processDateMethod()` synchronized, but that would have unnecessarily locked the listener registry methods during event delivery. In cases where a large number of listeners are present, that action could cause performance problems. Instead, the lock is placed only during the Vector copy by using the synchronized keyword in line 172.

Lines 175 –177 iterate through the copy of the Vector, calling the `dateChanged()` method in each of the registered listeners. Recall that "date changed" is the only event type associated with the DateEvent class. If DateEvent had more than one event type, it would have been necessary to ask the DateEvent for the type and then call the correct listener method based upon the response.

5. Call the event processor method (fire the event), where appropriate.

   In the Calendar2 Bean, the `processDateEvent()` method is called any time the selected date is changed. In listing 15.6, the method is called in both line 76 at the end of the `setDate()` accessor method, and in line 150 after a day of month button is clicked.

```
076         processDateEvent(new DateEvent(this, calendar.getTime()));
```

```
150         processDateEvent(new DateEvent(this, calendar.getTime()));
```

6. Create one or more listeners for your new event.

   Each listener must implement the event listener interface created in step 2 above. In listing 15.9, the Listener2 Bean implements the DateListener interface.

```
015   public class Listener2 extends TextField
016                               implements Serializable, DateListener
```

Lines 23–29 contain the `dateChanged()` method, which receives the DateEvent instance as a parameter.

```
023       public synchronized void dateChanged(DateEvent evt) {
024           // Get the Date value from the DateEvent
025           // and display it in the text field.
026           Date date = evt.getDate();
027           SimpleDateFormat df = new SimpleDateFormat("MM/dd/yyyy");
028           setText(df.format(date));
029       }
```

By calling the `getDate()` method of the DateEvent class in line 26, the listener can obtain the Date value represented by this event.

7. Register the event listeners with the Bean.

   In the CalendarFrame2 application (listing 15.10), this occurs in line 35:

```
035            cal.addDateListener(listener);
```

   This completes the steps for creating and implementing a new event in a Bean. This is the same event processing model that you learned in Chapter 14—the only difference is that you have to implement it yourself instead of enabling the AWT classes to do the work for you.

To summarize what's been covered so far, three scenarios have been explored for emitting events from a Bean:

- The Bean emits native JDK 1.1 events as a result of genuine AWT events being fired. The Scope Bean is an example of this. When the user moves the mouse over the Bean, mouse events are emitted.

- The Bean emits native JDK 1.1 events that are created from within the Bean and posted to the system event queue. The Calendar1 Bean is an example of this. When the user clicks a "day of the month" button, the program fabricates a MouseEvent and posts it to the system event queue. The superclass of the Calendar1 Bean is Canvas, so it knows how to process mouse events.

- The Bean emits a non-JDK 1.1 event. The Calendar2 Bean is an example of this. Several items had to be created to achieve this, including a special event class, an event type, an event listener interface, event listener registry methods, and an event processing method.

The last scenario presented is the case in which the Bean emits a native JDK 1.1 event but the event is not supported by the particular class chosen from which to derive the Bean.

Implementing AWT Event Processing Methods

As shown previously, the Calendar1 Bean is derived from the Panel class, which contains all the methods necessary to register mouse event listeners and to deliver mouse events. But what if you want the Calendar1 Bean to emit an AWT event, such as the semantic ActionEvent, not supported by the Panel class?

In this case, you must implement a few other things yourself, including the `addActionListener()` method, the `removeActionListener()`method, and the `processActionEvent()` method. The steps involved are a subset of the steps used previously to create and implement your own event class:

1. Design the new event.

   This step is not necessary, because the ActionEvent class already exists.

2. Design a listener interface for the event.

   This step is not necessary, either, because the ActionListener interface already exists as well.

3. Create the event listener registry and associated methods in the Bean.

   In this case, the listener is the ActionListener. Because a Canvas doesn't have the `addActionListener()` or `removeActionListener` methods, you must create them:

```
public synchronized void addActionListener(ActionListener dl) {
    actionListeners.addElement(dl);
}
```

```
public synchronized void removeActionListener(ActionListener dl) {
    actionListeners.removeElement(dl);
}
```

   You also must create a Vector (or other data container) to hold the references to the listeners:

```
   protected Vector actionListeners = new Vector();
```

4. Create an event processor method for the new event listener type.

   The event processing method that corresponds to ActionListener is the `processActionEvent()` method, which should be created in the Bean:

```
protected void processActionEvent(ActionEvent evt) {
       Vector list;
       // Make a copy of the listeners vector, in case listeners are
       // added or removed while events are being delivered.
       synchronized(this) {
           list = (Vector)actionListeners.clone();
       }
       for (int i=0; i<list.size(); i++) {
           ((ActionListener)list.elementAt(i)).actionPerformed(evt);
       }
   }
```

5. Call the event processor method (fire the event), where appropriate:

```
processActionEvent(new ActionEvent(this, ActionEvent.ACTION_PERFORMED,
"DateChange"));
```

   The "DateChange" string is the command name given to this action event. The listener can decide which action to take, based upon the command name.

6. Create one or more listeners for your new event.

   The listener must implement ActionListener and have an `actionPerformed()` method. This was covered previously.

7. Register the event listeners with the Bean.

This step is accomplished by calling the `addActionListener()` method with a reference to the desired listener. This was covered previously.

As you can see, this process is quite similar to the process of implementing your own events.

You now know how to make your Bean emit any kind of event, whether supported by the Bean's parent class or not. Before leaving this chapter, some advanced features of Beans will be discussed.

Using Advanced Features of Beans

You can develop Java Beans with the information already covered in this chapter. The following topics must be covered, however, to give your Java Beans more flexibility and functionality:

- Bound and constrained properties
- Introspection
- Property editors

Note You should also be aware of another topic related to property editors: *customizers*, which enable you to create a wizard with which the user of a builder tool can edit the properties of your Bean. This concept is beyond the scope of this book, however. For more information on customizers, consult the documentation in the BDK.

Bound and Constrained Properties

Earlier in the chapter, the types of properties were introduced. This section discusses two special kinds of properties:

- A *bound property* notifies a set of listeners whenever the value of the property changes. This is very useful when implementing a *data-view* architecture: When the data changes, each view of the data is notified so that each view can make the corresponding change.
- A *constrained property* asks permission from a set of listeners to make a value change. If any of the listeners object, an exception is thrown that informs the constrained property that permission to make the change was denied.

The Scope Bean examined earlier in the chapter has been modified to demonstrate how to create and use a bound property.

A Bound Property Example: Scope2, Coords, and Bar

Listing 15.11 depicts a Java Bean named Scope2, which contains a bound property named "coordString." When the user moves the mouse over the Bean, the Scope2 Bean exhibits the same behavior as the Scope Bean did. The Scope2 Bean also notifies any registered property change listeners of the change. The registered property change listeners in this case are:

- The Coords Bean in listing 15.12. This Bean displays a string that represents the coordinates at which the mouse cursor is positioned.
- The Bar Bean in listing 15.13. This Bean is a bar graph that displays either the x or y coordinate of the mouse cursor. The coordinate displayed depends on whether the Bar Bean's "horizontal" property is true.

Listing 15.14 depicts the ScopeFrame2 application, which displays the Scope2 Bean, the Coords Bean, a horizontal Bar Bean, and a vertical Bar Bean.

Listing 15.11

```
Line=================Java Source=================
//////////
// Scope2.java  A Java Bean that has bound properties
//
// Author: James L. Weaver  JDK 1.1 beta1
//////////
package chapter15.code.scope2;

```

```
import java.awt.*;
import java.awt.event.*;
import java.beans.*;
import java.io.Serializable;

public class Scope2 extends Canvas implements Serializable
{
    protected int xCoord = 0,
                  yCoord = 0,
                  ticks = 8;
    protected String coordString = "0,0";

    // Enlist the help of a class that registers and notifies
    // PropertyChangeListener objects of changes.
    protected PropertyChangeSupport changes =
              new PropertyChangeSupport(this);

    public Scope2() {
        // Enable mouse and mouse motion events to be processed.
        enableEvents(AWTEvent.MOUSE_MOTION_EVENT_MASK |
                     AWTEvent.MOUSE_EVENT_MASK |
                     AWTEvent.COMPONENT_EVENT_MASK);
        setSize(200, 200);
    }

    // The presence of both a setTick and a getTick cause the
    // Introspector to assume there is a read/write "tick" property.
    public void setTicks(int ticks) {
        this.ticks = ticks;
    }

    public int getTicks() {
        return ticks;
    }

    // The presence of both a setCoordString and
    // setCoordString cause the Introspector to assume there
    // is a read/write "coordString" property.
    public void setCoordString(String newCoordString) {
```

continues

Listing 15.11, Continued

```
        // Save the old value & update the current value.
        String oldCoordString = coordString;
        coordString = newCoordString;

        // Notify listeners that the bound property changed.
        changes.firePropertyChange("coordString",
                                   oldCoordString,
                                   newCoordString);
    }

    public String getCoordString() {
        return coordString;
    }

    public void addPropertyChangeListener(PropertyChangeListener l)
    {
        // Offload the task to the PropertyChangeSupport class.
        changes.addPropertyChangeListener(l);
    }

    public void removePropertyChangeListener(PropertyChangeListener l)
    {
        // Offload the task to the PropertyChangeSupport class.
        changes.removePropertyChangeListener(l);
    }

    public void paint(Graphics g) {
        int tickSize = 5;
        int xMax = getSize().width -1;
        int yMax = getSize().height -1;
        int xRes = xMax/ticks;
        int yRes = yMax/ticks;

        // Draw the crosshairs
        g.setColor(Color.red);
        g.drawRect(0, 0, xMax, yMax);
        g.drawLine(xCoord, 0, xCoord, yMax);
```

```
            g.drawLine(0, yCoord, xMax, yCoord);

            // Build and draw the coordinate string.
            setCoordString(new Integer(xCoord) + "," +
                           new Integer(yCoord));
            g.drawString(getCoordString(), tickSize, yMax - tickSize);

            // Draw the tick marks.
            for (int i=0,x=0; i<ticks; i++,x+=xRes) {
                g.drawLine(x, 0, x, tickSize);
                g.drawLine(x, yMax - tickSize, x, yMax);
            }
            for (int i=0,y=0; i<ticks; i++,y+=yRes) {
                g.drawLine(0, y, tickSize, y);
                g.drawLine(xMax - tickSize, y, xMax, y);
            }
        }

        // When the mouse moves, update the display.
        protected boolean processMouseMotionEvent(MouseEvent e) {
            if (e.getId() == MouseEvent.MOUSE_MOVED) {
                xCoord = e.getX();
                yCoord = e.getY();
                repaint();
            }
            super.processMouseMotionEvent(e);
            return false;
        }

        // When the mouse exits the Scope2 Bean area,
        // set coordinates to 0,0.
        protected boolean processMouseEvent(MouseEvent e) {
            if (e.getId() == MouseEvent.MOUSE_EXITED) {
                xCoord = 0;
                yCoord = 0;
                repaint();
            }
            super.processMouseEvent(e);
            return false;
```

continues

Listing 15.11, Continued

```
124         }
125     }
```

Lines 22 and 23 of listing 15.11 (Scope2.java) create an instance of the PropertyChangeSupport class:

```
022         protected PropertyChangeSupport changes =
023                     new PropertyChangeSupport(this);
```

PropertyChangeSupport is a convenience class that handles the details associated with maintaining a registry of property change listeners and notifying the listeners of a property change. PropertyChangeSupport, which is a class in the java.beans package, has three methods:

- void `addPropertyChangeListener(PropertyChangeListener)`
- void `removePropertyChangeListener(PropertyChangeListener)`
- void `firePropertyChange(String, Object, Object)`

Figure 15.5 depicts how bound properties work and how PropertyChangeSupport methods support bound properties.

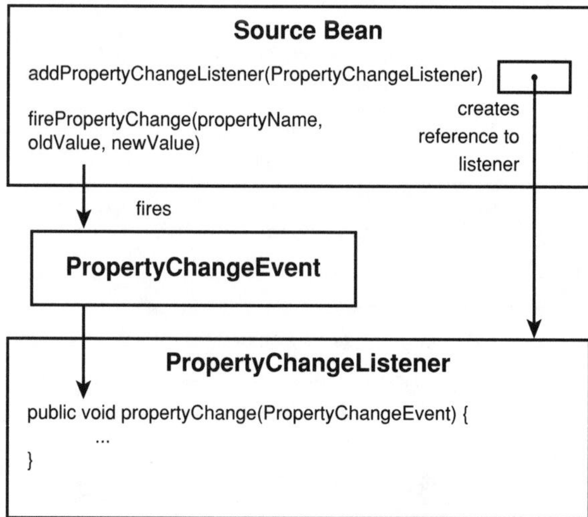

Figure 15.5
Bound Properties and supporting PropertyChange-Support methods.

The `addPropertyChangeListener()` method adds a PropertyChangeListener to the registry. The `removePropertyChangeListener()` method removes a PropertyChangeListener from the registry. The `firePropertyChange()` method calls the `propertyChange()` method of each registered PropertyChangeListener, passing a PropertyChangeEvent instance that contains the following:

- The name of the property that has changed. To access this, call the `getPropertyName()` method of the PropertyChangeEvent instance.
- The property's old value. To access this, call the `getOldValue()` method of the PropertyChangeEvent instance.
- The property's new value. To access this, call the `getNewValue()` method of the PropertyChangeEvent instance.

To use PropertyChangeSupport, you can either derive a class from it or make an instance of it. The Scope2 Bean uses an instance of PropertyChangeSupport, because Scope2 is already derived from Canvas. The constructor argument is a reference to the Bean that contains the bound property or properties.

Lines 46–56 contain the `setCoordString()` accessor method. In lines 53–55, the `firePropertyChanges()` method of the PropertyChangeSupport class is called, which notifies all the listeners of the property change. If the last two arguments are the same, this method is smart enough not to notify the listeners.

Lines 62–72 provide an `addPropertyChangeListener()` method and a `removePropertyChangeListener()` method that registers and deregisters property change listeners. Within each of these methods, the corresponding `PropertyChangeSupport` method is called, which maintains the registry.

The Coords Bean in listing 15.12 is a PropertyChangeListener that displays the current coordinates of the Scope2 Bean.

Listing 15.12

```
Line=================Java Source=================
//////////
// Coords.java  Demonstrates a Java Bean
// that is also a PropertyChangeListener.
//
// Author: James L. Weaver  JDK 1.1 beta1
//////////
package chapter15.code.scope2;

```

continues

Listing 15.12, Continued

```
09   import java.awt.*;
10   import java.awt.event.*;
11   import java.beans.*;
12   import java.io.Serializable;
13
14   public class Coords extends TextField implements Serializable,
15                                                    PropertyChangeListener
16   {
17       public Coords() {
18           super("??????", 10);
19           setEditable(false);
20       }
21
22       public void propertyChange(PropertyChangeEvent e) {
23           setText((String)e.getNewValue());
24       }
25   }
```

Lines 14 and 15 of listing 15.12 (Coords.java) indicate that the Coords Bean is a PropertyChangeListener.

Lines 22–24 are called whenever a property change event is fired on a Bean with which this instance is registered. In line 23, the new property value is retrieved from the PropertyChangeEvent instance and displayed.

The Bar Bean in listing 15.13 is a PropertyChangeListener that displays a bar graph of a dimension of the Scope2 Bean.

Listing 15.13

```
Line=================Java Source=================
//////////
// Bar.java  Demonstrates a Java Bean
// that is also a PropertyChangeListener.
//
// Author: James L. Weaver  JDK 1.1 beta1
//////////
package chapter15.code.scope2;

import java.awt.*;
```

```
import java.awt.event.*;
import java.beans.*;
import java.io.Serializable;

public class Bar extends Canvas implements Serializable,
                                          PropertyChangeListener
{
    Dimension totalSize;
    boolean horiz;
    int barLength;

    public Bar() {
        totalSize = new Dimension(0,0);

        // Default to horizontal bar.
        this.horiz = true;
        barLength = 0;

        setSize(100, 25);
    }

    // Bar can either be horizontal or vertical. The presence of
    // a setHorizontal() and an isHorizontal() defines a
    // read/write boolean "horizontal" property.
    public void setHorizontal(boolean horiz) {
        this.horiz = horiz;
    }

    public boolean isHorizontal() {
        return horiz;
    }

    public void propertyChange(PropertyChangeEvent e) {
        if (e.getPropertyName().equals("coordString")) {
            // Find out the dimensions of the source component
            totalSize = ((Component)e.getSource()).getSize();

            // Retrieve and parse the coordinate of interest.
            String coords = (String)e.getNewValue();
```

continues

Listing 15.13, Continued

```
49             if (horiz) {
50                 barLength = Integer.parseInt(coords.substring(0,
51                                         coords.indexOf(',')));
52             }
53             else {
54                 barLength = Integer.parseInt(coords.substring(
55                                         coords.indexOf(',') + 1));
56             }
57         }
58         repaint();
59     }
60
61     public void paint(Graphics g) {
62         int scaledBar;
63         setForeground(Color.blue);
64         g.drawRect(0, 0, getSize().width -1,
65                          getSize().height -1);
66         try {
67             // The "try" block is to protect against
68             // divide by zero error. Calculate length that the
69             // filled in bar should be.
70             if (horiz) {
71                 scaledBar = barLength * getSize().width
72                                              / totalSize.width;
73                 g.fillRect(0, 0, scaledBar, getSize().height -1);
74             }
75             else {
76                 scaledBar = barLength * getSize().height
77                                              / totalSize.height;
78                 g.fillRect(0, 0, getSize().width -1, scaledBar );
79             }
80         }
81         catch (Exception e) {
82         }
83     }
84 }
```

Lines 14 and 15 of listing 15.13 (Bar.java) indicate that the Bar Bean is a PropertyChangeListener as well.

Lines 34–36 contain the `setHorizontal()` accessor method for the horizontal property. If this is set to true, the Bar Bean is a horizontal bar graph that displays the relative value of the Scope2 Bean's x-axis. If the horizontal property is false, the Bar Bean is a vertical bar graph that displays the relative value of the Scope2 Bean's y-axis. Lines 38–40 contain the other horizontal property accessor method.

Lines 42–59 contain the `propertyChange()` method. In line 43, the event's `getPropertyName()` method is called to determine which property was changed. If the coordString property changed, the String is parsed to obtain the coordinate of interest, based upon the Bar Bean's orientation. After calculating and updating drawing-related values, the `repaint()` method is called to update the Bar Bean's display.

The ScopeFrame2 application in listing 15.14 creates, displays, and wires together a Scope2 bean, a Coords Bean, and two Bar Beans:

Listing 15.14

```
Line==================Java Source==================
//////////
// ScopeFrame2.java  Frame in which to run the Scope
// Java Bean.
//
// Author: James L. Weaver  JDK 1.1 beta1
//////////
package chapter15.code.scope2;

import java.awt.*;
import java.awt.event.*;
import java.beans.*;

public class ScopeFrame2 extends Frame {

    Scope2 scope;
    Coords coords;
    Bar hBar, vBar;

    public ScopeFrame2() {
        super("Scope2 Java Bean Demo");

        setLayout(new BorderLayout());
```

continues

Listing 15.14, Continued

```
        addWindowListener(new Wadapt());
        setSize(300, 300);

        scope = new Scope2();

        // Set the "ticks" property of the Scope Bean.
        scope.setTicks(8);

        // The Scope2 Bean will fill most of the Frame.
        add("Center", scope);

        // Create and add the Coords Bean.
        Panel pn = new Panel();
        add("North", pn);
        coords = new Coords();
        pn.add(coords);

        // Create and add a horizontal Bar Bean.
        Panel ps = new Panel();
        add("South", ps);
        hBar = new Bar();
        hBar.setSize(100, 25);
        hBar.setHorizontal(true);
        ps.add(hBar);

        // Create and add a vertical Bar Bean.
        Panel pe = new Panel();
        add("East", pe);
        vBar = new Bar();
        vBar.setSize(25, 100);
        vBar.setHorizontal(false);
        pe.add(vBar);

        // Wire the Beans together by adding the Coords Bean
        // as a property change listener to the Scope2 Bean
        // and the Bar Beans.
        scope.addPropertyChangeListener(coords);
        scope.addPropertyChangeListener(hBar);
```

```
61            scope.addPropertyChangeListener(vBar);
62
63            setVisible(true);
64        }
65
66        public static void main(String args[]) {
67            ScopeFrame2 menuFrame = new ScopeFrame2();
68            return;
69        }
70    }
71
72    class Wadapt extends WindowAdapter
73    {
74        public void windowClosing(WindowEvent evt) {
75            evt.getWindow().setVisible(false);
76            evt.getWindow().dispose();
77            System.exit(0);
78        }
79    }
```

The ScopeFrame2 application in listing 15.14 creates an instance of and displays a Scope2 Bean, a Coords Bean, and two Bar Beans (one of each orientation). In addition, the application sets some initial properties in each.

Lines 59–61 register the Coords and Bar Beans as property change listeners of the Scope2 Bean. As a result, when the mouse cursor moves over the Scope2 Bean, the coordinates are displayed and graphed by the Coords and Bar Beans.

Figure 15.6 depicts the ScopeFrame2 user interface.

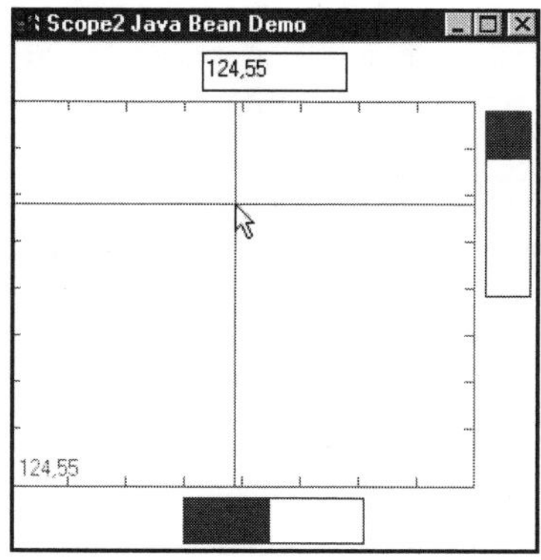

Figure 15.6

The ScopeFrame2 application.

Figure 15.7 shows the Scope2, Coords, and Bar Beans in the BDK BeanBox.

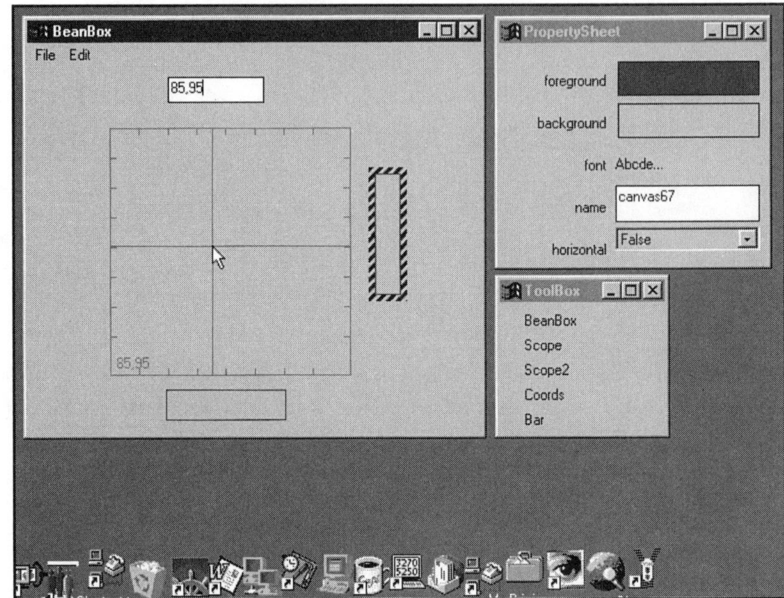

Figure 15.7

The Scope2, Coords, and Bar Beans in the BDK BeanBox.

Implementing Constrained Properties

A constrained property requires the blessing of its listeners before its value may be changed. This is very similar to the concept of bound properties in that a property change event is sent out to the listeners when a constrained property changes. The difference is that if any registered listener vetoes the change by throwing a Property VetoException, the change doesn't occur. To restrict the days that can be selected in the Calendar2 Bean to valid working days, for example, a listener could be created that vetos any changes that don't meet that criteria.

The VetoableChangeSupport class, which is similar to the PropertyChangeSupport class, handles the details associated with maintaining a registry of vetoable change listeners and notifying the listeners of a property change. This class also notifies each listener that a change is being withdrawn because a listener vetoed the change. VetoableChangeSupport, which is a class in the java.beans package, has three methods:

- void `addVetoableChangeListener(VetoableChangeListener)`
- void `removeVetoableChangeListener(VetoableChangeListener)`
- void `fireVetoableChange(String, Object, Object)`

Figure 15.8 depicts the process by which constrained properties work and how VetoableChangeSupport methods support constrained properties.

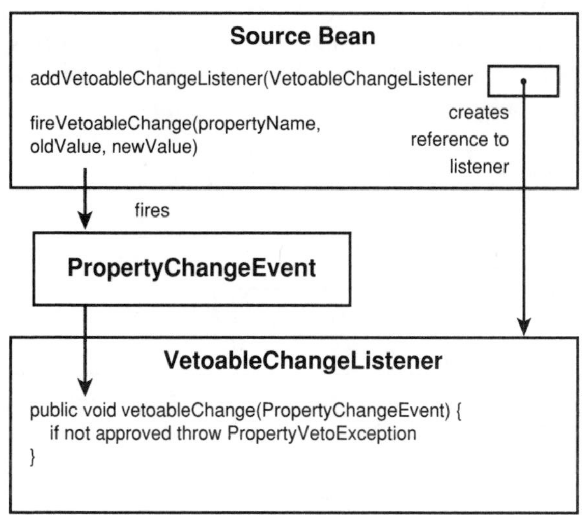

Figure 15.8

Constrained properties and supporting VetoableChange-Support methods.

The `addVetoableChangeListener()` method adds a VetoableChangeListener to the registry. The `removeVetoableChangeListener()` method removes a Vetoable-ChangeListener from the registry.

The `fireVetoableChange()` method calls the `vetoableChange()` method of each registered VetoableChangeListener, passing a PropertyChangeEvent instance. If any VetoableChangeListener throws a PropertyVetoException, then the `fireVetoableChange()` method calls the `vetoableChange()` method of each registered VetoableChangeListener again, this time with the original property. The `fireVetoableChange()` method then throws a PropertyVetoException so that the caller can catch it or relay it up the calling chain. Generally, you should allow the property accessor method to throw this exception so that the caller trying to set the property obtains the exception. This way, the caller can tell that the change was unsuccessful.

As with PropertyChangeSupport, to use VetoableChangeSupport you can either derive a class from it or create an instance of it.

The next section covers another advanced Beans topic—introspection.

Java Bean Introspection

A builder tool requires some way of identifying and analyzing the properties, events, and methods that are contained in a Java Bean. The process that JavaSoft has designed for this purpose is called *Bean introspection.*

The Introspector class, which is included in the java.beans package, provides a common mechanism for builder tools and applications to analyze a Java Bean. A few other classes in the java.beans package are used in conjunction with the Introspector class when doing Bean introspection. These are shown in figure 15.9, and the following discussion examines these classes. In addition, the introspection process uses a low-level mechanism, called the Java Core Reflection API, to identify an object's fields and methods. Figure 15.9 shows the java.beans classes that support introspection.

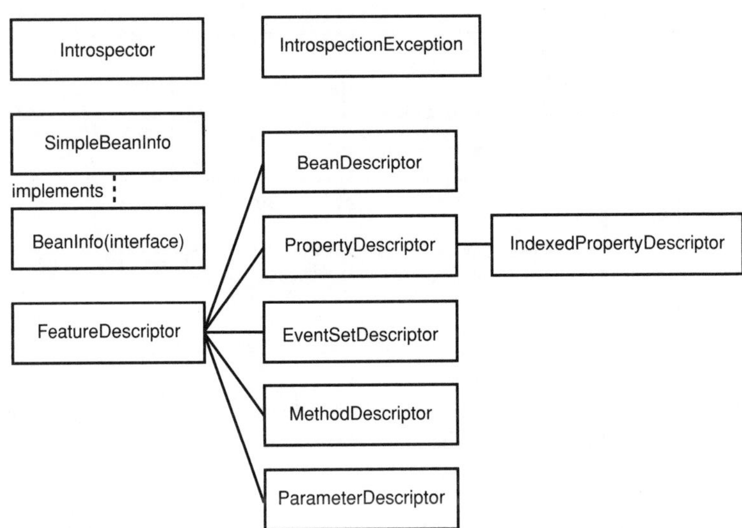

Figure 15.9
java.beans classes that support introspection.

As mentioned earlier in this chapter, a developer can define the properties, events, and methods to be exposed to the builder tool in two ways:

- Implicitly, through the use of design patterns
- Explicitly, via the BeanInfo interface

Design patterns for properties, events, and methods were described previously in the chapter. The BeanInfo interface is explained next.

The BeanInfo Interface

You can explicitly define which properties, events, and methods are exposed by providing a class that implements the BeanInfo interface. The name of this class is the name of the Bean with BeanInfo added to the end. Therefore, the BeanInfo class for the Calendar2 Bean is named Calendar2BeanInfo. Typically, this BeanInfo class is placed in the same package as the Bean, which is the first place that the Introspector looks.

To perform the introspection process on a Bean, call the static `getBeanInfo()` method of the Introspector class, and supply the name of the class to be analyzed. You also can supply the name of the superclass at which to stop the analysis. The Introspector performs the following high-level steps during the introspection process:

1. Looks for the associated BeanInfo class.
2. If one is found, obtains the explicit property, event, method, and other Bean information by calling methods of this class.
3. For any methods that supplied explicit information, uses that information and goes to step 5. For methods that didn't supply explicit information, continues with step 4.
4. Uses design patterns to discover implicitly defined properties, events, and methods.
5. Moves to the superclass of the class being analyzed.
6. If the top of the class hierarchy has been reached, or if the top class specified in the two-argument version of the `getBeanInfo()` method has been reached, then stops. Otherwise, returns to step 1.

Table 15.1 describes the methods of the BeanInfo interface referred to in steps 2 and 3. Many return values of these methods are instances of the classes in figure 15.9.

TABLE 15.1
Methods in the BeanInfo Interface

Method	Description
BeanDescriptor getBeanDescriptor()	Returns a BeanDescriptor instance that contains overall information about the Bean. Returns null if no explicit information is available.
PropertyDescriptor[] getPropertyDescriptors()	Returns an array of PropertyDescriptor instances that contain information about the Bean's proper ties. Returns null if no explicit information is available.
int getDefaultPropertyIndex()	Returns the index of the PropertyDescriptor array returned by `getPropertyDescriptors()` that should be treated as the default in a builder tool. Returns –1 if there is no default.

continues

Table 15.1, Continued
Methods in the BeanInfo Interface

Method	Description
EventSetDescriptor[] getEventSetDescriptors()	Returns an array of EventSetDescriptor instances that contain information about such elements as the Bean's events and listener methods. Returns null if no explicit information is available.
int getDefaultEventIndex()	Returns the index of the EventSetDescriptor array returned by `getEventSetDescriptors()` that should be treated as the default in a builder tool. Returns –1 if there is no default.
MethodDescriptor[] getMethodDescriptors()	Returns an array of MethodDescriptor instances that contain information about the Bean's methods. Returns null if no explicit information is available.
Image getIcon(int)	Returns an image object that can be used to represent the Bean in a builder tool. The argument is a constant that represents the image resolution and the presence of color. These constants are ICON_COLOR_16x16, ICON_COLOR_32x32, ICON_MONO_16x16, and ICON_MONO_32x32. Returns null if no icons are available.
BeanInfo[] get AdditionalBeanInfo()	Returns references to additional BeanInfo instances that can supply explicit information about this Bean.

So, to provide explicit information, you provide a class that implements the BeanInfo interface. If you want to provide explicit information about the Bean's properties, for example, you would implement the `getPropertyDescriptors()` method that returns an array of PropertyDescriptor instances. Because the class implements the BeanInfo interface, you also must supply an implementation for all the other BeanInfo methods, returning null when design patterns should be used.

SimpleBeanInfo, a convenience class shown in figure 15.9, implements all the BeanInfo methods. Unless overridden, these methods return null (or in some cases –1, as shown in table 15.1). You can extend your BeanInfo class from SimpleBeanInfo and only override the methods for which you want to supply explicit information. The next section contains an example of associating icons with a Bean by using the SimpleBeanInfo class.

Associating Icons with a Bean

Listing 15.15 depicts a Calendar2BeanInfo class that extends the SimpleBeanInfo convenience class described previously. The icons associated with the Bean are the only explicit information provided. Therefore, only the `getIcon()` method is overridden.

Listing 15.15

```
Line=================Java Source=================
01   //////////
02   // Calendar2BeanInfo.java  Demonstrates an overridden
03   // SimpleBeanInfo class. The only thing overridden is
04   // the getIcon() method so that a builder tool will
05   // display the icon for this bean.
06   //
07   // Author: James L. Weaver  JDK 1.1 beta1
08   //////////
09   package chapter15.code.scope2;
10
11   import java.awt.*;
12   import java.beans.*;
13
14   public class Calendar2BeanInfo extends SimpleBeanInfo {
15
16       public Image getIcon(int iconKind) {
17           if (iconKind == BeanInfo.ICON_COLOR_16x16) {
18               java.awt.Image img = loadImage("CalendarIcon16.gif");
19               return img;
20           }
21           else if (iconKind == BeanInfo.ICON_COLOR_32x32) {
22               java.awt.Image img = loadImage("CalendarIcon32.gif");
23               return img;
24           }
25           else {
26               return null;
27           }
28       }
29   }
```

The Introspector calls the `getIcon()` method four times, once with each BeanInfo constant mentioned in the `getIcon()` method of table 15.1. Lines 18 and 23 return the corresponding images for ICON_COLOR_16x16 and ICON_COLOR_32x32, but ICON_MONO_16x16 and ICON_MONO_32x32 return null. You only have to supply icons for a Bean if you want to control how the builder tool represents your Bean in a toolbox. If you supply just one icon, it is recommended that it be an ICON_COLOR_16x16.

The Introspector also calls every other method in the BeanInfo interface, to which the Calendar2BeanInfo class responds, "Go get implicitly defined information using design patterns."

As you have seen, the introspection process uses a Bean and an optional BeanInfo object as input. The output of the introspection process consists of another BeanInfo object that fully describes the properties, events, methods, icons, and overall information about the Bean. The next section shows how to use this created BeanInfo object to extract information about the Bean.

On the CD

The xmnbean Utility

Listing 15.16 (xmnbean.java) depicts an example of how you can accomplish the following actions:

- Initiate the introspection process
- Use the output of the introspection process to display information about the Bean

Note This utility uses the same java.beans classes and methods that a builder tool uses to examine a Bean.

Listing 15.16

```
Line=================Java Source=================
//////////
// xmnbean.java  Utility to examine
// (do introspection on) a Java Bean
//
// Author: James L. Weaver  JDK 1.1 beta1
//////////
package chapter15.code.xmnbean;

import java.io.*;
import java.beans.*;
```

```

public class xmnbean
{
    static String classStr;
    protected BeanDescriptor bd;
    protected PropertyDescriptor pd[];
    protected EventSetDescriptor ed[];
    protected MethodDescriptor md[];
    FileWriter fw;
    PrintWriter pw;

    public xmnbean() throws Exception {
        fw = new FileWriter("beaninfo.txt");
        pw = new PrintWriter(fw);

        // Load the Bean's class and create a Class object
        // to represent it.
        Class bean = Class.forName(classStr);

        // Introspect the Bean and store results in
        // a BeanInfo object.
        BeanInfo bi = Introspector.getBeanInfo(bean);

        // Get general Bean information from BeanDescriptor.
        bd = bi.getBeanDescriptor();
        pw.println("Bean name: " + bd.getName());
        pw.println("Bean class: " + bd.getBeanClass());
        pw.println("");

        // List all bean properties.
        pw.println("==== Properties: ====");
        pd = bi.getPropertyDescriptors();
        for (int i=0; i<pd.length; i++) {
            pw.println("Name: " + pd[i].getName());
            pw.println("    Type:   " + pd[i].getPropertyType());
            pw.println("    Getter: " + pd[i].getReadMethod());
            pw.println("    Setter: " + pd[i].getWriteMethod());
        }
        pw.println("");
```

continues

Listing 15.16, Continued

```
50
51          // List all bean events.
52          pw.println("==== Events: ====");
53          ed = bi.getEventSetDescriptors();
54          for (int i=0; i<ed.length; i++) {
55              pw.println("Event Name: " + ed[i].getName());
56              pw.println("    Add Listener Method: " +
57                          ed[i].getAddListenerMethod());
58              pw.println("    Remove Listener Method: " +
59                          ed[i].getRemoveListenerMethod());
60              md = ed[i].getListenerMethodDescriptors();
61              for (int j=0; j<md.length; j++) {
62                  pw.println("    Event Type: " + md[j].getName());
63              }
64          }
65          pw.println("");
66
67          // List all bean methods.
68          pw.println("==== Methods: ====");
69          md = bi.getMethodDescriptors();
70          for (int i=0; i<md.length; i++) {
71              pw.println(md[i].getName());
72          }
73          pw.println("");
74
75          pw.close();
76      }
77
78      public static void main(String args[]) throws Exception {
79          classStr = args[0];
80          xmnbean x = new xmnbean();
81      }
82  }
```

This application takes the fully qualified name of the Bean to be examined as the command line argument, such as “chapter15.code.calendar2.Calendar2.”

The `main()` method in lines 78–81 puts this argument into a static variable and creates an instance of this application’s class.

Lines 15–18 contain some java.beans classes from figure 15.9. These are returned from BeanInfo methods, as shown in table 15.1. Notice that all these classes are derived from the FeatureDescriptor class, which provides some methods common to these classes.

Lines 19 and 20 contain two java.io classes new to JDK 1.1 that support internationalization by writing 16-bit Unicode characters.

Lines 23 and 24 indicate that the output from this program will be stored in the beaninfo.txt file. Feel free to modify this application to accept a command line argument that specifies an output file, as well as any other modifications you want to make.

The static `Class.forName()` method in line 28 loads the Bean and returns a Class object that represents the Bean.

Line 32 is the most powerful line in the program. This line calls the static `getBeanInfo()` method of the Introspector class, which performs the entire introspection process. All builder tools and applications should use this method to perform introspection because it provides a single consistent mechanism. This method returns a BeanInfo object that fully describes the properties, events, methods, icons, and overall information about the Bean. The rest of this application interrogates this BeanInfo object to retrieve and display this information.

Line 35 begins the interrogation by calling the BeanInfo object's `getBeanDescriptor()` method, which appeared in table 15.1. This returns a BeanDescriptor instance that is queried for the Bean name in line 36 and the Bean class in line 37.

Line 42 calls the BeanInfo object's `getPropertyDescriptors()` method, which returns a PropertyDescriptor array. Lines 44–48 print the name, property type, and accessor methods for each property in the array.

Line 53 calls the BeanInfo object's `getEventSetDescriptors()` method, which returns an EventSetDescriptor array. Lines 55–59 print the name and registry methods. Line 60 calls the current EventSetDescriptor object's `getListenerMethodDescriptors()` method, and line 62 prints the listener method names (event types) for each event in the array.

Finally, line 69 calls the BeanInfo object's `getMethodDescriptors()` method, which returns a MethodDescriptor array. Line 71 prints the name of each method in the array.

Try running the utility with some of this chapter's example Beans as the argument. You may be surprised at how many properties, events, and methods the xmnbean utility identifies. This is because the Introspector checks the superclasses for the design patterns as well. The minimumSize property, for example, shows up in the Calendar2 Bean because of the presence of the `getMinimumSize()` method in the Component class.

This section covered Java Bean introspection. The next advanced topic to cover is property editors.

Property Editors

You may have noticed the difference between the number of properties that appear in the BDK BeanBox property sheets and the number identified by the xmnbean utility for a given Bean. One reason for this discrepancy is that the BDK doesn't know how to edit certain properties. This will be the case for any builder tool, because any Bean developer can create a new property type.

To solve this problem, you can create a *property editor* that knows how to edit a given property type.

Listing 15.17 (DateEditor.java) is a property editor for the date property of the Calendar2 Bean. This property is of type `java.util.Date`. The standard naming convention is to take the property type and add Editor to it, hence the name DateEditor. When the property sheet is displayed for the Calendar2 Bean, the presence of this DateEditor class enables the date property to be displayed and edited on the property sheet.

Listing 15.17

```
Line==================Java Source=================
//////////
// DateEditor.java  A property editor for date fields
//
// Author: James L. Weaver  JDK 1.1 beta1, BDK 1.1 beta 2
//////////
//package chapter15.code.calendar2;

// Put this DateEditor in the same directory as the
// other BeanBox property editors so that the BeanBox
// can find it.
package sun.beans.editors;

import java.util.*;
import java.beans.*;
```

```

public class DateEditor extends PropertyEditorSupport {

    // This method returns a Java code fragment to initialize
    // the property.
    public String getJavaInitializationString() {
        int month, day, year;
        Date dt = (Date)getValue();
        month = dt.getMonth();
        day = dt.getDay();
        year = dt.getYear();

        String str = "new Date(" +
                     year + "," +
                     month + "," +
                     day + ")";
        return str;
    }

    // This is called when the builder tool wants to display the
    // current property value on the property sheet. It builds and
    // returns a human editable string to be displayed.
    public String getAsText() {
        int month, day, year;
        GregorianCalendar greg = new GregorianCalendar();
        greg.setTime((Date)getValue());
        month = greg.get(Calendar.MONTH);
        day = greg.get(Calendar.DATE);
        year = greg.get(Calendar.YEAR);

        String str = (month + 1) + "/" +
                     day + "/" +
                     year;
        return str;
    }

    // This is called whenever the builder tool wants to retrieve
    // the property value from the property sheet. It parses the
    // displayed string and calls setValue() with an object of
```

continues

Listing 15.17, Continued

```
54        // the property type.
55        public void setAsText(String text)
56                    throws java.lang.IllegalArgumentException {
57            int month, day, year;
58
59            try {
60                month = Integer.parseInt(text.substring(
61                                  0, text.indexOf('/'))) -1;
62                day = Integer.parseInt(text.substring(
63                                  text.indexOf('/') + 1,
64                                  text.lastIndexOf('/')));
65                year = Integer.parseInt(text.substring(
66                                  text.lastIndexOf('/') + 1));
67                GregorianCalendar greg = new GregorianCalendar();
68                greg.set(Calendar.MONTH, month);
69                greg.set(Calendar.DATE, day);
70                greg.set(Calendar.YEAR, year);
71
72                // getTime() returns Date, which is the property type
73                setValue(greg.getTime());
74            }
75            catch (Exception e) {
76                throw new java.lang.IllegalArgumentException(text);
77            }
78        }
79    }
```

In line 11, this class is put into the sun.beans.editors package, the same location of the other property editors for the BDK beanbox. Two other possibilities exist for ensuring that a builder tool can locate a property editor:

- Register the property editor class by using the static `registerEditor()` method of the java.beans.PropertyManager class. To use this method, supply two Class objects: one that represents the Java type to be edited, and one that represents the property editor class. When using this registry mechanism, it is not necessary to follow the standard property editor naming convention—still, this is recommended.
- Use the standard property editor naming mechanism, and put the property editor class in the same package as the Bean class.

In line 16, the DateEditor class is derived from the PropertyEditorSupport class. The PropertyEditorSupport class provides methods that the property editor class can override. Three of these methods are overridden in the DateEditor class:

- `String getJavaInitializationString()`
- `String getAsText()`
- `setAsText(String)`

Lines 20–32 override the `getJavaInitializationString()` method. This method is called if the builder tool needs to generate code to initialize the value of this property.

Lines 37–49 override the `getAsText()` method. This method is called when the builder tool wants to display the current property value as a String on the property sheet. The method builds and returns a string that the user can edit.

Lines 55–78 override the `setAsText()` method. This method is called when the builder tool wants to take the String entered in the property sheet and update the property value. The method parses the displayed string and calls `setValue()` with an object of the property type.

Figure 15.10 shows the BDK BeanBox PropertySheet for Calendar2.

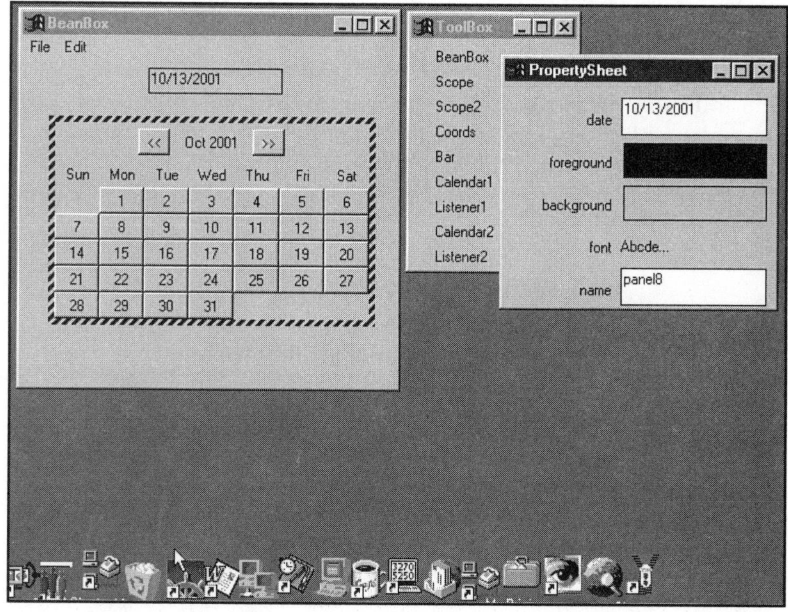

Figure 15.10

The Calendar2 Bean and Property Sheet in the BDK BeanBox.

Creating JAR Files

JAR file stands for Java Archive file, a feature new to JDK 1.1. JAR files were introduced mainly to speed up the downloading of class files associated with applets. Applets frequently contain many class files, image files, and so on. Before JAR files existed each of these files were downloaded separately with the Web browser initiating a time consuming HTTP connection request for each file. With JAR files you can compress all the files associated with an applet and put them all in one file. This reduces the number of HTTP requests to one, and the total size of the download is substantially reduced. To take advantage of this feature, use the ARCHIVES attribute of the HTML APPLET tag as shown in Chapter 8, "Creating Java Applets."

Another reason that JavaSoft introduced JAR files is to provide a standard, convenient way to package Java Beans. A JAR file can contain all the files that make up a Bean, and a JAR file may contain more than one Bean. This way, Java Bean developers can distribute their Beans via JAR files, and builder tools can extract the Beans from a JAR file at development time. A complex Bean may have a default state saved in the JAR file as well so that a developer who uses the Bean may start out with those defaults.

JAR files use the same format as ZIP files and have a *manifest file* that describes the contents of the JAR file. Each entry in a JAR file may be digitally signed so that their origin can be authenticated.

Jar Archive Tool

JavaSoft has provided a utility called the *Java Archive Tool* that enables you to package files into a JAR file and extract files from a JAR file. The Java Archive Tool (commonly referred to as the *jar tool*) is a Java application that uses classes from the new java.util.zip package. To invoke the jar tool, enter **jar** at the command line followed by one or more parameters. The first parameter is one or more of the options in table 15.2.

TABLE 15.2
Jar Archive Tool Command-Line Parameters

Parameter	Description
t (for table)	Lists the contents of a JAR file from standard input or a JAR file specified by the "f" option.
f (for file)	Specifies that the second parameter contains the JAR file to be processed. To list the contents of my.jar, for example, the command would be: `jar tf my.jar`

Parameter	Description
v (for verbose)	Specifies that verbose output be generated to `stderr`.
c (for create)	Creates a new JAR file on standard output, or in a file specified by the "f" parameter. The files and directories to be archived are specified as command line parameters. Directories are processed recursively. To archive all the files, for example, in the current directory and subdirectories to my.jar with verbose output, the command would be: `jar cvf my.jar *`
m (for manifest)	By default, a manifest file is made when creating a JAR file. You can use the "m" option to add to the contents of the manifest file by supplying a file that contains the desired content. This is useful for indicating which class files are Java Beans.
x (for extract)	Extracts files from the JAR file from standard input or a JAR file specified by the "f" option. Files extracted are specified as command line parameters. By default, all files are extracted. To extract all files from my.jar, for example, the command would be: `jar xf my.jar`

For more information on the jar tool, see the following Web page:

```
http://java.sun.com/products/JDK/1.1/docs/guide/jar/index.html
```

An Example of Using JAR Files with Beans

In this section, a JAR file is created (using the jar tool) that contains the Scope Bean from earlier in the chapter, as well as the state of the Scope Bean. The state will be saved through a mechanism called *serialization,* which is explained in Chapter 16, "Remote Method Invocation and Object Serialization."

Listing 15.18 (program ScopeJar.java) is an example how you can save the state of, or serialize, a Bean to a file. It also shows how you can restore the state of the Bean from that serialized object file. This application displays the Scope Bean and presents the user with three buttons:

- The "Serialize" button saves the state of the Bean to a serialized object file.

- The "Instantiate" button removes the Scope Bean from the display. It then creates another Scope Bean instance from the serialized object file.
- The "Set" button enables you to set the "ticks" property of the Scope Bean. The change is reflected immediately in the Bean.

To demonstrate saving and restoring state:

1. Note the value of the "ticks" property.
2. Click the Serialize button, which saves the Bean to the Scope.ser file.
3. Enter a new number for the "ticks" property (say 12) and click the Set button.
4. Click the Instantiate button. The state of the serialized Bean is restored, as indicated by the "ticks" property.

The Scope.java listing is not repeated here. It is the same as in listing 15.1 except for the package statement in line 6 that has been changed to:

```
06   package chapter15.code.scopejar;
```

Figure 15.18 shows the ScopeJar application's display.

Listing 15.18

```
Line=================Java Source=================
//////////
// ScopeJar.java  Serialize/instantiate a Scope
// Java Bean.
//
// Author: James L. Weaver  JDK 1.1 beta1
//////////
package chapter15.code.scopejar;

import java.awt.*;
import java.awt.event.*;
import java.io.*;
import java.beans.*;

public class ScopeJar extends Frame implements ActionListener {

    Scope scope;
    Button cerealEyes,
```

```
            instantiate,
            btnTicks;
    TextField txtTicks;

    public ScopeJar() {
        super("Scope Java Bean Serialization");

        setLayout(new BorderLayout());
        addWindowListener(new Wadapt());
        setSize(300, 300);

        scope = new Scope();
        scope.setTicks(8);
        add("Center", scope);

        Panel ps = new Panel();
        add("South", ps);

        cerealEyes = new Button("Serialize");
        cerealEyes.addActionListener(this);
        ps.add(cerealEyes);

        instantiate = new Button("Instantiate");
        instantiate.addActionListener(this);
        ps.add(instantiate);

        txtTicks = new TextField("8", 5);
        ps.add(txtTicks);

        btnTicks = new Button("Set");
        btnTicks.addActionListener(this);
        ps.add(btnTicks);

        setVisible(true);
    }

    public static void main(String args[]) {
        ScopeJar menuFrame = new ScopeJar();
        return;
```

continues

Listing 15.18, Continued

```
    }

    public void actionPerformed(ActionEvent e) {
        if (e.getSource() == cerealEyes) {
            write("Scope.ser");
        }
        else if (e.getSource() == instantiate) {
            remove(scope);
            read("Scope.ser");
            add("Center", scope);
            txtTicks.setText(new Integer(scope.getTicks()).toString());
            validate();
        }
        else if (e.getSource() == btnTicks) {
            scope.setTicks(Integer.parseInt(txtTicks.getText()));
            scope.repaint();
        }
    }

    public void write(String filename){
        try {
            FileOutputStream   f = new FileOutputStream(filename);
            ObjectOutputStream s = new ObjectOutputStream(f);
            s.writeObject(scope);
            s.flush();
        }
        catch (IOException e){
            System.out.println("Exception while Writing");
            return;
        }
    }

    public void read(String filename)
    {
        try {
            ClassLoader cl = Class.forName(
                "chapter15.code.scopejar.Scope").getClassLoader();
```

```
094             scope = (Scope)Beans.instantiate(cl, filename);
095         }
096         catch (Exception e){
097             System.out.println("Problem instantiating Scope");
098         }
099     }
100 }
101
102 class Wadapt extends WindowAdapter
103 {
104     public void windowClosing(WindowEvent evt) {
105         evt.getWindow().setVisible(false);
106         evt.getWindow().dispose();
107         System.exit(0);
108     }
109 }
```

Lines 29–31 create an instance of the Scope Bean, set the "ticks" property to 8, and add the Bean to the "Center" of the BorderLayout controlled frame.

When the Serialize button is clicked, line 61 calls the `write()` method contained in lines 76–87 which serializes the Bean to a file.

Note Object Serialization is explained in Chapter 16, "Remote Method Invocation and Object Serialization."

When the Instantiate button is clicked:

Line 64 removes the current Scope Bean instance from the frame.

Line 65 calls the `read()` method contained in lines 89–99 to create an instance of a Scope Bean from the serialized object file. These lines will be covered in a moment.

Line 66 adds the new Scope Bean instance to the frame.

Line 67 uses the `getTicks()` accessor method to get the ticks property of the new Scope Bean. It then displays this value in the text field.

In the `read()` method:

Lines 92 and 93 identify the class loader that loaded the Scope class.

Line 94 uses the `instantiate()` method of the java.beans.Beans class to make an instance of the Scope Bean from the Scope.ser file. The first parameter is the class loader, and the second is the name of the serialized object file, in this case Scope.ser. This is the same mechanism that a builder tool uses to load the state of a Bean.

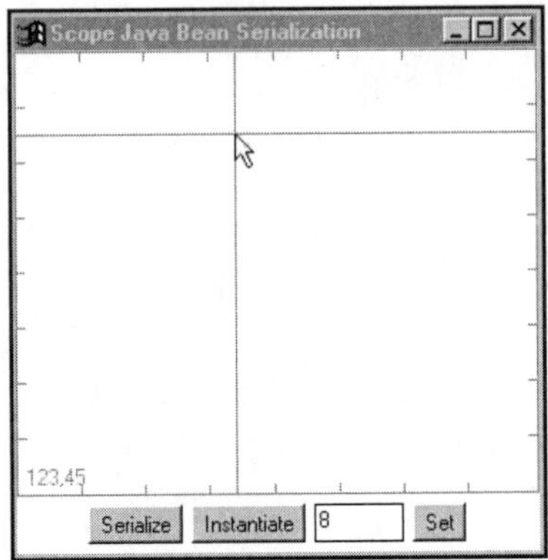

Figure 15.11
ScopeJar application display.

Using the Jar Tool to Package the Scope Bean

The steps for packaging a bean in a JAR file are as follows:

1. Create a file that supplies additional information to the manifest file.

   The additional information to be supplied is that the Scope.class file is a Java Bean. We'll arbitrarily name this file manifest.tmp, which contains the following lines:

```
Manifest-Version: 1.0
Name: chapter15/code/scopejar/Scope.class
Java-Bean: True
```

2. Run the jar tool to create the JAR file.

   Assuming that the default directory is at the base of the chapter15/code/scopejar path, and that the Scope.class and Scope.ser files are the only files in the chapter15/code/scopejar directory, execute the following command:

```
jar cfm scope.jar manifest.tmp chapter15/code/scopejar/*
```

   This creates a JAR file named scope.jar by using manifest information from manifest.tmp and containing the files in the chapter15/code/scopejar directory.

This JAR file can now be used directly by a builder tool, or the files can be extracted and used by an application similar to the way that ScopeJar does.

Summary

This chapter focused on the new Java component architecture known as Java Beans. It defined Java Beans and discussed the most important features: properties, events, and methods. Several examples demonstrated how you can build your own Beans and emit the desired events. Advanced topics, such as bound properties and introspection, were covered as well.

The next chapter covers the design goals and capabilities of Java Remote Method Invocation (RMI) and how to develop Java programs that use RMI. This chapter also discusses Object Serialization, how serialization enables RMI, and how serialization enables persistent Java objects.

CHAPTER 16

Remote Method Invocation and Object Serialization

A distributed application is one whose functionality is dispersed over more than one execution platform. Several approaches exist to enable you to develop distributed applications with Java. Included among these approaches are JDBC, Java IDL, and Java RMI:

- *JDBC (Java Database Connectivity)* is a standard SQL database access API. Chapter 17, "JDBC," covers JDBC in more detail.
- *Java IDL* enables Java to access network servers by using the Interface Definition Language defined by the Object Management Group. The Java IDL API did not make it into the JDK 1.1 release, and is beyond the scope of this book. Look for it in future JDK releases.
- *Java RMI (Remote Method Invocation)* is an API that enables a Java program running on one platform to invoke the methods of a Java program running on a different platform.

This chapter explores the design goals and capabilities of RMI and discusses how to develop Java programs that use RMI. You also will learn about a technology called Object Serialization that both helps enable RMI and provides a way to make Java objects persistent. A persistent object is one whose state can be saved to persistent storage, such as a magnetic disk.

Understanding Java RMI

Java RMI enables you to develop applications that consist of Java objects distributed over more than one platform. RMI enables objects in one Java Virtual Machine (VM) to call methods on objects residing in other Java VMs. Java primitive data types, objects that come with the JDK, and objects that you create all can be both passed as parameters and returned from these methods. Because RMI is included in the JDK 1.1 as a core library, you can count on it being supported on any JDK 1.1 compliant implementation of the *Java Platform.*

The Java Platform is an implementation of the Java VM and Java APIs on a given hardware or software platform. Currently, the JDK 1.0.2 implementation of the Java Platform is available for virtually every major operating system and browser, so any Java program that uses the JDK 1.0.2 API should work properly on any of these 1.0.2 compliant implementations. A JDK 1.1-compliant implementation of the Java Platform is becoming ported to virtually all the major hardware and software platforms.

Purpose for RMI

Java RMI was created as a pure Java solution for applications that have a distributed objects design, in which objects can communicate with each other by invoking each other's methods. Java applications have always had the capability to communicate with each other through the sockets protocol, which is a widely used communication protocol. By using sockets, applications can implement distributed functionality by sending requests and data back and forth. This approach is very low-level, however, and requires an application-level communication protocol that each application understands. An *application-level communication protocol* is an agreed-upon format for communicating data between two processes in a distributed application.

RMI's essential purpose is to provide an abstraction that enables an application designer to invoke methods on remote objects instead of having to communicate at a lower level. As a result, distributed applications written in Java can be completely object-oriented and thus can be designed with object-oriented tools and methods.

This means that objects can be placed on the network in the most practical location rather than in one Java VM address space. An object, for example, could reside on the same node as a relational database and provide services that make use of the underlying database.

RMI Design Goals

The RMI designers at the JavaSoft business unit of Sun Microsystems developed the following design objectives for RMI:

- To make the process of invoking remote objects as similar as possible to that of invoking local objects.
- To avoid completely disguising the locality of objects, and to enable client code to treat objects differently, where appropriate.
- To maintain the type safety and security of the native Java environment.
- To be extensible, so that later enhancements, such as replicated objects, would fit neatly into the overall architecture.
- To enable callbacks from servers to applets.
- To make the task of developing distributed applications as simple as possible.

The RMI implementation of JDK 1.1 has basically achieved these goals. How well these features can be implemented in actuality, however, will only become apparent as the Java development community gains more experience with them.

Overview of RMI Architecture

Two models will offer an overview of the RMI architecture. The first model, illustrated in figure 16.1, shows the flow of a remote method invocation. The second model, shown in figure 16.2, displays a block diagram of the RMI architecture.

Remote Method Invocation Flow

Figure 16.1 illustrates an overview of the process that occurs when a Java program calls a method located in a remote object.

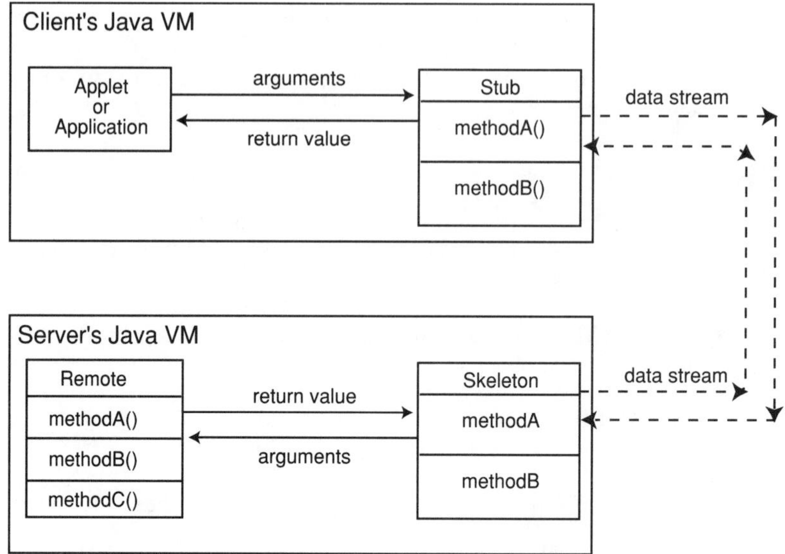

Figure 16.1
RMI application flow.

The following steps provide a behind-the-scenes look at how this process works:

1. The Java program calls a method of an object that represents the remote object, which is called a *stub.* The stub contains a method for each of the methods (that are allowed to be remotely invoked) in the remote object. These methods have the same name, parameters and return value as their counterparts.

The *stub* is sometimes referred to as the proxy, because it accepts method calls on behalf of the remote object.

2. The stub packages the arguments of the method into a stream that can be communicated through the network. This process is called *marshaling* and uses a *marshal stream.* During this process, the Java Object Serialization services serialize primitive data types and objects passed as arguments to the method. Object Serialization will be covered later in this chapter.

3. The *skeleton* is an object that resides in the remote VM and is the counterpart to the stub. Each remote object has a stub/skeleton pair. This skeleton unmarshals the arguments from the marshal stream and calls the method in the remote object with those arguments.

Note

Three architectural layers (see fig. 16.2) are involved in creating, sending, and receiving the marshal stream, which is discussed in the next section.

4. When the method returns, the skeleton marshals the return value (or exception, if an error occurred) onto a marshal stream and then sends the value back to the stub.

5. The stub unmarshals the return value and returns it to the original caller.

As you can see, the semantics of calling the stub are similar to those of calling a local object because the stub acts as a proxy for the remote object.

The Three Layers of the RMI System

As figure 16.2 illustrates, RMI uses three conceptual layers to support the flow just described:

- The Stubs/Skeletons Layer
- The Remote Reference Layer
- The Transport Layer

Each layer provides services to the layer above it, and the application code that uses RMI sits above the top layer.

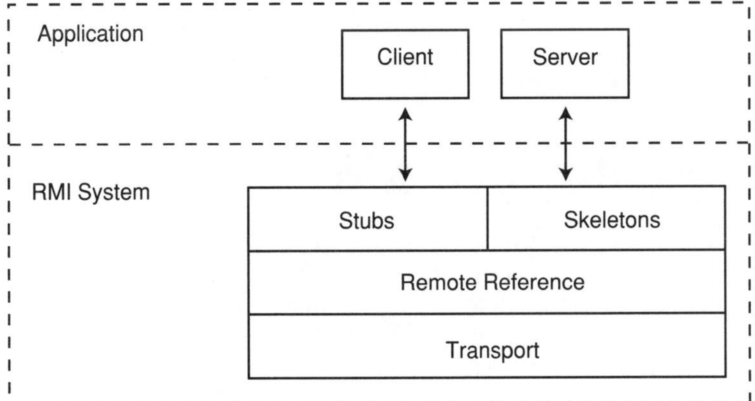

Figure 16.2
RMI system layers.

When a client invokes a remote method, the call flows down through the layers and is transformed as it goes to create a data stream that travels across the transport. The call then is reconstituted as it moves up through the layers on the server-side, where it emerges as a call to the remote method. The results of the invocation make the reverse journey, and control finally returns to the calling code in the client. Each layer has different responsibilities:

- The *Stubs/Skeletons Layer* consists of the stubs and skeletons described in the previous section. Stubs and skeletons perform complementary functions and form the interface between the RMI services and the code that calls and implements remote objects. Both objects are responsible for marshaling the arguments and unmarshaling return values. Stubs and skeletons are generated by the *rmic compiler*, which stands for *remote method interface compiler*, and will be used later in this chapter.

- The *Remote Reference Layer* provides a consistent interface to the stubs and skeletons above. This layer also hides the details of the specific remote reference semantics. The remote server object, for example, may actually be a set of replicated objects. In this case, the Remote Reference Layer is responsible for communicating with each of the replicated objects. The Remote Reference Layer also provides the marshal stream, into which the stub marshals the arguments.

- The *Transport Layer* handles the connectivity and provides a channel between the Java Virtual Machines (VMs), which contain the clients and remote objects. Each remote object can be referenced by the combination of an *endpoint* and an *object identifier*. This combination is called a *live reference*. The endpoint refers to a specific Java VM, and the object identifier refers to a specific remote object within that VM. The transport layer maintains a table of the remote objects in a Java VM.

The following section builds on the previous explanation of the RMI application flow and system layers, and provides a practical, hands-on example using RMI.

Developing with Java RMI

Now that you have a basic understanding of RMI, you will create a simple applet based upon the HelloGuiWorld applet from Chapter 13, "The New, Improved AWT: GUI Components, Containers, and Layout Managers," to demonstrate how you can develop Java programs that use RMI. The first version of this new applet (HelloApplet1) accesses a local object. This applet will be transformed step-by-step into an applet that accesses the object remotely.

The HelloApplet1 Applet

Listing 16.1 (HelloApplet1) also can be found on the CD accompanying this book.

Listing 16.1 illustrates the code of the HelloApplet1 applet, which is based upon the HelloGuiWorld applet in Chapter 13. Recall that when the button is pressed in this applet, the label toggles between displaying "Hello GUI World!" and " Goodbye!".

The main difference between the HelloGuiWorld and this HelloApplet1 applet is that the code that toggles the greeting back and forth from “Hello GUI World!” to “Goodbye!” has been moved into a separate class. This was done so that the class can be transferred to a different Java VM to demonstrate RMI. This class, named GreetingGen, is defined in lines 45–69. Figure 16.3 depicts the applet’s display.

Listing 16.1

```
Line=================Java Source=================
01   //////////
02   // HelloApplet1.java Example of transforming an applet
03   // into the RMI model.
04   //
05   // Author: James L. Weaver  JDK 1.1 beta
06   //////////
07   package chapter16.code.hello_remote1;
08
09   import java.awt.*;
10   import java.applet.*;
11   import java.awt.event.*;
12
13   public class HelloApplet1 extends Applet
14                              implements ActionListener{
15
16       Button pushButton;
17       Label greetingLabel;
18       GreetingGen gener;
19
20       public void init() {
21
22           pushButton = new Button("Push");
23           add(pushButton);
24
25           // Add an event "listener" for when an action
26           // event happens to this button. The
27           // actionPerformed method of the listener will
28           // be called.
29           pushButton.addActionListener(this);
30
31           greetingLabel = new Label("Hello GUI World!");
```

continues

Listing 16.1, Continued

```
        add(greetingLabel);

        gener = new GreetingGen();
    }

    // This method is called when the Button is clicked.
 public void actionPerformed(ActionEvent e) {
       greetingLabel.setText(gener.makeGreeting(greetingLabel.getText()));
        // Take next line out when bug in JDK 1.1 beta is fixed
       greetingLabel.repaint();
    }
}

class GreetingGen {
    // This class is responsible for generating a greeting.
    // It will later be converted to a class that can
    // be instanced to function as a remote object.

    String helloString;
    String goodbyeString;

    public GreetingGen() {
        // Set up the two greeting possibilities
        helloString = new String("Hello GUI World!");
        goodbyeString = new String("Goodbye!");
    }

    String makeGreeting(String lastGreeting) {
        String newGreeting;

        // Toggle between the two greetings
        if (lastGreeting.equals(helloString))
           newGreeting = goodbyeString;
        else
           newGreeting = helloString;
        return newGreeting;
    }
}
```

This is the associated HTML:

```
<HTML>
<HEAD>
<TITLE> Hello Remote World </TITLE>
</HEAD>
<BODY>
<APPLET CODEBASE="../../.."
        CODE="chapter16.code.hello_remote1.HelloApplet1.class"
        WIDTH=300 HEIGHT=100>
</applet>
</BODY>
</HTML>
```

As a quick review of this applet, a button and a label are created and placed on the applet in lines 22–32. Line 29 associates an event listener with the pushButton. Here, the event listener is the `actionPerformed()` method in line 38.

In line 34, an object is created from the GreetingGen class, which is defined in lines 45–69. This class contains one method, named `makeGreeting()`, which takes a String argument that contains the current greeting being shown. The `makeGreeting()` method returns a String that contains the new greeting to be shown.

Figure 16.3
HelloApplet1 applet display.

The applet now will be split apart and transformed into a distributed application that uses RMI.

Transforming HelloApplet1 to Use RMI

Figure 16.4 shows the following classes, which will be created to change the HelloApplet1 applet into the distributed HelloApplet2:

- **GreetingGen** is an implementation class that defines the interface for the remote object.
- **GreetingGenImpl** is the class from which the remote object is created.

- **GreetingGenImpl_Stub** is the stub, or proxy, class that the applet calls.
- **GreetingGenImpl_Skel** is the skeleton class with which the stub communicates to make the call to the remote object.

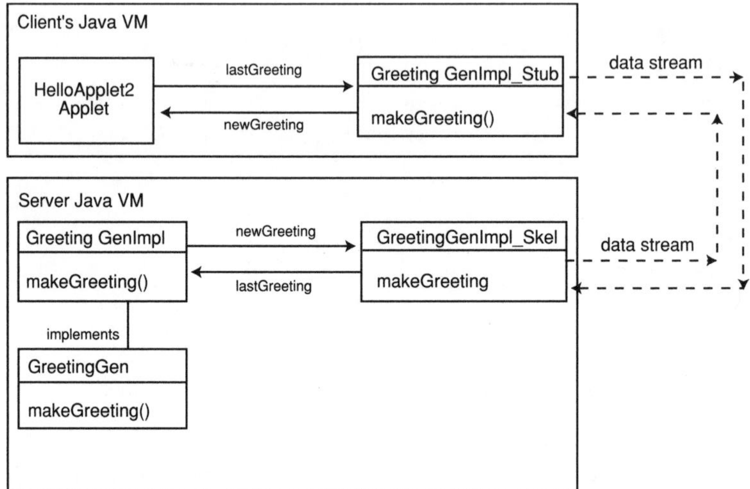

Figure 16.4
HelloApplet2 classes.

The following steps transform and execute the applet:

1. Code the GreetingGen interface, based upon the existing GreetingGen class.
2. Code the GreetingGenImpl class, based upon the existing GreetingGen class.
3. Modify the applet by making it invoke methods of the remote GreetinGenImpl class instead of invoking methods of the GreetingGen class.
4. Compile the files with javac.
5. Using the rmic compiler, generate the GreetingGenImpl_Stub and GreetingGenImpl_Skel classes.
6. Start the RMI registry.
7. Start the remote server and register the remote object.
8. Run the applet.

On the CD

This example, HelloApplet2, can be found on the accompanying CD.

Listings 16.2, 16.3, and 16.4 illustrate the HelloApplet2 applet and server components described in this section—the GreetingGen interface and the GreetingGenImpl class.

The sections following the listings demonstrate each of the above steps to transform the HelloApplet1 applet into the HelloApplet2 applet and server components.

Listing 16.2

```
Line==================Java Source==================
//////////
// HelloApplet2.java Example of transforming an applet
// into the RMI model.
//
// Author: James L. Weaver
//////////
package chapter16.code.hello_remote2;

import java.awt.*;
import java.applet.*;
import java.rmi.*;
import java.awt.event.*;

public class HelloApplet2 extends Applet
                            implements ActionListener{

    Button pushButton;
    Label greetingLabel;

    GreetingGen obj;

    public void init() {
        pushButton = new Button("Push");
        add(pushButton);

        // Add an event "listener" for when an action
        // event happens to this button. The
        // actionPerformed method of the listener will
        // be called.
        pushButton.addActionListener(this);

        greetingLabel = new Label("Hello Remote World!");
        add(greetingLabel);

```

continues

Listing 16.2, Continued

```
        try {
            obj = (GreetingGen)Naming.lookup("//" +
                getCodeBase().getHost() + "/GreetingServer");
        } catch (Exception e) {
            System.out.println("HelloApplet2: an exception occurred:");
            e.printStackTrace();
        }
    }

    // This method is called when the Button is clicked.
    public void actionPerformed(ActionEvent evt) {
        try {
            greetingLabel.setText(
            obj.makeGreeting(greetingLabel.getText()));
            // Take next line out when bug in JDK 1.1 beta is fixed
            greetingLabel.repaint();
        }
        catch (java.rmi.RemoteException e) {
            System.out.println("Error calling remote method");
            e.printStackTrace();
        }
    }
}
```

Listing 16.3

```
Line=================Java Source=================
//////////
// GreetingGen.java  Interface for an RMI
// remote object.
//
// Author: James L. Weaver   JDK version: 1.1
//////////
package chapter16.code.hello_remote2;

public interface GreetingGen extends java.rmi.Remote {
    String makeGreeting(String lastGreeting)
            throws java.rmi.RemoteException;
}
```

Listing 16.4

```
Line=================Java Source=================
//////////
// GreetingGenImpl.java  Implementation of an RMI
// remote object.
//
// Author: James L. Weaver   JDK version: 1.1
//////////
package chapter16.code.hello_remote2;

import java.rmi.*;
import java.rmi.server.UnicastRemoteObject;

class GreetingGenImpl
        extends UnicastRemoteObject
        implements GreetingGen
{
    String helloString;
    String goodbyeString;

    public GreetingGenImpl() throws RemoteException {
        super();

        // Set up the two greeting possibilities
        helloString = new String("Hello Remote World!");
        goodbyeString = new String("Goodbye!");
    }

    public String makeGreeting(String lastGreeting)
                    throws RemoteException {
        String newGreeting;

        // Toggle between the two greetings
        if (lastGreeting.equals(helloString))
            newGreeting = goodbyeString;
        else
            newGreeting = helloString;
        return newGreeting;
```

continues

Listing 16.4, Continued

```
    }

    public static void main(String args[])
    {
        // Create and install the security manager
        System.setSecurityManager(new RMISecurityManager());

        try {
            GreetingGenImpl obj = new GreetingGenImpl();
            System.out.println("Binding to GreetingServer");
            Naming.rebind("GreetingServer", obj);
            System.out.println("GreetingGenImpl bound");
        } catch (Exception e) {
            System.out.println("GreetingGenImpl.main exception");
            e.printStackTrace();
        }
    }
}
```

This is the associated HTML:

```
<HTML>
<HEAD>
<TITLE> Hello Remote World </TITLE>
</HEAD>
<BODY>
<APPLET CODEBASE="../../.."
        CODE="chapter16.code.hello_remote2.HelloApplet2.class"
        WIDTH=300 HEIGHT=100>
</applet>
</BODY>
</HTML>
```

Code the GreetingGen Interface

Each remote object must have a remote interface, which declares the methods that can be called by the client application. Listing 16.3 is the GreetingGen interface, which is the interface for the GreetingGenImpl remote object. The next section examines this interface.

Line 9 extends the GreetingGen interface from the Remote interface in the java.rmi package. All remote object interfaces must extend the java.rmi. Remote interface:

```
09   public interface GreetingGen extends java.rmi.Remote {
```

The remote interface also must be public, so that the client can access it.

Lines 10 and 11 specify the method in the remote object that can be called by a client:

```
10       String makeGreeting(String lastGreeting)
11               throws java.rmi.RemoteException;
```

In this simple example, only one method exists, but a remote object can have as many methods as required. The remote object also can contain methods that aren't specified by the remote object interface, but these cannot be invoked by a client. Each method in the interface must declare that it throws java.rmi.RemoteException for the client to handle remote exceptions or pass them on.

In addition to RemoteException and Remote, the RMI examples in this chapter use a few other classes and interfaces in the java.rmi and java.rmi.server packages. The additional classes are:

- **RemoteObject**—The superclass for all remote objects.
- **RemoteServer**—The superclass for all remote servers.
- **UnicastRemoteObject**—A specific type of remote server.
- **Naming**—A mechanism for obtaining references to remote objects.
- **RMISecurityManager**—Defines the RMI stub security policy for applications.

Figure 16.5 illustrates these classes, which will be covered shortly.

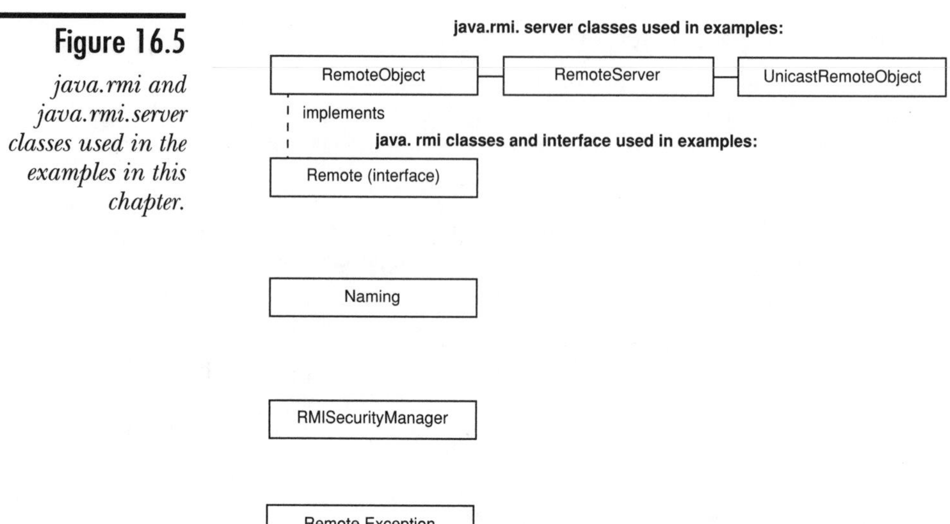

Figure 16.5 *java.rmi and java.rmi.server classes used in the examples in this chapter.*

Now that the remote object interface has been coded, let's create the implementation class for the remote object.

Code the GreetingGenImpl Implementation Class

Each remote object must have an implementation class. In this example, the GreetingGenImpl class is the implementation class (see listing 16.4).

Lines 12–14 show that this remote object implements GreetingGen, which was created in the last section:

```
12   class GreetingGenImpl
13           extends UnicastRemoteObject
14           implements GreetingGen
```

A remote object can implement any number of remote interfaces.

Line 13 extends GreetingGenImpl from the UnicastRemoteObject class, which is an RMI class that supplies server functionality so that you don't have to. Specifically, this class is used when the server has a non-replicated remote object, which is the usual case. As shown in figure 16.5, UnicastRemoteObject is derived from RemoteServer, which is derived from RemoteObject. In the future, remote servers will be extended from other subclasses of RemoteServer. These subclasses will implement servers with different semantics than the UnicastRemoteObject class provides. These semantics are part of the Remote Reference Layer in figure 16.2.

In line 19 in listing 16.4, the constructor declares that it throws RemoteException. This declaration must be done so that if a problem occurs when creating the remote server, the client can gracefully handle the exception:

```
19      public GreetingGenImpl() throws RemoteException {
20          super();
```

Line 20 (listing 16.4) calls the constructor of the super class, which is UnicastRemoteObject. This action causes the server to begin listening for requests. Note that it is not necessary to explicitly call `super()`, because the super class constructor is called by default.

Lines 27–37 (listing 16.4) contain the `makeGreeting()` method. The arguments and return type must be identical to the corresponding method in the GreetingGen interface class examined previously, and the `makeGreeting()` method must throw RemoteException:

```
27      public String makeGreeting(String lastGreeting)
28                      throws RemoteException {
29          String newGreeting;
30
31          // Toggle between the two greetings
32          if (lastGreeting.equals(helloString))
33              newGreeting = goodbyeString;
34          else
35              newGreeting = helloString;
36          return newGreeting;
37      }
```

The remaining server-side modification adds a `main()` method to this class so that it can run as a server and also have the opportunity to register its availability to remote clients.

Line 42 in the `main()` method creates and installs a security manager for this server:

```
42          System.setSecurityManager(new RMISecurityManager());
```

RMISecurityManager is one of the java.rmi classes identified in figure 16.5. This class is derived from java.lang.SecurityManager, and it ensures that the classes this server loads will not harm the server or the platform on which the server runs. Setting a security manager is necessary for the server to be able to dynamically load classes.

Line 45 (listing 16.4) creates an instance of the remote object:

```
45              GreetingGenImpl obj = new GreetingGenImpl();
```

You can create one or more instances of a remote object.

Line 47 in listing 16.4 registers this remote object with an RMI registry that runs on the remote platform:

```
47              Naming.rebind("GreetingServer", obj);
```

This RMI registry is a part of the RMI system and can be started with the *rmiregistry* utility. The RMI registry is sometimes called a *bootstrap registry,* because it is used to find a reference to the first object, which in turn provides references to other objects on the remote platform. The RMI registry should be restarted each time you make a change to a remote object's interface that is registered with the RMI registry.

The Naming class is used to register, or *bind,* this object with the RMI registry. In this case, the static method `rebind()` is used. The `rebind()` method has two arguments: a URL name assigned to this object, and an object reference. The object reference was created in line 45 during construction. As you'll see in the next section, a client can use the static `lookup()` method of the Naming class to gain a reference to the desired remote object, which is actually a reference to the stub in the client's VM.

Because the hostname and port aren't specified in the name passed by the `Naming.rebind()` method in line 47, the `rebind()` method assigns defaults. The default for hostname is the current host, and the default for the port number is the same one to which the rmiregistry utility defaults: 1099.

That takes care of the remote object, so we will now turn to the client modifications.

Modify the Applet to Call Remote Methods

The following two areas in the client code require changes:

- Getting a reference to the remote object
- Handling remote exceptions

In HelloApplet1, the client simply could refer to the GreetingGen object: The client knew where it was because the client created the object. In the remote case, however, obtaining a reference to a GreetingGen requires knowing the name of the instance of GreetingGen (many could exist), and handling the situation where one doesn't exist.

For simplicity, this example uses a single name that is known at compile time to both the client and server. This name, "GreetingServer," is passed as part of the URL formatted argument of the `Naming.lookup()` method in lines 36 and 37 (listing 16.2):

```
36              obj = (GreetingGen)Naming.lookup("//" +
37                  getCodeBase().getHost() + "/GreetingServer");
```

The rest of the argument in the `Naming.lookup()` call consists of the hostname of the RMI registry in which to identify this object's name. In the HelloApplet2 example, the RMI registry exists on the same platform from which the applet was retrieved. Because this is an applet, the host from which it was retrieved is returned from a call to `getCodeBase().getHost()`.

Lines 38–41 (listing 16.2) provide exception handling code, to be used when an exception occurs while calling the `Naming.lookup()` method.

```
38          } catch (Exception e) {
39              System.out.println("HelloApplet2: an exception occurred:");
40              e.printStackTrace();
41          }
```

`Naming.lookup()` returns a reference to the remote object, which is actually the stub that represents the remote object. If the call is successful, and if a remote object that implements GreetingGen is registered, then the reference to that object is used to invoke its methods, just as in the local version.

Notice that the Naming class is used in both the remote object and the client. The remote object uses it to bind the object to a name in the RMI registry, and the client uses it to look up a reference to the remote object by supplying a name. Table 16.1 lists the methods in the Naming class:

TABLE 16.1
Methods in the Naming Class

Constructor/Method	Description
void bind(String, Remote)	Binds the specified name to the remote object in the RMI registry
void rebind(String, Remote)	Rebinds the specified name to the remote object in the RMI registry; Replaces the existing binding, if already bound
void unbind(String)	Unbinds the specified name from a remote object reference
String[] list(String)	Returns an array of names that are currently bound in the RMI registry
Remote lookup(String)	Returns a reference to the remote object that is bound to the specified name

Notice that in line 36 of listing 16.2, the reference returned from `Naming.lookup()` is cast to GreetingGen; in line 20 of listing 16.2, the object reference is declared as a GreetingGen. With remote references, you always use the interface (in this case GreetingGen), not the implementation class (in this case GreetingGenImpl), as the object reference type.

```
20        GreetingGen obj;
```

Lines 46–55 (listing 16.2) contain a call to the method in the remote object, as well as the exception handling code:

```
46            try {
47                greetingLabel.setText(
48                        obj.makeGreeting(greetingLabel.getText()));
49                // Take next line out when bug in JDK 1.1 beta is fixed
50                greetingLabel.repaint();
51            }
52            catch (java.rmi.RemoteException e) {
53                System.out.println("Error calling remote method");
54                e.printStackTrace();
55            }
```

Because the object is remote, many more ways exist in which method invocations can fail. As a result, the client must add some extra code in the form of exception handlers for remote exceptions. In this example, exception handlers simply report that an exception occurred, but in a real application, they should be tied to recovery procedures.

The following sections describe how to compile and run this example. When platform-specific instructions exist, they will be given from a Windows 95/NT perspective, so translate them into instructions specific to your platform.

Compile the Java Files

Follow these steps to compile the Java files:

1. The three Java files (HelloApplet2.java, GreetingGen.java, and GreetingGenImpl.java) should be placed in a directory whose path ends in \chapter16\code\hello_remote2. The CLASSPATH should be set to include the directory within which this path is rooted. This is because the package name for the classes to be created is chapter16.code.hello_remote2. (This step is explained from a Windows 95/NT perspective.)

2. Make sure that your PATH includes the java\bin directory, because this directory contains the utilities (javac, rmic, rmiregistry, and appletviewer) used in these steps. (This step is explained from a Windows 95/NT perspective.)

3. Using the javac compiler in the JDK (1.1 beta or later), execute the following command:

```
javac *.java
```

This will produce the associated .class files for the three classes just described.

Generate the Stub and Skeleton Classes

The utility named *rmic*, included with JDK 1.1, creates the stub and skeleton classes for a given implementation class. The rmic utility operates upon the .class file, not the .java file. Execute the following command:

```
rmic chapter16.code.hello_remote2.GreetingGenImpl
```

This will create the GreetingGenImpl_Stub.class and GreetingGenImpl_Skel.class files.

Start the RMI Registry

To start the RMI registry on Windows 95/NT, use the *rmiregistry* utility by executing the following command:

```
start rmiregistry
```

On UNIX, you would execute the following:

```
rmiregistry &
```

This starts the RMI registry on the default port, which is 1099. The RMI registry services any number of applications that request remote object references on the assigned port.

Start the Remote Object Server

To start the remote object server that registers the remote object, execute the following command, replacing *yourhost* with the hostname of your http server, and *yourcodebase* with the codebase in which the stub class can be found. In this case, *yourcodebase* must equate with the directory in which \chapter16\code\hello_remote2 is rooted. The trailing forward slash on the URL is required.

```
start java -Djava.rmi.server.codebase= http://yourhost/yourcodebase/
➥chapter16.code. hello_remote2.GreetingGenImpl
```

Setting the java.rmi.server.codebase property is essential because when the server starts up, it checks to see if the appropriate stub class exists where this property indicates that it does. References to the remote server then can include the URL of the stub class so that it can be downloaded, in case it is not available in the client's CLASSPATH.

Run the Applet

After the remote object server successfully starts and binds to the RMI registry, the message generated in line 48 of GreetingGenImpl.java will be displayed in the system output. This indicates that GreetingGenImpl was successfully bound to the RMI registry.

Now you can start the Applet Viewer with the URL of the HelloRemote2.html file.

Passing Objects in Remote Methods

The HelloApplet1 and HelloApplet2 examples provide a simple demonstration of how you can create distributed Java applications with RMI. The RMI system does most of the work for you, including passing objects in remote methods. In lines 47 and 48 of HelloApplet2.java (listing 16.2), the call to `makeGreeting()` returns a String object that `greetingLabel.setText()` uses to cause the greeting to be displayed.

```
47             greetingLabel.setText(
48                     obj.makeGreeting(greetingLabel.getText()));
```

Because `makeGreeting()` is a method of a remote object, the String object had to be serialized by the RMI system. Many Java classes included in JDK 1.1 can be serialized, so in the above example, nothing special had to be done to enable the String object to be passed as a return value.

To make sure that a class can be serialized, you must implement the java.io.Serializable interface. The Planets application in the next section demonstrates how you can create a serializable class and pass objects of that class as the return value of a remote object.

The Planets Application

Listings 16.5, 16.6, 16.7, and 16.8 contain the code for the Planets application. This application consists of:

- A client applet named PlanetsApplet2 (listing 16.5). This applet demonstrates how to pass serialized objects.
- A remote object interface class named PlanetsInfo (listing 16.6). This is the interface for the remote PlanetsImpl object.
- A remote server class named PlanetsImpl (listing 16.7). This remote object manages the Planet objects and returns them to the client applet upon request.
- A class named Planet, which will be returned from the remote object to the client (listing 16.8). Instances of the Planet class represent each of the nine planets in our solar system.

Listing 16.5

```
Line=================Java Source=================
//////////
// PlanetsApplet2.java  Applet that demonstrates passing
// serialized objects.
//
// Author: James L. Weaver   JDK version: 1.1 beta
//////////
package chapter16.code.planets_rmi;

import java.awt.*;
import java.applet.*;
import java.rmi.*;
import java.awt.event.*;

public class PlanetsApplet2 extends Applet
                             implements ActionListener{

    TextField planetNum;
    Button infoButton;
    TextArea stats;

    int numPlanets = 0;
    String planetName = new String();
    int numMoons = 0;
    boolean rings = false;

```

continues

Listing 16.5, Continued

```
    PlanetsInfo obj;

    public void init() {
        try {
            obj = (PlanetsInfo)Naming.lookup("//" +
                getCodeBase().getHost() + "/PlanetServer");
        } catch (Exception e) {
            System.out.println("PlanetsApplet2: an exception occurred:");
            e.printStackTrace();
        }
        try {
            numPlanets = obj.getNumPlanets();
        }
        catch (java.rmi.RemoteException e) {
            System.out.println("Error calling remote method");
            e.printStackTrace();
        }

        setLayout(new BorderLayout());
        Panel p = new Panel();

        p.add(new Label("Planet Number 1-" + numPlanets + ":"));
        planetNum = new TextField(null, 3);
        infoButton = new Button("Info");
        p.add(planetNum);
        p.add(infoButton);
        add("North", p);

        stats = new TextArea();
        add("Center", stats);

        infoButton.addActionListener(this);
    }

    // This method is called when the Button is clicked.
    public void actionPerformed(ActionEvent evt) {
        String text = new String();
        Planet planet = null;
```

```
        int pnum = 0;
        try {
            pnum = Integer.parseInt(planetNum.getText());
        }
            catch (Exception e) {
        }
        if (pnum > numPlanets || pnum < 1 ) {
            stats.setText(planetNum.getText() + " is not a valid planet #");
            return;
        }
        try {
            planet = obj.getPlanet(pnum-1);
        }
        catch (java.rmi.RemoteException e) {
            System.out.println("Error calling remote method");
            e.printStackTrace();
        }
        stats.setText("Planet Name:      " + planet.getName() + "\r\n");
        stats.appendText("Number of Moons: " + planet.getMoons() + "\r\n");
        if (planet.hasRings())
            stats.appendText("Has Rings:        Yes");
        else
            stats.appendText("Has Rings:        No");
    }
}
```

Listing 16.6

```
Line=================Java Source================
//////////
// PlanetsInfo.java  Interface for an RMI
// remote object.
//
// Author: James L. Weaver   JDK version: 1.1 beta
//////////
package chapter16.code.planets_rmi;

public interface PlanetsInfo extends java.rmi.Remote {
    int getNumPlanets() throws java.rmi.RemoteException;
    Planet getPlanet(int num) throws java.rmi.RemoteException;
}
```

Listing 16.7

```
Line=================Java Source=================
//////////
// PlanetsImpl.java  Implementation of an RMI
// remote object.
//
// Author: James L. Weaver   JDK version: 1.1 beta
//////////
package chapter16.code.planets_rmi;

import java.rmi.*;
import java.rmi.server.UnicastRemoteObject;

class PlanetsImpl
        extends UnicastRemoteObject
        implements PlanetsInfo
{
    Planet planets[] = new Planet[9];

    public PlanetsImpl() throws RemoteException {
        super();

        // Populate the planets array
        planets[0] = new Planet("Mercury",0, false);
        planets[1] = new Planet("Venus",0, false);
        planets[2] = new Planet("Earth",1, false);
        planets[3] = new Planet("Mars",2, false);
        planets[4] = new Planet("Jupiter",16, true);
        planets[5] = new Planet("Saturn",18, true);
        planets[6] = new Planet("Uranus",15, true);
        planets[7] = new Planet("Neptune",8, true);
        planets[8] = new Planet("Pluto",1, false);
    }


    public int getNumPlanets() throws RemoteException
    {
        return planets.length;
```

```
    }

    public Planet getPlanet(int num) throws RemoteException
    {
        return planets[num];
    }

    public static void main(String args[])
    {
        // Create and install the security manager
        System.setSecurityManager(new RMISecurityManager());

        try {
            PlanetsImpl obj = new PlanetsImpl();
            System.out.println("Binding to PlanetServer");
            Naming.rebind("PlanetServer", obj);
            System.out.println("PlanetsImpl created and bound");
        } catch (Exception e) {
            System.out.println("PlanetsImpl.main exception");
            e.printStackTrace();
        }
    }
}
```

Listing 16.8

```
Line=================Java Source=================
//////////
// Planet.java  A class that represents a planet
// in the RMI demonstration.
//
// Author: James L. Weaver   JDK version: 1.1 beta
//////////
package chapter16.code.planets_rmi;

class Planet implements java.io.Serializable
{
    private String name;
    private int moons;
```

continues

Listing 16.8, Continued

```
    private boolean hasRings;

    public Planet(String name, int moons, boolean hasRings) {
        this.name = name;
        this.moons = moons;
        this.hasRings = hasRings;
    }

    public String getName() {
        return name;
    }

    public int getMoons() {
        return moons;
    }

    public boolean hasRings() {
        return hasRings;
    }
}
```

This is the associated HTML:

```
<HTML>
<HEAD>
<TITLE> Planets Applet 2 </TITLE>
</HEAD>
<BODY>
<APPLET CODEBASE="../../.."
        CODE="chapter16.code.planets_rmi.PlanetsApplet2.class"
        WIDTH=300 HEIGHT=300>
</applet>
</BODY>
</HTML>
```

As shown in figure 16.6, which follows this code walkthrough, the applet asks the user to enter a number associated with a planet in our solar system, with 1 representing Mercury and 9 representing Pluto. When the user clicks the Info button, the information associated with the desired planet is displayed in the text area. To accomplish this, an object that represents the desired planet is passed as a return value from the remote object to the client. The client calls a method of the planet object, which is now local, to get information about that planet.

To see how this works, first look at the PlanetsInfo interface, which is shown in listing 16.6. This is the remote interface class for the PlanetsImpl class. Two methods can be called by the client, as shown in lines 10 and 11 (listing 16.6):

```
10      int getNumPlanets() throws java.rmi.RemoteException;
11      Planet getPlanet(int num) throws java.rmi.RemoteException;
```

The `getNumPlanets()` method returns the number of planets in our solar system. The `getPlanet()` method returns a Planet object that corresponds to the num argument.

Listing 16.7 shows the PlanetsImpl class, which is the implementation of the remote object. Line 16 creates an array that refers to nine instances of the Planet class, which represents each of the planets.

```
16      Planet planets[] = new Planet[9];
```

Lines 22–30 (listing 16.7) populate the array with Planet objects that know their name, number of moons, and whether or not they have rings encircling them.

```
22          planets[0] = new Planet("Mercury",0, false);
23          planets[1] = new Planet("Venus",0, false);
24          planets[2] = new Planet("Earth",1, false);
25          planets[3] = new Planet("Mars",2, false);
26          planets[4] = new Planet("Jupiter",16, true);
27          planets[5] = new Planet("Saturn",18, true);
28          planets[6] = new Planet("Uranus",15, true);
29          planets[7] = new Planet("Neptune",8, true);
30          planets[8] = new Planet("Pluto",1, false);
```

When the `getNumPlanets()` method is called, it returns the length of the planets array.

```
34      public int getNumPlanets() throws RemoteException
35      {
36          return planets.length;
37      }
```

When the `getPlanet()` method is called, it returns the specified array element, which is a reference to the desired Planet instance.

```
39      public Planet getPlanet(int num) throws RemoteException
40      {
41          return planets[num];
42      }
```

Listing 16.8 shows the Planet class. For a class to be passed as a parameter or a return value, it must implement the java.io.Serializable interface, as shown in line 9.

```
09   class Planet implements java.io.Serializable
```

The Serializable interface has no methods, but its presence enables the class to be serialized.

The Planet class has three methods—shown in lines 21, 25, and 29 of listing 16.8—that the client can call to get information about the planet that a given instance represents:

```
021         public String getName() {
```

```
025         public int getMoons() {
```

```
029         public boolean hasRings() {
```

Listing 16.5 shows the client applet that uses the methods of the remote object and the Planet objects that it contains. After gaining a reference to the remote object, the client attempts to call the `getNumPlanets()` method of that object in line 37.

```
37                  numPlanets = obj.getNumPlanets();
```

The returned number is used in line 47 to build the string that prompts the user to enter a planet number.

```
47              p.add(new Label("Planet Number 1-" + numPlanets + ":"));
```

In line 75 (listing 16.5), the number (decreased by 1) that the user inputs into the TextField is passed to the `getPlanet()` method of the remote object.

```
75                  planet = obj.getPlanet(pnum-1);
```

The specified Planet instance is then serialized, marshaled, and sent as a return value from the server's VM to the client's VM. In lines 81–86, the methods of that instance are called locally to populate the TextArea with information about the planet that the instance represents.

```
        stats.setText("Planet Name:      " + planet.getName() + "\r\n");
        stats.appendText("Number of Moons: " + planet.getMoons() + "\r\n");
        if (planet.hasRings())
            stats.appendText("Has Rings:        Yes");
        else
            stats.appendText("Has Rings:        No");
```

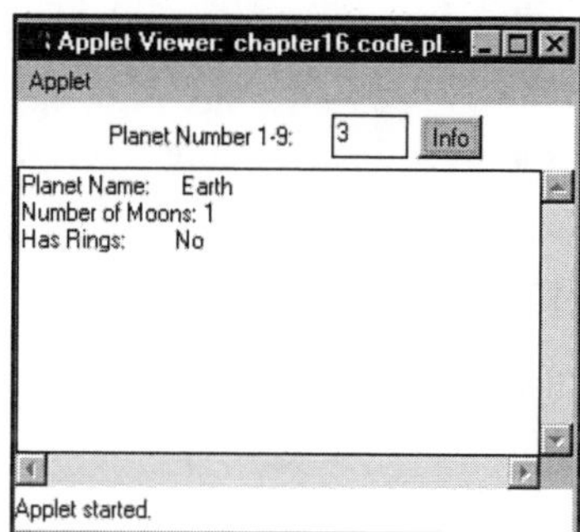

Figure 16.6
PlanetsApplet2 applet display.

The Java RMI system makes it fairly easy to build Java applications that have objects distributed over more than one Java VM. Object Serialization plays a big role in enabling Java RMI.

Understanding and Using Object Serialization

As you have seen, you can make a class serializable by implementing the java.io.Serializable interface. Also, extending a class from one that is serializable makes the extended class serializable. This section discusses Object Serialization in more detail.

Purposes for Object Serialization

Object Serialization services were created for two main reasons:

- Support for RMI (as already covered).
- Object persistence, which is the capability to save objects to a form of persistent storage, such as a magnetic disk.

One factor of object serialization that may not be immediately appreciated is that not only do the objects explicitly mentioned need to be serialized, but any objects that they refer to also must be serialized. Thus, it is not sufficient simply to copy the fields of an object for that object to be serialized. Starting with the initial object, it is possible to describe all the references with a graph, which, in this case, is a map of the references that objects have to one other. The entire graph of objects must be serialized.

Suppose that, for example, in the Planets example above, the Planet class contains an array of references to objects that each represent a hypothetical Moon class. To pass the entire Planet object to the client, it must serialize not only the Planet object, but also all the Moon objects that are referenced by the Planet object.

Using Object Serialization for Persistence

To provide the necessary functionality, object serialization services have been implemented to extend the DataInputStream and DataOutputStream classes from the java.io package. Because DataInputStream and DataOutputStream classes can deal only with primitive types, two complementary classes have been added: ObjectOutputStream and ObjectInputStream. These classes serialize an object or a graph of objects to a datastream, and deserialize (reconstruct) an object or a graph of objects from a stream.

Although the ObjectInputStream and ObjectOutputStream classes were created mainly to support RMI, they also make it easy to add persistence to Java objects. In other words, the new classes add the capability for objects to persist beyond a particular invocation of the program that creates and uses them. This often means getting objects to save themselves to files on a disk and to read themselves back later.

The next section builds on the Planets application that we've been working with, and illustrates the necessary steps to make the PlanetsImpl class persistent.

The Persistent Planets Application

To demonstrate the power and simplicity of serializing objects to disk, the PlanetsImpl class will be made persistent. Doing so will make the data available even when the server process is stopped and restarted.

Some new functionality has been added to the user interface. A new Bump button enables the user to increase the number of moons associated with a given planet. When the user presses this button, the following occurs:

- The newly added `bumpMoons()` method of the Planet object is called to increase the number of moons.

- The updated Planet object is passed to the newly added `setPlanet()` method of the PlanetsImpl remote object, demonstrating the capability to pass a local object to a remote object.
- The `setPlanet()` method calls the newly added `write()` method, which writes all the Planet objects to the disk of the remote server. Note that when the server is started, it reads the Planet objects from this file by using a newly added `read()` method.
- An event is posted that simulates the Info button being pressed. The updated number of moons now are immediately visible on the applet's display.

Listings 16.9, 16.10, 16.11, and 16.12 contain the code for this modified Planets application. Figure 16.7 shows the applet's display.

Listing 16.9

```
Line==================Java Source=================
//////////
// PlanetsApplet3.java  Applet that demonstrates passing
// and saving/loading serialized objects.
//
// Author: James L. Weaver   JDK version: 1.1 beta
//////////
package chapter16.code.planets_ser;

import java.awt.*;
import java.applet.*;
import java.rmi.*;
import java.awt.event.*;

public class PlanetsApplet3 extends Applet
                           implements ActionListener{

    TextField planetNum;
    Button infoButton, bumpButton;
    TextArea stats;

    int numPlanets = 0;
    String planetName = new String();
    int numMoons = 0;
```

continues

Listing 16.9, Continued

```
    boolean rings = false;

    PlanetsInfo obj;
    Planet planet = null;
    int pnum = 0;

    public void init() {
        try {
            obj = (PlanetsInfo)Naming.lookup("//" +
                getCodeBase().getHost() + "/PlanetServer3");
        } catch (Exception e) {
            System.out.println("PlanetsApplet3: an exception occurred:");
            e.printStackTrace();
        }
        try {
            numPlanets = obj.getNumPlanets();
        }
        catch (java.rmi.RemoteException e) {
            System.out.println("Error calling remote method");
            e.printStackTrace();
        }

        setLayout(new BorderLayout());
        Panel p = new Panel();

        p.add(new Label("Planet Number 1-" + numPlanets + ":"));
        planetNum = new TextField(null, 3);
        infoButton = new Button("Info");
        bumpButton = new Button("Bump");
        p.add(planetNum);
        p.add(infoButton);
        p.add(bumpButton);
        add("North", p);

        stats = new TextArea();
        add("Center", stats);

```

```
        infoButton.addActionListener(this);
        bumpButton.addActionListener(this);
    }

    // This method is called when the Button is clicked.
    public void actionPerformed(ActionEvent evt) {
        if (evt.getSource() == infoButton) {
            String text = new String();
            try {
                pnum = Integer.parseInt(planetNum.getText());
            }
                catch (Exception e) {
            }
            if (pnum > numPlanets || pnum < 1 ) {
                stats.setText(planetNum.getText() +
                        " is not a valid planet #");
                return;
            }
            try {
                planet = obj.getPlanet(pnum-1);
            }
            catch (java.rmi.RemoteException e) {
                System.out.println("Error calling remote method");
                e.printStackTrace();
            }
            stats.setText("Planet Name:      " +
                            planet.getName() + "\r\n");
            stats.appendText("Number of Moons: " +
                            planet.getMoons() + "\r\n");
            if (planet.hasRings())
                stats.appendText("Has Rings:        Yes");
            else
                stats.appendText("Has Rings:        No");
        }
        if (evt.getSource() == bumpButton) {
            if (planet != null) {
                planet.bumpMoons();
                try {
```

continues

Listing 16.9, Continued

```
                    obj.setPlanet(pnum-1, planet);
                }
                catch (java.rmi.RemoteException e) {
                    System.out.println("Error calling remote method");
                    e.printStackTrace();
                }
                EventQueue.getEventQueue().postEvent(new ActionEvent)
➥infoButton,
                        ActionEvent.ACTION_PERFORMED, null));
            }
        }
    }
}
```

Listing 16.10

```
Line=================Java Source=================
//////////
// PlanetsInfo.java  Interface for an RMI
// remote object.
//
// Author: James L. Weaver   JDK version: 1.1 beta
//////////
package chapter16.code.planets_ser;

public interface PlanetsInfo extends java.rmi.Remote {
    int getNumPlanets() throws java.rmi.RemoteException;
    Planet getPlanet(int num) throws java.rmi.RemoteException;
    void setPlanet(int num, Planet pl)
            throws java.rmi.RemoteException;
}
```

Listing 16.11

```
Line=================Java Source=================
//////////
// PlanetsImpl.java  Implementation of an RMI
// remote object.
//
```

```
// Author: James L. Weaver   JDK version: 1.1 beta
//////////
package chapter16.code.planets_ser;

import java.io.*;
import java.util.*;
import java.rmi.*;
import java.rmi.server.UnicastRemoteObject;


class PlanetsImpl
        extends UnicastRemoteObject
        implements PlanetsInfo
{
    Vector planets;
    String file = "planets.dat";

    public PlanetsImpl() throws RemoteException {
        super();

        read(file);
    }


    public int getNumPlanets() throws RemoteException
    {
        return planets.size();
    }

    public Planet getPlanet(int num) throws RemoteException
    {
        return (Planet)planets.elementAt(num);
    }

    public void setPlanet(int num, Planet pl) throws RemoteException
    {
        planets.setElementAt(pl, num);
        write(file);
    }
```

continues

Listing 16.11, Continued

```

    public void read(String filename)
    {
        try {
            FileInputStream in = new FileInputStream(filename);
            ObjectInputStream s = new ObjectInputStream(in);
            planets = (Vector)s.readObject();
        }
        catch (FileNotFoundException e){
            planets = new Vector();
            System.out.println("No input file found; Creating one.");

            // Populate the planets Vector
            planets.addElement(new Planet("Mercury",0, false));
            planets.addElement(new Planet("Venus",0, false));
            planets.addElement(new Planet("Earth",1, false));
            planets.addElement(new Planet("Mars",2, false));
            planets.addElement(new Planet("Jupiter",16, true));
            planets.addElement(new Planet("Saturn",18, true));
            planets.addElement(new Planet("Uranus",15, true));
            planets.addElement(new Planet("Neptune",8, true));
            planets.addElement(new Planet("Pluto",1, false));
            return;
        }
        catch (IOException e){
            System.out.println("Exception while Reading");
            return;
        }
        catch (ClassNotFoundException e){
            System.out.println("ClassNotFoundException while Reading");
            return;
        }
    }

    public void write(String filename){
        try {
            FileOutputStream   f = new FileOutputStream(filename);
            ObjectOutputStream s = new ObjectOutputStream(f);
            s.writeObject(planets);
```

```
            s.close();
        }
        catch (IOException e){
            System.out.println("Exception while Writing");
            return;
        }
    }

    public static void main(String args[])
    {
        // Create and install the security manager
        System.setSecurityManager(new RMISecurityManager());

        try {
            PlanetsImpl obj = new PlanetsImpl();
            System.out.println("Binding to PlanetServer3");
            Naming.rebind("PlanetServer3", obj);
            System.out.println("PlanetsImpl created and bound");
        } catch (Exception e) {
            System.out.println("PlanetsImpl.main exception");
            e.printStackTrace();
        }
    }
}
```

Listing 16.12

```
Line=================Java Source=================
//////////
// Planet.java  A class that represents a planet
// in the RMI demonstration.
//
// Author: James L. Weaver   JDK version: 1.1 beta
//////////
package chapter16.code.planets_ser;

class Planet implements java.io.Serializable
{
    private String name;
```

continues

Listing 16.12, Continued

```
    private int moons;
    private boolean hasRings;

    public Planet(String name, int moons, boolean hasRings) {
        this.name = name;
        this.moons = moons;
        this.hasRings = hasRings;
    }

    public String getName() {
        return name;
    }

    public int getMoons() {
        return moons;
    }

    public boolean hasRings() {
        return hasRings;
    }

    public void bumpMoons() {
        moons++;
    }
}
```

This is the associated HTML:

```
<HTML>
<HEAD>
<TITLE> Planets Applet 3 </TITLE>
</HEAD>
<BODY>
<APPLET CODEBASE="../../.."
        CODE="chapter16.code.planets_ser.PlanetsApplet3.class"
        WIDTH=300 HEIGHT=300>
</applet>
</BODY>
</HTML>
```

To make the planets persistent, two methods have been added to the PlanetsImpl class in listing 16.11:

- A `read()` method, contained in lines 45–76
- A `write()` method, contained in lines 78–89

Nothing special defines the names `read()` and `write()`, but they do not appear in the PlanetsInfo interface. This means that they can be called only from methods running in the same Java VM as the PlanetsImpl object, not from the client applet across the network. The methods are part of only the local interface of PlanetsImpl, not its remote interface.

Reading Objects from an ObjectInputStream

In the `read()` method, lines 48 and 49 (listing 16.11) create an ObjectInputStream from a FileInputStream. The FileInputStream specifies the name of the file from which the object is to be read.

```
048                 FileInputStream in = new FileInputStream(filename);
049                 ObjectInputStream s = new ObjectInputStream(in);
```

If the file is found, the `readObject()` method of the ObjectInputStream reads the Vector object that contains references to all the planets. The method then reads all the referenced planet objects.

```
050                 planets = (Vector)s.readObject();
```

Note this change made to the PlanetsImpl class: The Planet objects are contained by a Vector, not an array. This change was made because `readObject()` returns a reference to an object, not an array. Although it is possible to treat an array like an object, demonstrating this process would unnecessarily complicate this example.

Because the return type of `readObject()` is an Object, it must be cast to the proper class, which in this case is Vector.

If the file containing the Vector of planet references isn't found, the exception handling code in lines 52–67 (listing 16.11) are executed to create a Vector and populate it with planets.

```
052             catch (FileNotFoundException e){
053                 planets = new Vector();
054                 System.out.println("No input file found; Creating one.");
055
056                 // Populate the planets Vector
```

```
057             planets.addElement(new Planet("Mercury",0, false));
058             planets.addElement(new Planet("Venus",0, false));
059             planets.addElement(new Planet("Earth",1, false));
060             planets.addElement(new Planet("Mars",2, false));
061             planets.addElement(new Planet("Jupiter",16, true));
062             planets.addElement(new Planet("Saturn",18, true));
063             planets.addElement(new Planet("Uranus",15, true));
064             planets.addElement(new Planet("Neptune",8, true));
065             planets.addElement(new Planet("Pluto",1, false));
066             return;
067         }
```

Lines 68–75 (listing 16.11) catch other possible exceptions to the operations attempted in lines 48–50.

```
068         catch (IOException e){
069             System.out.println("Exception while Reading");
070             return;
071         }
072         catch (ClassNotFoundException e){
073             System.out.println("ClassNotFoundException while Reading");
074             return;
075         }
```

The `readObject()` method, the most useful method of the ObjectInputStream class, is used to read an object from the stream. This method can be overridden in a serializable class to provide a non-default way of reading the object.

You can use the methods defined by the DataInput interface (covered in Chapter 12, "Networking with Java") to read primitive types from the stream as well. For more information on the methods of the ObjectInputStream class, refer to the following Web page:

`http://java.sun.com/products/JDK/1.1/docs/api/java.io.ObjectInputStream.html`

To read objects from a stream, the objects first must be written. The next section covers this process.

Writing Objects to an ObjectOutputStream

In the `write()` method, lines 80 and 81 (listing 16.11) create an ObjectOutputStream from a FileOutputStream. The FileOutputStream specifies the name of the file to which the object will be written.

```
080                 FileOutputStream   f = new FileOutputStream(filename);
081                 ObjectOutputStream s = new ObjectOutputStream(f);
```

The `writeObject()` call in line 82 (listing 16.11) writes the Vector object to the stream. Because this Vector object references nine Planet objects, and because the Planet objects are serializable, the Planet objects are written to the stream as well. Line 83 closes the stream, writing any buffered information to the file.

```
082                 s.writeObject(planets);
083                 s.close();
```

The `writeObject()` is the most useful method of the ObjectOutputStream class. This method is used to write an object to the stream, and it can be overridden in a serializable class to provide a non-default way of writing the object.

The fields that are not written by `writeObject()` are static and transient fields, as well as references to non-serializable objects.

You can use the methods defined by the DataOutput interface (covered in Chapter 12) to write primitive types to the stream as well. For more information on the methods of the ObjectOutputStream class, refer to the following Web page:

http://java.sun.com/products/JDK/1.1/docs/api/java.io.ObjectOutputStream.html

Now that we have covered reading and writing serializable objects, let's examine the rest of the changes to the application.

Other Changes to the Planets Application

When the PlanetsImpl (listing 16.11) remote server starts up, line 25 in the constructor calls the `read()` method, examined previously.

```
025             read(file);
```

This creates the Vector and the Planet instances, either deserialized from a file or created from scratch, if the file isn't found.

In lines 31 and 36 the `getNumPlanets()` and `getPlanet()` methods are changed to reflect the use of a Vector instead of an array.

```
031             return planets.size();
```

```
036             return (Planet)planets.elementAt(num);
```

Lines 39–43 contain a new method, named `setPlanet()`, which the client calls after incrementing the number of moons in a Planet by clicking the Bump button.

```
039     public void setPlanet(int num, Planet pl) throws RemoteException
040     {
041         planets.setElementAt(pl, num);
042         write(file);
043     }
```

The updated Planet is passed from the client to this remote method, and the Planet object is placed into the Vector at the specified index in line 41. The `write()` method, examined previously, is called in line 42 to save the states of the Vector and Planet objects. Note that in a "real" application, you probably wouldn't want to save an entire file of data each time one portion of it changes.

The `setPlanet()` method must be added to the PlanetsInfo interface as well, because the client must invoke it remotely. This is shown in lines 12 and 13 of listing 16.10.

```
12      void setPlanet(int num, Planet pl)
13              throws java.rmi.RemoteException;
```

In the Planet class (listing 16.12), the `bumpMoons()` method was added to increase the number of moons.

```
public void bumpMoons() {
    moons++;
}
```

In the client applet (listing 16.9), note the portion of code that handles a bumpButton click:

```
        if (evt.getSource() == bumpButton) {
            if (planet != null) {
                planet.bumpMoons();
                try {
                    obj.setPlanet(pnum-1, planet);
                }
                catch (java.rmi.RemoteException e) {
                    System.out.println("Error calling remote method");
                    e.printStackTrace();
                }
                EventQueue.getEventQueue().postEvent(new ActionEvent)
➥infoButton,
                        ActionEvent.ACTION_PERFORMED, null));
            }
        }
```

Line 97 calls the `bumpMoons()` method of the Planet object that was received from the remote object. Line 99 calls the `setPlanet()` method of the remote object, passing the updated Planet object.

To cause the display to reflect the updated number of moons, lines 105 and 106 simulate the user clicking on the Info button. This is achieved by posting an ActionEvent for the infoButton to the EventQueue. The EventQueue is part of the new Delegation Event Model, which was covered in Chapter 14, "The New, Improved AWT: Menus, Events, and More New Features."

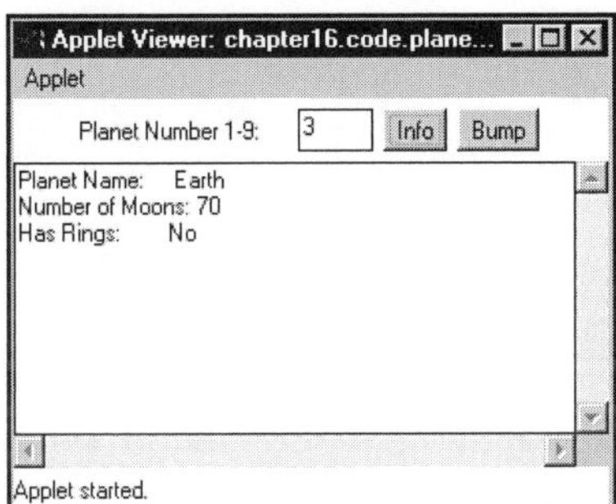

Figure 16.7
PlanetsApplet3 applet display.

Summary

In this chapter, you learned about Java RMI, its architecture, purpose, and design goals. You also learned about Object Serialization, how it enables RMI and object persistence, and how to develop applications that use RMI and Object Serialization.

The next chapter explores JDBC, another technology that enables distributed Java applications.

CHAPTER 17

JDBC

In December 1995, when Java first became a household name, Java public relations materials promised that Java would excel in two areas. The first, Web page enhancement, has been shown not only through animation applets, but also through such useful examples as dynamically updating content. The second area in which Java was prophecied to excel was in database access. Every client-server developer dreams of being able to write once and deploy anywhere (on any architecture running any operating system), and Java was said to fulfill this dream.

The claim of Web page enhancement came to fruition early, but the second claim of database access has only recently begun to appear. Although third-party proprietary solutions exist for Java database access, JavaSoft has adapted the Microsoft ODBC standard in its Java Database Connectivity (JDBC) Application Programming Interface.

This chapter focuses on databases in general, as well as writing Java code to access those databases by using the JDBC. The text first offers a lesson in database 101 and then explores the features of this API, including relevant code examples. In addition, the chapter evaluates alternative (third-party) technologies for database access from Java applications and presents the compelling reasons for the widespread acceptance of JDBC over proprietary solutions.

Database 101

As with any technology, relational database technology carries with it a series of acronyms, special terms, and intimidation. This first section presents an overview of relational database technology, but it is simply an introduction and should not be taken as anything more. The information presented here is sufficient to get you up and running with relational databases, but remember that becoming an expert on relational database technology takes years of work. As an incentive, those experts usually command six-figure salaries, so if you really enjoy what you learn in this section, you might consider becoming an expert on the technology.

Logical Placement of Information

For the most part, database technology involves storing and retrieving information in a logical manner. To start the discussion on database technology, table 17.1 defines a series of terms used when discussing databases.

Table 17.1
Databases 101—Important Terms

Term	Definition
Table	Data in a database is divided into a number of tables, each of which stores related pieces of information. A *table* can be treated as a giant grid of information.
Relations	Data in this category is unique to a given table but identical between two or more tables. A *relation* is used to identify related rows in different tables.
Schema	A *schema* consists of the set of all tables and their relations for a given database.
Row	A *row* contains the series of entries unique for the value of a given variable.
Column	Data is defined within a *column.*
Cell	A unique entry in a table, a *cell* occurs where the column and row meet at one location.

A Real-Life Example

Figure 17.1 illustrates a database schema for a simple student-tracking database. The names in the top half of the boxes indicate names for the tables, the names in the bottom half of the boxes indicate column names, and the lines between boxes indicate the rows that join the tables together; these joining rows are relations.

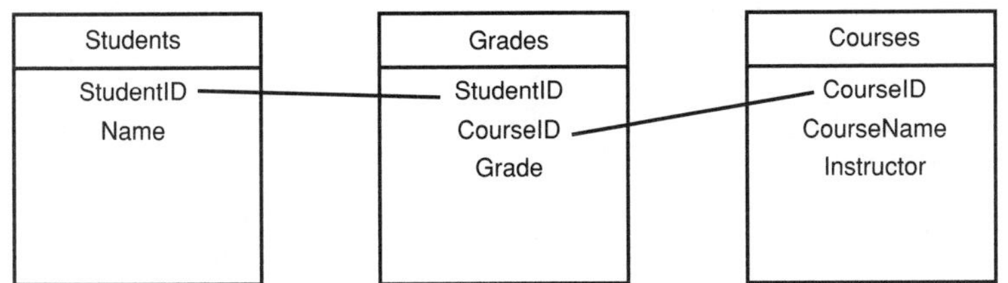

Figure 17.1

A simple database schema.

The following example describes how the tables would be used: If you wanted to find out all students who received an A in course number 00042, you would select, from the Grades tables, all entries in the StudentID column where the "CourseID" column equals 00042 and the Grade column equals A. At this point, you have a set of Student IDs indicating students who received As in course 00042. To find out their names, you would select, from the Students table, all entries in the Name column where the corresponding ID exists in the set of IDs found in the first search.

SQL: The Lingua-Franca of Databases

To perform the searches discussed in the preceding paragraph, use the language called Structured Query Language (SQL, often pronounced sea-quill). For the most part, you can get by with knowing the following five SQL reserved words: SELECT, INSERT, UPDATE, DELETE, and AND. It may seem that language developers often make aspects of their language difficult to use, but with SQL, this is not the case.

You probably can make some very well-educated guesses about the purpose of these reserved words; after you read the five examples below, you will fully understand their use.

SELECT

The SELECT reserved word is used to construct statements that find a specific part of a large data set. With figure 17.1, for example, you could use the SELECT keyword to select all the courses taught by Professor Simmons. The syntax of a SELECT statement follows:

```
SELECT <column name>, <column name>, <column name>,…
FROM <table name>
WHERE <condition>
```

Given this general form, the preceding example SELECT statement would be created as follows:

```
SELECT CourseID, CourseName
FROM Courses
WHERE Instructor = "Simmons"
```

INSERT

The INSERT reserved word is used to create a new row within a table. The syntax of an INSERT statement follows:

```
INSERT <value>, <value>, <value>, …
INTO <table name>
```

Continuing with the example of Professor Simmons, a time may come when the Professor signs up to teach a new class. Assuming that this new class is ID 00756 and has the name "Sweating Off Those Pounds," the following is the correct SQL to add the class to the Courses table:

```
INSERT 00756, "Sweating Off Those Pounds," "Simmons"
INTO Courses
```

Note It is important to note that the values inserted into the table are mapped directly onto the values in the table that gains new values. This means that the first entry in the set of affected values is inserted into the first column of the new row. The second value is inserted directly, of course, into the second column of the new row. This process continues until all values are inserted.

UPDATE

The UPDATE reserved word is used to change one or more values in an existing row. The general syntax of an UPDATE statement follows:

```
UPDATE <table name>
SET <column name> = <new value>
WHERE <condition>
```

To apply this situation to our continuing saga of Professor Simmons, the correct SQL to change the professor of "Sweating Off Those Pounds" from Simmons to Leno is as follows:

```
UPDATE Courses
SET Professor = "Leno"
```

```
WHERE CourseID = 00756
```

Of course, an equally valid alternate form would be the following:

```
UPDATE Courses
SET Professor = "Leno"
WHERE CourseName = "Sweating Off Those Pounds"
```

DELETE

The DELETE reserved word is used to construct statements that delete one or more rows from a given table. The correct syntax follows:

```
DELETE <table name>
WHERE <condition>
```

Let's return to the example of Professor Simmons. Suppose that one day the Professor decides to leave academia to pursue a career producing workout videos. Given this situation, all courses taught by him would have to be removed from the COURSES table. The correct SQL to remove these rows follows:

```
DELETE Courses
WHERE Professor = "Simmons"
```

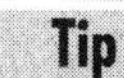

When dealing with this statement, remember that it deletes an entire row. To delete individual cells in a given row, use the UPDATE keyword to change the value of the cell in question to a blank value.

AND

In the above sections on the various SQL reserved words, all operations were performed on a single table. This, however, ignores the fact that relations between tables are maintained. For this reason, the AND reserved word is used to perform operations on two or more tables. Remember that the beginning of this chapter introduced the example of selecting the names of all students who had received an A in the course with ID 00042. By using both the SELECT and AND reserved words, the correct SQL to extract all student names who received an A in the course with ID 00042 follows:

```
SELECT Students.Name
FROM Students, Grades
WHERE Grades.Grade = "A"
AND Students.StudentID = Grades.StudentID
```

The preceding example introduces two new concepts: First, the management of multiple tables. Secondly, the use of multiple conditions in the WHERE clause. Perhaps most noteworthy about this statement is the new notation used when specifying columns. Because column names must only be unique for a table rather than the entire schema, it is necessary to indicate the exact table to which each column belongs. It is for that reason that the notation `<table name>.<column name>` is used.

One final note on the AND reserved word: Some situations exist where this word is used for operations on one table. To select, for example, all courses where the student with ID 00011 received an A, the following SQL is used:

```
SELECT CourseID
FROM Grades
WHERE Grade = "A"
AND StudentID = 00011
```

To expand on this example, use the following SQL to select the names of the courses where the student with ID 00011 received an A:

```
SELECT Courses.CourseName
FROM Courses, Grades
WHERE Grades.Grade = "A"
AND Grades.StudentID = 00011
AND Courses.CourseID = Grades.CourseID
```

Now that we've covered the basics of databases, it's time to relate databases to the topic at hand, JDBC.

Introducing JDBC

As the beginning of this chapter indicated, Java's cross-platform capabilities lead one to realize that some technology for accessing relational databases from a Java application (or applet) is necessary. This technology is the Java Database Connectivity Standard (JDBC).

What is JDBC?

JDBC is intended as a call-level SQL interface that provides Java programmers with a uniform interface to a wide range of relational databases. JDBC is similar in concept to Microsoft's Open Database Connectivity (ODBC) API, which has become the standard for relational database access. Because virtually all database engines offer access using the ODBC standard, and because the JDBC standard enables Java code to perform ODBC calls, it is easy to understand why JDBC is preferred over other non-open propitiatory standards.

What Does JDBC Do?

As you noted when studying SQL at the beginning of this chapter, SQL is an excellent language for managing data when stored in a series of tables. The primary function of JDBC is managing data stored in tables. To fulfill this function, JDBC defines Java classes to represent such elements as database connections, SQL statements, result sets, and metadata. These classes and interfaces are written in Java, so they provide a natural interaction with relational databases.

JDBC Release Information

The JDBC 1.1 version is currently available. This version, included in JDK 1.1 (Java Development Kit), can be downloaded as a compressed .tar file or a .zip file from the following Web page:

```
http://splash.javasoft.com/jdbc/index.html
```

Although this site includes the .java and the .html files for the API, it does not include any database drivers. A database driver acts as a middleman between your executing Java code and the relational database. For JBDC to work properly, the relational database being used must either provide a native implementation of JDBC or there must be a driver available for that database in question. The topic of database drivers is elaborated on later in this chapter. The JDBC 1.1 specification is available from the JavaSoft site as a postscript or acrobat file.

Examining the Application Programming Interface of JDBC

Instead of using methods that take many parameters to control a wide range of behavior, the Java core classes have been designed to use different methods to perform different tasks. The JDBC API maintains this pattern.

Components

Figure 17.2 illustrates the key components of the API. The drivers shown in the figure are examples of driver names.

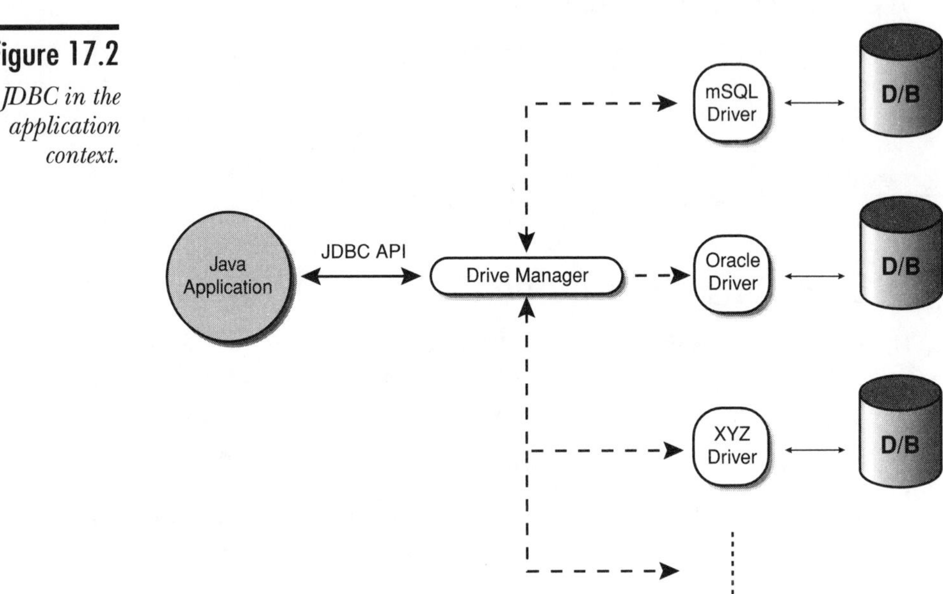

Figure 17.2
JDBC in the application context.

This list summarizes the key components that the following sections discuss:

- Driver Manager
- Drivers
- Native-API Partly Java Drivers
- Net-Protocol All-Java Drivers
- Native-Protocol All-Java Drivers
- JDBC-ODBC Bridge

Driver Manager

Where drivers provide the interface between the application and the vendor-specific DBMS, the Driver Manager controls the interaction between the application and the driver being used. It can support multiple drivers connecting to different Database

Management Systems (DBMSs). In addition, the Driver Manager loads the requested driver and provides support for the managing database connections.

JDBC Drivers

Many vendors currently offer JDBC drivers. The following Web site contains a list of these vendors:

```
http://splash.javasoft.com/jdbc/jdbc.drivers.html
```

Drivers can be written in Java so that they can be downloaded along with an applet. Drivers also can be implemented by using native methods to connect to database access libraries. JavaSoft requires that a driver support at least ANSI SQL-92 Entry Level functionality to pass the JDBC compliance tests.

In general, the drivers should provide implementations of the abstract classes specified in the JDBC API. Each database driver should provide a class that implements the java.sql.Driver interface. This interface is used by the java.sql.DriverManager class to locate a driver for a particular database URL. In addition, each driver must provide implementations of the following interfaces:

- java.sql.Connection
- java.sql.Statement
- java.sql.PreparedStatement
- java.sql.CallableStatement
- java.sql.ResultSet

Drivers can be classified as indicated in the following sections.

Native-API Partly Java Drivers

This type of driver maps JDBC calls to calls on the client-API for Oracle, Sybase, Informix, DB2, or other DBMSs. This driver also requires some binary code to be loaded on each client machine. Among its uses, the driver can be utilized when corporations want to develop Java applications and at the same time leverage their existing investment in DBMSs that do not have ODBC drivers. Because the driver maps the JDBC calls to client-API calls, the Java application does not need to contain native DBMS access code.

Net-Protocol All-Java Drivers

This type of driver is considered to be the most flexible type. It translates JDBC calls to a DBMS-independent net protocol, which then can be translated to a vendor-specific DBMS protocol by a server. The key component in this setup is a piece of middleware that sits between the client and the server. Due to the restriction that Java applets cannot connect back to a host other than the one which served the applet itself, this setup becomes a perfect solution. The middleware can sit at the server, and communicate between the applet and the DBMS.

Native-Protocol All-Java Driver

This driver type translates JDBC calls to the network protocol used by the vendor-specific DBMSs. DBMS vendors serve as the source for these drivers because many of the protocols used in this scenario are proprietary. Using these drivers is a feasible solution for intranet access because they enable a direct call from the client machine to the DBMS server.

The JDBC-ODBC Bridge

The Open Database Connectivity (ODBC) interface is Microsoft's solution for a DBMS-independent database access. ODBC, however, is not appropriate for direct use from Java applications because it is a C interface. Calls from Java programs to native C code involve certain drawbacks that would impact the security, implementation, robustness, and automatic portability of these applications. Some ODBC binary code and, in some cases, database client code must be loaded on each client machine that uses this driver. As a result, this driver works well on a corporate network or in a three-tiered architecture where application server code is written in Java.

JDBC is based on the X/Open SQL Call Level Interface, which is also the basis for ODBC. Due to the similarities of the two specifications, the JDBC-ODBC bridge is quite small and efficient. The bridge, a joint development of JavaSoft and Intersolv, translates JDBC calls to those that can be understood by ODBC clients at a C language level.

The JDBC-ODBC bridge provides backward compatibility to a wide range of databases that have released ODBC drivers, but do not have released JDBC drivers. Because ODBC drivers have been out for years and are available for virtually any system, chances are there is an ODBC driver for any system with which you may come into contact. The fact, however, that JDBC is so new means that this is not the case for JDBC. JDBC has been designed to be efficiently implemented on ODBC, so the bridge offers a way to use ODBC from Java. The bridge package, sun.jdbc.odbc, is available for the Solaris and NT/Win95 platforms and can be downloaded from the following Web page:

```
http://splash.javasoft.com/jdbc/index.html
```

The JDBC Driver Test Suite

JavaSoft and Intersolv have jointly developed a JDBC driver test suite that nicely profiles the capabilities of a JDBC driver. This test suite is an attempt to ensure the portability of applications across different JDBC drivers. As of now, it is not intended as a driver certification.

The JDBC Test Harness and the JDBC Test Suite are available for download at the following Web page:

```
http://splash.javasoft.com/jdbc/index.html
```

Both are needed to test a JDBC driver.

Interfaces and Classes

The JDBC API contains a collection of interfaces that enable the primary functions of opening and managing connections to particular DBMSs, executing SQL statements, and processing the results. The JDBC API also adds functionality in the form of cursors, transaction management, dynamic database access, and metadata. Three exception handling classes, which are essential to any robust application, are also provided. The java.sql package contains the following interfaces:

- Driver
- Connection
- Statement
- CallableStatement
- PreparedStatement
- ResultSet
- DatabaseMetaData
- ResultSetMetaData

The java.sql package contains the following classes:

- DriverManager
- DriverPropertyInfo
- Date

- Time
- Timestamp
- Types

The following are the exception classes:

- DataTruncation
- SQLException
- SQLWarning

Figure 17.3 illustrates the interaction between the commonly used interfaces and classes.

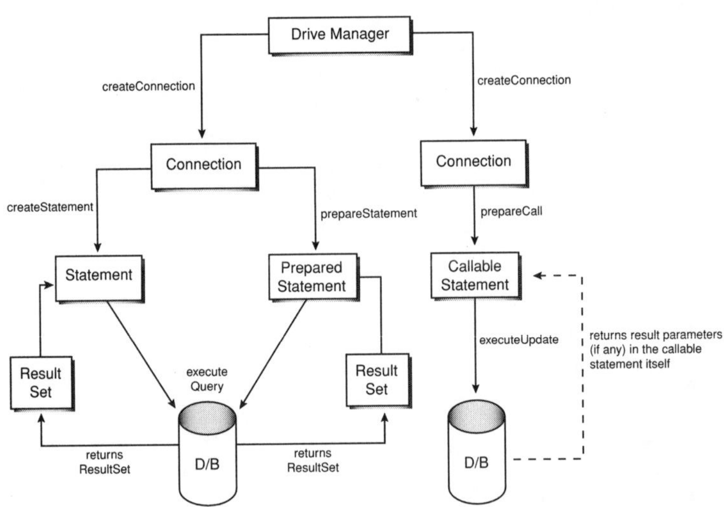

Figure 17.3
Interaction between interfaces and classes.

The following sections describe the interfaces and classes and explain their commonly used methods and data members. Although a complete listing of all the data members and methods is beyond the scope of this chapter, the sections detail the most important ones.

To obtain a complete listing of all data members and methods, refer to the following Web page:

```
http://www.javasoft.com/products/JDK/1.1/docs/api/Package-java.sql.html
```

The java.sql.Driver Interface

As with all Java interfaces and classes, the Driver interface extends the Object class. Each driver should provide a class that implements the Driver interface. When a Driver class is loaded, it should create an instance of itself and register with the Driver Manager. The following section discusses some commonly used methods of the Driver interface.

The acceptsURL() Method

This method returns true if the driver is capable of opening a connection to an URL (passed as a parameter). The method accepts the URL of the connecting database.

The connect() Method

This method attempts to make a database connection to a URL object (passed as a parameter). An additional parameter, a Properties object, can be used to pass a list of name-value pairs as connection arguments. Usually, the username and password are passed in the Properties parameter.

The driver returns null if it realizes that it cannot connect to the given URL. If the connection is successful, the driver returns a Connection object that represents a connection to the URL. Finally, the driver raises a SQLException if it has trouble connecting to the database.

The getPropertyInfo() Method

With this method, a user interface tool can obtain a list of properties that are needed from the user to connect to a database. Depending on what the user has supplied so far, more than one call to this method might be necessary.

This method accepts the URL of the connecting database, as well as a Properties object as a parameter that indicates the proposed information to be sent while opening a connection.

The method returns an array (possibly an empty one) of DriverPropertyInfo objects that describes the potential properties to be supplied by the user. The method also can throw a SQLException if it has trouble connecting to the database.

The jdbcCompliant() Method

This method ascertains whether the driver is a JDBC COMPLIANT(TM) driver. A driver returns a true value only if it passes the JDBC Compliance tests. To be JDBC COMPLIANT(TM), a driver must provide full support for the JDBC API and SQL 92 Entry Level.

The java.sql.Connection Interface

The public interface Connection extends the Object class. A Connection represents a data access and manipulation session with a particular database. Within this session, SQL statements can be executed, returning result sets. The following sections describe some widely used methods.

The close() Method

Certain situations may warrant an immediate release of the Connection's database resource and JDBC resources instead of waiting for them to be automatically released. The `close()` method provides these functions. Errors occurring during the execution of this method throw a SQLException.

The commit() Method

By default, changes are automatically committed after each statement is executed. In case the auto-commit feature has been disabled, explicitly call `commit()` to save the changes to the database to ensure that they won't be lost. This method also releases any database locks currently held by the Connection; it throws a SQLException in case of an error.

The rollback() Method

This method discards all the changes made since the last `commit()` or `rollback()` call. It also releases any database locks held by the Connection.

The createStatement() Method

This method returns a new Statement object that can be used to execute SQL statements without parameters. This method throws a SQLException in case of an error.

The prepareStatement() Method

This method returns a new PreparedStatement object containing the precompiled statement passed as a parameter. This object can be used to repeatedly execute the precompiled statement. This method accepts a SQL statement. This method throws a SQLException in case of an error.

The prepareCall() Method

This method returns a new CallableStatement object containing the precompiled SQL statement, the `prepareCall()` method accepts as a parameter a String object containing a SQL statement. This method throws a SQLException in case of an error.

The setAutoCommit() Method

This method, accepts a Boolean parameter and enables an application to specify whether its SQL statements should be automatically committed or grouped into transactions that are terminated by a `commit()`or `rollback()` call. The auto-commit mode is the default for new connections.

The java.sql.Statement Interface

The Statement interface extends the Object class. Classes that implement the Statement interface execute SQL statements that are static by nature and obtain results following their execution. Results are in the form of ResultSet objects; however, there can be only one ResultSet object open for each Statement object at any time. This means that if multiple ResultSets are required by the application, each must be generated by a corresponding Statement object.

The following sections discuss the most widely used methods of this interface.

The close() Method

This method can be used when it is necessary to release a Statement's database resource and other JDBC resources immediately, instead of waiting for the Statement to be automatically closed. The `close()` method throws a SQL Exception if an error occurs.

The execute() Method

This method executes a SQL statement—passed to it as a parameter—that can return multiple results. The return value, either a Boolean true or false, indicates the form of the first result. If the return value is true, the next result is a ResultSet. A return value of false indicates either that no more results exist or that the next result is an update count. You then can use the `getResultSet()`, `getMoreResults()`, or `getUpdateCount()` methods to retrieve any subsequent results. A SQL Exception is thrown in case of an error.

The executeQuery() Method

This method executes a SQL statement (passed as a parameter) that returns a single ResultSet object. A SQL Exception is thrown in case of an error.

The executeUpdate() Method

This method executes SQL UPDATE, DELETE, or INSERT statements. A SQL statement is passed as a parameter, and a row count is returned for these statements.

Such SQL statements as SQL DDL statements, which do not return anything, also can be executed. These statements return a value of 0. In case of an error, a SQL Exception is thrown.

The getResultSet() Method

This method returns the result of the current statement, in the form of a ResultSet object. This method should be called only once for each result. A SQL Exception is thrown in case of an error.

The getMoreResults() Method

This method moves to the next result of a Statement object. A value of true is returned if the next result of the Statement is a ResultSet. If the next result is an update count, or if no more results exist, a value of false is returned.

The java.sql.PreparedStatement Interface

The interface PreparedStatement extends the Statement interface. Because SQL statements require compilation by the DBMS, it is a good idea to precompile, and store in a PreparedStatement object any statements that are going to be used more than once. The object can be used many times to execute the statement efficiently. The following sections describe some of the most widely used methods of this interface.

The clearParameters() Method

In general, parameter values persist during repeated executions of the SQL stored in a Statement object. Setting a parameter's value clears its previous value automatically. To immediately release the resources used by current parameter values, however, use the `clearParameters()` method. This method throws a SQL Exception in case of an error.

The setXXX() Methods

The `setXXX()` methods that are used for setting the IN parameter values must specify types compatible with the defined SQL type of the input parameter. The `setInt()` method, for example, should be used if the SQL type of the IN parameter is Integer. *XXX* stands for the various data types that are supported.

The java.sql.CallableStatement Interface

The public interface CallableStatement extends the PreparedStatement interface. This interface provides the functions that execute SQL-stored procedures.

A CallableStatement can return one or multiple ResultSets. JDBC provides a SQL escape for stored procedures; this enables a uniform call to all relational DBMSs. The escape syntax contains two forms, one of which includes a result parameter. The result parameter must be registered as an OUT parameter when it is used. The other parameters can be used for input, output, or both.

Parameters are referred to by number in a sequential manner, beginning with 1.

The set methods inherited from PreparedStatement are used to set the IN parameter values. All OUT parameter types must be registered before the execution of the stored procedure. The following sections describe the most commonly used methods of the CallableStatement interface.

The getXXX() Methods

The `getXXX()` methods are used to obtain the values of the OUT parameters after execution of the stored procedure.

The registerOutParameter() Method

This method must be called before executing a stored procedure call to register the java.sql.Type of each OUT parameter. The parameterIndex parameter indicates the number of the parameter. A value of 1, for example, indicates the first parameter is being referenced, while a value of 2 indicates the second parameter. The sqlType parameter is a SQL-type code defined by java.sql.Types. This method throws a SQL Exception in case of an error.

Note When reading the value of an OUT parameter, you must use the `getXXX()` method whose Java type *XXX* corresponds to the parameter's registered SQL type.

The registerOutParameter() Method

This version of the registerOutParameter method is used for registering Numeric or Decimal OUT parameters. The first two parameters are the same as in the previous version of the method. A third parameter (an int) represents the number of digits to the right of the decimal point. Its value should be greater than or equal to zero. This method throws a SQL Exception in case of an error.

The wasNull() Method

An OUT parameter can have the value of SQL NULL. The `wasNull()` method returns true if the last value read was SQL NULL. This method throws a SQL Exception in case of an error.

Note You must first call `getXXX()` on a parameter to read its value and then call `wasNull()` to determine if the value was SQL NULL.

The java.sql.ResultSet Interface

The public interface ResultSet extends the Object class. The table of data that is generated by the execution of a Statement can be accessed through a ResultSet object.

The ResultSet object maintains a cursor that points to its current row of data. Initially, the cursor points to a location before the first row. Then, the table rows can be retrieved in sequence by using the "next" method.

The `getXXX()` methods retrieve the values in the columns of a particular row. Within a row, the values of the columns, which are numbered sequentially beginning from 1, can be randomly accessed—either by column index numbers, or column names. The JDBC driver attempts to convert the data to the specified Java type; the driver then returns a suitable Java value for the `getXXX()` methods.

When a Statement object is re-executed or used to retrieve the next result from a sequence of results, the current ResultSet is automatically closed. This also happens when the Statement that generated the ResultSet is closed.

The following sections describe the ResultSet interface's most widely used methods.

The getMetaData() Method

The ResultSetMetaData object, returned by the `getMetaData()` method, provides the number, types, and properties of a ResultSet's columns. The `getMetaData()` method throws a SQL Exception in case an error occurs.

The close() Method

This method is used when the application wants to release a ResultSet's database resource and JDBC resources immediately instead of waiting for the ResultSet to close by itself. This method throws a SQL Exception to indicate an error condition.

The next() Method

A ResultSet is initially positioned before its first row. To access the rows of the ResultSet, successive calls must be made to the `next()` method. The first call to `next()`, for example, makes the first row of the ResultSet the current row. This method throws a SQL Exception in case of an error.

The `next()` method returns true if the new, current row is a valid row. The method returns false if no more rows exist. This functionality is achieved by using a cursor.

Working with a Cursor

The idea of a cursor should be familiar to most programmers who have worked with a database. A *cursor* can be thought of as a pointer or iterator pointing to or indexing into a set of tuples. A *tuple* is a record in a database table that has values for the fields in the table. In the JDBC API, a cursor is an iterator indexing into a ResultSet.

Cursors are very useful when dealing with multitupled ResultSets because cursors can extract information from each row in the ResultSet. When a ResultSet is first created, the cursor points to the first row of data, which is referred to as the current row. The `next()` method of the ResultSet interface then iterates through the ResultSet and advances the position of the cursor to the next row of data.

The current version of JDBC provides only rudimentary support for cursors. To obtain the name of the cursor, use the `ResultSet.getCursorName()` method, which returns the name as a String object. The row of a ResultSet object currently identified by a cursor can be updated or deleted by a positioned update or delete that uses the name of the cursor.

Tip Not all commercially available DBMSs support positioned updates and deletes. Instead, the programmer must use the `DatabaseMetaData.supportsPositionedUpdate()` and `DatabaseMetaData.supportsPositionedDelete()` methods to confirm that the underlying DBMS does, in fact, support them. The Oracle DBMS, for example, supports positioned updates and deletes.

Developers who have worked with ODBC-style cursors should be aware that JDBC does not support scrollable cursors or enable the placement of bookmarks. The "Querying the Database" section of the example scenario discussed later in this chapter illustrates proper cursor use.

The java.sql.ResultSetMetaData Interface

The public interface ResultSetMetaData extends the Object class.

The java.sql.DatabaseMetaData Interface

The public interface DatabaseMetaData extends the Object class.

The java.sql.DriverManager Class

The DriverManager class extends the Object class. This class controls the interface between the application and a set of JDBC drivers. The DriverManager class also provides a set of services for managing the drivers.

During its initialization, the DriverManager class tries to load the driver classes that are referenced in the "jdbc.drivers" system property. If this property exists, it should have a colon-separated list of driver names. The DriverManager class attempts to load each named Driver class. By modifying this property, a user can choose the JDBC drivers to be used by his application. A program also can load JDBC drivers at runtime. A Driver class, for example, can be explicitly loaded by using the standard `Class.forName()` method. To load the imaginary.sql.iMsqldriver class, use the following line of code:

```
Class.forName("imaginary.sql.iMsqlDriver");
```

The following sections describe the methods of the DriverManager class.

The getConnection() Method

The `getConnection()` method attempts to establish a connection to the specified database URL. If the method is successful, it returns a Connection object, which represents the connection to the database URL. If an error occurs, a SQL Exception is thrown.

The method has three different forms:

- `Connection getConnection(String DatabaseURL)`: This causes the DriverManager class to try to select an appropriate JDBC driver from the drivers that are registered.

- `Connection getConnection(String DatabaseURL, Properties Props)`: This form accepts a Properties type parameter, which specifies a list of string name-value pairs. Usually, a user and password property should be included.

- `Connection getConnection(String DatabaseURL, String UserName, String UserPassword)`: With this form, the username and password are explicitly passed as parameters instead of being included in a Properties object.

The registerDriver() Method

To register itself with the DriverManager, a newly loaded Driver class should call this method. In the case of an error, a SQL Exception is thrown.

The getDriver() Method

This method causes the DriverManager object to attempt to load a driver that understands a particular database URL. If such a driver is present and is registered, the method returns a Driver object. This Driver object represents a JDBC driver that can connect to the database URL. This method throws a SQL Exception if an error occurs.

The getDrivers() Method

To obtain a list of JDBC drivers that the current caller can access, use the `getDrivers()` method. This method returns an Enumeration object containing all the currently loaded JDBC drivers that are accessible to the caller.

The deregisterDriver() Method

The DriverManager class also can deregister drivers from the list of registered drivers. This method drops the driver from the DriverManager's list. Applets, however, can deregister only drivers from their own class loader. In the event of an error, this method throws a SQL Exception.

The java.sql.DriverPropertyInfo Class

The DriverPropertyInfo class, which extends the Object class, is primarily of interest to advanced programmers who require or want to explore various connection properties. This class enables an interaction with a driver and provides properties for connections.

The constructor of this class accepts the name of the property (as a String) and the current value of the property (as a String). The current value of the property may be null. The following list describes the variables for the DriverPropertyInfo class:

- ***choices:*** This array contains the possible values for a property, if the value can be selected from a set of values.
- ***description:*** This variable provides a brief description of the property; it can have a null value.
- ***name:*** This variable supplies the name of the property.
- ***required:*** If this variable is set to true, a value must be supplied for the property during `Driver.connect()`. Otherwise, the property is optional.
- ***value:*** This variable indicates the current value of the property. This value depends on a combination of the information supplied to `getPropertyInfo()`, the Java environment, and driver-supplied default values. If no value is known, it can be null.

The java.sql.Date Class

This class is essentially an extension of the java.util.Date class. Functions have been added to enable JDBC to identify this class as a SQL DATE value. The class contains formatting and parsing operations to support the JDBC escape syntax for date values.

The documentation provided by JavaSoft recommends against the use of the full facilities of the underlying java.util.Date class. The `setHours()` method, for example, would give a java.sql.Date value that would not compare properly with other SQL Date values, because a SQL Date consists of just a day, a month, and a year. The following sections describe the methods and constructors of the java.sql.Date class.

Constructors for the java.sql.Date Class

The constructor for this class has the following two forms:

- `Date(int year, int month, int day)`: This constructs a date from the supplied parameters.
- `Date(long datevalue)`: This constructs a date by using a time value in milliseconds.

Methods of the java.sql.Date Class

The java.sql.Date class has the following methods:

- `String toString()`: This method returns a String in the "yyyy-mm-dd" format.
- `Date valueOf(String datestring)`: This method accepts a String in the form "yyyy-mm-dd" and returns a corresponding Date object.

The java.sql.Time Class

This class adds to the functionality provided by the java.util.Date class, enabling JDBC to identify it as a SQL TIME value. Formatting and parsing operations have been added to support the JDBC escape syntax for time values.

Once again, the JavaSoft documentation recommends against the use of the full facilities of the underlying java.util.Date class. The `setMonth()` method, for example, obtains a java.sql.Time value that would not compare properly with other Time values. The following sections describe the constructors and methods of the java.sql.Time class.

Constructors for the java.sql.Time Class

The java.sql.Time Class constructor has the following two forms:

- `Time (int hour, int minute, int second)`: This constructs a Time object from the specified parameters.
- `Time (long timevalue)`: This constructs a Time object by using the timevalue, provided in milliseconds.

Methods of the java.sql.Time Class

The java.sql.Time class has two methods:

- `Time valueOf (String timevalue)`: This method accepts a String in JDBC time-escape format "hh:mm:ss" and then converts it to a Time object.
- `String toString()`: This method returns a String in "hh:mm:ss" format.

The java.sql.Timestamp Class

This class is an extension of the java.util.Date class. Modifications enable JDBC to identify this as a SQL TIMESTAMP value. With its new capabilities, this class now can hold the SQL TIMESTAMP nanos value and perform formatting and parsing operations that support the JDBC escape syntax for timestamp values.

This class is actually a combination of a java.util.Date and a separate nanos value. The *nanos,* which are fractional seconds, are separate from the integral seconds, which are stored in the java.util.Date component. To obtain a time value that includes the fractional seconds, convert the nanos to milliseconds and add this value to the value returned by the `getTime()` method.

Constructors for the java.sql.Timestamp Class

The constructor for the java.sql.Timestamp class has the following two forms:

- `Timestamp(int year, int month, int date, int hour, int minute, int second, int nanosecond)`: This constructs a Timestamp object by using the values supplied as parameters.
- `Timestamp(long timevalue)`: This constructs a Timestamp by using a time value in milliseconds.

Methods of the java.sql.Timestamp Class

The java.sql.Timestamp class has the following methods:

- `Timestamp valueOf(String timeStampStr)`: Accepts a String in the timestamp format "yyyy-mm-dd hh:mm:ss.fffffffff" and returns a corresponding Timestamp object.
- `String toString()`: Returns a String in the "yyyy-mm-dd hh:mm:ss.fffffffff" format.
- `int getNanos()`: Returns the Timestamp's fractional seconds part.
- `void SetNanos(int nanovalue)`: Sets the Timestamp's nanos value.
- `boolean equals(Timestamp ts)`: Tests Timestamp values for equality. This method compares the current Timestamp with the supplied Timestamp value. It returns true if the values are equal, or false if they are not.
- `boolean before(Timestamp ts)`: Determines if the current Timestamp object is earlier than another Timestamp value. This method accepts the Timestamp value, ts, to compare with the current Timestamp object. It returns true if the current Timestamp object's value is before ts; otherwise, false is returned.
- `boolean after(Timestamp ts)`: Determines if the current Timestamp object is later than another Timestamp value. This method accepts the Timestamp value, ts, to compare with the current Timestamp object. It returns true if the current Timestamp object's value is after ts.

The java.sql.Types Class

The Types class extends the java.lang.Object class and defines constants used to identify SQL types. The actual type constant values are equivalent to those in XOPEN.

The section "Mapping SQL Data Types to Java Data Types," which occurs later in this chapter, presents a detailed mapping of SQL types to Java types.

The java.sql.DataTruncation Class

The DataTruncation class extends the java.sql.SQLWarning class. When JDBC truncates a data value unexpectedly, it either reports a DataTruncation warning for a read process or throws a DataTruncation exception for a write process.

The SQL state for a DataTruncation is "01004."

The following sections describe the constructor and methods for the java.sql.DataTruncation class.

Constructor for the java.sql.DataTruncation

This constructor has the following form:

```
DataTruncation( int index, boolean param_truncated, boolean read_truncated, int
dataSize, int dataTransferredSize)
```

The index parameter is the index of the column or parameter value. The param_truncated parameter is true if a parameter value was truncated. If the truncation occurred for a read process, the read_truncated value is true. The dataSize variable indicates the original size of the data. The size of the data after truncation is indicated by dataTransferredSize.

Methods of the java.sql.DataTruncation Class

The java.sql.DataTruncation class has the following methods:

- `int getIndex()`: Returns the index of the column or parameter that was truncated. The return value is –1 if the column or parameter index is unknown. In this case, the parameter and read fields of the DataTruncation object should be ignored.
- `boolean getParameter()`: Returns true if the truncated value was a parameter; if a column value was truncated, false is returned.
- `boolean getRead()`: Returns true if the value was truncated when read from the database. This method returns false if the data was truncated during a write.
- `int getDataSize()`: Returns the number of bytes that should have been transferred. The value is –1 if the size is unknown. If data conversions were being performed, the number returned can be an approximation.
- `int getTransferSize()`: Returns the number of bytes that were actually transferred. If the size is unknown, the return value is –1.

The java.sql.SQLException Class

The java.sql.SQLException class extends the java.lang.Exception class. The SQLException class provides information about a database access error.

Each SQLException class provides the following kinds of information:

- A string that describes the error. This string, which is used as the JavaException message, is available via the `getMessage()` method.

- A vendor-specific integer error code. This is usually the actual error code that is returned by the database being accessed.

- A SQLState string that is in accordance with the XOPEN SQLState conventions. The acceptable values of this string are described in the XOPEN SQL specification.

- A chain to the next Exception. This chain can be used to obtain more information about the error.

The following sections describe the constructors and methods for the java.sql.SQLException class.

Constructors for the java.sql.SQLException Class

The constructors of this class follow:

- `SQLException()`: This constructs a SQLException object. The reason and SQLState attributes of the object default to null, and the vendorCode attribute defaults to zero.

- `SQLException(String reasonForException)`: This constructs a SQLException with a reason. The SQLState attribute, however, defaults to null, and the vendorCode attribute defaults to zero.

- `SQLException(String reasonForException)`: This constructs a SQLException with a reason and a SQLState. The reasonForException attribute describes the exception, and the SQLState attribute is an XOPEN code for the exception. The vendorCode attribute, however, is set to zero.

- `SQLException(String reasonForException, String SQLState, int vendorCode)`: This constructs a fully specified SQLException.

Methods of the java.sql.SQLException Class

The java.sql.SQLException class consists of the following methods:

- `int getErrorCode()`: This returns the vendor-specific exception code.

- `String getSQLState()`: This returns the SQLState, defined in the XOPEN specification.

- `SQLException getNextException()`: This method is used to obtain the next exception that is chained to the current exception.

- `void setNextException(SQLException nextSQLException)`: This adds a SQLException to the end of the chain.

The java.sql.SQLWarning Class

The java.sql.SQLWarning class extends the java.sql.SQLException class. The SQLWarning class provides information about a database access warning. When a method of an object causes a warning to be reported, the warning is chained to that object. The following sections describe the constructors and methods for the java.sql.SQLWarning class.

Constructors for the java.sql.SQLWarning Class

The constructors for this class have the following forms:

- `SQLWarning()`: This constructs a SQLWarning with the reason and SQLState attributes set to null; the vendorCode attribute is set to zero.
- `SQLWarning (String reasonForWarning)`: This constructs a SQLWarning with a reason. The SQLState attribute, however, defaults to null, and the vendorCode attribute defaults to zero.
- `SQLWarning(String reasonForWarning, String SQLState)`: This constructs a SQLWarning with values for the reason and SQLState attributes. The vendorCode attribute defaults to zero.
- `SQLWarning(String reasonForWarning, String SQLState, int vendorCode)`: This constructs a SQLWarning object with a reason that describes the warning, a SQLState that is an XOPEN code identifying the warning, and a vendorCode that is a vendor-specific warning code.

Methods of the java.sql.SQLWarning Class

The java.sql.SQLWarning class consists of the following methods:

- `SQLWarning getNextWarning()`: This returns the SQLWarning object chained to the current SQLWarning object.
- `void setNextWarning(SQLWarning nextwarning)`: This adds a SQLWarning object to the end of the chain.

Because both SQL and Java have an existing data type structure, it is necessary to have an agreed mapping between the two. This next section discusses the mapping of SQL data types to Java data types.

Mapping SQL Data Types to Java Data Types

Before assigning data that is retrieved from a database to application variables, be sure that it is assigned to compatible types. Also, to store and retrieve parameters and recover results returned after the execution of SQL statements, make sure that enough type information is available to the program.

A mapping of SQL data types to Java data types makes this conversion clear. Table 17.2 illustrates the default Java mapping for common SQL data types.

Table 17.2
Common SQL Data Types

SQL Type	Java Type
TINYINT	byte
SMALLINT	short
INTEGER	int
BIGINT	long
REAL	float
FLOAT, DOUBLE	double
NUMERIC, DECIMAL	java.lang.Bignum
BIT	boolean
BINARY, VARBINARY, LONGVARBINARY	byte[]
CHAR, VARCHAR, LONGVARCHAR	String
DATE	java.sql.Date
TIME	java.sql.Time
TIMESTAMP	java.sql.Timestamp

The documentation provided by JavaSoft mentions that the Java data type does not require exactly the same form as the SQL data type. Java, for instance, does not have any fixed length arrays, so variable-length Java arrays can be used to represent both fixed and variable-length SQL arrays.

Also, Java strings have been used, although they do not match any of the SQL CHAR types exactly.

The following list details some of these mappings:

- TINYINT↔byte. Represents an 8-bit value, so that it can be mapped to Java's byte type.
- SMALLINT↔short. Represents a 16-bit value, so that it can be mapped to Java's short type.
- INTEGER↔int. Represents a 32-bit value, so that it can be mapped to Java's int type.
- BIGINT↔long. Represents a 64-bit value, so that it can be mapped to Java's long type.
- REAL↔float. Must support 7 digits of mantissa precision, so that it can be mapped to the float type in Java.
- FLOAT↔double. Must support 15 digits of mantissa precision.
- DOUBLE↔double. Must support 15 digits of mantissa precision.
- NUMERIC↔java.lang.Bignum. Represents fixed point numbers when absolute precision is required. This type is often used for currency values.
- DECIMAL↔java.lang.Bignum. Represents fixed point numbers when absolute precision is required. This type is often used for currency values.

Note Both the NUMERIC and DECIMAL SQL data types are mapped to java.lang.Bignum extended precision number type, which is provided in JDK 1.1. Moreover, simple strings and arrays of characters can be used to access DECIMAL and NUMERIC values. In this way, Java programmers can use `getString()` to retrieve a NUMERIC or DECIMAL result.

- BIT↔boolean. Maps directly to the boolean type in Java. It can be used to indicate a 0 or 1 value.
- BINARY↔byte[]. Can be expressed as a byte array in Java. Java programmers do not need to distinguish between the three SQL byte arrays: BINARY, VARBINARY, and LONGVARBINARY.
- VARBINARY↔byte[]. Can be expressed as a byte array in Java.

- LONGVARBINARY↔byte[]: Can be expressed as a byte array in Java. The LONGVARBINARY SQL type can be used to return multimegabyte data values, so that it can be retrieved as a Java input stream. Programmers then can read data from the stream in the chunk size that they prefer.
- CHAR↔String. Can be expressed as a String type in Java. Java programmers do not need to distinguish between the CHAR, VARCHAR, and LONGVARCHAR SQL data types because they can be expressed identically in Java.
- VARCHAR↔String. Can be expressed as a String type in Java.
- LONGVARCHAR↔String. Can be expressed as a String type in Java. The LONGVARCHAR SQL type can be used to store multimegabyte strings. By retrieving a LONGVARCHAR value as a Java input stream, programmers can retrieve the value in chunks. Java streams can be used for Unicode, as well as ASCII data.
- DATE↔java.sql.Date. Consists of a day, month, and year. For SQL DATE information, java.sql.Date can be used. The hour, minute, second, and millisecond fields of the base class java.util.Date are set to zero.
- TIME↔java.sql.Time. Consists of hours, minutes, and seconds. For SQL TIME information, java.sql.Time can be used. The year, month, and day fields of the base class java.util.Date are set to 1970, January, and 1, respectively. This signifies the "zero" date in the Java epoch.
- TIMESTAMP↔java.sql.Timestamp. Consists of both DATE and TIME, as well as a nanosecond field. For SQL TIMESTAMP information, you can use java.sql.Timestamp, which also has a nanosecond field.

This section discusses the mapping of results and parameters whose types are known at compilation time. Some applications may not have knowledge of the database schema that they access at the time they are compiled, so JDBC provides support for complete dynamically typed data access.

Exploring JDBC Metadata Capabilities

Metadata is information about both the data in the database and the database itself. This information is invaluable when determining the nature of the data and the capabilities of the database. The initial design of JDBC used complex methods in core JDBC classes to implement metadata features. This approach was, however, discarded and replaced by two additional interfaces in JDBC release 1.10, and carried forward into the current JDK 1.1 release. JDBC provides database application programmers with two interfaces that provide a wide range of metadata functions. These interfaces are java.sql.DatabaseMetaData and java.sql.ResultSetMetaData.

The DatabaseMetaData Interface

DatabaseMetaData provides metadata about the database itself. The methods of this interface generally return their results in java.sql.ResultSet objects. Because this section discusses only a few of the most commonly used features of Database MetaData, you can refer to the JavaSoft Web site at the following Web page for a complete reference document:

```
http://splash.javasoft.com/jdbc/html-0110/java.sql.DatabaseMetaData.html#_top
```

The following are some of the most commonly used methods in the DatabaseMetaData interface:

- `URL getURL()`: Obtains the Uniform Resource Locator (URL) of the database. The URL is returned as a Java String object, if it can be determined. A SQLException is thrown if the URL cannot be determined.
- `String getUserName()`: Returns the username that is known to the database as a Java String object. The method throws a SQLException if the username cannot be determined.
- `int getMaxConnections()`: Provides the maximum number of active connections that the database can support. An integer representing the maximum number of connections is returned.
- `ResultSet getTables(String CatalogName, String SchemeNamePattern, String TableNamePattern, String TableTypes)`: Searches for tables matching the TableNamePattern and the specified TableTypes (for example, Table, System Table, View, and so on) in the catalog (specified by CatalogName). This method also searches for all the schema matching SchemaNamePattern. It returns a ResultSet containing the descriptions of all the tables matching the above-mentioned criteria. Each row in the ResultSet describes a single table. The user can iterate through the ResultSet to obtain table descriptions.

Warning Not every method of this interface can be completely implemented by all database drivers. Database vendors or third-party driver providers can implement only the most commonly used methods. Any method that is not implemented throws a SQLException if the method is invoked.

The ResultSetMetaData Interface

The ResultSetMetaData interface is probably more commonly used than the DatabaseMetaData interface. The ResultSetMetaData interface gives an application programmer information about the ResultSet obtained from a query. The programmer can use this interface to determine properties of the columns in a ResultSet.

The following list describes important methods of this interface:

- `int getColumnCount()`: Obtains the number of columns in the ResultSet. This method returns an integer that equals the number of columns.
- `String getColumnName(int Column Number)`: Obtains the actual name of a column, given the column number in a ResultSet.
- `int getColumnType(int Column Number)`: Returns the SQL type of the column indicated by Column_Number. SQL types are defined in java.sql.Types. Refer to table 17.2 for a list of SQL types and their mapping to corresponding Java data types.
- `boolean isCurrency(int Column Number)`: Checks whether the value in the column specified by using Column_Number is a currency (cash) value or not. This method, which returns a true or false value, is quite useful in financial applications.
- `String getTableName(int Column Number)`: Obtains the name of the table to which the column represented by Column_Number belongs. This method then returns the name of the table in a Java String object.

Other methods can determine whether a particular column can only be read, if it can be written, or if a search can be specified by using the column.

Implementing JDBC

So far, this chapter has presented information to familiarize you with JDBC. Now it's time to put this knowledge to work. This section presents a real-life scenario that uses JDBC to create a corporate Web site, and takes you step-by-step through the implementation procedure.

Background Information

Based in Atlanta and Macon, Georgia, H2O Inc. is an up-and-coming dealer of water pumps of all kinds. With growing competition, H2O decided that they needed to target a wider market, including the entire state of Georgia, by using the World Wide Web. Company officials were convinced that Web shopping would bring in an unprecedented amount of revenue because their company would become more visible and more accessible from distant places.

H2O, however, faced certain problems. The offices in Atlanta and Macon had grown independently, creating differences in the way each of the offices stored information. The Atlanta office maintained their inventory database on Oracle (`http://www.oracle.com`), whereas the smaller Macon office maintained its database on mSQL (Mini SQL—for full details refer to `http://www.minmet.uq.oz.au/msqljava/`), a lightweight database engine.

To enable their Web shoppers to view the entire inventory contained collectively within both offices, the company designed an application with Java and JDBC.

The following sections demonstrate how JDBC and Java were used to create a Web shopping site.

System Overview

Figure 17.4 presents a system overview of the Web shopper site. From this figure, it is evident that the application must read the databases at both sites and combine the information to give a complete picture to the prospective customer.

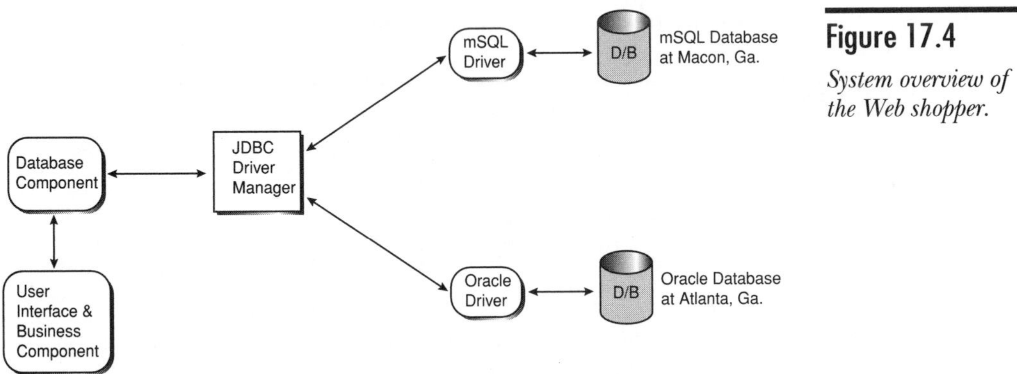

Figure 17.4

System overview of the Web shopper.

Assume that the application uses JDBC API 1.11. H2O obtained Oracle and mSQL JDBC drivers from JDBC driver vendors. The application is logically composed of two units: a user interface combined with a business logic component coded with Java, and a database component coded with the JDBC API.

H2O's aim is to first provide a list of the available water pumps from which the shopper can make a selection. This can be followed by such information as price and inventory, as well as update operations, such as ordering a particular water pump.

System Implementation

Because this chapter mainly targets JDBC, the discussion focuses on the database component of the system. The implementation can be done in a series of systematic steps, as follows:

1. Connecting to the database.
2. Querying the database.
3. Updating operations.
4. Closing statements and connections.

The following sections explore the process step by step.

Step One: Connecting to the Databases

The first step in any database application involves establishing a connection to the databases that contain information pertinent to the application. The following code creates a connection to the database at Macon, Georgia.

Listing 17.1

```
Line===================Connecting to the Database at Macon=====================
DriverManager myManager = new imaginary.sql.iMsqlDriver();
String url = "jdbc:msql://www.H2OMacon.com:4333/Shopdb";
Connection con = myManager.getConnection(url, "nobody",                ""); 
```

The first line of code creates an instance of the mSQL JDBC driver provided by Imaginary (refer to `http://www.imaginary.com/~borg/Java`). The application communicates with the mSQL database by using the previously mentioned mSQL JDBC driver. Another way to inform the DriverManager about a Driver class is to use the following standard Class.forName method:

```
Class.forName("imaginary.sql.iMsqlDriver");
```

The second line of code creates a String object with the value of the location of the H2O Macon office database. This String object is required to create a Connection object, and it follows the naming convention defined in JDBC specifications. Here, the substring "jdbc" informs the server that the protocol to be used is JDBC. The substring "msql" defines the subprotocol, and `//www.H2OMacon.com:4333/Shopdb` specifies the database name "Shopdb" and the server name.

Note The value 4333 is the MSQL_PORT for non-root access on UNIX systems.

The third line of the code actually creates the connection by using the location specified by String URL and logging in as user "nobody" with an empty password parameter. This entire section of code must be placed within a try block to catch any SQLException that may be thrown during the execution of this code. A SQLException is thrown if a connection could not be established.

Other ways exist to obtain a database connection. One way is to use the Driver interface to obtain a connection. For the same effect as the previously defined piece of code, implement the code in listing 17.2.

Listing 17.2

```
Line=============Alternative Method of Connecting to a Database=============
        Properties props = new Properties();
        props.put("server","www.H2OMacon.com:4333");
        props.put("user","nobody");
        props.put("password","");
        Driver msqldr = new imaginary.sql.iMsqlDriver();
        String url = "jdbc:msql://www.H2OMacon.com:4333/Shopdb";
        connection1 = msqldr.connect(url,props);
```

Here, the connection is obtained by asking the mSQL JDBC driver to create a connection to the given URL by using the given properties. In essence, both segments of code achieve the same result—they create a connection.

The next action involves creating a connection to the database in the Atlanta office of H2O. This can be accomplished by using a JDBC driver for Oracle (refer to `http://www.weblogic.com/`—this is an Oracle JDBC driver offered by WebLogic Technologies) or by using the JDBC-ODBC bridge. The code lines in listing 17.3 use jdbcKona, a JDBC driver offered by WebLogic for connecting to Oracle, Sybase, and MS SQL databases.

Listing 17.3

```
Line===============Connecting to the Database at Atlanta====================
        Properties props = new Properties();
        props.put("user",     "nobody");
        props.put("password", "");
        props.put("server",   "www.H2OAtlanta.com/inventory");
        try {
```

continues

Listing 17.3, Continued

```
         Connection connection2 =
➥DriverManager.getConnection("jdbc:weblogic:oracle", props);
            }
         catch (SQLException e) {
         System.out.println("Error message " + e.getMessage();
         }
```

Now that both the connections are set up, it is time to query the database.

Step Two: Querying the Database

H2O must present to the prospective customer the list of all the different kinds of water pumps available at both sites of the company. The solution involves running queries against both databases and then combining the results for an overall picture. Listing 17.4 illustrates the queries in code.

Listing 17.4

```
Line=====================Querying the Databases=============================
     Statement stmt1 = connection1.createStatement();
     ResultSet set1 = stmt1.executeQuery("SELECT * from SHOP_MACON ORDER BY
➥Pump_Id");
    // Pump_Id is the primary key which represents a unique pump
    // identification number
     Statement stmt2 = connection2.createStatement();
     ResultSet set2 = stmt2.executeQuery("SELECT * from SHOP_ATLANTA ORDER
➥BY Pump_No");
    // Pump_No is essentially same as Pump_Id but was named
    // differently by the Atlanta database designers.
```

After executing the preceding two statements, all the unique tuples from each site are stored in ResultSets, set1, and set2. The `executeQuery()` method of Statement interface is usually used to execute a non-update query. You also can use java.sql.PreparedStatement for this purpose. A PreparedStatement can be used to specify IN parameters to query statements. IN parameters are used to dynamically change the query statement as required. If, for example, the prospective shopper was interested only in pumps that cost less than a particular value, it might be efficient to have a PreparedStatement with IN parameters, as shown in the following line of code:

```
  PreparedStatement stmt3 = connection1.prepareStatement("SELECT *FROM
➥SHOP_MACON WHERE (Pump_Cost < ?)");
```

The question mark symbolizes an unknown IN parameter. To determine all the pumps that cost less than 500 dollars, the following lines of code can be used:

```
30   stmt3.setInt(1, 500);
31   ResultSet set3 = stmt3.executeQuery();
```

Line 30 sets the value of the first IN parameter to an integer value of 500. If there had been more than one "?" symbol in the PreparedStatement, this would mean that more than one IN parameter exists. The parameter number (the first argument that is sent to the `setInt` method) is used to set one of the IN parameter values while using one of the `setXXX` methods (*XXX* stands for such values as Int, String, or Byte) that is defined for the PreparedStatement interface.

To modify the above query to search for pumps costing less than 1,000 dollars, change the IN parameter, as shown in the following lines of code:

```
30     stmt3.setInt(1, 1000);
31     ResultSet set4 = stmt3.executeQuery();
```

ResultSet set4 now contains all the pumps costing less than 1,000 dollars. As the previous examples illustrate, PreparedStatements are an efficient way to code dynamically changing queries.

Let's return to H2O's Web shopping system. The ResultSets from querying both databases have been obtained, but these results must be processed correctly to give the Web shopper a complete picture. It is perfectly possible that the number of attributes (columns) in ResultSets set1 and set2 vary and that the names of the corresponding attributes are also different. As a result, the application programmer may need to obtain the names of the attributes for processing the obtained data. This can be achieved by using the ResultSetMetaData interface, as shown in the code in listing 17.5.

Listing 17.5

```
Line====================Using ResultSetMetaData===============================
ResultSetMetaData rset1 = set1.getMetaData();
int num_columns_in_set1 = rset1.getColumnCount();
 String[] col_names1 = new String[num_columns_in_set1];
 for (int iterator=0; iterator<num_columns_in_set1; iterator++) {
     try {
          col_names1[iterator] = rset1.getColumnName(iterator);
          }
      catch (SQLException e) {e.getMessage()}
     }
```

Line 32 first defines a ResultSetMetaData object, and line 33 then uses the metadata object to obtain the number of columns in the result. The application programmer can use the `getColumnName()` method of the metadata object to determine the column names of the attributes in ResultSet set1. This information can be used for printing purposes, such as generating a report header.

Assume for simplicity that the Web shopper is to be presented with three attributes from each table—Pump_Id in set1 and Pump_No in set2, Pump_Name in set1 and Pump_Label in set2, and Pump_Cost in set1 and Pump_Price in set2.

Furthermore, also assume that these attributes are columns numbered one, two, and three respectively in the actual tables—hence, they are numbered similarly in the ResultSets.

The following code in listings 17.6 and 17.7 extracts the required information from the ResultSets set1 and set2.

Listing 17.6

```
Line===============Navigating through the set1 ResultSet Object================
41 while (set1.next()) {
42      String  Pump_ID = set1.getString(1);
43      String  Pump_NAME = set1.getString(2);
44      float   Pump_COST = set1.getFloat(3);
45      Process_Row(Pump_ID, Pump_NAME, Pump_COST);
46      }
```

The ResultSet object is automatically assigned a cursor at the time of its creation. The name of the cursor can be obtained by using the `getCursorName()` method of the ResultSet interface. To obtain the names and prices of the pumps satisfying the query, it is necessary to iterate through the ResultSet by using the `next()` method, which advances the cursor's position by one. Similarly, the results from ResultSet set2 also must be read. This can be accomplished by implementing the code in listing 17.7.

Listing 17.7

```
Line===============Navigating through the set2 ResultSet Object================
47 while (set2.next()) {
48      String  Pump_ID = set2.getString("Pump_No");
49      String  Pump_NAME = set1.getString("Pump_Label");
50      float   Pump_COST = set1.getFloat("Pump_Price");
51      Process_Row(Pump_ID, Pump_NAME, Pump_COST);
```

```
    // Process_Row is a method that combines the results
    // from the two tables.
     }
```

Note that the column names are used to index into each row in the ResultSet directly. Although this process produces much more readable code, it is not as efficient as using column indexes to index into each row.

Step Three: Furthering the Scenario with Update Operations

The Java component of the system displays the information requested by the Web shopper and then offers the shopper an opportunity to place an order.

Assume that the Web shopper decides to purchase two HG55-E (Pump Id) High-Power Water Pumps. After carefully considering the buyer's location, the business logic component decides that the pumps should be delivered to the customer from the Atlanta unit of H2O. The database must be updated to reflect the potential sale, as illustrated in listing 17.8.

Listing 17.8

```
Line===================Updating the Database at Atlanta===================
Statement stmt4 = connection2.createStatement();
String query = new String("UPDATE SHOP_ ATLANTA SET Pump_Units = Pump_Units
➥-2 WHERE Pump_Id = ");
     // Pump_Units represents the number of pumps available in
     // the inventory at that given instant.
query.concat(selected_Pump_Id);
          //Selected_Pump_Id represents the String object containing
          //the Id of the pump the shopper wants to buy.
try {
     return_code = stmt4.executeUpdate(query);
     }
catch (SQLException e) {
     System.out.println(e.getMessage());
     }
```

As listing 17.8 illustrates, the `executeUpdate()` method of Statement interface is used to execute SQL statements that can make some changes to the database. This includes UPDATE, INSERT, DELETE, and DDL (Data Definition Language) commands.

The execution of the code in listing 17.8 does not indicate that the transaction has been completed. H2O must mail the Web shopper an invoice, and the shipping office must be informed of the requested delivery. The entire logic associated with these processes can be handled by the stored shipping_and_invoice procedure, which takes these parameters: Selected_Pump_Id, Quantity_Purchased, User_Name, and User_Address.

The following code calls the stored shipping_and_invoice procedure.

Listing 17.9

```
Line=====================Calling a Stored Procedure==========================
try {
      CallableStatement call_stmt = connection1.prepareCall("{ ? = call 67
➥shipping_and_invoice(?, ?, ?, ?)}");
      }
catch (SQLException e) {}
call_stmt.registerOutParameter(1, java.sql.Types.Bit);
call_stmt.setString(2, Selected_Pump_Id);
call_stmt.setInt(3, Quantity_Purchased);
call_stmt.setString(4, User_Name);
call_stmt.setString(5, User_Address);
try {
      call_stmt.executeUpdate();
      }
 catch (SQLException e) {}
 boolean successful = call_stmt.getBoolean(1);
 if (successful)
      send_user_message("Transaction successful!");
          // send_user_message displays a message on the screen
else
      send_user_message("Transaction failed!");
```

To execute a stored procedure, you must use the CallableStatement interface, which extends the PreparedStatement interface used earlier. The CallableStatement object is created by using the `prepareCall` method of the Connection object. (The `prepare Call` method takes a special escape sequence, so refer to `{call ....}`. The curly braces form an escape sequence that instructs the driver and the Driver Manager that this is a stored procedure.)

Line 69 uses a version of the call statement that returns a result value, which is indicated by the first question mark "?". Every result value must be registered as an OUT parameter with the CallableStatement. This is accomplished by using the registerOutParameter, as shown in line 69. The java.sql.Types.Bit data type has been used because the stored procedure is expected to return a Boolean value. Line 69 has several "?" symbols apart from the result value. Here, these are used as IN parameters.

Actually, these values can be used as either IN or OUT parameters. If used as OUT parameters, they must be registered with the CallableStatement in a manner similar to the result value. The IN parameters are specified by using the `setXXX` (*XXX* represents such values as Int and String) methods of the PreparedStatement interface. The four IN parameters that are required for this procedure are set between lines 70 and 73. The command `call_stmt.executeUpdate();` actually executes the CallableStatement.

Tip Some drivers may send the call statement to the database when the `prepareCall()` method is invoked. Others wait until the `executeUpdate()` method of the CallableStatement is invoked. As a result, it is good programming practice to try to catch exceptions for both the `prepareCall()` and `executeUpdate()` methods.

The statement, `boolean successful = call_stmt.getBoolean(1)` from line 81 extracts the Boolean value returned by the stored procedure to determine whether the transaction was successful. The last four lines of code are fairly straightforward.

Step Four: Cleaning Up

Now that the transaction has been completed, it is good practice to release all resources that the application may have obtained. Each of the Statement objects used can be released by using the `close()` method. The following code, for example, releases the resources held by Statement object, stmt1:

```
stmt1.close();
```

This process should be repeated for each Statement object created by the application.

Finally, the database connections should be released. This is also achieved by using the `close()` method. The following, for example, closes Connection object, connection1, and releases the resources held by this connection:

```
connection1.close();
```

Overall, JDBC aided H2O in creating the desired Web shop by leveraging their system infrastructure by using this modern technology.

Comparing JDBC with Existing Database Access Technologies for the World Wide Web

Using the World Wide Web as a medium for business prompted many technologies that enable database access over the Web. Of particular note among these technologies is Common Gateway Interface, or CGI, as it is popularly known. This section compares the JDBC approach to some of the existing Web-based database access technologies, namely the following:

- CGI scripts
- Java API for databases
- Vendor tools for database access from the Web

CGI Scripts

Common Gateway Interface scripts are a common and widely used technology that can be used to access a database from the Web and interact with databases on a server. These scripts can be implemented by using a variety of languages, including C, C++, Perl, and Python. Scripts interact with a user through the medium of HTML documents and present their output information by creating HTML documents live.

Prior to Java and JDBC, CGI scripts epitomized the term "dynamic" Web interaction. CGI scripts could communicate with a database on a server by using either an Application Programming Interface (API) or an embedded SQL. The scripts could present the required information to the user by using a well-understood and easy-to-use medium—HTML.

CGI scripts, however, also have several shortcomings. Because CGI scripts cannot truly provide dynamic content—they actually run on the back-end server—the server bears the complete responsibility of all the required computation. This produces fat servers, servers with heavy amounts of processing, and thin clients, machines that process virtually no data, which are not desirable system characteristics.

In contrast, the combination of JDBC and Java is a truly dynamic duo. The client performs processing while the server is used only when actual database access is required. Furthermore, the Java API includes a package called java.awt, which is devoted to the creation and manipulation of graphical components. (AWT stands for Abstract Windowing Toolkit.) The java.awt package provides a more flexible and powerful means of designing user interfaces; HTML, although simple to use, lacks some of the features provided by java.awt.

Most importantly, CGI scripts are known to be weak security links in a system. In comparison, JDBC provides a more secure environment. Remember, though, that the JDBC is relatively new, so not everything is known about it yet.

Information regarding CGI security issues can be found at `http://www.cerf.net/~paulp/cgi-security`.

With client/server design issues, JDBC offers a much better approach than CGI scripts, for the following reasons:

- JDBC does not have the problem of a fat server and thin client.
- JDBC can be used with any DBMS that provides a JDBC driver. JDBC also can be used with any DBMS that can be accessed through an ODBC driver. This can be accomplished by using the JDBC-ODBC bridge (provided by JavaSoft and Intersolv).
- JDBC provides metadata about the SQL query results.

Java API for Databases

An increasing number of databasevendors may provide a Java API for database access. MsqlJava, a Java API for mSQL, is one example(refer to `http://www.minmet.uq.oz.au/msqljava/`). By using a Java database API produces a seamless integration of database access code within the application, so that it is a more desirable approach than CGI scripts.

Using a Java database API, however, restricts the application to the particular DBMS for which the Java API is provided. This factor renders JDBC as the better option. Furthermore, not many DBMSs come with a Java API. (To this author's knowledge, mSQL is the only DBMS that provides a Java API.)

Vendor Tools for Database Access from the Web

Some DBMS vendors provide tools for Web access. Microsoft's SQL Server Web Assistant, a non-CGI solution for database access from the Web, serves as one example (refer to `http://www.microsoft.com/msdn/sdk/platforms/doc/backoff/sqldrop/hydra/admin/src/adminwn_4.htm`). The Web Assistant is mainly used to create HTML pages on a prescheduled, triggered basis. For more information on how to use Microsoft SQL Server in the Internet environment, refer to `http://www.microsoft.com/sql/sqlinet1.htm`.

Using these kinds of tools limits the Web application, however, to a particular DBMS or a particular vendor, which is not a desirable characteristic of any application.

As with any new technology, only time will show what will become of it. It is hoped that JavaSoft will aid in Object to relational mappings; currently, however, JDBC is a strong API for developing client/server applications in Java.

Moving Forward: JDBC's Future Direction

JavaSoft intends to provide a higher-level API over JDBC that will target transparent objects and relational mapping, as well as enable the mapping of Java objects to one or more relational database tables. JavaSoft also plans to enhance the capabilities of the JDBC API to include increased cursor support and other useful features. Currently, JavaSoft has plans for a Java Transaction Service API that will be designed to enable Java programs to complete transactions across multiple databases (refer to `http://splash.javasoft.com/jdbc/jdbc.databases.html`).

Other Database Access Technologies for Java

Other non-relational DBMS-based options may be available to Java application programmers who want to introduce persistence to their applications. The options presented in the following sections are Persistence through Object Serialization and ODMG Java Object Database Standard.

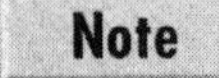

Objects that exist beyond the life of the program that created them are called *persistent* objects.

Object Persistence Using Object Serialization

For small applications, the amount of data involved may not be sufficient to warrant the use of a DBMS. In such situations, it may be optimal to use Object Serialization to emulate database functions such as persistence.

Object Serialization involves mapping objects into an object output stream and then reconstructing these objects from an object input stream.

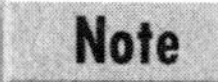

Serialization has been mainly utilized for serializing objects into a byte stream for communication via sockets in Java Remote Method Invocation.

Most common Java objects can be serialized by using the Object Serialization system (`http://www.javasoft.com/products/JDK/1.1/docs/guide/serialization/index.html`). Serialization of user-defined classes requires the implementation of either the Serializable or Externizable interface. The difference between these two interfaces is that the object stream for Serializable objects contains sufficient information for reconstructing an object from the stream, whereas Externizable objects are solely responsible for their external formats and reconstruction.

Serialization can be used for persistence by creating files of objects. These files can be used instead of databases, but it becomes the responsibility of the programmer both to save all the objects in files (using serialization) before quitting the program and to read these objects from files before starting execution again. The overheads involved are quite considerable and increase rapidly with growing numbers of application objects. An example of providing persistence for Java objects is Persistent Java (`http://copeland.smartchoice.com/~laforge/index.html#Introduction`), created by Bill la Forge. Serialization has been used for persistence in other languages, such as C++, using products such as the Tools h++ Class Library from RogueWave Software, Inc. (refer to `http://www.roguewave.com/products/tools/toolsfund.html`).

ODMG Java Object Database Standard

Object Database Management Group (ODMG) and JavaSoft created a new working group in February 1996. The goal of this working group is to define an object database standard for Java. Object databases are ideally suitable to represent Java objects in a transparent and seamless manner. Key concepts of the standard include:

- Transparent persistence
- Persistence by reachability
- Multiple implementations of Java binding
- Addition of classes to Java to implement the complete ODMG object model

Transparent persistence involves making active instances of Java objects persistent without modifying existing code. Persistance by reachability requires that all objects that can be reached from any root object be made persistent at commit-time. The Java environment must be enhanced to fully comply with the ODMG object model. This requires that classes and constructs such as collections, relationships, transactions, and databases be added to Java.

Currently, some products are designed for object-database support for Java. These products include ObjectStore PSE (persistent storage engine) from ObjectStore and POET for Java from POET. These products, however, do not claim to be compliant with the new ODMG Java standard for object databases.

Online References

For more information on topics relating to JDBC, you may find the following sites useful:

`http://splash.javasoft.com/jdbc`—This site provides the official JDBC documentation from JavaSoft. The JDBC 1.10 specification and API are available for download at this site.

`http://www.imaginary.com/~borg/Java`—The mSQL JDBC Driver, and its documentation, are available at this site. This site also has links to MsqlJava and mSQL home pages.

`http://www.weblogic.com/`—This home page of WebLogic, Inc. provides JDBC drivers for several leading relational DBMSs, such as Oracle, Sybase, and Microsoft SQL Server. WebLogic's JDBC drivers can be downloaded for trial use from this site.

Summary

This chapter provided an overview of the aims and functions of JDBC, and the documentation of the JDBC API should prove to be a valuable guide. The real-world implementation scenario showed how JDBC is used to achieve better integration and flexibility for a corporate enterprise, and you can extend the insight provided to other environments as well. A comparison of JDBC with competing technologies showed a perspective that can be used when you make decisions. As it evolves to provide wider functionality, JDBC certainly is a technology worth watching and following.

CHAPTER 18

Servlets and the Java Web Server

This chapter covers servlets, the newest aspect of Java networking. Servlets are the server-side equivalents of applets—Java programs designed to execute in an environment provided by a Web server. Originally intended as a Java-style replacement for Common Gateway Interface (CGI) programs, servlets are supported as an extension package to JDK 1.1 and use a Java-based HTTP server that implements the newly defined Servlet API. Like applets, servlets can be automatically downloaded to the server, and untrusted servlets run in a secured environment. Unlike applets, servlets have no graphical user interface and do not use the AWT classes; all user interaction is by way of the browser. In this chapter, you are also introduced to the basic features of the Java Web Server and learn how to construct your own servlets with the Servlet API.

Note Because the Java Web Server is being released after JDK 1.1, this chapter covers the Servlet API at the time of the JDK 1.1 release—concentrating on the essentials of Servlet programs and the features expected in the final product. Because the examples are based on the Servlet API alpha 2 release, some examples may need minor corrections to work with the final product release. The latest information on the Servlet API and the Java Web Server can be found at `http://java.sun.com/products/java-server/`.

Introducing Servlets

The obvious question since the introduction of Java and the HotJava browser, with its client-side applets, has been, "What can Java do for the server-side?" Java applets facilitate the addition of specialized functions, such as intelligent forms, to a Web page; with servlets, developers may add custom Java processing functions to the server with the new Servlet API definitions, which extend Web server functionality. Servlets are just the beginning of a standard way to develop object-oriented, portable, strongly typed Web applications that can be used in any server supporting this API.

The following section explains servlets in relation to applets, and explains the purpose of the Servlet API. It also presents an overview of the uses of servlets.

Comparing Servlets and Applets

Before going into detail about servlets and the new Servlet API, it's important to understand the differences between servlets and applets. Servlets and applets are compared in table 18.1.

Table 18.1
Comparison of Servlets and Applets

Servlet	Applet
Subclass of GenericServlet	Subclass of Applet or HttpServlet
Runs in a server	Runs in a browser
Must be thread-safe	Generally single thread per applet
Uses Web browser for user interface	Uses AWT for user interface

Servlet	Applet
If downloaded to server, controlled access to files and network	If downloaded to browser, no access to files and network access back only to serving host
If local to server, full access	Access to local files browser-dependent to files and network

Servlet API Goals

The Servlet API is the standard Java interface between Web servers and HTTP-processing programs. Servlets execute in a special environment provided by a Web server that supports the new Servlet API. This environment supplies all the resources servlets need to run, and a security model to maintain system integrity. This approach is similar to the controlled execution environment provided by Web browsers for applets. The Servlet API has the following attributes:

- **Ease of use and understanding.** The Servlet API provides the same HTTP information as is available through CGI variables, simplifying the conversion of existing CGI programs to servlets.
- **High performance.** The Servlet API eliminates the overhead of starting an external CGI program to serve each request; it enables servlets to perform practically all server operations, including basic file serving.
- **Platform independence.** Like applets, servlets run on any server platform that provides a Java Virtual Machine supporting the Servlet API.
- **Transport independence.** The Servlet API has base classes that are independent of the transport protocol used to carry Web content and subclasses that are specific to HTTP. Specific versions of the Servlet API can be developed for future Web transport protocols.
- **Secure and safe.** Untrusted servlets run in a secured environment, as described in the "Untrusted Servlet Security Sandbox" section later in the chapter, which protects access to the network and other local resources. Trusted servlets have full access to local resources.

Java's Servlet API has a significant advantage over CGI in terms of performance, transport independence, and security. The differences between servlets and CGI programs are highlighted in table 18.2.

Table 18.2
Comparison of Servlet API and CGI

	Servlet	CGI Program
Language	Java	Any programming language
Invocation	Direct method call	Run program
Parameters	From ServletRequest methods	From environment variables
Runtime Checks	Java Virtual Machine	Language specific
Security	Java Security Manager	Operating system specific

What You Can Do with Servlets

Servlets have all the power and flexibility of Java programs; any Java function or package that does not use the AWT (remember there is no graphical user interface) can be used. Trusted servlets, for example, have full access to read and write files. You can use the JDK 1.1 internationalization package to construct localized HTML dynamic content, the Java Database Connectivity (JDBC) package to access databases, and a Remote Method Invocation (RMI) or Common Object Request Broker Architecture (CORBA) package to get information from other machines. The only restriction on servlets' use of Java packages is that the package must support multithreading or be thread-safe; otherwise the servlet must provide thread safety as described in the "Writing Servlets" section of this chapter.

Because the Servlet API is specified in Java, instead of a procedure language, as done by other server extension interfaces, you get the benefits of object-oriented development in building your server extensions. As an example of the power and flexibility of servlets, the Java Web Server uses servlets to handle file requests, manage file caches, and construct error response pages. All HTTP processing is handled by a different core servlet shipped with the product, depending on the operation performed or information requested. The use of servlets for all Web server operations makes a very flexible Web platform. Server administrators, for instance, can easily subclass the file serving servlet to collect statistics on files requested and track user information, or administrators can subclass the error response servlet to return specialized error messages.

Examining the Servlet API

The Servlet API is defined by the classes in the java.servlet and java.servlet.http packages. A utility package to assist in dynamically generating HTML, java.servlet.html, is also provided. Figure 18.1 shows the java.servlet.* packages, classes, and their relationships. Together, these packages specify the following:

- The generic behavior of servlets independent from the Web transport protocol
- Additional facilities available to HTTP-specific servlets
- Support for programmatic creation of HTML pages as a hierarchical structure of HTML elements

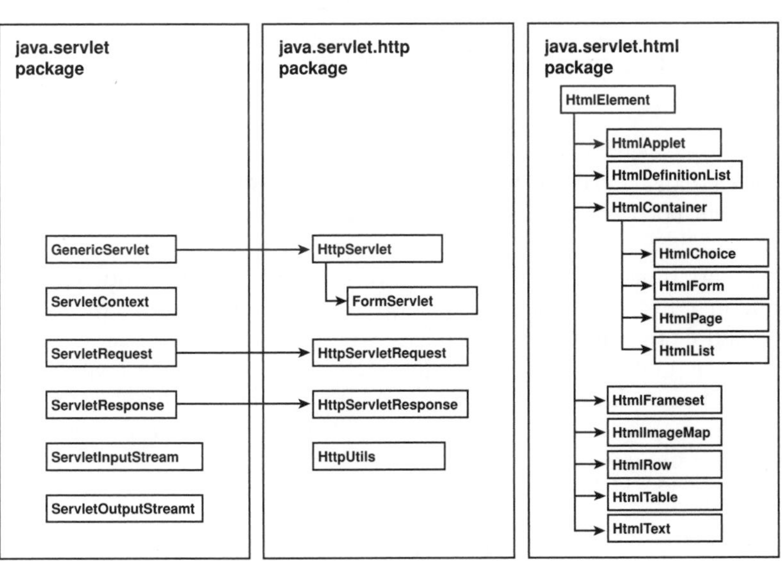

Figure 18.1

The Servlet API classes.

The following sections cover the methods that comprise the Servlet API. Developers may have access to additional vendor-specific classes and servlets that are proprietary to a given server. Any such extensions would be covered by server-specific documentation.

The java.servlet Package

The java.servlet package defines the operation of servlets from a protocol-independent perspective. At this level, the protocol used to access the servlets could be HTTP, a network file system protocol, or another transport protocol. Servlets designed to operate as a Java Web Server server-side-include use the classes in this package. The four interfaces and three implementation classes in this package are described in more detail in the following sections.

Methods of the Servlet Interface

Servlet is the highest level, generic interface class. It defines four basic methods that accomplish the following: initialize the servlet, destroy the servlet, service a request, and return an information string. You override the `init()` method if your servlet needs to perform any initialization after it is loaded. You access the initialization parameters specified for your servlet by calling `getInitParameter()` or `getInitParameters()`. For the Java Web Server, these parameters are stored in the servlet.properties file and can be changed by using the server administration servlet.

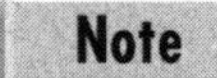

The names of configuration-related files are those used by the Java Web Server; other servers may use different file names. You should always use the defined interfaces and not attempt to directly access the configuration files.

The actual servlet work is performed in the `service()` method. You must code your `service()` method in a thread-safe manner because concurrent requests for the same servlet result in multiple threads executing your `service()` method. The easiest way to be thread-safe is to not modify any object instance variables and only to use parameters of the `service()` call. Alternatively, you can add the `Synchronized` modifier to your declaration of `service()` to restrict access to one thread at a time. Table 18.3 lists the Servlet interface methods.

Table 18.3
Methods of the Servlet Interface

Method	Description
void init(ServletStub)	Initialize a servlet.
void destroy()	Free allocated resources when the servlet class is unloaded.
void service(ServletRequest, ServletResponse)	Process the incoming request and create the outgoing response.

Method	Description
String getServletInfo()	Return an information string that describes the servlet.

A subclass of Servlet uses a ServletContext object, described in the following section, to obtain information about the server's environment and to call various server utility routines.

Methods of the ServletContext Interface

The ServletContext interface defines methods that the servlet can use to interact with its operating environment. The relationship between a Servlet and the methods of the ServletContext is similar to the one between an Applet and an AppletContext. The facilities provided to a servlet are currently limited to getting MIME types, translating path names, finding other servlets, and logging information. These methods are listed in table 18.4.

TABLE 18.4
Methods of the ServletContext Interface

Method	Description
String getMimeType(String)	Returns the MIME type of the specified file by matching the file name suffix against entries in the mime.properties file.
String getRealPath(String)	Applies the alias rules in the alias.properties file to the specified virtual path and returns the corresponding real path; null is returned if the translation fails.
String getServerInfo()	Returns a string identifying the name, version, and platform of the server software.
Servlet getServlet(String)	Returns a servlet of the given name.
Enumeration getServlets()	Returns an enumeration of all the servlets currently loaded in the server. This enumeration includes the calling servlet.
void log(Servlet, String)	Writes a message to the servlet log for a given servlet.

Methods of the ServletRequest Interface

The ServletRequest interface class defines methods used to obtain information about the servlet request independent of the actual transport protocol used between the client and the server. The request must be carried by an Internet transport protocol, such as HTTP.

The request can include parameters or content information. The servlet can determine the length of any content sent with the request by using `getContentLength()`. The servlet can also obtain the content encoding type by using `getContentType()`. When content is available, the servlet can read it using a HttpInputStream obtained from `getInputStream()`. Table 18.5 lists the methods available in the ServletRequest interface.

TABLE 18.5
Methods of the ServletRequest Interface

Method	Description
String getRemoteAddr()	Returns the IP address of the client that sent the request.
String getRemoteHost()	Returns the fully qualified hostname of the agent that sent the request.
String getServerName()	Returns the hostname of the server that received the request.
int getServerPort()	Returns the port number on which this request was received.
String getProtocol()	Returns a string identifying the protocol and version.
String getParameter(String)	Returns the value of the specified parameter for the request.
Hashtable getParameters()	Returns a hashtable of all the parameters of this request.
String getContentType()	Returns the MIME type of any data included with the request, or null if the MIME type is not specified in the request header.

Method	Description
int getContentLength()	Returns the size of the data included with the request, or –1 if a length is not specified in the request header.
ServletInputStream getInputStream()	Returns an input stream for reading any data included with the request.

Methods of the ServletResponse Interface

The ServletResponse interface defines a general way to create the response to the service request. At this generic level, the response is content with only a MIME identifier and optional length. To write the actual content of the response, the servlet calls `getOutputStream()` to get a ServletOutputStream and then makes the necessary `print()` calls to compose the response. Table 18.6 lists the methods of ServletResponse.

TABLE 18.6
Methods of the ServletResponse Interface

Method	Description
void setContentType(String)	Sets the MIME type of the response.
void setContentLength(int)	Sets the content length for the response.
ServletOutputStream getOutputStream()	Returns an output stream used for writing response data to the client.

Methods of the GenericServlet Class

In general, the GenericServlet class is a base implementation class for any transport-independent servlet, and specifically it is used for any servlet that can be invoked from a server-side include. GenericServlet implements the Servlet interface, supplying a base implementation of the required methods, and provides convenient access to information from the servlet's ServletContext. In addition to implementing `init()`, `destroy()`, `service()`, and `getServletInfo()` methods required by the Servlet interface, GenericServlet provides the following methods, listed in table 18.7:

Table 18.7
Methods of the GenericServlet Class

Method	Description
String getInitParameter(String)	Returns the value of an initialization parameter of the servlet as specified in either the servlet.properties file or as an attribute in the <servlet> tag for server-side includes servlets.
Hashtable getInitParameters()	Returns a name/value pair hashtable of the initialization parameters of the servlet.
ServletContext getServeletContext()	Returns the servlet context.
void log(String)	Logs a message into the servlet log file.

Methods of the ServletInputStream Abstract Class

ServletInputStream is an abstract subclass of InputStream that defines the `readLine(byte[], int offset, int count)` method, which reads bytes into the byte array starting at the offset until either the array is filled or a newline character is read.

Methods of the ServletOutputStream Abstract Class

ServletOutputStream is an abstract subclass of OutputStream that is similar to a PrintStream, but only defines methods to print the most commonly used network data types (`ints`, `longs`, and `Strings`). You must convert other data types by using the `toString()` method before printing to the ServletOutputStream. The implementation of ServletOutputStream handles conversion from internal Unicode encoding of characters to US-ASCII (generally used by Internet protocols). This class also defines methods to print and terminate the line with the Internet-standard CR/LF combination. Table 18.8 lists the methods of the ServletOutputStream class.

Table 18.8
Methods of the ServletOutputStream Class

Method	Description
void print(int)	Prints an integer.
void println(int)	Prints an integer followed by a CRLF.
void print(long)	Prints a long integer.

Method	Description
void println(long)	Prints a long integer followed by a CRLF.
void print(String)	Prints an ASCII string.
void println(String)	Prints an ASCII string followed by CRLF.
void println()	Prints a CRLF.

The java.servlet.http Package

The java.servlet.http package supports servlets that specifically use HTTP. HTTP provides additional request information and response features than what is available to generic servlets. This package contains two interface classes, two implementation classes, and the implementation of a servlet class intended to be subclassed. These HTTP-specific classes are:

- HttpServlet
- HttpServletRequest
- HttpServletResponse
- FormServlet
- HttpUtils

All are described in the following sections.

HttpServlet Abstract Class

You subclass HttpServlet, itself an abstract subclass of GenericServlet, to implement your HTTP-specific servlets. HttpServlet handles the cast conversion between the generic ServletRequest and ServletResponse objects, and their HTTP-specific subclasses HttpServletRequest and HttpServletResponse. You override the `service (HttpServletRequest, HttpServletResponse)` method in your servlet class to perform the servlet processing function. Table 18.9 lists the methods of the HttpServlet class.

Table 18.9
Methods of the HttpServlet Class

Method	Description
void service(ServletRequest, ServletResponse)	Performs the cast conversion between generic and HTTP-specific request and response objects. Normally you should not override this method.
void service(HttpServletRequest, HttpServletResponse)	Override to accept HTTP service requests.

HttpServletRequest Interface Class

HttpServletRequest is a subclass of ServletRequest that handles request information, other than content identification, contained in an HTTP request header. Beyond that of the base ServletRequest, the information available from HttpServletRequest falls into four general categories:

- General information about the request
- Information concerning the URL
- Authentication-related information
- Access information to the original HTTP header

The exact information that is available when using these calls is described in the following sections.

General Request Information

These methods provide you with general information about the request, including the name of the method used to access the data and any query information. This group includes the `getMethod()` and `getQueryString()` methods. The parameters of the request are obtained by using the `getParameters()` method, defined in `ServletRequest`.

URL Information

These methods provide you with information about the requested URL, its major components, and its local translation.

Authentication-Related Information

The servlet provides you with some very weak access control by using name and address information about the client as provided by `getHostName()` and `getHostAddress()`. The type of HTTP-level authentication in use is available using `getAuthType()`. For connections running in basic mode, `getRemoteUser()` returns the user identification.

Access to HTTP Request Header Fields

`HttpServletRequest` provides you with a means to get direct access to the HTTP request header fields to get information not explicitly supported by an `HttpServletRequest` method. Examples include user-agent, referer, preferred languages, accepted content encodings, and client-state (cookie) information, as well as any non-standard header fields.

Instead of using an enumerator, the `getHeader()` and `getHeaderName()` methods take an index into the header. An index of 0 retrieves the first header field; null is returned if the index is greater than the number of fields available. You can also access request header fields by name, which happens to be the easiest approach. In this case, the request header is searched for a matching field name and returns the field value. Use `getHeader()`, `getIntHeader()`, or `getDateHeader()` depending on the desired data conversion.

Table 18.10 summarizes the methods of the HttpServletRequest class.

TABLE 18.10
Methods of the HttpServletRequest Class

Method	Description
String getMethod()	Returns the method used in the request.
String getQueryString()	Returns the part of the URI following the '?'.
String getRequestURI()	Returns the request URI.
String getServletPath()	Returns the part of the request URI that refers to the servlet being invoked.
String getPathInfo()	Returns optional, extra path information following the servlet path, but preceding the query string.
String getPathTranslated()	Returns extra path information translated to a real path by using the alias.properties rules.

continues

Table 18.10, Continued
Methods of the HttpServletRequest Class

Method	Description
String getRequestPath()	Returns the part of the request URI that corresponds to the servlet path plus the optional, extra path information.
String getAuthType()	Returns the authentication scheme of the request, or null if none.
String getRemoteUser()	Returns the name of the user making this request or null if the name is not specified.
String getHeader(int)	Returns the value of the *n*th header field or null if fewer than *n* fields.
String getHeaderName(int)	Returns the name of the *n*th header field or if fewer than *n* fields.
String getHeader(String)	Returns the value of a header field.
int getIntHeader(String, int)	Returns the value of an integer header field after converting the string to an int. If the field is not found, it returns the default value.
long getDateHeader(String, long)	Returns the value of a date header field after converting the string to a date. If the field is not found, it returns the default value.

HttpServletResponse Interface Class

The HttpServletResponse is a subclass of ServletResponse and provides you with the mechanisms to create an HTTP response header. These mechanisms are used for the following four purposes:

- To set the response status
- To add arbitrary response header fields
- To create an error response
- To redirect the request to another URL

Creating normal, error, and redirect responses using the HttpServletResponse object is described in the following sections.

Setting the Response Status

The HTTP response header includes a status number indicating the success, redirection, or failure of the request. The return status defaults to 200 or OK. If an error is returned or OK is not the correct status, the servlet can specify both an error code and some descriptive text. If only an error code is given, the code is translated into a standard status text string. The most common response status numbers are the following:

200	Success
204	No new information
300	Resource has moved to a new location
301	Redirect query to new URL
304	Document has not been modified
403	Access prohibited
404	Resource not found

Specifying Non-Standard Header Fields

Your servlet can add any field to the response header by using one of the `setHeader()` methods, enabling you to add non-standard header fields not supported by HttpServletResponse. Provide the name of the header field (without a colon) as the first argument and the data as the second argument. Variants of setHeader are defined for String, int, and Date parameters. Successive calls to set the same header field overwrite the previous value and do not add multiple copies of the field. For example, calling:

```
setHeader("refresh", 30);
```

would add a refresh response header field with a value of 30; this instructs the browser to automatically reload the page in 30 seconds.

Returning Error Responses

HttpServletResponse provides two methods to create and send standard error responses. To return an error, your servlet calls `sendError()` with a status code and an optional explanatory message. The page is titled and has a header that indicates the status code and a standard text message based on the status code. The optional explanatory message is inserted into the body of the returned page. For example, calling:

```
sendError(404, "Couldn't find it!")
```

would create a returned page that has a title and H1 header of `"404 Not Found"` and `"Couldn't find it!"` as the text.

Returning Redirect Response

`HttpServletResponse` also provides a method to create and send a standard redirect response. Calling `sendRedirect()` creates and sends a `"302"` (Moved Temporarily) response. Pass a string that indicates the new location of the page. The string should be a URL because it is placed in the returned page as a link. However, `sendRedirect()` does not check to see if the string is actually a correctly formatted URL. If you have a URL object already, convert it to a string by using `toString()` before calling `sendRedirect()`.

Table 18.11 summarizes the methods associated with the HttpServletResponse class.

Table 18.11
Methods of the HttpServletResponse Class

Method	Description
void setStatus(int)	Sets the response status code.
void setStatus(int, String)	Sets the response status code and explanatory text.
void setHeader(String, String)	Sets the named header field to the indicated value.
void setIntHeader(String, int)	Sets the named integer header field after converting the value to a String.
void setDateHeader(String, long)	Sets the value of the named date field after converting the long into an Internet-standard date-time string.
void unsetHeader(String fieldname)	Removes the named header field from the response.
void sendError(int)	Sends an error response using the specified status code and standard explanatory message.
void sendError(int, String)	Sends an error response using the specified status code and detailed explanatory message.

FormServlet Class

The FormServlet class is the only servlet class that is specified as part of the Servlet API, hence it is available in all Web servers that support servlets. You can build forms processing servlets by subclassing FormServlet and overriding the `sendResponse()` method. The `sendResponse()` method handles form information and generates a response. When the `sendResponse()` method is called, the FormServlet's `service()` method has already accomplished the following:

- Verified the HTTP method as GET or POST
- Retrieved the form information from either the URL for a GET request or from the content of the request for a POST
- Stored the form information as a hashtable of name/value pairs

The FormServlet class extracts the form information from either the query string for GET requests, or the content for POST requests, making the differences between GET and POST invisible to your servlet. An example construction of your own form processing servlet is provided in the "Handling HTML Forms" section of this chapter.

Refer to table 18.12 for a summary of methods of the FormServlet class.

TABLE 18.12
Methods of the FormServlet Class

Method	Description
String getServletInfo()	Returns a String containing information about your servlet.
void service(HttpServletRequest, HttpServletResponse)	Override if special request processing is required.
void sendResponse (HttpServletResponse, Hashtable)	Override this method to supply code to process the form and generate a response.

HttpUtils Class

The HttpUtils class is a set of static utility routines that are useful in building servlets. In the Alpha 2 release, the only method defined is `parseQueryString(String)`. This method builds a hashtable of name/value pairs based on parsing a query string. Your servlet can use the name (as the key) in the `Hashtable.get()` method to retrieve the value string.

The java.servlet.html Package

The third package included with the Servlet API is java.servlet.html. This package includes thirteen HTML support classes that provide operations for assembling HTML elements, such as tables, image maps, and forms. From these elements, you can build an HTML page as a hierarchical list of HTML commands and text elements, and then write out the completed page to a ServletOutputStream. The classes of this package are listed in table 18.13.

Note The HTML generation support provided in the Alpha 2 release is fairly limited. This package is likely to change significantly for the final release.

Table 18.13
HTML Creation Classes

Class	Description
HtmlElement	Supports the basic HTML element interface definition.
HtmlText	Supports text enclosed by tags.
HtmlContainer	Supports a list of HtmlElements enclosed by tags.
HtmlApplet	Supports the applet HTML tag with width and height specification.
HtmlChoice	Supports the select HTML tag.
HtmlDefinitionList	Supports the dl, dt, and dd HTML tags.
HtmlForm	Supports building HTML forms comprised of input fields, check boxes, radio buttons, text areas, selections, and submit buttons.
HtmlFrameset	Supports frameset HTML tag.
HtmlImageMap	Supports client-side image map HTML tags.
HtmlList	Supports the ul and ol HTML list tags.
HtmlPage	Supports building a Web page comprised of a header and body areas.
HtmlTable	Supports building of tables from row elements.
HtmlRow	Supports the HTML to define a row of a table.

All the classes in this package implement the HtmlElement interface, which enables you to specify text for the HTML tag and write the resulting HTML to an output stream. By creating objects that represent the various HTML tags and calling methods to add data and attributes to the tags, you can generate the most common HTML elements and avoid some simple errors, such as ending tags in the wrong order. It may, however, be simpler to hand-generate the HTML, particularly for simple, static pages. The examples in the section "Writing Servlets," which follows, make use of the classes from the java.servlet.html package to generate dynamic response pages.

The methods in this package do not automatically add double-quotes to enclose literal strings used as HTML attributes. You must add double quotes if your string has embedded spaces or other special control characters.

The parameter layout of these methods is similar for all classes. The first parameter is the information that is to be added to the HtmlElement. Overloaded methods are often defined to handle the addition of Strings, HtmlElements, or Vectors.

The second parameter is either the tag or attributes for a tag implied by the method. `HtmlContainer.addLink()`, for example, implies an "a" tag, so the second parameter is interpreted as attributes of the tag. When using tags, do not include the '<', '>', or '/' characters in the tag string; these characters are automatically supplied where needed. Multiple tags are specified by using a comma-delimited string.

These HTML support classes do not check the actual HTML to verify that the tags and keys are legal and used correctly. They only ensure that the tags are terminated in the correct order.

Writing Servlets

The Servlet API provides an environment that makes writing servlets very easy. All servlets must implement the java.servlet.Servlet interface. The easiest way is by subclassing either GenericServlet or HttpServlet; regular HTTP-processing servlets subclass HttpServlet and server-side-include servlets subclass GenericServlet. When an HTTP request is received, the server translates the URL into a reference to a specific servlet class. If this is the first request for the servlet, the servlet class is dynamically loaded, and its `init()` method is called to perform any necessary servlet-specific initialization. In most cases, the servlet has already been loaded, in which case its `service()` method is just called.

Note that several different threads can concurrently execute the `service()` method of the same servlet object. A single instance of the FileServlet object, for example, serves all requests to load files. Consequently, servlets must be designed to operate in multithreaded environments. The easiest way to ensure this is to store all information about the request being processed in local variables rather than store it as instance variables in the servlet object. For cases in which access to a single resource must be controlled, you must use the standard Java synchronization techniques based on the `Synchronized` keyword. In most cases, you can simply add the `Synchronized` modifier to the declaration for `service()`, or `sendResponse()` and effectively modify the servlet to serve only one client at a time. Of course, limiting access to a single thread (that is, handling client requests one at a time) may reduce performance.

The following sections contain examples of a simple HelloWorld servlet and a forms processing servlet.

HelloWorldServlet

This section shows how to build a simple servlet that outputs "Hello World" and displays a table of the various HTTP information available from the request. To run this example servlet on the Java Web Server, you must specify the following:

- A rule that translates the URL (/helloworldservlet) to the name of the servlet (helloworldservlet).
- The class name for the servlet code (HelloWorldServlet).
- The addition of the servlet to the list of servlets loaded at startup.

You can reconfigure the server by using the administration servlet or by editing the configuration files as described in table 18.15. After compiling the servlet, copy the .class file into the /servlet directory, which is the default location of servlet code.

Table 18.15
Configuration Changes Needed to Run the "Hello World" Servlet with the Java Web Server

File	Change	Additions
rules.properties	add	/helloworldservlet= helloworldservlet
servlet.properties	edit	servlets.startup= file cgi invoker admin error helloworldservlet
	add	helloworldservlet.code=HelloWorldServlet

The code in listing 18.1 (HelloWorldServlet.java on the CD-ROM accompanying this book) subclasses HttpServlet, overrides the `service()` method, and uses the HTML support classes to generate the response.

Listing 18.1

```
Line=================Java Source=================
import java.io.*;
import java.servlet.*;
import java.servlet.html.*;
import java.servlet.http.*;

public class HelloWorldServlet extends HttpServlet {
  public void HelloWorldServlet() {
  }

  public String getServletInfo() {
    return "This servlet displays a hello message.";
  }

  public void service (HttpServletRequest req, HttpServletResponse res)
    throws ServletException, IOException {
  ServletOutputStream out = res.getOutputStream();
  res.setContentType("text/html");
  HtmlPage page = new HtmlPage("Hello World");
  page.add("Hello World", "h1");

  HtmlTable tbl = new HtmlTable("Border");
  tbl.addHeader("Parameter");
  tbl.addHeader("Value");
  nextRow(tbl, "Server name", req.getServerName());
  nextRow(tbl, "Server port", req.getServerPort());
  nextRow(tbl, "Client host", req.getRemoteHost());
  nextRow(tbl, "Client addr", req.getRemoteAddr());
  nextRow(tbl, "Protocol", req.getProtocol());
  nextRow(tbl, "Method", req.getMethod());
  nextRow(tbl, "Request URI", req.getRequestURI());
  nextRow(tbl, "Request path", req.getRequestPath());
  nextRow(tbl, "Servlet path", req.getServletPath());
```

continues

Listing 18.1, Continued

```
33      nextRow(tbl, "Path info", req.getPathInfo());
34      nextRow(tbl, "Translated path", req.getPathTranslated());
35      nextRow(tbl, "Query String", req.getQueryString());
36      nextRow(tbl, "Authorization", req.getAuthType());
37      nextRow(tbl, "Remote user", req.getRemoteUser());
38      nextRow(tbl, "Content length", req.getContentLength());
39      nextRow(tbl, "Content type", req.getContentType());
40      page.add(tbl);
41
42      tbl = new HtmlTable("Border");
43      tbl.addHeader("Header Field");
44      tbl.addHeader("Value");
45      int index = 0;
46      String fieldname;
47      while ((fieldname = req.getHeaderName(index)) != null) {
48        nextRow(tbl, fieldname, req.getHeader(index));
49        index++;
50        }
51      page.add(tbl);
52      page.write(out);
53      }
54
55      void nextRow(HtmlTable tbl, String name, String value) {
56      tbl.newRow();
57      tbl.addData("<strong>" + name + ":</strong>");
58      if (value != null)
59        tbl.addData("<em>" + value + "</em>");
60      }
61
62      void nextRow(HtmlTable tbl, String name, int value) {
63      nextRow(tbl, name, Integer.toString(value));
64      }
65  }
```

Lines 6–13 in listing 18.1 indicate that the servlet is using HTTP and define a servlet information method. Regular servlets subclass HttpServlet, but server-side-includes servlets subclass GenericServlet. The actual work of the servlet is performed in lines 14–53 in the `service()` method where you output a hello message and information from the HTTP request. The processing steps are described next:

1. Prepare the response header.

   The first step is setting the response header information. The servlet can create its response by using the HttpServletResponse passed to the `service()` method. Alternatively, to have complete control of the response contents, you can reset the HttpServletResponse and write the response header directly to the ServletOutputStream. Before calling `service()`, the server sets the HttpServletResponse status to 200 or "OK," the "Date:" header field is set to the current date and time, and the "Server:" header field is set to identify the server. If there is an error or OK is not the correct status, the servlet can specify both an error code and some descriptive text. If only an error code is given, the code is translated into a standard status text string. Normally, you would not change these values. Because the default values are appropriate for this response, you just use the HttpServletResponse object.

   As shown on line 17, you need to identify the type of data contained in the response by specifying the MIME type as follows:

   ```
   17    res.setContentType("text/html");
   ```

   This declares the response should be interpretted by the browser as text formatted as HTML. Along with specifying the content type, you may optionally specify the content length.

2. Get the output stream.

   In line 16, to write the content, the servlet calls `getOutputStream()` to get a ServletOutputStream as follows:

   ```
   16    ServletOutputStream out = res.getOutputStream();
   ```

3. Create the HTML page object, title, and header.

   You can create your HTML either manually by using `print()` statements, or by using any HTML support package, such as the one provided as part of the Servlet API. For this example, you use the HTML generation classes from java.servlet.html and on lines 18 and 19 create a new HtmlPage with an H1 header.

4. Display the request information as a table.

   Lines 21–40 display the information available from the HTTP request as a table. You allocate an HtmlTable object and add column headers and rows of data. Finally, write the contents of the table to the output stream.

5. Display the HTTP header fields as a table.

Lines 42–50 display the HTTP request header fields as a table. Again, you allocate an HtmlPage object and add column headers and rows of data. Note how you iterate the request headers using an index. You can also get field contents by using the name of the header field.

6. Transmit the response.

   Finally, write the HTML for the page to the ServletOutputStream. The response header that you created in step 1 is automatically written to the ServletOutputStream before your first write is handled.

   Lines 55–64 define methods to help create the table. A sample of the output of the servlet is shown in figure 18.2.

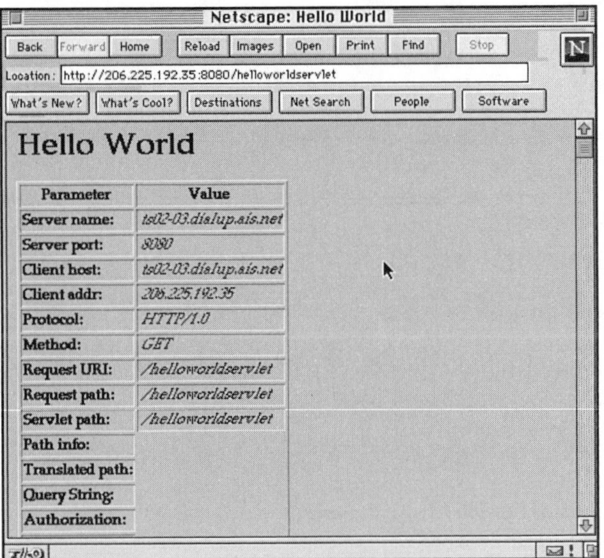

Figure 18.2
Sample HelloWorldServlet output.

Handling HTML Forms

When using HTML forms, the browser extracts the information entered into the form by the user and sends it to the server as either a GET or POST request. Because form processing is such a common servlet activity, the Servlet API includes a built-in Servlet class specific for forms handling the FormServlet class.

In the following example, the PlanetsApplet remote method invocation example in Chapter 16, "Remote Method Invocation and Object Serialization," is rewritten as a servlet. This servlet implements a simple form that supports querying of planet information and incrementing the number of moons; the planet information is stored as a serialized object. To run this example servlet on the Java Web Server, you must specify the following:

- A rule that translates the URL in the generated HTML (/planets) to the name of the servlet (planets).
- The class name for the servlet code (PlanetsServlet).
- The initialization parameter that identifies the file containing planetary information.
- The addition of the servlet to the list of servlets loaded at startup.

You can reconfigure the server by using the administration servlet or by editing the configuration files as described in table 18.16. After compiling the servlet, copy the .class files into the /servlet directory, which is the default location of servlet code.

TABLE 18.16
Configuration Changes Necessary for Running PlanetsServlet Example on Java Web Server

File	Change	Additions
rules.properties	add	/planets=planets
servlet.properties	edit	servlets.startup= file cgi invoker imagemap admin proxy error planets
	add	planets.code=PlanetsServlet planets.initArgs=\ file=servlets/planetlist

The code in listing 18.2 (PlanetsServlet.java on the CD-ROM accompanying this book) subclasses FormServlet, overrides the `sendResponse()` method, and uses the HTML support classes to generate the response.

Listing 18.2

```
Line==================Java Source==================
import java.io.*;
import java.servlet.*;
import java.servlet.html.*;
import java.servlet.http.*;
import java.util.*;

// the Planet object holds the information about a given planet
class Planet implements Serializable {
  private String name;
  private int moons;
  private boolean hasRings;

  public Planet(String name, int moons, boolean hasRings) {
    this.name = name;
    this.moons = moons;
    this.hasRings = hasRings;
  }

  public String getName() {
    return name;
  }

  public int getMoons() {
    return moons;
  }

  public boolean hasRings() {
    return hasRings;
  }

  public synchronized void bumpMoons() {
    moons++;
  }
}

public class PlanetsServlet extends FormServlet {
  Vector planets;
```

```
  String file;

  public void PlanetsServlet() {
  }

  public String getServletInfo() {
    return "This servlet displays information about the planets.";
  }

  //initialize the planet information table
  public void init() throws ServletException {
    Hashtable ht = getInitParameters();
    if (ht != null) {
      file = (String)ht.get("file");
      if (file != null)
        read();
      else
        setupPlanets();
      }
    else
      setupPlanets();
  }

  // Populate the planets Vector
  void setupPlanets() {
    planets = new Vector();
    planets.addElement(new Planet("Mercury",0, false));
    planets.addElement(new Planet("Venus",0, false));
    planets.addElement(new Planet("Earth",1, false));
    planets.addElement(new Planet("Mars",2, false));
    planets.addElement(new Planet("Jupiter",16, true));
    planets.addElement(new Planet("Saturn",18, true));
    planets.addElement(new Planet("Uranus",15, true));
    planets.addElement(new Planet("Neptune",8, true));
    planets.addElement(new Planet("Pluto",1, false));
  }

  void read() {
    try {
```

continues

Listing 18.2, Continued

```
      FileInputStream in = new FileInputStream(file);
      ObjectInputStream s = new ObjectInputStream(in);
      planets = (Vector)s.readObject();
    }
    catch (FileNotFoundException e) {
      setupPlanets();
      return;
    }
    catch (IOException e){
      log("Planets.read: Exception while Reading");
      return;
    }
    catch (ClassNotFoundException e){
      System.out.println("ClassNotFoundException while Reading");
      return;
    }
  }

  //synchronize in case multiple clients concurrently call "bump"
  synchronized void write() {
    try {
      FileOutputStream f = new FileOutputStream(file);
      ObjectOutputStream s = new ObjectOutputStream(f);
      s.writeObject(planets);
      s.close();
    }
    catch (IOException e) {
      System.out.println("Exception while Writing");
      return;
    }
  }

  int getNumPlanets() {
    return planets.size();
  }

  Planet getPlanet(int num) {
    return (Planet)planets.elementAt(num);
```

```
}

public void sendResponse(HttpServletResponse res, Hashtable params)
  throws IOException {
  ServletOutputStream out = res.getOutputStream();
  res.setContentType("text/html");
  HtmlPage page = new HtmlPage("Planet Information");
  page.add("Planet Information", "h1");

  String planetnumber = (String)params.get("planet");
  HtmlForm form = new HtmlForm("/planets", "GET");
  form.add("Planet number 1 - " + getNumPlanets() + ":  ");
  if (planetnumber != null)
    form.addTextField("planet", "size=3 value=" + planetnumber);
  else
    form.addTextField("planet", "size=3");
  form.addSubmitButton("name=action value=Info");
  form.addSubmitButton("name=action value=Bump");
  page.add(form);

  try {
    if (planetnumber != null) {
      int index = Integer.parseInt(planetnumber) -1;
      Planet p = getPlanet(index);
      String action = (String) params.get("action");
      if ("Bump".equalsIgnoreCase(action)) {
        p.bumpMoons();
        write();
      }
      HtmlTable tbl = new HtmlTable("Border");

      // add name of planet
      tbl.newRow();
      tbl.addData("Planet Name:");
      tbl.addData(p.getName());
      // add number of moons
      tbl.newRow();
      tbl.addData("Number of Moons:");
      tbl.addData(Integer.toString(p.getMoons()));
```

continues

Listing 18.2, Continued

```
154            // add if had rings
155            tbl.newRow();
156            tbl.addData("Has Rings:");
157            tbl.addData((p.hasRings() ? "Yes" : "No"));
158            page.add(tbl);
159          }
160          page.write(out);
161        }
162        catch (NumberFormatException e) {
163          page.add("<hr>");
164          page.add(planetnumber + " is not a valid planet #", "h2");
165          page.write(out);
166        }
167        catch (Exception e) {
168          page.add("<hr>");
169          page.add("Error: " + e, "h2");
170          page.write(out);
171        }
172      }
173    }
```

Lines 8–34 in listing 18.2 declare a Planet object that holds the information about a planet and, because it implements Serializable, can be stored to and read from a file. The only difference from the Planet class definition in the Chapter 16 example is the need to declare the `bumpMoons()` method as synchronized to ensure thread-safe operation.

Lines 36–46 declare the servlet as a subclass of FormServlet. The servlet's `init()` method (lines 47–59) is called once when the servlet is loaded to initialize any information needed by the servlet. Each service request is handled by a separate thread that accesses a single instance of the servlet; any instance variables set up by the `init()` method are shared by these service threads. Line 49 accesses the initialization parameters of the servlet:

```
049      Hashtable ht = getInitParameters();
```

Only one parameter, "file," is defined that specifies the file name of the file that holds the information about the planets. Lines 50–58 initialize the planet information either from this file or by using predefined information. Lines 62–73 define the `setupPlanets()` method to initialize the use of predefined information, and lines 75–93 define a `read()` method to initialize the use of a Vector of Planets object stored in a file.

Lines 96–107 define a method to write the updated planet information to the file. This method is declared as synchronized to ensure that only one thread at a time attempts to write-out the information. Because the `init()` method is only called once at initialization, synhronization is not necessary for the `read()` method.

Lines 109–115 define methods to get planet information and to determine the number of planets. Because the underlying Vector operations are thread-safe, further synchronization is not necessary.

The essence of the servlet is the `sendResponse()` method, defined in lines 117–172. The `sendResponse()` method is called by the FormServlet's `service()` method to perform the form's processing and to create the response. Because the FormServlet superclass has already stored the form information in a hashtable, performing forms handling is a simple matter of retrieving data from the Hashtable and processing it. For this example, processing is simply determining the planet number and creating the HTML to display the information as follows:

1. Prepare the response header and get output stream.

   To create the response, set values in the HttpServletResponse object and write to the output stream defined by lines 119 and 120:

   ```
   119     ServletOutputStream out = res.getOutputStream();
   120     res.setContentType("text/html");
   ```

   You must always specify the content-type on responses that include data.

2. Create the HTML response page.

   Allocate an HtmlPage to help construct the HTML response page and add a level-one header as shown in lines 121 and 122:

   ```
   121     HtmlPage page = new HtmlPage("Planet Information");
   122     page.add("Planet Information", "h1");
   ```

   Lines 124–133 create the HTML for the form. This form consists of an input text field to hold the planet number and two buttons labeled “Info” and “Bump.”

The HTML creation classes are a simplification of the complete language; you are required to manually create HTML code for attributes not supported by the classes.

3. Process forms action request.

Lines 135–160 perform the form's processing and create the response. Lines 124 gets the planet number from the form and lines 137 and 138 convert that number into a reference to the planet object. Lines 139–143 process the "Bump" action command.

Lines 144–157 create an HTML table to display the planet information and then adds rows for planet name, number of moons, and has-rings indication. After you finish building the table, add the table to the page, and then write the HTML for the complete page to the output stream:

```
160        page.write(out);
```

The first write to the ServletOutputStream triggers a write of the HTTP response header to the output stream. Even though the ServletOutputStream is buffered, you do not need to call the `flush()` method; the server automatically calls the stream's `flush()` method.

Lines 162–171 catch exceptions and return errors to the requester. This completes the PlanetsServlet. Figure 18.3 shows the output of the servlet. The following section describes the Java Web Server in more detail.

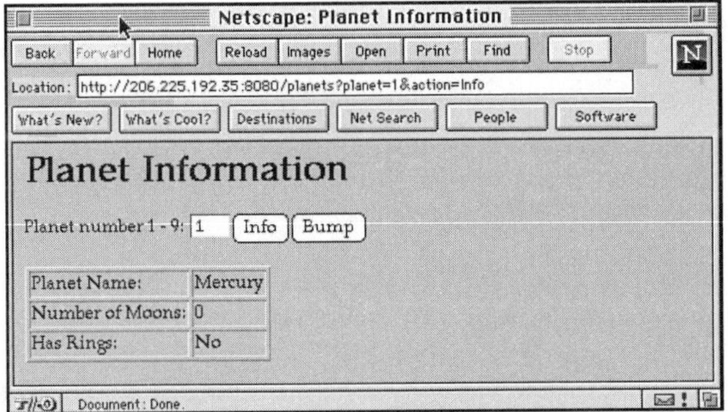

Figure 18.3
PlanetsServlet output.

Using the Java Web Server

Just as Sun needed to implement the HotJava browser to develop the Java language and applet environment, a server environment is needed to develop, test, and demonstrate the Servlet API. The new Java Web Server fulfills these needs and represents a reference implementation of the Servlet API. The server is completely written with Java technology and operates on any Java-compliant server platform. The next section provides you with a quick introduction to the Java Web Server.

Setting up the Java Web Server

As is the case with most servers, a variety of parameters need to be set for proper server operation when using the Java Web Server. Fortunately, the default parameter values can be used in most cases. You can reconfigure the server either by editing the configuration files or by using the administration servlet. In most cases, you use the servlet because it ensures correct formatting of the configuration file entries. Because this servlet will likely change for the final release, the following section explains the entries in the underlying configuration files. Each configuration file entry corresponds to a command in the administration servlet.

The configuration files, all kept in the /admin subdirectory, are in the Properties class file format. Properties is a subclass of Hashtable that defines a mechanism to load and store the contents of a hashtable to a file. Each line in the file corresponds to one key/value entry in a Hashtable and is comprised of key string separated from a value string by the equality (=) character. The server's TCP port, for example, is specified by the following entry in the httpd.properties file:

```
server.port=8080
```

Three configuration files are related to servlet operation that are of interest to the administrator or servlet developer:

- Path translation rules—rules.properties file
- File alias table—aliases.properties file
- Servlet control and init parameters—servlet.properties file

These files are explained further in following sections.

In addition to configuration information directly related to servlets, the Java Web Server supports virtual hosting, proxy operation, and an access control scheme. Virtual hosting enables the administrator to establish multiple, logically disjointed HTML document collections on one physical server. Unless you closely inspect the IP address of the servers, you are probably unaware that different virtual hosts are served by one physical server. Compare IP addresses because even the IP host names of virtual hosts are distinct. Proxy services supports operation through a security firewall and provides local caching for proxied files.

Server access control is supported by a scheme of security realms, users and groups, and access control lists. The related files are as follows:

- Access control lists—acl.properties file
- General security configuration—security.properties file
- User and group identification files stored within the realm directory

The next section focuses on the configuration aspects related to servlets.

Path Translation Rules

The rules.properties file defines the translation rules for converting an URL request to the name of the servlet that handles the request. An example file is as follows:

```
/=file
/cgi-bin=cgi
/imagemap=imagemap
/servlet=invoker
/admin/adminservlet=admin
/loganalyzer=loganalyzer
```

The string to the left of the equals sign (=) is matched against the requested URL; the longest match, starting from the left of the requested URL, is used in the translation. The string on the right of the = is the name of the servlet to handle the request. The string "/" to the left on the first line specifies the default mapping as "file," which provides the usual HTTP file and directory service.

If you want to replace one of the standard, built-in servlets, such as "file," with your own custom version, do not change the name of the servlet in the rules.properties file—instead change the class to be loaded for the servlet named "file" in the servlet.properties file. Internally, the server code provides you with special processing based on the name of the servlet. The name in the rules.properties file is treated as a description of the service.

Alias Table

The Java Web Server provides you with an aliasing mechanism to translate the requested path information into another string. For files, the FileServlet uses the rules in the alias.properties file to map the shorthand pathname specified in an URL to a full file pathname. Use aliases as a way to accomplish the following:

- Eliminate typing long URLs
- Hide your internal directory structure
- Temporarily fix broken links when reorganizing directories and moving files

An example alias.properties file follows:

```
/=public_html
/cgi-bin=cgi-bin
/admin=admin/html
/doc=doc
/applet=servlets
/icons=icons
/~user=/home/$user/public_html
```

The string to the left of the = is matched against the requested URL; the longest match, starting from the left of the requested URL, is used in the translation. The string to the right of the = is the file name of the file. The last line defines the familiar shorthand for a user's directory, "~user," which actually refers to "/home/user/public_html."

Servlet Control Parameters

The servlet.properties files contain all the information needed to load and initialize any named servlet. You can specify three different parameters for each servlet: a codebase, code class name, and initialization parameters. They take the form of the following entries, respectively:

- <servletname>.codebase=URL
- <servletname>.code=classname
- <servletname>.initArgs=name/value pairs

You need to specify the codebase if the class is not in the current CLASSPATH. The name/value pairs from initArgs can be accessed by the servlet by calling the `getInitParameter()` method to get the value of a specific parameter or `getInitParameters()` to get a hashtable of all arguments.

A special entry, `servlets.startup`, lists the servlets to be automatically loaded at server start-up time. An example of a servlet.properties file is as follows:

```
servlets.startup= file cgi myservlet error
file.code=sun.server.http.FileServlet
cgi.code=sun.server.http.CgiServlet
error.code=sun.server.http.ErrorServlet
myservlet.code=specialsyservlet.class
myservlet.initArgs=param1=value1, param2=value2,\
  param3=value3
```

Note You use the backslash (\) character to indicate a line continuation.

Processing HTTP Requests

The Java Web Server is built by using the Java Server Development Toolkit and has a main thread that accepts incoming connections on a ServerSocket as defined by the server.port configuration parameter, deploys the actual service processing to a handler thread, and loops back to accept additional connections. The handler threads are allocated from a pool of service threads to reduce the overhead of thread allocation for each request. By using a different thread to handle each connection, the server can service several clients concurrently. Server connection processing and request handling is shown in figure 18.4.

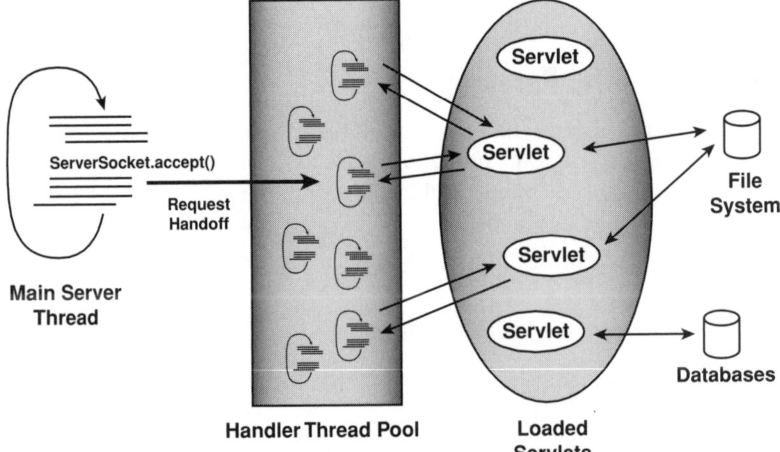

Figure 18.4
Server request handling.

To handle a request, the HTTP server carries out the following tasks:

1. Creates an HttpServletRequest object from the information in the HTTP request header. This object performs the same functions as the environment variables used to communicate request information to CGI programs.

2. Applies the path translation rules found in the rules.properties file to convert the URL into the name of the appropriate servlet. All URLs are converted into a servlet name; the longest matching rule is used to perform the translation.

3. Verifies access permission to the resource according to the information in the acl.properties file. If your file service and invocation servlets do not use the standard names "file" and "invoker" they will need to implement their own access checking.

4. Translates the servlet name according to the information in the servlet.properties file into a full pathname, such as URL, codebase, or class name information that specifies how to load the servlet.

5. Loads and, if necessary, initializes the servlet. Every HTTP request either invokes a servlet or returns an error. Initialization parameters for each servlet can be specified in the servlet.properties file; these parameters are passed to the `init()` method after the servlet is loaded but before the `service()` method is called.

6. Creates an HttpServletResponse object with basic response information, such as the server identification and current time.

7. Calls the servlet's `service()` method passing the request and response objects as arguments.

8. Completes the transaction by ensuring the response is sent and, if appropriate, the connection is closed.

This process is shown in figure 18.5.

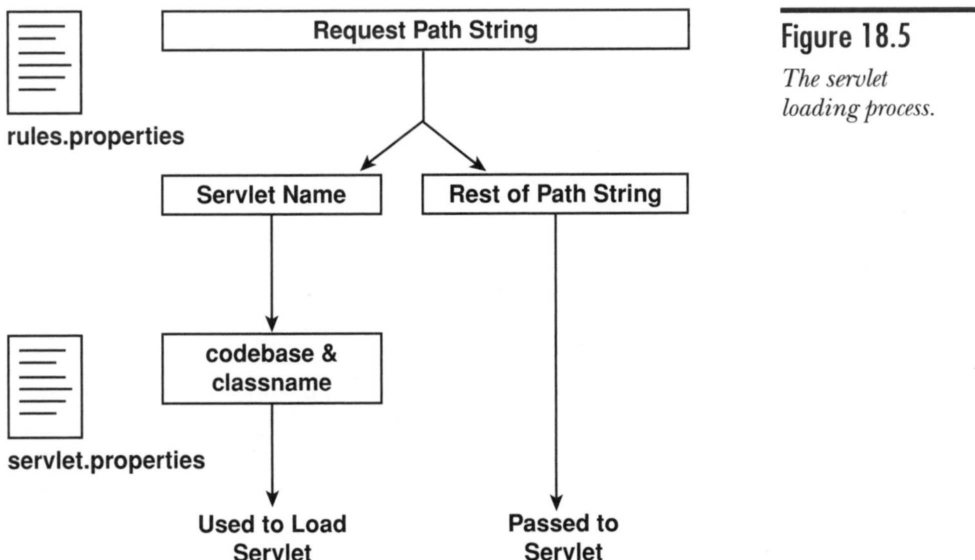

Figure 18.5

The servlet loading process.

Because servlets can be identified by a full URL, servlets can be downloaded from the network, in a way similar to applets, and executed on the server. The upcoming section "Untrusted Servlet Security Sandbox" describes how such servlets are handled.

Providing Security

As Web servers expand their roles from simply providing users with access to publicly available documents to becoming the center of workgroup and enterprise computing, security becomes increasingly important. Not all files, directories, or servlets should be accessible to anyone who knows the URL. The Java Web Server, for example, has a built-in administration applet/servlet pair that enables an administrator to reconfigure the server; obviously access to this servlet must be controlled. You may want to control access to Web pages in the same manner that file servers provide read-access controls for files. The security model of Web servers resembles the security measures found on traditional file servers and shared computers.

Security Features

The Java Web Server offers a variety of security and protection mechanisms for your server. These are based on HTTP's security features, the Secure Sockets Layer (SSL), and the security mechanisms inherent in Java's protected Virtual Machine environment. The server's authentication modes are specified on an individual file or servlet basis.

The Java Web Server supports the following security mechanisms:

- Basic HTTP username/password authentication
- Digest authentication
- Secure sockets layer
- Access control lists

Untrusted Servlet Security Sandbox

For running untrusted servlets, the Java Web Server provides a secured environment that isolates the untrusted servlet from the rest of the HTTP server. Trusted servlets execute on a thread in the main server's thread group. Untrusted servlets execute in a thread group separate from the server's group. The use of a separate thread group prevents a servlet from trying to interfere with the main processing task. The untrusted servlet environment limits access to network resources, files, and server configuration information by adding a servlet security manager that checks for risky operations and blocks them. Execution of untrusted servlets is shown in figure 18.6.

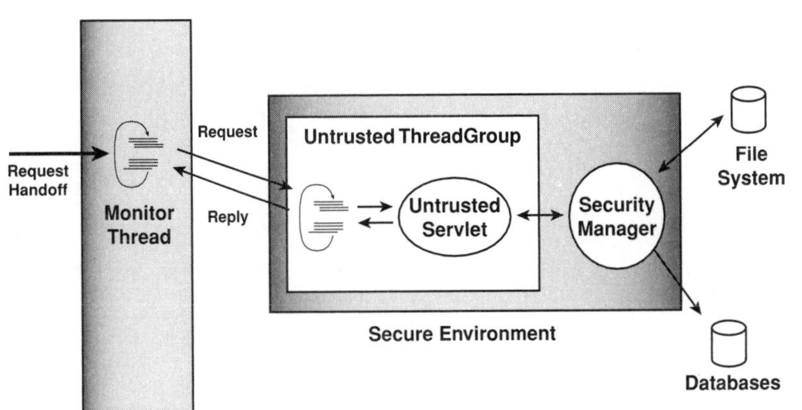

Figure 18.6

Untrusted servlet handling.

Built-In Servlets

Because the Servlet API is efficient and powerful, many of the features often coded directly into an HTTP server are implemented as servlets in the Java Web Server. This use of servlets simplifies the base server code and enables server administrators and users to customize server features by providing additional servlets. Because of the object-oriented nature of the Servlet API, you can subclass existing servlets to create new servlets customized for your application. The Java Web Server includes several standard servlets to provide the functions commonly available in HTTP servers. These core servlets are as follows:

- File servlet (FileServlet) accesses files and directories
- Server-side include servlet (SSIncludeServlet) processes server-side include files
- Error servlet (ErrorServlet) creates custom error responses
- Invoker servlet (InvokerServlet) invokes an arbitrary servlet
- Imagemap servlet (ImagemapServlet) handles image maps on the server
- CGI invoker servlet (CGIServlet) runs CGI programs
- Administration servlet (AdminServlet) performs administrative tasks

Generally, the standard servlets are not really designed to be subclassed; in the interest of efficiency, most provide only public `service()` and `sendResponse()` methods. The FormServlet, however (part of the Servlet API and discussed in detail in the section at the beginning of this chapter), and the ErrorServlet are designed to be modified to perform custom forms processing and to provide custom error messages.

FileServlet

The FileServlet provides you with the normal static content file serving functions expected of an HTTP server. The URL path translation rules are set to default requests not handled by other servlets to the FileServlet. The FileServlet only supports GET and HEAD requests; an error is returned for any other HTTP method. If the requested file is a directory, the servlet returns the contents of a Welcome file residing in the requested directory. The default name of the Welcome file is index.html. If the Welcome file is not found, the servlet returns a formatted directory listing. You can change the name of the Welcome file by adding a welcome="pagename.html" entry to httpd.properties.

If a file is requested, the servlet determines the correct content type by matching the file extension against those in the mime.properties file. The FileServlet has an internal cache to hold the contents of frequently requested documents. If the file size is less than a configured value, the file is read into an internal buffer and cached. The file caching size is specified by the ramcache.entry.size entry in the httpd.properties file; the default value is 8,000 bytes.

If the MIME type of the file is "java-internal/parsed-HTML," the content type is set to "text/html" and the FileServlet calls the server-side include servlet for additional processing of the file. By default, the extension of files that contain server-side includes is .shtml, as specified in the mime.properties file.

Server-Side-Include Servlet

If the MIME type of the file is "java-internal/parsed-html," the SSIncludeServlet further processes the file to resolve any references to servlets embedded in the document. By default, these files have extensions of .shtml. As the document is written to the client, the SSIncludeServlet scans for the newly defined <servlet> HTML tag. When this tag is encountered, the servlet identified in the attributes of the tag is invoked and its output is sent to the client in place of the <servlet> </servlet> HTML element. You can invoke any servlet as a server-side include and you can invoke any server-side include servlet as a regular HTTP servlet by using the InvokerServlet. Of course, whether or not the output is meaningful depends on the exact servlet combination.

The server-side includes supported by SSIncludeServlet are not the same as that supported by many other HTTP servers, such as NCSA and Netscape, that embed server-side include commands inside HTML comments. The Java Web Server-supported server-side includes can only be used to invoke servlets and to insert the output into the current document. The syntax for invoking servlets follows:

```
<servlet name=Name code=Code.class codebase=CodeBase
initParam1=initArg1 initParam2=initArg2…>
<param name=param1 value=val1>
```

```
<param name=param2 value=val2>
.
.
.
</servlet>
```

The server first tries to invoke the servlet with the name provided in the name field. If this fails or if no name is provided, the server attempts to load the servlet based on the code and codebase fields. Any remaining attribute fields within the <servlet> tag are passed as initialization parameters to the servlet. If the server loads the servlet and a name was specified, the server keeps the servlet loaded so that the next time the servlet is accessed it is not reloaded. If no name is specified, the server reloads the servlet each time it is accessed.

After the servlet is ready to execute, the server calls the `service()` method of the servlet. The name/value pairs specified in the HTML file with the <param> tag are accessible to the servlet by using the standard `getParameter()` and `getParameters()` methods on the ServletRequest object passed to the servlet in the `service()` method. Everything the servlet writes to `ServletResponse.getOutputStream()` is also written to the client as part of the client's requested document.

Error Response Servlet

When you call HttpServletResponse's `sendError()` method with only a status code to return an error to the requester, the ErrorServlet is actually invoked to create and send the error reply. The built-in ErrorServlet returns either a simple error reply message generated by translating the status number into a standard error text string, or it returns the contents of a file from the preconfigured error page directory (the error.directory servlet `init()` parameter). The files in the error directory are named by adding the .HTML extension to the status code; for example, the message for "not found" (code 404) is contained in the file 404.html.

By implementing the creation and transmission of error response pages as a servlet, Java Web Server provides great flexibility in handling error responses. You can easily replace the built-in servlet with your own customized error response servlet.

InvokerServlet

The InvokerServlet processes HTTP requests to explicitly invoke a servlet instead of implicitly invoking a servlet as a result of path translation. In the default server configuration, the InvokerServlet is triggered by a /servlet in the requested URL. The rest of the URL characters occurring after /servlet are presumed to identify the name of the servlet to be executed.

ImagemapServlet

The ImagemapServlet handles the server-side processing of image maps that are specified by using an extension of standard NCSA map files. A server-side image map is specified in an HTML file by placing `<IMG>` inside the `<A HREF=...>` tag instead of text description of the link. The following HTML, for example, is used to place an image map in a document:

```
<A HREF="http://<server-host-name>/imagemap/<map-file-name>">
<IMG SRC="<image-file>" ISMAP>
</A>
```

Image map files can reside anywhere HTML documents are permitted to reside. The ImagemapServlet supports image map files that are in standard NCSA format, with some extensions to provide better support for text-only browsers.

CGIServlet

To enable backward compatibility with existing CGI programs, Java Web Server has a built-in servlet, CGIServlet, that functions as a bridge between the Servlet API and CGI. The translation of servlet requests to CGI is feasible because all the necessary information is available through the Servlet API.

AdminServlet

Online server administration is performed by AdminServlet. By using this servlet, the administrator can perform all the server's configuration functions without ever having to manually edit configuration files. Also, the use of an administration servlet ensures that changes to multiple configuration files are correctly completed.

The following is a partial list of the functions performed with the AdminServlet:

- Restart or shut down the server.
- Change operating parameters, such as the server port.
- Vary parameters that affect server performance, such as timeouts and file cache size.
- Control event logging.
- Specify file and servlet name aliases.
- Control virtual host properties.
- Configure proxy operation.

- Set up user and group access control information.
- Administer access control lists and specify the resource to which they apply.
- Identify the servlets loaded at server startup.

Summary

This chapter has introduced servlets and explained their functionality as well as the Servlet API. The basics of the Java Web Server were also explained. The Servlet API and the Java Web Server covered in this chapter are only beginning steps toward defining a radically new architecture in server software. Taken to its logical conclusion, servlets can evolve into the server-side equivalent of application components, and the Servlet API can become the future of server software component architecture—a Java Beans for the server. This new architecture goes beyond simply replacing CGI programs—it completely changes server implementations. The Java Web Server shows how an HTTP server can be remolded to use servlets to significantly increase flexibility and customization. As the servlet technology matures, more standard servlets will be defined, such as standard servlet bridges to databases; and new server-side technologies, such as JDBC, will be first introduced as servlets.

INDEX

Symbols

A

B

C

D

E

F

G

H

J

K

L

M

P

Q - R

T

U

V

W

X - Y - Z

Getting Started with the CD-ROM

This page provides instructions for installing software from the CD-ROM.

Windows 95/NT 4 Installation

Insert the disc into your CD-ROM drive. If autoplay is enabled on your machine, the CD-ROM setup program starts automatically the first time you insert the disc.

If setup does not run automatically, perform these steps:

1. From the Start menu, choose Programs, Windows Explorer.
2. Select your CD-ROM drive under My Computer.
3. Double-click SETUP.EXE in the contents list.
4. Follow the on-screen instructions that appear.
5. Setup adds an icon named CD-ROM Contents to a program group for this book. To explore the CD-ROM, double-click on the CD-ROM Contents icon.

How To Contact New Riders Publishing

If you have a question or comment about this product, there are several ways to contact New Riders Publishing. You can write us at the following address:

New Riders Publishing
Attn: Publishing Manager
201 W. 103rd Street
Indianapolis, IN 46290

If you prefer, you can fax New Riders Publishing at 1-317-817-7448.

To send Internet electronic mail to New Riders, address it to `support@mcp.com`.

You can also contact us through the Macmillan Computer Publishing CompuServe forum at `GO NEWRIDERS`. Our World Wide Web address is `http://www.mcp.com/newriders`.

Technical Support:

If you cannot get the CD/Disk to install properly, or you need assistance with a particular situation in the book, please feel free to check out the Knowledge Base on our Web site at **http://www.superlibrary.com/general/support**. We have answers to our most Frequently Asked Questions listed there. If you do not find your specific question answered, please contact Macmillan Technical Support at **(317) 581-3833**. We can also be reached by email at **support@mcp.com**.